THE ENGLISH
RELIGIOUS LEXIS

THOMAS CHASE

Texts and Studies in Religion
Volume 37

THE EDWIN MELLEN PRESS
Lewiston / Queenston

Library of Congress Cataloging-in-Publication Data
Chase, Thomas.
    The English religious lexis.
    (Texts and studies in religion ; v. 37)
    Bibliography; p.
    Includes index.
    1. English language--Lexicology. 2. English
language--Semantics. 3. Theology--Terminology.
4. Christianity--Terminology. I. Title. II. Series.
PE1583.C5 1988 423'.028 87-31377
ISBN 0-88946-826-5

PE
1583
.C5
1988

This is volume 37 in the continuing series
Texts & Studies in Religion
Volume 37 ISBN 0-88946-826-5
TSR Series 0-88946-976-8

The Edwin Mellen Press
Box 450
Lewiston, New York
USA 14092

The Edwin Mellen Press
Box 67
Queenston, Ontario
CANADA L0S 1L0

Printed in the United States of America

To my mother
and in memory of my father

Preface

This book began some years ago as a contribution to the *Historical Thesaurus of English* project in the Department of English Language at Glasgow University. The aim of the *Historical Thesaurus* project is a simple one, though the work involved is vast: to provide a semantically-based classification of the English vocabulary from earliest times to the present.

The classification of the religious lexis presented here will, with modifications, form part of the *Historical Thesaurus*. I attempt to demonstrate that the classificatory devices found here, which stem from a structural approach to language, will be valid for other lexical fields. Chapter 1 outlines the idea of lexical fields in general, their primary divisions, and the means of ordering groups of lexical material within them. Under the governing semantic relationship of hyponymy, several classificatory devices developed for the religious lexis are discussed. Chapter 2 is devoted to an explanation of the classification. In it are discussed the conventions employed to display low-level subordination within the lexical field, and it considers in turn each of the subfields of the present classification. Chapter 3 comprises the five subfields of the classification. Chapter 4, by providing definitions of and a commentary on selected lexical items and categories, seeks to justify their placement and provide information about the lexis. Chapter 5 provides basic historical and etymological data from the religious lexis.

Semantic classification is a notoriously dangerous exercise. There are few clear-cut rules. What seems to one the obvious way to classify a given set of words is to another utterly wrong. This classification is entirely my own work, and I am conscious of many controversial points in it. Nonetheless, I offer it in the hope that it might provoke discussion. Though it is mainly an exercise in lexical semantics which employs the religious lexis as a body of data, I trust that scholars in fields other than that of linguistics will find it of interest. In particular, students of religion and historians of ideas will find much information about the way in which speakers of English over the centuries have viewed aspects of religion and have encoded their views in language.

During my stay in Glasgow from 1980 to 1983 I enjoyed the guidance of Leslie W. Collier, Christian Kay, and Professor M. L. Samuels. From their close attention and constructive criticism this work has benefited greatly. In preparing the book for publication, I am indebted to Glasgow University and Oxford University Press for permission to use *Historical Thesaurus* archives, and to Luther College, University of Regina, for providing several grants administered by the Social Sciences and Humanities Research Council of Canada. Funding for the *Historical Thesaurus* project has been received from the British Academy, the Axe-Houghton Foundation, the Vogelstein Foundation, and the Leverhulme Trust. Mrs Pamela Vickruck assisted in the preparation of early stages of the typescript. Kirsten Costain undertook the arduous tasks of proofreading the classification and preparing the index. I owe a large debt to the Computing Services department of the University of Regina: to Mr Gregor Larson for his help with software, and especially to Mr Dale Anderson, whose detailed knowledge of document preparation systems was shared generously from beginning to end of this project.

T.C.
University of Regina
January 1988

Table of Contents

Schedule of categories in classification - vii
Abbreviations, typographical conventions, and dating - xxi

Chapter 1 - Lexical Subordination   1

I. The lexical field   1
II. The role of the headword   11
III. Subordination within categories   19
IV. Two other low-level classificatory devices   29
    a. 'Family tree' and 'locomotive' progressions   29
    b. Conceptual alphabetization   32
V. Lexical gaps   33

Chapter 2 - Introduction to the Classification   36

System of subordination   43
Organization of subfields   51
R1   51
R2   56
R3   59
R4   64
R5   70

Chapter 3 - The English Religious Lexis   73

R1 - Belief, Doctrine, and Spirituality   73
R2 - Churches, Sects, and Religious Movements   148
R3 - The Institutional Church   197
R4 - Worship, Ritual, and Practice   256
R5 - Artefacts   347

Chapter 4 - Notes to the Classification   389

R1   389
R2   414
R3   429
R4   448
R5   463

Chapter 5 - Historical and Etymological Data   483

I. Historical data   485
II. Etymological data   491
III. Combined historical and etymological data   497
IV. Unreplaced Old English compounds   500

Bibliography   503
Index   513

Schedule of Categories
in Classification

R1 - Belief, Doctrine, and Spirituality

R1.1.0. Faith 73
R1.1.1.0. Creed 74
R1.1.1.1. Kinds of creed 75
R1.1.2. Doctrine 75
R1.1.3. Tradition 76
R1.1.4. Communion 77
R1.1.5.0. Religion 77
R1.1.5.1. A Religion/Church 78
R1.1.5.2. Kinds of religion 80
R1.1.6. Orthodoxy 80
R1.1.7. Heterodoxy 81
R1.1.8. Free-thought 82
R1.1.9. Superstition 82
R1.1.10. Heresy 82
R1.1.11.0. Paganism 84
R1.1.11.1. Paganization 86
R1.1.12.0. Atheism 86
R1.1.12.1. Atheization 87
R1.1.13.0. Conformity 88
R1.1.13.1. Non-conformity 88
R1.1.13.2. Recusancy 89
R1.1.14. Apostasy 89
R1.1.15.0. Sectarianism 90
R1.1.15.1. Sectarianization 90
R1.1.15.2. Bigotry 91
R1.1.15.3. Schism 91
R1.1.16. Catholicity 91

R1.2.0. Scripture general 92
R1.2.1.0. Bible 92
R1.2.1.1.0. Text of Bible 94
R1.2.1.1.1. Kinds of texts 94
R1.2.1.1.2. Canon 95
R1.2.1.1.3. Textual criticism 95
R1.2.1.1.4. Versions of text 96
R1.2.1.2.0. Divisions of the Bible 97

R1.2.1.2.1.0. Old Testament 97
R1.2.1.2.1.1. Divisions of Old Testament 98
R1.2.1.2.1.2. Genesis – R1.2.1.2.1.18. Jeremiah 99
R1.2.1.2.2. Apocrypha 100
R1.2.1.2.3.0. New Testament 101
R1.2.1.2.3.1. Gospel 101
R1.2.1.2.3.2. Acts of the Apostles 102
R1.2.1.2.3.3. Epistle 102
R1.2.1.2.3.4. Book of Revelations 102
R1.2.1.3. Biblical personages 103
R1.2.1.4. Biblical places 104
R1.2.1.5. Biblical events 104
R1.2.2. Hebrew scripture 106
R1.2.3. Non-Judæo-Christian scriptures 107

R1.3.0. Patristics 108
R1.3.1. Fathers of the church 108
R1.3.1.1. Individual fathers 108
R1.3.1.2. Patristic writings 109
R1.4.0. Law 109
R1.4.1. Canon law 109
R1.4.2. Jewish law 110
R1.4.3. Islamic law 111
R1.5.0. Theology 112
R1.5.1. Kinds of theology 113
R1.5.2. Departments of theology 114

R1.6.0. Holiness 116
R1.6.1.0. Saint 117
R1.6.1.1. Particular saints 118
R1.6.1.2. Canonization 119
R1.6.1.3. Discanonization 120
R1.6.2.0. Consecration 120
R1.6.2.1. Reconsecration 121
R1.6.2.2. Blessing 121
R1.6.3. Unholiness 122
R1.7.0. Piety 123
R1.7.1. Sanctimoniousness 124
R1.7.2. Misdevotion 125
R1.7.3. Impiety 126

R1.8.0. Spirituality 126
R1.8.1.0. Soul 127

R1.8.1.1. Transmigration 128
R1.8.1.2. Regeneration 129
R1.8.1.3. Doctrines concerning the soul 130
R1.8.2.0. Unspirituality 131
R1.8.2.1. Secularization 132
R1.8.3.0. Contemplation 132
R1.8.3.1. Self-examination 133
R1.8.3.2. Quietism 133
R1.8.4. Rapture 133
R1.8.5.0. Mysticism 134
R1.8.5.1. Mystery 134
R1.8.5.2. Mystical significance 135
R1.8.5.3. Otherworldliness 135
R1.8.6.0. Inspiration 135
R1.8.6.1. Prophecy 136
R1.8.6.2. Vision, manifestation 137
R1.9.0. Grace 137
R1.9.1. Doctrines concerning grace 138
R1.9.2. Merit 139
R1.9.3. Righteousness 139

R1.10.0. Sin 140
R1.10.1. Kinds of sin 142
R1.11.0. Atonement 143
R1.11.1. Doctrines concerning atonement 144
R1.12.0. Salvation 144
R1.12.1. Doctrines of salvation 145
R1.13.0. Reprobation 147

R2 - Churches, Sects, and Religious Movements

R2.1.0. Judaism 148
R2.1.1. Jewish groups and sects 148

R2.2.0. Christianity general 150
R2.2.0.1. Conversion to Christianity 153
R2.2.0.2. Lack of Christianity 153
R2.2.0.3. Opposition to Christianity 154

R2.2.1. Major early Christian sects 154

R2.2.1.1. Antidicomarian 154
R2.2.1.2. Arianism 154
R2.2.1.2.1. Kinds of Arianism 154
R2.2.1.3. Collyridianism 155
R2.2.1.4. Docetism 155
R2.2.1.5. Donatism 155
R2.2.1.5.1. Kinds of Donatism 155
R2.2.1.6. Gnosticism 155
R2.2.1.6.1. Kinds of Gnosticism 155
R2.2.1.7. Manicheism 156
R2.2.1.7.1. Kinds of Manicheism 156
R2.2.1.8. Monophysitism 157
R2.2.1.8.1. Kinds of Monophysitism 157
R2.2.1.9. Nestorianism 157
R2.2.1.10. Pelagianism 158
R2.2.1.10.1. Kinds of Pelagianism 158
R2.2.1.11. Photinianism 158
R2.2.1.12. Sabellianism 158

R2.2.2.0. Orthodoxy 158
R2.2.2.1. Orthodox groups and sects 159
R2.2.3.0. Roman Catholicism 159
R2.2.3.1. Roman Catholic groups and sects 161
R2.2.3.2. Conversion to Roman Catholicism 163
R2.2.3.2.1. Freeing from Catholicism 163
R2.2.3.3. Anticatholicism 163

R2.2.4.0. Protestantism general 164
R2.2.4.0.1. Conversion to Protestantism 164
R2.2.4.0.1.1. Freeing from Protestantism 165
R2.2.4.0.2. Fundamentalism 165
R2.2.4.0.3. The Reformation 165
R2.2.4.0.3.1. Pilgrimage of Grace 165
R2.2.4.0.3.2. Counter-Reformation 165
R2.2.4.1.0. Anglicanism 165
R2.2.4.1.1.0. Anglican groups and divisions 166
R2.2.4.1.1.1. Broad-churchism 166
R2.2.4.1.1.2. Continuationism 166
R2.2.4.1.1.3. Henricianism 166
R2.2.4.1.1.4. High-churchism 166
R2.2.4.1.1.5. Lollardy/Wyclifism 166
R2.2.4.1.1.6. Low-churchism 167
R2.2.4.1.1.7. Reunionism 167

R2.2.4.1.1.8. Tractarianism 167
R2.2.4.1.2. Anglicanization 167
R2.2.4.2.0. Antitrinitarianism 168
R2.2.4.2.1. Antitrinitarian groups and sects 168
R2.2.4.3.0. Arminianism 168
R2.2.4.3.1. Arminian groups and sects 169
R2.2.4.3.2. Arminianization 169
R2.2.4.4.0. Baptistry 169
R2.2.4.4.1. Baptist groups and sects 169
R2.2.4.5.0. Calvinism 171
R2.2.4.5.1. Calvinist groups and sects 171
R2.2.4.5.2. Calvinization 171
R2.2.4.6.0. Lutheranism 171
R2.2.4.6.1. Lutheran groups and sects 172
R2.2.4.6.2. Lutheranization 172
R2.2.4.7.0. Mennonism 172
R2.2.4.7.1. Mennonite groups and sects 172
R2.2.4.8.0. Methodism 173
R2.2.4.8.1. Methodist groups and sects 173
R2.2.4.8.2. Methodization 174
R2.2.4.9.0. Moravianism 174
R2.2.4.9.1. Moravian groups and sects 174
R2.2.4.10.0. Mormonism 174
R2.2.4.10.1. Mormon groups and sects 175
R2.2.4.11.0. Plymouth Brethrenism 175
R2.2.4.11.1. Darbyite groups and sects 175
R2.2.4.12.0. Presbyterianism 175
R2.2.4.12.1. Presbyterian groups and sects 176
R2.2.4.12.2. Presbyterianization 177
R2.2.4.13.0. Puritanism 178
R2.2.4.13.1. Puritan groups and sects 178
R2.2.4.13.2. Puritanization 178
R2.2.4.14.0. Quakerism 179
R2.2.4.14.1. Quaker groups and sects 179
R2.2.4.14.2. Quakerization 179
R2.2.4.15.0. Salvationism 179
R2.2.4.16.0. Waldensianism 180
R2.2.5. Various (anti-)Christian groups 180

R2.3. Non-Christian Religions 190
R2.3.1.0. Buddhism 190
R2.3.1.1. Buddhist groups and sects 190
R2.3.2.0. Confucianism 191

R2.3.3.0. Hinduism 191
R2.3.3.1. Hindu groups and sects 191
R2.3.3.2. Sanskritization 192
R2.3.4.0. Islam 192
R2.3.4.1. Islamic groups and sects 193
R2.3.4.2. Islamization 194
R2.3.5.0. Lamaism 195
R2.3.6.0. Mithraism 195
R2.3.6.1. Mithraicization 195
R2.3.7.0. Odinism 195
R2.3.8.0. Shinto 195
R2.3.8.1. Shintoization 195
R2.3.9.0. Taoism 195
R2.3.10.0. Zoroastrianism 195
R2.3.10.1. Zoroastrian groups and sects 196
R2.3.10.2. Zoroastrianization 196
R2.3.11. Miscellaneous non-Christian groups 196

R3 - The Institutional Church

R3.1.0. Church government 197
R3.1.1. Kinds of church government 198
R3.1.2. Ecclesiastical authority 201
R3.1.3.0. Ecclesiastical discipline 201
R3.1.3.1. Ecclesiastical court 201
R3.1.4.0. Council 203
R3.1.4.1. Kinds of council 203
R3.1.4.2. Historical councils 204
R3.1.4.3.0. Chapter 205
R3.1.4.3.1. Member of chapter 205
R3.1.4.3.2. Cathedral cleric general 206

R3.2.0. Clergyman general 206
R3.2.1.0. Clerical superior general 208
R3.2.1.1.0. Pope 209
R3.2.1.1.1. Antipope 211
R3.2.1.1.2. Individual popes 211
R3.2.1.1.3. Papal offices, officials 211
R3.2.1.1.4. Papal documents 213
R3.2.1.2. Patriarch 213

R3.2.1.3. Cardinal 214
R3.2.1.4. Primate 215
R3.2.1.5. Metropolitan 215
R3.2.1.6. Archbishop 215
R3.2.1.7. Primus 216
R3.2.1.8.0. Bishop 216
R3.2.1.8.1. Kinds of bishop 218
R3.2.1.8.2. Bishop's officials 220
R3.2.1.9. Archpriest 220
R3.2.1.10. Archdeacon 220
R3.2.1.11. Dean 221
R3.2.1.12. Various superiors 221

R3.2.2.0. Priest 222
R3.2.2.1. Kinds of priest 223
R3.2.3. Rector 226
R3.2.4. Parson 227
R3.2.5. Pastor 227
R3.2.6. Vicar 228
R3.2.7. Curate 228
R3.2.8. Chaplain 229
R3.2.9. Confessor 229
R3.2.10. Preacher 230
R3.2.11.0. Deacon 231
R3.2.11.1. Subdeacon 232
R3.2.11.2. Epistoler 232
R3.2.11.3. Levite 232
R3.2.12.0. P in minor orders general 232
R3.2.12.1. Acolyte 232
R3.2.12.2. Lector 233
R3.2.12.3. Exorcist 233
R3.2.12.4. Ostiary 233
R3.2.13. Other clergy 233

R3.3. Religious 235
R3.3.0. Religious general 235
R3.3.1. Religious superior 237
R3.3.2.0. Monk 239
R3.3.2.1. Nun 240
R3.3.2.2. Anchorite 240
R3.3.2.3. Cœnobite 241
R3.3.2.4. Friar 241
R3.3.2.5. Monastic functionary general 242

R3.3.3.0. Religious order general 243
R3.3.3.1. Augustinian 243
R3.3.3.2. Benedictine 244
R3.3.3.3. Carmelite 245
R3.3.3.4. Dominican 245
R3.3.3.5. Franciscan 246
R3.3.3.6. Jesuit 246
R3.3.3.7. Trinitarian 247
R3.3.3.8. Greek religious 247
R3.3.3.9. Religio-military religious 247
R3.3.3.10. Other religious 248

R3.4. Laity 250
R3.4.0. Layman general 250
R3.4.1. Lay functionary general 252
R3.4.2. Lay brother/sister general 255
R3.4.3. Lay association 255

R4 - Worship, Ritual, and Practice

R4.1. Worship 256
R4.1.0. Worship 256
R4.1.1. Kind of worship general 258
R4.1.2.0. Ritual general 260
R4.1.2.1. Kinds of rite 264
R4.1.3. Part of service general 265
R4.1.4.0. Service music general 269
R4.1.4.1.0. Hymn 269
R4.1.4.1.1. Kinds of hymn 270
R4.1.4.2. Plainchant 272
R4.1.4.3.0. Psalm 272
R4.1.4.3.1. Kinds of psalm 273
R4.1.5.0. Liturgical year 274
R4.1.5.1. Sabbath 274
R4.1.5.2.0. Feast, festival 275
R4.1.5.2.1. Specific Christian seasons and feasts 277
R4.1.5.2.2. Jewish seasons and feasts 284
R4.1.5.2.3. Other seasons and feasts 285
R4.1.5.3. Fast general 285
R4.1.6.0. Canonical hours general 286

R4.1.6.1. Other services 287
R4.1.7. Church-going 287

R4.2. Sacrament 288
R4.2.0. Sacrament general 288
R4.2.1.0. Baptism 289
R4.2.1.1. Kinds of baptism 291
R4.2.2.0. Confession 292
R4.2.2.1.0. Penitence 293
R4.2.2.1.1. Impenitence 294
R4.2.2.2. Absolution 295
R4.2.2.3.0. Penance 295
R4.2.2.3.1. Remission of penance 296
R4.2.3. Confirmation 296
R4.2.4.0. Communion 297
R4.2.4.1.0. Mass 299
R4.2.4.1.1. Kinds of mass 300
R4.2.4.2. Eucharistic doctrines 301
R4.2.5. Marriage 303
R4.2.6.0. Order general 304
R4.2.6.1.0. Ordination 305
R4.2.6.1.1. Unfrocking 306
R4.2.6.2. Vocation 306
R4.2.6.3. Induction 306
R4.2.6.4. Seminary 307
R4.2.6.5. Monastic profession 308
R4.2.7.0. (Extreme) unction 309
R4.2.7.1. Funeral 310
R4.2.7.2. Vigil 311
R4.2.7.3. Commemoration 311

R4.3.0. Prayer 311
R4.3.1. Kinds of prayer 313
R4.4. Good works 316
R4.5.0. Preaching 316
R4.5.1. Evangelization 318
R4.5.2. Catechesis 319
R4.5.3.0. Proselytization 320
R4.5.3.1. Mission 320
R4.5.3.2. Revival 321
R4.5.4.0. Conversion 321
R4.5.4.1. Moral conversion 322
R4.5.4.3. Unconversion 323

R4.6. Pilgrimage 323
R4.7. Crusade 324

R4.8.0. Sacrifice 324
R4.8.1. Kinds of sacrifice 326
R4.8.2. Propitiation 327
R4.9.0. Cleanness (ceremonial) 328
R4.9.1. Purification 328
R4.9.2. Tonsure 329
R4.9.3. Circumcision 330
R4.10.0. Sacrilege 330
R4.10.1. Blasphemy 331
R4.10.2. Iconoclasm 332
R4.10.3. Clerical misbehaviour 332
R4.10.4. Controversy 333

R4.11.0. Vow 333
R4.11.1. Covenant 334
R4.11.2. Non-jurancy 334
R4.12.0. Martyrdom 335
R4.12.1. Confession 335
R4.13. Exorcism 336
R4.14.0. Excommunication 336
R4.14.1. Imprecation 338
R4.14.2. Interdict 338
R4.15. Other practices 338

R4.16.0. Benefice 341
R4.16.1. Kinds of benefice 342
R4.16.2. Advowson 344
R4.16.3. Simony 345
R4.16.4. Other financial matters 345

R5 - Artefacts

R5.1. Property general 347
R5.2.0. Land general 347
R5.2.1. Structures of/in land 348

R5.3.0. Sanctuary/holy place general 348
R5.3.1. Temple 349

R5.3.2. Principal place of worship 350
R5.3.3. Church/place of worship 350
R5.3.4. Chapel 351
R5.3.5. Synagogue 352
R5.3.6. Shrine 352
R5.3.7. Other 353
R5.3.8. Construction/measurement 353

R5.4. Parts of buildings 353
R5.4.0. Division of building general 353
R5.4.1. Door 353
R5.4.2. Narthex/portico 354
R5.4.3. West end 354
R5.4.4. Antenave 354
R5.4.5. Nave 354
R5.4.6. Aisle 354
R5.4.7. Crossing 354
R5.4.8. Transept 354
R5.4.9. Screen 355
R5.4.10. Choir 355
R5.4.11. Chancel/sanctuary 355
R5.4.12. Holy of holies 355
R5.4.13. Altar rail 355
R5.4.14. Pavement 355
R5.4.15. Gradual 355
R5.4.16.0. Altar/communion table 355
R5.4.16.1. Parts of altar 356
R5.4.17. Retrochoir 357
R5.4.18. Apse 357
R5.4.19. Ambulatory 357
R5.4.20. Crypt 357
R5.4.21. Triforium 357
R5.4.22. Clerestory 357
R5.4.23. Gallery 357
R5.4.24. Bell-tower 357
R5.4.25. Baptistry 358
R5.4.26. Sacristy/vestry 358
R5.4.27. Chapel 358
R5.4.28. Oratory 358
R5.4.29. Other 359

R5.5. Monastic property 359
R5.5.0. Monastic property general 359

R5.5.1.0. Monastic land 359
R5.5.1.1. Monastic estate 359
R5.5.2.0. Monastery/convent 359
R5.5.3. Parts of monastery 360
R5.5.4. Hermitage 361
R5.6. Clerical residences 361
R5.6.0. Clerical residence general 361
R5.6.1. Other 361

R5.7. Furniture 362
R5.7.0. Furniture general 362
R5.7.1. Ark of the covenant 362
R5.7.2. Bell 362
R5.7.3. Canopy 362
R5.7.4. Confessional 363
R5.7.5. Font 363
R5.7.6. Lectern/pulpit 363
R5.7.7. Matraca 363
R5.7.8. Seat 364
R5.7.8.1. Pew 364
R5.7.9. Sepulchre 365
R5.7.10. Stations of the cross 365
R5.7.11. Holy water stoup 365
R5.7.12. Tabernacle 365
R5.7.13. Table 365
R5.7.14. Other 365

R5.8. Implements 366
R5.8.0. Implement general 366
R5.8.1. Vessel general 366
R5.8.2. Ampulla/chrismatory 366
R5.8.3. Aspergillum 366
R5.8.4. Calefactory 367
R5.8.5. Cauldron 367
R5.8.6. Cruet 367
R5.8.7. Cup 367
R5.8.8. Fistula 367
R5.8.9. Grail 367
R5.8.10. Holy water vessel 367
R5.8.11. Incense holder 367
R5.8.12. Laver (Jewish) 367
R5.8.13. Libatory 367
R5.8.14. Paten 367

R5.8.15. Piscina 368
R5.8.16. Pyx 368
R5.8.17. Thurible 368
R5.8.18. Other 368

R5.9. Cloths, carpets, cushions 370
R5.9.1. Altar cloth 370
R5.9.2. Eucharistic cloth 371
R5.9.3. Sudarium 371
R5.9.4. Veil 371
R5.9.5. Prayer carpet 371
R5.9.6. Cushion 371

R5.10. Portable shrines, relics 372
R5.10.1. Portable shrine 372
R5.10.2. Relic 372

R5.11. Vestments 372
R5.11.0. Vestment general 372
R5.11.1. Particular functionaries' attire 373
R5.11.2. Outergarments 374
R5.11.3. Neck and shoulder garb 375
R5.11.4. Headgear 376
R5.11.5. Sartorial appurtenances 376
R5.12. Monastic garb 377
R5.12.0. Monastic garb general 377
R5.12.1. Monk's garb 377
R5.12.2. Nun's garb 377
R5.12.3. Belonging to order wearing white habit 377
R5.12.4. Items of attire 377
R5.13. Lay garments and headgear 378
R5.13.0. Lay garment general 378
R5.13.1. Items of attire 378
R5.14. Pilgrims' garb 379
R5.14.0. Pilgrims' garb general 379
R5.14.1. Items of attire 379

R5.15. Consumables 379
R5.15.1. Bacon 379
R5.15.2. Cake 379
R5.15.3. Candle 380
R5.15.4. Easter-egg 380
R5.15.5.0. Eucharistic elements 380
R5.15.5.1. Bread 380

R5.15.5.2. Wine 381

R5.15.6. Herb 381

R5.15.7. Incense 381

R5.15.8. Oil 382

R5.15.9. Palm frond 382

R5.15.10. Paper 382

R5.15.11. Soma 382

R5.15.12. Water 382

R5.16. Books 382

R5.16.0. Book general 382

R5.16.1. Service book general 382

R5.16.2. Lectionary 384

R5.16.3. Breviary/office book 384

R5.16.4. Music books 385

R5.16.5. Other books 385

R5.16.6. Miscellaneous 386

R5.17. Symbols 386

R5.17.0. Symbol general 386

R5.17.1.0. Image 386

R5.17.1.1. Christian image 387

R5.17.1.2. Non-Christian images 388

Abbreviations, Typographical Conventions, and Dating

a	adjective, *ante*
adv	adverb
advphr	adverbial phrase
arch.	archaic
bibl.	in biblical use
c	*circa*
colloq.	in colloquial use
contempt.	contemptuous use
controv.	in controversial use
deris.	in derisive use
derog.	in derogatory use
dial.	dialectal
dict.	in dictionary
eccl.	ecclesiastical
erron.	erroneous use
fig.	in figurative use
GkCh	Greek (Orthodox) Church
hist.	in historical use
host.	hostile
hum.	humorous
joc.	jocular
L	Latin
MedL	Medieval Latin
n	noun
N	Northern dialect
nattrib.	attributive noun
ncoll.	collective noun
nf	feminine noun
npl	plural noun
nphr	noun phrase
NT	New Testament
occas.pl.	occasionally in plural sense
OE	Old English
OE(L)	Old English, from Latin
OT	Old Testament
p	person, someone
pa	participial adjective
pl	plural
poet.	in poetic use
pseudo.arch.	pseudo-archaic

q	quotation
RCCh	Roman Catholic Church
s	source
Sc	Scottish
Sc.eccl.hist.	Scottish ecclesiastical history
sing.	singular
transf.	transferred sense
v	verb (unmarked for transitivity)
va	verb absolute
vi	intransitive verb
vn	verbal noun
vpass	passive verb
vphr	verb phrase
vrefl	reflexive verb
vt	transitive verb
x	something
xp	something or someone
XR	cross-reference (see category specified)

(2q1s) following date	two quotations from one source
(1) following date	one citation only
? by date	date uncertain
? preceding lexical item	meaning uncertain
+ preceding OE item	*ge-* prefix optional
ð	Old English character ð

In the classification, Old English lexical items are italicized, as are unnaturalized loanwords. In the text, all lexical items referred to as such are italicized. Meanings, concepts, and definitions are enclosed in quotation marks. Unless otherwise stated, all definitions are from the *OED*.

1545(1) one citation only, from 1545

1563/87– first citation dated 1563/87; item remains in use

1588–(1840) first citation dated 1588; last citation dated 1840, but item is judged not obsolete

xxii

1415 + 1826–(1870) no citations between 1415 and 1826; item is judged not obsolete

a1300–c1375 *N. and Sc.* citations, all of Northern or Scottish provenance, from a1300 to c1375

c1449–a1548 + c1650*Sc.* c1650 citation *only* of Scottish provenance

c1500*Sc.* **+ 1597–** c1500 citation *only* of Scottish provenance

1488–1681 + 1821–*hist.* item in use from 1488 to 1681; from 1821 citation onward, use is historical

Chapter One
Lexical Subordination

I. The Lexical Field

The classification of the English religious lexis which forms the central part of this work is based upon a structural approach to the vocabulary of natural language. Such an approach is termed 'structural' because it attempts to organize the vocabulary by means other than the semantically unmotivated alphabetical ordering characteristic of standard dictionaries. If alphabetical organization, together with other semantically unmotivated methods, is abandoned,[1] and conceptual or referential meaning chosen as the property of lexical items to be used to classify a given lexical set, the framework that emerges is one composed of the sense-relations existing between individual items and between groups of items.

This approach, focusing on sense-relations between lexical items isolated from syntactic contexts, is at odds with the bulk of semantic research carried out over the last three decades. The dominance of transformational-generative grammar, in which semantics is inseparable from syntax, has resulted in a neglect of lexical semantics *per se*. Indeed, semantics has proved itself the transformationalists' greatest single

---

[1] Other semantically unmotivated methods of organization are, if hardly viable, at least imaginable, *e.g.* a list based on phonological features.

stumbling-block; the indeterminacy and elusiveness of lexical meaning remain in large measure intractable to the highly systematized devices evolved for the description of syntactic structures by the transformationalists.[2]

It remains, then, to attack semantic problems from a different standpoint. According to Geckeler, "the first task of structural semantics is to build up a paradigmatic type of semantics, *i.e.* word semantics, and ...any attempt to work seriously on combinatorial semantics, *i.e.* sentence semantics or even text semantics, must turn out to be premature unless linguists have first established a solid base of word semantics."[3] Classification of lexical fields, as an essential part of structural semantics, can thus be seen as necessarily anterior to syntactical semantics. An understanding of the nature of the lexis—of nominative function—is needed before analysis of the predicative function of syntactically-ordered linguistic material.

Unlike alphabetical ordering, where no lemma occupies a superordinate or governing position over other lemmata, a conceptually based classification of a given lexical set entails the construction of a complex framework with sense-relations existing, if we can use the metaphor of three-dimensional space, on vertical, horizontal, and lateral axes.[4] This framework forms a

---

[2]Cf. Janet Fodor, *Semantics: Theories of Meaning in Generative Grammar* (Cambridge, Massachusetts: Harvard University Press, 1980); R. H. Robins, *A Short History of Linguistics* (London: Longman, 1979), pp. 228–229; Geoffrey Sampson, *Schools of Linguistics: Competition and Evolution* (London: Hutchinson, 1980), pp. 157–158.

[3]'Structural Semantics,' in Eikmeyer and Reiser (eds.), *Words, Worlds, and Contexts* (Berlin and New York: de Gruyter, 1981), p. 381. Cf. also N. G. Komlev, *Components of the Content Structure of the Word* (The Hague and Paris: Mouton, 1976), p. 152: "The solution of many important questions in linguistics depends essentially on the elucidation of questions related to lexical meaning... One of the immediate tasks of linguists working in the field of semantics is the regularization of existing semantic facts and laws. It appears to us that in the attainment of these goals a decisive role is played by the systemization of the content components of the word as the most important unit of language and speech."

[4]For a simplified illustration of concepts viewed metaphorically as occu-

whole, a system of sense-relations which, though by no means independent of other systems also constructed around lexical material from a natural language, is nonetheless seen as having an identity of its own.

The boundaries of the system are at times vague and difficult to define. Indeterminacy and overlapping, problems often associated with the meanings of individual lexical items, are also characteristic of lexical fields. The lexical field "religion," for example, overlaps with many, among them "morality," "myth," "(non-religious) ritual observances," and others. Some components of a field are felt to be central, others peripheral, and the inclusion or exclusion of items at the periphery will at times perhaps seem arbitrary.[5] Yet a strong and obvious bond exists between the constituent lexical items. Such a system is called a *lexical field*.[6] The term *lexical field* is preferred to *conceptual field* or *semantic field* because it makes no claim to the universality sometimes implied by the last two. Lexical items themselves are the materials for classification, rather than the philosophically disputed concepts they represent. A further caution deriving from the important distinction between conceptual or semantic and lexical fields is stated by Baldinger:

---

pying three-dimensional space, see C. E. Osgood et. al., *The Measurement of Meaning* (Urbana and London: University of Chicago Press, 1957), p. 244. On graphic representation of conceptual systems, see Kurt Baldinger, *Semantic Theory* (Oxford: Basil Blackwell, 1980), pp. 104–108.

[5] General agreement on items in the centre of a field and uncertainty about those on the periphery are analogous to results obtained from studies of the meanings of individual denotata, such as that of Berlin and Kay on colour terms in various languages. For a brief and useful account, see Geoffrey Leech, *Semantics* (Harmondsworth: Penguin, 1981), pp. 24–25 and 233–236.

[6] A simple definition offered by A. Ballweg-Schramm is that "the lexical field is a structured set of lexical items which, in at least one of their meanings, can be related to a common concept" ('Some Comments on Lexical Fields and their Use in Lexicography,' in Eikmeyer and Reiser, *op. cit.*, p. 464).

A conceptual system which depends on a given language would be no more than a tautology and could not serve as a starting-point for onomasiological studies. A conceptual system has to be 'supranational,' that is, independent of any given language. The fact that many languages may not have words to express this conceptual system does not make the system void. There are any number of possible conceptual systems, but it must be remembered that we cannot construct total conceptual systems, but only partial ones.[7]

Lexical fields, on the other hand, are based on a monolingual, and in the present case diachronic, sample.

Though von Humboldt was among the first to posit the idea that a natural language is an organic system, an entity composed of smaller systems which are themselves composed of many sub-systems, Saussure provided the real impetus for research in field theory with his insistence that the *signifié* or concept carried by any given word assumed its *valeur* or meaning only by virtue of its relationships with meanings occupying nearby semantic space.[8] A lexical field is thus the product

---

[7]Baldinger, *op. cit.*, p. 125. Cf. also Suzanne Ohman, 'Theories of the Linguistic Field,' *Word* 9 (1953), 128: "The distinction between conceptual and lexical fields ...seems somewhat problematic. Trier himself, understandably, does not always keep these two types clearly separated. Conceptual fields can hardly be defined independently of language ...It is only by contrasting corresponding lexical fields in various actual languages, whether temporally or sociologically distinct, that one can visualize a conceptual field existing apart from language and divisible in different ways."

[8]Ferdinand de Saussure, *A Course in General Linguistics* (trans. Wade Baskin) (New York: Philosophical Library, 1959). For a brief account of field theory, see N. C. W. Spence, 'Linguistic Fields, Conceptual Systems, and *Weltbild*,' *Transactions of the Philological Society* (1961), 87-106. Spence calls for a pragmatic approach to field theory, which he says has thus far "generally been applied in too rigid a way and [has] sometimes been completely misapplied, to produce mere pseudo-structures." Also useful are Adrienne Lehrer, *Semantic Fields and Lexical Structure* (Ams-

of the relationships between its constituent parts, and these constituent parts have little signification if viewed apart from the tangle of relationships both within and without the field of which they form the nodes. [9]

If a lexical field is the composite of interactions between its parts, how is it first conceived as a unit? In seeking to determine the shape and extent of a field, does one begin with individual constituents and build up a picture of the field itself, or does a vague idea of the field's extent provide the starting point from which one gradually determines its nature? Given the size of vocabularies of most natural languages, the former approach does not recommend itself. A lexical field is first conceived as a lexical set whose referents (both concrete and abstract) make up a conceptual unit. As noted above, 'core' items at the centre of the field are most readily agreed upon, while peripheral items are seen differently by different people. Like their corresponding concepts, the referents are bound by a characteristic set of relationships both syntagmatic and paradigmatic. These relationships are embodied in the perception of the natural world (elements, organisms, colours) and of social phenomena evolved by man (hierarchical structure, warfare, religion). To go further and claim that such relationships exist (at least in the case of the natural world) outside the conceptual systems of the human mind would be to enter the

---

terdam: North-Holland, 1974); N. G. Komlev, *op. cit.*, pp. 139–142; and Suzanne Ohman, *op. cit.*, 123–134. A good summary may be found in John Lyons, *Semantics* (Cambridge: Cambridge University Press, 1977), I, pp. 267–268.

[9] Another way of looking at this is provided by Eugene A. Nida, *Componential Analysis of Meaning* (The Hague and Paris: Mouton, 1975), p. 32: "To determine the linguistic meaning of any form contrasts must be found, for there is no meaning apart from significant differences. If all the universe were blue, there would be no blueness, since there would be nothing to contrast with blue. The same is true for the meanings of words. They have meanings only in terms of systematic contrasts with other words which share certain features with them but contrast with them in respect to other features."

nominalist controversy.[10] This is quite unnecessary: for purposes of semantically based classification, it is requisite only that the relationships are perceived by the speakers of a natural language and are thereby reflected in the structure of that language.

Once an idea of the field is established, it is necessary to specify its chief divisions, the subfields which together f. m a coherent whole. Let us take the lexical field of "gar...s" as an example. Though largely self-contained, it has links with neighbouring fields such as "pastimes" and "amusements," and is itself a part of the larger conceptual domain we might label as "recreation." Within the lexical field "games" several groupings are immediately distinguishable whose extent and importance merit the label *subfield*, such as "players," "equipment," and "rules." Thus far, then, we can hypothesize that the field "games" exists, that it has several component parts, and that it is itself part of a larger conceptual complex ultimately falling under a superordinate at the top of the paradigm, probably labelled "social activity." So much can be determined without recourse to means more specialized than ordinary introspection. It is the classifier's specialized task to go further, to attempt to justify a more careful and detailed systematization of the lexical field and to display the relationships that exist between its constituent parts. Some methods developed for this purpose are discussed below and are embodied in the classified lexical field set out in chapter 3.

It is well at this point to state clearly a caution in regard to the "systematization" inherent in lexical classification. An approach such as this, based on general extralinguistic knowledge, is open to criticism. Baldinger, speaking of the classificatory system of Hallig and von Wartburg, criticizes it on

---

[10]Cf. John Lyons, *Introduction to Theoretical Linguistics* (Cambridge University Press, 1968), p. 443: "Acceptance of the structural approach in semantics has the advantage that it enables the linguist to avoid commitment on the controversial question of the philosophical and psychological status of 'concepts' or 'ideas.'"

the grounds of "naive realism" and deems it to represent nothing more than "a kind of man-in-the-street ontology *(Ontologie des Durchschnittsmenschen)."* [11] But what, it might be asked, serves better? *A priori* attempts to organize lexical fields on the basis of Trierian symmetry and discreteness are an impossibility. Experience shows that to approach a lexical field with a minutely detailed plan for the disposition of its subfields and divisions is to doom oneself to failure. Any classification must grow out of the relevant lexical field rather than be imposed upon it. Because lexical fields are reflections of the immensely complex conceptual systems of the human mind, it is futile to hope that a single plan of classification can be applied to any field at random. A classifier commences by setting to the task of sifting through the definitions of his lexical material and, bearing in mind his hypotheses about the extent and general shape of the field, works until recognizable patterns emerge. It must also be stressed that the classification of a lexical field, as the work of an individual, is bound to be idiosyncratic to a degree: "There is evidence for the view that semantic structures can be looked at in a variety of ways" [12] might seem a truism, but it is a truism of which we need frequent reminder. Put in a more uncompromising form, "it is impossible to have a semantic classification that is uniquely and eternally valid."[13]

Broadly speaking, lexical fields can be seen to possess three levels. The first level is that of subfields, the limited number of large groupings into which a lexical field is divided. In the classification of the religious lexis, five subfields were established.[14] The second level comprises the disposition of

---

[11]Baldinger, *op. cit.*, p. 119; see also Lyons (1977), *op. cit.*, I, pp. 300–301.

[12]Adrienne Lehrer, *op. cit.*, p. 18. Lest it be thought that this point is too obvious, Lehrer reminds us of the work of Trier, whose highly systematized approach to field theory attracted much serious attention earlier this century.

[13]A. Ballweg-Schramm, *op. cit.*, p. 462.

[14]For a discussion of the extent of these subfields, see chapter 2.

components and component groups within the subfields, and represents the 'great middle' of the lexical field. The third and lowest level covers close meaning relations between quasi-synonyms and cognate lexical items of different parts of speech. We can specify the levels at which systematization is likely to be of most use. Obviously, the initial determination of lexical fields, which involves the partition of the lexis, is aided by a moderate degree of syntagmatic systematization. Much of this will be based on common knowledge of the conceptual universe. But the most workable application of systematization is to be found at the lowest levels of the paradigm, in relationships between head noun and semantically dependent modifiers, between process or action nouns and their relevant verbs. At this level lexical relations are not necessarily much influenced by the nature of the lexical field of which they form a part: these relations are similar, if not identical, across a large part of the lexis. Of the parts of a lexical field, the great middle, representing the intermediate stages of hyponymic structure, remains most intractable. In chapter 2, the reader will find a discussion of various problems encountered in the disposition of material within a subfield (see, for example, the discussion of R4.16. BENEFICE on p. 69.) The variety of sense-relations at this level, a phenomenon not of language *per se* but of the conceptual system it represents, requires considerable flexibility on the part of the classifier, flexibility that at times appears to degenerate into inconsistency. [15] Yet only a high degree of flexibility permits a valid structuring of the middle level of a lexical field.

The overall organization of a lexical field, based on the relation of unilateral implication (that is, all material to some degree 'implies' the superordinate), is hierarchical, with degrees of subordination and stages of sub-grouping all organized under a superordinate term (in the present classification, "religion"). This superordinate is an abstraction in the sense that no imme-

---

[15] Baldinger, *op. cit.*, pp. 115–118.

diate hyponymic relation holds between it and all lexical constituents in its field. No one would argue that the sense of the
verbal noun *shriving* ("the hearing of confessions") classified
at R4.2.2.0. CONFESSION does not belong in a classification
of the lexical field "religion," but in what sense can *shriving*
be seen as a hyponym of *religion?* John Lyons, who is responsible for the introduction of the term *hyponym*, defines it first
as the relation of "inclusion" and then as that of "unilateral
implication."[16] Standard hyponymic relation is exemplified by
the set *tulip:flower*, where *tulip*, by virtue of the fact that it
denotes a certain kind of flower, is a hyponym of *flower*, the
general term or superordinate. No such direct relation obtains
between *shriving* and *religion*. At best, if one were to subject
shriving to componential analysis, one of its semantic components would be 'religion.' Because of the amount of conceptual
space between *shriving* and *religion*, 'religion' is characterized
as a redundant component of the former term, a component
unlikely to appear in immediate analysis, but present nonetheless in its conceptual structure.[17] This is true for all of the
lexical constituents of the lexical field "religion": though the
process of analysis in many cases would be time-consuming,
its product would be a set of component-strings each of which
contains the archisememe 'religion.' [18]

Because this relation of indirect or distant inclusion is quite
distinct from that between *tulip* and *flower* (which characterizes some well-defined middle level relations within a field), it
is better given a distinct label. *Hyponymy* is thus reserved for
relations of direct inclusion (*e.g. priest:clergyman*), whereas
the governing headword of a field is called an *archisememe*.
This allows the term *superordinate* to be confined to sets existing within a closely bounded semantic area, and suggests the

---

[16]Lyons (1968), *op. cit.*, pp. 453, 455.

[17]Cf. Geoffrey Leech, *op. cit.*, pp. 110–113.

[18]The term 'archisememe' is borrowed from the work of Pottier. See
Eugenio Coseriu and Horst Geckeler, *Trends in Structural Semantics*
(Tubingen: Gunter Narr, 1981), pp. 41–42.

differing natures of the two relations.

Under the abstract archisememe, then, exist a number of subfields. Both the number and nature of subfields are, as mentioned, a function of the constituents of the lexical field undergoing classification. We can immediately reject the extreme structuralist position (such as that espoused by Trier) that subfields, like the fields that they compose, should be of roughly uniform dimensions and should be completely self-contained and well-defined (*i.e.* each field possesses unambiguous boundaries which do not overlap with those of neighbouring fields). A cursory examination of any large lexical set will demonstrate the impossibility of maintaining this position. Boundaries of fields can be indistinct and fluctuating; lexical material, as mentioned, occasionally has good claim to a place in the structure of more than one field. [19] The five subfields of "religion" are distinct, yet each of them is related to and sometimes overlaps with the other four. Each required a structure developed from its own lexical constituents, though some low-level classificatory devices are common to all.

The lexical field "religion" covers a large conceptual space dealing with one of the most pervasive and enduring of social phenomena. It encompasses a wide range of referents, from the most abstract of theological concepts to simple concrete nouns referring to specific implements employed in ritual and ceremonial observances. Its five-part structure was determined after an examination of lexical material, and represents a notional approach, based on information provided by *OED* definitions of the lexical items, to the problem of establishing a coherent classificatory framework of the lexical field. The sizes of the five subfields vary widely: R4 WORSHIP, RITUAL, AND PRACTICE contains more than twice the number of lexical items of R2 CHURCHES, SECTS, AND RELIGIOUS MOVEMENTS. Their

---

[19] For a discussion of indeterminacy, see Baldinger, *op. cit.*, pp. 28–29, and John Lyons, *Language and Linguistics* (Cambridge: Cambridge University Press, 1981), p. 148.

hierarchical structures differ as well: the material in R5 ARTE-FACTS can, with the possible exception of R5.17. SYMBOL, be conveniently subsumed under the superordinate term "religious artefact," while no comparable superordinate exists for the constituents of R1 BELIEF, DOCTRINE, AND SPIRITUALITY.

These facts demonstrate the divergent nature of subfields within a lexical field, and argue for a view of fields that is flexible, that takes full cognizance of the influence which lexical constituents have on the shape of the field of which they are a part, and that recognizes that even apparently basic features of field construction (such as an identifiable superordinate) are inevitably a function of the relationships between constituents.

II. The role of the headword

One of the thornier problems in semantic theory concerns the relationship between a noun and its set of paronymic or derivative adjectives, adverbs, and verbs (*e.g. holiness, holy, holily, holy (vt)*).[20] The chief difficulty is to determine which part of speech is conceptually prime, and which may thus be said to have semantic primacy over its paronyms. Semantic primacy, it should be noted, is not necessarily a concomitant of etymological primacy; etymological base forms, from which paronyms are derived, are not necessarily semantic primes. *Holiness*, for example, is etymologically a derivative of *holy*, yet *holiness* possesses semantic primacy in the structure of this classification. It is also necessary to determine whether the relationship between semantic primacy and a part of speech is constant so that, for example, in any given set of paronyms, we can assume that one part of speech, be it noun, verb, or adjective, is

---

[20]Cf. George Miller, 'Semantic Relations among Words,' in Morris Halle, Joan Bresnan, and George A. Miller (eds.), *Linguistic Theory and Psychological Reality* (Cambridge, Massachusetts, and London: The MIT Press, 1978), p. 112; see also John Lyons (1977), *op. cit.*, I, pp. 230ff.

invariably the prime term from a conceptual standpoint.

If the problem is approached from the perspective of componential analysis, no answer is immediately forthcoming. All standard proposals for sets of semantic components involve entities which (though they are themselves abstractions) bear resemblance to the májor parts of speech, such as nouns, verbs, and adjectives.[21] In fact, it is not possible to construct formulæ describing even moderately complex concepts without the use of semantic components possessing the characteristics of particular parts of speech.

Another approach involves assigning primacy to whichever part of speech in a paronymic set is most frequently attested. Chafe advances this possibility: "there is a correlation between frequency of occurrence and the property of being basic or underived which reflects ultimately a greater cognitive salience of the state as opposed to the process."[22] The present classification embodies a system in which nouns constitute the set of headwords to which concepts denoted by other parts of speech are subordinated. An examination of the full complement of unindented headwords will show that there are no exceptions to this rule in any part of the classification. The reasons for the

---

[21] See John Lyons (1968) op. cit., pp. 470-482; Lyons (1977) op. cit., pp. 326, 328–335; Nida, op. cit., Anna Wierzbicka, Semantic Primitives (Frankfurt: Athenaum Verlag, 1977); Ruth M. Kempson, Semantic Theory (Cambridge: Cambridge University Press, 1977), pp. 18–20; Leech, op. cit., pp. 89–122; C. Kay and M. L. Samuels, 'Componential Analysis in Semantics: Its Validity and Applications,' Transactions of the Philological Society (1975), 49–79. A list of thirty-six primitives in Kay and Samuels contains fewer than ten 'nominal' primitives. Aside from this difficulty, componential analysis would seem to be ill-suited to a field such as "religion." Even proponents concede that its application to large concrete areas of the vocabulary is unprofitable, for it involves an "embarrassing" number of primitives (see Kay and Samuels, 50). There is the further difficulty of reaching agreement on the nature and validity of semantic components themselves; cf. Lyons (1968), pp. 472–475, and Lyons (1977), pp. 328–335.
[22] Wallace Chafe, Meaning and the Structure of Language (Chicago and London: The University of Chicago Press, 1970), p. 122.

employment of such a convention are twofold. First, *Historical Thesaurus* format requires the separation of parts of speech;[23] second, if separate parts of speech are to be coherently classified, a nominal headword provides the most capacious superordinate and thus arguably the most basic conceptual unit for fields of this nature. This is not necessarily the case for all lexical fields. Work in other fields suggests that the nature of the field determines the choice of headword. Adjectives or verbs may thus prove themselves more suitable for certain fields.

In earlier versions of the classification, limited experimentation in even closer association of paronyms was carried out, but this approach (which, for example, made an adjectival paronym immediately subordinate to the noun from which it is derived, and similarly immediately subordinated participial adjectives and verbal nouns derived from a verb to that verb) unsatisfactorily obscured the relations between paronymic and nonparonymic terms of the same part of speech. Disadvantages outweighed advantages; the necessity consistently to separate parts of speech became clear.

The conceptual primacy of the noun is by no means universally accepted. Chafe, for example, presents a hypothetical two-part structure of the conceptual universe, one part composed of states and events and represented by verbs, the other, represented by nouns, composed of things. "Of these two, the verb will be assumed to be central and the noun peripheral."[24] But his bias toward sentence semantics is displayed in one of the reasons he cites to support his assumption: "in every language a verb is present semantically in all but a few marginal utterances."[25] While the latter assertion is difficult to gainsay with regard to sentence semantics, the conceptual primacy of the verb is highly dubious in the context of lexical fields and the relations between field constituents. There is the additional

---

[23]Cf. chapter 2.
[24]Chafe, *op. cit.*, p. 96.
[25] *Ibid.*

difficulty that verbs tend to have a wider spread of meaning than nouns. Since the vast bulk of the lexicon denotes things as opposed to states, most lexical fields are composed of "thing-words." It is not, therefore, illogical to employ lexical items denoting things as the primary organizational tool in these fields.

In most areas of the present classification, then, the head-word reflects the noun's inherent conceptual primacy. *Holiness* is thus treated as conceptually more basic than *to consecrate, to sanctify, to holy,* though morphologically it is a de-adjectival abstract noun; similarly, *worship* is treated as more basic than *to worship.* A difficulty then arises in R4 WORSHIP, RITUAL, AND PRACTICE, which contains a large proportion of terms denoting processes and actions. In a subfield such as this it is arguable that in some specific instances verbs possess conceptual primacy over nouns (*e.g.* that the intransitive verb *cneowlian/kneel* is conceptually as well as etymologically more basic than the verbal noun *kneeling* or its latinate synonym *genuflexion*).[26] The number of such cases is limited. For purposes of retrievability and consistency, the sense-relation here has been inverted, and the conceptually derivative verbal noun made the headword, with the verb subordinated to it. This arrangement can perhaps be criticized for artificiality, but it represents the most satisfactory solution to the problem. It can thus be said that semantic primacy is not a characteristic of only one part of speech, and that the choice of nouns to provide headings for a classification involves in some instances modification of the sense-relations between various parts of speech. This further demonstrates a point made earlier in connection with the construction of lexical fields: only a flexible approach can cope with the variety of relations present in every lexical set.

If the noun is to serve as category headword, to what degree

---

[26]The verbal noun is attested only from the beginning of thirteenth century.

does nominal referential indeterminacy affect category structure? No claim is made in this classification for absolute synonymy between category constituents. Familiar difficulties in
defining synonymy have led certain scholars (such as Bloom-
field) to insist that synonymy does not exist, that natural languages permit no such redundancy. Nida, on the other hand,
offers a looser view of synonymy: synonyms, he says, are words
that "can be substituted one for the other in at least certain
contexts without significant changes in the conceptual content
of an utterance," though he admits that they "are almost never
substitutable one for the other in any and all contexts."[27] The
Bloomfieldian view is perhaps valid in its own terms, but it is
unnecessarily restricted, particularly for purposes of thesaurus
construction. If it were adopted, collocation of lexical items
with identical referents would not be possible because of varia-
tions in connotative meaning; even ordinary dictionary definitions would be difficult to achieve.[28] For purposes of classification, identity or near identity in cognitive meaning is sufficient
evidence of synonymy. Both introspection and experience suggest that cognitive synonymy is perceived to exist in varying
degrees. These degrees exist over a wide range of shades of
signification, on the one hand approaching (but only rarely
attaining) what Lyons calls "complete and total" synonymy,
which requires terms that are "interchangeable in all contexts"
and which manifest "equivalence of both cognitive and emotive sense,"[29] and on the other embodying a loose association
between closely related referents whose discreteness has been
blurred as a result of lack of knowledge of the referents or the
gradual vitiation of the relationship between a lexical item and
its referent. An example of nearly total synonymy is the re-

[27]Nida, *op. cit.*, p. 18.
[28]See, however, R. A. Waldron, *Sense and Sense Development* (London:
Andre Deutsch, 1979), pp. 55–58; Roy Harris, *Synonymy and Linguistic
Analysis* (Oxford: Basil Blackwell, 1973); Lyons (1968) *op. cit.*, pp. 446–
453; Baldinger, *op. cit.*, pp. 212-253.
[29]Lyons (1968), *op. cit.*, p.448.

lationship obtaining between *strinkle* (c1425–1559) and *dashel* (1502–1540), two of the twenty-three constituents of R5.8.3. ASPERGILLUM. The former item appears in English dialects of the North and East, the latter in the South and Southwest. As dialectal variants, the two cannot be said to be interchangeable in all contexts, though their cognitive meanings are identical, and the emotive (or associative) meanings, difficult to specify, are probably very limited. Closer to our own time, the musical terms *improvisation* and *extemporisation* exist in a relationship which also approaches the ideal of total synonymy. With regard to cognitive meaning, they are interchangeable in the lexical field "music," and, so far as the writer has been able to determine, manifest no difference of register (though they could well have varying connotations for individual speakers).[30] The more relaxed view of synonymy offered by Nida characterizes relations between constituents of most categories in this classification. *Divine, man in black,* and *snub-devil* all have the referent "cleric, clergyman," and thus the same cognitive meaning, leading to their classification in R3.2.0. CLERGYMAN GENERAL. Their connotative meanings, however, are quite distinct, and the contexts in which each might be found vary widely. There is, as well, the loose synonymy consequent upon misunderstanding of the discreteness of two referents. An example is found in vernacular usage with the occasional interchangeability of *priest* and *minister* (which in careful usage exist in paradigmatic relation to each other)

---

[30]There is evidence of the gradual restriction of each item to a region. British usage seems to favour *extemporisation,* while North American usage supports *improvisation* (as indeed does French for the cognate term). The objection has been raised that *improvisation* in British musical usage carries connotations of being 'makeshift' or 'second-best'; this is supported by the *Penguin English Dictionary,* which in part glosses *improvise* as "compose or perform according to spontaneous fancy without preparation" and *extemporise* as "compose and perform simultaneously." Yet it should be noted that several of the standard textbooks on the subject of improvisation in music employ the term *improvisation* (perhaps reflecting French usage) with no pejorative implication.

or *minister* and *clergyman* (where the first is a hyponym of the second). In sum, a broad view of synonymy is necessary for lexical classification. To attempt distinctions of Bloomfieldian severity in a classification of a lexical field would be nearly impossible even on a synchronic basis, and quite unattainable if the lexical sample is diachronic.[31] In their place, an extended view of cognitive synonymy provides a ready framework for the classification; it makes its construction possible and ensures a high degree of retrievability; nor is the user misled by false expectations.[32] What might be lost in a doomed quest for absolute synonymy within individual categories is gained in the creation of a usable framework.

If this is true of the nominal head category, it is also true of the subordinate adjectival, adverbial, and verbal categories. Such being the case, what can be said of the relationship between them? Implicit in the superordinate-hyponym relation is the notion of governance; the headword governs to some extent the interpretation of lexical material subsumed under it. This concept of governance is made explicit in the present classification by the category tags which serve to describe the contents of a particular line and to locate that concept within the structure of a category. No claim to an unvarying relationship between 'governor' and 'governed' can be made. As has been demonstrated above, the constituents of the head category themselves exist in varying relations to one another. For subordinate parts of speech this is equally the case, if not more so. An example will be found at R1.6.0. HOLINESS. There

---

[31] Cf. Stephen Ullmann, *The Principles of Semantics* (Glasgow: Jackson, 1951), p. 154: "In semantics, the existence of spatio-temporal regularities is in most cases extremely hard to demonstrate, and their very possibility is still doubted by many scholars.... One might... say that if diachronistic linguistics at large is isolative in its methods, then diachronistic semantics is even more so, to the point of becoming outright atomistic."

[32] Lyons (1968) *op. cit.*, p.447: "It may be worth pointing out that the practical utility of reference works such as *Roget's Thesaurus* depends upon a prior knowledge of the language on the part of the person using them."

are fourteen constituents in the nominal head category. In the main subordinate adjectival category, labelled CHAR BY, there are forty-three constituents. Of the fourteen head category constituents, five are derived from the *holy/hallow* base, seven from the *sancti-/sacro-* base, and two from *blessed.* In addition, there are four adjectival constituents from disparate sources, including a borrowing from the Moslem tradition *(Kramat).* The basic cognitive meanings of both nouns and adjectives are sufficiently clear to allow their placement in the present categories. But there are a number of sense-components in the category which are not shared by all constituents. *Sacrosanctity,* for example, carries in some contexts the connotation of "inviolability," and can thus be seen as a slightly 'stronger' synonym for *holiness.*[33] Thus *sacrosanctity* cannot be said to maintain a superordinate relation with constituents of the subordinate adjectival category which is identical to that maintained by *holiness.* Each exists in a set of idiosyncratic relations with adjectival constituents; this set fluctuates over time and, indeed, from speaker to speaker.

Such a variety of relations within the confines of a single small category does not invalidate the entire classificatory procedure. It is salutary to repeat that an attempt to attain perfect one-to-one correspondence, to eliminate all ambiguity from the categories, is bound to fail. The relations between constituents of head and subordinate categories are fluid, reflecting the nature of the conceptual domain. What this classification provides is a system that combines an adequate degree of specificity, allowing fine distinctions to be made where they are possible, with the adaptability and capacity required by the lexis. The degree of specificity of the present classification far exceeds that found, for example, in Roget; equally, it avoids the overfine distinctions that characterize analyses of very small lexical samples (*e.g.* those of Trier on the intellectual field in Middle High German, or the many studies of

---

[33]See also the notes in chapter 4 to this part of the classification.

limited sets of kinship terms carried out by anthropological linguists) and which would be of little use if applied to a sample comprising several thousand constituents.

III. Subordination within categories

Among the most widely applicable features of the present classification are those found at the lowest levels of the hierarchy. These low-level (or microclassificatory) devices embody several basic sense-relations characteristic of many areas of the vocabulary of natural languages: agent noun, derivative adjectival and adverbial forms, performative verbs. So small is the amount of semantic space between a head noun and these subordinate concepts that the nature of the lexical field impinges little on their relations. They are a feature of the present classification most likely to be of use in classifying other lexical fields, and for this reason some discussion of them will be useful.[34]

Since microclassificatory devices are concerned with sense-relations rather than semantic components, the difficulty of defining the nature of semantic components or 'particles of meaning' is avoided. In some ways the devices employed in the classification are similar to parts of Carnap's theory of meaning postulates, which, according to Lyons, "can be defined for lexemes as such, without making any assumptions about atomic concepts, and ... can be used to give a partial account of the sense of a lexeme without the necessity of providing a total analysis."[35] Hyponymy is the governing sense-relation in Carnap's theory: it is hyponymic relations that the present microclassificatory devices display.

Basic hyponymic relations are those characterized as "kind of (x)" or "part of (x)," where (x) represents the superordinate.

---

[34]For an explanation of the system of full stops employed in the classification to display lexical subordination at low levels, see chapter 2.

[35]John Lyons, *Language, Meaning and Context* (London: Fontana, 1981), p. 93; see also Geoffrey Leech, *op. cit.*, pp. 117–118.

Patriarch is thus a hyponym of *clerical superior* by virtue of the fact that a patriarch is a kind of clerical superior. In the classification of the religious lexis, this basic hyponymic relation is usually placed so as to be a part of the system of numbered category heads. "Patriarch," together with "pope," "cardinal," "archbishop," and others are assigned numbered categories (R3.2.1.1. – R3.2.1.12.) under the superordinate category R3.2.1.0. CLERICAL SUPERIOR GENERAL. In some instances, however, the basic hyponymic relation is located at a lower level in the classification, and is thus covered by an unnumbered category tag specifying the kind or part of the superordinate term referred to. At R1.1.10. HERESY, for example, the three lexical items *buggery, buggerage,* and *archheresy* all share the referent "extreme heresy," by definition a hyponym of "heresy" itself. The three items are thus specified as hyponyms of *heresy* and are classified as immediately subordinate to the numbered head category, before personal nouns such as those specified as P CHAR BY. (If the number of kinds of head concept is large, a separate subordinate category is established; see chapter 2.)

First among the nouns referring to persons is the sense-relation labelled by the category tag P CHAR BY, "person characterized by (x)," where (x) is the concept contained in the headword category. Together with its parallel subordinates P PERF ("person performing") and P UNDERGOING ("person undergoing"), it subsumes most of the nouns in the classification referring to persons. The sense-relation is that of the embodiment or manifestation in a person of the concept carried in the superordinate category. At R1.7.1. SANCTIMONIOUSNESS, for example, among the nineteen constituents of the line labelled P CHAR BY is the standard noun *hypocrite,* defined as "one who falsely professes to be virtuously or religiously inclined." *Hypocrisy* is defined as "the assuming of a false appearance of virtue or goodness, with a dissimulation of real character or inclinations, especially in respect of religious life or belief."

Viewed from the standpoint of their sense-components, these definitions are nearly identical, with that of *hypocrite* carrying an added marker for the concept of "person." The category tag P CHAR BY is a transform of this relation, for it makes explicit the semantic primacy of abstract concept over the embodiment of that concept in a person. In this case "hypocrisy" is the governing concept; P CHAR BY indicates merely that the constituents of the line it heads are personal embodiments of the governing concept.

This is one of the most basic sense-relations; P CHAR BY specifies it adequately, without unnecessarily limiting its scope or applicability. Such is also the case with the agent noun tag P PERF (*e.g. propitiator* under the headword *propitiation*) and the patient noun tag P UNDERGOING (*e.g. catechumen* under the headword *catechesis*). These are found largely in R4 WORSHIP, RITUAL, AND PRACTICE, with its high proportion of action and process nouns, and often co-occur. In R4.1.2.0. BAPTISM, for example, they specify two of the five lines containing nouns which refer to people subordinate to the head concept "baptism." Personal agent nouns usually exist in greater number than personal patient nouns, a fact indicating the greater conceptual prominence of the former. Scattered throughout the classification are several dozen other personal noun tags, some of which occur only a few times and some of which are unique. In the case of R4.2.1.0. BAPTISM, for example, there are additional lines labelled CANDIDATE FOR PERSON SPONSORING (A) PERSON UNDERGOING and PERSON DEFERRING B [*i.e.* "*baptism*"] UNTIL HIS DEATHBED.[36] Of these, the last is unique, the second highly restricted, and the first, though not rare, is not widespread. (In the fifteen-thousand item religious vocabulary, the category tag CANDIDATE FOR occurs approximately half a dozen times.) Another example of

---

[36]A category tag like this one with the head concept redundantly carried in it (shown in the classification by means of a single upper-case character) is *ipso facto* unlikely to have parallels elsewhere.

the effect of head concept meaning on low-level sense-relations is found at R4.4. GOOD WORKS, where the noun *workmonger* and three cognitive synonyms (referent: "person expecting to be justified by good works") are constituents of the line P EXPECTING TO BE JUSTIFIED BY. This sense-relation has only one or two analogues in the lexical field of religion; it is unlikely that many further analogues will be found outside that field. Such a phenomenon at low levels is the unavoidable concomitant of variety in sense-relations, which itself reflects the variety of extralinguistic activities.

Among subordinate categories devoted to non-personal noun forms outside the basic hyponymic link "kind of" or "part of" discussed earlier, the semantic spread is somewhat wider, owing to a considerably greater number of possible sense-relations. The common sense-relation here is "y char by (z)," where (z) represents the concept contained in the head category (*e.g.* R1.1.10. HERESY, the tag CHURCH/SECT CHAR BY). Such a link is, of course, heavily affected by the nature of the head concept, and the classification shows a large number of unduplicated category tags of this kind. Of even greater variety are the unique non-personal noun categories associated with some abstract head concepts. Under the superordinate "salvation" (R1.12.0.), for example, subordinate non-personal noun categories include TESTING OF P FOR WORTHINESS OF, INWARD KNOWLEDGE OF, TENDENCY TO PROMOTE, PREDESTINATION TO, and several more. Inevitably the tags reflect *OED* definitions, but limited experimentation proved the difficulty of reducing such links to a more standardized calculus or set of formulæ, both because of the variety of these sense-relations (of which the examples provided are only a small range), and because of the danger of twisting their meanings. At this level, small gains made in the area of uniformity are more than offset by increased complexity of the category tag and a consequent obscuring of the sense. Perhaps the danger lies not in the presence of a large number of non-personal subordinate category tags in the classification as a whole, but in their proliferation under the governance of a single headword. A large number of parallel subordinates of this kind presents to the reader an unwieldy clump of material whose sole justification for collocation is its several links with the head concept. Under the headword *baptism* at R4.2.1.0., for example, the following non-personal category tags appear:

Baptism
.rite of
.rite preceding
.consecration of font prior to
.consecration of water used in
.time of
.vow of
.renunciation of devil, world, and flesh at
.spiritual relation between sponsor and baptizee at

With the exception of the first two category tags, it is difficult to establish anything other than an arbitrary order among them, given the disparity of their sense-components. The list leaves an impression of shapelessness. This example, however, is an unusual one. From the evidence of the religious vocabulary, an unstructured complement of subordinate categories rarely exceeds five or six (except in R5 ARTEFACTS, where a different set of sense-relations prevents confusion) and does not represent an impenetrable tangle.

A similar situation characterizes subordinate adjectival categories.[37] Two category tags (CHARACTERISTIC OF and CHARACTERIZED BY) between them subsume the greater proportion of adjectival material throughout the classification. The balance is classified under a variety of tags, some of moderate

---

[37]In addition to standard treatments on relations between adjectives and their base nouns (*e.g.* Lyons 1977), an interesting account may be found in C. S. Lewis, *Studies in Words* (Cambridge: Cambridge University Press, 1967), p. 27.

frequency and some unique. The two main adjectival tags are discussed first, and a consideration of some of the less well-attested follows.

CHARACTERISTIC OF and CHARACTERIZED BY occur with roughly equivalent frequency in most parts of the classification. Few *OED* definitions of adjectives contain either phrase; for the most part the dictionary prefers the description "of or pertaining to." CHARACTERISTIC OF signifies that relation in a looser way and at the same time covers similar adjectival sense-relations. One of the most basic in the conceptual structure, the relation is used for both abstract and concrete areas of the vocabulary. Its simplest function is seen in cases such as the noun/adjective pair *transept/transeptal* (R5.4.8.), where the adjective carries almost exactly the same sense-components as its base noun, with an additional marker distinguishing it as an adjective (another way of describing this is to remember that the adjective in most if not all conceivable uses can be replaced by substituting the noun used attributively, *i.e. transept-X*). Without commencing a disquisition upon the symbiotic bond between syntax and semantics, we can see that this sense-relation, as well as being basic, is one of the closest possible, with very little semantic space separating the two terms. In addition to the concrete areas of the lexis, it is present in abstract areas, particularly those covering actions or processes. At R4.8.2., for example, there is the pair *propitiation/propitiatory*; once again, in most contexts the adjectival form can be replaced by the noun used attributively without damage either to meaning or to syntax.[38]

At another level of abstraction, CHARACTERIZED BY replaces CHARACTERISTIC OF as the principal adjectival tag. The reason lies with the concept denoted by the base noun: we speak not so much of the abstract concept as of things or persons who manifest that abstraction. Thus the common ad-

---

[38]Admittedly the substitution is not felicitous from the stylist's point of view.

jectival sense-relation in these cases is not centred on the base noun to the extent seen with CHARACTERISTIC OF. In conceptual terms, weighting is given not to the abstract concept but to its modifying effect on the entity to which it is applied. In R1.8.2.0. UNSPIRITUALITY, for example, there are classified under the adjectival tag CHAR BY some thirty-nine items of wide etymological provenance, none of which can be said to stand in a sense-relation to the superordinate that could be labelled CHARACTERISTIC OF. The semantic focus is on the relationship between object noun and relevant abstraction, not on the abstract concept itself, as is the case with adjectival items subsumed under the tag CHARACTERISTIC OF. This may be demonstrated by attempting substitution: *unspirituality-man* is an unsatisfactory replacement for *unspiritual man* on both syntactical and semantic grounds.

Though it is not a common occurrence, both sense-relations can exist under a single superordinate. Thus, in R1.12.0. SALVATION, *redemptional* and *soterial* refer directly to the concept of "salvation, redemption," while adjectives such as *safe, chosen,* and *elect* refer to entities (in this case, persons or groups of persons) which partake of or are characterized by the head concept.

What of other adjectival sense-relations? Outside the preceding two standard classes exist several, the natures of which are responsive to the superordinate concept. Depending on the class, the constituents are morphologically formed from ordinary adjectival suffixes (*-able, -izing*) or are the product of an independent adjective combined with the superordinate term (*e.g. sin-sick* "sick with sin" and *sin-wood* "mad with sin" in R1.10.0.). Some are the result of compression (*e.g. unreclaimed* "unreclaimed from sin").

The variety is sufficiently wide to enable a parallel to be drawn with subordinate noun classes: though most of the material can be subsumed under a limited number of constantly recurring category tags, the remainder is spread un-

evenly across a number of rare or unique category tags. Part
of this is due to the nature of the superordinate term, but a
more productive source of adjectival variation is, as mentioned,
the possibility of combining almost any neutral adjective or
adverb with a noun or another adjective to produce a new
compound. Such is the case with the "sin" adjectives mentioned above and with adjectives such as *pan-ecclesiastical* and
pan-denominational ("representing an entire church or denomination"), *intra-ecclesiastical* ("existing or occurring within a
church"), and *mystico-religious* ("mystically religious"). Again,
the question of meaning might almost be seen to be secondary:
many such terms express concepts which are usually expressed
phrasally, thus making them mere stylistic or syntactic variants. But the fact remains that they must be classified as
adjectives, and they thereby account for some of the rarer category tags.

Adverbial categories are of a much narrower scope, and
can be subsumed, almost without exception, under the standard tag IN MANNER OF.[39] This tag echoes the *OED* formulaic
gloss on adverbs, "in an *x* manner," where *x* is the related base
adjective. *Mystically*, for example, is subordinated to the superordinate *mysticism* at R1.8.5.0.; its full category description
is "in the manner of mysticism," which reflects the *OED* gloss
"in a mystic manner or sense." Because this sense-relation
is constant to a high degree, it might be asked why, given the
system of subordination in the classification, could adverbs not
be made semantically subordinate to their corresponding adjectives, instead of being made parallel subordinates with the
adjectives under the superordinate. There is a case to be made
for this approach; in addition to the problem of morphologically unrelated items, however, a policy of strict separation of

---

[39]Cf. R. H. Robins, *op.cit.*, p.124. Speaking of Port Royal grammatical
systems, Robins says that "structural interpretations of the functions of
certain classes of words may be noticed. Adverbs are no more than an
abbreviation of a prepositional phrase (*sapienter*, wisely = *cum sapienta*,
with wisdom)."

parts of speech prevents it. Like the relation between many adjectives subsumed under the tag CHARACTERISTIC OF and their corresponding nouns, the relation between most adverbs and their companion adjectives is very close.

Verbal categories in the classification further bear out the pattern established by other parts of speech: a great majority of verbs are classifiable under several recurring tags. Chief among these are TO PERFORM and TO UNDERGO, indicating respectively the active, performative function and the passive, patient function. They account for a high proportion of verbs in the present classification, and adequately locate these terms within the conceptual framework of a category. The sense-relations they represent are so transparent as to require little comment. Other verbal categories are, however, worthy of note. Among these are the causative (category tags TO CAUSE, TO PRODUCE) and the converse (category tag TO REVERSE). Causative verbs in this classification most often are associated with abstract concepts such as spiritual states or experiences. In R1.8.4. RAPTURE, for example, the transitive verb *ecstasy* is a subordinate causative verb (category tag TO PRODUCE) whose putative non-personal subject is regarded as inducing the state or experience referred to by the head concept "rapture." A similar sense-relation, except that both subject and object are usually personal, is that indicated by the category tag TO IMBUE WITH *(e.g.* the transitive verb *hereticate* in R1.1.10.). In some instances in R1 and in many in R2, it refers to the processes of inculcating a particular dogma (active) or subscribing to that dogma (passive). This sense-relation is attested in most of the lexically well-represented denominations found in R2.

The privative (TO DEPRIVE OF) is found in both abstract and concrete areas of the vocabulary; constituents of these classes are characterized by the standard privative prefixes *un-* and *de-*.

Within the framework for nouns, adjectives, adverbs, and

verbs outlined above, opposition has been found a satisfactory device only when treated with a degree of freedom.[40]
To employ opposition rigidly results in a classification riddled
with unnecessary gaps and which, though perhaps better constructed on logical grounds, insufficiently reflects the real pattern of sense-relations in the lexis. Morphologically-embodied
opposition (*i.e.* negatives and privatives formed morphologically from a neutral or positive base form, such as *unholy*
from *holy* and *unspiritual* from *spiritual*, rather than by means
of non-specific syntactical devices) occurs unevenly. In abstract areas of the vocabulary, opposition is indicated both
morphologically and by means of morphologically unrelated
pairs (*e.g. belief/atheism, believer/atheist*). Morphologically-
embodied opposition is easily dealt with in the present classificatory structure through use of standard negative and privative
category tags such as NOT and ABSENCE OF. This approach
is most satisfactory in cases in which the negative member of
the pair is conceptually less prominent and lexically less well-
attested than the semantically neutral or positive superordinate term. Where such is not the case, and the negative term
is well attested or has special significance, a separate subordinate category for the negative has been established. Without
disrupting the overall set of sense-relations, this method allows
a cluster composed of a negative or privative concept and its
accompanying lexical items a separate node close to the overall superordinate. Examples of this arrangement are found at
R1.6.3. UNHOLINESS and R1.8.2.0. UNSPIRITUALITY.

Thus far we have considered only bipolar pairs of opposition. Complex conceptual systems often have a number of steps
between the two extremes, the system thus forming a gradable
scalar structure.[41] Since relations between constituents of a

---

[40]On opposition, see Leech, *op. cit.*, pp. 99–108; Lyons (1977) *op. cit.*,
I, pp. 270–287; Nida, *op. cit.*, pp. 107–110; C. K. Odgen, *Opposition*
(Bloomington: Indiana University Press, 1967).

[41]A standard example of scalar progression is of course the base, comparative, and superlative forms of adjectives. See Lyons (1977) *op. cit.*, I,

scalar system are entirely dependent on the concepts contained therein, no single pattern can be put forward as a model to which all should conform. Indeed, idiomatic reactions to even a single set of concepts could result in widely varying orderings. R1.1.0. FAITH to R1.1.12.0. ATHEISM is a loose scalar system subsuming, on the one hand, lexical material referring to religious belief, and, on the other, a complete lack of it. Within these boundaries are ranged concepts covering kinds of faith (codified, proper, and dubious), faith perverted to some degree (free-thought, superstition), and faith seen to be unambiguously perverse (heresy, paganism). Few of these are clear-cut: there is considerable semantic overlapping in some areas, making possible the interchange of some items.

The classificatory devices discussed above have demonstrated themselves capable of dealing with the bulk of the material in the lexical field "religion," and promise to be of use in the classification of other fields. Nonetheless, there remains a residue of lexical material which is not adequately treated by techniques. Below, two further devices aimed at this residue are outlined.

IV. Two other low-level classificatory devices

a. 'Family tree' and 'locomotive' progressions

Related to the idea of a scalar progression is the 'family tree' or genealogical method of ordering certain lexical sets. It applies to material denoting groups and movements which have an historical relationship with one another, and as such forms the basic classificatory framework of R2 CHURCHES, SECTS, AND RELIGIOUS MOVEMENTS and R3.3.3. RELIGIOUS ORDERS. These semantic areas are almost entirely given over to proper

pp. 271–279.

nouns. From a conceptual standpoint, proper nouns are very nearly impossible to classify, owing to their lack of ordinary conceptual content.[42] The classifier is forced to rely on extralinguistic criteria of which, in this case, only historical fact provides a set of relationships on which a classification can be based. As is discussed in chapter 2, historical data on the provenance of the various groups serves to provide a set of 'genealogical' superordinates and subordinates in which the lexical material can be located. Vertical and lateral relations are set out plainly, demonstrating the flexibility of the classificatory system. In a complete classification of the lexis, sets such as this will appear with some regularity (*e.g.* in the field of politics); the present system would seem to be capable of ordering this material in an easily retrievable yet not counterintuitive form.

Another area unamenable to a strictly conceptual approach is that comprising parts of a concrete entity.[43] In the classification of the lexis, this type of part-whole relation is represented by lexical material referring to buildings and parts of buildings. Unlike proper nouns, most lexical items denoting parts of buildings are at least quasi-generic, and thus possess identifiable meaning. The difficulty they present is of a different kind. What are the relationships between building parts, and can these relationships be used to form a classificatory frame-

---

[42] Nida (*op. cit.*, p. 25) says proper nouns possess "only reference and not meaning." For a discussion of semantic difficulties associated with proper nouns, see J. R. Searle, 'The problem of proper names,' in Danny Steinberg and Leon Jakobovits (eds.), *Semantics* (Cambridge: Cambridge University Press, 1971), pp. 134–141. Also of value are Paul Ziff, *Semantic Analysis* (Ithaca, New York: Cornell University Press, 1960), pp. 86–87 (Ziff casts doubt on whether proper nouns can be regarded as words at all); Benson Mates, *On the Semantics of Proper Names* (Lisse: Peter de Ridder, 1975); and N. G. Komlev, *op. cit.*, pp. 102–103.

[43] The human body represents a special case. On the classification of body parts, see Irené A. W. Wotherspoon, *A Notional Classification of Two Parts of English Lexis* (University of Glasgow B. Litt. thesis, 1969), chapters 3 and 4.

work? A complete set of relationships is difficult to produce, even for the most common lexical constituents. If the parts of an average house are listed, for example, it is easy to group items such as "kitchen" and "dining room," but it is difficult to determine a comparable link between "dining room" and "sitting room," or between "hallway" and "bedroom." If on such a simple level consistent and useful relationships are not evident, the difficulties are compounded when a classifier seeks to deal with larger or less familiar structures.

Church buildings are both larger, less familiar, and more complex. Classification based on function is unworkable owing to the fact that most areas in church buildings can be employed for more than one purpose, and few functions are confined exclusively to a single well-defined area (in other words, there is no constant relationship between function and area of building). Of methods for organizing their many parts into a coherent framework, the 'locomotive' appeared to be the least of possible evils.[44] It represents a progression in which distinct building parts, accorded equivalent status in the category (*i.e.* they are assigned the same degree of subordination), are classified in the order they might be encountered on a walk around the building. Beneath them are subsumed only 'parts of parts' (*e.g.* parts of an altar are subordinated to *altar*) and lexical offshoots formed by parts of speech such as adjectives.

There are several possible objections to this method. It is indeed arbitrary, in that another person might make his progression differently, thus altering the order of the subordinate categories. Further, building parts away from the main area of the structure (in the case of a church, for example, upper parts such as the triforium, and neighbouring or associated structures such as church houses and chapter houses) are not easily integrated into the progression. These objections have weight, but it appears that if 'locomotive' organization is not used in these cases, only conceptual alphabetization remains.

---

[44]Cf. Miller's notion of locative inclusion (Miller, *op. cit.*, p. 79).

Like the problems presented by proper nouns, those posed by parts of specialized concrete entities will recur with varying frequency throughout the lexis. The 'locomotive' principle, as set out in the present classification, is a useful means of dealing with these problems.

b. Conceptual alphabetization

There remain restricted areas of the lexis where any sort of a conceptually-based, historically-based, or extralinguistically-based classification is simply not applicable, because no links exist between the lexical items in these areas other than the underlying one relating them as kinds or varieties of their superordinate. Such is the case in R1.2.1.4. BIBLICAL PLACES, R1.6.1.1. PARTICULAR SAINTS, R2.2.5. VARIOUS (ANTI-)CHRISTIAN SECTS AND MOVEMENTS, and several other categories in the present classification. In these areas the semantic relations might be said to exist (returning to the metaphor employed earlier) in two rather than three dimensions: particular saints, for example, are subsumable under the superordinate "saint," but their relations with one another, if they exist at all, are indeterminate and of no value to the classifier. The same difficulty obtains in R4.15. OTHER PRACTICES, a list of actions which have no appreciable relation with preceding categories in R4.

Such categories represent miscellaneous lexical material, a sprinkling of items with a clear link to the overall archisememe (in this case, "religion"), but with no place in the general classificatory framework.[45] They are fewest in conceptual fields covering well-defined and highly-systematized entities of lim-

---

[45]For a transformational-generative approach to this difficulty, see J. J. Katz and J. A. Fodor, 'The Structure of a Semantic Theory,' *Language* 30 (1963), 170–210. Katz and Fodor propose the term *marker* for those semantic components sufficiently systematic to form part of a framework, and the term *distinguisher* for random components. The dichotomy has been roundly attacked from both within and without the generative camp.

ited extent; in large lexical fields comprising material from both abstract and concrete sources, they are a contained but persistent problem.

It appears that the only adequate method of dealing with such essentially miscellaneous material is conceptual alphabetization. It allows for limited low-level subordination, so that an alphabetized concept can have its own small complement of related terms (usually paronyms) expressing adjectival or verbal functions. Items in a category of alphabetized concepts are parallel subordinates. The method of ordering facilitates retrieval but in itself implies no subordination. It will be seen that this method of organization can provide but little information about constituent lexical items, simply because the sense-relations between them are tenuous. This does not mean, however, that categories organized this way are of no value: on the contrary, each category contains the available complement of synonymous or quasi-synonymous items, and their interest is increased further when the lexis being classified is drawn from a diachronic sample, as in the present classification.

V. Lexical gaps

A classification based on successive hyponymic subordination can be expected to contain some lexical gaps, defined as "the absence of a lexeme at a particular place in the structure of a lexical field."[46] The possibility of their presence is increased by the fact that the *OED* is restricted in its coverage to the written as opposed to the spoken language. An appreciable number of lexical items might thus have eluded the lexicographers because they are unattested in print. These facts notwithstanding, the total number of lexical gaps in the present classification, representing probably no more than a half of one per cent of the number of category tags (excepting gaps in parts of R2, which

---

[46]Lyons (1977) *op. cit.*, I, p. 301.

are discussed below), is very low. A common source of lexical gaps is the practice of maintaining relatively consistent classificatory structures at low levels. In the subordinate category R1.1.12.1. ATHEIZATION, for example, the two constituents are the noun *atheizer* and the transitive verb *atheize*. There are no attested occurrences of the process noun *atheization*, yet it occurs in the heading of the category because it is necessary to sustain the pattern of process nouns in this section of R1 (*e.g. paganization, sectarianizing*, both of which are attested) and provides the superordinate to which its paronyms can be subordinated. No damage is done to the fabric of sense-relations: unattested forms occur when required in the metalanguage of category tags.

By morphological and semantic criteria there is no reason why *atheization* should not occur. Its absence may be due to its absence in print, as mentioned above, or by an omission in *OED* sampling. An example of a genuine gap in the vocabulary (at least to the writer's knowledge) can be found at the head of R4.1.3. PARTS OF SERVICE, where there is no discoverable term denoting the concept "any part of a church service," thus depriving this category of a lexical realization of its superordinate concept.

The largest number of gaps occurs in parts of R2 CHURCHES, SECTS, AND RELIGIOUS MOVEMENTS, where the attempt to provide a consistent class of category heads, in this case the *-ism* nouns denoting a particular doctrine or group, resulted in some unnecessary lacunæ. As is pointed out in chapter 2, many of these groups failed to reach a status deserving of the importance signified by the *-ism* suffix, and are attested only in the form of personal nouns (*-ist, -ian*, etc.). The entirely alphabetical section R2.2.5. VARIOUS (ANTI-) CHRISTIAN SECTS AND MOVEMENTS is designed to avoid most of these gaps by allowing either the personal noun or the group name to serve as headword.

This concludes the general discussion of field construction

and classificatory devices. Chapter 2 provides a description of the composition of the five subfields in the classification of the religious lexis, and an account of the system of category tags employed to display hyponymic relations and semantic subordination.

Chapter Two
Introduction to the
Classification

The present classification of the English religious lexis is drawn from the *Historical Thesaurus of English* archive maintained in the Department of English Language, Glasgow University.[47] This archive employs as its temporary system of ordering the nine hundred and ninety classes of *Roget's Thesaurus of English Words and Phrases*.[48] Sixteen classes are primary sources

---

[47] On the need for a historical thesaurus, see Gustaf Stern, *Meaning and Change of Meaning* (Göteborg: Elanders Boktrycheri Aktiebolag, 1931), p. 3; Stephen Ullmann, *Semantics* (Oxford: Basil Blackwell, 1962), pp. 254–256; and M. L. Samuels, 'The Role of Functional Selection in the History of English,' *Transactions of the Philological Society* (1965), 15–40. For an account of the Glasgow *Historical Thesaurus* project, see L. W. Collier and C. J. Kay, 'The Historical Thesaurus of English,' *Dictionaries* 2/3 (1982/3), 80–89; J. A. Roberts, 'The English Historical Thesaurus,' *Nottingham Linguistic Circular* 11 (1982), 20-28; C. J. Kay, 'The Historical Thesaurus of English,' in R. R. K. Hartmann (ed.), *LEXeter '83 Proceedings* (Tubingen: Max Niemeyer, 1984), pp. 87–91; C. J. Kay and T. J. Chase, 'Constructing a Thesaurus Database,' *Journal of Linguistic and Literary Computing,* (forthcoming).

[48] Robert Dutch (ed.), *Roget's Thesaurus of English Words and Phrases* (London: Longman, 1962; rev. 1982 by S. M. Lloyd). For the purposes of *Historical Thesaurus* classificatory work, an additional category (numbered 1001) has been established, subsuming lexical material referring to parts of the body.

for material in the lexical field of religion, *viz.:*

- 973 Religion
- 974 Irreligion
- 975 Revelation
- 976 Orthodoxy
- 977 Heterodoxy
- 978 Sectarianism
- 979 Piety
- 980 Impiety
- 981 Worship
- 982 Idolatry
- 985 Churchdom
- 986 Clergy
- 987 Laity
- 988 Rituals
- 989 Canonicals
- 990 Temple

In addition, a substantial number of non-religious classes have been searched for religious material assigned to them because of close semantic links (*e.g.* "sin" in 616 EVIL and 934 WICKEDNESS; "penance" in 939 PENITENCE and 941 ATONEMENT). Such a search was required not only because of the varying approaches to Roget taken by *Historical Thesaurus* compilers, but also because of the indeterminacy of parts of Roget's classification. The additional classes are:

74 Assemblage	84 Unconformity	85 Number
86 Numeration	88 Unity	90 Duality
91 Duplication	92 Bisection	93 Triality

94 Triplication	95 Trisection	96 Quaternity
97 Quadruplication	98 Quadrisection	99 Five and over
102 Fraction	132 Young person	133 Old person
160 Power	164 Production	183 Space
184 Region	185 Place	186 Situation
191 Inhabitant	192 Abode	194 Receptacle
218 Support	222 Crossing	226 Covering
228 Dressing	247 Angularity	255 Concavity
258 Smoothness	259 Roughness	267 Land travel
268 Traveller	269 Water travel	270 Mariner
271 Aeronautics	272 Transference	273 Carrier
274 Vehicle	275 Ship	281 Direction
301 Food	333 Friction	335 Fluidity
337 Liquefaction	339 Water	340 Air
341 Moisture	343 Ocean	344 Land
345 Gulf	346 Lake	347 Marsh
348 Plain	349 Island	350 Stream
351 Conduit	352 Wind	359 Mineral
360 Life	361 Death	362 Killing
363 Corpse	364 Interment	365 Animality
369 Animal husbandry	370 Agriculture	371 Mankind
372 Male	373 Female	379 Heat
380 Cold	381 Calefaction	382 Refrigeration
383 Furnace	384 Refrigerator	385 Fuel
386 Taste	387 Insipidity	388 Pungency
389 Condiment	390 Savouriness	391 Unsavouriness
392 Sweetness	393 Sourness	410 Melody
411 Discord	412 Music	413 Musician
414 Musical instruments	420 Luminary	441 Spectator
442 Optical instrument	447 Intellect	449 Thought
451 Idea	461 Experiment	465 Measurement
485 Belief	486 Unbelief	487 Credulity
500 Sage	531 Messenger	534 Teaching
537 Teacher	539 School	547 Indication
551 Representation	553 Painting	554 Sculpture

555 Engraving	556 Artist	589 Book
594 Drama	615 Good	616 Pursuit
644 Goodness	645 Badness	646 Perfection
647 Imperfection	648 Cleanness	649 Uncleanness
651 Disease	655 Deterioration	658 Remedy
665 Danger signal	686 Agent	687 Workshop
689 Management	690 Director	692 Council
708 Party	709 Dissension	710 Concord
713 Defence	718 War	721 Submission
722 Combatant	723 Arms	727 Success
728 Failure	729 Trophy	733 Authority
741 Master	761 Request	764 Promise
789 Thief	790 Booty	791 Barter
792 Purchase	793 Sale	794 Merchant
795 Merchandise	796 Mart	797 Money
809 Price	837 Amusement	844 Ornamentation
866 Repute	868 Nobility	894 Marriage
895 Celibacy	897 Benevolence	898 Malevolence
899 Malediction	903 Benefactor	904 Evildoer
909 Forgiveness	913 Right	917 Duty
929 Probity	930 Improbity	933 Virtue
934 Wickedness	937 Good man	938 Bad man
939 Penitence	940 Impenitence	941 Atonement
945 Asceticism	946 Fasting	961 Condemnation
1001 Parts of the body		

The necessity for a search of many of these categories is obvious: lexical material referring to the concept "catechist," for example, could as well be placed in 537 TEACHER as in 973 RELIGION. A thorough search of a substantial portion of the *Historical Thesaurus* archive ensures as well that properly numbered but misfiled slips are brought to light.[49]

---

[49]The search conducted for this classification indicates that the number of misfiled slips is not substantial and does not present serious difficulty. A large number of the preceding non-religious categories were searched by

The present classification of the religious lexis thus contains the great bulk of the available material drawn from the
Oxford English Dictionary and its supplements, augmented by
Old English religious vocabulary drawn from the dictionaries
of Bosworth and Toller, and Clark Hall.[50]

A notable omission from the classification is material subsumed in the archive under Roget categories 965 DIVINENESS,
966 GODS IN GENERAL, 967 PANTHEON, 968 ANGEL, 969
DEVIL, 971 HEAVEN, and 972 HELL. There are two reasons
for this omission, one pragmatic and one theoretical. Prag-
matically, the inclusion of this material would have expanded
the classification by approximately a further three thousand
items, making completion of the project within the stipulated
time difficult.[51] Theoretically, a valid distinction can be made
between religion as an intellectual and social activity arising
from belief in the existence of a supernatural order, and the
supernatural order itself, consisting (in conceptual terms at
least) of beings, states, and places. In practice the distinction
can be maintained with a fair degree of rigour, though it is not
absolute. Items denoting Armageddon, the Scala Cæli, and
the Apocalypse are found in R1.2.1.4. and R1.2.1.5., for example, owing to their importance in scripture and in Christian
doctrine. During final editing of the *Historical Thesaurus*, this

department staff at Glasgow engaged in work supported by the MSC and
YOP programmes; for this assistance I am very grateful.

[50] James Murray et al. (eds.), *A New English Dictionary on Historical
Principles* (Oxford: Oxford University Press, 1884–1921); R. W. Burchfield
(ed.), *A Supplement to the Oxford English Dictionary*, Volume I A-G, Volume II H-N, Volume III O-Scz, Volume IV Se-Z (Oxford: Clarendon Press,
1972, 1976, 1982, and 1986); J. Bosworth and T. Northcote Toller, *An
Anglo-Saxon Dictionary* (London: Oxford University Press, 1921), and *Additions and Corrections* by A. Campbell (Oxford: Oxford University Press,
1972); John R. Clark Hall, *A Concise Anglo-Saxon Dictionary* (fourth edition with supplement by Herbert D. Meritt, Cambridge: Cambridge University Press, 1960).

[51] Work on the classification was done during a three-year Glasgow University doctoral fellowship.

material will be removed from the present classification and integrated with the lexical field "the supernatural," now being classified by Dr Reinhard Gleissner of the University of Regensburg. Such will also be the case with material from the two Roget classes 983 SORCERY and 984 OCCULTISM.

The classification comprises some fifteen thousand lexical items organized into five hundred and twelve numbered categories, which in turn are divided into five large subfields:

- R1 – BELIEF, DOCTRINE, AND SPIRITUALITY
- R2 – CHURCHES, SECTS, AND RELIGIOUS MOVEMENTS
- R3 – THE INSTITUTIONAL CHURCH
- R4 – WORSHIP, RITUAL, AND PRACTICE
- R5 – ARTEFACTS

A decision on the nature and extent of the five subfields was made early in the project, following a preliminary examination of lexical material; the boundaries fixed upon then have for the most part remained stable.[52] R5 ARTEFACTS is the most self-sufficient of the five, with a minimum of cross-references to other subfields. There are strong links between R4 WORSHIP, RITUAL, AND PRACTICE and R1 BELIEF, DOCTRINE, AND SPIRITUALITY, though they share only two archive classes as a source of material. R3 THE INSTITUTIONAL CHURCH is moderately independent, though there are a number of cross-references between clerics and their functions (*e.g.* between R3.2.12.3. EXORCIST and R4.13. EXORCISM, R3.2.9. CONFESSOR and R4.2.2.0. CONFESSION). R2 CHURCHES, SECTS,

---

[52]One class which caused considerable difficulty is R4.16.0. BENEFICE, which was originally placed with the concepts of "ordination" and "induction" in R3 THE INSTITUTIONAL CHURCH. When, however, it was decided to establish a section in R4 containing lexical material referring to the various sacraments, "ordination" (and "induction") had to be placed therein; "benefice," semantically linked with both "ordination" and "induction," thus followed them into R4.

AND RELIGIOUS MOVEMENTS stands alone as an entire subfield consisting of a catalogue of proper names, though it is far from being devoid of interest either from the semanticist's standpoint or from that of the historian of ideas (see, for example, the high incidence of polemical terms in R2.2.3.0. ROMAN CATHOLICISM, or the shifting attitudes toward Islam reflected in the constituents of R2.3.4.0. ISLAM).

Inevitably, the five-part division entails occasional difficulties, as in the cases of particular instances of abstract concepts and of the relation of function to functionary. An example of the latter case is that mentioned above in connection with R3 cross-references, the relation between R3.2.12.3. EXORCIST and R4.13. EXORCISM. One of the most constant sub-categories in the classification is that labelled P CHAR BY ("person characterized by"), or, where the headword is a noun denoting action or process, P PERF ("person performing"). The many appearances of these category tags display the close semantic link between a process noun and its agent or subject, and demonstrate the viability of the link employed as a standard classificatory device. In some cases, however, maintaining consistency in the overall five-part structure of the classification means that low-level devices such as this are temporarily abandoned and replaced by a cross-reference. Inclusion of lexical material denoting "exorcist" in R3.2.13. MINOR ORDERS, for example, was necessary because the office of exorcist is one of the minor orders in the Latin church, and the structure of R3.2. is based on the hierarchy of that church. A cross-reference within R4.13. EXORCISM directs the reader to R3.2.12.3. EXORCIST, unambiguously pointing to the agent nouns and, in the process, imparting the additional information that the office of exorcist is one of the minor orders of the church.

Specific instances of abstract concepts are more problematic. In R2 CHURCHES, SECTS, AND RELIGIOUS MOVEMENTS, the lexemes referring to the concept of "conversion to a specific religion" form a recurring subordinate category (R2.2.0.1.,

R2.2.3.2., R2.2.4.0.1., R2.2.4.1.2., R2.2.4.3.2., R2.2.4.5.2., R2.2.4.6.2., R2.2.4.8.2., R2.2.4.12.2., R2.2.4.13.2., R2.3.3.2., R2.3.4.2., R2.3.6.1., R2.3.8.1., and R2.3.10.2.); yet the abstract concept "conversion" is found at R4.5.4.0. This apparent anomaly is due to the fact that the diagnostic components of these items have equal weight: *christianization*, for example, denotes "the process of becoming Christian, the adoption of Christian doctrine and dogma," and thus must be subordinated to the head concept "Christianity," while *conversion* (with no specification as to which religion) must be grouped with such closely-related concepts as "evangelization," "catechesis," and "proselytization," which are found in R4 together with other religious activity.

Having briefly discussed two difficulties inherent in the choice of the present five-part structure, we can now consider the system employed to display lexical subordination. A discussion of features recurring at lower levels of the classification is provided in chapter 1 as part of the explanation of classificatory systems developed for this project.

System of subordination

The system of subordination employed in the present classification displays semantic dependence by means of the convention of full stops preceding subordinate category tags. The ordering of subordinate categories in itself inplies no subordination, but follows a flexible order which is outlined below. All subordinate categories preceded by one full stop beneath a head category are thus, for the purposes of the classification, parallel subordinates. Further subordination is indicated by the use of additional full stops. The following compressed example will serve as an illustration of the system:

R1.7.3. Impiety: *bismernes, godscyld, godwrecnes, ...*
.**instance of:** impiety 1529–

.p char by: *lahbreca*/law-breaker OE+c1440–, ...
..pl/coll: the ungodly 1526–(1847)
.char by: *æwbræce, arleas, godscyldig,* ...
.in manner of: *arleaslice, unæwfæstlice,* ...
.to imbue with: undevout *vt* c1440(1)
.to treat with: unreverence *vt* 1553+1642

In this example, several features which appear throughout the classification are shown.[53] The category number (R1.7.3.) serves to locate the concept in the framework of the classification as a whole: "R1" is the subfield BELIEF, DOCTRINE, AND SPIRITUALITY; ".7" indicates the class "piety" within the subfield; ".3" locates the specific concept "impiety" within the class. Taken together, these stages of classification are the macroclassificatory stage.

Turning to the specific concept "impiety" and the nouns, adjectives, adverbs, and verbs associated with it, we come to the microclassificatory stage. Head categories in the classification are always noun categories: the basis for the rule has been discussed in chapter 1 and, though perhaps somewhat contentious from the standpoint of semantic theory, there can be no doubt that it provides a stable framework for classification, a framework possessing the added advantage of a high degree of retrievability. Thus constituent nouns in this numbered head category refer to the basic concept of "impiety." Cross-references at the end of the head category direct the reader to related concepts elsewhere in the classification. The degree of relatedness between cross-referenced concepts varies considerably, from near equivalence (such as exists between "impiety" and "unholiness") to an interesting link (such as that between *artolatry* in R4.1.1. KIND OF WORSHIP and *wafer-god* in R.15.5.1. BREAD.

---

[53]The ellipses at line ends indicate only that lexical items have been dropped in this example to save space. For the full lexical complement, see R1.7.3. in the classification.

The parallel subordinates INSTANCE OF, P CHAR BY, CHAR BY, IN MANNER OF, TO IMBUE WITH, and TO TREAT WITH are distinguished by a single full stop preceding the category tag, and follow the general order agreed upon in the *Historical Thesaurus* project: nouns first, followed by adjectives, adverbs, and verbs.[54] It is worth stressing again that the placement, for example, of CHAR BY (an adjectival tag) beneath P CHAR BY (a nominal tag) is a convention and indicates *per se* no semantic dependence or subordination of the former to the latter: in other words, the order itself is arbitrary and semantically indifferent.

Among subordinate noun categories, those referring to persons are treated first, followed by those referring to things and qualities. An exception to this general rule is the occasional interpolation of nominal categories containing lexemes referring to instances of the head concept, or to varieties thereof. R1.7.0. PIETY provides an instance of this:

R1.7.0. Piety
.instance of
.of many forms
.p char by

In some categories the number of kinds of the main concept has required the establishment of a separate subordinate category. A case in point is R4.3.0. PRAYER. Following standard procedure, the first category tags in this class would have been as follows:

R4.3.0. Prayer
.instance of
..together
.kind of
.p perf , etc.

---

[54]See the list of recurring category tags at the beginning of the book.

Since, however, there are almost forty kinds of prayer listed in the classification, a separate subordinate category (R4.3.1. KINDS OF PRAYER) was established; this procedure has the advantage of maintaining a reasonable distance between head concept and subordinate adjectives, adverbs, and verbs, thereby facilitating the generation of category descriptions. Thus in R4.3.0. material which would have been found in the line marked KIND OF above has been placed in R4.3.1.; other lines in R4.3.0. remain undisturbed and in the conventional order.

The number of subordinate nominal categories referring to persons is relatively small; most important among these are PERSON PERFORMING, PERSON UNDERGOING, PERSON CHARACTERIZED BY, PERSON BELIEVING IN, and PERSON ADVOCATING. If there are sufficient plural or collective nouns, they are given a separate category; this is also the case with "feminine" nouns (*priestess*, *preacheress*), which are separated from the main nominal category if numbers warrant. Should the subordinate nominal category refer to an impersonal object, quality, or thing, that object, quality, or thing is either specified directly or represented by an x. Those specified directly present no difficulty in interpretation:

R1.8.2.0. Unspirituality
.p char by
..pl/coll
.thought char by
.act char by

If, however, x appears in the category tag, the referent of the noun has been left unspecified by the *OED* or Bosworth-Toller. In R1.6.3. UNHOLINESS, the lexeme *unholy* 1831+1837 is the sole constituent of a line headed by the category tag XP CHAR BY; the *OED* definition of this item is simply "an unholy person or thing."[55] In R1.6.2.0. CONSECRATION, the category

---

[55]The two citations are as follows: 1831 (Carlyle), "How many other Unholies has your covering Art made holy, besides this Arabian Whinstone!";

tag X PERFORMING indicates that the sole constituent of the line (*sanctifier* 1753+1829) is to be glossed as "something that sanctifies."

Subordinate adjectival categories cover a wide semantic range. Chief among them are the tags CHAR OF ("characteristic of") and CHAR BY ("characterized by"), but there are many others whose nature is largely determined by the head category to which they are subordinated. As an example, the following extract from R1.8.1.0. SOUL illustrates both the possible range of the adjectival tags and the manner in which the head category determines their nature:

R1.8.1.0. Soul
.char of
.endowed with
.. not
.endowing with
.(of p:)unwell in
.(of S:)alive
.(of S:)dead

A smaller but equally interesting set of adjectival categories is found at R1.8.0., subordinated to the head concept "spirituality":

.char by
..surpassingly
.uplifted with
.(of x:)delightful because of

Again, at R1.6.0. HOLINESS, we find a still different complement of adjectival categories, largely the result of the Old English love of compounding:

.char by

1837 (also Carlyle), "All Phenomena of the spiritual land: Dignities, Authorities, Holies, Unholies!"

..**equally:** *efenhalig*
..**very:** *đurhhalig*
..**infinitely:** *eallhalig*/all-holy OE–
..**eternally:** ever-blessed a1711–

Participial adjectives ending in -*ed* have been classified wherever possible under main adjectival headings, rather than subordinated to the verb. Lexical items such as *divined, celebrate,* and *divinified* are thus grouped with the main adjective *holy.* Participial adjectives of this kind of course carry with them the component [HAVING GONE THROUGH THE PROCESS OF (VERBAL NOUN)], whereas *holy* refers to no process and in itself indicates nothing of a previous non-divinized or unbeatified state. Grouping participial adjectives with the main adjectives does, however, eliminate the need for an additional category, and manifests the close semantic link between the two kinds.

Subordinate adverbial categories are fewer in number; the tag IN MANNER OF designates the majority of the adverbial categories. Verbs, too, are largely confined to standard transitive and intransitive senses: TO PERFORM and TO UNDERGO between them designate most of the verbal categories, though wider ranges do occasionally occur (*e.g.* R1.1.5.1. CHURCH, where TO FORM INTO, TO DEPRIVE C OF ITS CHARACTER, TO IMBUE WITH PRINCIPLES OF, TO BECOME UNITED TO, TO PLAY THE, and TO SANCTION BY AUTHORITY OF all appear). R4 WORSHIP, RITUAL, AND PRACTICE contains nearly all of the action- and process-nouns in the classification, yet the vast majority of verb categories therein are identified by one of the two tags mentioned above.

We have noted that the conventional order of parts of speech within a category is noun, adjective, adverb, verb. There is an important and systematic exception to this rule, an exception that reflects the classification's conceptual basis. Let us examine a part of the category R1.10.0. SIN. After the headword "sin" and the nominal tags covering concepts such as "instance of" and "person characterized by," there is the

following block of material at the beginning of the adjectival
tags (the actual lexical constituents are included here for the
sake of clarity):

.**char by:** *firenfremmende, firenful, firengeorn, firensynnig,*
  firenwyrcende, gyltlic, higesynnig, læne, synfah, synlic,
  synscyldig, synwyrcende, wamscyldig, wamwyrcende,
  forsyngod/forsinned OE–c1200, *synig*/sinny OE–c1475,
  synnful/sinful OE–, plightful 13..(1), ysunged/ysinged
  13..– 1387, ysinwed al400(1), sin-soiled 1593–, peccant
  1604–, sinning 1609–, piacular 1610–, peccable 1633(1),
  piaculous 1646–1661, peccanimous 1656–1668 +
  1922–1939 (*Joyce*), piaculary a1670(1)
..**condition of being:** sinfulhead c1250–a1400, sinfulness
  14..–, peccancy 1656–
...**the impressing of p with sense of his:** convincing
  1615–1642
....**char by:** convicting 1876(1)
....**to perform:** convict *vt* 1526–1624 + 1862–, convince *vt*
  1648 + a1853–
...**undergoing:**
....**condition of having undergone:** convincement 1617–,
  conviction 1675–1678 + 1821
  .**capable of:** *etc.*

In the doubly- and triply-subordinate categories following
CHAR BY there are both nouns and verbs, an apparent violation of the established order. With CAPABLE OF we return to
tags designating adjectives. The reason for the interpolation of
non-adjectival material in the midst of a set of adjectives is that
the principle of separation of parts of speech within the classification is not allowed to override the more important principle
that closely-related concepts should be placed together. In
this example, *sinfulhead* c1250–al400 (reading backward from
the category tags) is glossed as "the condition of being characterized by sin"; one step and a subordination further, the

verbal noun *convincing* 1615–1642 is glossed "the impressing of a person with a sense of his condition of being characterized by sin." By means of successive subordinations an important sense-relationship is thus clearly and unambiguously displayed. A strict separation of lexical items by parts of speech would have widely separated the items classified above, and would have required long category tags at the appearance of each separate part of speech.

Generating category descriptions for twice- and thrice-subordinate category lines by means of reading backward through the relevant set of tags may seem clumsy or difficult, but it is a system that works well when readers accustom themselves to it. In some cases, if the category tags do not seem to yield a clear description, it is helpful to substitute one of the lexical constituents in place of one or more tags. To take a simple example, in R1.1.14. APOSTASY we find the following (the sample is condensed):

R1.1.14. Apostasy: apostasy c1380–
.p char by: *apostata*/apostate *OE(L)–*
.char by: apostate 1382–
..not: unapostatized 1684 *(2qls)*
...condition of being: unapostatizedness 1684(1)

Using category tags, the following description of *unapostatizedness* is generated: "condition of being not characterized by apostasy"—clear, but somewhat infelicitous. If, however, the sole constituent of the doubly-subordinate category line ..NOT is substituted for the balance of the category tags, a description is produced at once. This is a simple example, but it gives some indication of the flexibility of the system and its usefulness in cases of three-, four-, and five-fold subordination.

A certain amount of freedom in reading category tags is requisite: the plural inflection, for instance, may be required, or the order in which the tags are read may vary from a simple retrogression. In the following example, the head category tag should be read second rather than last:

R1.1.11.1. Paganization
.a second time:
..to perform: repaganize *vt* 1685(1)

(*i.e.*, the description of *repaganize* is "to perform paganization a second time"). In certain cases, the 'governing' property of head concepts is allowed to carry over the boundaries of numbered categories: this is common where the KIND OF category is sufficiently large to be assigned a separate number. In R1.10.1. KINDS OF SIN, for example, the main list is a series of alphabetically ordered tags:

Actual
First
Formal *etc.*

In these cases, the head concept to be applied is that of the preceding numbered category.

We have discussed briefly the sources of the classification, its primary divisions, and the devices employed in it to display lexical subordination. To complete the introduction, we will describe the internal organization of each of the primary divisions or subfields.

Organization of subfields

R1 - Belief, Doctrine, and Spirituality

R1 is divided into thirteen classes, which fall into six groups:
R1.1. FAITH
R1.2. SCRIPTURE
R1.3. PATRISTICS, R1.4. LAW, R1.5. THEOLOGY
R1.6. HOLINESS, R1.7. PIETY, R1.8. SPIRITUALITY
R1.9 GRACE
R1.10. SIN, R1.11. ATONEMENT, R1.12. SALVATION, R1.13. REPROBATION

R1.1. FAITH contains lexical material referring to the abstract concepts of "faith" and "religion," to those of "codified faith" and various attitudes thereto, and finally to states consequent upon the adoption or denial of a form or forms of faith ("conformity," "apostasy," "sectarianism," and "catholicity"). The interpolation of R1.1.2. DOCTRINE and R1.1.3. TRADITION between R1.1.1. CREED and R1.1.4. COMMUNION might seem odd until it is remembered that "communion" in the present sense of "agreement in codified faith" requires as a logical necessity "agreement in doctrine and (partially if not wholly) in tradition" as well. There are close links between R1.1.0. FAITH and R1.1.5.0. RELIGION, demonstrated by the duplicate entries of the two Old English lexemes *æ(w)* and *æwfæstnes* and of *lay* a1225–1599. R1.1.5.1. A RELIGION/CHURCH, following general practice, is subordinated to R1.1.5.0. RELIGION as referring to a type or instance of the concept embodied in the superordinate category; it serves as well as the superordinate of R2 CHURCHES, SECTS, AND RELIGIOUS MOVEMENTS.

R1.1.6. ORTHODOXY to R1.1.11. PAGANISM subsumes lexical material referring to judgements made regarding the validity of religious doctrines. The historical identification in the English-speaking world of Christianity with orthodoxy is apparent in these categories (*e.g. the faith* a1300– in R1.1.6. and R2.2.0., and the equation of *maumetry* ("Islam") with *paganism* in R1.1.11.0.). The concepts of "heathenism," "paganism," and "idolatry" are grouped together under the heading of R1.1.11.0. PAGANISM, though some might dispute the degree of synonymy existing between them. "Paganism" and "heathenism" can be classified under the same rubric on the basis of circularity of definition; [56] *idolatry* is defined as "the worship of idols or images 'made with hands'; more generally, the paying or offering of divine honours to any created object," and thus, it might be argued, should be placed in a separate

---

[56]The *OED* glosses *heathen* as "pagan" and *pagan* as "heathen."

category. In practice, however, *idolatry* has been subject to the referential indeterminacy that characterizes pejorative language in general. Typical of this usage is the 1781 citation from William Cowper's *Hope*, which speaks of "the gross idolatry blind heathens teach." R1.1.12.0. ATHEISM contains items referring to the concept not of "lack of correct belief" but of "lack of any belief." *Agnosticism* might seem out of place here, as current usage tends to assign it a referent verging on "incomplete atheism"; it is better defined, however, as the belief that the "existence of anything beyond and behind natural phenomena is unknown and (so far as can be judged) unknowable, and especially that a First Cause and an unseen world are subjects of which we know nothing," a definition which, though less uncompromising than that assigned to *atheism*, in fact amounts to much the same thing.

R1.13.0. CONFORMITY to R1.1.16. CATHOLICITY comprises material covering various concepts concerned with conditions following upon the adoption or repudiation of specific faiths. In R1.1.16. CATHOLICITY, the presence of five Old English adjectives in the sense "catholic, universal" where there are no Old English nouns appears an anomaly; *anlic, eallic,* and the like, however, appeared in widely-disseminated vernacular translations of religious documents, including the Apostle's Creed (which contains the phrase *et unam sanctam catholicam et apostolicam Ecclesiam)*; the abstract concept "universality" was not employed in this context.

The six constituents of R1.2.0. SCRIPTURE GENERAL refer to the sacred writings of any religion, and thus act as superordinates for this class. R1.2.1.3. BIBLICAL PERSONAGES, R1.2.1.4. BIBLICAL PLACES, and R1.2.1.5. BIBLICAL EVENTS contain material assigned to the archive classes searched in the preparation of this classification. As such, they are incomplete: coverage of the events of Christ's earthly life in R1.2.1.5., for example, is scanty. Most lexical material denoting biblical persons, places, and events is located in category 965 of the

Historical Thesaurus archive, and will form part of the classification of gods and divinities being undertaken by Dr Gleissner in Regensburg (to whose classification the material gathered here will be conjoined in the published *Historical Thesaurus*). R1.3.0. PATRISTICS, R1.4.0. LAW, and R1.5.0. THEOLOGY comprise lexical material whose referents are concerned with the interpretation, development, and application of doctrine revealed in or based on scripture. R1.5.1. KINDS OF THEOLOGY is concerned with systems or schools of theological speculation whose genesis is associated with a particular place or person; R1.5.2. DEPARTMENTS OF THEOLOGY lists several foci of theological research.

From R1.6.0. HOLINESS to the end of R1 is classified the lexis of the spiritual states seen to be part of religion, and behaviour consequent upon the presence or absence of such spiritual states. R1.6.0. HOLINESS contains a section (R1.6.1.0 – R1.6.1.3.) concerned with saints (as "people characterized by holiness") and the processes leading to sainthood or the removal thereof. Lexical material denoting the process of investing someone or something with holiness is classified at R1.6.2.0 CONSECRATION. This concept is of considerable importance in the lexical field of religion, and has links with several other concepts, including R4.9.1. PURIFICATION and, less immediately, with R4.2.6.1.0. ORDINATION and R4.2.6.5. MONASTIC PROFESSION.

R1.7.0. PIETY subsumes three concepts, "devotion," "piety," and "fear" (this last in the sense of "fear proceeding from an awareness of the power and omniscience of God"). Two Old English lexical items in the category, *æwfæstnes* and *arfæstnes*, embody the link between "piety" and "firmness in religion" or "religiousness" (*cf.* R1.1.5.0.).

Spirituality, in the sense classified at R1.8.0., is defined as "the quality or condition of being spiritual; attachment to or regard for things of the spirit as opposed to material or worldly interests," and as such is distinct from both "religiousness" and "piety." R1.8.1.0. SOUL to R1.8.1.3. DOCTRINES CONCERNING THE SOUL comprises lexical material referring to the soul, its transmigration and regeneration, and doctrines associated with it.

From R1.8.3. CONTEMPLATION to R1.8.6.2. VISION, MANIFESTATION are classified lexical items denoting types of spiritual activity. These categories have substantial links with lexical material outside the field of religion. In particular, the constituents of R1.8.6.1. PROPHECY are only a part of presumably a much larger field.

R1.9. GRACE is remarkable as a relatively independent yet central concept in the lexical field of religion. Cross-references to the sacraments draw attention to the ecclesiastical means of imparting grace; others to Calvinism and Arminianism indicate the central role played by grace in the doctrines of these two religious traditions. Yet the network of semantic relationships around "grace" is very much less complex than that surrounding concepts of equivalent importance in religion, such as "holiness" or "piety"; the two concepts most closely related ("merit" and "righteousness") are here subordinated to the head category, and have only a moderately-sized representation in the lexis.

R1 concludes with the classification of "sin," amendment of sin ("atonement"), and the two final states, "salvation" and "reprobation."[57] Once again complex relations link material classified here with material outside the lexical field of religion. "Sin" is bound up with the concept of "evil" (indeed, "sin" might be defined briefly as "evil or wrong seen from a religious perspective") and "salvation," though less closely, is related to "life characterized by goodness."

---

[57] "Heaven," "hell," "purgatory," and "limbo," it should again be noted, are to be classified together with gods and divinities; the task has been undertaken by Dr Gleissner.

R2 - Churches, Sects, and Religious Groups

This subfield largely comprises proper names, and subsumes lexical material denoting religious denominations.[58] There are three large divisions in R2:

R2.1. JUDAISM
R2.2. CHRISTIANITY
R2.3. NON-JUDÆO-CHRISTIAN RELIGIONS

Though far smaller in terms of lexical representation, Judaism is placed in the classification before Christianity because it antedates and gave birth to the latter (*cf.* also the notes to this section in chapter 4). The huge preponderance of lexical material in this section referring to Christian groups yet again witnesses to the close relation between Christianity and the English-speaking world. Globally, Christianity is only one among several large religions, each with a proliferation of sects; yet in the English vocabulary Christianity is far more extensively represented, its lexis larger than those of all other religions combined.

Within R2.2.0. several groupings of categories can be distinguished. R2.2.0. to R2.2.0.3. includes lexical items referring to the general concept of Christianity and to movement toward and away from it (R2.2.0.1. CONVERSION TO CHRISTIANITY, R2.2.0.2. LACK OF CHRISTIANITY, and R2.2.0.3. OPPOSITION TO CHRISTIANITY). R2.2.1.0. to R2.2.1.12. lists the major early Christian sects; those early sects not found here are included at R2.2.5. VARIOUS (ANTI-)CHRISTIAN SECTS AND MOVEMENTS. Since the decision for inclusion either here at R2.2.1. or at R2.2.5. was based on information gained from the *OED* definitions and citations by one who has no special familiarity with the history of early Christian sectarianism, certain placements are bound to prove controversial; why, it might be asked, place the Collyridians in R2.2.1. while consigning the

---

[58] R2 does not include religious groups composed solely of ordained members. These are found in R3 (R3.3.0. – R3.3.10., R3.3.4.3.).

Photians to R2.2.5.? The main criteria for inclusion at R2.2.1. are, first, historical prominence, and, second, evidence of at least a moderate degree of 'spread' (that is, a substantial number of adherents). Groups not fulfilling these criteria are placed in R2.2.5.

R2.2.2. Orthodoxy stands alone, the result of the first great schism within Christianity, which produced the Eastern churches. Roman Catholicism (R2.2.3.) takes precedence among Western branches of Christianity on the basis of both age and size. Within this category and the subcategories that follow, several recurring classificatory devices become evident. As elsewhere in the classification, the KINDS OF subcategory follows immediately upon the head category. A heavily represented category such as R2.2.3. ROMAN CATHOLICISM possesses additional subordinates (covering the concepts of "conversion to and from Catholicism" and "anticatholicism" similar to those of a class (*cf.* R2.2. CHRISTIANITY).

The classification of Protestant sects and churches from R2.2.4.0. to R2.4.16.0. is organized alphabetically. A system of classification based on a 'family tree' (*i.e.* on the historical relationships between sects) was planned at an earlier stage, but proved unworkable because of the rapid and frequently random proliferation of denominations in the sixteenth and seventeenth centuries. Such a system would, for example, have subordinated Presbyterianism to Calvinism; the number of direct relationships like this is, however, limited, and many denominations of more or less independent genesis (*e.g.* Moravianism) would of necessity have been relegated to R2.2.5.

The system eventually arrived at and employed here assigns to each of sixteen major Protestant groups a subordinate category number (from R2.2.4.1. to R2.2.4.16.). To each of these is further subordinated a complement of identifiable descendants, offshoots, or divisions. An example of the former is the subordination of Wee Frees in R2.2.4.12.1. to Presbyterianism, and of the latter the subordination of Tractarianism in

58 INTRODUCTION TO THE CLASSIFICATION

R2.2.4.1.1.8. to Anglicanism.
As immediate subordinates to the category R2.2.4.0. PROTESTANTISM GENERAL, the four subordinate categories R2.2.4.0.2. FUNDAMENTALISM, R2.2.4.0.3. THE REFORMATION, R2.2.4.0.3.1. PILGRIMAGE OF GRACE, and R2.2.4.0.3.2. COUNTER-REFORMATION might seem strangely placed. Fundamentalism, a school of religious thought characterized by its uncompromising insistence on inerrant scripture as the only source of authority in religion, has been closely associated with Protestantism and can be said to have provided part of the impetus for the Reformation and thus for the genesis of Protestantism itself. The Reformation, Pilgrimage of Grace, and Counter-Reformation are historical occurrences, one well-defined and the other two vast movements still, some claim, taking place today. The present placement of these subordinate categories can be justified on the grounds of indisputable semantic links with the superordinate category.

ANTITRINITARIANISM appears out of place as the category tag for R2.2.4.2.0., the sole constituent of which is *Unitarianism*. It was chosen as superordinate because it denotes "doctrine of Christian denomination which rejects the concept of a tripartite godhead," and thus provides a heading to which, among several others, Binitarianism and Tetratarianism can be subordinated.

There are strong links between several of the groups listed here and systems of church government or ecclesiastical polity set out in R3.1.1. Notable among these groups are R2.2.4.12.0. PRESBYTERIANISM and, to a lesser extent, R2.2.4.1.0. ANGLICANISM.

In R2.2.5. VARIOUS (ANTI-)CHRISTIAN SECTS AND MOVEMENTS are listed alphabetically over one hundred and sixty sects (or representatives thereof) which have no apparent relationship to groups represented in preceding numbered categories. Either the doctrine (denoted by a noun ending in *-ism*) of the sect or a member (denoted by a noun ending in *-ist,*

-*ian*, -*er*, and the like) can serve as category tag. For consistency and clarity in preceding numbered categories the -*ism* noun is always employed as the category tag; where such a noun is not attested in the lexis it has been coined to serve as part of the metalinguistic structure of category tags. In the present section, however, with a large number of poorly-attested, small subcategories, the consistent use of either the -*ism* or the -*ist* noun as category tag would have resulted in an inordinately large number of empty lines; a more flexible approach was called for, and the present system satisfies this need without sacrificing either clarity or concision.

Exactly the same arrangement prevails in R2.3. NON-CHRISTIAN RELIGIONS. Ten major religions are assigned category numbers, and to each of them are subordinated their respective sects and divisions. Once again, because no familial relationship exists between them, the ten major denominations are listed alphabetically with R2.3., as are the eighteen religions in R2.3.11. MISCELLANEOUS NON-CHRISTIAN SECTS AND GROUPS.

R3 - The Institutional Church

This subfield accommodates the structure of ecclesiastical authority, the temporal as opposed to the spiritual aspect of the church. It is divided into four classes:

R3.1. CHURCH GOVERNMENT
R3.2. CLERGYMAN
R3.3. RELIGIOUS
R3.4. LAYMAN

R3.1.1. KINDS OF CHURCH GOVERNMENT lists the various models of ecclesiastical polity, and is followed by categories containing lexical items denoting the concepts of "authority" and "discipline" in church affairs. Immediately subordinate to R3.1.3.0. ECCLESIASTICAL DISCIPLINE is the concept of "ecclesiastical court," as the embodiment and instrument of the abstract concept "discipline." There are two groups of church courts; the first is composed of those examples attached to a clerical superior (pope, archbishop, bishop), and the second of those associated with the Presbyterian system of church government. The three listed papal courts —Curia, Inquisition, and Rota— have differing remits, but each is concerned with the exercise of authority in a defined sphere, the Curia in the governance of the church as a whole, the Inquisition with the suppression of heresy, and the Rota with the application of doctrine and canon law to matters such as the annulment of marriages. Courts associated with the local curia or chanceries of metropolitans and ordinaries are now largely part of history, though individual features of them still exist, such as the diocesan chancellor (in the Anglican church now usually a layman, in the Roman Catholic a priest). Presbyterian church courts are classified in ascending order of authority, from the general assembly, which bears responsibility of governance of the national church and the maintenance of doctrine therein, to kirk-sessions, exercising their authority within the confines of individual parishes.

R3.1.4.0. COUNCIL brings together lexical items denoting a variety of assemblages of ecclesiastical authorities. *Synod*, as defined by the *OED*, serves as one superordinate of this category, though it seems usually to be associated with a council of bishops (note, however, the more specific Old English term *biscopseonod*). R3.1.4.3. CHAPTER classifies a specific kind of council, that associated with a cathedral or collegiate church and comprised of ordained members usually in possession of an ecclesiastical living. R3.1.4.3.1. CATHEDRAL DIGNITARIES is subordinated to the concept of "chapter" because the dignitaries referred to are usually, though not invariably, members of the chapter.

R3.2.0. CLERGYMAN GENERAL marks the beginning of the second large class within R3. Its constituent lexical items serve as superordinates for the class as a whole (though it should be noted that the use of a number of these lexical items to refer to members of the hierarchy would be unidiomatic). Items referring specifically to the concept of "priest," defined as "clergyman with sacrificial function," are reserved until R3.2.2.0., though most speakers would probably use constituents of the present category to denote "priest" (*i.e.* the relation between *clergyman* and *priest* is one of hyponymy rather than synonymy; *cf.* chapter 1.).

With this category, too, begins a pattern of subordinate categories which contains lexical items referring to the office, authority, and territory of individual clerics. Another recurring category tag is WIFE OF, the constituents of which more often than not are intended to be humorous (*e.g. archbishopess, archdeaconess*). The order established is head noun followed by KINDS OF (though, as with the category "prayer" and others, in the case of "bishop" the number of kinds required a separate subordinate category), OFFICE OF, TENURE OF OFFICE OF, SEE OF, and various other subordinate nouns.

The organization of subordinate categories within R3.2. is based on the hierarchical principle, with superiors preceding subordinates. Since the very large majority of terms in this class denote functionaries of the Western Christian church in one or another of its branches, the choice of the Western Christian hierarchy to provide a classificatory framework is an obvious one. The hierarchy is clear in its overall structure, though several individual placings deserve comment. "Patriarch" is placed before "cardinal" on the basis of the former's historical importance and attachment to major ancient bishoprics, though patriarchs themselves are now usually members of the College of Cardinals. Even though most present-day archbishops are metropolitans, "metropolitan" has been separated from "archbishop" because elevation to an archbishopric does not presuppose the assumption of metropolitan authority (those curialists, for example, who are given archiepiscopal rank and with it one of the now defunct North African sees have no metropolitan authority); a further anomaly exists in the Greek Church, where metropolitan authority can be possessed by bishops as well as archbishops. "Primus," though a tiny category of only two constituents, requires separate treatment: it cannot be subsumed under either "metropolitan" or "archbishop" because the primus (a figure apparently unique to the Scottish Episcopalian Church) has no metropolitical or archiepiscopal authority. His pre-eminence is purely ceremonial.

R3.2.3. RECTOR, R3.2.4. PARSON, and R3.2.5. PASTOR might have been classified together, as the three terms tend to be used by different traditions and in various locales to mean much the same thing, the incumbent of a parish. This notwithstanding, it seemed better to assign each of them a separate category to display the small but real differences between them. A rector, for example, is a clergyman in canonical authority over a parish and in possession of any living or livings attached to that parish; *parson*, however, carries with it no such specificity, and *pastor* emphasizes a particular function of the incumbent of a parish – the spiritual oversight of a congregation. These distinctions were clearly visible in the nineteenth century, from which period many of the *OED* citations are drawn; it would appear, however, that current popular usage treats the terms with a degree of interchangeability that suggests the future relationship between them will be near synonymy.[59]

R3.2.11.1. SUBDEACON and R3.2.11.2. EPISTOLLER are here treated separately, though the principal function of the subdeacon is to read the epistle at public worship. Once again the reason for the separation is historical and denominational: a relationship of identity between the two has not held at all times and in all places.

At R3.3.3.0. begins the classification of religious orders. A choice of ordering principles was available for this section, rang-

---

[59]See also the notes in chapter 4 to these categories.

ing from a classification based on date of foundation and relative length of existence to purely alphabetical organization. The plan finally adopted was the 'family tree' mentioned earlier in connection with Protestant sects and churches (R2.2.4.). There it proved unworkable, owing to the random genesis of many sects in post-Reformation times, but here it provides a clear organizational principle, and provides added information about relationships between orders at a glance. Nine superordinate categories were established:

R3.3.3.1. AUGUSTINIAN

R3.3.3.2. BENEDICTINE

R3.3.3.3. CARMELITE

R3.3.3.4. DOMINICAN

R3.3.3.5. FRANCISCAN

R3.3.3.6. JESUIT

R3.3.3.7. TRINITARIAN

R3.3.3.8. GREEK RELIGIOUS

R3.3.3.9. RELIGIO-MILITARY RELIGIOUS

To these superordinates are subordinated religious orders which are offshoots, adaptations, or reformulations of the original monastic rule. A glance at the table of contents will show, for example, that the Antonine order (subordinated to "Augustinian") is an offshoot or adaptation of the Augustinian order. Further degrees of subordination display further steps in the process of adaptation of a particular monastic rule: the compressed example below shows that the Trappistines are an offshoot of the Trappists, themselves a reformed branch of the Cistercians, who in turn are a branch of the Benedictine order:

R3.3.3.2. BENEDICTINE

.CISTERCIAN

..TRAPPIST

...TRAPPISTINE

Both R3.3.3.8. GREEK RELIGIOUS and R3.3.3.9. RELIGIO-MILITARY RELIGIOUS are small categories wherein the organization is alphabetical.

R4 - Worship, Ritual, and Practice

R4 falls into four large classes:
R4.1. WORSHIP
R4.2. SACRAMENT
R4.3. PRAYER – R4.15. OTHER PRACTICES
R4.16. BENEFICE

The first class subsumes lexical material denoting practices directly concerned with the worship of a divinity, thus including all ritual not specially directed to a sacramentary or supplicatory end. Music is also included here as a parallel subordinate category to "parts of service," as the bulk of religious music is designed to be employed in the context of a service of worship. The various liturgical feasts and seasons find a place in R4.1. WORSHIP on account of their intimate connection with varying forms of service and types of ritual intended for performance on specific occasions.

R4.1.3. PARTS OF SERVICE is organized on the sequential basis of a progression from beginning to end of a service. The service employed is the eucharistic rite of the Western Christian church. Obviously details of service vary somewhat from denomination to denomination, but the broad outline remains remarkably constant, from the opening ritual of procession, greeting, confession, and absolution, through the readings from scripture and various parts of communion ritual, to post-communion ceremonies and the return of the clergy to the sacristy or vestry. R4.1.4. SERVICE MUSIC contains only those items with a direct reference to church music; cross-reference to the classification of the full musical lexis in the *Historical Thesaurus* is presupposed, and much of the material contained in the present classification might well be duplicated there, in particular those items contained in R4.1.4.0. SERVICE MUSIC

GENERAL. Items in the superordinate category of R4.1.4.1.0. HYMN denote the concept of "religious song" in its most general sense, and thus serve as superordinates for the subordinate category R4.1.4.1.1.

R4.1.5. THE LITURGICAL YEAR subsumes lexical material referring to named occasions in the ecclesiastical calendar. After subordinate categories devoted to the concepts of "sabbath" and "feast/festival" in general, observances are classified sequentially according to the framework provided by the Christian liturgical year. R4.1.5.2.1. SPECIFIC CHRISTIAN SEASONS AND FEASTS thus begins with the season of Advent and ends with feastdays falling in November and early December. Where possible, individual feasts are subordinated to the liturgical seasons containing them (*e.g.* Mid-Lent Sunday is subordinated to the season Mid-Lent), but in certain cases this relationship has been bypassed for reasons of clarity and in order to avoid a potentially confusing amount of subordination. The category description of *Shrove-Tuesday*, for example, is (reading from the relevant category tags) "Tuesday in the Sunday, Monday, and Tuesday of the first week of the period following the Sunday before Lent," a description which, though accurate, has perhaps reached the edge of opacity. Moveable feasts, which paradoxically are those fixed on an unchanging date of the civil calendar, are inserted into the classification at appropriate points.[60]

Because of the differing liturgical years established by non-Christian denominations, R4.1.5.2.2. JEWISH SEASONS AND FEASTS follows the Jewish pattern of seasons and festivals, while the very scanty lexical representation from non-Judæo-Christian traditions in R4.1.5.2.3. led to the use of alphabeti-

---

[60]Fixed or immoveable feasts are those occurring on a certain day of the week (*e.g.* Easter Thursday, Easter Sunday), while moveable feasts are those fixed for a particular date which falls on varying days of the week from year to year (*e.g.* the Feast of St James on 25th July). John Lyons discusses calendrical organization (a "cyclical set") in his *Semantics* (Cambridge: Cambridge University Press, 1977), I, p. 290.

zation as the method of ordering this material.

R4.1.5.3. FAST might at first glance seem to belong to a later part of R4—that dealing with practices—but its placement here as a subordinate of R4.1.5. THE LITURGICAL YEAR can be defended on the ground that its constituents refer to the days on which or seasons in which fasting occurs. Additionally, the establishment and observation of ecclesiastical fasts is rightly considered a branch of heortology (defined as "the science which has for its subject the origin, meaning, growth, and history of the religious feasts and seasons of the Christian year").

R4.1.6. CANONICAL HOURS is organized chronologically, beginning with the earliest service of the day and concluding with the last. "Vespers" and "evensong" have been treated as synonyms, though it can be argued that this has not been the case at all times and in all places.

With R4.2. SACRAMENT we arrive at the second of the four large groups within R4. As is the case elsewhere in the classification, such a concept, chosen as a superordinate, is treated in its broadest sense and fullest extent so as to provide a maximum of classificatory utility. Various Christian denominations hold that only one or two sacraments ought to be recognized as such; others deny the existence of any. Here the full Latin complement of seven sacraments is used to form a framework for this section, built according to the temporal order in which the sacraments are received, from baptism at birth to extreme unction at point of death. One branching of the progression occurs at R4.2.5. MARRIAGE and R4.2.6. HOLY ORDERS, where (for purposes of the progression only!) a choice of one or the other sacrament is necessarily made.

The substantial number of cross-references following R4.2.1.0. BAPTISM hints at the centrality of this concept in Christian thinking and its considerable semantic overlap with "regeneration," "conversion," and the like.

To R4.2.2. CONFESSION are subordinated the closely-related concepts "penitence," "impenitence," "absolution," "penance," and "remission of penance." R4.2.4.0. COM-MUNION contains lexical material denoting a wide range of concepts concerning the eucharist, the Roman Catholic form thereof, and eucharistic doctrine. Though, as noted earlier, the Latin eucharistic service provides the framework for R4.1.3. PARTS OF SERVICE owing to its comprehensiveness and relative prominence among rites, lexical material denoting the eucharistic service itself is classified in the present category as the liturgical manifestation of the abstract concept "eucharist." Lexical material denoting "mass" is merely a subset of the latter, and is thus placed in the subordinate categories R4.2.4.1.0. and R4.2.4.1.1. Eucharistic doctrines grouped at R4.2.4.2. are placed in alphabetical order after lexical material denoting the dogma of Christ's presence in the eucharist. Though an attempt was made to organize the doctrines on a semantic basis, very few of the sense-components of these items were shared widely enough to permit such a classification.

"Marriage" is a concept whose strong links with the lexical field of religion are the result of long custom and usage rather than of any organic relationship. Some religions view marriage as a sacrament, others merely as a ceremony, and marriage ceremonies conducted on a civil basis without reference to the church or its ministers are increasingly common. R4.2.5. MARRIAGE is thus limited in its coverage to areas of the lexis denoting the ceremonies, conventions, and requirements of marriage performed as an ecclesiastical ordinance, whether sacramental or not. Nonetheless, many items present here will doubtless be duplicated in or removed to the classification of "courtship," "engagement," and "marriage" in their non-religious context.

Ordination can be considered as the sacrament of marriage for ecclesiastics; the ordinand takes vows binding him to the church in a way similar to that by which a husband is bound to a wife. This relationship is made explicit in the case of nuns, who are (or were) said to be "brides of Christ." Thus the orderly progression of sacraments in R4.2., as mentioned earlier, branches at this point. Subordinate to the head concept are categories containing related matter which denotes concepts such as "unfrocking," "vocation," "induction," and "seminary."

The last of the sacraments is extreme unction, classified at R4.2.7. As is pointed out in the notes accompanying the classification, *unction* denotes "the anointing with oil of a person," and is not necessarily connected with last rites, as it is used in other ceremonies such as baptism, confirmation, and ordination as well. Yet the fact remains that the action of anointing is a central part of last rites, whereas it is only one of the several ritual observances employed in connection with the three sacraments mentioned above. Unmodified or further unspecified uses of *unction* in most cases refer to the last rites, and so the present classification, wherein all words referring to this concept are grouped in R4.2.7., is seen as defensible. "Funeral" is subordinated to "extreme unction" because in itself it is not a sacrament, but a service of prayer and commemoration in which the deceased person's soul may be commended to God. Also subordinate to "extreme unction" are the two quasi-liturgical procedures of "vigil" and "commemoration," both referring to specific instances of the abstract concepts which are the primary denotata of these nouns.

From R4.3. to R4.15. are classified various ecclesiastical practices. There is a fair amount of disparity between them, but groupings are evident (*e.g.* R4.3. PRAYER and R4.4. GOOD WORKS, R4.6. PILGRIMAGE and R4.7. CRUSADE). The referent of R4.3. PRAYER is understood to be "prayer" in its general, non-liturgical sense; the concept "liturgical prayer" is subsumed in R4.1. WORSHIP, though several constituents of R4.3.1. KINDS OF PRAYER have a liturgical use or setting. The paucity of material in R4.4. GOOD WORKS is perhaps a reflection of the vagueness and indeterminacy of this concept:

specific good works are more likely to be mentioned (for an indication of some of these, see the notes to the classification), but in themselves they form a part of the religious lexis.

At R4.5. is classified lexical material referring to activities directed toward the publication and acceptance of religious truth and doctrine. "Preaching" is the central concept in this area, and is most fully represented in the lexis. *Evangelization* more specifically refers to the preaching of Christianity, and the subordinate categories that follow refer to various aspects of the process of spreading religious doctrines as well as to activities associated with it.

"Sacrifice" is another central concept in the Judæo-Christian tradition as well as in other religions; hence the heavy lexical representation and the wide provenance of that representation, particularly among constituents of R4.8.1. KINDS OF SACRIFICE. Cross-references to such concepts as "atonement," "eucharist," and "purification" display the links between "sacrifice" in its general sense and metaphorical uses of the concept (such as "eucharist") as well as ends to which sacrifice is directed (such as "atonement" and "purification"). "Propitiation" is subordinated to "sacrifice" because it is an activity almost exclusively associated with "sacrifice," and possesses few links with other parts of the religious lexis.

R4.10. contains lexical material referring to actions directed against religion, its ritual manifestations and artefacts, and to actions prejudicial to good order within the church as a corporate body.

At R4.16. is grouped the lexis of religious financial matters. The larger part of this lexis refers to benefices and associated matters. In earlier drafts of this classification, "benefice" was placed in R3 THE INSTITUTIONAL CHURCH, but its dubious claim to inclusion in that subfield and the fact that it did not fit well into its hierarchical structure combined to suggest removal to its present place in R4. Subordinated to it are the concepts of "right of presentation to church living" (*advowson*), "wrongful sale of church office" (*simony*), and the alphabetical listing of miscellaneous financial matters.

R5 - Artefacts

This subfield is divided into six groups:
R5.1. - R5.6. BUILDINGS
R5.7. - R5.10. FURNITURE AND IMPLEMENTS
R5.11. - R5.14. CLOTHING
R5.15. CONSUMABLES
R5.16. BOOKS
R5.17. SYMBOLS

Constituents of R5.1. PROPERTY GENERAL serve as superordinates for the entire subfield with the exception of symbols, which though artefacts cannot be considered as property.

The proportion of lexical material of non-Christian provenance is higher in this than in any of the other subfields of the present classification, an anomaly which has to some extent affected the shape of R5. Though Christianity has proven itself highly original in much of the doctrinal field, it displays a genius for adapting to its own purposes artefacts of other, antecedent religions. Since this is a diachronic classification covering the full chronological span of the language, an amount of referential indeterminacy (particularly at the earlier periods) is difficult to avoid. Many Old English lexemes denoting pre-Christian temples, for example, were taken over at later stages to refer to Christian structures. The plan adopted has been to make no primary distinction (*i.e.* a distinction embodied in a head category) on the basis of religious provenance: non-Christian material will be found side by side with Christian. Thus, for example, *heafodstede* is classified with *halignes/holiness* in R5.3.0., and *gesele* with *cirice/church* in R5.3.3.

R5.4. PARTS OF BUILDINGS is organized according to a

"locomotive" principle (see chapter 1) which classifies lexical material referring to the various parts of buildings according to the order in which the referents themselves might be encountered by a person entering a church through the main door at the liturgical west end and proceeding eastward through the nave and sanctuary. The hypothetical building whose parts form subordinate category headings in this class is a Christian church of large proportions built on the standard medieval cruciform plan. Such a choice is justifiable on the grounds that the great bulk of lexical material is rendered classifiable by this framework, and that its 'retrievability' factor is high.[61]

In many of the categories that follow a semantic organization except on the broadest level has proved unworkable. In R5.6., for example, the broad-level grouping brings together lexical items referring to the habitations of various clerics, but as no semantic link exists between them (other than the features "habitation" and "of cleric") a structure employed elsewhere (the hierarchical plan of R3) is used again here to provide a framework. Such is also the case in R5.11.1. PARTICULAR FUNCTIONARIES' ATTIRE. Where other structures are not applicable, such as in R5.11.2. OUTERGARMENTS and R5.11.3. NECK AND SHOULDER GARB, only the broad grouping stands, and category tags are organized alphabetically.

The constituents of R5.15. CONSUMABLES (for which there is no superordinate) are organized alphabetically. Palms find a place here because they are burned to produce ashes used in Ash Wednesday ceremonies marking the start of Lent; Chinese joss-paper is also included because it is burned during religious observances.

---

[61]Though, as noted earlier, a considerable proportion of the R5 lexis is of non-Christian provenance, this is not the case in R5.4. PARTS OF BUILDINGS, wherein most of the material is Christian. A quick glance at the dates of words in this class shows that many were either employed for the first time or revived after long disuse in the nineteenth century, a phenomenon which reflects the general revival of interest in ecclesiology associated with the Tractarian movement in England (cf. chapter 5).

R5.16. Books begins with books used in the services of the church, books which contain the formulæ of public worship. These are followed by lectionaries and then breviaries and office books, the latter being employed by clerics for their private devotions. Music books are organized alphabetically, as in the small remaining group of books that fit into none of the preceding categories.

R5 closes with a list of symbols whose names appear in Bosworth-Toller and the *OED*. As has been discussed in chapter 1, a section such as this presents the classifier with a problem: how does one deal with a loosely-structured group of lexical items which have very few or only one feature in common (here, the feature "image")? For the sake of ease of reference, R5.17.1. has been divided into Christian and non-Christian parts.

Chapter Three
The English Religious Lexis

R1.1. Faith

R1.1.0. Faith: *æ(w)*, *æwfæstnes*, *+leafa*/(y)leve OE–c1330, belief
c1175–, lay a1225–1599, fay a1300–1596, troth
c1300–1432/50, trow c1300+1883*arch.*, truth 13..–1500/20,
faith c1382–, believing 1523–(1825), vay 1586–1602 *S.dial.*

> XR R1.1.5.0. Religion
> R1.9.3. Solifidianism
> R1.12.1. Nudifidian

.**absolute:** implicit faith 1610–, implicit
reverence/belief/confidence 1610–

.**entrusted by God to xp:** depositum 1582–(1732)

.**resting on demonstrative evidence:** sciential faith c1456(1)

.**unreasoning:** collier's faith 1581-1680

> XR R1.1.9. Superstition

.**without works:** workless *a* 1532–1653

> XR R4.4. Good Works

.**p char by:** truand a1300(1), trower c1300(1), lever c1340(1),
priest 1382–1810, acknowledger 1535–1678, believer 1549–,
professor 1597– *now chfly. Sc. and U.S.*, credent 1638(1),
affier a1641(1), faithfullist 1653(1), *bhakta* 1828– *Hindi*

..**pl/coll:** *geleafful, geleafsume*

..**office of:** priesthood 1897(1)

..weak: weakling 1548–, pettyfidian 1647(2)

.char by: *geliefed, getreowful,* +*leaffull*/leafful OE–a1250, beliefful c1175–1548, trowing a1300–1483, faithful a1300–(1759), faithed c1374–1545, believing c1440–, feable/fiable 1483(1), professant 1621–1643, professing 1675–

..condition of being: *getreowfulnes,* faithfulness 1388–, belieffulness 1548+1853

.with: faithfully 1401–1607, believingly 1643–(1854)

.lack of susceptibility to: untenderness a1658+1680

..char by: untender a1658–a1812

..with: untenderly 1651(1)

.theory/science of: pistiology 1900(1)

.flame of: faith-fire 1890– *fig.*

.to have: *geliefan*/yleve *v* OE–c1400, trow *vi* 1200–1573, believe *vi* c1200–, believe *vt* 1297–, trow *vt* 1340–1513, believe *va* 1377–

.to produce: *to geleafsuman vphr*

.to provide xp with standard of: faith *vt* 1547–1553

R1.1.1.0. Creed (codified faith): *creda*/creed OE(L)–, *geleafa, credo (L)* c1175–, troth c1200–1481, creance 1393–1669, symbol 1490–, confession 1536–, persuasion 1623–, Shema(h) 1706– *Jewish,* Shahada(h) 1885– *Moslem*

> XR R1.5.2. Symbolics
> XR R4.1.3. Creed

.p adhering to: creedsman a1834+1887

.char of: symbolical 1745–, symbolic 1867–, cre(e)dal 1868–

.(of p:)believing all: omnifidel 1848(1)

.(of xp:)without: creedless 1827–, confessionless 1883–

..condition of being: creedlessness 1838–

.(of x:)expressed in: symbolized 1912(1)

.article of: article c1230–

..(of xp:)furnished with: articled 1868(1)

..to furnish with: article *vt* 1826(1)

.word from, asserting doctrine of procession of Holy Ghost:

filioque 1876–
.**repetition of:** creed 1425+1808
.**books/documents stating:** standards *npl* 1841–

.**formulation of:** confessionalism 1876–
..**to perform:** symbolize *vt* 1895–

.**indifference to:** latitudinism 1667+1685, indifferentism 1827–,
anythingarianism 1851(1), adiaphorism 1866+1881
XR R1.1.16. Catholicity
XR R2.2.4.1.1.1. Broad-churchism
..**p char by:** politic 1589–1633, politique 1609–, adiaphorist
1645–1710, politician 1656–1681, latitudinarian 1662–,
anythingarian a1704–, indifferentist 1807–
..**x char by:** adiaphoron 1652–1865
..**char by:** adiaphoron 1553+1587, adiaphorist 1882(1)

R1.1.1.1. Kinds of creed
Apostles': belief c1175–(1840), symbol 1490–, Apostles' Creed
a1658–
Athanasian: Athanasian 1586–
.**p adhering to:** Athanasian 1724–, Athanasianist 1873(1)
.**principles of:** Athanasianism 1777(1)
Irish: Irish articles 1877+1967
Nicene: Nicene creed 1567–, Nicæan creed 1706–
XR R4.1.3. Creed
.**p adhering to:** Nicenian 1663(1), Nicæan 1860(1), Nicene
1882(1), Nicenist 1891(1)

R1.1.2. Doctrine

R1.1.2. Doctrine: *lar*/lore OE–1838, belief a1225–, doctrine
1382–, dogma 1791–
XR R1.4.0. Law
.**instance of:** doctrinals *npl* 1619–(1876), dogma 1638–,
dogmatism 1803–(1871)
XR R1.5.2. Dogmatics
.**char of:** *larlic*, doctrinal 1570–, dogmatical 1627–, dogmatic

1706–

.in manner of: dogmatically 1630–, doctrinally 1633–

.p holding extravagant: notionist 1652–(1869)
.holy: *haligdom*
.leading: faith-mark 1822(1)
.new: new lights *npl* 1650–1744 + 1785–*Sc*
..p adhering to: dogmatist 1577/87–1797
.commonly accepted but unauthoritative: pious opinion
    1865(1)
.char by denial: negativism 1824–, negatism 1885(1)
..p adhering to: negationist 1856–, negativist 1873–

R1.1.12.0. Atheism

.moderate interpretation of: minimizing 1874(1), minimism
    1874–
..p char by: minimizer 1867–
..char by: minimizing 1875(1), minimistic 1897(1)
..to engage in: minimize *vi* 1875–
.rigorous interpretation of: maximism *no quots.*

XR R2.2.3.1. Ultramontanist

..p char by: maximizer 1868–
..char by: maximistic 1888(1)
..to engage in: maximize *vi* 1875–

.judicious handling of: economy 1833–(1885)
..char of: economical 1833 + 1864, economic 1851(1)
.stress on: doctrinality 1846(1), doctrinalism 1869 + 1894

XR R1.1.6. Orthodoxism

..p char by: doctrinalist 1860(1)

.indication that book is free from error in: *nihil obstat*
    1886–

R1.1.3. Tradition

R1.1.3. Tradition: tradition 1551–

XR R1.4.2. Mishnah

.relating to teachings of Christ: paradosis 1950–

.p upholding: traditioner 1646–(1868), traditionist 1666-(1872), traditionary 1727/41–1732, traditionalist 1875–

XR R4.1.2. Ritualist

.char of: traditionalistic 1874(1)

.excessive reverence for: traditionalism 1860–, traditionism 1864 + 1896

..to manifest: traditionize *vi* 1840(1)

R1.1.4. Communion

R1.1.4. Communion (agreement in codified faith): *gemænscipe, gemana, ðeodraden,* fellowred a1300–a1400, communing a1300–1509, common a1300–a1631, fellowship a1300–, commoning c1340(1), brotherhead c1380+1382, communion c1386–, brotherhood 1388-(1865), sodality 1600–, consent 1635–1709, *koinonia* 1907– *Gk.*

XR R1.1.16. Catholicity
R4.14.0. Excommunication

R1.1.5. Religion

R1.1.5.0. Religion: *æ(w), æwfæstnes, geleafa,* lay a1225–1599, law a1225–1685, religion a1225–, rite c1375–1567, opium of the people 1926–

XR R1.1.0. Faith

.char of: *æwfæstlic,* religious 1538–, religionary a1691–(1867), religio- 1894– *comb.form*

.char by: *æwfæstlic,* religious a1225–, serious 1796–

XR R1.7.0. Piety

..state of being: religiosity 1382–, religiousty 1388-1475, religiousness 1450/1530–

.parallel to: parareligious 1966–

.without: unreligioned 1674(1), religionless 1750–

.in manner of: *æwfæstlice,* religiously 1382–

.description of: hierography 1656 + 1877

.history of: hierology 1883(1)
..p versed in: hierologist 1839–
.literature about: hierology 1854–
.to imbue with: religionate *vt* 1676(1), religionize *vt* 1830–
.to affect: religionize *vi* 1716 + 1853

R1.1.5.1. A Religion/Church: *æfterfylgung, geleafa, +laðung,
cirice*/church OE–, kirk c1200– *Sc. and N.*, spouse c1200–
fig., lore a1225–c1550, law a1225–1685, religion a1300–, faith
c1325–, hirsel c1375+1880 *fig.; Sc. and N.*, sect c1386–, set
1387–1538, lear c1440(1), schism c1511–, profession 1526–,
congregation 1526/34–1708, segregation 1563+1605,
communion 1565–, sex 1575/85–1707, *hortus conclusus* 1624–
fig., confession a1641(1), sectary 1643–1764, dispensation
1643/7–, judg(e)ment 1653–1687, churchship 1675(1),
persuasion 1727–, denomination 1746/7–, connexion
1757–(1859), covenant 1818–1867, sectarism 1821(1), cult
1901–
.visible: church visible 1562-(1858)
.invisible: church invisible 1561–, church mystical 1594(1)
.militant: church militant 1538–
.mother: mother-church 1574–
.secret: para-church 1870–
.small: under-faction 1642+1667, under-sect 1653+1682,
sectiuncle 1851(1)
.triumphant: church triumphant 1552(1)

.char of: *ciriclic*/churchly OE–, church c1200–, ecclesiastic 1483–,
ecclesiastical 1538–, churchlike 1593(1), ecclesial 1649–,
ecclesiastico- 1685– *comb.form*, denominational 1838–,
church-wise 1847(1), cultic 1898–, cultual 1906+1912
..condition of being: ecclesiasticalness 1659(1), ecclesiasticism
1862–, churchiness 1884–, churchliness 1887(1)
..not: unchurchlike 1642–, unchurchly 1858+1883
.strongly smacking of: churchish 1786–1852, churchy 1864–
                                    XR R2.2.4.1.0. Anglicanism
.included in: in the bosom of the church a1600–, inchurched
a1658–1702

..not: churchless 1834/5–
.without: churchless 1641–1662, unchurched 1870+1889
.existing/occurring within: intra-ecclesiastical 1840(1)
.representing entire: pan-ecclesiastical 1888(1),
    pan-denominational 1892–
.between several: inter-church 1905 + 1926,
    inter-denominational 1920(1), transdenominational 1972–

.in manner of: *godcundlice*, ecclesiastically 1588–, church-wise
    a1626–1635, denominationally 1845(1), cultically 1953(1)

.status of: factory 1641(1–*Milton*), churchship 1645–a1716,
    churchdom 1659–(1851)
.usage of: church-way 1647–1689
.matters concerning: ecclesiastics *npl* a1619–1738, ecclesiasticals
    npl 1641–1710, spirituals *npl* 1647–
..char of: spiritual 1338–, spirital 1390(2)

.membership in: *ciricgemana, cristendom*, church-membership
    1651–, church-communion 1653–1746
..p having: sister *nf* c1449–, church-member 1653–(1705),
    churchman 1677–, church-woman *nf* 1722–, zioner 1760(1),
    churchite 1811–1848
...in diocese: diocesan 1502–(1839), diocesener a1626(1)
..certificate of: letter of communion 1697(1), communion letter
    a1711(1)

.p adhering to same: *brođor*/brother OE–, co-religionist
    1842–(1862), co-religionary 1861(1)
.p believing in all: omnist 1839(1)
.p desiring union of all: unionist 1852–(1869)
                               XR R1.1.16. Catholicity

.subjection to influence of: churching 1856(1)
.proclamation of: apostleship 1855(1)
.doctrine of multiplicity of: polychurchism 1883–
..char of: polychurch 1883(1)
.excessive devotion to: churchism 1768–, churchianity 1837–,
    ecclesiolatry 1847–, ecclesiasticism 1862–

.science of: ecclesiology 1837–

..p **studying:** ecclesiologist 1841–(1884)
..char **of:** ecclesiological 1847–(1883), ecclesiologic 1882(1)
.to **form into:** church *vt* 1659(1), enchurch *vt* 1681–1702
.to **deprive C of its character:** dischurch *vt* 1629–1656,
    non-church *v* a1769(1)
.to **imbue with principles of:** churchify *v (no quots.)*
..**having undergone:** churchified 1843–
.to **become united to:** be reconciled to *vpass* 1639–1769,
    reconcile (oneself) to *vrefl* 1689(1)
.to **play the:** church it *vphr* 1619(1)
.to **sanction by authority of:** canonize *vt* 1393–(1869)
..**having been:** *godcund*
...**not:** churchless 1884(1)

R1.1.5.2. Kinds of religion
.**affected/excessive:** religiosity 1799–
                                    XR R1.7.1. Sanctimoniousness
..**char by:** religiose 1853–
.**institutional:** institutionalism 1862–
..p **char by:** institutionalist 1920+1957
..**char by:** institutional 1908–
.**natural:** natural religion 1675–
.**nature-based:** naturalism 1866–(1894), nature-religion 1877(1)
                                    XR R1.5.1. Natural theology
..p **char by:** naturalist 1587–(1864), naturian 1621–1633
..**char by:** naturalist 1830(1), naturalistic 1840–(1884),
    naturalized 1858–
.**influenced by politics:** politico-religious *a* 1754–
..p **char by:** politico-religionist 1835(1)
.**revealed:** revealed religion 1719–

R1.1.6. Orthodoxy

R1.1.6. Orthodoxy: *rihtgeleafa, rihtgeleaffulnes,* the faith
    a1300–, truth c1375–, soundness 1583–, orthodoxy 1630–,
    orthodoxism 1644(1), orthodoxness 1644–1709,

orthodoxalness 1654(1), orthodoxality 1660–1726,
symmetricalness 1684(1)
.**instance of:** orthodoxies *npl* 1871–(1874)

.**p char by:** faithful 1571–1849, orthodox 1587–1797, orthodoxist
1857(1)
..**pl/coll:** the faithful 1558–(1848)
...**list of:** diptychs *npl* 1640–(1882/3)
.**p professing:** orthodoxian 1621–

.**char by:** *geleafful, rihthycgende, rihtgeleafful, rihtlyfend,*
rihtgelyfed, rihtgelyfende, rihtwuldriende, wuldorlic, riht/right
OE–1648, catholic c1500–, sound 1526–, catholical 1556(1),
orthodoxastical 1563/87–1577, orthodoxical 1577–, orthodox
1581–, orthodoxal 1585/7–1819, symmetral 1660–1685,
hardshell 1838–, hardshelled 1842–, observant 1902–,
bienpensant 1923– *Fr.*

.**in manner of:** *rihtgeleaffullice, rihtlice,* soundly 1574–1676,
orthodoxally 1606 + 1834, orthodoxly c1615–, orthodoxically
1834–

.**emphasis on:** orthodoxism 1828–
XR R1.1.2. Doctrinalism
.**Vincentian:** Vincentian *a* 1875–
.**1539 Act testing:** Six Articles 1655 + 1862
.**to display:** be sound on (x) *vphr* 1856– *colloq.; orig. U.S.*

R1.1.7. Heterodoxy

R1.1.7. Heterodoxy: heterodoxy 1659–, heterodoxness 1664–,
unorthodoxy a1704–(1879), cacodoxy a1864(1)

.**instance of:** heterodox 1619–1691, heterodoxy 1652/62–

.**p char by:** heterodox 1647(1)

.**char by:** heterodox 1637/50–, heterodoxal c1645–1674,
heterodoxical 1651–(1821), unorthodox 1657–, cacodoxical
1693+1880, cacodox 1716(1), cacodoxian 1716(1)
XR R1.1.2.3. Unapostolic

.in manner of: heterodoxly 1664–

R1.1.8. Free-thought

R1.1.8. Free-thought: free-thinking ?1692–1773, free-thought
  1711–

.p char by: free-thinker ?1692–

.char of: free-thinking 1726–
.char by: free-thinking a1716 + 1750

R1.1.9. Superstition

R1.1.9. Superstition: *scinnlac,* superstitiosity c1400–1520,
  superstition 1538–, collier's faith 1581–1680
                                        XR R4.1.2.1. Mummery
.instance of: freit a1300–(1868), superstition 1402–

.p char by: bigot 1598–1664, superstitionist 1651–

.char of: superstitious c1386–
.char by: superstitious 1526–, superstitional 1683+c1850,
    ?freightful 1716(1), freity 1788+1818 *Sc.*
..quality of being: superstitiousness 1526–

.in manner of: superstitiously 1552–

.to treat (x) with: superstitiate *vt* a1688(1)

R1.1.10. Heresy

R1.1.10. Heresy: *gedwildæfterfylgung, gedwola, gedwolspræc,
  scinnlac, treowleasnes, dwild*/dwild OE–c1200, heresy
  a1225–, misbelief a1225–, sect 13?–a1727, misbelieving
  1340–1644, irreligion 1592–1655, steal-truth 1628(1),
  Manich(a)eism 1894–
.extreme: buggery 1330(1), buggerage 1538(1), arch-heresy
  1668(1)

.p char by: *gedwildman, +dwola, +dwolmann, toslitere,*
eretic/heretic OE–, erite c1175(1), dwale c1200–c1250,
bugger/bougre 1340*2q1s,* erege 1340(1), landleaper
1377–1565, buggeress *nf* c1450(1), misbeliever 1470/85–1868,
landloper 15..(1), zendik 1842(1-*Moslem*), zendician
1845(1-*Moslem*)
..chief: arch-heretic 1528–1659 + 1858, heresiarch 1624–
XR R3.2.1.8.1. Dwolbiscop

..who denies his H: negative 1731(1)
..p capturing: heretic-taker 1563/87(1)
.p purveying: heresy monger 1872(1)
.p fighting: heresimach 1824(1)

.church/sect char by: synagogue (of Satan) 1464–1688 + 1874

.char by: *dwellic, gedwol, dwollic, dwoligenlic, sliten, widerweard,*
dwal-kenned c1200(1), misbelieved a1225–1494, dwale
c1250(1), misbelieving c1330–, landleaping 1377(1), heretic
1382–, heretical 1532–, sinistral 1545–1547, sinistrous
1560–1632, unsound 1597–(1680), servetian 1655(1),
manichæistic 1924 + 1932
..condition of being: hereticalness 1681–

.in manner of: irreligiously 1577(1), heretically 1661–

.description of: heresiography 1645–, heresiology 1874–
..p producing: heresiologist/-er 1710–, heresiographer 1822–
.search for: heresy hunting 1882(1), heretic hunting 1895(1)
..p engaging in: heresy-hunter 1765–, heresy ferret 1814(1)
.(of the Inquisition:)delation of heretics to secular power:
relaxation 1826 + 1894
XR R3.1.3.1. Inquisition

..to perform: relax *vt* 1838+1853

.burning of heretics: Bonnering 1613–1627, heretic burning
1895(1)
.the determining whether x is char by: qualification 1826(1)
.the pronouncing (xp) as char by: heretication 1685–
..p performing: hereticator 1685–
..to perform: beheretic *vt* 1539 + 1656, hereticate *vt* 1629–,
hereticize *vt* 1830(1)

.to imbue (xp) with: hereticate *vt* 1731 + 1832
.to fall into: lapse *vi* 1611–(1667)

R1.1.11.0. Paganism

R1.1.11.0. Paganism: *deofolgield, feondgyld, hǣðengield, idelgild, idelnes, ungeleafsumnes, wigle, wigweorðung, hǣðenscipe*/heathenship OE–c1205, *hǣðennes*/heatheness(e) OE–1848, *hǣðendom*/heathendom OE–, idolatry c1250–, maumetry a1300–1577/87 + a1654*hist.*, fornication a1340–(1860), whoredom c1380–, prepucy 1382(1-*transf.*), prepuce c1400–1582 *(transf.)*, paganism 1433–, imagery c1440–1624, paynimhood c1470(1), gentility 1526–1650, superstition 1526–, superstitiousness 1526–, uncircumcision 1526–, mahometry 1530–1579, idolry 1535(1), whoring 1535–a1638, paganity 1548–(1866), idololatry 1550 + a1641, gentilism 1577–, heathenry 1577–, uncircumcisedness 1583 + a1639, idolatrousness 1583–1764, paganry 1583 + 1866, irreligion 1598–, infidelity 1603 + 1613, heathenism 1605–, idolism 1608 + 1816, ethnicism 1613–1851, misreligion 1623–1648, idolomania 1624 + 1660, idolomany 1624 + 1654, iconolatry 1624–, baalism a1625–(1862), image-worship 1628–, idolizing 1637 + 1677, irreligiousness 1643(1), idol-worship 1667–, pagod-worship 1719(1), ethnicity 1772(1), symbololatry 1828 + 1888, irreligionism 1843(1), old religion 1848(1), baal-worship 1863(1), gentiledom 1869(1), triology 1894(1)
.instance of: maumetries *npl* c1340–1563/87, infidelity 1542/5 + 1652, heathenism 1843 + 1860

XR R1.7.3. Impiety
R5.17. Symbol, image

..minor: after-paganism 1664(1)

.p char by: *deofolgielda, hǣðengilda, hǣðen(a)*/heathen OE–, saracen c1250–1552, payen c1290–a1550, paynen 13..(1), ?wanbody 1303(1), ethnic c1375–1728, pagan c1375–, idolater c1380–, miscreant 138.– *arch.*, paynim 1382–1848, idolaster c1386–1616, gentile 1390–(1844), maumeter c1440–1496,

infidel 1470/85–, maumet-worshipper 1483(1), serve-image
1530(1), heathenist 1551–1570, image-worshipper 1563–1565,
giaour 1564– *Moslem*, baalist a1603–1642, idolatress *nf* 1613–,
idolist 1614–, iconolater 1654–, baalite 1639 + 1821, caffre
1680–1817 *Moslem*, iconodulist 1716–, irreligionist a1779–,
kaffir 1790–1865 *Moslem*, goy 1841– *Jewish*, iconodule 1893–
..who is king: *hæðencyning*
..pl/coll: *hæðendom, hæðenfolc, ðeoda*/thedes OE–a1175,
hæðennes/heathenesse OE–(1828), *da hæðen*/the heathen
OE–, paynim c1250–14.., heathenhede a1300(1), ?saracen
a1300–1303, ging a1300–a1340, payeny/payenie a1300–a1530,
payemy c1300(1), the nations a1340–1656, paynimry
1382–1483 + 1835–1886, paynimy 1481(1), pagany
a1533–1594, gentility 1546–1582, the faithless 1577(1),
gentilism a1638–1654, paganism 1640–c1650, pagandom
1853–, heathendom 1860–, heathenry a1890(1)

.char by: *godgildlic, hearglic, ðeodisc, hæðenisc*/heathenish
OE–(1774), *hæðen*/heathen OE–, misbelieved a1225–1494,
payen a1300–1513, paynim c1320–(1899) *arch. or poet.*,
miscreant c1330–1865, payeme c1375–c1400, uncircumcided
1382(1-*Wyclif*), uncircumcised a1400–(1825), heathenly
1415–1591, ethnic c1470–(1873), miscredent 1480(1), gentile
1494–1789, profane 1500/20*Sc.* + 1560–, whorish 1535–1711,
idolous 1546(1), maumetrous 1546(1), ethnical 1547–1762,
ethnish 1550 + 1563, gentilish 1550–1651, idololatrical
1550–1679, idolatrical 1550–1796, idolatrous 1550–, infidel
1551–, gentilical 1573–1600, paganical 1573–1678, irreligious
1575/85–1634, idolish 1577/87–1641, heatheny 1580(1),
superstitious 1582–a1704, paganish 1583–1718, pagan c1586–,
idol 1600–, gentilic 1604 *(2q1s)*, gentilitious 1613(1),
idolatrizing 1614 + 1817, mahound 1624 *(2q1s)*, misreligious
1625(1), paganizing 1631–, gentilizing a1638–(1819),
idololatrous a1642(1), infidelious 1648 + 1652, baalitical
1659(1), national 1662(1), idolatric 1669–(1887), baalish
1690(1), idololatric a1711(1), paganized 1732–, infidelical
1802 + 1864, gentilized 1827–, greekish 1851(1), unselect
1882(1), paganistic 1933–, goyish 1959– *Jewish*

XR R4.2.1.0. Unbaptized
..**not:** unpagan 1614(1), unidolatrous 1841 + 1881

.**in manner of:** superstitiously 1552–, heathenishly 1561–,
   ethnically 1563–1587, idolatrously 1583–, paganly
   1659–(1835), paganically 1664–1678, paganishly 1825(1),
   infidelly 1844(1)

.**time/place where P prevails:** *hædendom, hædenscipe,*
   hædennes/heatheness OE–(1828), barbary 1480 + 1513

.**to practise:** idolatrize *vi* 1592–(1706), gentilize *vi* 1593–1680 +
   1814–, idol *vt* 1598–1644, idolize *vt* 1598–, idolize *vi* 1631–,
   paganize *v* 1640–, ethnicize *vi* 1663(1), heathenize *v* 1681–,
   infidelize *vi* 1876(1)
.**to deprive (xp) of:** unidolatrize *vt* 1659(1)

R1.1.11.1. Paganization: paganizing 1652–, paganization 1863–
.**p performing:** paganizer 1727/41–
.**to perform:** paganize *vt* 1615–, heathenize *v* 1681–, gentilize *vt*
   1827–, infidelize *vt* 1836 + 1847
.**to undergo:** paganize *v* 1640–

.**a second time:** repaganizing 1685 + 1701, repaganization
   1888(1)
..**p performing:** repaganizer 1672(1)
..**char by:** repaganized 1854(1)
..**to perform:** repaganize *vt* 1685(1), anapaganize *vt* 1831(1)

R1.1.12.0. Atheism

R1.1.12.0. Atheism: *geleafleasnes, geleafleast/-lyst, ungeleafful,*
   ungeleafsum, ungetreownes, unbelief c1160–, untruth c1380
   (2q1s), untroth c1380–c1400, unbelieffulness 1382(1- *Wyclif),*
   unreligiosity 1382(1), irreligiosity 1382–1612, unfaithfulness
   1388–1561, unbelieving a1400–, doubt c1400–, unfaith 1415 +
   1826–(1870), infidelity 1509–(1875), incredulity 1532–1619,
   atheonism c1534(1), unbelievingness 1561 + 1581,
   irreligiousness 1577–, unreligiousness 1579(1), atheism 1587–,

faithlessness 1605–, discredence 1626–(1849), doubting
a1628–, disbelieving 1644(1), discredit 1647–(1868),
atheisticalness 1654 + 1667, diffidelity 1659(1), disbelief
1672–, atheisticness 1691(1), scepticism 1800–, nothingism
1809/10–1884, nihilism a1817–, infidelism a1834(1-*Coleridge*),
agnosticism 1870(1), disfaith 1870(1), know-nothingism 1871
+ 1881, nothingarianism 1872–1894, no-Goddism 1931(1)

.p char by: *ungelyfen(d)*, infidel 1526–, unbeliever 1526–,
nullifidian 1564/78–, atheist 1571–, sceptic 1638–, disbeliever
1648–, scorner ?1651–, scoffer 1691–, sceptic-Christian
1711(1), nothingarian 1789–, nihilist 1836/7–, no-religionist
1838(1), netheist 1855–, agnostic 1870–, know-nothing 1871
+ 1875, nescient 1872–, nothingist 1890(1), bush baptist
1902–1959 *Austral. slang*, no-Goddite 1952(1)

..pl/coll: the faithless 1577 + 1944

.char by: *geleafleas, +treowleas, ungeleafful, ungeleafsum,
ungelyfed, ungetreowe, untriwe,* unbelieved c1200–c1450,
faithless a1300–, untruthful c1375+1456, unbeliefful
c1380–c1430/40, unfaithful 1382–(1800), unreligious 1382–,
untrothful a1400(1), unbelieving a1400–, out of belief
1493(1), godless 1528–, irreligious 1561–, incredulous
1579–(1829), atheistical 1588–, athean 1611–1625, atheal
1612(1), atheous 1612–1792, beliefless 1612 + 1849,
nullifidian 1627–, atheistic 1634–, nihilistic 1857–,
know-nothing 1860–, agnostic 1873–, nescient 1876(1),
agnostical 1884–, no-God 1933(1)

.in manner of: unreligiously c1535 + 1847, irreligiously
c1630–(1769,) atheistically 1655–, unbelievingly 1685–(1850),
agnostically 1882(1)

.to manifest: untrow *vi* c1200(1), discredit *vt* 1559–, disbelieve *vt*
1644–, atheize *vi* 1678(1), disbelieve *vi* 1834(1)

R1.1.12.1. Atheization:
.p performing: atheizer 1678(1)
.to perform: atheize *vt* 1678–1865

R1.1.13.0. Conformity

R1.1.13.0. Conformity: conformity 1622–
.p char by: conformitan 1603–1622, conformitant 1621–1662,
　　regular 1632(1), conformist 1634–
..pl/coll: conformity 1672(1)
..occasional: occasionalist 1705(1)

.char by: conformable 1597–1861, conformitant 1632–1641,
　　conformist 1641–, conform 1663–1711, conforming 1681–
.to manifest: conform *vi* 1619–

R1.1.13.1. Non-conformity: dissent 1585–, nonconformity
　　1618–, inconformity 1633–, unconformity 1635–a1667,
　　dissentaneousness 1652(1), dissenting 1655(1),
　　nonconformitancy a1670(1), nonconforming 1682–1716,
　　dissension 1708–1807, dissenterism 1809 + 1847,
　　nonconformism 1844–, dissentism 1859(1), dissenterage
　　1866(1-*Carlyle*)
　　　　　　　　　　　　　　　　XR R1.1.7. Heterodoxy
.p char by: unconformitant 1605 + 1629, nonconformitan
　　1618–1647, non-conformer 1619–1676, non-conformist 1619–,
　　nonconformitant 1627–a1670, inconformist 1633–, dissenter
　　1639–, unconformist 1640 + 1653, fanatic 1644–1833 *hostile*,
　　disagreer a1660(1), non-consenter 1661(1), nonconformist
　　1672–, withdrawer 1677 + 1823, meeting-house man 1711(1),
　　shit-sack 1769–1785 *hostile*, recusant 1777–, dissident
　　1790–(1874), meetinger 1810–, chapel-goer 1842(1),
　　speckle-belly 1874(1-*slang*)
..pl/coll: separation 1599–1710, meeting-folks 1835(1)
..of Liverpool: Octagonian *a* 1813(1)
..Protestant: sectary 1556–, separator 1607–?1684, separatist
　　1608–, Protestant dissenter 1672–1839
　　　　　　　　　　　　　　　　XR R1.1.15.0. Sectarianism
..rural: pantiler 1856–1889
..Russian: Raskolnik 1799–
　　　　　　　　　　　　XR R2.2.2.1. Russian Orthodoxy

.char by: dissentious a1568–1676, unconformitant 1605 + 1629, unconformable 1611–(1861), unconformed a1631 + 1676, unconforming 1641–(1825), nonconformist 1641–, dissenting 1644–, nonconforming 1646–, unconformitable 1647(1), unconform 1653 + 1676, fanatical 1678–1703, non-consenting 1680–1805, unconformist 1688(1), pantile 1715–1785, nonconformistical 1808(1), dissident 1837(1-*Carlyle*), dissenterish 1841 + 1864, chapel 1946– *colloq.*

.in manner of: nonconformistically 1891(1)

.to imbue with: dissenterize *vt* 1838+1856
.to manifest: dissent *vi* c1553–

R1.1.13.2. Recusancy

R1.1.13.2. Recusancy: recusance 1597–, recusancy c1600–
.p char by: recusant 1552/3–, refuser 1610–1687
.char by: refusant 1577(1), recusant 1611–

R1.1.14. Apostasy

R1.1.14. Apostasy: *fleamlast, frætgenga, onwegacyr(red)nes, widersacung, widersæc,* apostasy c1380–, perversion 1388–, recidivation c1420–1693, residuation 1534(1), backsliding 1552–(1865), resiluation 1577/81(1), apostatizing 1659(1), apostating 1660(1), perverting 1680(1), apostatism 1814(1)

.p char by: *aflieged, hindergenga, widersaca, apostata*/apostate OE(L)–, postate 1387–1483, apostatrice *nf* 1546(1), backslider 1581–(1873), pervert 1661–(1879)
..from Judaism: meshum(m)ad 1892–

.char by: forraught c1200(1), apostate 1382–, apostasied 1393(1-*Gower*), departed c1511(1), apostatical 1532–, apostatate 1536–1629, apostatic 1583 + 1841, apostatous 1588(1), collapsed 1609–1626, apostatized 1629 + 1827, apostated 1642–1680, apostatizing 1652 + 1880, apostating a1656(1), backsliding 1816(1), backslidden 1871(1)

..**not:** unapostatized 1684 (*2q1s*)

...**condition of being:** unapostatizedness 1684(1)

.**in manner of:** pervertedly 1816–

.**to promote:** *framgewitan v,* pervert *vt* 13..–, apostatize (from/to)
    vi 1552–(1839), apostatize *vi* 1611–

.**to manifest:** *widersacian v,* backslide *vi* 1581–(1835)

R1.1.15.0. Sectarianism

R1.1.15.0. Sectarianism: separatism 1641–, sectarism
    1643–1835, sectarianism 1817–, denominationalism
    1855–(1870), sectism 1864–, separationism 1875 + 1886
    denominationality 1892(1)

.**p char by:** sectator 1541–, sectary 1556–, swermer 1585/7(1),
    swermerian 1585/7(1), sectuary 1592–1654, separator
    1607–?1684, separatist 1608–, sectist 1612–1654, separate
    1612–1659, separist 1616–1700, seeker 1617–1836, sectarist
    1618–1833, opinionist 1623–1760, seekerness 1657(1),
    sectarian 1827–, come-outer 1855– *U.S.,* denominationalist
    1870(1), disjunctionist 1872(1), seekerist 1884(1)
                XR R1.1.13.1. Protestant non-conformist

.**char of:** sectarian 1649–, separatist 1864–

.**char by:** sectary 1590–1798, separatistical 1610(1), separistical
    1633(1), separistic 1653(1), separate 1680 + 1686, separating
    1734(1), sectarial 1816–, separatist 1830(1), separatistic
    1830–, denominational 1838–, separatical 1846(1), societyish
    1863(1)

.**in manner of:** denominationally 1845(1), sectarianly 1853(1)

R1.1.15.1. Sectarianization: sectarianizing 1908(1)

.**char by:** sectarianizing 1909(1)

.**to perform:** sectarianize *vt* 1846/9–, denominationalize *vt*
    1869–(1893), sectionalize *vt* 1890/1(1)

.**to manifest:** separate *vi* 1595–, sectarianize *vi* 1842–

R1.1.15.2. Bigotry: bigotry a1674–, bigotism 1681 + 1705
.p char by: bigot 1661–
.char by: bigoted 1645–, bigotish 1652(1), narrow-throated 1674–,
   bigotic(al) 1678(2)
.in manner of: bigotly 1646(1), bigotically 1678(1), bigotedly
   1831(1)

R1.1.15.3. Schism: *toslitnes,* schismacy 1387(1), schism 1390–,
   segregation 1555–1683, concision 1557–a1716, scissure
   1634–1654
                                        XR R2.2.4.0.3. Reformation
.instance of: ?schism 1644(1)
..formal: formal schism ?1656(1)

.p char by: schismatic 1377–, schismat(e) c1450(*3q2s*),
   conventicler 1590–1862 *hostile,* conventiculist 1637(1-*hostile*),
   conventicleer 1647–1716 *hostile,* sectarian 1654– *now hist.,*
   schismatist 1754–(1895)
.p founding: schismarch 1657(1)

.char by: schismatic c1440–, schismatical a1548–, schismic
   1608+1614, schismatizing 1657+1712, schismaticating
   1712(1), separated 1869(1)
..condition of being: schismaticalness 1664–1718

.in manner of: schismatically 1554–

.the accomplishing of: secession 1660–
..to perform: schismatize *vt* 1645(1)
..to undergo: schize *vi* 1596(1), schismatize *vi* 1601–, schism *vi*
   1604–1645, secede *vi* 1797–

R1.1.16. Catholicity

R1.1.16. Catholicity: universality ?1559–(1874), catholicness
   1605–1674, catholicship 1653(1), catholicism 1656–(1796),
   œcumenicity 1840–, catholicity 1841–, unsectarianism
   1866(1), œcumenicality 1869(1), undenominationalism
   1883(1), ecumenism 1948–

.p supporting: undenominationalist 1884(1), unsectarian 1888(1),
    ecumenist 1964–
.p belonging to church claiming: catholic c1425+1594–

.char by: *anlic, eallic, eallgeleaflic, geleaflic, gemæne,* universal
    1483–, catholic 1526+1642, catholic 1532–, œcumenical
    1563/87–, œcumenic 1588–(1840), schismless 1641(1),
    unsectarian 1847–, œcumenian 1865(1), undenominational
    1871+1885
..not: uncatholic 1660–
...condition of being: uncatholicalness 1695(1)

.in manner of: œcumenically a1751–, undenominationally 1906(1)

.to promote: unsectarianize *vt* 1836(1)

                                    XR R4.2.4.0. Intercommunion

R1.2. Scripture

R1.2.0. Scripture general: *fyrngewrit, halig gewrit*/holy writ
    OE–, Holy Write 1303–1551, scripture 1581–, sacred writ
    1593(1), sacred book 1781(1)

R1.2.1.0. Bible: *seo halge gesegen, Godes boc*/God's book
    OE–(1635), *bibliodece*/bibliotheca OE(L) + 1879, *halig
    gewrit*/Holy Writ OE–, *gewrit(u)*/writ OE–, book c1200–,
    Bible a1300–, (the) (holy) scripture a1300–, Holy Write
    1303–1551, the (sacred/holy) writings 1340–, holy lettrure
    1377(1), the (holy) scriptures 1382–, gospel 1393–1483,
    escripture 1489(1-*Caxton*), theology 1494(1), oracles 1548–,
    word 1553–, the write 1567(1), sacred writ 1593(1), sacred
    letters a1604(1), *Kitab* 1652– *Arab.*, sacred book 1781(1), the
    sacred volume 1850–, the good book 1896(1)

.p writing: penman (of God) 1601–1741+1875
.p revising: revisionists *npl* 1881+1885

.char of: theologal 1484–1610, theological 1526–, scripturely
    1549+1597, theologic 1605–1637, scriptural 1641–, biblic
    1684–c1811, biblical 1790–, biblico- *comb. form* 1800–(1869),

testamentary 1849 + 1905
> XR R1.2.2. Targumic

..quality of being: scripturality 1831–, biblicality 1851–,
scripturalness 1874–

..to render (x): scripturalize *vt* 1858(1)

..not: unscripturely 1549(1), scriptureless 1563–, unscriptural
1653–, unscripture 1697(1), unbiblical 1828–

...quality of being: unscripturalness 1677 + 1868, unscripturality
1733 + 1827

...to render (x): unscripture *vt* 1690(1)

.subjected to: biblicized 1865(1)

.warranted by: scriptured 1606(1), scripture-proof 1641 + 1647

.devoted to study of: philobiblical 1880(1)

.learned in: scriptured 1532 + 1533

.in manner of: scripturely 1532(1), scripturally 1679–, biblically
1838(1)

..not: unscripturally 1824(1)

.reading of: scripturing 1588(1), bible-reading 1827 + 1863
> XR R4.5.1. Evangelization

..p char by: bibler 1538 + 1625, bible-reader 1538 + 1874, biblist
1562 + 1653, scripture-reader 1625–, bible-clerk 1626(1),
?scripturalist 1725(1), bible-student 1853(1), bible-woman *nf*
1859–
> XR R1.2.1.1. Textualist

..char by: bible-reading 1849(1)

..vigorous/aggressive: bible-punching 1933(1)

...p char by: bible-pounder 1889–1923, bible-puncher 1917 +
1938, bible-thumper 1923 + 1942, bible-banger 1942– *Austral.
and N.Z.*, bible-basher 1945 + 1958 *Austral. and N.Z.*

...char by: bible-bashing 1944(1), bible-pounding 1951(1),
bible-punching 1961(1), bible-banging 1964(1)

.devotion to: scripturism 1864–

.denial of authority to: antiscripturism 1661(1)

..p char by: antiscripturian 1645(1), antiscripturist 1647–1731

..char by: antiscripturian 1613(1), antiscriptural 1677 + 1856

R1.2.1.1.0. Text of Bible: text 13..–(a1668)

.**passage of:** *gewrit(u)*/writ OE–a1200, stead c1175–1557, text
    1377–, scripture 1382–(1864), verse 1560–, parcel 1570–1655
.**volume of:** text 1387–1536 + 1883*hist.*, Bible 1468–, text-book
    1861–1877, *textus* 1874–

.**p learned in:** scripturian 1599–, textuary 1608–(1879), textualist
    1629–, textuist 1631–1700, scripturist 1661–
                          XR R1.2.1.0. Scripture-reader
.**char of:** textual c1470–, textuary 1646–
.**conforming to:** textual 1614–

.**exact meaning of Hebrew/Greek:** verity 1535–1771

.**strict adherence to:** textuality 1836–1888, bibliolatry 1847(1),
    grammatolatry 1847–, biblicism 1851 + 1874, scripturalism
    1858–, textualism 1863–, biblism 1879(1)
                          XR R1.2.1.1.3. Literalism
                          R2.2.4. Fundamentalism
..**p char by:** ink-divine 1604(1), textual 1614(1), text-man
    1619–1702, scripturist 1624 + 1737, scripturary 1659(1),
    scripturarian 1678 + 1718, textuary 1727/41 + 1828,
    bible-bigot 1766–1820, bible-moth 1789 + 1820, bibliolatrist
    1826(1), biblist 1836(1), biblicist 1837 + 1862, bibliolater
    1847(1), scripturalist 1857(1), textualist 1885(1)
..**char by:** textual 1613(1), textuary 1613(1), scripturian 1826(1),
    bibliolatrous 1865(1)
.**opinion that T is sufficient guide:** gymnobiblism 1826(1)
..**p char by:** gymnobiblist 1844(1)
..**char by:** gymnobiblical 1834(1)

R1.2.1.1.1. Kinds of texts
Four parallel versions: tetraples *npl* 1684–1705, *tetrapla npl*
    1831/3(1)
Six parallel versions: *hexapla npl* 1613–
.**char of:** hexaplar 1828 + 1882/3, hexaplarian 1845(1), hexaplaric
    1894(1)
Eight parallel versions: *octapla npl* 1684–

R1.2.1.1.2. Canon: canon 1382–

XR R1.2.1.2.1.6. Deuteronomy

R1.2.1.2.2. Apocrypha

R1.2.1.2.3.0. Antilegomena

R1.2.1.2.3.3. Canonical epistle

.char of/by: canonial a1225(1), canonized 1382(1), ruler a1390(1), canonical a1568–(1862), canonic 1634/46–(1835)

..condition of being: canonicalness 1638–1747, canonicity 1797–(1849)

..not: apocrypha 1387–1690, apocryph(e) 1548(1), uncanonized 1548 + 1860, acanonical 1753(1), uncanonical 1835 + 1884

.primary:
..char of: protocanonical 1629–(1849)
.secondary:
..char of: deuterocanonical 1684–

.action of making into: canonizing 1651(1)
..to perform: canonize *vt* 1593–

.action of excluding from:
..to perform: discanonize *vt* 1605–1660, discanon *vt* 1608(1)

R1.2.1.1.3. Textual criticism
Criticism: textualism 1888–

XR R1.5.2. Isagogics

Interpretation:
.allegorical: allegory 1382–, allegorizing 1579 + 1677
..p char by: allegorizer 1824(1)
..char of: allegoric 1388 + 1549, allegorical 1528–, allegorizing 1860(1)
..to employ: allegorize *vt* 1724–, allegorize *vi* 1782(1)
.literal:

XR R1.2.1.1.0. Textualism

R2.1.1. Karaitism

..p char by: literalist 1644–, text-man 1647(1)
..char by: literal 1382–, literalistic 1875–
..in manner of: literally 1533–
.mystical: anagogy 1519–, spiritualizing 1649–, spiritualization

1820(1), anagogue 1849(1)

XR R1.8.5.2. Mystical significance

..Jewish tradition of: *cabbala* 1521–, cabal 1616–1663

.p char by: spiritualizer 1698–, mysticist 1860(1)

..char by: mystical 1526–(1860), anagogical 1528–

..in manner of: spiritually 13..–1559, anagogically 1553/82 + 1875

..to employ: spiritualize *vt* 1645–, mysterize *vt* 1650(1)

.tropological: tropology 1583–

XR R2.2.5. Tropics

..char by: tropologic c1380–, tropological 1528–

..in manner of: tropologically 1549–

R1.2.1.1.4. Versions of text

Authorized Version (1611): Authorized Version 1824(1), King James('s) Translation / Version 1835–, law-Bible 1847(1)

Bishops' Bible (1568): Bishops' Bible 1835(1)

Coverdale Bible (1539): Great Bible 1553 + 1835–

Douai Bible: Douai (-Bible) 1837–

Geneva Bible (1560): Geneva Bible c1570–, Geneva Testament 1678(1-*Dryden*), Breeches Bible 1835(1)

'He' Bible (1611): He Bible 1878–

Montanian interlinear version: interlineary 1659 + 1677

Revised Version: R. V. 1896(1)

Revised Standard Version: R. S. V. 1961–

'She' Bible (1611): She Bible 1878(2)

Treacle Bible: Treacle Bible 1899(1)

Vernacular Bible: (the) open Bible 1837 + 1908

Vinegar Bible: Vinegar Bible 1834–

Vulgate Bible: Vulgate 1815–

.char of: Vulgar 1535–1691 + 1823, Vulgate 1609–

.edition of: Vulgate 1865(2)

.interlinear gloss in: interlineary 1685(1)

.Clementine: Clementine *a* 1843(1)

.Henten's: Hentenian *a* 1902 + 1930

.Hieronymian: Vulgar 1613–1711, Vulgate 1728–

..char of: Vulgar 1535–1691 + 1823

.pre-Hieronymian: Vulgate 1728 + 1855, *Vetus Itala* (no quots.)
.Sixtine: Sixtine *a* 1843–
.Syriac: Syriac 1644–, Peshito/-itta *a* 1793–

R1.2.1.2.0. Divisions of the Bible
Testament: *ægecydnes, gecydnes,* testament a1300–, will a1893(1)
.char of: testamental 1621(1), testamentary 1849 + 1905
                       XR R1.2.1.0. Scriptural
.included in: testamented 1907(1)
.quality/nature of: testamentalness 1669(1)
Book: book c1200–

R1.2.1.2.1.0. Old Testament: *ægesetnes, seo hundseofontige*
    gefadunge, ealde lagu/old law OE–1542, Bible a1300–1850,
    Old Testament c1340–, Moses and the Prophets 1382(1), the
    Law and the Prophets 1382–1611, Septuagint 1633–, LXX
    1662–, O.T. 1892(1)
                       XR R1.2.2. Targum
.70 Greek translators of: septuagint(s) *n (pl)* 1563–1684, the
    seventy 1614–
.student of: septuagintalist 1850(1)
.char of: Old Testamentaire a1671(1-*Sc.*), septuagintal 1760–
.xp in OT foreshadowing xp in NT: type 1607–, *anagogue*
    1849(1), *figura* 1959(1)
.opinion that OT foreshadows Xtianity: Cocceianism 1886(1)
..p holding: Cocceian 1685–(1818)
..char of: Cocceian 1860(1)
.Mosaic dispensation within: *ealde lagu*/old law OE–1542,
    lagu/law OE–, Moses' law a1300(1), Torah 1577–, Mosaical
    law 1563 + 1615, Mosaic law 1701(1), law-covenant 1803(1)
                     XR R1.2.2. Pentateuch
                     R2.2.5. Antinomianism
..moral part of: moral law 1551–(1819)
                   XR R1.2.1.2.3.1. New Law
...char of: moral c1380–(1819)
...fact of belonging to: morality 1656–a1662
..p expounding: *ælærend, ælareow,* lawyer 1526(1), law-worker

1577(1), law-preacher 1645(1), legalist 1646–
                                    XR R1.7.1. Hypocrite
                                    R2.1.1. Pharisee
..char of: legal ?a1500–, lawish 1560–1654, Mosaical 1563–,
    Mosiac 1662–, Moschical 1687(1)
                                    XR R1.2.1.4. Sinaic
...condition of being: Mosaicity 1885–
..accepting: nomian 1800(1)
..principles of: legalism 1838–, Mosaism 1845–
..study of: ?law-work 1645–(1860)
.decalogue within: *tienbebod, woruldriht, lagu*/law OE–1719,
    Godes lagu/God's law OE–c1380, the (ten) commandments
    c1280–, law of God 1382–a1548, ten words 1382–1650 +
    1884, decalogue 1382–, ten precepts 1494–1564, testimonies
    1535–1611, the (ten) commands 1552–1642
..as inscribed in stone: witnessing a1340–1382, witness
    1530–1535
..one of: commandment c1325–, statute c1381–1707, ?law-word
    1645(1), command 1667(1)
...that is to be interpreted literally: literal *a* 1561–1605
..p expounding: decalogist 1650–(1889)

R1.2.1.2.1.1. Divisions of Old Testament
Pentateuch: the Law 1382–1611, Pentateuch 1530–
.char of: Pentateuchal a1846–
.Samaritan text of: Samaritan 1627–1653
                                    XR R1.2.2. Hebrew Scriptures
Hexateuch: Hexateuch 1878–
.char of: Hexateuchal 1889 + 1892
.priestly code within: priests' code 1891(1), priestly code 1899–
..writer of: priestly writer 1905(1)
.section of: sedra 1907–

Heptateuch: Heptateuch 1678–

Octateuch: Octateuch 1607–
manuscript/edition of: Octateuch 1976–

R1.2.1.2.1.2. Genesis: *cneorisboc, gecyndboc, Genesis*/Genesis
  OE(L)–
.**char of:** Genesitic 1856–, Genesiac(al) 1877–
.**account of Creation therein:** hexaëmeron a1593–
..**p believing:** Mosaist 1887(1)
..**p holding restitutionalist theory of:** restitutionalist 1888(1)
..**p holding visionist theory of:** visionist 1888(1)
..**p holding epochist theory of:** epochist 1888(1)
.**promise implied by curse upon serpent in:** *protevangelium*
  1874–, protevangel 1875–

R1.2.1.2.1.3. Exodus: *Exodus*/Exodus OE(L)–, Exode a1225(1)

R1.2.1.2.1.4. Leviticus: *ďenungboc*, Leviticus c1400–
                                          XR R4.1.2.0. Ritual
.**char of:** Levitical 1540(1)

R1.2.1.2.1.5. Numbers: Numery c1400–1574, Numbers c1400–

R1.2.1.2.1.6. Deuteronomy: *seo æftera æ, æteræ*, Deuteronomy
  1388–
.**p writing:** deuteronomist 1862–
                                          XR R1.2.1.1.2. Canon
.**char of:** deuteronomical 1533–, deuteronomic 1857–,
  deuteronomistic 1862–

R1.2.1.2.1.7. Judges: Judges 1579 + *mod.*

R1.2.1.2.1.8. Kings: the Books of Kings 1382–(1611)

R1.2.1.2.1.9. Chronicles: Paralipomena a1340–1706, Chronicles
  1545–

R1.2.1.2.1.10. Wisdom Books: Wisdom Books c1200 + 1887,
  Wisdom literature 1887(1)
.**char of:** sapiential 1568–(1880)

R1.2.1.2.1.11. Wisdom: Sapience 1362–1563, the Book of
  Wisdom 1430/40(1), the Wisdom of Solomon 1611(1), the
  Wisdom 1875–
                                          XR R1.2.2. Wisdom literature
.**char of:** Sophia 1904(1), Sophian 1904(1)

R1.2.1.2.1.12. Ecclesiasticus: Ecclesiasticus *no quots.*, the
Wisdom of Jesus the son of Sirach 1611(1)

R1.2.1.2.1.13. Psalms: *saltere*/psalter OE–, *sealmas*/Psalms
OE–1382 + 1581–, psalm-book c1200(1), psalm-song
c1200(1), psalter-book c1200–1545, psalmody 1471(1),
Psaltery 1628(1), Book of Psalms 1817(1), Psalms of David
1817(1)

XR R4.1.4.3.0. Psalm
.**part of:** nocturn 1483–1548/9, spell 1579–a1653
.**one of:** *dryhtleoð, hearpsang, sang, sealmcwide, sealmleoð,*
sealmlof, sealmsang, sealm/psalm OE–, theody 1867(1)
.**set of fifty:** *fiftig* OE
.**char of:** psalmic 1835–
.**composed as:** ?psalmed 13..(1)

R1.2.1.2.1.14. Proverbs: *bispellboc, cwidboc*, the Book of
Proverbs 1303–

R1.2.1.2.1.15. Ecclesiastes: Ecclesiastes a1300–
.**Solomon as author of:** the ecclesiast 1873(1)

R1.2.1.2.1.16. Song of Solomon: *brydlic gewrit*, love-book
a1225(1), *cantica npl* a1300–1577, Song of Songs 1382–,
Canticles *npl* 1526–(1845), Song of Solomon 1568–

R1.2.1.2.1.17. Isaiah:
.**char of:** Isaianic 1882 + 1898, Isaian 1883 + 1896
.**Isaiah as author of:** evangelical prophet 1547–(1853), evangelic
prophet 1683(1)
.**deutero:** Second Isaiah 1881–

R1.2.1.2.1.18. Jeremiah:
.**char of:** Jeremianic 1880–

R1.2.1.2.2. Apocrypha: *dyrngewrit, tweonigendlicu gewritu npl,*
ipokrephum 13..(1), Apocrypha 1539–
XR R1.2.1.1.2. Canon
.**part of:** *dyrngewrit*, apocryphal 1661–1677
.**char of:** apocrypha *a* 1387–1690, apocryph(e) 1548(1- *Coverdale)*,
apocryphal 1615–, apocryphous 1677(1)
.**p supporting inclusion of in Bible:** apocryphalist 1834(1)

R1.2. SCRIPTURE 101

R1.2.1.2.3.0. New Testament: *niwe gewitnes, seo niwe æ, seo niwe gewitnes, godspellboc*/gospel-book OE–1530, New Testament c1340–, testament 1500/20 + 1831–(1888), new covenant 1587 + 1796, the Christian volume 1785(1)
.p following: testament-man 1819(1)
.p maintaining that NT was written in pure Greek: purist 1835–
.char of: new testamental 1838(1)
.Curetonian Syriac version of: Curetonian 1861 + 1904
..char of: Curetonian 1861 + 1904
.Muratorian canon of: Muratorian canon 1855(1), Muratorian fragment 1855–
.1582 English translation of: Rhemish *a* 1589–, Rhemist-English *a* a1653(1)
.parts of whose canonicity is in dispute: antilegomena 1847–
XR R1.2.1.1.2. Canon

R1.2.1.2.3.1. Gospel: *cristes æ, cristes boc, godspel*/gospel OE–, vangel a1340–a1578, evangel a1340–(1884), wangel c1375– *Sc. and N.*, evangely 1382–1683, vangelie a1390(1), *evangelium* 1541–(1850)
XR R4.5.1. Evangelization
R5.16.2. Lectionary

.p writing: *godspellere*/gospeller OE–1674 + 1933, *evangelista*/evangelist OE–, gospelwright c1200(1)
..char of: evangelistic 1845–
.one of: *cristes boc, godspel*/gospel OE–, evangely 1393–1530, evangel c1400–(1866), spell 1579–a1653
..synoptic: synoptic 1858(1)
...p writing: synoptist 1860–
...char of: synoptic 1841–, synoptical 1875(1), synoptistic 1879(1),
..Matthew's:
...char of: Matthean 1897 *2q1s*,
..Mark's:
...char of: Marcan 1902–, Marcan 1909–
...great omission in: great omission 1911–
..Luke's:
...char of: Lucan 1876–

...**great insertion in:** great insertion 1911–
..**apocryphal, of James the Less:** *protevangelion* 1715–(1851)
..**harmony of four:** diatesseron 1803–(1887), monotessaron
    1831–1882, tetrevangelium 1898–
XR R1.5.2. Harmonistics

.**char of:** *godspellic, godspellisc,* evangelical 1553–1751, evangelic
    1594–, gospellary 1679(1)
.**such as is contained in:** gospel-like 1549–(1671)
..**not:** ungospel-like 1574–1674
.**(of p:) devoted to:** gospel-like 1553–1671
.**devoid of:** gospelless 1882/3–
.**in accordance with:** gospelly 1545 + 1678, gospel-like 1576 +
    1671, evangelically 1624–(1772), evangelicly 1678(1)
..**not:** inevangelicly 1683(1)
.**message of:** *word*/word OE–
.**truth of:** gospel-truth 1647 + 1738
.**earliest utterance of:** *see R1.2.1.2.1.2. Protevangelium*
.**faithfulness to:** evangelicalness 1645(1), evangelicity 18.. +
    1839, evangelism 1842 + 1888, evangelicality 1857(1)

R1.2.1.2.3.2. Acts of the Apostles: Deeds of the Apostles
    c1380–1533, apostle a1400–1794

R1.2.1.2.3.3. Epistle: *pistol*/pistle OE(L)–1551, epistle a1225–
XR R5.16.2. Lectionary
.**canonical:** canonial epistles a1225(1), canonized epistles 1382(1),
    canon 1483–1502, canonical 1561(1), canonical epistle 1755(1)
.**catholic:** catholic epistle 1582–(1855), general epistle 1611(1)
.**pastoral:** pastoral epistles *npl* 1836(1), pastorals *npl* 1901–
.**James's:**
..**char of:** Jacobic 1871(1), Jacobean 1883 + 1898
.**St Paul's to the Romans:** Romans c1420–

R1.2.1.2.3.4. Book of Revelations: Apocalypse c1230–, Book
    of Showing(s) a1300(1), Book of Privity/-ies a1300–c1380,
    Book of Sights 1340(1), pocalips 1377–a1440, the Revelation
    (of St John) c1400–, Revelations 1656–, (Book of)
    Revelations 1691–
XR R1.2.1.5. Biblical events

.**St John the Divine as author of:** apocalyptic 1629(1),
revelationist 1657–, apocalypt 1834(1), apocalyptist 1835–
.**char of:** apocalyptical 1633–a1638 + 1858, apocalyptic 1663–

R1.2.1.3. Biblical personages
Apostle: *ealdorđegn, postol*/postle OE–1533, *apostol*/apostle OE–,
apostoless *nf* c1410 + 1652
.**pl/coll:** *đa twelf*/the twelve OE–, *đa twelf apostalas*/the twelve
apostles OE–
.**chief:** *ealdorapostol,* arch-apostle 1726(1), pillar apostle 1882/3–
.**fellow:** *efenapostol*
.**land's:** *eđelboda*
.**char of:** *apostolic*/apostly OE + a1520, apostolical 1548–,
apostolic 1549–
..**quality of being:** apostolicness 1632(1), apostolicalness
1664–1680, apostolicity 1832–
...**claim to:** apostolicism 1864(1)
..**not:** unapostolic 1675–(1876), unapostolical 1837(1)
.**(of x:)immediately following:** subapostolic 1880–
XR R1.1.7. Unorthodox
.**in manner of:** apostolically 1641 + 1845
..**not:** unapostolically 1868 + 1884
.**office of:** *apostolhad*/apostlehood OE–(1483)*(poet. and arch.),*
apostleship 1526–(1697), apostolate 1642(1)
.**succession of:** apostolical succession 1836–
XR R3.2.1.8. Bishop
..**p maintaining:** apostolical 1839(1), successionist 1846–

7 deacons (Acts vi): the seven 1382–
Disciple: *discipul*/disciple OE(L)–, discipless *nf* 1382–1548
70 disciples (Luke x): the seventy 1520–1681/6
70 elders: septuagints 1564(1)
Holy innocents: (holy) innocents a1340–
John the Baptist: *fulwihtwer, fulluhtere*/fulcnere OE–c1200,
Baptist c1200–
XR R4.2.1.0. Baptist
.**p following:** Johannite 1659(1)
.**char of:** Johannine 1874(1)

Three Kings: the Three Kings c1200–(1583), the Magi 1377–,
    wise men 1382–, sages 1667(1)
Maccabee: Maccabee 1375–, Maccabean 1845(1)
.char of: Maccab(a)ean 1821–
Murderer of Christ: kill-Christ 1647(1)

R1.2.1.4. Biblical places
Armageddon: Armageddon 1896
                                    XR R1.2.1.5. Apocalypse
Heavenly/ideal city: Jerusalem 1382–, the new Jerusalem 1959–
Jerusalem: Holy City 1382–(1844)
Mount of Olives: Olivet c1275–
Holy Sepulchre: the holy sepulchre c1200–, the sepulchre
    1362–1486, holy grave a1455–c1511, holy sepulture 1525(1)
Mount Sinai: Sinaic *a* a1769–, Sinaitic *a* 1786–
                         XR R1.2.1.2.1.0. Mosaic dispensation
Scala Cæli: Scala Cæli 1549–(1626)
Via dolorosa: *via dolorosa* 1878–, *via crucis* 1894–

R1.2.1.5. Biblical events
Annunciation: Annunciation c1440–
Nativity: nativity a1300–
Mystical incident in Christ's life: mystery 1655–
                                XR R1.8.5.0. Mysticism
Christ's discourses: sermon c1250–
.on attaining greater moral perfection: counsel (of perfection)
    c1380–
Christ's beatitudes: blessings c1400 + 1588, macarism a1860–
Christ's non-gospel sayings: logion 1875–, agrapha *npl* 1890–
.(of x:) containing: logian 1909–(1921)
Last Supper: the (last) supper 13..–, cene c1320–1491, maundy
    1377–1640, the holy supper c1421(1), maundy-supper 1532(1)
Christ's anguish at Gethsemane: agony 1382–
Scourging of Christ: flagellation 1426–1703
Crucifixion: *rodehengen,* rood-pine c1200(1), sacrifice c1375–,
    Cross c1380–, Crucifixion 1858–
Passion: passion c1175–
Ascension: *upastigennes,* Ascension c1315–
.char of: ascendental 1858(1)

Second coming: second advent 1736(1), Parousia 1875–

Apocalypse: *se* micla/mæsta dæg, day of wrath a1300(1), pocalips 1377–a1440, day of the Lord 1382–(1583), day of doom c1386(1), the last day a1400–, day of judgment a1533–, the great day 1583–(1746/7), fifth monarchy 1657–1731, kingdom-come 1848–(1873), *eschaton* 1935–

> XR R1.2.1.2.3.4. Book of Revelations
> R1.2.1.4. Armageddon

.p believing in: millenary 1561–, chiliast 1611–, milliary 1650(1), millenar 1654(1), fifth monarchy men *npl* 1657–1731, millenian 1657/83–(1827), millen(n)ist 1664–1795, millenarian a1674–, fifth-monarchist 1736–1832/4, millennianite a1845(1), millenniumite 1837(1), eschatologist 1877(1)

..following Nepos: Nepotian 1641(1)

.char of: apocalyptic 1663–, fifth-monarchical 1679–1705

.doctrine of: chiliasm 1610–, chilianism 1645(1), eschatology 1844–, apocalypticism 1884–, apocalyptism 1889–, apocalyptic 1898–

..char of: eschatological 1854–

..char by: chiliastical a1638(1), chiliastic 1675–

..in manner of: chiliastically 1882(1)

.doctrine that A is now taking place: realized eschatology 1936–

..p holding: presentist 1878(1)

.doctrine that A has taken place:

..p holding: preterist 1843–(1860)

..char of: preterist 1878–

.doctrine that A is taking place:

..p holding: presentist 1878(1)

.doctrine that A will take place:

.p holding: futurist 1842–

.doctrine that 2nd coming will precede A: premillenarianism 1844(1), premillennialism 1848–

..p char by: premillenarian 1844–, premillennialist 1848–

..char by: premillenarian 1844–

.doctrine that 2nd coming will follow A: postmillenialism 1879(1)

..p char by: postmillenialist 1851(1), postmillenarian 1886(1)
.doctrine of sexmillenary duration of world: sexmillenarian *a*
    1851(1)
Joys of Mary: Joys of Mary a1310–(1674)

R1.2.2. Hebrew Scripture

R1.2.2. Hebrew Scripture
Hebrew (Aramaic) Old Testament: Targum 1587–
                    XR R1.2.1.2.1.0. Old Testament
.char of: Targumic a1873–
.translator of: Targumist 1642–
                    XR R1.8.6.1. Nabi
..char of: Targumistic 1890(1)
.marginal emendation in: *Keri* 1644–

Pentateuch: Testimony 1382–1667, Mosaical law 1563 + 1615,
    Torah 1577–, Mosaic law 1701(1)
                    XR R1.4.2. Rabbi
.char of: Mosaical 1563–, Mosaic 1662–
..not: unmosaic 1644 + 1868
.x belonging to: mosaicals *npl* 1643(1)

Hexateuch: Hexateuch 1878–
.author of, using Elohim: Elohist 1862–
..char of: Elohistic 1841–, Elohimic 1871–, Elohim 1875–
.author of, using Jehovah: Jehovist 1844–, Jahvist 1892(1)
                    XR R1.5.0. Adonist
..char of: Jehovistic 1841–, Jahvistic 1885 + 1894

Wisdom literature:
                    XR R1.2.1.2.1.10. Wisdom books
.char of: Sophian 1904(1)

Megillah: Megillah 1650–

Pseudepigrapha: *pseudepigrapha npl* 1884–

Masorah: Mas(s)ora(h) 1613
.p contributing to: Mas(s)orete 1587–
..pl/coll: Mas(s)ora(h) 1723–

..**char of:** Masoretical a1693–, Mas(s)oretic 1701–

Hagiographa: *Kethubim npl* 1690 + 1892–, hagiographa *npl*
    1583–, hagiography 1812(1)
.**char of:** hagiographal 1657–, hagiographical *"17th c."*,
    hagiographic 1888–
.**p writing:** hagiographer 1656–

Genizah: genizah 1897–

R1.2.3. Non-Judæo-Christian scriptures

R1.2.3. Non-Judæo-Christian scriptures
Granth: Granth 1798–
Jataka: Jataka 1828–
Koran: Alcoran 1366–1796, Koran 1625–, Kitab 1652–, Qur(')an
    1876–
XR R2.3.4.0. Hafiz, Alcoranist
.**section of:** sura 1661–
..**first:** *fatiha(h)* 1821–
.**char of:** Alcoranish 1634–1762, Alcoranal 1652(1), Koranic 1811–,
    Alcoranic 1857 + 1859, Qur(')anic 1905–
.**to make into:** alcoran *vt* a1678(1)
Purana: Purana 1696–
.**char of:** Puranic 1809–
.**(of x:)subsequent to:** post-Puranic 1862(1)
Shaster: Shaster/Shastra 1630–
.**char of:** S(h)astraic 1961–
Tantra: Tantra 1799–
.**char of:** Tantric 1905(1)
.**doctrine of:** Tantrism 1882–
Veda: Vedam 1734–1794, Veda 1776–
.**division of:** upanishad 1805–
..**principal:** rig-veda 1776–, rgveda 1886/7–
...**char of:** rig-vedic 1881–, rgvedic 1962–
...**student of:** vedist 1896(1)
..**third:** Samaveda 1798–, Saman 1843–

.version of, in continuous text: Samhita 1805–
.text from: mantra 1808–, gayatri 1845–
Zend-Avesta: Zend-Avesta 1630–, Zend 1715–, Avesta 1856–
.part of: Gatha 1862–
..char of: Gathaic 1891(1)

R1.3. Patristics

R1.3.0. Patristics: patrology 1600–, patristics 1847–
.p studying: patristic 1842(1)
.char of: patrological 1716(2), patristical 1831–, patristic 1837/9–,
    patrologic 1890(1)
.system based on: patristicism 1864–

R1.3.1. Fathers of the church: *fæder, forðfæder,* heahfæder,
    the Fathers (of the Church) 1340–, church-father 1856(1)
.distinguished by learning: doctor(s) 1303–(1552)
.who wrote in Greek: Greek fathers 1711–(1838)
.char of: patristical 1849–, patristic 1874–
..condition of being: patristicalness 1836(1)
.in manner of: patristically 1882(1)
.compilations of opinions of: (the (four) book(s) of) the
    sentences 1387–1682
..p compiling: sententioner 1545 + 1581, sententiary a1603–,
    sententiarist 1677(1)
.series of extracts from writings of: *catena* 1644–
..p compiling: catenist 1880(1)
.worship of: patrolatry 1846(1)

R1.3.1.1. Individual fathers
Thomas Aquinas: the Angelic Doctor 1657(1)
.doctrine of: Thomism 1727/41–
..p following: Thomist 1533–
..char of: Thomistical 1533–1715, Thomist 1845–, Thomistic
    1881–
Ignatius: Ignatian *a* 1832 + 1846
Isidore: Isidorian *a* 1882/3–

Origen:
.char of: Origenical 1600(1), Origenian 1661–, Origenic 1678(1)
.p following: Origenist 1546–
..char of: Origenistic 1853–
.doctrine of: Origenism 1727/8–
XR R1.2.1.1.3. Scriptural interpretation

.to follow: origenize *v* 1886(1)

R1.3.1.2. Patristic writings
Centuries: Centuries *npl* 1606(1)
.p compiling: century-writer 1626–1684, centurist 1636–1686,
    centuriator 1660–
Collations: Collations *npl* c1200–
Didache: Didache 1885–(1891)

R1.4. Law

R1.4.0. Law: *æriht, lagu*/law OE–, lay a1225–1599, common law
    of the church c1380(1)
XR R3.1.2 Ecclesiastical authority

R1.4.1. Canon law: *canonas npl* OE(L), *preostlagu*, the canon
    a1300–1601, canon law c1340–, decretal right 1489(1),
    pontifical law 1651–1758
XR R1.1.2. Doctrine

.professor of: canonistre 1362–1382, canonist 1542–(1868),
    canoneer 1641–1681
..char of: canonistic 1645–(1861)
.part of: *canondom, canonic, canon*/canon OE–
XR R5.16.5. Maniple of the curates

.principles of: canonism 1622(1)
.char of: canonistical 1865(1)
.char by: *preostlic, regollic, riht, rihtgeset, canonic*/canonic
    OE(L)–, spiritual 1474–1642, canonial 1502(1), canonical
    1570/6–(1868)
..condition of being: canonicalness 1638–(1747)
..not: uncanonical 1632–, incanonical 1637 + 1648, uncanonic

a1711 + 1868
.in manner of: *regollice,* canonly 1502(1), canonically
    1529–(1837), canonially 1581(1)
..not: uncanonically 1713–(1865)

.papal decrees forming part of: decretals *npl* 1377–, cretals *npl*
    c1380(1) decretal *ncoll* 1531 + 1563/87
                 XR R3.2.1.1.4. Papal documents
..p versed in: decretistre 1393(1), decretist c1400-(1871),
    decretary 1581(1), decretalist 1710(1)
..one of: decretal c1330–
..sixth book added to: sext 1656–
..char of: decretaline 1600–1708
..in manner of: decretally 1621–(1726)

..papal constitution not included in: extravagant 1502–(1882),
    extravaganite 1549(1)
...char of: extravagant 1387–(1885)

R1.4.2. Jewish law: Talmud 1532–
.p learned in: *rabbi*/rabbi OE–, talmudist 1569–, rabbin
    1579–(1852), talmudic 1624–a1656, Morenu 1650–, *Talmid*
    Chacham 1863–, rebbe 1881–, rav 1892–, Lamdan 1907–
                  XR R1.2.2. Masorete
..pl/coll: rabbin 1826–(1860), rabbinate 1881–
..Sephardic: haham 1676–

..char of: rabbinic 1612–, rabbinical 1622–, rabbinish 1652(1),
    rabbinic 1678(1)
..before: pre-rabbinical 1977(1)
..in manner of: rabbinically 1684–
..office of: rabbiship 1669–, rabbinate 1702(1), rabbinship 1852(1)
...period of: rabbinate 1890(1)
..government of: rabbindom 1889–
..personality of: rabbinship 1599(1)
..doctrine of: rabbinism 1652–, talmudism 1883 + 1896
...p adhering to: rabbinist 1599–
                  XR R2.1.1. Karaite
...char of: rabbinistical 1599–1676, rabbinitic 1884(1), rabbinistic

1888(1)
...study of: rabbinics 1905–
...to imbue with: rabbinize *vt* 1835–
...to adopt: rabbinize *vi* a1641–1652
..argumentation char of: *pilpul* 1894–

.p judging: dayan 1880–
.p interpreting: *writere*/writer OE–, scribe 1377–
                                        XR R2.1.1. Pharisee
..pl/coll: scribedom 1863(1)
..char of: scribistical 1600(1), scribal 1863–, sopheric 1888(1)
..authority of: sopherism 1890(1)
..teaching/literature of: scribism 1657–

.char of: Talmudistical 1593–, Talmudical 1605–, Talmudic 1611–,
    Talmudistic 1642–1781

.scroll of: *sefer torah* 1650–
.substance of: tradition c1380–, Mishna(h) 1610–
                                        XR R1.1.3. Tradition
..char of: Mishnical 1718(1), Misniac 1723(1), Misniacal 1723(1),
    Mishnic 1867–, Mishnaic 1878–
..writer of: Tanna 1718–, Tannaite 1919–
...char of: Tannaitic 1905–, Tannaite 1950–
..binding precept in: *Halachah* 1856–
...p writing: Halachist 1882(1)
...char of: Halachic 1856 + 1878
.later part of: Gemara 1613–
..char of: Gemaric 1723–
.legendary element of: Haggadah 1856–
..p writing/versed in: Haggadist 1882 + 1891
...char of: Haggadistic 1856 + 1882
..char of: Haggadic 1866 + 1881, Agadic 1878 + 1881, Haggadical
    1882/3(1)
..in manner of: Haggadically 1920(1)
.in oral tradition: Oral Law 1733–

R1.4.3. Islamic law: Sharia 1855–
.p learned in: talisman 1599–1668, mullah 1613–, *moolvee* 1625–,
    mujtahid 1815–, *ulema* a1843–

..pl/coll: *ulema* 1688(1)

R1.5. Theology

R1.5.0. Theology: divine 1303–c1400, divinity c1305–, theology
1362–
.p studying: *dryhtwurða*, diviner 1377–1552, theologue
c1425–1859, theologian 1483–, theologician c1560–, theologer
1588–(1849), theologist a1638–(1857), divine 1662–,
theologant 1678(1), theological 1866(1)
..attached to cathedral: theologal 1638 + 1872, canon
theologian 1885(1)

XR R3.1.4.3. Chapter
..of the Latin church: Latinist a1568 + 1964–
..who is also jurist: theologo-jurist a1843(1)
..learned: doctor a1375–(1871), cherubim 1547–1638, worthy
1605–1611
..non-Christian: diviner 1387(1), divine 1387–1587, theologian
1603 + 1904, theologer 1609–, theologist a1638–(1816),
theologizer 1685–1693
...Jewish adonist: adonist 1753(1)

XR R1.2.2. Jehovist
...Mohammedan: talisman 1599–1668, mullah 1613–, softa 1613–,
ulema a1843–
....pl/coll: *ulema* 1688(1)
...learned in the Shasters: Shastri c1645–

XR R1.2.3. Shaster
..petty: theologaster 1621–(1888), theologastric 1894(1), theologist
1900(1)
..p who is not: atheologian 1603(1)

.char of: theologic 1477–(a1876), theological 1603–
..not: untheological 1641–
.in manner of: theologically 1611–
.matters of: theologicals *npl* a1626 + 1774, theologicks *npl*
1728(1)
.speculation in: theologization a1529(1)
.hatred char discussions of: *odium theologicum* 1758–

.**knowledge of/skill in:** divinityship 1762(1)
..**char by:** godly-learned 1545–1611
.**statement of:** theologoumenon 1891–
.**opposition to:** atheology 1678 + 1878
..**char by:** atheological a1641 + 1880
..**with:** atheologically a1641(1)
.**to treat (x) with:** theologize *vt* 1649 + 1873
.**to speculate/reason with:** theologize *vi* 1656–

R1.5.1. Kinds of theology
.**a:** theology 1669–, theologism 1867–
.**Antiochene:**
..**p adhering to:** Antiochene 1845–, Antiochian 1867–
..**char by:** Antiochian 1840(1), Antiochene 1884–
.**of Thomas Aquinas:** *see R1.3.1.1. Thomism*
.**astro-theological:** astro-theology 1882(1)
..**char of:** theoastrological 1833(1)
.**of Karl Barth:** Barthianism 1934(1)
..**p adhering to:** Barthian 1931(1)
..**char by:** Barthian 1929–
.**biblical:** biblical theology 1846–
.**false:** pseudo-theology 1940–
.**based on myth:** mytho-theology 1927 + 1932
.**natural:** natural theology 1677–, physico-theology 1712–
                              XR R1.1.5.2. Natural religion
..**as illustrated by study of stones:** lithotheology 1869–
..**p adhering to:** physico-theologist 1825(1)
..**char by:** physico-theological 1675–
..**geology combined with:**
...**char of:** theogeological 1852(1)
.**mythology combined with:** theomythology 1858 + 1868
.**non-Christian:** theology 1662–, divinity 1669–
..**p adhering to:** *see R1.5.0. Theologian*
.**of St Paul:** Paulism 1823(1), Paulinism 1857–
..**p adhering to:** paulian 1609(1), pauline 1740(1), paulite
        1839(1), paulinist 1882(1), paulinian 1883(1)
..**char by:** paulian 1638(1), pauline 1817–, paulinistic 1860–,

paulinian 1874–
..**to follow:** paulinize *vi* 1865(1)
.**of St Peter:** Petrinism 1857(1)
..**p adhering to:** Petrinist 1922(1)
.**philosophy combined with:**
..**char of:** theophilosophic 18.. + 1901
.**process:** process theology 1971–
..**p char by:** process theologian 1974–
.**rationalistic:** new light 1650–(1806), neologism 1827–,
    rationalism 1824–, neology 1834–, neologianism 1846–,
    modernism 1901–

XR R1.8.5.1. Rationalism

..**p adhering to:** rationalist 1647–, new light a1734–, neologist
    1827–, neologian 1846–, modernist 1907–
..**char by:** new light 1732–, neologic 1797 + 1828/32, neologous
    1812(1), neologistic 1827 + 1936, neological 1827–,
    rationalistic 1830–, neologian 1831–, modernistic 1909 + 1924
..**in manner of:** neologically 1847(1)
.**of Robert of Melun:**
..**p adhering to:** robertine 1846 + 1906
.**scholastic:** school-divinity 1594–(1840), scholasticism 1756/82–
..**p adhering to:** school-doctor 1528–1609, schoolman a1540–,
    school-divine 1594–
.**of Duns Scotus:** Scotism a1871–
..**p adhering to:** Scotist 1530–
..**char by:** Scotistical 1600 + 1716, Scotist 1884–
.**synthetic:** pantheology 1656–

R1.5.2. Departments of theology
Apologetics: apologetics a1733–, apologetic 1882(1)
.**p studying:**
..**17th century Catholic:** methodist 1686–
Catechetics: catechetics 1849–

XR R4.5.7. Catechesis

Didactics: *didache* 1936–
Dogmatics: dogmaticals 1605 + 1716, dogmatic 1845–(1894),
    dogmatics 1845–

.p studying: dogmatician 1846–

> XR R1.1.2. Doctrine

Harmonistics: harmonistic(s) 1875 + 1886

> XR R1.2.1.2.3.1. Tetrevangelium

Irenics: irenics 1882/3 + 1890
.char of: irenical 1660–
Isagogics: isagogic(s) 1864–

> XR R1.2.1.1.3. Textual criticism

Liturgics: liturgics 1882–

> XR R4.1.2.0. Liturgy

Meta-theology: meta-theology 1957–
.p studying: meta-theologician 1967(1)
.char of: meta-theological 1969(1)
Moral theology: moral theology 1727/41–, casuistry 1725–
.p studying: casuist 1609–, casuistess *nf* 1865(1)
.char of: casuistical 1649–
.char by: casuistic 1660–
.in manner of: casuistically 1678–
.laxist: laxism 1895(1)
..p studying: laxist 1865–
.probabiliorist: probabiliorism 1845–
..p studying: probabiliorist 1727/41–
.probabilist: probabilism 1842–
..p studying: probabilist 1657–
..char of: probabilistic 1864(1)
.rigorist: rigorism 1882(1)
..p studying: rigorist 1715–
.tutiorist: tutiorism 1885(1)
..p studying: tutiorist 1845–
Mystical theology: mystical theology 1613–(1844), mystic
   theology 1639–(1854)

> XR R1.8.5. Mysticism

Pastoral theology: poimenics 1883–
Symbolics: symbolism 1846 + 1907, symbolics 1847–, symbolic
   1864(1)

> XR R1.1.1.0. Creed

Typology: typology 1845–(1882)

> XR R5.17. Symbol

.p **studying:** typologist 1841–(1898)

R1.6. Holiness

R1.6.0. Holiness: *haligdom*/halidom OE–a1626,
halignes/holiness OE–, blessedhede a1300 + 1340, holihede
a1300–1340, holite 14..(1), sanctitude c1450–(1870/4),
sanctimony 1540/1–1725, sanctity 1601–, spirituality
1613/18(1), sacrosanctity 1650–(1900), sacredness 1681/6–,
hallowedness 1828 + 1866, sacrosanctness 1876(1), sacrality
1958–

XR R1.6.1.0. Saintliness

R1.7.0 Piety

.**of mind:** sanctanimity 1801 + 1873

.**instance of:** *haligdom, halig*/holy OE–, sanctitudes *npl* 1552(1),
sanctities *npl* 1597–(1856)

.**p char by:** *see R1.6.1.0. Saint*

.**obligations/feelings char by:** sanctities *npl* 1849–(1894)

.**odour of:** odour of sanctity 1756–

.**capable of:** sanctifiable 1894(1)

..**condition of being:** sanctifiableness 1894(1)

.**char by:** *gebletsod, gasthalig, gesælig*/seely OE–c1400,
gehalgod/hallowed OE–, *halig*/holy OE–, blessed c1200–,
blissful a1225–1534, saint a1300–1710, benedight a1300–c1460
+ a1890, sacred 13?–, devout c1380–1659, divine c1380–,
dedicate c1386–1814, consecrate c1386–1667 + 1887, sacrate
1432/50–a1572, sanctificate c1485–1538, sacrificed 1504(1),
sacre 1513–1577/87, sanctified 1525–, happy 1526–1700,
reverend 1563–1693, vowed 1585–1691, devoted 1594–(1829),
anointed 1597(1), devote 1597–1667, consecrated 1599–,
dedicated c1600–(1805), sacrosanct 1601–, sanctimonious
1604–1801, religious 1611–(c1820), sacrosanctious 1621(1),
divined 1624(1), celebrate 1632(1), divinified 1633–,
sacrosanctified a1693(1), sanctimonial 1721–1773, divinized
1839(1), sacramented 1851–(1886), sacral 1882–, sanct 1890
+ 1895, sacramented 1914(1), *Kramat* 1947–(*Moslem*)

XR R1.6.1.0. Saintly

R1.7.0. Pious

..equally: *efenhalig*
..very: *đurhhalig*
..infinitely: *eallhalig*/all-holy OE–
..eternally: ever-blessed a1711–

.in manner of: *haliglice*/holily OE–, saintly 1532 + 1653,
   sanctifiedly 1633(1), sacredly 1694 + 1884

.the honouring of (xp) because of: *halgung*/hallowing OE–
XR R4.1.0. Worship
..to perform: *halgian v*, +*bletsian*/bless *vt* OE–, sanctify *vt*
   c1450–1611, saint *vt* 1652–1657

R1.6.1.0. Saint: *sanct (L), wuldormaga/-mago, halga*/hallow
   OE–1647, *halig*/holy OE + 1548–1648, saint a1300–, saintess
   nf 1449–(1865), *santa nf* a1450(1), ?sainty a1529(1), holy one
   1535–, she-saint *nf* 1537–, *Mar* 1694–, *rishi/richi* 1766–
.pl/coll: *ealle halga*/all-hallow(s) OE–, blessed/blest c1200–(1863),
   sanctified *ncoll* 1620(1), sainthood 1818(1), saintdom *ncoll*
   1862(1)
..list of: rubric a1611–(1813)
.great:
..friend of: synascete 1850(1-*GkCh*)
.guardian: patron c1380(1)
.married female: matron 1519*Sc.* + 1862
.non-Christian: saint 13?–(1876)
..Buddhist, of highest rank: *bodhisat(tva)* 1828–, Mahatma
   1855–, ar(a)hat 1870–, Lohan 1878–
...state of: ar(a)hatship 1870–, bodhisat(tva)ship 1889–
..Hindu: Maharishi 1785–, rishi 1808–, siddha 1846–
XR R1.8.6.0. Inspiration
..Moslem: pir 1672–, weli / wely 1819–
...having local cult: sheikh 1613–
.petty: saintrel c1440 + 1653, saintling 1622–(1854)

.char of: *halig*/holy OE–, saint c1175–, life-holy c1200–c1440,
   sanctified c1485–, saintish 1529–(1840), saintlike c1580–,
   sainted 1598–(1848), sancteous 1631(1), savoury 1642 +

1731, saintly 1660–
XR R1.6.0. Holiness

..**condition of being:** sanctity c1394–, sainthood 1550–, saintship 1631–(1866), saintliness 1837–, saintdom 1842 + 1887
..**and heroic:** hagi-heroical 1829–
..**not:** saintless a1603(1), unsaintly 1659–, unsaintlike 1681 + 1891
...**condition of being:** unsaintliness 1887–
.**(of x:)peopled with/haunted by:** besainted 1865(1)
.**in manner of:** saintedly c1789(1)

.**types of:**
..**char of:** hagiotypic *a* 1886–
.**rule of:** hagiarchy 1826–
.**worship of:** hagiolatry 1808–, hierolatry c1814–
XR R4.1.1. Dulia

..**p char by:** hagiolater 1875(1)
..**char by:** hagiolatrous 1841–
.**madness of/for:** hagiomania 1797–
.**literature about:** hagiology 1807–, hagiography 1821–, hagio-romance 1843–, saintology 1848 + 1892, hierology 1890(1)
XR R5.16.2. Synaxarion

..**p writing:** hagiologist 1805–, hagiographist 1817(1), hagiographer 1849–, saintologist 1885(1)
XR R3.3.3.6. Bollandist

..**char of:** hagiographic 1819–, hagiologic 1826(1), hagiographical 1864–, hagiological 1872–
.**celestial crown of:** aureole c1220–1502 + 1884, *aureola* 1483–(1702), glory 1646–, halo 1646–, nimbus 1727/38–, gloria 1784 + 1866, gloriole 1844–, nimb 1849–
..**provided with:** haloed 1791–, nimbed 1849–, nimbused 1852–
..**to provide with:** halo *vt* 1801–

.**to act/live as:** saint *vi* c1460–(1880)

R1.6.1.1. Particular saints
Ambrose: Ambrosian *a* 1609–
Anthony: Tantonie *a* 1594(1)

Augustine: *see R1.9.1. Augustinianism*
Columba:
.**disciple of:** Columban 1879(1)
.**char of:** Columban 1879–
Cuthbert:
.**disciple of:** *haliwere(s)folc*/haliwerfolk *ncoll* OE–1430 +
    1816–*hist.*
Cyprian: Cyprianic *a* 1695–1696 + a1861–
Dominic: Saint Sunday 1490– *local*
Felicitas:
.**seven sons of:** seven brethren c1450–1588
Francis: the Assisian 1870–
.**char of:** Assisian 1870–
Ignatius: *see R1.3.1.1. Ignatius*
Isidore: *see R1.3.1.1. Isidore*
Jerome:
.**char of:** Hieronymian 1884(1), Hieronymic 1889(1)
XR R1.2.1.1.4. Vulgate

John Chrysostom:
.**disciple of:** Johannite 1680 + 1681
John the Divine: *see R1.2.1.2.3.4. Revelationist*
Mamertius, Pancras, Gervais: ice saints *npl* 1895–
National saints: seven champions 1596–1735
XR R1.6.1.0. Guardian saint

Patrick: Patrician *a* 1872–
Paul:
.**x char of:** Paulinism 1927(1)
XR R1.5.1. Paulinism

Peter: *see R1.5.1. Petrinism*
Thomas Aquinas: *see R1.3.1.1. Thomas Aquinas*
Vincent de Paul:
.**char of:** Vincentian 1934(1)
Walpurgis: Walpurgis 1823–

R1.6.1.2. Canonization: canonizing c1380–(1727), canonization
    c1380–, sanctification 1526-(1876), sainting 1563/83–a1668,
    beatification 1626-(1864), canonication a1641(1), apotheosis

1651–, consecration 1677(1), beatitude 1847 + 1865
.p performing: canonizer 1588–(1821)
.performing: canonizing 1869(1)
.having undergone: canonized c1440–, canonizate 1538–1565,
    enskied 1603–(1858), besainted 1615 + 1711, incalendared
    1622(1), sainted 1631–1855, beatified 1650–(1852)
..not: unsainted a1642–
.char of p attaining 1st degree of: worshipful 14..–1483,
    venerable 1432/50–
.to perform: +*halgian*/hallow *vt* OE–, saint *vt* 1375–, canonize *vt*
    c1380–, sanctify *vt* 1390–(1865), shrine (p) for a saint *vphr*
    1530–1599, portess *vt* 1570(1), rubricate *vt* 1570 + 1638, holy
    vt 1578–1622, calendar *vt* 1594–1842, beheaven *vt* 1601 +
    1609, besaint *vt* a1603–1680, templify *vt* 1615 + 1690 *fig.*,
    beatify *vt* 1629–, beatificate *vt* a1636 + 1655, besanctify *vt*
    1826(1)

R1.6.1.3. Discanonization: discanonization 1811(1)
.char by: unsainted 1851(1)
.to perform: unsaint *vt* 1572–, uncanonize *vt* 1607–1751, dissaint
    vt 1612(1), discanonize *vt* 1797(1)

R1.6.2.0. Consecration: *eallhalgung, segnung,*
    +*bletsung*/blessing OE–c1205, *halgung*/hallowing OE–,
    benison a1300–(1828), dedication 1382–(1776), consecration
    1382–, dedifying 1494(1), sanctification 15?–1832, devotion
    1502–, sanctifying 1526–(1727/41), holy-making 1535(1),
    dedicating 1535–(1611), consecrating 1591–1641, sacring 1610
    + 1613, devouement 1611(1), devotement 1621–(1852),
    sacration 1627/77–1628, devoting 1640–(1677), sequestration
    1654 + 1681, devote 1659(1), dedicature c1850(1),
    sacralization 1918–
                                    XR R1.6.1.2. Canonization
                                       R1.6.2.2. Blessing
                                       R4.9.1. Purification
                                       R4.10.0. Desecration
.of a church: *cirichalgung, ciricmærsung, templhalgung,*

church-holy c1440(1), church-hallowing 1516–1565,
consecration 1570/6–, consecrating 1641(1)
.of salt: *sealthalgung*
.of water: *wæterhalgung*

XR R4.2.1.0. *Fantbletsung*
.p performing: *gehalgigend,* hallower 1382–1607, holy-maker
c1546(1), consecrator 1552–
.x performing: sanctifier 1753 + 1829
.performing: hallowing c1175–, sacrand 1508(1), sanctifying
1586–, sanctificative 1607(1), consecrating 1642–, sacring
1644(1)
.in manner of: sanctifyingly 1847(1)
.to perform: *gefreolsian v, +bletsian*/bless *vt* OE–,
+halgian/hallow *vt* OE–, bensy *vt* c1315(1), sacre *v*
c1380–(1644), dedie *vt* c1430–1549, consecrate *vt* 1460–,
dedify *vt* 1482–1494, sanctify *vt* 1483–, consacre *vt*
1491–a1618, dedicate *vt* 1530–(1885), sequester 1533–1697,
devove *vt* 1567–1808, celebrate *vt* 1584(1), devote *vt* 1586–,
vow *vt* 1600(1), set apart *vphr* 1604–, devout *vt* 1605–1651,
devow *vt* 1621(1), inaugurate *vt* 1638–1847, behallow *vt*
1648(1), sanctificate *vt* a1677 + 1883, sanctize *vt* 1691(1),
sacrify *vt* 1819(1-*nonce*), sacrament *vt* 1829–1844, sacralize *vt*
1933

XR R1.6.2.2. To bless
..beads: pardon *vt* 1524–1553

XR R4.2.2.3.1. Indulgence
R5.8.18. Rosary
..a church: consecrate *vt* 1568–

R1.6.2.1. Reconsecration: reconsecration 1763–(1847),
rededication 1883–
.char of: rededicatory 1896(1),
.char by: rededicate 1839/48(1)
.to perform: reconsecrate *vt* 1611–(1684), rededicate *vt* 1703–,
resanctify *vt* 1675 + 1847, rehallow *vt* a1711–(1855)

R1.6.2.2. Blessing: *bletsung*/blessing OE–, benison

a1300–(1828), benediction 1432/50–, *benedicite* 1610–(1823),
   beation 1652(1)

                                        XR R1.6.2.0. Consecration
                                        XR R4.15. Sign of the Cross
.with special efficacy: *halgung*
..without: cardinal's blessing 1702–1758
.of bread: *hlafsenung*
..and wine: kiddush 1753– *Jewish*
.given on departure: ?leave-giving 1450/1530(1)
.asked at table: *beodfers*, benedicite a1225 + 1725–, grace a1225–
                                        XR R4.3.1. Prayer before meal

.char of: benedictory 1710–, benedictional 1902(1)
.char by: *gebletsod*, blessed c1200–, benedight a1300–c1460 +
   a1890
                                        XR R1.6.0. Consecrated
..by a priest: priested 1603(1)
..not: *ungebletsod*, unsained a1275–(1881), unblessed 1340–
...state of being: unblessedness 1549 + 1881
.in manner of: benedictionally 1911(1)

.to perform: *geeadigan vt*, *+bletsian*/bless *vt* OE–, sacre *vt*
   c1380–1644
                                        XR R1.6.2.0. To consecrate
..amply/profusely: bebless *vt* 1598–1799
..bells: baptize *vt* 1655(1)
                                        XR R5.7.2. Bell

R1.6.3. Unholiness: unholiness 1534–, unblessedness 1549 +
   1881, unsanctifiedness 1634(1), unsanctity a1639 + 1838,
   unsanctification a1684(1), unhallowedness 1899(1)
                                        XR R1.7.3. Impiety
                                        R1.8.2.0. Unspirituality
                                        R1.10.0. Sin
                                        R4.10.0. Profanation
.xp char by: unholy 1831 + 1837
.char by: *ful*, *un(ge)halgod*/unhallowed OE–, *unhalig*/unholy OE–,
   unblessed 1340–, unsacred 1382–(c1440), unconsecrate
   1529–1673 + 1850, unconjured 1546(1), unsanctified

1570–(1855), unconsecrated 1579–, unhallowed 1588'–, disholy
1593 + 1596, indivine 1603(1), unholied 1603 + 1649,
insacred 1665(1)
.in manner of: unholily 1561–, unsanctifiedly 1650(1)
.process of investing (xp) with: unhallowing c1554–(a1859),
unsanctification 1804(1)
XR R3.3.4.0. Laicization
..char of: unsanctifying a1859(1)
..to perform: unholy *vt* a1555(1), unsanctify *vt* 1594–(1862),
common *vt* 1621 (*2q1s*)
XR R4.10.0. Desecration

R1.7. Piety

R1.7.0. Piety: *æwfæstnes, arfæstnes, estfulnes, wilsumnes,
wynsumnes,* love-eie a1225(1), life-holiness a1225–1393,
devotion a1225–, godfrightihead c1250(1), reverence c1290–,
pity 1340–1483, devoutness 1377–, love-dread c1380–c1440,
fear c1400–, godliness 1531–, piety 1604–, devoteness 1606(1),
piousness 1623–1692 + 1817, theopathy 1748–(1881),
devoteeism 1828–(1852), pietism 1829–, *bhakti* 1832–,
devotionality c1849 + 1850, devotionalism 1859–(1883), pi
c1870– *slang, bhakti-yoga* 1959(1)
XR R1.1.5.0. Religion
R1.6.0. Holiness
.instance of: devout 1649(*1-Milton*), piety 1652–, spirituality
1676(1)
.of many forms: polypiety 1647(1)
.p char by: *godes freond*/friend of God OE–c1375, servant (of
God) a1300–, devoto 1599–1712, devotive 1608(1), devout
1616–1675, devotress *nf* 1624–1689, devoter 1634(1), devota
nf 1644 + 1685, devotee 1645–, devotary 1646 + a1670,
devotor 1648(1), devotionist a1656–1755, devotesse *nf*
1658(1), devotionary 1660–a1670, devote 1660–1779, devotist
1675(1), devotionair a1734(1), devotionalist 1736–(1829),
pietist 1767–, devotioner 1883(1)
..only temporarily: temporary 1619–1647

.char by: *æfremmende, æfyllende, æwfæst, arfæst, arfæstlic,*
    cristen, estful, estig, estlic, godcund, godcundlic, hold,
    godfyrht/godfright OE–c1200, *god*/good OE–(a1661), seely
    a1225–c1450, devote 1225–1651 + 1839, devout 1297–,
    gracious a1300–1757, ghostly a1340–1483, piteous
    c1380–1570, spiritual 1382–, pitiful c1449–1570, pie c1450(1),
    inward c1450–1694, ?evangelic 1460/70(*2q1s*), godly 1526–,
    servantly 1561–a1603, timorate 1570(1), godful 1593(2),
    fearful 1597–, pious 1602–, heavenly-minded a1656–,
    theopathetic 1748–(1878), godfearing 1835–, fire-spirited
    1839(1), theopathic 1846–(1899), unctional 1849 + 1864,
    interior 1854–, sacramental 1874–1877, pi 1891(1-*slang*)
                                    XR R1.1.5.0. Religious
..popishly: pope-holy 1633(1)
                                    XR R1.7.1. Sanctimoniousness
.in manner of: *arfæstlice, estfullice, holde, holdlice, wilsumlice,*
    piteously c1305–1382, devotely c1325–1588, devoutly c1325–,
    devoutement a1400(1), godly 1530–1631 + 1871, godlily
    1548–(1798), divinely 1594–1682, piously 1611–, godfearingly
    1899(1)
                                    XR R1.1.5.0. Religiously
.to lead a life char by: walk with God *vphr* a1629(1)
.'melting' of soul because of intense: liquefaction 1526–a1711
..(of soul:)to undergo: liquefy *v* 1483–1502
                                    XR R1.8.1. Soul

R1.7.1. Sanctimoniousness: *hiwung,* hypocrisy a1225–,
    pope-holy ?a1366–a1518, ?sauntering c1440(2), pope-holiness
    1528–1583, hypocrism 1591(1), lip-holiness 1591(1),
    lip-religion 1597(1), pharisaism 1601–, lip-devotion 1607(1),
    sanctimony a1618–(1871), lip-worship 1630–(1862),
    sanctimoniousness 1679–, unction 1692 + 1817–,
    sanctification 1760/72(1), goodiness 1810–, pietism 1829–,
    goodyism 1842–, lip-reverence c1843(1), Mawwormism
    1850(1), lip-homage 1858(1), devil-dodging 1861(1),
    goody-goodyism 1881–, goody-goodyness 1884(1), unctuosity
    1884 + 1885, Pecksniffery 1885–, piosity 1922–

XR R2.2.4.13. Puritanism

.p char by: *ælareow,* hypocrite a1225–, lip-gospeller 1558(1), saint
1563–, pharisee 1589–, separatist 1620–(1866), canter
1652–(1848), cant 1725–, pietist 1767–, holy Willie
1785*(Burns)* + 1916–, devil-dodger 1791–, creeping jesus
c1818– *slang,* Mawworm 1850–(1899), goody-goody 1873–,
lip-Christian 1882(1), high-liver 1888(1), plaster saint 1890–,
goody-good 1904(*2q1s*), christer 1924– *U.S. slang*

XR R1.2.1.2.1.1. Legalist
R2.1.1. Pharisee

..pl/coll: unco guid 1786– *Sc.*
.talk char by: lip-labour 1538–1788/92, lip-labouring 1549(*2q1s*),
lip-work 1649–, canting 1659–1771, cant 1709–

XR R4.5.0. Preaching
R4.3.0. Prayer

.char by: pope-holy 1377–1589, pie c1450 + 1932–, as holy as a
horse 1530(1), hypocritish 1530–1641, pharisaical 1531–,
hypocritic 1540–(1848), hypocritical 1561–, hypocritely
1574(1), horse-holy 1589(1), sanctified 1600–(1860),
sanctimonious 1603–, pharisaic a1618(1), bible-bearing
1624(1), lip-holy 1624(1), canting 1663–(1864), unctuous
1742–, pietical 1782(1), pietistical 1800(1), goody 1830–,
goody-good 1851–, Pecksniffian 1851–, goodyish 1864(1),
pietic 1865(1), goody-goody 1871–, maw-wormish 1883(1),
pietistic 1884(1), maw-wormy 1885(1), devil-dodging 1886(1),
pietose 1893(1), pi 1891–, holier-than-thou 1912–,
antimacassar 1913–, holy 1916–

XR R1.1.5.2. Religiose

.in manner of: hypocriticly 1541(1), hypocritically 1548–,
sanctimoniously 1622-, sanctifiedly 1641(1), cantingly
1695–(1840), unctuously 1864–, pietistically 1884(1),
Pecksniffianly/-ingly 1914–
.to manifest: play the pope-holy *vphr* a1555(1), cant *vt* 1641(1),
cant *vi* 1678–(1856), Pecksniff *vi* 1903(1)

R1.7.2. Misdevotion: misdevotion 1612–1649
.char by: misdevout 1610–1651, misdevoted 1612/15(1)

R1.7.3. Impiety: *bismernes, godscyld, godwrecnes, unmiltsung,*
unpity a1340 + c1400, impiety a1340–, undevotion
c1340–1565, unpiteousness 1382(*2q1s*), unpiteousty 1382(1),
undevoutness c1440(1), ungodliness 1526–, indevotion 1526–,
godlessness 1553–, devoutlessness 1576(1), impiousness 1599
+ 1695, unpiety 1675(1), indevoutness 1842(1), unblessedness
1881(1)

> XR R1.1.11.0. Paganism
> R1.6.3. Unholiness
> R4.10.0. Sacrilege

.instance of: impiety 1529–

.p char by: *lahbreca*/law-breaker OE + c1440–, servant (of
devil/sin) a1340–a1770, fire-brand 1340–1560, member of
Satan c1375(*1-Sc.*), malignant 1597–1617

..pl/coll: the ungodly 1526–(1847)

.char by: *æwbræce, arleas, godscyldig, godwræc, hæðen,
lahbrecende, unrihtwis*/unrighteous OE–, hinderful
c1200–1569, undevote a1300 + a1340, unpiteous
c1374–c1400, undevout a1395–, indevout c1450–, ungodly
1526–, profane c1560 + 1666–, impious 1575/85–, ungodded
1579–1687, unhallowed 1588–, godless 1632–, devoteless
1650–1738, undivine 1685–(1860), indevote a1742(1),
unctionless 1842(1), god-forsaken 1856–, indevotional
1865(1), *link* 1889–1902 *Yiddish*

> XR R4.1.5.0. Sabbath-breaking

.in manner of: *arleaslice, unæwfæstlice, unrihtlice,* hinderfulliche
c1200(1), undevoutly 1377–(1647), unpiteously 1382(*2q1s*),
ungodly 1526–1606, ungodlily 1583–(1860), impiously 1597–,
indevoutly 1694(1), undivinely 1884(1)

.to imbue with: undevout *vt* c1440(1)

.to treat with: unreverence *vt* 1553 + 1642

R1.8. Spirituality

R1.8.0. Spirituality: *gastedom, gæstedom,* spiritualty
1377–?a1500, spirituality 1500/20–, spiritual-mindedness
1647–

XR R1.6.0. Holiness
R1.7.0. Piety
R1.8.4. Rapture

.p char by: spiritual 1532(1)
.strength char by: armature 1542–1682 + 1865
.wisdom char by: sapience c1430–1614
.improvement char by: edification 1382–, edifying 1509–(1705), building 1604(1)
..char by: edificative c1410–1634/46, edifying 1526–, edifiable 1526(1), edificant 1642 + 1655, edificatory 1649–
..in manner of: edificatively ?c1530(1), edifyingly 1662–
..to produce: edify *vt* 1340–, enhance *vt* c1380–1526, exhance *vt* a1450(1), build *vt* 1526(2)
..to receive: receive *vt* a1300–1597
..to profit from: edify *vi* 1636–a1670

.char by: *gastbrucende, gastcund, sawolcund, gastlic*/ghostly OE–, spiritual 1377–, espiritual c1386–1477, spritual c1420–1789, spretual 1498–1554/9, spiritually-minded 1526–(1844), spiritualized 1651–, spirituous 1712(1), spiritualizing 1845(1)
..surpassingly: angelical c1555–1560 + 1837, trans-spiritualized 1683(1)
.uplifted with: uplifted c1454–
..condition of being: upliftedness 1893(1)
.(of x:)delightful because of: savoury c1449–(1855)

.in manner of: *gastlice*/ghostly OE–1619, spiritually 13..–1559, spritually 1526(1)

.the endowing with: spiritualization 1809–
..to perform: spiritualize _*vt* 1631–
.belief in: spiritualism 1836–, animism 1880(1)
.discipline char by: exercitation 1398 + c1425, exercising 1548(1)
XR R4.1.0. Worship
..p char by: exerciser 1686(1), exercist 1715(1), exercitant 1858 + 1890
..char by: exercitate c1425(*2q1s*), exercised 1552–(1841)

R1.8.1.0. Soul: *sawol*/soul OE–, spirit c1375–

.condition of being: soulhood 1882(1), soulship 1893(1)

.char of: souly c1400–1727, soulish c1550–(1886), soul-like
    1654–(1899), soular 1825(1), soulical 1845–(1875)

.endowed with: souled c1400(1), soulified 1662(*2q1s*), ensouled
    18.. + 1865

..not: soulless 1553–(1897)

.endowing with: ensouling 1826 + 1868

.(of p:)unwell in: soul-sick 1598–

.(of S:)alive: vital 1807(1)

.(of S:)dead: dead 1382–

.in manner of: soul-like 1845(1)

.working of God within: motion 1526–(1760/72)

XR R1.7.0. Liquefaction

.final state of advancement for: unitive way / road / life 1649–

.final liberation of: *moksha* 1785– *Hindi*, *mukti* 1785– *Hindi*

XR R1.8.1.1. Transmigration

.destruction of: annihilation 1753 + 1876, *fana* 1867– *Sufi*

XR R1.8.1.3. Annihilationism

..to perform: annihilate *vt* 1634–(1728)

.(of God:)to visit: *secan*/seek *vt* OE–c1366

.to endow with: soul *vt* c1386 + 1646, ensoul *vt* 1652–

.to put/take into: ensoul *vt* 1633–(1881)

.to commit S to God: recommand *vt* c1380–a1533, recommend
    vt c1400–, recommit *vt* 1521(1)

.(of S:)to live: live *vi* c1375–1611

.(of S:)to die: die *vi* 1340–(1627)

R1.8.1.1. Transmigration: transanimation 1574–(1871),
    metempsychosis c1590–, transmutation 1594(1),
    transmigration 1594–, commigration 1613(1), metemsychose
    1630 + 1786, transincorporation 1810–(1843)

XR R1.8.1.0. Moksha

.soul char by: transmigrant 1882(1)

.doctrine of: transmigrationism 1868(1)

..p believing in: metemsychosist 1834–, transmigrationist
    1884–(1903)

.char of: transmigrative 1727–(1844), transmigratory 1816–(1893), metempsychosic 1905(1)

.char by: metempsychosed 1594–(1843), transmigrant 1654 +
1888, transmigrated 1682 + 1754, transmigratory 1693 +
1898, metempsychosal 1848(1), metempsychic 1886(1)

.in manner of: transmigratively 1818–(1819)

.to perform: metempsychose *vt* 1594–, transanimate *vt*
1608–a1641, metempsychize *vt* 1618(1), metempsychosize *vt*
a1843(1)

R1.8.1.2. Regeneration: +*edniwung, edsceaft,* regeneration
c1420–, reparation 1447–1725, gain-birth c1550(1),
regeneracy 1626–(1853), rebirth 1837–, reawakening 1862(1),
reawakenment 1886(1)

XR R1.9.1. Synergism, Monergism
R4.2.1.0. Baptism

.p char by: child of God c1200–(1850), regenerate a1569–1652

.char of: regeneratory 1803–1831, regenerative 1839/52–

.char by: regenerate 1526–, uprising 1585 + 1633, regenerated
1594–, reborn 1598–, regenerative 1839/52–, twice-born
1849–(1902)

XR R4.5.4.1. Converted

.(of x:)causing: regenerating 1681(1)

.to perform: +*cwician v, geliffæstan v, geliffæstian v,* renew *vt*
1382–, regener *vt* 1456–c1500, regender *vt* 1532 + 1533,
regenerate *vt* a1557–

.to undergo: be born again *vphr* 1382 + 1611, regenerate *vi*
1786(1)

.absence of: unregeneracy 1622–, unregeneration 1625–,
irregeneracy 1641(1), irregeneration a1654 + 1657,
unregeneratedness 1664(1)

..p char by: unregenerate c1625 + 1627

XR R3.3.4.0. Layman

..human nature char by: old man 1382–1733

XR R4.5.4.3. Inconversion

..char by: carnal c1510–1865, unregenerated 1579–(1826),
unrenewed 1579–(a1866), unregenerate 1612–, irregenerate

1657–
..causing: unregenerating 1657(1)

R1.8.1.3. Doctrines concerning the Soul
Animism: animism 1832–(1864), psychism 1890(1)
.p holding: animist 1864(1)
.char of/by: animistic 1871–
.in manner of: animistically 1884–
Annihilationism: annihilationism 1881(1)
XR R1.8.1.0. Annihilation
R1.13.0. Reprobation
.p holding: annihilationist 1875–
Appropriationism:
.p holding: appropriationist 1862(1)
Conditionalism: Conditionalism 1895–
.p holding: Conditionalist 1895–
Creationism: creationism 1847–
XR R1.8.1.3. Traducianism
.p holding: creationist 1882(1)
Mortalism: mortalism 1646(1), thanatism 1900–(1902)
.p holding: mortalist 1646–1757, mortalian 1647(1),
    anti-eternitarian 1746(1), thanatist 1902(1)
Nullibism: nullibism 1681(1)
.p holding: nullibist 1662–(1803), nullubist 1668(1)
Pre-existencism:
.p holding: pre-existentiary 1682–1698, pre-existerian 1837(1),
    pre-existencist 1883(1)
Psychopannychism: psychopannychism 1877(1)
.subject of: psychopannychy 1642 + 1847
.p holding: psychopannychite 1642 + 1682, soul-sleeper
    1645–1727, psychopannychist 1659(1), psychopannychian
    1872(1)
.char of: psychopannychistic 1891(1)
Soularism:
.p holding: soulary 1643(1)
.char of: soulary 1643(2)
Thnetopsychism: thnetopsychism 1882/3(1)

Traducianism: traducianism 1843–(1893)
XR R1.8.1.3. Creationism

.p holding: traducter 1682(1), traducianist 1872(1), traductionist 1889(1)

.char of: traducianist 1872(1), traducian 1880–(1884)

Transmigrationism: *see R1.8.1.1. Transmigrationism*

R1.8.2.0. Unspirituality: *woruld*/world OE–, worldlyship c1380(1), worldliness c1380–, secularity 1395–, siecle c1400–c1450, worldlihood c1449(1), mundanity 1502 + 1647–, secularness 1530(1), carnality 1548–, carnalness 1549(1), civility 1549–1649, rudiments of the world 1557–1665 + 1881, earthly-mindedness 1608–1691, temporalness 1611(1) worldly-mindedness a1628–, unspiritualness 1642–(1863), Sadducism 1647–1778, Sadduceeism 1661–(1872), unspirituality 1842 + 1863, materialism 1850–, secularism 1851–, terrestrialism 1856(1), this-worldliness 1872–(1887), temporalism 1872–, despiritualization 1874(1), this-worldism 1883(1), this-worldness 1930(1)
XR R1.1.12.0. Atheism
R1.6.0. Unblessedness
R2.1.1. Sadduceeism

.p char by: man of the world 1535–1749, worldling 1549–, earthling 1615–, this-worldian 1830(1), secularist 1851–, earth-man 1860–(1947), hylicist 1880 + 1893
XR R1.8.1.2. Unregenerate

..pl/coll: world 1362–(1738)
XR R3.3.4.0. Laity

.thought char by: *woruldgeđoht*

.act char by: dispirituality 1684(1)

.world char by: world-spirit 1850(1)

.char by: *giemleas, woruldcund, flæslic*/fleshly OE–, *woruldlic*/worldly OE–, world c1175–14.., of the world('s) c1200–1533, secular c1290–, worldish 13..–, timely 1340–a1615, uttermore 1395(1), mundane 1475–, seculary 1480(1), profane 1483–, carnal c1510–(1865), unghostly 1526–, human a1533–, sensual 1557–1677, mundial c1560*Sc.*

+ 1619, subcelestial 1561–, worldly-witted 1563 + 1845, civil
1592–1830, earthly-minded 1593–1670, worldly-minded
1601–, lay 1609–a1668, mundal 1614–1631, unspiritual 1643–,
wilderness *nattrib* 1651–1719, worldly-handed 1657(1),
timesome 1674(1), outward 1674(1), apsychical 1678(1),
secularized 1683–, choical 1708 + 1914, worldling 1720 +
1845, secularizing 1825–, timeous 1855(1), Sadducee 1857(1),
secularistic 1862–, apneumatic 1864(1), Sadduceeic 1875(1),
this-worldly 1883(1) this-world 1889(1), secular-minded
1899–

.in manner of: *giemeleaslice, woruldcundlice, woruldlice*/worldly
OE–, unghostly a1400/50(1), carnally 1527–1714, civilly
1577–(1853), worldward 1583–1651, secularly 1840–,
worldwards 1845(1), materialistically 1852(1), unspiritually
1871(1)

R1.8.2.1. **Secularization:** secularization 1706–, deconsecration
1867–, laicizing 1884–, naturalization 1897(1), desacralization
1959–
.p **performing:** secularizer 1887(1), laicizer 1891(1)
.to **perform:** *giemeleasian v,* worldlify *vt* 1612(1), secularize *vt*
1711–, unspiritualize *vt* a1716(1), temporalize *v* 1828(1),
despiritualize *vt* 1840–, laicize *vt* 1870–, deconsecrate *vt*
1876–, desacralize *vt* 1964–
.to **reverse:** unsecularize *vt* 1816–(1897)

R1.8.3.0. **Contemplation:** *upgemynd,* contemplation a1225–,
meditation a1340–, meditating 1645(1), recollection
1669–(1869), recollectedness a1699–, *recueillement* 1845–,
mantra 1962–
.highest **state of:** *samadhi* 1795–
.p **char by:** contemplative a1340–(1864), silentiary 1611–, ascetic
1673–

XR R3.3.2.2. Hermit
.life **char by:** contemplative life c1340–(1670), contemplative
14..(1), recollection 1642(1)
.char **by:** contemplative c1340–, recollected 1650–

..not: unrecollected 1850(1)
.to perform: medite *vi* 1483(1), meditate *vi* 1560–, recollect *vt* 1669–(1862)

R1.8.3.1. Self-examination: self-examination 1647–, examen 1651–(1885)

XR R4.2.6.1. Ordination
.p char by: self-examiner 1710(1), self-examinant 1825(1)
.char by: self-examining 1710(1)

R1.8.3.2. Quietism: quietism 1687–, Molinism 1720–(1868)

XR R1.8.5.0. Mysticism
.p char by: quietist 1685–, Molinosist 1727/52–1797, Molinist 1868(1)
.char of: quietistic 1850–

R1.8.4. Rapture: *estfulnes,* rapture 1629–, ecstasy a1652– *now hist. or allus.,* fanaticism 1652–, fanatism 1680–1800, ze(a)lotism 1716–, religionism 1791–, seraphism 1846(1), ecstasis 1874(1), rapturousness 1880(1)

XR R1.7.0. Piety
.pretended: seraphicism 1676(1)
..p char by: seraphicalist 1659(1)
.p char by: Canaanite 1611(1), zealist 1614–1638, zeal 1614–1647, zelant 1625 + 1885, religionist 1653–, spiritato 1659–1678, ecstatic 1659–18.., rapturist 1663(1), votary a1700–, religioner 1820 + 1852, subject 1820(1), voteen 1830/2– *Irish,* zelator 1867(1) Cananæan 1881(1)
..marked with stigmata: stigmatist 1880(1), stigmatic 1885(1)
..char of: vowed 1665(1), zealot 1670–

XR R4.11.0. Vow
.char by: *estful,* frenetic c1540–, phrenetic 1565–, seraphical 1581–1742/3, ecstatical 1600–1678, ecstatic c1630–, ecstasied 1649–1787, seraphic 1659–, phrenetical 1663–1674, rapturous 1678–, synagoguish 1690(1), solid 1740–(1769), religionistic 1889(1)
.in manner of: *estfullice,* zealously 1644(1), ecstatically 1664–,

rapturously 1664–
.to produce: ecstasy *vt* 1624(1)

R1.8.5.0. Mysticism: mysticism 1736–
                                        XR R1.5.2. Mystical theology
                                            R1.8.3.2. Quietism
                                    R2.1.1. Chasidism, Therapeutism
                                        R2.2.1.4. Gnosticism
                                            R2.3.4.1. Sufism
.false: pseudo-mysticism 1964(1)
..p char by: pseudo-mystic 1961(1)

.p char by: *mystes* 1676–, mystic 1679–, myst a1693–1856

.char by: +*ryn(e)lic*, misty c1380–1570, mystic 1382–, mysterial
    1528 + 1675, mystical 1529–, mysterious 1624–
..condition of being: mysticalness 1608–(1816), mysteriousness
    1649–, mysticity 1760–, mysticality 1834–, mysticness 1912(1)
..and religious: mystico-religious 1834–
..not: unmystical 1862 + 1899

.in manner of: *geryn(e)lice*, in his mystery c1315(1), through his
    mystery ?a1400(1), mysterially c1425(1), in mist c1430 +
    1667, mysticly c1450 + 1868, in (a) mystery 1526–1628,
    mystically 1552–

R1.8.5.1. Mystery: *gastgeryne*, privity a1225–1470, mist
    13..–c1430 + 1667, mystery 1382
                                        XR R1.2.1.5. Mystery
.of God's existence: *mysterium tremendum* 1923–
.relating to bull and serpent: tauro-serpentine *a* 1855(1)
.which is essential feature of all religion: numinous 1923–,
    numinosum 1938–
..excessive reverence for: thaumatolatry 1827(1)

.char of: +*ryn(e)lice*, misty c1380–1570, mystic 1382–, mysterial
    1528 + 1675, mystical 1529–, mysterious 1624–, telestic
    1678–1822
..condition of being: mysticalness 1608–(1816), mysteriousness

1649–, mysticity 1760–, mysticality 1834–, mysticness 1912(1)
.**creating:** mysterifical 1607(1)
.**in manner of:** mysteriously a1716–(1738)

.**initiation into:** mystagogy 1579–
..**p conducting:** mystagogue a1550–, mysteriarch 1656 + a1839–,
hierophant 1677–
...**char of:** hierophantic 1775–
..**char by:** mystagogical 1624–(1853), mystagogic 1631–
..**in manner of:** mystagogically 1836(1)

.**system of doctrine concerning:** mysteriosophy 1894–
.**rationalization of Christian:** nominalism 1836(1), rationalism
1827–

XR R1.5.1. Neologism
..**p char by:** rationalist 1647–, nominalist 1654–
..**char of:** rationalist 1828–, rationalistic 1830–, nominalistic 1863–
..**in manner of:** rationalistically 1847 + 1869

R1.8.5.2. Mystical significance: mistihede a1400(1)
XR R1.2.1.1.3. Anagogy
.**ability to understand:** *anagogue* 1706–1751, anagogy
1727/51(1)
XR R1.8.6.0. Inspiration
..**char of:** anagogic 1388 + 1677–

R1.8.5.3. Otherworldliness: otherworldliness a1834–,
disattachment 1860(1), otherworldism 1894(1)
.**char by:** otherworldly 1880–

R1.8.6.0. Inspiration: *ætywednes, ætywung, bierht(u), inlihtnes,
onblawnes, onbryrdnes, onlihting, onlihtnes,
on(ge)wrig(en)nes, wuldorword,* inspiration 1303–, revelation
1303–, illumination c1340–, illustration c1375–1653, revealing
1375–, oracle c1384–, information 14..–1559, gospel 1481 +
1878, aspiration a1534 + a1535, illuminating c1561(1),
entheos 1594–1782, enthusiasm 1603–1807, flame-light
1611(1), inspirement 1616 + 1677, respiration 1622(1),

spiration 1628–1686, irradiation 1633–, income 1647–a1708,
theopneustian 1660(1), afflatus 1665–(1873), entheasm
1751(1), *prana* 1830–, inflation 1835(1), theopneusty 1847(1),
inflatus a1861(1), theopneustia 1894(1)

XR R1.2.1.2.3.4. Book of Revelations
.by Holy Ghost: embreathing 1548(1), embreathement 1854(1)
..the coming of: Pentecost 176.–

.p char by: *inlihtend, onlihtend, wita,* seer 1382–, illuminate
1600–, enthusiastic 1610–1707, enthusian 1621–1707,
enthusiast a1641–1700, inspirado 1664(1), alumbrado
1671(1), inspired 1749(1), Maharishi 1785–, *muni* 1785–, *rishi*
1808–, Mahatma 1855–

XR R1.6.1.0. Hindu saint
.p believing in: inspirationist 1846–, revelationist 1888(1),
revelationer 1898(1)

.char by: *awrigen, +ryn(e)lic,* inspired c1450–, illumined 1526 +
1727/41, godly-wise 1532–1633, revealed 1562–, illuminate
1563–, enthusiac 1603(1), enthusiastic 1603–(1849),
illuminated 1606–, entheate c1630 + 1640, enthean 1635 +
1652, theopneust 1647–(1885), illuminative 1649–,
enthusiastical a1652(1), enthusiast 1681 + 1742, entheous
1682(1), revelational 1701–, entheastic 1794(1), theopneustic
1827 + 1847, theophanic 1882/3–(1886), inspirational 1888 +
1899, theophanous 1909(1), Beatrician 1943–
..not: natural 1526–, uninspired 1690–
..capability of being: inspirability 1869(1)
.endowed with like gift of: fellow-inspired 1685(1)
.in manner of: inspiredly 1591–, entheastically 1794(1)

.to produce: *onbryrdan v, onwreon v,* inspire *vt* a1340–, illumine
vt c1340–1554 + 18.., reveal *vt* c1375–, aspire *vt* 1532–1633,
illuminate *vt* 1538–(1875), enlighten *vt* 1577–(1877)

R1.8.6.1. Prophecy: *witegung*/witieng OE–c1200, prophecy
a1225–, prophetism 1701–
.instance of: prophecy a1300–, message 1546–
..book containing: *witegungboc*

.p char by: *boda, witege (nf), witegestre (nf), witega*/witie
OE–a1225, prophet c1175–, prophetess *nf* a1300–, sibyl *nf*
a1300–, ?secretary 1599–a1727, *mlimo* 1896–
..pl/coll: prophecy 13..(1), prophets 1382–, prophethood 1875–
..office of: prophetship 1642–, prophethood 1840–
..greater O.T.: major prophets 1660(1)
XR R1.2.1.2.1.0. Old Testament
..lesser O.T.: minor prophets 1654–(1860)
XR R1.2.1.2.1.0. Old Testament
..Hebrew O.T.: *nabi* 1877–
XR R1.2.2. Targum
...adherence to: nabi'ism 1922(1)
..Micah: Morasthite a1390–
..ancient Celtic: *euhages npl* 1609–(1827)
..Indian: sad(d)hu 1845–, his sadhuship 1914(1)
...principles of: sadhuism 1903–
..char of: prophetly 1547/64(1)
..without: prophetless 1900–

.char of: prophetical 1456–, prophetic 1604–, fateful 1715/20–
.in manner of: prophetically 1577–(1856), propheticly 1656 +
1704

.to perform: *witegian*/witie *v* OE–c1200, *bodian*/bode *vt*
OE–1771, prophesy *vt* 1377–(1847), prophesy *vi* 1382–,
prophet *vi* c1450(*2q1s*), prophetize *vi* 1588–1715

R1.8.6.2. Vision, manifestation
Beatific vision: beatifical vision 1605(1), beatific vision
1639–(1869)
Third divine manifestation: bethphany/-ie 1635–(1883)
Manifestation of Christ: Christophany 1846–
Manifestation of God/a god: theophany a1633–, theophanism
1849(1)

R1.9. Grace

R1.9.0. Grace: *ar, est, (Godes) giefu,* grace c1325–

XR R2.2.4.3.0. Arminianism
R2.2.4.5.0. Calvinism
R4.2.0. Sacrament

.proportionate/efficient: efficacious grace a1679(1), congruous
grace 1683(1)

XR R1.9.1. Congruity

.sufficient: sufficient grace 1728–

.char by: gracious a1300–1757, graceful c1420–1611, engraced
1874(1)

XR R1.6.0. Holy

..condition of being: grace 1382–, state of grace 1754–
.full of teaching about: gracy 1661(1)

XR R4.5.1. Evangelization

.p holding that G can be lost: executifidian a1656(1)
.p holding that G is conditional: conditionalist 1678(1)
.continuance in: perseverance a1555–
..on part of those elected to eternal life: perseverance of the
saints 1628(1)
..to manifest: persevere *vi* 1751(1)
.moment regarded as propitious for reception of: sacrament
of the present moment 1921–

.to endow (xp) with: engrace *vt* 1610 +1874, grace *vt* 1634–1701
+ 1961, graciousize *vt* 1701(*2q1s*)

XR R4.2.0. Sacrament

R1.9.1. Doctrines concerning grace
Augustinianism: Augustin(ian)ism 1830–

XR R1.12.1. Predestinarism

.p holding: Augustinian 1860(1)
.char by: Augustinian 1674 + 1851
Condignity: condignity1554–(1842), condignness 1581(1)

XR R4.4. Good works

Congruity: congruence a1541–1635, congruity 1553–(1856),
congruism 1885(1)

XR R1.9.0. Congruous grace
R4.4. Good works

.**p holding:** congruist 1727/51–
.**char by:** congruistic 1867(1), congruist 1885(1)
Molinism: Molinism 1669(1)
.**p holding:** Molinist 1655–(1859)
.**char by:** Molinistic 1669(1)
Monergism: monergism *no quots.*

XR R1.8.1.2. Regeneration

.**p holding:** monergist 1867/80(1)
Synergism: synergism 1764–
.**p holding:** synergist 1657–
.**char by:** synergistical 1657–1772, synergistic 1818–

R1.9.2. Merit: merit a1225–

XR R4.4. Good works

.**possession of:** meritoriousness 1639–
.**concern for, with regard to salvation:** merit-mongering
    1845(1-*contempt.*), meritmongery 1856(1-*contempt.*)

XR R1.12.0. Salvation

..**p char by:** merit-monger 1552–(1846), merit-worker 1577(1),
    merit-merchant 1647(1) *(all contemptuous)*
..**char by:** merit-monging 1611(1)
..**in manner of:** meritorily c1400–c1449, meritoriously 1502–a1716

.**to earn:** merit *vt* 1543–

R1.9.3. Righteousness: *rihtwisnis*/righteousness OE–, justice
    1534–1622
.**civil:** civility 1619–a1640
..**p char by:** civilian 1619–1645, civilist 1626(1)
...**pl/coll:** *domfæst*
..**char by:** *rihtwis*/righteous OE–, civil 1619–1676
..**in manner of:** civilly 1592–1608, civil 1642(1)

.**imputation of R of Christ:** imputation 1545–
..**p char by:** imputarian 1668(1)

.**p holding that man can himself attain:** justiciary
    1532–a1716, self-justiciary 1644–1692, self-justifier 1655(1),

justiciar 1772(1)
..with assurance of salvation: fiduciary 1654–(1864)
XR R1.12.0. Salvation
..char of: justiciary 1615–a1665

.the attainment of: justifying 1382 + a1769, justification 1526–
..doctrine of J by faith alone: solifidianism 1628–
XR R1.12.0. Salvation
...p char by: solifidian 1596–
...char of: solifidian 1605–
...char by: solifidian 1628–
..char of: justifying 1526–
..deprived of: unjustified 1651–(1828)
..in manner of: justifyingly 1711(1)
..to deprive of: unjustify *vt* 1646 + 1654

R1.10. Sin

R1.10.0. Sin: *forwyrht, gylting, syngung*/sinning OE–, *synn*/sin
OE–, plight c1200–c1375, culp(e) 1377–1601, offension
1382–1388, peccation 1862(1)
XR R1.7.3. Impiety
R1.13.0. Reprobation
.instance of: *syndæd, synleahtor, synn*/sin OE–, debt
a1225–(1858), piacle 1644–1676 + 1880, peccancy 1648–
..unamended: *unbeted a*, unbet *a* c1200 + a1300

.p char by: *agyltend, mangewyrhta, mansceaða, manwyrhta,
synnecge nf, synnigiend, wiðercora, synfull*/sinful OE–c1400,
synnfull/sinful *npl* OE–1624, sunegild *nf* c1230(1), sinner
c1325–, sinneress *nf* 1382–1647, peccant 1621 + 1803,
evil-liver 1846 + 1887
..condition of being: sinnership c1750–

.char by: *firenfremmende, firenful, firengeorn, firensynnig,
firenwyrcende, gyltlic, higesynnig, læne, synfah, synlic,
synscyldig, synwyrcende, wamscyldig, wamwyrcende,
forsyngod*/forsinned OE–c1200, *synnig*/sinny OE–c1475,
synnful/sinful OE–, plightful 13..(1), *ysunged*/ysinged

13..–1387, ysinwed a1400(1), sin-soiled 1593–, peccant 1604–,
sinning 1609–, piacular 1610–, peccable 1633(1), piaculous
1646–1661, peccanimous 1656–1668 + 1922–1939 (*Joyce*),
piaculary a1670(1)

..condition of being: sinfulhead c1250–a1400, sinfulness 14..–,
peccancy 1656–

..very: *heahsynne*

...the impressing of p with sense of: convincing 1615–1642

....char by: convicting 1865(1)

....to perform: convict *vt* 1526–1624 + 1862–, convince *vt* 1648 +
a1853–

...undergoing:

....condition of having undergone: convincement 1617–,
conviction 1675–1678 + 1821

.capable of: sinnable 1662 + 1863

..condition of being: sinnableness 1863(1)

.mad with: sin-wood c1250(1)

.sick with: sin-sick 1609–

..condition of being: sin-sickness 1633(1)

.(of soul:)sooty with: sooty 1655–1680

.hardened in: clumsed/clumst a1340–1340, obdurate c1440–,
obdured 1585–, obfirmed 1597–1637

XR R4.2.2.1.1. Impenitent

.unreclaimed from: unreclaimed 1602–, unreconciled 1711(1)

..condition of being: unreclaimedness 1646(1)

.in manner of: sinfulliche/sinfullike c1200–c1450, sinfully a1300–,
sinningly 1647–1674

.in direction of: sinward 1377–

.tendency to: sinningness 1863(1)

.desire to: *synnlust, synræs*

XR R1.8.1.2. Unregeneracy

.burden of: *synbyrden*

.foulness of: *synrust*

.snare of: *syngrin*

.woe of: *firenearfeðe*

.sorrow for: contrition a1300–, contriteness 1692 + 1755

..**char by:** contrite a1340–, contrited 1483–1821, contritional
1648(1)
..**with:** contritely 1829–

XR R4.2.2.1.0. Contrition

..**imperfect:** attrition c1374–
...**char by:** attrite 1625 + 1817

.**to commit:** *asyngian v, +firenian v, firentacnian v, scyldigian v,*
*gesyngian v, +syngian/*sin *vi* OE–, sin *vt* c1315 + 1682–
..**by looking:** mislook *vi* c1200–1390
...**process of:** mislook 1390(1)
..**by thinking:** misfeel *vi* c1200(1), misthink *vi* a1225 + 1615
..**by taking pleasure:** mislike *vt* c1200(1)
.**to surpass in:** outsin *v* 1606–1772
.**to promote:** *forsyngian v*
.**to act as p char by:** sinner it *vphr* 1735 + 1880
.**to bring self into/beyond a state by:** sin (oneself)
into/beyond *vphr* 1665–a1716
.**to force (xp) away by:** sin away *vt* 1684–1694 + 1860
.**(of S:)to grow grave:** aggrege *vi* c1400(1)

R1.10.1. Kinds of sin:
Actual: actual sin c1315–

XR R1.10.1. Original sin

First: *frumdysig*
Fleshly: body-sin a1240(1)
Formal: formal sin 1641(1)

XR R1.10.1. Material sin

Against the Gospel: gospel-sin 1647(1)
Material: material sin *no quots.*
Mortal: *deadfiren, firensynn, grimman, heafodgilt, heafodleahter,*
heafodsynn, heahsynn, morðor, deadly sin a1225–, mortal sin
1426–, scape ?c1590 + 1671, cardinal sin 1611(1-*Shakespeare*)
.**p char by:** deadly sinner 1622(1-*Donne*)
..**in fourth rank:** pentient 1704 + 1850 *(early ch.)*
.**char of:** *heafodlic/*headly OE + 1388, deadly a1225–(1819),
mortal 1426–
..**condition of being:** mortality 1532–1681

.in manner of: deadly c1225–1579, mortally 1526–1662

Original: *frumscyld,* fall of man a1300(1), flesh a1300–, original
  sin c1315–, birth-poison 1528(1), birth-sin 1562 + 1842, lapse
  1659–1768/74

.innate corruption of human nature due to: depravation
  1577–1725, original pravity 1618(1), depravement 1677(1),
  depravedness 1715(1), depravity 1757–(1874), natural pravity
  1847(1)

.p believing in: lapsarian 1928–

..not: antilapsarian 1674(1)

.p believing OS is inherited: traducianist 1858(1)

..char of: traducianistic 1882/3(1)

.p believing in possibility of second: relapsarian 1700(1)

.char of: lapsarian 1954–

.char by: collapsed a1640–1667

Predominant: predominant 1633–1699

Private: house-sin 1645(1)

Venial: venial c1380–1671, peccadilian 1529–1569, escape
  1576–1678, peccadillo 1591–, peccadill 1621–1736, peccadillie
  1660(1)

.pl/coll: venialia *npl* 1654(1), sins of daily incursion *npl*
  a1655–1737

.char of: *medmicel, miltsigendlice,* venial a1300–

R1.11. Atonement

R1.11.0. Atonement: *betnes, bot*/boot OE–a1240 + 1844*hist.*,
  satisfaction a1300–(1885), reconciliation 13..–, atonement
  1526–, contentation 1535–1656

                                        XR R4.8.0. Sacrifice

.p char by: the redeemed *npl* 1535–1753, the ransomed *npl*
  1611–(1846)

.p making A for others' sins: satisfactory 1587(1), sin-eater
  1686/7 + 1860

.char by: satisfactory 1547–, atoning 1814(1)

..condition of being: reconcilableness 1757(1)

.to perform: content *vt* 1548(1), atone *vt* a1677–

R1.11.1. Doctrines concerning atonement
Calvinist doctrine of:
.p holding: atonementist 1836(1)
Grotian doctrine of: Grotianism 1920(1)
.char of: Grotian 1864–
Satisfactionist doctrine of: satisfaction theory 1932–
.p holding: satisfactionist 1668–(1858)
Stancarian doctrine of:
.p holding: Stancarian 1565–1655, Stancarist 1882/3(1)

R1.12. Salvation

R1.12.0. Salvation: *aliesing, hals, halwendlica, halwendnes, hreddung, læcedom, liesing, aliesedness*/alesedness OE–c1175, *aliesendnes*/alesendness OE–c1230, *aliesnes*/alesness OE–c1230, *halnes*/healness OE–c1250, *geliesnes*/lesness OE–1340, *hæl(u)*/heal OE–1578, *hælđ*/health OE–, berrhless c1200(1), salvation a1225–, saving a1300 + a1340, buying a1300–c1410, soul-heal a1300–1560, safety a1300–1675, savement 13?–1485, predestination a1340–, redemption a1340–, safeness a1375–c1440, election 1382–, soul-health 1390–a1618

> XR R1.9.2. Merit-mongering
> R1.9.3. Fiduciary

.p char by: chooseling a1300(*3q1s*), israelite 1382–1699, predestinate 1529–, elect 1532–1646, comprehensor 1653–a1710, Zionite 1675(1), sanctificationist 1868(1)
..pl/coll: *scæp*/sheep OE–, chosen c1200–, heritage a1340–, Israel 1382–, peculiar people/nation 1494–(1738), peculiar 1609–1659, election 1611(1)
..condition of being: peculiarity 1661–1777, Israelism 1684(1)

.char of: redemptional 1840–(1854), soterial 1879(1)
.char by: safe a1300–1562, saved a1300–, withboght 1340(1), chosen 1382–, ransomed c1400–c1440, redempt a1450 + c1500, elect 1526–, elected 1548+ 1550, Israelistic 1684(1), redeemed 1648–(1866)
..not: *see R1.13.0. Reprobate*

.causing: saving a1300–, safe-making 1579(1), salvifical
    1581–1678, salvific 1591–a1711, redemptory 1602(1),
    redemptive 1647–, electing 1674(1), redeeming 1754(1)
.capable of: salvable 1667–(1888), saveable a1706(1), redeemable
    1768/74(1)
..condition of being: saveableness 1638(1), salvability
    1654–(1868), salvableness 1727(1), redeemableness 1892(1)

.in manner of: savingly 1629–(1877)

.testing of p for worthiness of: probation 1526–
.way of: *riht wæg*/right way OE–, *bhakti-marga* 1937– *Hindi,*
    jnana-marga 1877– *Hindi*
                    XR R4.4. *Karma-marga*
..p devoted to: *jnani* 1885– *Hindi*
.inward knowledge of: inner light 1856–
.tendency to promote: savingness a1658 + a1677
.predestination to: predestination a1374–
.history of: *heilsgeschichte* 1938–, salvation history 1959–
.teaching laying stress on: salvationism 1883 + 1902
.doctrine of: soterialogy 1768/74(2), soteriology 1864–
..char of: soteriological 1879–

.to perform: *aliesan*/alese *v* OE–c1250, save *vt* a1225–, ransom *vt*
    a1300–, redeem *vt* c1460–, elect *vt* a1617–, unsin *vt* c1629–
.to predestinate to: predestine *vt* c1380–, predestinate *vt* c1450–

R1.12.1. Doctrines of salvation
Absolutism: absolutism 1753–(1775)
Apocatastasis: apocatastasis 1867–
Auto-soterism: auto-soterism 1909(1)
.char of: auto-soteric 1894–
Infralapsarianism: *see R1.12.1. Sublapsarianism*
Nationalism: nationalism 1836–
.p char by: nationalist 1846(1)
.char of: nationalizing 1836(1)
.as applied to England: Anglo-Israelitism 1876–,
    British-Israelism 1920(1)
..p char by: Anglo-Israelite 1875–, British-Israelite 1934 + 1948

..char of: British-Israel 1907(1)
Nudifidianism:
.p char by: nudifidian 1648–a1653
Particularism: particularism a1828–, particular redemption
    1847(1), partialism 1864(1)
                          XR R2.2.4.4.1. Particular Baptists
.p char by: particularist 1727/41–, limitarian 1844–1852,
    partialist 1864(1)
.char of: particularistic 1886 + 1956
Predestinarianism: predestinarianism 1722–, predeterminism
    1888(1)
                          XR R1.9.1. Augustinianism
                               R2.2.4.3. Arminianism
.p char by: predestinator 1579–1812, predestinatian 1630(1),
    predestinatist 1630(1), predeterminant 1660(1),
    predestinarian 1667–, predeterminer a1678(1),
    predestinationist 1894(1)
.char of: predestinary 1599 + a1662, predestinarian a1638–(1843),
    predestinatian 1685(1)
.char by: predestinate c1380–(1833), predestinated 1737/69(1)
Postdestinarianism:
.p char by: post-destinarian 1700(1), submortuarian 1700(1)
Restorationism: restorationism 1834–, restitutionism 1896(1)
.p holding: restitutionalist 1773–, restorationist 1834 + 1892
Sublapsarianism: infralapsarianism 1847 + 1865,
    sublapsarianism 1865–
                          XR R2.2.4.5.0. Calvinism
.p char by: sublapsarian 1656–, infralapsarian 1731–
.char of: sublapsarian 1660–, sublapsary 1728(1), postlapsarian
    1733 + 1950–, infralapsarian 1775–
Supralapsarianism: supralapsarianism 1775–
                          XR R2.2.4.5.0. Calvinism
.p char by: supralapsarian 1633–, supra-creatarian 1660(2),
    superlapsarian 1668–a1679, supralapsary 1728(1)
.char of: supralapsarian 1633–, supralapsary 1755(1),
    superlapsarian 1807/8(1)
Terminism: terminism 1882/3(1)
.p char by: terminist 1727/41–(1860)

.char of: terministic 1860+ 1882/3
Universalism: universalism 1805–
.p char by: universalist 1626–
.char of: universalist 1810–(1877), universalian 1853(1),
    universalistic 1847 + 1887

R1.13. Reprobation

R1.13.0. Reprobation: tinsel a1300–c1375 *Sc. and N.,*
    damnation a1300–, damaing c1400–1707, damnement
    1480(1), reprobation 1532–, accursedness 1583–1674,
    preterition 1621–(1862), non-election 1651–, tartarization
    1819(1)

> XR R1.8.1.0. Annihilation
> R1.10.0. Sin
> R4.14.0. Excommunication

.p believing in: reprobatarian 1657(1), reprobationer 1692(1)
.p char by: fire-brand 1340–1560, reprobated 1535(1), reprobate
    1545–, preterite 1864(1)
..pl/coll: reprobate 1563–

.char of: reprobatarian 1676(1), preteritive 1836(1)
.char by: *fæge, fordemed, fordon, widercoren,* damned 1393–, lost
    a1533–(1818), condemned 1543–1588 *Sc.,* reprobate 1561–,
    devoted 1611–(1862), unsaved 1648–(1866), damning 1655(1),
    reprobated 1668 + 1782, non-elect 1674–, unelected 1836(1)
.worthy of: damnable 1303–(1882/3)
.in manner worthy of: damnably c1386–(1786)

.doctrine of: tartarology 1867 + 1868

.to cause: *anidran v, fordon*/fordo (into/to) *v* OE–a1200,
    fordeman/fordeem *vt* OE–c1320, damn *vt* a1325–, condemn *vt*
    1375–(1563), destroy *vt* c1380–1611, reprobate *vt* 1526–,
    pretermit *vt* 1608(1), tartarize *vt* 1675 + 1819, tartarus *vt*
    1856(1)
.to suffer: leese *vi* c1175(1), lose *vi* c1175(1), perish *vi* c1250–, be
    lost *vphr* a1533–(1861)

R2 - Churches, Sects, and Religious Movements

R2.1. Judaism

R2.1.0. Judaism: Jewhead a1300(1), Jewry 13..–1552, Judaism 1494–, Jewship 1535 + 1549, Jewishness 1549–1627, Jewism 1579–(1800), Israelitism 1626(1), Jewhood 1851(1), Jewdom 1869–

.p char by: Jew c1275–, synagogist c1662(1), sabbatizer 1683(1), smouse 1705–1785 *derog.*, smouch 1765– *derog.*, sheeny 1816– *derog.*, yid 1890– *derog.*, hebe/heeb 1932– *derog.*

..pl/coll: *Judeas,* Jewry c1330–, (men of) the circumcision 1382–1839

.char by: *Judeisc,* circumcis c1250(*2q1s*), Judaical c1470–a1769 + 1875, circumcised 1604–1802, Judaic 1611–, phylactered 1738(1-*fig.*), Jehovistic 1885(1)

..not: unjewish 1822 + 1892

.in manner of: Jewly 1382(1), Jewishly 1558–1661, Judaically 1582–a1714

.the following of: Judaizing 1626(1), Judaism 1641–
..p char by: Judaizer 1631–, Judaist 1846–
..char by: Judaizing 1704 + 1884, Judaistic 1833 + 1880
..to engage in: judaize *vi* 1582–

R2.1.1. Jewish groups and sects
Ashkenazim: Ashkenazim *no quots.*, Tudesco/-a 1897–
Assidæanism:
.p char by: Assidæan/-ean/-ian 1382 + 1611
Chasidism: Chas(s)idism 1893–
.p char by: (C)has(s)id 1812–, Assidæan/-ean/-ian 1834(1)
..not: Mitnagged 1904–
.char by: (C)has(s)idic 1918–
Canaanism: makebox[1in]

XR R1.8.4. Fervour

.p char by: zealot 1537–, zelotist 1593–1640, Canaanite 1611(1),
  zelator 1644(1), Cananæan 1881(1), zelatrice/-ix *nf*
  1890–(1902)
.char by: zelotical 1630–1694, ze(a)lotic 1657–
Essenism:
                                        XR R1.8.5. Mysticism
.p char by: Essee c1380–1613, Essene 1553–
.char by: Essenical a1641(1), Essenic 1832/4–(1879), Essenizing
  1875(1), Essenian 1878(1)
Falashaism:
.p char by: Falasha *sing. or coll.* 1710–
Genism:
.p char by: Genist 1613 + 1882
Hebra: Hebra 1880–
Herodianism:
.p char by: Herodian 1382–
.char by: Herodian 1633–
Karaism: Karaitism 1727/41(1), Karaism 1882/3(1)
                    XR R1.2.1.1.3. Scriptural interpretation
.p char by: Karaite 1727/41–
Leviticalism: Levitism 1879(*2q1s*), Leviticism 1888(*2q1s*),
  Leviticalism 1892–
                                        XR R4.1.2.0. Ritual
.p char by: Levite a1300–
.char by: Levitic 1632–, Levitical a1665–
.in manner of: Levitically 1641–
.quality of: Leviticality 1621(1-*nonce*), Leviticalness 1639(1)
Maimonism:
.p char by: Maimonist 1881(1), Maimonidean 1882/3(1)
.char by: Maimonidean 1864–
Mizrachism:
.p char by: Mizrachi *npl* 1911–
Nazarism:
.p char by: Nazarean 1577–, Nazarite 1661(1), Nazarene 1689–
                                        XR R2.2.5. Ebionitism
Orthodoxy: Orthodoxy 1888–
.p char by: Orthodox 1889–
.char by: Orthodox 1853–

Pharisaism: Pharisaism 1610–

XR R1.7.1. Sanctimoniousness

.p char by: *ieldewita, sundorhalga, fariseus*/pharisee OE–,
Pharisian c1394–1567

XR R1.2.1.2.1.1. Legalist

.char by: *fariseisc*, Pharisaical 1538–, Pharisaic 1643–, Pharisæan
1645 + 1891, Pharisaist 1918(1)

Reform: Reform Judaism 1892–

.p char by: reformer 1855–, reform Jew 1870–

.char of: reformed 1844–

.association supporting: Reform Party / Association 1843–

Sadducism: Sadducism 1635(1), Sadduceeism 1845–(1891)

XR R1.8.2.0. Unspirituality

.p char by: *rihtwisend, saduceas*/Sadducee OE–, Sadduce(æ)an
1547–1678

.char by: Sadduce(æ)an 1593–(1880), Sadducaical 1601 + 1702,
Sadducaic 1840 + 1883

Sephardism:

.p char by: Sephardi 1851–

.char by: Portuguese 1662–, Spanish 1817–, Sephardic 1866–,
Spanish-Jewish 1948–

Territorialism:

.p char by: territorialist 1905–(1909)

Therapeutism: Therapeutism 1854(1)

XR R1.8.5. Mysticism

.p char by: Therapeutæ *npl* 1681–(1856), Therapeutics *npl*
1847(1), Therapeuts *npl* 1865(1)

.char by: Therapeutic 1681–(1875)

R2.2. Christianity

R2.2.0. Christianity general: *cristennes, Godes lage,
cristendom*/Christendom OE–(1649), *godspel*/gospel OE–,
the faith a1300–, Christianity 1303–, the cross c1325– *fig.*,
Christ's profession c1375 + c1380, the way c1382–,
Christenhood c1449(1), Christianism 1576–1801/15

XR R1.1.6. Orthodoxy

.of a sort: Christianism 1674– *contempt.*
.false/spurious: pseudo-Christianity 1685–(1865)
..p char by: pseudo-Christian 1579(1)
..char by: pseudo-Christian 1664(1)
.fervently evangelical: Jesus *nat* 1970–
XR R4.5.1. Evangelization
.Judaizing: concision *ncoll* 1557–
.'muscular': Muscular Christianity 1857–
..p char by: Muscular Christian 1858–
..char by: Muscular Christian 1970(1)
.paganized: pagano-Christianism 1667(1)
..p char by: pagano-Christian 1680(1)
..char by: pagano-Christian 1668(1)
..to render (x): pagano-Christianize *vt* 1681–1685
.rational: rational Christianity 1750–
.religionless: religionless Christianity 1953–
.universal:
..char by: pan-Christian 1868(1)
XR R1.1.16. Catholicity

.p char by: *cristenmann*/C(h)ristenman OE–1523,
   cristen/Christen OE–1530, *lim*/limb OE–1607 *fig.*, member
   of Christ 13..–1582 *fig.*, disciple c1380–, saint 1382–(1847),
   Nazarene 1382–, Christian 1526–, Nazarite 1535 + 1656,
   cross-bearer 1540(1-*fig.*), Nazrani 1583– *Moslem*, Galilean
   1611–(1776) *contempt.*, Nazaritan 1625 + 1632, goy 1841–
   Jewish, shiksa *nf* 1892– *Jewish*
..pl/coll: *ða cristnan, gelaðung, halig cirice*/holy church OE–1642,
   cirice/church OE–, *sion*/Zion OE–, Christendom
   a1131–(1866), body of Christ c1200–(1611), Christianity
   a1300–1631, mother 1377–1833, general church 1380–c1394,
   Peter's barge c1440(1), mother church c1460–1827,
   congregation 1526–1583, catholic church 1559–1685 + *mod.*,
   gentiledom a1638 + 1878, St Peter's ship 1678(1), church
   catholic 1839(1), priest 1897(*2q1s* - *fig.*)
XR R1.1.16. Catholicity
XR R1.1.5. Church
...in earliest times: primitive church 1526–1795, early church

1875(1)

....**member of:** primitive 1600–1686

....**char of:** primitive 1685(1)

...**part of:** Christendom c1205–c1330, Christianity 1831–

XR R1.1.5. Church

R3.3.4. Congregation

...**priestly office of:** priesthood 1897(1)

..**fellow-:** *gebroðor, efencristen*/even-Christian OE–1602

..**according to Bible standard:** Bible-Christian 1744 + 1788 (*both Wesley*)

..**ancient Roman:** Romans *npl* a1390–a1704

..**Spanish, conforming to Moslem customs:** Mozarab 1788 + 1840

...**char of:** Mozarabic 1706–1863, Gothic 1867–

XR R2.3.4. Islam

..**condition of being:** *cristendom*/Christendom OE–1681, Christianity 1303–, Christiandom 1585(1), Christianimity 1637(1), Christianness a1660(1)

..**description of:** Christianography 1635 + a1647

.**char by:** *cristenlic, cristlic, geleafful, cristen*/Christen OE–1623 + 1640*dial.*, evangelic 1502–(1866), evangelical 1531–(1875), Christian 1553–, Christianlike 1574–1841, Christianly 1620–1841

XR R1.1.16. Orthodoxy

R1.2.1.2.3.1. Gospel

..**somewhat:** Christianish 1882(1)

..**somewhat less than:** infra-Christian 1906 + 1917

.**befitting:** Christianable 1889–(1926) *colloq.*

.**prior to:** pre-Christian 1861(2), pre-Christianic 1883(1)

.**subsequent to:** post-Christian 1864–

.**in manner of:** *geleaflice, geleaffulice,* Christenly c1386–1553, Christianly 1538–1850, Christianlike 1593–1632

.**toward:** faithward 1886(1)

.**time/place where C prevails:** *cristendom*/Christendom OE + 1389–(1849), Christianity 1303–c1650, Christdom 1463/82(1), the Christian commonweal 1559–1603, Christiandom a1670–1762/71

R2.2.0.1. Conversion to Christianity: Christening
a1300–c1340, enchristianation 1654(1), Christianization
1833–1847, Christianizing 1859(1)

> XR R4.2.1. Baptism
> R4.5.1. Evangelization
> R4.5.4. Conversion

.**p carrying out:** Christianizer 1806(1)

.**to carry out:** *cristen*/christen *vt* OE–1644 + 1880, Christian *vt*
 1586–1684, Christianize *vt* 1593–1851

..**having undergone:** christened c1200–1728, christianized
 1671–1767, christianizing 1806(1), evangelized 1816–(1819)

..**again:** rechristianize *vt* 1792–(1851)

.**to undergo:** christianize *vi* 1598–1823

.**p having undergone:** christianizer 1652(1-*derog.*)

..**Hindu:** rice-Christian 1816–

..**medieval Spanish Jew or Muslim:** marrano 1583–1645 +
 1900–

R2.2.0.2. Lack of Christianity: unchristenness c1548(1),
 unchristianity 1652–, unchristianness 1648/9 + 1667

> XR R1.1.11. Paganism
> R1.1.12. Atheism

.**char by:** *uncristen*/unchristen OE–1553, unchristened c1330–,
 faithless 1534–1628, unchristian 1555–, unchristenlike
 1570(1), unchristianed 1579(1), unchristianlike 1610–(1866),
 unchristianly 1643/5 + 1645, unevangelized 1775–

.**in manner of:** unchristenly 1535 + a1568, unchristianly 1547–,
 unchristianlike 1701–1784

.**act of endowing (xp) with:** unchristianizing 1853(1),
 de-christianizing 1869(1), dechristianization 1882(1)

..**(of xp:)having undergone:** unchristianized 1636(1),
 unchristening 1659(1)

..**to perform:** unchristian *vt* 1633–1712, unchristen *vt*
 1643/5–1718, unchristianize *vt* a1714(1), dechristianize *vt*

1834–(1884)

State of having ceased to be C: after-Christianity 1906(1)
.p char by: after Christian 1911(1)
.char by: after Christian 1886–

R2.2.0.3. Opposition to Christianity: antichristianism 1590–,
   antichristianity 1661–(1731)
.p char by: antichristian 1621–(1801)
.char by: antichristian 1587–, antichristianized 1701(1)
.in manner of: antichristianly 1596–
.to denounce (xp) as char by: antichristian *vt* a1718(1)

R2.2.1. Major early Christian sects
R2.2.1.1. Antidicomarian: Antidicomarian *n* 1532(1),
   Antidicomarianites *npl* a1625–(1751)

R2.2.1.2. Arianism: Arianism a1600–
.p char by: Arian 1532–, Arianizer c1680 + 1842, Eusebian
   1730/6 + 1838, Exucontian 1844–(1877)
.char by: *arrianisc*, Arian 1642–, Arianistical 1791(1), Eusebian
   1882/3(1)
.professing: Arianizing ?c1760 + 1845
.to convert to: Arianize *vt* 1803(1)
..p performing: Arianizer c1680 + 1842
.to follow: Arianize *vi* 1605 + 1845

R2.2.1.2.1. Kinds of Arianism
Anomœan:
.p char by: Anomœan 1526–, Hetero(o)usian 1874–
.char by: Hetero(o)usian 1678 + 1790, Anomœan 1683–
Eunomian:
.p char by: Eunomian c1449–
Homoean:
.p char by: Homoean 1896–
.char by: Homoean 1833–
Semi-Arianism: Semi-Arianism 1819–, the Homoiousion 1833–,
   Homoiousions 1969(1)

.p char by: semi-Arian a1616–1756/9, Lucianist 1727/41–,
   Homoiousian 1732–, Collucianist 1753–1855
.char by: Homoiousian 1683–, semi-Arian 1781 + 1833, Lucianic
   1882–

R2.2.1.3. Collyridianism:

XR R4.1.1. Mariolatry

.p char by: Collyridian 1565–
.char by: Collyridian 1827–1833

R2.2.1.4. Docetism: Docetism 1846–
.p char by: Docetes *npl* 1781–, *Docetæ npl* 1818/21–(1831/3),
   Docetists *npl* 1880(1)
.char by: Docetic 1846–(1855)
.in manner of: docetically 1887–

R2.2.1.5. Donatism: Donatistry 1564(1), Donatism 1588–
.p char by: Donatist c1460–, Rogatist 1565–, Donatian 1627(1)
.char by: Donatistical 1581 + 1645, Donatistic 1828–, Donatist
   1861–

R2.2.1.5.1. Kinds of Donatism
Rogatist:
.p char by: Rogatian 1524–, Rogatist 1565–, Rogatianist 1608(1)

R2.2.1.6. Gnosticism: Gnosticism 1664–

XR R1.8.5. Mysticism

.p char by: Gnostic 1585/7–
.char by: Gnostical 1828–, Gnostic 1838–
.to imbue (xp) with: gnosticize *vt* 1842–
..p performing: gnosticizer 1875(1)
.to adopt: gnosticize *vi* 1664 + 1840

R2.2.1.6.1. Kinds of Gnosticism
Archontic:
.p char by: Archontic 1586–(1751)
Basilidian:
.p char by: Basilidian 1586 + 1860
.char by: Basilidian 1877(1)
Cerinthian:

.p char by: Cerinthian 1585/7(1)
.char by: Cerinthian 1576–
Encratite: *see Severian below*
Heracleonite:
.p char by: Heracleonite a1555–
Mandæan:
.p char by: Sabian 1797 + 1883, Mandean 1875–
.char by: Sabian 1859–(1886), Mandean 1883–
Marcosian:
.p char by: Marcosian 1587–
.char by: Marcosian 1708(1)
Priscillian: *see R2.2.1.7.1. Priscillian*
Saturnian:
.p char by: Saturnian 1598 + 1607
Secundian:
.p char by: Secundian 1765(1)
Serpentian: Ophism 1865(1), Ophitism 1875(1)
.p char by: Ophian 1678 + 1882/3, Ophite 1692–, Serpentinian
    1758(1), Serpentian 1841(1)
.char by: Ophic 1865–, Ophitic 1865–
Sethian:
.p char by: Sethian 1721–, Sethinian 1723–1728, Sethite 1765–
Severian: Encratism 1885(1)
.p char by: Encratite 1587–, Severite 1607(1), Severian 1607–
Valentinian: Valentinianism 1875–
.p char by: Valentinian c1449–
.char by: Valentinian 1579–

R2.2.1.7. Manicheism: Manich(a)eism 1626–, Patarinism
    1854(1)
.p char by: Manichee a1380–(1842), Manich(a)ean 1556–,
    Catharist 1600–1832, Patarin/Patarene 1727/41–,
    Manichæist 1880(1)
.char by: Manich(a)ean 1638–(1855)
.to imbue (xp) with: manich(a)eanize *vt* 1865(1)
.to adopt: manich(a)eanize *vi* 1838(1)

R2.2.1.7.1. Kinds of Manicheism

Bagnolian:
.p char by: Bagnolians *npl* 1727/51 + 1847
Hydroparastate:
.p char by: Hydroparastates *npl* 1730/6 + 1853
Paternian:
.p char by: Paternian c1449–
Paulician: Paulicianism 1764(1)
.p char by: publican 1481–1855, Paulician 1727/41–
.char of: Paulician 1840(1)
Priscillian: Priscillianism 1620–
.p char by: Priscillianite 1585/7–1676, Priscillianist 1594–1834,
    Priscillian 1680(1)
.char of: Priscillianist 1887–

R2.2.1.8. Monophysitism: Monophysitism 1837–
.p char by: Monophysite 1698–
.char by: Monophysite 1788–, Monophysitic 1823–

R2.2.1.8.1. Kinds of Monophysitism
Coptic:
.p char by: Copt 1615–(1849), Coptite 1678(1)
.char by: Coptic 1678–(1849), Coptite 1680(1)
Jacobitic: Jacobitism 1882/3(1)
.p char by: Jacobite c1400–1645 + 1867, Jacobin 1517–1768
.char of: Jacobin 1727(1)
Julian:
.p char by: Julianist 1698 + 1874
Severian:
.p char by: Severian 1698–. Severite 1716(1)
Themistian:
.p char by: Themistians *npl* 1874–(1883)
Theodosian:
.p char by: Theodosian 1788–(1874)
Theopaschite:
.p char by: Theopaschite 1585–, Theopaschist 1887(1)

R2.2.1.9. Nestorianism: Nestorianism 1612–
.p char by: Nestorine c1400(1), Nestorian c1449–, Nestorianizer

1888(1)
.char by: Nestorian 1565–
.to follow: Nestorianize *vi* 1895(1)

R2.2.1.10. Pelagianism: Pelagianism 1583–
.p char by: Pelagian 1532–
.char by: Pelagian 1579–
.to incline to: pelagianize *vi* 1625–1674
..inclining to: pelagianizing 1629 + a1861
..p performing: pelagianizer 1674(1)

R2.2.1.10.1. Kinds of Pelagianism
Cælestian:
.p char by: Celestine *no quots.*, Celestian 1532(1)
Semi-Pelagianism: semi-Pelagianism 1626–
.p char by: semi-Pelagian a1600–
.char by: semi-Pelagian 1626–(1845)

R2.2.1.11. Photinianism: Photinianism 1655 + 1865
.p char by: Photinian 1648–
.char by: Photinian 1720–

R2.2.1.12. Sabellianism: Sabellianism 1668–(1907), Modalism
　　1859–
.p char by: Sabellian 1402–(1850), Modalist 1832(1)
..following Marcellus: Marcellian 1607–1727/41
.char by: Sabellian 1577–(1848), Modalistic 1878–, Modalist
　　1897(1)
.to follow: Sabellianize *vi* 1833 + 1840

R2.2.2. Greek Orthodoxy

R2.2.2.0. Orthodoxy: Greekery 16ᴇ0(1 -*contempt.*)
.p char by: Greek c1380–, Grecian 1547–1766, Easterling
　　1561–1649, Orientalist 1683(1), fermentarian 1775(1),
　　Prozymite 1850– *hostile*, Eastern 1865(1), Orthodox 1888(1)
　　　　　　　　　　　　XR R5.15.5.1. Unleavened bread
..pl/coll: Greek Church 1560–, Orthodox Church 1772–

.char by: Greek 1560–, Grecian a1600(1), Greekish 1606–1639,
   Orthodox 1679–
.char of all parts of: pan-orthodox 1888(1)
..principle of union between: pan-orthodoxy 1900 + 1902

R2.2.2.1. Orthodox groups and sects
Abyssinian:
.p char by: Abyssinian 1735–
Armenian:
.p char by: azymite 1727/51–, Armenian 1875(1)
Non-united:
.char of: non-united 1777–
Russian:
.p char by: Russian 1585/7–, Russie 1607(1), Russ 1607 + 1635
.following Nikon: Nikonianism 1957(1)
..p char by: Nikonian 1874 + 1888
...not: Raskolnik 1723–, Old Believer 1814–, *Starover* 1861–, Old
   Ritualist 1885–
..char by: Nikonian 1877(1)
Ruthenian:
.p char by: Ruthenian 1863 + 1886
Theodosian:
.p char by: Theodosian 1860 + 1874
Uniate:
.p char by: Melchite 1619–, Uniat(e) 1833–, United Greek 1849 +
   1863, Melkite 1902–, Malkite 1909(1)
.char of: Uniat(e) 1855–

R2.2.3. Roman Catholicism

R2.2.3.0. Roman Catholicism: Rome c1380–, papistry 15..–,
   popishness 1530–1657, Popery a1534–, Popistry 1545(1),
   mass-monging 1552–1612 *contempt.*, antichristianity
   1555–1670 *hostile*, antichristianism 1588–(1849) *hostile*,
   Babylonism 1610 + 1645 *hostile*, Catholicism 1613/17–,
   Romanality 1637(1), Catholicship 1674(1), Romanism 1674–,
   pseudo-Catholicism 1679(1-*hostile*), Roman Catholicity 1806

+ 1965, Roman Catholicism a1823–, Catholicity 1830–(1868), popism 1840(2), Romishness 1864 + 1886, papacy 1914(1-*erron.*), old religion 1934–

XR R3.2.1.1.0. Papacy

.p char by: Romanist 1523–, antichristian 1531–1753 *hostile*, papist 1534– *now hostile*, Roman 1547–, Popestant a1550–1551 + 1880, flesh-maker 1550(1-*contempt.*), mass-monger 1550–1826 *contempt.*, Pope-catholic c1554–1570, popeling 1561–1705, Babylonian 1564 + 1795 *contempt.*, Catholic 1570–, pope-worshipper 1579(1), papane 1581(1), Cartholic 1582(1-*derisive*), Cacolike/-leek 1582–1626 *derisive*, papistic 1589(1), Romist 1592–1821, pseudo-Catholic 1601–1647 *hostile*, papish 1604–1802 + 1828-*dial.*, romish *npl* 1605 + 1625, Roman Catholic 1605–, Romish Catholic 1606–1689 + 1826, papal 1611(1), popinian 1613(1), romulist 1620(1), papalin(e) 1624–1784, papicolist 1633–1644, papagan 1641(1), Romist Catholic 1661(1), papalina *nf* 1671(1), red-letter man 1677(1), azymite 1727/51–, papalist 1750–, R. C. *abbrev.* a1762–, craw-thumper 1785 + 1873 *slang*, Catholicist 1812(1), papisher 1823–1836 *dial.*, romanite 1839(1), western 1860–, Latin 1867–, Romanensian 1885 + 1891, mick(ey) 1924– *derog.*, pape 1935– *Sc. and Ulster - hostile*, Roman candle 1941–, tyke 1941– *Austr. and N.Z. slang*, left-footer 1944– *slang*, Teague/Taig 1971– *Ulster*

..coll: Antichrist c1370–, Mother Church c1380–, Whore (of Babylon) 1530–, Church Malignant 1542/5–1659, Latin Church 1560–1654, West 1586–, Western Church 1628–, Scarlet Whore 1648–1709, Red Letter 1679–c1688, Scarlet Lady 1807–(1873), Scarlet Woman 1816–(1867), Lady of Rome 1858(1), Lady of Babylon 1860(1)

..not: non-Catholic 1793–1859 + 1971–, uncatholic 1865(1)

..from birth: cradle-Catholic 1952–

..chief: arch-papist 1554–(1636)

..orthodox: Trentist 1601(1), Tridentine a1836–a1882

.p favouring: romanizer 1844–

.char of: popish 1528– *hostile*, romish 1531–, antichristian 1532–

hostile, pontifical 1533(1), babylonical 1535(1-*hostile*),
Roman 1535–, papistical 1537–, papistic 1545–, papish
1546–(1898), west 1553–1628, Catholic 1554–, Latin 1560–,
babylonish 1590 + 1654, Romanish 1591–, papal c1592–1814,
pseudocatholical 1601(1), mass-monging 1607 (1-*contempt.*),
romified 1609 + 1613, pseudocatholic 1610–1613 + 1908,
papizing 1612(1), babylonic 1614(1), romulian 1614(1),
Roman Catholic 1614–, pontificial 1621–1684, pontifician
1625–1817, Romanist 1635–, babylonian 1637 + 1790,
papized 1639(1), papagan 1647–1679, Romanical 1663(1),
Romanistical 1684(1), popish-like 1689–1705, western 1699–,
Catholic 1791–, papicolar c1810(1), Romanistic 1829–,
papalized 1879(1), papalistic 1886(1)
..**not**: uncatholic 1601–, acatholic 1809–, non-catholic 1823–,
unromanized 1847 + 1861
.**drawn toward**: romanized 1610–1628 + 1870, romized 1655(1),
romeward 1851 + 1887, romanensian 1885–

.**in manner of**: Catholically 1526–, popishly 1538–, Catholicly
1542–1853, papistically 1572–, malignantly 1645(1-*hostile*),
romishly 1658 + 1682, papistly 1716(1),
Roman-Catholic(al)ly 1793–
.**toward**: romanly 1606 + 1899, romeward 1864–, romewards
1866(1)

.**trait indicative of**: catholicism 1609–(1842)
.**fondness for**: Roman fever 1877–

R2.2.3.1. Roman Catholic groups and sects
Baianism: Baianism 1733 + 1928 *see also Jansenism below*
.**p char by**: Baianist 1733(1)
.**char by**: Baianist 1936(*3q1s*)
Cisalpinism: Gallicanism 1858–, Cisalpinism 1886(1)
.**p char by**: Gallicanist 1715 + 1882/3, Cismontanes *npl* 1858(1),
Gallican 1882(1)
.**char by**: Gallican 1633–, Cisalpine 1792–
English Catholicism: Anglo-Romanism 1866(1)
.**p char by**: English Catholic 1584–, Anglo-Roman c1840–

..**of Queen Mary's reign:** Marian 1868–
..**in 17th c., outwardly conforming:** schismatic 1584–(1877),
  church-papist 1601–1682, church-catholic 1627(1)
...**char of:** schismatical 1582(1)
..**of pre-Reformation stock:** Old Catholic 1846–
..**who aims at conversion of England:** ransomer 1890–
German Catholicism:
.**p char by:** German Catholic 1871–
Inopportunism:
.**p char by:** inopportunist 1880–
.**char by:** inopportunist 1888 + 1895
Jansenism: Jansenism 1656–

                                      XR R3.3.0. Port-royalist
.**p char by:** Jansenian 1653 + 1657, Jansenist 1664–
.**char by:** Jansenistical 1745 + 1756, Jansenistic 1837 + 1882/3,
  Jansenist 1860(2)
Mariavism:
.**p char by:** Mariavite 1906–
Maronism:
.**p char by:** Maronite c1511–

                                       XR R2.2.5. Monothelitism
Old Catholicism:
.**p char by:** Old Catholic 1871–
Opus Dei: Opus Dei 1954–
.**p char by:** *Opusdeista* 1974(1)
Padroadism:
.**p char by:** padroadist 1890(1)
Ribbonism: Ribandism 1848 + 1888, Ribbonism 1848–, Ribbon
  Society/Association 1866(1)
.**p char by:** Ribbonman 1813–, Ribandman 1820 + 1858,
  Ribandist 1823(1)
.**char by:** Ribbon *attrib.* 1818–(1857)
Sillonism: Sillonism 1910–
.**p char by:** Sillonist 1910–
Slavonic:
.**char of:** Galgolitic 1861(1)
Transmontanism:
.**p char by:** ultramontane 1592–1855, ultramontanist 1855(1)

.char by: transmontanian 1624(1), transalpine 1794(1)
.in manner of: transalpinely 1826(1)
Ultramontanism: ultramontanism 1827–(1878), infallibilism 1870
+ 1895, Vaticanism 1875–
XR R3.1.3.1. Vatican

.p char by: ultramontanist 1826–(1885), Vaticanist 1846–,
infallibilist 1870–, ultramontane 1873–(1882)
XR R1.1.2. Maximizer

.char by: ultramontane 1728–(1873/4), infallibilistic 1890(1),
Vaticanist 1892–
.process of endowing (xp) with: ultramontanizing 1893(1)
Universalism:
.p char by: universalist 1644(1)

R2.2.3.2. Conversion to Roman Catholicism: poping
1608(1), catholicizing 1826–, papizing a1843(1), papalization
1843(1), papalizing 1882(1), romanization 1893(1),
catholicization 1905–
XR R4.5.4.0. Conversion

.p perf: papalizer 1842(1)
.char by: romanizing 1624–, latinizing 1853(1)
.to carry out: inromanize *vt* 1620(1), popify *vt* a1670–1746,
latinize *vt* 1682–, papisticate *vt* 1746(1), papalize *vt* 1839–,
romanize *vt* 1851 + 1862, catholicize *vt* 1865(1)
.to undergo: catholicize *vi* 1611 + 1853, papalize *vi* 1624–,
romanize *vi* 1637–, pope *vi* c1916–
.a second time: re-romanization 1882/3(1)
..to carry out: re-romanize *vt* 1606 + 1882/3

R2.2.3.2.1. Freeing from Catholicism: uncatholicizing 1822(1)
.char by: uncatholicized 1863(1)
.to carry out: decatholicize *vt* 1794–(1889), uncatholicize *vt/refl*
1806 + 1842

R2.2.3.3. Anticatholicism: no-popery *no quots.*
XR R1.1.15. Sectarianism

.p char by: anti-Catholic 1780–, No-Poperist 1827(1)

.char by: anti-papal 1639-, anti-Catholic 1665 + 1823, No-Popery
   attrib. 1827-

R2.2.4. Protestantism

R2.2.4.0. Protestantism general: gospel 1552 + 1565, the
   religion 1577-a1674, reformity 1606(1), Protestantism 1649-,
   Protestancy 1655-1822

.p char by: evangelical 1532-(1878), gospeller 1533-, Protestant
   1539-, evangelic 1616-1758, religionary 1683-1760, Prot
   1725-, reformed 1741(1), gospellist 1845(1), Prod 1942-
   Ulster, Proddy dog 1954- *Ulster - hostile*
.pl/coll: (the) reformed *npl* 1588-1772, Protestantism 1662/3-,
   Protestantdom 1676 + 1896, Protestantcy 1711(1)
..who attends Mass: mass-gospeller a1555(1)
..of episcopal church: prelate-protestant 1680 (1-*hostile*)
..of Saxony: Saxonian a1600(1)

.char by: evangelical 1532-, Protestant 1539-, evangelic
   1583-1792, Protestantical 1592 + 1612, Protestantish 1680 +
   18.., Proddy 1961- *Ulster,* Prod 1977-
..and rejecting good works and sacraments: evangelical
   1791-, evangelic 1812-(1874), evangelican 1847(1),
   evangelistic 1848(1)
                                    XR R1.12.0. Salvation
..of British ultra-protestant groups: Orange 1795-
..not: unprotestantlike 1641(1), unprotestant 1841 + 1881
..common to all: pan-protestantism 1898(1)

.in manner of: evangelically 1532(1), protestantly 1659(1),
   protestantishly 1685(1)
..of sects rejecting good works and sacraments:
   evangelically 1890(1)

R2.2.4.0.1. Conversion to Protestantism: protestanization
   1880 + 1977
.to carry out: protestantize *vt* 1834-
..p perf: protestantizer 1908(1)

.to undergo: protestantize *vi* 1851–

R2.2.4.0.1.1. Freeing from Protestantism: unprotestantizing
    1841(1)
.char by: unprotestantizing 1847(1)
.to perform: unprotestantize *vt* 1833–1895

R2.2.4.0.2. Fundamentalism: Fundamentalism 1920–
                              XR R1.2.1.1. Textualism
.p char by: fundamentalist 1922–
.char by: fundamentalist 1922–
..Exeter Hall: Exeter Hall *attrib.* 1849–1888
.parts of U.S. reputed to adhere to: Bible Belt 1926–

R2.2.4.0.3. The Reformation: the New Learning c1550–1732,
    the Reformation 1563–
                              XR R1.1.15.3. Schism
.char of: reformed 1563–, reformational 1861–
..not: unreformed 1788 + 1892
.before: pre-Reformation 1868–
.after: post-Reformation 1850–
.advocate of: reformitor 1537(1), reformator 1538–1657, reformer
    1561–, reformist 1589–, reformatist 1620–1653
.new: re-reformation a1631–1690

R2.2.4.0.3.1. Pilgrimage of Grace: Pilgrimage of/for Grace
    1536–
R2.2.4.0.3.2. Counter-Reformation: Counter-Reformation
    1840–

R2.2.4.1.0. Anglicanism: Protestancy 1604–1687, Church of
    Englandism 1818–1865, Anglicanism 1838–
                              XR R3.1.1. Episcopacy
.p char by: Protestant 1608–, Anglican a1797–
..pl/coll: English Church 1532/3(1), Church of England 1534–,
    church people 1928(1)

.**char by:** Anglican 1635–, episcopal 1752–, episcopalian 1768–,
    churchy 1843–, church 1853–(1861)
..**of all parts of:** pan-Anglican 1867–
..**not:** unanglican 1842(1)

R2.2.4.1.1.0. Anglican Groups and Divisions
R2.2.4.1.1.1. Broad-churchism: Broad Church 1853–
                                        XR R1.1.1.0. Indifferentism
.**p char by:** Broad-churchman 1878–
..**pl/coll:** Broad Church 1853–

R2.2.4.1.1.2. Continuationism:
.**p char by:** continuationist 1891(1)

R2.2.4.1.1.3. Henricianism: Henricianism 1900 + 1903

R2.2.4.1.1.4. High-churchism: High Church 1702–,
    High-Churchship 1720(1), High-flying 1730(1),
    High-Churchism 1823–, High-Churchmanism 1829(1),
    Laudism a1834–1841, Anglo-Catholicism 1838 + 1842,
    Canterburianism 1848(1), Laudianism 1872(1),
    High-Churchmanship 1874–
.**p char by:** high-flyer/-flier 1680–, high-churchman 1687–,
    Laudian 1710(1), Sacheverellite 1710(2), Laudist 1730(1),
    Anglo-Catholic 1842–, high-churchite 1848(1), high-churchist
    1868(1)
.**char by:** Canterburian 1570 + 1660, Laudian 1691– *mainly hist.,*
    high-flying 1695–, high church 1704–, high 1706/9–,
    Anglo-Catholic 1838–, high and dry 1853–
.**post-Restoration:**
..**char of:** Tantivy 1681–

R2.2.4.1.1.5. Lollardy/Wyclifism: Lollardy 1390–, Lollardry
    1414–, Lolling c1418(1), Lollery 1547–1620, Wycliffianism
    1668(1), Wyclif(f)ism 1675–, Lollardism 1823–, Wyclif(f)ry
    1896–
.**p char by:** Loller c1386–1556, Lollard 1390–, Wyclifan 1402(1),
    Known Men *npl* c1449 + 1563, Wyclif(f)ist c1449–, hooded
    man 1460(1), Wyclif(f)ian 1570–1717, Wyclif(f)ite 1580–,

Lollardist 1882(1)

.char by: Lollardy a1529 + 1888, Wyclif(f)ian 1720–, Wyclif(f)ist 1725(1), Wyclif(f)ite 1843–, Lollardizing 1865(1), Lollardian 1887(1)

R2.2.4.1.1.6. Low-churchism: Latitudinarianism 1676–(1867), Low Church 1702–, Hoadlyism 1800–, evangelicism 1807 + 1864, evangelism 1812–(1876), low-churchmanism 1829(1), evangelicalism 1831–(1884), peculiarism 1836–(1838), peculiarity 1838(1), low-churchism 1864(1), evangelicanism 1887(1)

.p char by: Protestant 1608–, latitude-man 1662(*2q1s*), Latitudinarian 1662–1705, low churchman 1702–(a1715), low-boy 1715(*2q1s*), Hoadlyite 1800(1), evangelical 1804–(1876), evangelic 1812(1), simeonite 1823–, peculiar 1837–, low churchman 1845(1), sim 1851–1883, recordite 1853–, evangelican 1876(1), kensitite 1898–(1936)

.char by: low church 1710–1714, Hoadlyan 1800(1), low 1854–, low church 1867(1)

R2.2.4.1.1.7. Reunionism: reunionism 1895(1)

.p supporting: reunionist 1866–

.char of: reunionistic 1867 + 1883

R2.2.4.1.1.8. Tractarianism: Tractism 1837–1844, Newmania 1838–, Newmanism 1838–, Puseyism 1838–, Tractarianism 1840–(1899), Oxford Movement 1841–, Oxfordism 1847–(1849)

.p char by: tractite 1834–1844, high-churchman 1835–, Oxfordist 1836(1), Newmanite 1837–, Puseyite 1838–1851, tractarian 1839–, tractator 1842–1844, Puseyist 1870(1)

.char by: Newmanite 1838–1841, tractarian 1840–(1896), tractite 1844(1), Puseyitical 1844–1845, Newmanic 1849(1), Puseyistical 1849–1850

..not: untractarian 1846(1)

.to incline to: newmanize *vi* 1836(1), tractarianize *vi* 1842 + 1880

R2.2.4.1.2. Anglicanization:

.to promote: anglicanize *vt* 1919–

R2.2.4.2.0. Antitrinitarianism: Unitarianism 1698–
.**p char by:** trinitarian 1565–1706, trinitary 1581(1), Unitarian
1687–, Racovian 1768/74(1), Bid(d)el(l)ian 1780 + 1882/3,
unicist 1807 + 1832 *both Coleridge*
.**char by:** Racovian 1652–a1861, unitarian 1687–, unitarianized
?1846 + 1893

R2.2.4.2.1. Antitrinitarian groups and sects
Binitarianism: Binitarianism 1928(1)
.**p char by:** Binitarian 1908(1)
.**char by:** Binitarian 1910 + 1928
Monarchianism: monarchianism 1841–, Theodotianism 1876(1)
.**p char by:** Praxean 1719–, monarchian 1765–, Theodotian
1853–(1874), Monarchianist 1872(1), Monarchist 1876(1)
.**char by:** monarchistic 1833(1), monarchian 1847–,
monarchianistic 1872(1), Praxean 1874(1)
Noetianism: Noetianism 1874(1)
.**p char by:** Noetian 1585–
.**char by:** Noetian 1719–
Remonstrant Synod: Remonstrant Synod 1830 + 1846
Socinianism: Socinianism 1643–, Socinism 1645(1)
.**p char by:** Socinian 1645–
.**char by:** Socinianized 1652–, Socinianizing 1655–, Socinian
1694–, Socinianistic 1884(1)
.**to promote:** socinianize *vt* 1695–
.**to adopt:** socinianize *vi* 1671(1)
Tetratarianism:
.**p char by:** Tetradites *npl* 1727/41–1882/3, tetratheite 1874(1)
XR R2.2.1.7. Manicheism

R2.2.4.3.0. Arminianism: Arminianism 1618–1674 + 1822
XR R2.2.4.8.1. Wesleyanism
.**p char by:** Arminian 1618–(1834)
XR R1.12.1. Postdestinarian
.**char by:** Arminian 1618–1674 + 1853, Arminianish a1700(1)

R2.2.4.3.1. Arminian groups and sects
Dutch Reformed:
.p char by: remonstrancer 1618 + 1716, remonstrant 1618–
.char by: remonstrant 1618–, remonstrantical 1619(1)
.document of: remonstrance a1662–1721
Manifestarian:
.p char by: manifestarian 1647–1689
Semi-Arminian:
.p char by: Amyraldist *no quots.*, methodist 1692(1)

R2.2.4.3.2. Arminianization:
.to promote: arminianize *vt* 1637–(1698), arminianize *vi*
1674–(1698)

R2.2.4.4.0. Baptistry: Anabaptistry 1553/87–(1709),
Catabaptistry 1574(1), Anabaptism 1577–1641 + 1856–,
Catabaptism 1655(1)
.p char by: Anabaptist 1532–(1856), rebaptizer 1552–1651,
Catabaptist 1561–1725 + 1864, dipper 1617–(1887), dopper
1620–1625 + 1881, wederdoper 1647(1), Baptist 1654–(1860),
waterman 1657(1), rebaptist 1673(1)
..pl/coll: Anabaptist 1586–(1883)
.char of: anabaptistical 1549–(1861), anabaptistic 1651 + 1774,
catabaptistical 1661(1), anabaptist 1708–(1858)

R2.2.4.4.1. Baptist groups and sects
Campbellite:
.p char by: Campbellite 1830–(1881), reformer 1831– *U.S.*, the
Disciples *npl* 1834–(1881)
Davidist:
.p char by: Davidist 1657–(1882/3), Davidian 1885(1), Davist
1885(1)
Dunkard:
.p char by: dunker 1756–(1886), dunkard 1784–(1896), Tumbler
1796(1)
Free-will:

.p char by: free will Baptist 1732

XR R2.2.4.3. Arminianism

Hardshell:

XR R2.2.4.5. Calvinism

.p char by: hardshell 1845–
.char by: hardshell 1838–, hardshelled 1842–
Hemerobaptist:
.char by: Hemerobaptist 1577–
Muncerian:
.p char by: Muncerian c1559–1560
Munster:
.p char by: Knipperdolling 1594–1690 + 1823*hist.*, monasterian
    1641(1)
.char by: monasterian 1650(1)
Old Baptist:
.p char by: Old Baptist (church) *ncoll* 1845 + 1889
Particular:

XR R1.12.1. Particularism

.p char by: Particular Baptists *npl* 1738–
Primitive:
.p char by: Primitive Baptist 1851–

Self-Baptist: XR R2.2.4.12. Congregationalism

.p char by: se-baptist 1610 + 1732
.char by: se-baptistic 1610(1)
Separatist:
.p char by: separatist 1645(1)
Seventh-Day:

XR R4.1.5.1. Sabbath

.p char by: Traskite 1618–1661, Traskist 1631–1694, Sabbatarian
    1645–(1820), Seventh-day man 1694(1),
    Saturday-sabbatharian 1705(1), Sabbat(h)arian 1719(1),
    Sabbatist 1857 + 1865
.char by: seventh-day 1684–
Shouter:
.p char by: shouter 1950–
Southern:
.p char by: Southern Baptist 1866–

R2.2.4.5.0. Calvinism: Calvinism 1570–, Huguenotism 1611 +
  1859, Genevanism 1625(1)
                                  XR R1.9.0. Grace
.p char by: Genevian 1564–c1719, Huguenot 1565–, Calvinist
  1579–, Calvinian 1582–1691, Genevan 1843–
                          XR R2.2.4.8.1. Whitefieldian
.char by: Calvinian 1566–(1862), Genevian 1573–1804,
  Calvinistical 1606–1853, Calvinish 1637(1), Huguenot 1682–,
  Calvinistic 1820–(1850), Calvinized 1824(1), Calvinizing
  1829(1), Genevan 1853–, Huguenotic 1897(1)
.in manner of: calvinistically 1674–1832

R2.2.4.5.1. Calvinist groups and sects
Cevennian:
.p char by: Camisar(d) 1703–
Gomarist:
.p char by: Gomarist 1674–
Hopkinsian: Hopkinsianism 1850(1)
.char by: Hopkinsian 1860–
Hyper-Calvinist: Hyper-Calvinism 1882/3(1)
.p char by: Hypercalvinian 1674(1), hyper 1856 + 1863 *hum.*,
  hyper-Calvinist 1856 + 1892
.char by: hyper-Calvinistic 1896(1)
Taylorist: Taylorism 1882/3 + 1885
Tylerist: Tylerism 1891(1)
Walkerite:
.p char by: Walkerite 1830(1)

R2.2.4.5.2. Calvinization:
.to perform: calvinize *vt* 1862(1)
.to undergo: calvinize *vi* 1659–1861
..p who does: Genevizer 1682–1692

R2.2.4.6.0. Lutheranism: Lutheranism 1560–, Lutherism
  a1695–, Lutherianism 1796(1)
.p char by: Lutheran 1521–, Lutherian 1526–1589, confessionist

c1568–1849, Martinist 1751(1), Lutherist 1883(1)
.char by: Lutheran 1530–, Augustan 1565–(1796), Lutheranic
    1848(*2q1s*)

R2.2.4.6.1. Lutheran groups and sects
Calixtin: Syncretism 1618–(1831)
.p char by: Calixtin(e) 1727/51–1826, Syncretist 1764–
Confessional:
.p char by: Confessional Church *ncoll* 1938–
Flacian:
.p char by: Flacian 1565–1847, substantialist 1657 + 1847,
    Flacianist 1872(1)
.char by: Flacian 1882/3(1)
Philippist: Philippism 1882/3(1)
.p char by: adiaphorist 1564–(1832), Philippist 1727/41–,
    Melancthonian 1863(1)
.char of: Melancthonian 1755–, Philippistic 1882/3(1)
Pietist: Pietism 1697–
Ubiquitist: Ubiquity 1579–1882/3, Ubiquitism 1617–1857,
    Ubiquitarianism 1885(1), Ubiquism 1891(1)
.p char by: Ubiquitary 1585/7–1709, Ubiquiter 1589 + a1599 *Sc.*,
    Ubiquitarian 1651–1874, Ubiquitist 1687(1), Ubiquist 1728 +
    1842
.char by: Ubiquitary 1599 + 1603, Ubiquitarian 1640–1882

R2.2.4.6.2. Lutheranization:
.to perform: lutheranize *vt* 1879(1)
..p who does: lutheranizer 1845(1)
.to undergo: lutheranize *vi* 1857(1)

R2.2.4.7.0. Mennonism: Mennonism 1684(1)
.p char by: Mennonite 1565–, Mennonist 1645–1866, Mennist
    1771 + 1869 *U.S.*, plain people *npl* 1904 – *U.S.*

R2.2.4.7.1. Mennonite groups and sects
Amish:

.p char by: Hooker 1880(1), Amish *ncoll* 1884(1)
.char by: Amish 1844–
Borborite:
.p char by: Borborite 1659–

R2.2.4.8.0. Methodism: Methodism 1739–1851, swaddling
    1759–1771/2 *slang*, Connexionalism 1883–
                                 XR R2.2.4.9.1. Inghamite
.p char by: Methodist 1733–, swaddler 1747–(1907) *slang*,
    Methody/-dee 1753–, bible-bigot 1766–1820 *contempt.*,
    bible-moth 1789 + 1820 *contempt.*
.char by: swaddling 1747–(1885) *slang*, Methodistical 1749–,
    Methodist 1766–, Methodistic 1791–1849, Connexional 1838–
.inclined to: Methodizing 1820–1842
.in manner of: Methodistically 1787–

R2.2.4.8.1. Methodist groups and sects
Huntingdonian:
                                 XR R2.2.4.5. Calvinism
.p char by: (Lady/Countess of) Huntingdon('s) Connexion *ncoll*
    1874–, Huntingdonian 1970(1)
.char of: Huntingdonian a1800(1)
Kilhamite:
.p char by: Kilhamite 1815 + 1860
Jumping: Jumperism 1800 + 1876
.p char by: Jumper 1774–
Primitive: Ranterism 1841(1), Primitivism 1907(1)
.p char by: Ranter 1823–1862, Primitive 1855–, Primitive
    Methodist 1860–
..pl/coll: Primitive Methodist Connexion 1812(1)
Sacramentarian:
.p char by: Sacramentarian 1732–1797
Separatistic:
.p char by: separate 1882/3(1)
Shouting:
.p char by: shouter 1820(1)

Wesleyan: Wesleyanism 1774–, Wesleyan Methodism 1796–,
    Wesleyism 1847–
                                 XR R2.2.4.3. Arminianism
.p char by: Wesleyan 1791–, Wesleyan Methodist 1796–,
    Wesleyite 1807(1)
..advocating separation from C of E: separatist 1859(1)
.char by: Wesleyan 1771–, Wesleyanized 1849–
Whitefieldian: Whit(e)fieldism 1879–, Whit(e)fieldianism 1915(1)
                                 XR R2.2.4.5. Calvinism
.p char by: Whitefieldian 1744(1), Whit(e)fieldite 1748–1786

R2.2.4.8.2. Methodization:
.having undergone:
..not: unmethodized 1751(1)
.to perform: methodize *vt* 1846(1)
.to undergo: methodize *vi* 1771(1)

R2.2.4.9.0. Moravianism: Herrnhutism 1753(1), Moravianism
    1829–, Herrnhutenism 1879(1), Herrnhutianism 1882/3(1)
.p char by: Moravian 1746–, Herrnhuter 1748–
..pl/coll: United Brethren 1702(1), Unity (of the Brethren)
    1780–(1865)
.char by: Moravian 1745–
.influenced by: Moravianized 1820(1)

R2.2.4.9.1. Moravian groups and sects
Inghamitism:
                                 XR R2.2.4.8. Methodism
.p char by: Inghamite 1839–

R2.2.4.10.0. Mormonism: Mormonism 1831–
.p char by: Mormon 1830–, Mormonite 1831–, Mormonist
    1842(1-*Dickens*), Mormoness *nf* a1861–(1906)
..pl/coll: Mormon Church 1838–, Latter-Day Saints 1842–(1851),
    Mormondom 1860–, Mormonry 1930(1)
..not: gentile 1847–

...on friendly terms with p char by: Jack Mormon 1845– *U.S.*
.p founding, and his successors: the prophet 1844–
.char by: Mormonite 1835–(1882), Mormon 1842–
..not: gentile 1861(*2q1s*)

R2.2.4.10.1. Mormon groups and sects
Danite:
.p char by: destroying angel 1838–(1943), Danite 1838–(1948)

R2.2.4.11.0. Plymouth Brethrenism: Plymouth-Brotherism
1848(1), Brethrenism 1865–, Plymouth-Brethrenism 1874 +
1879, Darbyism 1876(1), Plymouthism 1876–
.p char by: Plymouth sister *nf* 1860(1), Plymouthite 1876(1),
Plymouth brother 1879(1), Darbyite 1882/3–(1890),
Plymouthist 1885(1), Plym 1953– *colloq.*
..pl/coll: saints *npl* 1838–, Plymouth Brethren 1842–, Brethren
1886(1)

R2.2.4.11.1. Darbyite groups and sects
Open Brethrenism:
.p char by: Open Brethren *npl* 1879–

R2.2.4.12.0. Presbyterianism: Presbytery 1590–,
Presbyterianism 1644–, Presbyterism 1659 + a1670,
Presbyteering 1684(1)
XR R2.2.4.5. Calvinism
R3.1.1. Consociation

.full-blown: archpresbytery 1649(1-*Milton*)
.p char by: disciplinary 1585/7(1), disciplinarian 1585/7–1673 +
1886*hist.*, consistorian 1606–a1670 + 1889*hist.*, Presbyterian
1641–, Presbyterial 1647(1), Presbyterialist 1647(1),
Presbyter 1647–1827, kirkman 1650–, cloak-man 1680(1),
kirker 1680–(1893) *Sc.*, Presbyteer 1708(1), Knoxian 1714 +
1937
..pl/coll: Kirk a1674–

.char of: consistorial 1561*Sc.* +1593–, presbyterial 1592–1681/6 +
    1904, disciplinary 1593–1641, consistorian 1593–1660,
    disciplinarian 1593–1654 + 1889*hist.*, Scotican 1635–1844,
    allobrogical 1640 + 1646, Presbyterian 1641–, Presbyteral
    1651–, Scotized 1657 + 1711, Knoxian 1905–

XR R3.1.4. Presbyterian

..all: pan-Presbyterian 1877–
..not: unpresbyterated 1650 + 1656
.in manner of: presbyterially 1655(1), presbyterianly 1656–1691
    + 1894

R2.2.4.12.1. Presbyterian groups and sects
Burgher:
.p char by: Burgher 1766–
Cameronian:
.p char by: Cameronian 1691 + 1816*hist.*, reformed Presbyterian
    1701–, non-hearer 1853–(1855)
.char by: Cameronian 1693–, reformed Presbyterian 1806–
Congregationalist: Brownism c1617–(1732), independency
    1642–, independentism 1653–1665 + 1827, Congregationalism
    1716–(1861)

XR R2.2.4.4.1. Se-Baptist
R3.1.1. Church government

.American non-Calvinist: New England Theology 1899 + 1967
.p char by: Brownist 1583–, Barrowist 1589–(1884), Independent
    1644–, Congregational 1653(1), Congregationer 1654–a1670,
    Congregationist 1659(1), Congregationalist 1692–
.char by: Brownistical 1636–, congregational 1642–,
    independentish 1653(1)
.(of churches:)formed according to: congregated 1653–1799,
    independented 1659(1), congregate 1680(1)
.in manner of: congregationally 1887(1)
.to imbue with: congregationalize *vt* 1882(1)
Covenanting: *see R4.11.1. Covenant*
.p char by: Whig 1657–
.char by: Whig 1681–1732
Evangelical:

.p char by: high-flyer/-flier 1856 + 1897
.char by: wild 1778–a1830
Free Kirk:
.p char by: Free-Kirker 1881(1), Free Church/Kirk of Scotland
    ncoll 1843–
Glassite:
.p char by: Glassite 1772–
..**Sandemanian:** Sandemanian 1792–
...**char of:** Sandemanian 1766–
Hebridean: yellow stick 1861–(1880)
Morisonian: Morisonianism a1861(1)
.p char by: Morisonian a1861(1)
.char by: Morisonian 1878(1)
New School: New School 1806–
Relief:
.p char by: reliefer 1798(1), Buchanite 1846 + 1910, reliever 1895
    + 1897
..**pl/coll:** (the) relief 1764–, Relief Church 1767–
Rowite: Rowism 1846(1)
.p char by: Rowite 1834–1846
Secession: Secession 1733-, Secessionism 1899–
.**Antiburgher:** Antiburgher 1766–(1815)
.p char by: seceder 1758–
..**pl/coll:** secession 1782–
.char by: seceding 1758(1), secession 1838-, secessional 1838–
United:
.p char by: United Presbyterian 1874(1)
.char by: United Presbyterian 1847-, U. P. *abbrev.* 1865 + 1878
Wee Free:
.p char by: Wee Frees *npl* 1904(1), Wee Free Kirk *ncoll* 1904– *Sc.*,
    Wee Kirkers *npl* 1905(1)

R2.2.4.12.2. Presbyterianization
.**having undergone:**
..**not:** unpresbyterated 1650 + 1656
.**to perform:** kirkify *vt* 1661 + 1854, presbyterate *vt* 1702-,
    presbyterianize *vt* a1843–

.to incline to: presbyterianize *vi* c1878(1)

R2.2.4.13.0. Puritanism: precisianism 1573–1651, Puritanism
1573–, Catharism 1574–1838, Purantism 1602(1), cloak
1649–1663 *contempt.*, saintism 1691(1), perfectism 1830(1),
hot gospelling 1923– *slang*

> XR R1.7.1. Sanctimoniousness
> R2.2.4.16. Waldensianism
> R2.2.5. Novatianism

.not: impuritanism 1818 + 1892
.p char by: Catharite 1555(1), hot gospeller 1562 + 1874– *slang*,
precisian 1571–, Puritan 1572–, Catharan 1574–1656,
disciplinary 1585/7(1), disciplinarian 1585/7–1673 +
1886*hist.*, Catharist 1600–1832, Puritant 1607(1), saint
?1610–(1886), perfectist 1618–, Cathar(e) 1637–, prick-ear
1642(1), Catharinian 1657(1), Jacobite 1658(1), Methodist
1758–1834 *transf.*, wowser 1909– *Austral. slang*
..not: impuritan 1617–

.char of: precise 1566–1694 + 1827–1860, Puritan 1589–, pure
1598–1785, Puritanian 1600(*2q1s*), Puritant 1604(1),
Puritanic 1606–, Puritanical 1624–, kneeless 1631(1-*allus.,*),
precisianical a1652(1), catharistic 1838(1), patarin/-ene
1926–, hot-gospelling 1931–
..condition of being: precisianship 1573 + 1574/5, preciseness
1598–1790, holiness 1888– *orig. U. S.*
..not: hickory 1831–

.in manner of: puritanically 1706(1), puritanly 1897(1)

R2.2.4.13.1. Puritan groups and sects
Albigensianism:
.p char by: bugger/bougre 1340(*2q1s*), Albigenses *npl* 1625–,
Bonhomme 1751(1)
.char by: Albigensian 1604 + 1832–

R2.2.4.13.2. Puritanization:
.p perf: puritanizer 1847(1)

.to perform: puritanize *vt* 1648–
.to undergo: puritanize it *vi* 1625(1), hot-gospel *vt/i* 1952–

R2.2.4.14.0. Quakerism: Quakerism 1656–, Quaking 1669–1671,
   Quakery 1673–1688, Quakerdom 1824–1855
.p char by: meeter 1646–a1713, shaker 1648–1694, Quaker 1651–,
   trembler 1678–1820, friend 1679–, yea-and-nay man a1700(1),
   whaker 1700–1802 *dial.*, Quakeress *nf* 1721–1852, broad-brim
   1749–1863, yea-and-nay 1807(1), drabman 1860(1),
   shad-belly 1860(1- *U.S.*)
..not: unfriend 1828 + 1846
...pl/coll: world 1648–
.char by: quaking 1654–1755, Quakerly 1684–1829, Quakeristical
   1685(1), Quakerish 1743–, Quaker-like 1818–1838, Foxian
   1823(1), Quakerian 1827(1), Quakeric 1847(1), friendly
   1886(1)
..condition of being: Quakerishness 1785(1)
.in manner of: Quaker-like 1680(1), Quakerly 1684–, Quakerishly
   1886(1)

R2.2.4.14.1. Quaker groups and sects
Beaconite:
.p char by: Beaconite 1835–
Shaker: Shakerism 1818–,
.p char by: Shaker 1784–, Shaking Quaker 1784–, Shakeress *nf*
   1860–
..pl/coll: Shakerdom 1861(1)
..following Hicks: Hicksite 1839–

R2.2.4.14.2. Quakerization: Quakerization 1864(1)
.to perform: Quakerize *vt* 1825(1)

R2.2.4.15.0. Salvationism: Salvationism 1889(1)
.p char by: soldier 1876–, Salvationist 1882 + 1892, Salvation
   1889(*2q1s*), Salvationer 1889(1), Sally 1936–

..**female:** hallelujah-lass 1886 + 1965, lass 1886–, Salvation lassie
    1891–, poke-bonnet 1899(1), lassie 1906–
..**who is officer:** captain 1878–, lieutenant 1884–, major 1907–
..**pl/coll:** Salvation Army c1880–, (the) Sally 1915–, Sally Ann(e)
    1927–, Sally Army 1961–
.**char by:** Salvation Army 1881–

R2.2.4.16.0. Waldensianism: Vaudism 1855(1), Waldism
    1888(1)
.**p char by:** Waldensian 1604 + 1832–, insabbatist 1634 + 1804,
    Lyonist 1644–1727/41, Waldense 1888(1)
..**pl/coll:** Waldenses *npl* 1537–, Vaudois *npl* 1560–, Vaudese *npl*
    1781(1)
.**char by:** Waldensian c1645–, Vaudois 1830–, insabbatized
    1832(1), Vaudese 1882/3(2)

R2.2.5. Various (anti-)Christian groups

Acephali: Acephali *npl* 1625–1721, Acephalist 1659–1696
.**char by:** Acephalian 1586(1)
Adamitism: Adamitism 1831(1)
.**p char by:** Adamite 1628–1713
Adoptionism: Adoptionism 1874(1)
.**p char by:** Adoptionist 1847–(1874),
Agepamonite: Agepamonite 1850–, Agepamonian 1893–,
    Agepamone *ncoll* 1851–
Agnoetism: Agnoetism 1753(1)
.**p char by:** Agnoites/Agnoetes *npl* 1586–1775
Agonyclite: Agonyclite 1710(1)
Albigensianism: *see R2.2.4.13. Puritanism*
Alogian: Alogian 1675–1849
Angelist: Angelist 1651(1)
.**to incline to doctrine of:** angelize *vi* 1605(1)
Angelite: Angelite 1753–
Annihilationism: *see R2.2.5. Destructionism*
Anointer: Anointer 1677(1)

Anthropomorphite: Anthropomorphite 1561 + 1872
Antinomianism: Antinomianism 1643–, Antinomism 1658–1672
XR R1.4.0. Law
.p char by: Antinomic 1586(1), Antinomist 1632–1656,
    Antinomian 1645–
.char of: Antinomian 1645–
.to teach: antinomianize *vt/i* 1692–1707
.Ranting: Rantism 1665–1691, Ranterism 1673–1697
..p char by: Ranter 1651–(1856)
.Libertine:
..p char by: Libertine 1563/83–1589
.Huntingdonian:
..p char by: Huntingdonian 1815 + 1921
.Vanist:
..p char by: Vanist 1658–
Antipodist: Antipodist 1866(1)
Aphthartodocetæ: Incorruptibles *npl* 1727/41 + 1853
Apollinarianism: Apollinarianism 1877–
.p char by: Apollinarian 1586 + 1852, Apollinarist 1640–1702+
    1882
.char by: Apollinarian 1659(1)
Apostolic: Apostolic 1580–(1751), Dulcinist 1721 + 1884
Apotactite: Apotactite 1727/51–(1838)
Aquarian: Aquarian 1586 + 1751
XR R4.2.4. Eucharist
Arabian: Arabian 1670(1)
Arnoldist: Arnoldist 1669 + 1882
Artotyrite: Artotyrite 1586 + 1837
XR R4.2.4. Communion
Augustinian (Bohemian): Augustinian 1645(1)

Bardesanism: Bardesanism 1674 + 1751
Baxterian: Baxterian 1835 + 1839
Beardies: *see R2.2.5. Southcotians*
Bible-Christians: Bible-Christian a1860 + 1860, Bryanites *npl*
    1882/3(1)
XR R2.2.4.8.1. Wesleyan Methodism
Blue-Domeism: Blue-Domeism 1945(1)

.p char by: Blue-Domist 1952(1), Blue Domer 1961 + 1962
Boehmenism: B(o)ehminism 1656(1)
.p char by: B(o)ehmenist 1655 + 1824, Behmist 1731 + 1854,
    B(o)ehmenite 1846(1)
.char of: Behmenish 1739(1), B(o)ehmist 1912(1), Behmenistic
    1919(1), Behmenist 1961(1)
Bogomilism: Bogomilism 1887 + 1941
.p char by: Bogomil(e) 1841–, Bogomilian a1875(1)
.char of: Bogomilian 1852(1), Bogomilist 1887(1)
Bohemian: *see R2.2.5. Utraquism*
Brethren of the Common Life: Brethren of the Common Life
    1860(1)
Brethren of the Free Spirit: Brethren of the Free Spirit 1860(1)
Brotherist: Brotherist 1807(1)
Buchmanism: Buchmanism 1928–, Moral Rearmament 1938–
.p char by: Buchmanite 1928–(1936), Moral Rearmer 1956–
.char by: Buchmanite 1933(1)
Bush Brother: Bush Brotherhood *ncoll* 1903(1), Bush Brother
    1930 + 1950

Cainism: Cainism 1620(1)
.p char by: Cainite 1647–1764, Cainian 1657(1)
.char by: Cainitic 1882/3(1)
Calixtin: *see R2.2.5. Utraquism*
Capharnaism: Capharnaism 1828(1)
Carpocratite: Carpocration 1585/7–, Carpocratite 1579(1)
Cataphrygian: *see R2.2.5. Montanist*
Christadelphianism: Christadelphianism 1876(1)
.p char by: Christadelphians *npl* 1873–, Thomasite 1888(1)
.char by: Christadelphian 1876(1)
Christian Science: Christian Science 1863–
.p char by: Christian scientist 1881–
Clementine: Clementine 1883(1)
Collegian: Collegian 1727/51–1818, Collegiant 1764–1818
Convulsionism: Convulsionism 1870(1)
.p char by: convulsionary 1741–, convulsionist 1865–
.char by: convulsionary 1814–
.dancing:

..p char by: Dancers *npl* 1764–(1882/3)
.jerking:
..p char by: Jerker 1851 + 1889
.rolling:
..p char by: holy roller 1842–

Destructionism: annihilationism 1881(1)

XR R1.13.0. Reprobation
.p char by: Destructionist 1807(1), annihilationist 1875 + 1880
Disciplinant: flagellant 1563/87–, Disciplinant 1620–1766 + 1881,
    flagellist 1833 + 1926
Dominical: *see R2.2.5. Sabbatarianism*
Dulcinism: *see R2.2.5. Apostolic*

Ebionitism: Ebionitism 1780–(1882), Ebionism 1879 + 1880

XR R2.1.1. Nazarism
.p char by: Ebionite 1650–(1882)
.char by: Ebionitic 1833–(1882)
Endeavourer: Endeavourer 1893–(1900)
Enthusiast: Enthusiasts *npl* 1637 + 1639
Essenism: Essenism 1852–(1882)
.p following debased: Ossene 1863–
Euchite: Euchite 1585–(1882/3), Messalian/Massalian a1591–,
    Hesychast 1835–, Palamite 1859–
.char by: Messalian/Massalian 1597–, Palamite 1877–
Eutychianism: Eutychianism 1612 + 1846
.p char by: Eutychian 1556–(1882/3)
.char by: Eutychian 1579–(1724)

Faithism:
.p char by: faithist 1885–(1928)
Familism: Familism 1642–1765
.p char by: Family of Love *ncoll* 1579–1667, Family-lovist
    1589(1), Familist 1592–(1853)
..following Grindleton: Grindletonian 1641–1661
.char by: familistic 1646 + 1667, familistical 1653 + 1702
.in manner of: familistically 1653(1)

Grindletonian: *see R2.2.5. Familist*
Hallelujah: Hallelujah 1946 + 1955
Harmonist: Harmonist 1824 + 1875, Rappite 1832–1864, Rappist
    1845–
Henrician: Henrician 1579 + 1889
Hermesianism: Hermesianism 1847 + 1885
Hieracite: Hieracite 1585/7 + 1745
Holy roller: *see R2.2.5. Convulsionary*
Hussite: *see R2.2.5. Utraquism*
Hypsistarian: Hypsistary c1610(1), Hypsistarian 1727/41 +
    1882/3
.char by: Hypsistarian 1705(1)

Illuminati (Bavarian): Illuminati *npl* 1797–, Illuminates *npl*
    1906(1)
.char by: illuminated 1634–(1802), illuminized 1920(1)
.to teach doctrine of: illuminize *vt* 1828(1)
Illuminati (Spanish): Illuminati *npl* 1599–1749, *Alumbrado* 1749
    + 1847, Illumine 1794–, Illuminee 1800(1)
                                      XR R2.2.4.13.0. Puritanism
Incorruptibles: *see R2.2.5. Aphthartodocetæ*
Invisibles: Invisibles *npl* 1852(1)
Irvingism: Irvingism 1836 + 1876
.p char by: Irvingite 1836–, Catholic (and) Apostolic Church
    ncoll 1861–

Jehovah's Witnesses: Jehovah's Witness 1933–, Russellite *no*
    quots.
Joachimism: Joach(im)ism 1906–
.p char by: Joachimite 1797–, Joach(it)ist / Joachite / Joachimist
    1874–
Jocism: Jocism 1939(1)
.p char by: Jocist 1935–
Jordanite: Jordanite 1934–
Josephism: Josephism 1947(1), Josephitism 1950(1)
Jovinian: Jovinian 1585/7(1), Jovinianist 1864–
.char by: Jovinianish 1614(1)
Khlist: Khlist 1856–

Libertinism: *see R2.2.5. Antinomianism*
Luciferian: Luciferian c1555–
$\qquad$ XR R2.2.1.2.0. Arianism
.char by: Luciferian 1607–1865
Lullism: Lullism 1929–
.char by: Lullian 1653–1669 + 1933–

Macedonianism: Macedonianism 1642–1646
.p char by: Macedonian 1559–
Majorism: Majorism 1857–
$\qquad$ XR R1.12.0. Salvation
$\qquad$ R4.4. Good works
.p char by: Majorist 1874(1)
.char by: Majoristic 1845(1)
Marcionism: Marcionism 1882(1), Marcionitism 1894(1)
.p char by: Marcionite a1540–, Marcionist 1546–, Lucianist
$\qquad$ 1727/41–
.char by: Marcionitish 1874(1), Marcionitic 1875–, Lucianic 1882–
Martinism: Martinism 1879(1)
$\qquad$ XR R1.8.5.0. Mysticism
.p char by: Martinist 1871(1)
Materiarian: Materiarian 1678(1), Materialist 1702(1)
.char by: Materiarian 1678(1)
Messalian: *see R2.2.5. Euchite*
Millerism: Millerism 1843–
.p char by: Millerite 1846(1), Second Adventist 1878(1),
$\qquad$ Adventist 1883–
Monothelitism: Monothelitism 1685–1856, Monothelitism 1765–,
$\qquad$ Monotheletism 1850(1)
$\qquad$ XR R2.2.3.1. Maronite
.p char by: Monothelite 1430/40–1856, Monothelete 1880(1)
.char by: Monothelite 1619–1856, Monothelitic 1716–,
$\qquad$ Monotheletic 1885(1), Monotheletian 1887(1)
Montanism: Montanism 1597–
.p char by: Pepuzian 1565–1727/41, Montanist 1577–1833,
$\qquad$ Cataphrygian 1585/7–1750, Phrygian 1585/7 + 1837,
$\qquad$ Pepusite 1653(1)
.char by: Montanical 1607(1), Montanistical 1629–1660,

Montanistic 1645–1833, Montanist 1859(*2q1s*),
.**Tertullian:** Tertullianism 1702(1)
..**p char by:** Tertullianist 1710–1831/3
.**to follow:** montanize *vi* 1594–1840
Moral Rearmament: *see R2.2.5. Buchmanism*
Muggletonianism: Muggletonianism 1881(1)
.**p char by:** Muggletonian a1670–1868
.**char by:** Muggletonian 1729(1)

Nazarene (Hungarian): Nazarene 1886(1)
.**char by:** Nazarene 1680–1765
Nazarenism: Nazarenism 1892–
.**p char by:** Nazarene 1898–
.**char by:** Nazarene 1910–
Neighbourhood: Neighbourhood 1883(1)
New Thought: New Thought 1887–
.**p char by:** New Thoughter 1907–
Nicolaitanism: Nicolaitism 1669(1), Nicolaitanism 1882/3(1)
.**p char by:** Nicolaite 1382–1586, Nicolaitan 1526–
.**char by:** Nicolaitan 1874(1)
Novatianism: Novatianism 1574–
XR R2.2.4.13.0. Puritanism
.**p char by:** Novatian c1449–, Novatianist 1597–
.**char by:** Novatian 1630–
Nubians: Nubians *npl* c1400(1)

Old Christian Church: Old Christian (Church) 1849(1)
Opinionist: Opinionist 1693–1707
Origenist: Origenist 1647 + 1874, Origenian 1727/41(1)
Osiandrist: Osiandrian 1582–, Osiandrist 1725–
XR R1.11.0. Atonement
Overcomer: Overcomer 1882/3(1)
Oxford Groups Movement: Groupism 1933(1)
.**p char by:** groupist 1933–, grouper 1934–
..**pl/coll:** group 1928–

Passionist: *see R2.2.5. Patripassian*
Patrician: Patrician 1659–1727/41

Patripassianism: Patripassionism 1847(1)
.p char by: Patripassian 1579–, Passionist 1874(1)
.char by: Patripassian 1727/41–
.in manner of: patripassianly 1876(1)
Paulian: Paulian c1449–, Samosatenian 1597–1727/41, Paulianite
    1696(1), Paulinist 1696–
.char by: Samosatenian 1697–a1861
Peculiar People: Peculiar People *npl* 1875–(1901), Peculiar
    1876–(1893)
Pentecostalism: Pentecostalism 1932–
.p char by: Pentecostal 1904–, Pentecostalist 1925–
.char of: Pentecostal 1904–, Pentecostalist 1958–
Pepuzian: *see R2.2.5. Montanist*
Petrobrusian: Petrobrusian c1559–
Phantasiast: Phantasiast 1680–(1863), Phantasmatic 1701(1),
    Phantasmist 1823(1), Phantomist 1895(1)
.char by: Phantasiastic 1826(1)
Philadelphianism: Philadelphianism 1697(1)
.p char by: Philadelphians *npl* 1693–
.char by: Philadelphian 1693–
Photianism: Photianism 1854 + 1864
.p char by: Photian 1849–, Photianist 1948(1)
.char by: Photian 1850–, Photianist 1948–
Phrygian: *see R2.2.5. Montanist*
Pneumatomachy: Pneumatomachy 1889(1)
.p char by: Pneumatomachist 1654–, Pneumatomachian 1707–
.char of: Pneumatomachian 1915–

Ranterism: *see R2.2.5. Antinomianism*
Rappist: *see R2.2.5. Harmonist*
River Brethren: River Brethren *npl* 1854 + 1951
Rogerene: Rogerene 1754– *U.S.*

Sabbatarianism: Sabbatarianism 1673/4–
.p char by: sabbatary 1596 + 1621
..not: dominical 1861–(1884)
.char by: Sabbatarian 1654–
Sabbathaism: Sabbathaism 1882/3(1), Sabbatianism 1892–

.p char by: Sabbatian 1892–
.char by: Sabbatian 1892–
Sabbatian: Sabbatian 1708/22–(1882/3)
Sabian: Sabian 1661–1841
.char by: Sabian 1787–(1886)
Saducean: Saducean 1597(1), Sadducee 1680(1)
.char by: sadducizing 1707 + 1854
Samaritanism: Samaritanism a1641–1886
.p char by: Samaritan c1511–1799
Samosatenian: *see R2.2.5. Paulian*
Sampsæan: Sampsæan 1613 + 1875
Sandemanianism: Sandemanianism 1766 + 1822
.p char by: Sandemanian 1792 + 1882/8
.char by: Sandemanian 1810 + 1876
Schwenkfeldianism: Schwenkfeldianism 1579(1)
.p char by: Schwenkfeldian 1562–(1886), Swenkfeldian 1564–1796,
    Zuen(c)kfeldian 1565(1), Zwenckfeldian 1565(1), Swingfelter
    1792(1), Zwingfelter 1794(1), Schwenkfelder 1882/3–(1884)
Separatist: ?Separatist 1821(1)
Septembrian: Septembrian 1644(1)
Sepulchral Heretic: Sepulchral Heretic 1728(1)
Servetianism: Servetianism 1655(1)
.p char by: Servetian 1564–(1874)
Seventh-Day Adventist: Adventist 1843–, Seventh-day
    Adventists *npl* 1860–
Severian: *see R2.2.1.8.1. Monophysitism*
Sibyllist: Sibyllist 1605–, Sibyllianist a1641(1)
Simonianism: Simonianism 1887–
.p char by: Simonian 1585/7–, Simonist 1880(1)
.char by: Simonian 1883–
Skoptsism: Skoptsism 1911(1)
.p char by: Skoptsi *npl* 1856–
Smalcaldian:
.char by: Smalcaldic 1668–, Smalcaldian 1679–
Southcottian: New Israelite *no quots.*, Southcottian 1842–,
    Beardies *npl* 1875–, Sabbatharian 1882/3(1)
.char by: Southcottian 1843–
Stercoranism: Stercoranism 1728–

XR R5.15.5. Eucharistic elements
.p char by: Stercoranite 1579(1), Stercoranist 1686–, Stercorarian 1728(1), Stercorist 1872(1)
Stundism: Stundism 1888(1)
.p char by: Stundist 1878–
Swedenborgism: Swedenborgism 1807–(1863), Swedenborgianism 1863(1)
.p char by: Swedenborgian 1791–
.char by: Swedenborgian 1807–
Sweet Singers: Sweet Singers *npl* 1680–1732
Synusiast: Synusiast 1728(1)

Tatianist: Tatian 1585/7(1-*erron.*), Tatianist 1754/8–1862
Tertullianism: *see R2.2.5. Montanism*
Theophilanthrope: theophilanthrope 1801–1843
.char of: theophilanthropical 1801(1)
Thnetopsychism: Thnetopsychism 1882/3(1)
XR R1.8.1.3. Thnetopsychism
Thomæan: Thomæan 1727/41 + 1842
.char by: Thomæan 1727/41(1)
Tigurine: *see R2.2.5. Zwinglian*
Timist: Timist 1884(1)
Transcendentalism (New England): the Newness 1865–c1870
Triclavianism: Triclavianism 1838(1)
.p char by: Triclavian 1838(1)
Tropics: Tropics *npl* 1585/7(1), tropist 1727/41–1775
XR R1.2.1.1.3. Scriptural interpretation
Turlupins: Turlupins *npl* 1639–

Utraquism: Utraquism 1861 + 1892
XR R4.2.4.2. Eucharistic doctrine
.p char by: Bohemian 1579(1), Calixtin(e) 1710–1838, Utraquist 1836–(1881)
.char by: Bohemic 1612(1), Utraquistic 1894(1), Utraquist 1894 + 1900
Valesian: Valesian 1702–(1808)
Waterlander: Waterlandian 1765–, Waterlander 1860–
.char by: Waterlandish 1762(1)

Zionite: Zionite 1882/3–(1886)
Zwinglianism: Zwinglianism 1581–
.p char by: Zwinglian 1532–, Tigurine 1674(1), Zwinglianist
    1674–1745
.char by: Zwinglian 1565–, Tigurine a1651–1788

R2.3. Non-Christian Religions

R2.3.1.0. Buddhism: Buddhism 1801–
.p char by: Buddhist 1801–, Buddhite 1803 + 1816
.char by: Buddhic 1816 + 1817, Buddhist 1816–, Buddhistical
    1837 + 1860, Buddhistic 1841–
.in manner of: Buddhistically 1920 + 1921
.pan-: Pan-Buddhism 1902(1)
..char by: Pan-Buddhist 1902(1)

R2.3.1.1. Buddhist groups and sects
Hinayana ('lesser vehicle'): Hinayana 1868–, Theravada 1875–
    Hinayanism 1907(1)
.p char by: Hinayanist 1907–
.char by: Hinayanian 1956(1)
Hau-Hau: Hau-Hauism 1875 + 1914
.p char by: Hau Hau 1865–
Hoa Hoa: Hoa Hoa 1955–
Jainist: Jainism 1858(1)
.p char by: Jain(a) 1805–, Jainist 1816(1)
.char by: Jain(a) 1805–, Jainist 1893(1)
Jodoist:
.p char by: Jodo *ncoll* 1727–
Mahayana: Mahayana 1686–
.p char by: Mahayanist 1891–, Mahayanistic 1907–, Mahayanian
    1956–
Ritsu: Ritsu 1880–
Shin: Shinshu 1727 + 1896, Shin 1877–
Shingon: S(h)ingon 1727–
Soka Gakkai: Soka Gakkai 1953–

Soto: Soto 1893–
Tendai: Tendai 1727–

R2.3.2.0. Confucianism: Confucianism 1862–
.p char by: Confucian 1837–, Confucianist 1846–
.char by: Confucian 1847–, Confucianist 1884(1)

R2.3.3.0. Hinduism: Hinduism / Hindooism 1829–
.p char by: gentile 1555–1727, gentoo 1638–, Hindu/-doo 1662–
.char by: Hindu/-doo 1698–, Hinduic / Hindooic 1889 + 1893
.section of: *gotra* 1877–

R2.3.3.1. Hindu groups and sects
Brahmin: Brahmism 1813 + 1852, Brahminism/-inanism 1816–
.p char by: Brahmin/-man 1481–, Brahminee *nf* 1794–,
     Brahminist 1816(1)
..condition of: Brahminhood 1840–
.char by: Brahminical 1809–, Brahminic 1862 + 1865,
     Brahministic 1886(1)
Brahmoist: Brahmism 1852(1), Brahmoism 1857–
.p char by: Brahmoist 1870(1), Brahmo 1870 + 1927
.char of: Brahmic 1852–(1869)
Hare Krishnan: Hare Krishna 1968–
XR R2.3.3.1. Vishnuism
Krishnan: Krishna 1875–, Krishnaism 1885–
.p char by: Krishnaist 1889(1), Krishnaite 1889(1)
Lingamistic: *see R2.3.3.1. Sivaist*
Puranistic: Puranism 1882(1)
.p char by: Puranic 1878(1)
Sakti: Saktism 1877–
.p char by: Sakta/Sacta 1877–
Sikhist: Sikhism 1849–
.p char by: Seik 1781–1830, Sikh 1781–
..who is convert from Islam: Mazhabi 1849–
.char by: Sikh 1845–
Sivaist: Lingamism 1843(1), Siva-worship 1876–, Sivaism 1901–,

Shivaism 1931–

XR R4.1.1. Phallicism

.p char by: Saiva 1810–, S(h)aivite 1867–, Sivaite 1880–, Sivite 1882–, Shivaite 1958–

.char by: Saiva 1842–, S(h)aivite 1882–, Sivaist 1937–

Tantric: Tantricism 1959–

.p char by: Tantrist 1891(1), Tantrik 1956(1)

Vedaic: Vedism 1882–, Vedaism 1887(1)

Vishnuic: Vishnuism 1871–

.p char by: Vaishnava 1845– Vishnuite 1871–, Vishnuvite 1883–

.char of: Vaishnava 1876–, Vais(h)navite 1919–

Yogi: Yoga 1820–, Yogecism 1881(1), Yogism 1893(1)

.p char by: Yogi 1619–, Yogist 1881(1)

.Hatha-: Hatha-Yoga 1911–

..p char by: Hatha-Yogi(n) 1937–

.Karma-: Karma-Yoga 1896–

..p char by: Karma-Yogi 1896–

R2.3.3.2. Sanskritization: Sanskritization 1952–
.to undergo: Sanskritize *vi* 1952(1)

R2.3.4.0. Islam: Maumetry c1386–1638 + 1805, Mahometry 1481–1561 + 1804–1890, Turcism 1566–1721, Turkery 1585–1709, Turkism 1595–1660, Mahometism 1597–1793, crescent 16..– *allus.,* infidelity 1603 + 1613, Mahometanism 1612–1840, Mohammedry 1613(1), Mohammedism 1614–1850, *Mussulmanlik* 1625(1), Moorism 1627(1), Saracenism 1659–1907, Mussulmanism 1731–1865, Islamism 1747–, Ismaelism 1750 + 1799, Moslemism 1777–, Mohammedanism 1815–(1860), Islam 1818–

.all: Panislamism 1882(1), Panislam 1883(1)

..char by: Panislamic 1881–

.founder of: Mahound c1290–1849, Mahomet c1380–, Mohammed 1615–

.p char by: *Sarracene*/Saracen OE–, Mahomet 1508–1747, Mahometan 1529–1841, Turk a1548–1737, Mahometist 1553–1654, Mahomite 1559–a1618, Mussulman 1563/83–,

Ismaelite 1571–, Mahometician 1588(1), Moor 1588–1864,
Moslem / Muslim 1615–, Mahometant 1635(1),
Mussulwoman *nf* 1668–1854, Moorman 1698–, Unitarian
1708–, Mohammedan 1777–, Islamite 1821–, Moslemite
a1835(1)

..pl/coll: the faithful 1753–, the mosque 1779–1856
..fanatical: Assassins *npl* 1603–, *ghazi* 1753–, razakar 1948–
..who is convert from Hinduism: Khoja 1882–, She(i)kh /
Shaikh 1883–
..who knows Koran by heart: hafiz 1662 + 1819–
..who adheres to letter of Koran: Alcoranist 1753(1)
..who has made Mecca pilgrimage: Hadji / Hajji 1612–
..black: Black Muslim *no quots.*, Muslim 1961–
..Bulgarian: Pomak 1887–
.char by: circumcis c1250(2), Saracen a1300–(1862), Mahometical
1561–1713, Mahometish 1583(1), Mahometic 1585–1648/99,
turbaned 1591–(1895), Mussulmanlike 1599(1), Mahometan
1600–1850, Ismaelitish 1604(1), circumcized 1604–1802,
Saracenican 1607–1786, Ismaelitical 1613(1), Saracenical
1613–1768, Moorish 1613–, Mahound 1624(*2q1s*),
Mahometanical 1632(1), Mussulmanish 1638(1), Saracenic
1638–(1897), Mohammedan 1681–, Mussulman 1684–,
Sarazantic 1726(1), Moslem / Muslim 1777–, Islamic 1791–,
Islamitic 1791–, Islamitish 1799(1), Mussulmanic 1800–,
Saracenian 1818(1), Islamite 1847 + 1871, Ismaelitic 1884(1),
Islamistic 1893(1), Moslemic 1903(1)

R2.3.4.1. Islamic groups and sects
Black Muslim:
.p char by: Black Muslim 1960–
Drusic: Drusedom 1890(2)
.p char by: Drusian 1601–(1877), Druse 1786–
Hanifist: Hanifism 1877(1)
.p char by: Hanif 1734 + 1883
Kadarite:
.p char by: Kadarite 1727/41 + 1860
Karmathian:

.p char by: Karmathian / Carmathian 1819–
Motazilite:
.p char by: Motazilite 1727/41 + 1734
Muridist: Muridism 1866–
Shiite (unorthodox): Ismaelism 1852–, Shiism 1883–
.p char by: Ismaelite 1613 + 1839, Shiah 1626–, Shiite 1728–,
    Ismaelian / Ismailian 1839–, twelver 1876–
.char by: Ismaelian / Ismailian 1839–, Shiitic 1884(1)
Sufist: Sufiism 1817–, Sufism 1836–
                                      XR R1.8.5. Mysticism
.p char by: Sufian 1585(1), Sufi 1653–, Suffee 1698(1), Murid
    1815–, Sufist 1913(1)
.char by: Sufian 1698(1), Sufistic 1854(1), Sufiistic 1880(1), Sufic
    1884–
Sunni (orthodox): Sunn(i)ism 1892–
.p char by: Islam 1613 + 1814, Sunni 1626–, Sunnite 1718–, Hanif
    1734 + 1883, traditionist 1759–(1864), Islamist 1855 + 1895
..pl/coll: Sunni 1626–
.char by: catholic 1613 + 1625
.Hanafite:
..p char by: Hanafite 1880 + 1887
.Hanbalite:
..p char by: Hanbalite 1886 + 1887
.Shafiite:
..p char by: Shafiite 1838–
.Tau Sug: Tau Sug 1923–
Wahabiist: Wahabi(i)sm / Wahabeeism 1826–
.p char by: Wahabi / Wah(h)abee 1807–, Wahabite 1810–
.char by: Wahabite 1810–

R2.3.4.2. Islamization: Mohammedanizing 1875(1),
    Mohammedization 1906(1)
.to perform: mahometize *vt* 1585(*2q1s*), mahometanize *vt*
    1779(1), mohammedanize *vt* 1828/32 + 1903, moslemize *vt*
    1845–, Islamize *vt* 1846–
.to undergo: mahometize *vi* 1656(1)

R2.3.5.0. Lamaism: Lamaism 1817–, Lamism 1834(1),
    Lamanism 1852–(1867)
.p char by: Lamaite 1814(1), Lamaist 1889–
.char by: Lamaic 1827(1), Lamanical 1867(1), Lamaistic 1883(1)

R2.3.6.0. Mithraism: Mithraism 1822–, Mithraicism 1864–
.p char by: Mithraicist 1864–, Mithraist 1888–

R2.3.6.1. Mithraicization:
.char by: mithraicizing 1864(1), mithracizing 1876(1)
.to undergo: mithraize *vi* 1890–

R2.3.7.0. Odinism: Odinism 1848–, Wodenism 1891(1)
.p char by: Odinist *no quots.*
.char by: Odinist 1864(1), Odinic 1864–, Odinian 1869(1),
    Odinitic 1883(1)

R2.3.8.0. Shinto: Shinto 1727–, Xinto 1776(1), Shintoism 1857–
.p char by: Shintoist 1727–, Shinto 1829–
.char by: Shintoistic 1893(1), Shinto 1904(1)

R2.3.8.1. Shintoization:
.to perform: Shintoize *vt* 1895(1)

R2.3.9.0. Taoism: Tao 1745– Taoism / Daoism 1838–
.p char by: Taoist / Daoist 1838–
.char by: Tao 1831(1) Taoist / Daoist 1839–, Taoistic 1856–

R2.3.10.0. Zoroastrianism: Parseeism 1843–, Parsism 1849–,
    Zoroastrianism 1854–, Zoroast(e)rism 1862–, Zarathustrism
    1871(1), Mazdaism 1871–, Zarathustrianism 1886(1)
                                    XR R4.1.1. Pyrolatry
.p char by: Guebre 1687–, Mazdean 18..(1), fire-worshipper
    1806–, Zoroastrian 1811–, Zarathustrian 1871(1), Mazdaist
    1920–

216THE ENGLISH RELIGIOUS LEXIS

.char by: Guebrish 1687(1), Zoroastrian 1743–, Zoroastric
1854(1), Mazdean 1880(1), Zarathustric 1886(1),
Zarathustrian 1891(1)

R2.3.10.1. Zoroastrian groups and sects
Zendicist: Zendicism 1697–
.p char by: Zendik 1842(1), Zendician 1845(1), Zendikite 1877(1)

R2.3.10.2. Zoroastrianization:
.to perform / undergo: Zoroastrianize *vt/i* 1891(2)

R2.3.11. Miscellaneous non-Christian groups
Atenism: Atenism 1925–
Bahaism: Babism 1850–, Bahaism 1903–
.p char by: Babi/-bee 1850–(1896), Babist 1866–, Baha(')i 1889–,
Babite 1911(1), Bahaite 1914(1), Bahaist 1924(1)
Caodaism: Caodaism 1937–
.p char by: Caodaist 1953–
Cargo-cult: Cargo-cult 1949–
Coelicolism:
.p char by: Coelicolist 1856(1-*Newman*)
Druidism: Druidism 1715–(1879), Druidry 1868(1)
.p char by: Druidan 1509(1), Druid 1563–, Druidess *nf*
1755–(1827)
.char by: Druidish 1577 + 1723, Druid 1670–, Druidean 1678(1),
Druidical 1755–, Druidic 1773–
Fox-worship: fox-worship 1880(1)
Jahvism: Jahvism 1867–
.char by: Jahvistic 1874 + 1899
Kizilbash: Kizilbash 1960(1)
Macumba: Macumba 1939–
Metawileh: Metawileh 1799–
Mystery-religion: mystery-religion 1913–
Nat-worship: Nat-worship 1833–
.p char by: Nat-worshipper 1906 + 1923
Nature-religion: religion of nature 1902–

Osirism: Osirism 1906(1)
Peyotism: Peyotism 1934–, Peyote Cult 1920–
.p char by: Peyotist 1934–
Poro: *Poro* 1788–
Quetzalcoatlism: Quetzalcoatism 1934(1)
Rastafarianism: Rastafari / Ras Tafari 1955–, Rastafar(in)ism
    1955–, Rastafarianism 1968–
.p char by: Rastafarite 1953(1), Rasta 1955–, Rastafarian 1955–,
    locksman 1960 + 1966, Rastaman 1960–
..pl/coll: Rastafari(s) *npl* 1955–
.char by: Rastafarian 1963–
Rosicrucianism: Rosicrucianism c1740–, Rosicrucianity 1838(1)
.p char by: Rosicrucian 1624–, ?rose-knight 1838(1)
.char by: rhodostaurotic 1626(1-*Jonson*), rose-cross 1627(1),
    Rosicrucian 1662–
Samaritanism: Samaritanism a1641–
.p char by: *Samaritan*/Samaritan OE–
Sandee: Sande(e) 1803–
Santeria: *Santeria* 1950–
Scientology: scientology 1951–
.p char by: scientologist 1952–
Scythism: Scythism 1609–(1816)
Shamanism: shamanism 1780–
.p char by: shaman 1780–, shamanian 1802(1), shamanist 1842–,
    shamanite 1871(1)
.char of: shaman 1780–, shamanistic 1854–, shamanic 1899–
.to imbue (x) with: shamanize *vt* 1901(1)
Shango: *Shango* 1953–
Subud: Subud 1958–
Unification Church: Unification Church 1973–
Vegetarian: Vegetarian 1895–
Yezidi: Yezidi / Yezidee 1818–

R3.1. Church government

R3.1.0. Church government: church government 1594–
.particular form of: state (of things) 1387(2), platform

1573–(1882), way a1647–1750
.**science of:** ecclesiastics 1672(1)

R.3.1.1. Kinds of church government
Collegiality: collegiality 1965–
XR R3.2.1.1.0. Papacy

Conciliarism: conciliarism 1945–
XR R3.2.1.1.0. Papacy

.**p supporting:** conciliarist 1932–
.**before:** pre-conciliar 1967–
Congregationalism: congregationalism 1716–
XR R2.2.4.12.1. Congregationalism

Consociation: consociation 1641–1797, consociationism 1884(1)
XR R2.2.4.12.0. Presbyterianism

.**char by:** consociated 1669(1)
.**to employ:** consociate *vt* 1796(1)

Episcopacy: prelacy c1380–1850, prelatism 1611–1641,
  episcopality c1618(1), prelatry 1641(1-*Milton*), prelaty
  1641–1644 (3-*Milton*), episcopacy 1647–, episcopy 1660(1),
  bishopry 1665(1), Cathedral 1679(1), episcopalianism 1846–
XR R2.2.4.1.0. Anglicanism

.**p supporting:** bishopist 1590(1), cathedralist 1644–1661,
  episcoparian 1649–1691, prelatist 1659–(1827), episcopal
  1708–1823, episcopalian 1738–
..**not:** antipræsulist 1640(1)
.**char of:** episcopal 1651–, episcoparian 1691(1)
.**char by:** prelatical 1641–(1849), prelatish 1642(1), prelatic 1642–,
  episcopal 1752–, episcopalian 1768–
..**not:** unepiscopal 1659 + 1863, unprelatic 1858(1)

.**led by archbishops:** archiepiscopy 1642(1), archiepiscopacy 1642
  + 1678
.**in which bishops have monarchical authority:**
  monepiscopacy 1889–
..**char of:** monepiscopal 1891(1)
.**the bringing under authority of:** episcopizing 1768–(1881)
..**to perform:** episcopize *vt* 1767–(1868)

Erastianism: Erastianism 1681–, regalism 1869–, cæsarism
1876(1), territorialism 1882/3–(1888), cæsaro-papism 1890–
XR R3.1.1. Josephism
.p supporting: Erastian 1651–(1876), regalist 1894(1)

Establishmentarianism: statism 1609–c1660, establishmentism
1851(1), state-churchism 1862(1), establishmentarianism 1873
+ 1876
.instance of: parliament faith 1565(1), parliament religion
1565–1726, established church 1660–, parliament church
1711–1726, state-church 1726–, establishment 1731–,
law-church 1826–(1845), standing order 1861 + 1911 *U.S.*
.p supporting: parliamentarian 1613(1), malignant 1642 – *hostile*,
state-churchman 1845(1), establishmentarian 1846–
..pl/coll: statute congregation 1594(1), church-folk 1871(1)
.char by: establishmentarian 1847–
..not: unestablished 1885 + 1887
.opposed to: antimagistratical 1645–1669, antimagistrical 1692(1)
.the conferring of E on a church: establishment 1662/3–
.the removal of E from a church: disestablishment 1860–,
disestablishing 1869(1)
..p supporting: disestablisher 1869–(1885), disestablishmentarian
1885–
..to perform: disestablish *vt* 1838–
.the inclusion of non-conformists within: comprehension
1667/8–1855
XR R1.1.13.1. Non-conformity
R1.1.16. Catholicity
..1673 Act testing worthiness for: Test Act 1708–
...p supporting: test-monger 1687(1), test-man 1693(1), tester
1697(1)
.supporting: comprehensional 1687(1)

Febronianism: Febronianism 1856–
XR R3.1.1. Phyletism
.p supporting: Febronian 1884–
.char of: Febronian 1882–

Free-churchism: free-churchism 1884(1)

.**instance of:** free church 1869–
.**p supporting:** free-churchman 1847–

Hierocracy: hierarchy 1563/87–, hierocracy 1794–, theocracy
1825(1), hierarchism 1846–, priestdom 1871–
XR R3.1.1. Patriarchism
R3.2.2.0. Priestcraft
.**clergy involved in:** hierarchy 1619–, hierocracy 1828(1)
.**p supporting:** theocrat 1843–(1897)
XR R3.2.1.0. Clerical superior
.**char by:** hierarchical 1561–, hierarchal 1641–(1824), priest-ridden
1653–(1864), priest-rid 1664–1860, hierarchic 1681–,
hierocratical 1799(1), hierocratic 1851–
..**condition of being:** priest-riddenness 1653(1)
.**in manner of:** hierarchically 1624(1)

Josephism: Josephism 1880(1), Josephinism 1882/3 + 1891
XR R3.1.1. Erastianism
R3.3.3.10. Russian Josephite
.**char of:** Josephine 1882/3 + 1886

Morellianism: Morellianism 1676(1)
.**char of:** Morellian 1644(1)

Patriarchism: patriarchy 1641(1), patriarchism a1666–
XR R3.1.1. Episcopacy, Hierocracy
Phyletism: Phyletism 1900–
XR R3.1.1. Febronianism
Presbyterianism: *see R2.2.4.12. Presbyterianism*

Territorialism: territorialism 1873 + 1904 *Sc.*
.**instance of:** territorial church 1863(1-*Sc.*)
.**char of:** territorial 1822 + 1873 *Sc.*

Theocracy: theocracy 1622–, thearchy 1643 + 1863
.**instance of:** church-state 1676(1)
.**ruler of:** theocrat 1827–(1874)
.**char of:** theocratical 1690–(1863), theocratic 1741–(1865),
thearchic 1855–
.**in manner of:** theocratically 1827(1)

R3.1.2. Ecclesiastical authority: *lareowdom, onweald,* prelacy
a1340–1577, episcopy 1641(1-*Milton*), episcopacy 1659(1),
episcopé 1957 + 1963

XR R1.4.0. Law
.of the church in medieval Europe: *sacerdotium* 1955–
.p supporting: spiritualist 1651(1)
.char of: cathedral 1638–
.in position of: *in cathedrâ advphr* 1635–(1674)

R3.1.3.0. Ecclesiastical discipline: discipline 1549–
.char of: disciplinary 1593–(1719)
.to subject to: disciplinize *vt* 1659(1), discipline *vt* 1828 + 18..
Canonical obedience: canonical obedience 1621–(1869)

R3.1.3.1. Ecclesiastical court: chapter a1300–c1386 + 1726,
spiritual court 1498/9–, bum-court 1544–1583, Court
Christian 1628–(1863), ecclesiastical court 1681–, Court of
Christianity 1695–(1835), church-court 1839–

.of pope (Curia): Court of Rome c1290–1613, Pontifical 1628(1),
Curia 1840–, Vatican 1909–

XR R3.2.1.1.0. Pope
..member of: courtesan/-zan 1426–1563/87, chaplain of the Pope
1638(1), curialist 1847–
..char of: curial 1864–, curialistic 1870–, Vaticanic 1898(1),
Vaticanal 1899(1), Vaticanical 1908(1)
..under authority of: Vaticanized 1890(1)
..system of: curialism 1870–
..influence of: *Romanita* 1963(1)
..the bringing under authority of: Vaticanization 1873(1)
...to perform: petrinize *vt* 1883(1), Vaticanize *vt* 1896(1)
..study of: Vaticanology 1976 + 1982
...p perf: Vaticanologist 1975–

.of pope (Inquisition): Inquisition 1502–, faith-press 1624(1),
Holy Office 1727/41–

XR R1.1.10. Relaxation
..officer of: inquisitor 1545–, familiar 1560–

...**chief:** inquisitor-general 1659–, grand inquisitor 1852 + 1862
...**office of:** inquisitorship 1669 + 1840
.**of pope (Rota):** Rote 1528–1787, Rota 1679–
..**char of:** Rotal 1907(1)

.**of archbishop:** prerogative 1603(1), prerogative court
    1603–(1857), prerogative office 1716(1), court of audience
    1726–(1809), officiality 1742–

                        XR R3.2.1.6. Archbishop
..**of Canterbury:** (Court of) Arches 1297–(1863)
..**official of:** auditor 1640–(1726)
...**presiding:** official a1327–, official principal 1899–

.**of bishop:** consistory a1307–
..**place of:** consistory 1577–1645
..**official of:** apparitor 1528–, paritor 1530–, copist 1581–1587,
    tawny-coat 1591–1634
...**presiding:** chancellor c1400–
....**office of:** chancellorship 1726(1)
..**char of:** consistorial c1450*Sc.* + 1691–, consistorical 1611–1762,
    consistorian 1655(1)
..**in manner of:** consistorially 1752(1)

.**Presbyterian:** church-court 1839–
..**general assembly:** general assembly a1572–, comitial
    1593–1754, kirk-assembly 1752(1)
..**synod:** synod 1593–
...**char of:** synodal 1600–1640, synodalian 1702(1)
..**presbytery:** eldership 1557–(1885), seniory 1572–1589,
    presbytery 1578–, consistory a1593–, *classis* 1593–1796,
    colloquy a1672–, reformed presbytery 1744–1860, class
    1785(1), *colloque* 1846–, elderhood 1860(1)
...**district of:** presbytery 1581– *mainly Sc., classis* 1653–1761/2
...**char of:** consistorial 1561–, classical 1586–1848, presbyterial
    1592–, consistorian 1593–1660, presbyterian 1641–, classic
    c1645–1648, presbyteral 1651–

                    XR R2.2.4.12.0. Presbyterianism
...**in manner of:** classically 1680(1), presbyterially 1904(1)
..**kirk-session:** consistory a1593–, kirk-session 1717–

...**member of:** elder 1526–, ruling elder 1593–, lay-elder
1594–1827, elderling 1606(1-*contempt.*), presbyter 1615–1858,
eldress *nf* 1640–(1880)

....**fellow-:** compresbyter a1600–1637/50, sympresbyter
1671–a1677, copresbyter 1693–c1828

....**pl/coll:** eldership 1557–(1885), presbytery 1611–1853,
presbyterate 1641–, elderhood 1860(1), *presbyterion* a1886(1),
presbyterium 1896–

....**office of:** eldership 1577–(1655), presbytership 1597–,
presbytery 1604–1704, presbyterate 1642–

....**char of:** presbyteral 1611–, compresbyterial 1641(1)

....**(of x:)constituted of:** presbyteral 1611–, presbyterate 1853(1)

R3.1.4.0. Council: *gemot, sinoð*/synod OE(L) + 1387–, council
1125–, sene 1380–1609, synody a1548(1)

.**meeting-place of:** *sinoðstow*

.**decision/decree of:** synodal 1485–1765

XR R5.16.5. Synod book

.**char of:** *sinoðlic,* synodal c1450–, synodical 1561–, conciliary
1616–1702, synodic 1640–, synodatic 1661(1), conciliar
a1677–, synodial 1727(1)

.**in manner of:** synodically a1604–, conciliarly 1656–(1846),
synodally 1668(1)

R3.1.4.1. Kinds of council

American episcopal: convention 1785–

Church of England: church congress 1861–, church assembly
1919–

.**decennial:** Lambeth Conference 1867–

.**provincial:** convocation a1400–, provincial 1637/50–1654

..**ordinance of:** provincial a1529–1659

..**char of:** convocational 1641–

..**in manner of:** convocationally 1701(1)

Bishops': *bisceopseonoð*

.**letter from:** tractatorian letter 1672/5(*2q1s*), tractory

1709–1725, tractatory letter 1725(*2q1s*)
Cardinals': conclave 1625–

XR R3.2.1.3. Conclave
.char of: conclavical 1660(1), conclave 1681–1686
.(of p:)taking part in: in conclave 1524–
.with pope: consistory 1393–
..char of: consistorical 1611–1632, consistorial 1707–
..in manner of: consistorially 1624(1)
Congregational: consociation 1818–(1857)
Ecumenical:
.theology/doctrine of: œcumenicalism 1888

XR R1.1.16. Catholicity
Acting in name of entire church: virtual church 1646–1654
Jewish: council 1382–1638, Sanhedrim 1588–(1877)
.member of: Sanhedrist 1593 + 1879, Sanhedrinist 1880(1)
..chief: patriarch 1795–
.body of trustees in Sephardic: *mahamad* 1831–
Illegally assembled: conciliable 1521–1642, conciliabule 1817–
Irish episcopal:
.member of: synodsman 1870–
Legatine: legatine synod 1647(1)
Lutheran: consistory 1698–, *ministerium* 1881–
Mormon: (first) presidency a1853–1858
Parishioners': vestry 1589–, revestry 1631–
.char of: vestrical 1881(1), vestral 1884(2)
Presbyterian: *see R3.1.3.1. General assembly*
Self-elected: junto 1641–1716
Wesleyan: conference 1744–

R3.1.4.2. Historical councils
Chalcedon (AD 451): Chalcedonian *a* 1788–
.p supporting: Chalcedonian 1758(1), synodist
        1846(1-*disparaging*), synodite 1846(1-*disparaging*)
Ephesus (AD449): robber council / synod 1862 + 1865
Nicæa (AD 325 and AD 787): Council of Nicene 1387–1563,
        Nicene Council 1432/50–

XR R4.1.5.2.1. Quartodeciman

.char of: Nicene 1597–
Tridentine (AD 1542): Tridentine *a* 1561–, Trentish *a*
    1601–1675, Trentine *a* 1826–1851
.p supporting: Trentist 1601(1), Tridentine a1836–a1882
.in manner of: Tridentally 1842(1)
.to conform to: Tridentize *vi* 1826(1)
First Vatican (AD 1869/71): Vatican Council 1878–
Second Vatican (AD 1959/65): Second Vatican Council 1961–
                            XR R2.2.3.1. Ultramontanism

R3.1.4.3.0. Chapter: *capitol/-ul(a)*/c(h)apitle OE–1456,
    choir/quire c1300–1556, chapter c1305–, close a1587(1),
    cabildo 1924–
.church possessing: colleged kirk c1425(1-*Sc.*), college-church
    1513–1540, collegiate church 1514–a1674, collegial church
    1530–1670
..to form into: collegiate *vt* 1538–1848
.char of: canonic 1483(1), canonical 1579–, capitular 1611–(1861),
    capitulary 1774–(1861)
.in manner of: capitularly 1702–1761

R3.1.4.3.1. Member of chapter: *capitelari*/capitulary OE(L) +
    1694, *canonic*/canonic OE(L)–a1853, canon c1205–, canoness
    nf 1682–, chapterist 1716(1), capitular 1726–1761
                            XR R1.4.1. Canon law
                            R1.5.0. Canon theologian
.pl/coll: dignity 1486(1)
                            XR R3.1.4.3.0. Chapter
.assistant to: vicar 1387–, vicary 1432/50–1505, vicar choral
    1530/1–, lay vicar 1837–
.head: dean c1330–, warden 1429–1538, decan 1432/50–1538,
    provost 1560–1845, deaness *nf* 1759–(1878)
                            XR R3.2.1.11. Dean
..office of: deny 1340(1), deanery c1440–(1848), deanship
    1611–(1881),
..wife of: deaness 1848–(1884)
..assistant to: sudene 1362–a1529, southdean 1393(1), subdean

14..–
...**office of:** subdeanery 1579–
...**char of:** subdecanal 1846(1)
.**minor:** petty canon 1530–1769, domicellary canon 1727/51(1),
domiciliar 1761(1), minor canon 1862–
..**of St Paul's, London:** cardinal 1748–(1877)
.**numerary:** numerary canon 1726(1)
.**regular:** regular canon 1387–(1844), canon of the Order of St
Augustine c1400(1), black canon a1672 + 1722, regular
canoness *nf* 1682(1), canoness of St Augustine *nf* 1772(1)
.**residentiary:** residenter 1455 + 1719, residencer 1522 + 1628,
residentiary c1525–, canon residentiary 1632–, resident 1812
+ 1873, stagiary 1868–
..**non-:** non-residentiary c1630(1)
                                              XR R4.16.0. Non-resident
..**office of:** residentiaryship 1624–(1831)
.**secular:** secular canon 1297–(1868), secular canoness *nf* 1726(1)
.**supernumerary:** supernumerary canon 1726(1)
.**office of:** canonry 1482–, canonship 1534–1762, chanonie / canony
1641(1), canonicate 1652–1865
.**wife of:** canoness 1873(1)

R3.1.4.3.2. Cathedral cleric general: cathedralist 1644–1661
Chancellor: chancellor 1578 + 1884

Proctor: proctor 1586–
Scholaster: scholaster 1732 + 1793, scholastic 1844(1), scoloc
1852– *hist.*
                                              XR R4.16.1. Prebendary
Secondary: secondary 1436–, seconder 1898(1)
Seneschal: seneschal 1882(1)
Stallary: *see R3.2.6. Stallary*
Vicar Choral: *see R3.2.13. Vicar choral*

R3.2. Clergyman

R3.2.0. Clergyman general: *ciricend, ciricđen, clericmann,*

gefera, godes đeow, đegn, godes man/God's man OE–c1450,
cleric/clerk OE(L)–(1858), *preost*/priest OE–, secular
a1290–, minister c1315–, kirkman c1340–(1853) *Sc. and N.*,
churchman c1340–, divine c1380–, man of God 1382–(1814),
spiritual c1450–1682, reverend 1484–, ministrator 1523(1),
man of the church 1523–1530, *abbe* 1530–, tippet man
1550(1), clergyman 1577–, padre 1584–, your reverendship
1609–1739, cock 1614 + 1871*hist.*, cleric 1621–, cassock
1628–(1859), levite 1640–a1704 *contempt.*, gownsman
1641–(1855), teaching elder 1642 + 1735, ecclesiastic 1651–,
religionist 1653– his fathership 1670–, crape-gown-man
1682(1), man in black 1692(1), revd. *abbrev.* 1693–, crape
1699–1754, soul-driver 1699–(1846) *slang*, rookship
1710(1-*mock*), secularist 1716(1-*nonce*), rev. *abbrev.* 1721–,
autem jet 1737(1-*slang*), liturge 1737(1), his reverence 1762–,
snub-devil 1785(1-*slang*), soul-doctor 1785(1-*slang*),
crape-man 1826(1), officiator 1830–, clerical 1837–,
venerability 1842(1), officiant 1844–, liturgist 1848 + 1890,
rook 1859(1-*slang*), shovel hat 1859(1), ecclesiast
1866(1-*Newman*), clergywoman *nf* 1871–, ecclesiastical
1882/3(1), sky-pilot 1883–, joss-pidgin-man 1886–, josser
1887– *Austral. slang*, white-choker 1903– *slang*, sin-shifter
a1912– *slang*, sin-buster 1931(1-*U.S. slang*), *parch* 1944 +
1953 *Welsh*

.**office of:** *clerichad*/clerkhood OE + c1400–c1449 + 1849 *arch.*,
ministry 1382–, clergy c1400–1561, clerkship ?1488–1720,
ministration 1550(1), clergyship 1616(1), clericality 1660(1),
churchmanship c1680–, cassock 1687–1848, cloth 1701–1866,
clericature 1725–1867, clericate 1868(1)
.**rule of:** clericalism 1864–, clerisy 1870(1), clericism 1878(1)
XR R3.1.1. Hierocracy
..**p supporting:** clericalist 1881–
...**not:** anticlerical 1881–
....**char of:** anticlerical 1845–
..**the placing of x under:** clericalization 1907–
...**to perform:** clericalize *vt* 1886(1)

.**the service of:** church-service c1340(1), ministration(s) 1535–,

ministering 1566–, ministry 1623 + 1879, ministerialism
1884(1)
..char of: ministering 1654(1)
..to carry out: minister *vi* c1330–(1855)

.wife of: clergy-feme 1589(1), clergywoman 1820–1867 *hum.*
.child of: daughter / bairn / son / child of the manse 1855– *Sc.*

.char of: *folcisc, god,* secular c1290–, ruler a1380 + 1399, reverent
c1380–c1447, ruly c1450(1), ecclesiastical 1538–(1845),
ministerial 1561–, clerkly 1565–1861, clerical 1592–,
ecclesiastic 1603–(1820), cleric 1621–, clergical 1632–1641,
clergy a1635–1670, reverend 1645–, hieratical 1656–,
shovel-hatted 1832–, churchmanly 1841–1855, churchmanlike
1852–, hieratic 1866–
..condition of being: spiritualship 1670–1680, clerisy 1858(1),
clericity 1866(1), reverendship 1870(1), clericality 1877–
..not: unclerklike 1647(1), uncanonical 1747–(1867), unclerical
1870(1), unecclesiastical 1834 + 1870, unclerkly 1875 + 1895
.(of x:)provided with: clergy'd 1696(1)
..not: clerkless 1478/80(1), unministered 1657(1)
.(of x:)composed of C and laity: clerolaical 1599–1606
.in manner of: ministerially 1848(1), clerically 1876(1)
..not: unclerkly 1531(1), undivinely 1618 + 1657, undivinelike
1649(1), unecclesiastically 1766(1), unclerically 1883(1)

R3.2.1.0. Clerical superior general: *biscopealdor, ealdorsacerd,*
forebiscop, heafodbiscop, heahfæder, heahsacerd, hlaford,
heahbiscop/high-bishop OE–1551, *biscop*/bishop OE–1647,
prelate c1205–, prince of priests a1300–1388, emperor-clerk
138.(2-*Wyclif-contempt.*), pontifical ?a1400(1), dignity
c1450–(1865), patriarch 1477–1733, ?gentleman untrial
1486–1600, hierarch 1574–, presul 1577(1), church-governor
a1600–, archbishop 1600(1), *monseigneur* 1600–1660, aaron
1607(1), pontiff 1610–, sheikh 1613–, protomist 1635–1638,
monsignor(e) 1641–, prelatess *nf* 1642–, high-priestess *nf*
1645–, pontifex 1655(1), protarch 1656(1), dignitary 1672/3–,
hierophant 1677–, high(-)priest 1767–, ecclesiarch

1781–(1878), arch-pontiff 1790(1)
>   XR R3.1.1. Episcopacy, hierocracy
>   R3.2.1.8.0. Bishop
>   R3.2.1.12. Protopope

.pl/coll: prelacy 13..–1827, ?lords spiritual 1451–(1765), pontifical c1470(1), pontificality 1486(1), prelatry 1653 + 1879, prelature 1845 + 1855

.p adhering to: pontifical 1590(1), pontifician 1614–1691, pontificial 1631 + 1838

.p subject to: subject a1380–1552

.office of: *heahsacerdhad*, prelacy c1325–(1827), pontificals *npl* 1432/50–1621, officialship ?1461–1762, bishopric 1480(1), high-priesthood 1535–, pontifical 1567(1), prelateship 1570–1832, pontificality 1593–1651, prelature 1607–, prelaty 1641 + 1642, officiality a1662–, pontificacy 1665(1), prelation 1695(1), pontificate 1727/41–, officialty 1726(1), presulate 1853(1)

.char of: spiritual 1399–, pontifical c1440–(1775), prelately 1550(1), aaronical 1628(1), prelatical 1634–, prelatic 1649–, high-priestly 1849–, monsignorial 1876(1), prelatial 1886(1)

.char of CS acting like pope: papa-prelatical 1692(1)

..p adhering to p char by: papa-prelatist 1816(1)

..not: unprelatical 1647–(1857), unprelatic 1880(1)

.in manner of: prelatically 1641–a1659, pontifically a1711(1)

.to bring under authority of: prelatize *vt* 1641–

.to act as: prelate *vi* 1548/9–1656

R3.2.1.1.0. Pope: *domne (L), papa*/pape OE–1627, pope c1200–, apostoile 1205–c1440, vicar 1340–, antichrist c1370– *hostile*, universal bishop c1380–1728, servant of the servants of God c1386(1), vicar general 1390–1651, Holy Father c1400–(a1562), His Holy Fatherhood c1400–(1641), (His / Your) Holiness 1450–, vicegerent 1547/64–, papa 1559–, man of Rome 1581(1), bullman 1588(1), apostolicship c1593(1), bridge-maker 1611 + 1877, infallibleship 1613(1-*mock*),

popeship 1640– *hum.*, pontifex 1651 + 1851, decretaliarch
1656–1708, pontiff a1677–, infallibilityship 1679–1709 *mock*,
holyship c1680(1), his infallibility 1834 + 1886 *mock*
.**female:** popess 1529–, papess 1620–1866
.**petty:** popet 1550 + 1641 *contempt.*, popeling 1588– *contempt.*
.**as sovereign:** pope-king 1882(1)

.**office of:** *papseld/-setl, se micla had, papanhad*/popehood OE–,
  papdom/popedom OE–, *cægan*/keys OE–, the see
  c1330–(1840), apostaile c1380–c1400, poperiche 1387(2),
  popehead 1387–1556, papate 1390–1456, papacy 1390–,
  popeship c1440–, papality 1456–1661 + 1826, pontification
  1521(1), pontificacy 1529–1793, Apostolic See 1529–, See of
  Rome 1559–1616, power of the keys 1560(1), Catholic Seat
  1563(1), papalty 1577–1859, popedomship 1588(1),
  œcumenacy 1646(1), economacy 1651(1), chairship 1660(1),
  pontificate 1685–, Holy See 1765–, Roman See 1769(1), Papal
  See 1788(1)
..**tenure of:** popedom 1568–1741, pontificate 1685–
..**char of:** apostolical 1546 + 1864

.**government of:** papacy 1550–, papism 1550–, popedom 1641–,
  paparchy 1839/40–, papalism 1870–
                    XR R2.2.3.0. Roman Catholicism
                       R3.1.1. Collegiality, conciliarism
                       R3.1.4. Curia, inquisition, Rota
..**ecclesiastical polity resembling:** popedom 1545–
..**char of:** paparchical 1895(1)

.**claims of:** Petrine claims *npl* 1930(*2q1s*)
.**infallibility of:** infallibility 1624–
.**assumption of authority like that of:** popedom 1588–, popery
  1721–1735
..**p char by:** pope 1589–
.**worship of:** papolatry 1894(1)
..**p char by:** papolater 1913(1)
..**char by:** papolatrous 1894(1)
.**method of electing:** scrutiny c1450–, adoration 1599 + 1860,
  compromise 1726–

.**prelate regarded as possible:** *papabile* 1958–
..**char of:** papable 1592–1670 + 1900, *papabile* 1934–
.**to elect as:** impapase *vt* 1563/87(1)
..**again:** repope *vt* 1869(1)
.**x char of:** popeness a1684(1)

.**char of:** papal 1390–, pontifical 1447–, apostolic 1477 + 1844,
      antichristian a1532(1-*hostile*), popish a1540–1567, popelike
      1553–, papane 1581(1), popely a1600 + 1826, popizing
      1611(1), pontificious 1624–1638, popal 1651(1), papizing
      1692(1), pontific 1716–a1797, papist 1819(1), popan 1839(1)
.**in manner of:** popelike 1574(1), papally 1627–

.**to act as:** pope *vi* 1537–1646, papize *vi* 1629(1)

R3.2.1.1.1. Antipope: antipope 1579–
.**office of:** antipapacy 1670(1)

R3.2.1.1.2. Individual popes
Hildebrand (Gregory VII):
.**policy of:** Hildebrandism 1855–
                              XR R2.2.3.1. Ultramontanism
..**p supporting:** Hildebrandist 1680(1)
..**char of:** Hildebrandine 1659 + 1855, Hildebrandic 1837(1)
Liberius:
.**calendar attributed to:** Liberian calendar a1773–
.**catalogue of Ps up to and including:** Liberian catalogue
      1840–
Pius:
.**char of:** Pian 1916–
Sixtus V:
.**char of:** Sixtine 1843–
                              XR R1.2.1.1.4. Sixtine (Vulgate)
Urban VI:
.**p supporting:** Urbanist 1523 + 1855

R3.2.1.1.3. Papal offices, officials

Datary: Datary c1645–

XR R3.2.1.1.3. Prodatary, under-datary

Papal dioceses: suburbicaries *npl* 1665(1)

.char of: suburbicarian 1654–, suburbicary 1654–, suburbican
  1659–, urbic 1664(1), urbicary 1683–1728, suburbicarial
  1688(1), suburb 1813(1), suburban 1858(1)

Papal states: patrimony of St Peter 1601–1756/7

.ruler of: legate 1653–1756/7

.to return (x) to: reincamerate *vi* 1672(1)

Vatican (Curia): *see R3.1.3.1. Church court*

Abbreviator: *see Vice-chancellor*

Bullist: bullist 1587 + 1653

XR R3.2.1.1.3. Summist

R3.2.1.1.4. Bull

Chamberlain: camerlingo 1753(1)

Datary: datary 1527–(1825)

Legate: legate 1154–, ablegate 1890–

Nuncio: apocrisiary 1432/50–(1744), nuncio 1528–

.office of: nunciature 1652–, nunciate 1882/3(1)

..duration of: nunciature 1662–

Penitentiary: great / high / chief / grand penitentiary 1670–

.office of: penitentiaryship 1570–1716, penitentiary 1658–

Plumbator: plumbator 1677(1)

Prime Minister: padrone 1670(2)

.office of: padronacy 1670(1), padronage 1670(1), padronship
  1670(1)

Prodatary: prodatary 1880(1)

.assistant to: under-datary 1670(1)

XR R3.2.1.1.3. Datary

Protonotary: prot(h)onotary 1758–1845

.apostolical: prot(h)onotary (apostolic(al)) 1494–

Qualificator: qualificator 1688–1826, qualifier a1843–

XR R1.5.0. Theologian

Sacristan: sexton 1667–1728

Summist: bull-driver 1649(1), summist 1686–1694

XR R3.2.1.1.3. Bullist

R3.2.1.1.4. Bull

Vicar: Pope's vicar 1696–, papal vicar 1844–
.apostolic: *see R3.2.1.8.1. Vicar apostolic*
Vice-chancellor: vice-chancellor 1432/50–
.assistant to: abbreviator 1532–(1751), breviator 1546–(1751)

R3.2.1.1.4. Papal documents
Bull: bull 1297–, brevet 1362–
> XR R3.2.1.1.3. Bullist, plumbator, summist
> R4.2.2.3.1. Sabbatine bull
.pl/coll: bullary a1674–
.char of: bulled 1330 + 1610, bullish 1546(1)
.issuing: bulling 1624(1)
.leaden seal of: bull 1340–
.to issue: bull *vt* 1563/87 + a1670
..against (xp): embull *vt* 1589(1)
Encyclical: (papal) brief c1460–, breve 1536–, encyclical letter 1647–, encyclic letter 1824(1), encyclical 1837–, encyclic 1851–1864, *encyclica* 1888(1)
Motu Proprio: *motu proprio* 1848–
Provincial: provincial 1605(1)
Rescript: rescript 1528–
> XR R1.4.1. Decretals

R3.2.1.2. Patriarch: primate c1205–, patriarch c1300–, beatitude 1658–
> XR R3.2.1.4. Primate
> R3.2.1.6. Archbishop
.Abyssinian: *Abuna* 1635 + c1870, *Metran* 1850(1)
..office of: Metranate 1850(1)
.of Alexandria: pope 1636 + 1850
.arch-: arch-patriarch 1579(1)
.Armenian: Catholic 1612–1735, *Catholicos* 1625–
..office of: Catholicate 1878(1)
.of Constantinople:
..seat of: *Phanar* 1897–
..official attached to: referendary 1716(1), prothonotary 1835(1), chartophylax 1879–

.**office of:** patriarchy 1561–1657, patriarchship 1566–(1726),
   patriarchdom 1572–1641, patriarchate 1617–, patriarchacy
   1681(1)

.**char of:** patriarchal 1570–, patriarchical 1606–1670
.**(of x:)having:** patriarched 1632(1)

R3.2.1.3. Cardinal: cardinal 1125–, carnal a1528–1598 *derog.*,
   red(-)cap 1539 + 1609, red-hat 1598 + 1884*hist.*,
   purple-father 1615(1), eminence 1653–, eminency 1655–1670,
   prince of the (Holy Roman) Church 1901–
.**who has responsibility for particular area:**
   cardinal-protector 1670(1)
.**who acts as king:** king-cardinal 1613(1-*Shakespeare*)
.**pl/coll:** college c1425(1), College of Cardinals 1593–, conclave
   1613–1839, Sacred College *(no quots.)*
                                        XR R3.1.5.1. Conclave, consistory
..**met for papal election:** conclave 1625–
...**member of:** conclavist 1616 + 1656
....**p attending on:** conclavist 1656–
...**interest group within:** squadron 1670 + 1906
....**member of:** squadronist 1670(2)
...**char of:** conclavical 1660(1), conclave 1681–1686
...**(of p:)taking part in:** in conclave 1524–
..**having charge of church affairs:** congregation 1670–
...**char of:** congregational 1662(1)
...**with regard to foreign missions:** (Congregation of the)
      Propaganda 1718–
....**missionary attached to:** propagandist 1833(1)
                                        XR R4.5.3.1. Missionary

.**office of:** cardinality 1525–1616, cardinalship 1537–, (red) hat
   1597/8–, cardinalate 1645–(1839), the purple 1685–,
   cardinalric 1688(1)
.**system of:** cardinalism 1670–1849

.**char of:** cardinalish 1624(1), cardinalical 1650(1), cardinalitial
   1670–1849, cardinalitian 1716–1866, cardinalic 1886(1)
   cardinalatial 1888–

.to raise to rank of: cardinalate *vt* 1577–1620, cardinalize *vt*
1616 + 1921, incardinate *vt* 1862(1), enhat *vt* 1925(2)

R3.2.1.4. Primate: primate c1205–

XR R3.2.1.2. Patriarch

.office of: primalty c1330(2), primacy c1470–, primateship
1631–1799
.see of: prim acy 1552 + 1807 *both Sc.*
.char of: primal 1543(1), primatial 1623–, primatical a1677–,
primatic 1687–1826

R3.2.1.5. Metropolitan: metropolitan 1432/50–, metropolite
1578–
.Orthodox: eparch 1691 + 1882/3

.office of: metropolitanship a1638–, metropolitanate 1854–,
provincialate 1906(1)
.see of: province 1377–, metropolis 1535–1850, metropolie 1635(1),
metropolite 1635(1), metropole 1862–
..Orthodox: eparchy 1796–(1862), eparchate 1882/3(1)
..char of: provincial 1377–1851
...Orthodox: eparchial 1882/3(1)
..at level of: provincially 1628–1704

.char of: metropolitical 1541–, metropolitan a1548–, metropolical
1550(1), metropolitic 1555–1612, metropolic 1681/6(1)
.(of xp:)independent of jurisdiction of: autocephalous 1863 +
1881

.in manner of: metropolitically 1637–1834

R3.2.1.6. Archbishop: *ealdorbiscop, heahbiscop*/high-bishop
OE–1551, *arcebiscop*/archbishop OE–, erchevesque ?a1400(1),
arch-flamen c1425–1656, most reverend 1485 + 1727, your /
his grace 1500/20–, father 1508–, hierarch 1574–, arch-prelate
1594–1851
.of Canterbury: Canterburiness 1588–1589, Lambeth 1941–

.Orthodox: primate c1205–, exarch a1600–
.petty: archbishopling 1851(1)
.pl/coll: archiepiscopacy 1901(1)

.office of: *arcebiscopdom, arcehad, arcebiscophad*/archbishophood
  OE + c1449 + 1845, *arcebiscoprice*/archbishopric OE–, pall
  1538–, archbishopship 1556(1), archiepiscopalship 1606(1),
  grace 1631(*2q1s*), archiepiscopacy 1662 + 1848–,
  archiepiscopate 1792 + 1855
..Orthodox: exarchate 1876(1)
.see of: *arcebiscopstol, arcerice, arcestol, arcebiscoprice* /
  archbishopric OE–, arch-see 1612 + 1865, primacy
  1745–1867, archdiocese 1844–
..Orthodox: exarchate 1877(1)

.character of: archiepiscopality 1655(1)
.official at consecration of: high steward 115..(1)
.wife of: archbishopess 1781(1)

.char of: archiepiscopal 1611–, arch-prelatic(al) 1651 + 1882
.in manner of: archiepiscopally 1839–

.to make: archbishop *vt* 1836(1)
.to act as: archbishop it *vphr* 1692(1)

R3.2.1.7. Primus: *primus* 1860–
.office of: primus-ship 1899(1)

R3.2.1.8.0. Bishop: *domne (L), scirbiscop*/shire-bishop OE +
  1880*hist., biscop*/bishop OE–, bisp a1300(2) + 1330, ordinary
  c1380–, your discretion 1426–1555, diocesan c1440–, ordinar
  1465(1), my lord of (x) a1470–, right reverend 1492–, father
  1508–, patriarch 1517–1547 + 1885, bite-sheep 1553/87–1683
  hum., rocheter 1559(1), pope 1563–1570 *early ch.,* presul
  1577(1), rochet 1581–1678, diocesser 1606(1), monseigneur
  1610–, lawn sleeves c1640–1768/74, episcopant
  1641(1-*Milton*), diocesian 1715(1), lawn-man 1795(1-*derog.*),
  diocesiarch 1805(1), pair of lawn sleeves 1844(1), bish 1875–
  joc.

XR R3.1.1. Episcopacy

.pl/coll: prelacy 13..–1827, bishopdom 1641–1858, prelatry 1653 +
1879, episcopacy 1757–(1889), episcopate 1842–, prelature
1845 + 1855, episcopy 1874(1), episcopature 1884(1)

.a race of: *biscopcynn*

.office of: *biscopfolgod, biscophaddegnung, biscopscir,*
biscopdenung, healdnes, biscopdom/bishopdom OE + 1635,
biscophad/bishophood OE–(1849), mitre 1387/8–, bishopric
1394–1851, see c1450–, chair 1480–1867 *fig.,* bishopry
1535(1-*Sc.*), pontificality 1556–a1656, episcopality 1636 +
1647, lawn sleeves c1640–1768/74, episcopate 1641–,
episcopacy 1685 + 1869, lawn a1732–c1800 *fig., cathedra*
1863–1866

..tenure of: episcopacy 1660–(1844), episcopate 1868–

..succession of: *see R1.2.1.3. Apostolic succession*

.see of: *biscopscir, biscopseld, setl, stol, scir*/shire OE + 1338,
rice/riche OE + c1400, *biscoprice*/bishopric OE–(1777),
biscopstol/bishopstool OE–a1300 + 1868–(1876), siege
1297–1579, bishop-see 1330 + 1650, diocese c1330–, seat
1387–(1888), *eveschie* 1475(1), see 1534–, bishopwick 1570(1),
chair 1615–1647, parish 1709 + 1898 *hist.,* episcopate
1807–(1861), stake 1833– *Mormon, cathedra* 1863–1866

XR R3.2.1.5. Eparchy

..main city of: see 1534–1756/7

..p in: diocesan 1502–(1839), diocesener a1626(1)

..vacancy of: *sede vacante* 1589–1783

...during: *sede vacante* 1535–

...B administering S during: intercessor 1727/41(1)

..area within not subject to authority of B: peculiar
jurisdiction c1525–

...xp within: exempt 1532–1706, exaun 1678(1)

XR R3.2.2.1. Peculiar

...privilege establishing: exemption 1460–(1868)

...char of: exempt 1460–1726 + 1868*hist.,*

..char of: cathedral 1297–, diocesan 1450/1530–, cathedratic
1661–1725, cathedraical 1676(1), diocesian 1715(1), parochial
1861(1-*hist.*), diocesal 1880(1)

.personality of: bishopdom 1589(2)
.possessions of: episcopalia *npl* 1865–(1914)
.'worship' of: episcopolatry 1867 + 1882
.triennial visitation of B to his diocese: triennial 1640–1724
.letter from B to his diocese: mandate 1763–1824, pastoral
    (letter) 1865–
.public confirmation of appointment of B by pope:
    preconization 1692–
..to give: preconize *vt* 1692–
XR R4.2.6.1.0. Confirmation

.lawful entering into office of: succession 1565–
.act/fact of making: episcopofactory 1649(1), episcopization
    1861(1), episcopation 1872 + a1876
XR R4.2.6.1.0. *Biscophadung*

.char of: *biscoplic*/bishoply OE–1642, mitred c1380–, horned
    c1425–a1651, pontifical c1440–, episcopal 1485–, rochet 1554
    + 1641, bishoplike 1544–(1868), pontifical 1591–1769,
    pontifician 1645–a1709, lawny 1647–1742/8, episcopalian
    1822(2), rocheted 1842 + 1868
..not: unepiscopal a1661–, unbishoply 1865 + 1876
.enthroned as: cathedrated 1626(1)
.qualified for appointment as: episcopable 1676–(1884)
.not consecrated as: unbishopped 1601(1)

.in manner of: *biscoplice*, pontifically c1380–, bishoplike c1555 +
    1621, pontifically 1599–1681, episcopally 1680–

.to make: mitre *vt* c1380–c1440 + 1801–, bishop *vt* 1549–(1861),
    incathedrate *vt* 1635 + 1641, episcopize *vt* 1649–(1832),
    episcopate *vt* a1661(1), episcopalize *vt* 1823(1)
.to deprive (x) of: unbishop *vt* a1661(1)
.to act as: sit *vi* 1387–, episcopate *vi* 1641 + 1705, bishop (it)
    vphr 1655(*2q1s*), episcopize *vi* 1679–1820
XR R4.2.4.1.0. Pontificate

R3.2.1.8.1. Kinds of bishop
.of Alexandria: pope 1646 + 1850
.Anglican: superintendent 1554–1721, superintendentship 1565(1),

magpie a1704 + 1903 *derisive*

.coadjutor: coadjutor 1549–(1863), co-bishop 1726(1), coadjutator
1881(1)

..office of: coadjutory 1616–1725, co-episcopacy 1644(1),
coadjutorship 1668–

.of city: *burhbiscop*

.-elect: lite c1425–1497 *mainly Sc.*, bishop-elect / -designate 1751–

.fellow-: *efenbiscop*

.female: bishopess 1854 + 1880 *hum.*,

.heretical: *dwolbiscop*

.who acts as king: king-bishop 1890(1)

.missionary, of no fixed diocese: regionary bishop
1727/38–(1869)

XR R3.2.1.8.1. May bishop

..char of: portative 1550(1), utopian 1709(1)

.petty: bishoplet 1878(1)

.representing papal authority in a place: vicar apostolic
1766–, V. A. 1787–, vicar apostolical 1849(1)

..see of: vicariate 1818–

.who is a peer: Lords Spiritual *npl* 1451–(1765)

.who is a prince: prince-bishop 1867–

..see of German: stift 1637–1678 + 1819

.of same province: comprovincial 1642–

..char of: comprovincial 1593–

.Roman Catholic: spittle-bishop 1555(1-*hostile*)

.suffragan: *underðeod, leodbiscop*/lede-bishop OE–c1325, suffragan
c1380–, suffragan bishop / bishop suffragan 1475–,
under-bishop 1574(1), chorepiscopus a1600–1844 *early ch.*,
suffragant 1611(1), choral bishop 1636(*2q1s - early ch.*),
chorepiscope 1660(1-*early ch.*), suffraganean bishop 1704(1)

..office of: suffraganship 1549–a1661, suffragancy 1864(1)

..see of: lede-bishopric ?a1300(1), suffraganate 1879–

...char of: suffragan 1712–

..char of: chorepiscopal 1839– *early ch.*, suffraganal 1892(1),
suffraganeous 1904(1)

.titular: May bishop 1565(1-*opprob.*), tulchan *a* a1578–1859 *Sc.*,
titular bishop 1767 + 1885

XR R3.2.1.8.1. Regionary bishop

..in uncivilized/heretical country: *in partibus* 1687–
...char of: *in partibus* 1687–
.Wesleyan: superintendent 1784–

R3.2.1.8.2. Bishop's officials
Commissary: commissary 1362–, commissar c1475(1)
.office of: commissaryship 1563/87–1726
Consultor: consultor 1896–
Grand Vicar: grand vicar 1662–
.office of: vicariate 1611–a1773
Surrogate: surrogate 1603–
Syncellus: syncellus 1706–, syncellite 1720(1)
Thane: *ðegn*
.pl/coll: *biscopweorod*
Vicar capitular: vicar capitular 1846–
Vicar forane: vicar foreign 1825(1), vicar foran(e) 1888–, V. F.
    abbrev. a1912–

XR R3.2.1.11. Rural dean
Vicar general: chancellor c1400–, vicar general c1450–, provisor
    c1560–1841, V. G. *abbrev.* 1871 + 1922
.office of: vicar-generalship a1578–

R3.2.1.9. Archpriest: arch-flamen c1425–1656 + 1823,
    archpriest 1485–(1854), archpresbyter 1562–1610 + 1861–
.Roman: pontifex maximus 1777 + 1934–

.office of: archpriestship 1560–1691, archflamenship c1640(1),
    archpriesthood 1670 + 1881, archipresbyterate 1915–

.char of: archipresbyteral 1844(1)

R3.2.1.10. Archdeacon: *heahdiacon*/high-deacon OE + 13..,
    arcediacon/archdeacon OE–, archdean c1425–1634/46 *Sc.*,
    archdiacre c1450(1)

.office of: archdeaconship 1591 + 1755, archdeanery 1828(1-*hist.*),
    archdeaconry 1872(1), archdeaconate 1882(1)

.**district of:** archdeaconry 1555–1590 + 1847
.**wife of:** archdeaconess 1861(1)

.**char of:** archidiaconal 1651–1674 + 1849

R3.2.1.11. Dean: dean a1350–1514, dean rural c1450 + 1826,
   rural dean c1450–, pleban 1481(2-*Sc.*)

XR R3.1.5.3.1. Dean
R3.2.1.8.2. Vicar forane

.**area of:** deanery c1440–(1890), decanery 1538–1647, rural
   deanery 1642–, decanate 1835(1)
..**in certain cities (e.g. Exeter):** christianity 1587–,
   christenhood 1762(1)

.**char of:** ruridecanal 1861 + 1888

R3.2.1.12. Various superiors
Christian:
.**Lutheran:** superintendant 1560–
..**district of:** superintendency 1762–
.**Methodist:** leader 1743–1791
.**Mormon:** revelator 1867–
.**Presbyterian:** moderator 1563–
..**office of:** moderatorship 1641–
..**char of:** moderatorial 1867–
..**to act as:** moderate *vi* 1577–
.**Russian Orthodox:** *starets/-etz* 1923–
.**Salvation Army:** general 1883–
.**Wesleyan:** assistant a1791(1)

Non-Christian: *ealdormann,* prelate a1400–1601, pope c1400–

.**Buddhist:** dalai lama 1698–, panchea 1763–, rinpoche 1774–,
   grand lama 1807–, Thathanabang 1839–, teshu-lama 1876–
.**Druid:** arch-druid 1747–(1839)
.**Egyptian:** Sem 1882–
.**Greek:** protopope 1662–, *protopapas* 1682–1820, proto-presbyter
   1882/3(1)

XR R3.2.1.0. Hierarch
.Herculean: stephanophore 1624(1)
.Indian: gooroo / guru 1613 + 1810– destour 1630–(1878),
    mahant 1800–, *Sankaracharya* 1947–
.Islamic: mufti 1586–(1852), imam 1613–, sheikh-ul-islam 1686–,
    grand mufti 1695(1), Khilafat 1923(1)
.Jewish: *biscop, ealdorbiscop, heahbiscop,* high(-)priest 1382–
..deputy of: sagan 1625–(1904)
.ancient Roman: king-sacrificer 1601(1), king of the sacrifices
    1781(1)

R3.2.2.0. Priest: *æweweard, ciricdingere, clænsere, cleric (L),*
    clerus (L), sacerd (L), dingere, preost/priest OE–, beaupere
    c1300–1599, sir(e) c1380–1635, divine c1380–1791, Sir John
    c1386–1653, his/your paternity 1432/43–, your fatherhood
    1483–a1661, father 1529–, key-bearer a1540–, key-keeper
    1563/87(1), your priestdom 1588–1615, *sacerdos* c1590 +
    1930– *often pl.*, your priesthood 1593(1), presbyter
    1597–1846, ?flasher 1611 + 1736, *pere* 1619–, pater c1630(1),
    his fathership 1670–, sacerdote 1685(1), soggarth 1836– *Irish,*
    your priestship 1868(1), soutane 1890(1), joss-man 1913–
    slang
.pl/coll: *preostheap, preosthired, preostgesamnung,* clergy c1275–,
    priesthood 1377–, discretion 1486(1), sacerdos c1590(1),
    sacerdotage 1859 + 1875 *derisive*

.office of: *hadnotu, sacerdhad, preosthad*/priesthood OE–,
    priesthead a1300–1588, sanctuary c1380–1781 *fig.,* priestdom
    1528(1), flamenship 1600 + 1610, sacerdotal a1640(1),
    priestship 1642–1896, sacerdocy 1657/83–1877, long robe
    1762–, sacerdoce 1829 + 1926, priestism 1842– *hostile,*
    sacerdotalism 1847/54–(1880), sacerdotage 1884(1-*derisive*),
    sacerdotium 1931–
..p supporting: priestling 1720 + 1907, sacerdotalist 1865–(1896)
..exercise of: priestcraft 1483*Sc.* + 1900*nonce,* priesting
    1550–1641
..char of: sacerdotal 1871–(a1884)
..to subject to: sacerdotalize *vt* 1865–1899

.**disciplinary power of:** keys *npl* a1300–(a1711) *fig.*
..**char of:** key-bearing 1669(1)
.**craft/policy of:** priestcraft 1681–(1869)

XR R3.1.1. Hierarchy

.**wife of:** presbyteress 1546–1672/5, priestess 1709 + 1778 *colloq.*

.**char of:** *gehadod, sacerdlic,* sacerdotal c1400–, priestial c1449(1), priestly 1465–, priestlike c1470*Sc.* + 1559–(1831), priestish 1529–1569, priesterly 1535(1), sacerdotical 1641(1), ?hierographic 1658(1), priestal 1839 + 1848, hieratic 1859–

XR R4.2.6.1.0. Ordained

..**condition of being:** sacerdotality 1668(1), priestliness 1681–, sacerdotalness 1727(1)
..**and political:** hieraticopolitical 1685(1)
..**not:** unpriestly 1537–(1837), unsacerdotal 1847 + 1860
.**(of x:) without:** priestless 1297 + 1879–, unpriested 1548–1858

.**in manner of:** priestly c1400–1755, priestlike 1565 + 1611, sacerdotally 1836–
..**not:** unpriestly 1554(1), unsacerdotally 1834(1)

.**to make:** priest *vt* 1504–
.**to make (x) free of:** unpriest *vt* 1844(1)
.**to act as:** priest *vi* c1400–1509, priest it *vphr* 1642(1)

R3.2.2.1. Kinds of priest
.**Asian:** shaman 1698–
.**Aztec:** fire-keeper 1873(1)
.**who blesses bells:** bell-hallower 1549(1)
.**Brahmin:** *pedanda* 1817–
.**ancient British:** flamen c1330–1652, druidan 1509 + 1570, druid 1563–, druidess *nf* 1755–(1827)
..**one class of:** vates *npl* 1728–
..**char of:** druidish 1577 + 1723, druid 1670–, druidean 1678(1), druidic 1773–, druidical 1755–(1879)
.**Buddhist:** bonze 1588–, lama 1654–, bonzess *nf* 1860(1)
..**mendicant:** mendicant 1613–1848
.**chantry:** chaplain c1340–1602, chantry-priest 1480–, chanter 1483–1813, cantuarie-priest 1538(1), chanterist 1548(1),

cantarist 1800 + 1894

XR R3.2.8. Chaplain
..foundation for: chantry c1386–(1868), mansionary 1651(1), chapelry 1877(1)

.Chinese: joss-man 1948–
.of church: *ciricđegn, mynsterpreost*
.Egyptian: pastophor(us) 1658–, *setem* 1963–
..funereal: *c(h)olchyte* 1878–
..who kept temple seal: sphragistes 1847–
.fellow: *efenmæssepreost, efensacerd*
.female: *sacerd, nunne*/nun OE–1698, priestress 1480–1603, priest 1599–1614, presbyteress 1651–1682 + 1901, priestess 1693–
..office of: priestesshood 1841–
.ancient Greek: hierophant 1677–

XR R1.8.5.1. Hierophant
..female, who delivered oracles: pythoness 1823(1), *pythia* 1842–1844, pythian 1844(1)
.Hawaiian: kahuna 1886–
.heathen general: *biscop, heargweard, mæssepreost, sacerd* (L), priest c1200–, flamen c1400–1808, clergyman 1609–1693, divine 1611(1-*Shakespeare*), fetishe(e)r 1613–, baal-priest 1831(1), fetisheeress *nf* 1864(1)
..char of: flaminical 1641(1), flaminal a1693(1), flamineous 1846(2)
.high-: *see R3.2.1.0. Clerical superior general*
.Hindu: pujari 1813–
.ignorant: Sir John Lack-Latin c1534–1614, patrico a1550– *slang*, hedge-priest 1550–, tom pat c1700(1-*slang*)
..who performed irregular marriages: knit-beggar 1700(1), buckle-beggar a1700 + 1822, couple-beggar 1702–1944
.who is king: priest-king 1866–
.Maori: *tohunga* 1831(1)

.who celebrates Mass: *hiredpreost, mæsseđegn, weofodđegn, mæssere*/masser OE + 1543–1579 *later uses derisive*, *mæssepreost*/mass-priest OE–1686 + 1902, *preost*/priest OE–, altarer 1413(1), misser/-ar a1560–1604, massing-priest 1560–1656, sacrificer 1563 + 1848, Christ-maker 1581(1-*opprob.*), conficient 1614–1638, missalian 1624(1),

missalist 1624 + 1909, sacrificul(e) 1653(1), waiter at the
altar 1711(1), altar-thane 1753(1-*hist.*), celebrant 1839–,
president 1945–
XR R3.2.2.1. Roman Catholic priest

..annually for the dead: annueller c1386–a1528, annuary
1550(1)

..early in the morning: morn-priest 1466(1), morrow-mass priest
1494–1635, morrow priest 1563(1)

..office of: *mæssepreosthad*

..district of: *mæssepreostscir*

.Moslem: mufti 1586–(1852), shereef 1599–, imam 1613–, *alfaqui*
1615–1846

..office of: muftiship 1690(1), imamate 1727/41 + 1860, imamship
1895(1)

.neighbouring: *neahfæder*

.parish: parish priest a1300–, papa 1591– *Orth.Ch.*, parochian
1621–1715, *cure* 1655– *Fr.*, pope 1662– *Orth.Ch.*, paroecian
1725(1), parochial 1853(1), paroch 1900(1), rector 1923–
RCCh.
XR R3.2.3. Rector

..jurisdiction of: *preostscir*/priest-shire OE + 1844*hist.*,
ciricsocn/church-soken OE–c1200 + 1875*hist.*, parish 1292–,
?paroschen c1330(1), parishing c1450–1584 *N.dial.*,
parochin(e) 1500/20–1824 *Sc.*, charge 1530–, parishen
a1555–179., paroece 1564(2), parochrie 1581(1-*Sc.*)

...exempt from local bishop's authority: peculiar 1562–(1899)
XR R3.2.1.8.0. Exempt

...division of: chapelry 1591*Sc.* + 1669–, chapelcy 1594(1)

...matters concerning: parochialities *npl* 1871(1)

...absorption in duties of: parochialism a1884(1)

...action of making into: parochialization 1896(1)

....to perform: parochialize *v* a1846–

.....not: disparish *vt* 1593 + 1864

...to work in: parochialize *v* 1871–
XR R3.3.4.0. Parishioner

.petty: *see R3.2.2.1. Young priest*

.who officiates at rood altar: rood-priest 1516 + 1618

.Roman:
..Arval: Arval Brethren *npl* 1854(1)
..fetial: father patrate 1533(1), fetial / fecial 1533–
..flamen: flamen 1533–
...office of: flamen-ship 1600 + 1610
..pontifex: pontifex 1579/80–, pontifice 1603(1), pontiff 1626–
...office of: pontificate 1581 + 1868
...char of: pontifical 1579/80–, pontificial 1609(1), pontific 1644(1)
..Salian: Salian 1781(1)
...char of: Salarian 1598(1), Salian 1653–(1871)
..vestal: vestal virgin *nf* 1432/50–, vestal *nf* 1579/80–
.Roman Catholic: missary 1550–1657, pope's knight
      1558–(1872), popeling 1561–1705, greasling
      1583(1-*contempt.*), don 1600(1), ointling a1603(1), dom
      1716–, black-gown 1804 + 1872 *U.S.*
                                        XR R3.2.2.1. Mass-priest
.who is ruler: priest-ruler 1920(1)
.who ministered to p seeking sanctuary: grith-priest 1391(1)
.sacrificial: sacrifier 1382–1563, sacrificer 1547–(1865), sacrificulist
      1652(*3q1s*)
..office of: sacrificership 1562(1)
.Santerian: santero 1950–
.Shamanistic: Shaman 1698–
.subordinate: underpriest c1200(1)
.substitute: priest-in-charge 1941–
.village: *tunpreost*
.voodoo: papaloi 1884–
.young/petty: priestling 1629–(1866) *usu. contempt.*, priestlet
      1880– *usu. contempt.*, priesteen 1907(1-*Ulster*)

R3.2.3. Rector: *reccere*, person c1250–1625, parson c1325–,
      rector 1393–
.lay: lay rector 1778(1)
.of synagogue: *heahealdor*, archisynagogue 1582–1783
.of team ministry: team rector 1976(1)
.vice-: vice-rector 1629–
..office of: vice-rectorship 1856(1)

.**office of:** rectorship 1600–(1753)
.**wife of:** rectoress 1729–
.**char of:** rectoral 1658–1865, rectorial 1769–

R3.2.4. Parson: curate c1340–1886, curator 1362–c1450, parson
1588–, sir 1591 + 1869*dial.*, black-coat 1627–1870, spiritual
flesh broker a1700(1), finger-post 1785(1-*slang*
XR R4.16.1. Parsonage
.**duly presented and inducted:** parson imparsonee 1607–(1845)
.**new/petty:** parsonet 1834 + 1877
.**sporting:** sporting parson 1826–
.**who is also squire of parish:** squarson 1876–(1895)
.**pl/coll:** parsondom 1850–, parsonry 1876(1)

.**office of:** parsonship 1680(1), parsonhood 1834(1), parsonity
1844(1)
.**work of:** parsoning a1792–
.**lore about:** parsonology 1815–
.**worship of:** parsonolatry 1852(1)
.**wife of:** parsoness 1784–
.**child of:** parsonet 1812(1)

.**char of:** parsonly 1775–1776, parsonic 1785–, parsonical 1785–,
parsonish a1834–, parsonese 1860(1)
..**not:** unparsonical 1858 + 1889
.**possessing:** parsoned 1882(1)
.**in manner of:** parsonically 1750(1)

.**to make:** parsonize *vt* 1880(1)
.**to act as:** parsonize *vi* 1892(1)

R3.2.5. Pastor: *lareow, hierde*/herd OE–1549/62, shepherd
a1300–, herdman c1320–1553, pastor 1377–, angel
1382–(1839), flock-feeder 1545(1), domine a1679–a1711 +
1892, dominie 1824–(1887) *U.S.*
.**chief:** arch-pastor 1574 + a1600
.**female:** pastoress 1887(1)
.**incompetent:** pastorling 1624(1)

.**inducted to charge:** placed minister 1733–(1818)
.**joint:** co-pastor 1805–
..**office of:** co-pastorate 1881–
..**church in care of:** collegiate church 1726 + 1876, collegiation
     1887(1)
.**sub-:** under-shepherd 1669–
.**pl/coll:** pastorhood 1839(1), pastorate 1846–

.**office of:** pastorship 1563–, pastorage 1662(1), pastorate a1795–
.**duties of:** pastoralia *npl* 1959–
.**work of:** pastoring 1894(1)
.**church without:** widow church a1759(1)

.**char of:** *hierdelic,* pastoral 1526–, pastorly 1616–, angelical 1678
     + 1864
.**lacking:** pastorless a1711(1)
.**acting as:** pastoring 1623(1)

.**to provide x with:** pastorize *vt* 1882(1)
.**to act as:** pastoralize *vi* 1870(1), pastor *vi* 1872–

R.3.2.6. Vicar: vicar 1303–, vicaire c1395–1520, ficker 1589(*2q1s*)
                              XR R4.16.1. Vicarage
.**in cathedral:** stallar(y) 1561/2 + 1861– *Sc.eccl.hist.*
                              XR R3.1.5.3.2. Cathedral cleric
..**office of:** stallary 1612–1624 *Sc.*
.**in team ministry:** team vicar 1976–
.**temporal:** temporal vicar 1726(1)
.**pl/coll:** vicarage 1485–1505, prudence 1486(1)

.**office of:** vicaried 1388(1), vicary c1420–1712, vicariship
     c1430(1), vicarship 1534–, vicariate 1610–, vicarage
     1622–1734, vicarate 1883–
.**church of:** vicariate 1762(1)
.**wife of:** vicaress 1770–

.**char of:** vicarly 1596(1), vicarial 1744–, vicarish 1938–

R.3.2.7. Curate: curate 1557–, minister 1624(1)

.on horseback: cavalry curate 1894–(1898)

.vice-: vi-curate a1617(1)

.pl/coll: charge 1486(1)

.office of: *carfulnys,* cure (of souls) c1340–, curateship 1598–1684
+ 1861, curacy 1682–

> XR R4.16.1. Sinecure

.function of: curating 1831 + 1907

.char of: cured 1393(1)

> XR R4.2.6.3. Settled
> R4.16.1. Discured

.to act as: cure *vt* 1377–1581

R3.2.8. Chaplain: *preost, capellan*/chaplain OE(L)–, capellane
a1661–1827, chapel-man 1663(1), man-minister 1715(1)

> XR R3.2.2.1. Chantry-priest

.army: camp-chaplain 1679/88(1)

.chief: arch-chaplain 1614(1)

.college: conduct priest c1400–1474, conduct 1499–1587 + 1830

.who prays for the dead: soul-priest 1484–1606, soul-chaplain
1550(1)

.diocesan, who attends condemned criminals: ordinary
1696–1900

.domestic: *handpreost, hiredpreost,* trencher-chaplain 1589–1676
contempt., levite 1655–a1704 + 1849*hist.*

.who says Marian mass: Saint Mary priest 1446(1)

> XR R4.2.4.1.1. Marymass

.prison: prison chaplain a1902–

.at sea: holy joe 1874–, sky-pilot 1888–, sin bosun 1948–

.office of: chaplainship 1536–1846, scarf 1712–1844, chaplaincy
a1745–

R3.2.9. Confessor: *woruldscrift, scrift*/shrift OE–1638,
shrift-father a1225–1600 + 1853–*arch.*, father a1300–1505,
ghostly father 1300–1677, penancer 13..–1377 + 1865, shriver
1340–1661, confessor 1340–, penitencer a1350–1656 +

1840*hist.*, penitentiary 1483–, confessary a1619–a1656, *confessarius* 1661–1845, soul-friend 1891 + 1896

XR R4.2.2.2. Absolver

.**royal:** clerk of the closet 1530–1716

.**district of:** *scriftscir*/shrift-shire OE + 1838–*hist.*, shrift-district 1872(1-*hist.*)

..**properly assigned:** *rihtscriftscir*

.**char of:** confessorial 1855(1)

R3.2.10. Preacher: *æboda, bodere, bydel*/beadle OE–, speller a1200–a1300, preacher a1225–, sermoner c1325–, angel 1382–c1560 + 1860–, predicator 1483–1839, pulpit-man 1582–1681, predicant 1590– *now hist.,* pulpiter 1600–1681 + 1894, sermonist 1630–1844, sermoneer a1637(1), pulpiteer 1642–1861, preachman c1645–1727/8, pulpitarian 1654–1860, predicatory 1686(1), use-man a1716(1), preacher-man 1899– *U.S.,* preach 1968– *U.S.*

XR R3.3.2.4. Predicator
R4.5.0. Preaching
R4.5.1. Evangelist

.**Anglican, with no parish:** lecturer 1583–1844
.**assistant:** exhorter 1513/75–(1901)
.**Spanish cathedral:** magistral 1772(1)
.**with no charge:** stibbler 1721–1865 *Sc.,* licentiate 1854–1866
.**who divides his text:** text-divider 1670(1)
..**practice of:** text-dividing 1670(1)
.**dissenting:** tub-man 1642–1651, tub-preacher 1643–1719 + 1899*hist.,* tubster 1681–1700 *all contempt.*
.**female:** predicantess 1647–1662, preacheress 1649–, predicatress 1669(1)
.**Irvingite:** prophet 1560 + 1832–1854
.**Jewish itinerant:** maggid 1892–
.**lay:** green apron 1654–1705 *contempt.,* lay-preacher 1747–, local preacher 1772–
.**char by long sermons:** spin-text 1693–
.**Methodist itinerant:** local preacher 1772–, travelling preacher

1789–(1825), rounder 1820 + 1893, local 1824– *dial.,*
circuit-preacher / -rider 1830–(1909), rider 1884(2)
..**chief:** circuit-steward 1839(1)
..**district of:** circuit 1766–
..**char of:** travelling 1789(1)
..**to work as:** travel *vi* 1791–
.**Moslem:** khatib 1625 + 1821–
.**open air:** field-preacher 1688–1839, street preacher 1878–
                                        XR R3.3.3.10. Poor priest
.**who preaches to private congregation:** parlour-preacher
   1589(1)
.**Puritan:** prophesier 1631(1)
.**who preaches on Saturdays:** sabbatine preacher 1772(1)
.**who preaches violently:** thump-cushion 1827(1), dustman
   1877(1-*slang*)
.**who preaches only once a year:** strawberry preacher 1566(1)
.**pl/coll:** counting 1486(1), the pulpit 1570–

.**office of:** preachership a1656–
.**p in charge of selecting and approving:** trier 1655–1862

.**char of:** predicatory 1611–, predicant 1629–, predicatorial
   1772–1792

R3.2.11.0. Deacon: *diacon*/deacon OE(L)–, levite 1393–1604,
   gospeller 1506–, kirk-maister 1522 + 1572, *diacre* 1523(1),
   bead-master 1579(1), reliever 1582–1610 *Relief Ch.*
.**chief:** proto-deacon 1698(1), proto-diacon 1896(1) *both Orth.Ch.*
.**female:** deaconess a1536–
.**lay:** lay-deacon 1861–
.**newly-ordained:** ordinee c1330–
.**pl/coll:** deaconry a1679(1), diaconate 1891(1), deaconate 1892(1)

.**office of:** *decanhad, diacondenung, diaconhad*/deaconhood OE +
   1382–c1449, deaconhead c1400(1), deaconry 1483–(1824),
   deaconship 1565–(1849/53), diacony 1636(1), diaconate
   1727/51(1), deaconate 1882/3(1)

.**char of:** diaconal 1611–, deaconal 1890(1-*U.S.*)

.(of x:)possessing: diaconate a1679(1-*nonce*)

.to act as: diaconize *vi* 1644(1)

R3.2.11.1. Subdeacon: *underdiacon, subdiacon*/subdeacon
OE(L) + 1303–, sudekyn / sodeken c1315–1483, southdeacon
c1400–1563, tunicle 1554(1)

.office of: subdeaconry 1554–1587, subdeaconship 1615–,
subdiaconate 1725–, subdeaconhood 1728(1), subdeaconate
1878(1)

.char of: subdiaconal 1849(1)

R3.2.11.2. Epistoler: *pistolrædere,* subdeacon 1440–, pistler
a1529–a1640, epistoler 1530–(1862), epistler 16..–1667,
postiller 1891(1)

R3.2.11.3. Levite: *diacon*/deacon OE(L)–c1449, levite a1300–

.char of: levitical 1535–, Aaronical 1618(1), Aaronic 1874–(1879)

R3.2.12.0. P in minor orders general: *cleric*/clerk
OE(L)–1537, waiter at the altar 1648(1)
XR R4.2.6.0. Minor orders

.char of: *gemæne*

R3.2.12.1. Acolyte: *huseldegn, acolitus*/acolyte OE(L)–, colet
1382–1563 + 1760/5*Hist.,* waiter 1563(1), acolouthite
1599–1642, colliter 1669(1), acolythist 1726–1844

.bearing candle: *candelbora, taporberend,* cierge-bearer c1450(1),
taperer c1450–, cierger 1624(1), ceroferary c1650(1), cerofer
1884(1)

.bearing cross: crosier / crozier 1393–1586 + 1858, cross-bearer
1568–1840, crucifer 1574–

.bearing crozier: crosier / crozier c1380–1558

.assisting Greek patriarch: hieromnemon 1727/41(1)

.bearing holy water: holy-water clerk 1303–1660
XR R5.8.10. Cruet

.bearing incense: ship-bearer c1450(1), boat-bearer 1899 + 1918, boat-boy 1902(1)

XR R5.8.11. Navicula

.bearing paten: patener 1853–
.serving mass: server 1853–
..function of: serving 1757(1)
..char of: serving 1885(1)
..to work as: serve *vt* 1393–
.bearing thurible: thuribuler 1504–(1891), thurifer 1853–

XR R4.15. Incenser
R5.8.17. Thurible

.pl/coll: *hired*
.office of: acolyteship 1562(1)

R3.2.12.2. Lector: *rædere*/reader OE–, lister 1377–1555, lector 1483–, lecturer 1570–1647
.office of: lectorship 1605–, lectureship 1634–, lectorate 1876–

R3.2.12.3. Exorcist: *exorcista (L)*, *halsi(g)end, healsigend,* benet c1383–1553/87 + 1846, exorcist 1560–, priest benedict 1660(1)

XR R4.13. Exorcism

R3.2.12.4. Ostiary: *ciricweard*/church-ward OE–1131 + 1871, ostiary 1432/50–, ostiar 1588(1-*Sc.*)

XR R3.3.4.1. Church-officer, church-warden

R3.2.13. Other clergy
Annunciator: annunciator 1753–
Assistant: helper 1780–
Ceremoniarius: ceremoniarius 1865–
Dutch reformed cleric: *predikant* 1849–
Feretrar: feretrar 1463 + 1828, pheretrer 1555(1)

XR R5.3.6. Shrine

Irish country cleric: rum 1720 + 1729 *slang*
Irvingite cleric: prophet 1883(1)
Non-conformist cleric: prig a1704–1752 *slang*

Pardoner: pardoner 1362–, pardonister c1380–1496, questor 1387–, quester a1550–1707, pardon-monger 1570 + 1874/7, indulgentiary 1577 + 1617, quæstuary 1614–1664, indulgencer 1647(1), pardon-pedlar 1653(1), questman 1691(1), questionary 1820(1-*Scott*)

Precentor: *heahsangere,* arch-chanter 1387–1844, chanter 1483–, ruler of the choir 1485–a1538 + 1853-*arch.,* cantor 1538–, chanterer c1540(1), taker-up 1578(1-*Sc.),* precentor 1613–, praise-leader 1920(1-*Sc.*)

.**female:** precentrix 1706–, precentress 1892(1)

.**Jewish:** chazzan 1650–, cantor 1893–

.**office of:** chantership 1529–1809, precentorship 1819–, cantorship 1884(1)

.**to act as:** precent *vi* 1732–, rule *vt* 1898(1)

XR R4.1.4.0. Precent

.**deputy of:** *æftersingend,* subchantress *nf* 14..(1), subchanter 1515–, succentor 1642–

XR R4.1.4.0. Succent

..**office of:** subchantership 1546(1), succentorship 1691 + 1829

Presbyterian cleric: cloak 1649–1663, mas john ?1661–1826

Proselytizing Irish cleric: souper 1854–

XR R4.5.3.0. Proselytizer

Psalmist: psalmister 1387–1483, psalmist 1565–, psalmodist 1726(2),

Relief Church cleric: relief minister 1768(1)

Rome runner: Rome-runner 1362–1577 + 1895*hist.,* Rome-raiker 1535–a1585 *Sc.*

Cleric of rank to wear scarf: scarf-officer 1710/11(1), scarf-man 1711(1)

Stationar: stationar(y) 1868(2)

Versicular: versicular c1450(1)

Vicar choral: vicar choral 1587–, priest-vicar 1688–

XR R3.1.4.3.2. Cathedral cleric

Wesleyan retired cleric: supernumerary a1791–

Young/petty cleric: clergion c1325–c1400, clerkling 1863–

R3.3. Religious

R3.3.0. Religious general: *mynstermann,* closterer a1300(1),
religious c1330–, cloisterer 1340–1627 + 1818, professor c1420
+ 1761, votary 1546–, regular 1563–, conventual 1611–,
religionary 1663(1), co(n)venter 1671(1), conversant 1671(1),
conventualist 1762(*2q1s*), religioner 1812 + 1896

.pl/coll: *cirice, hired, hiwan, hiwræden, inhiwan/-higan,* religious
a1225–, convent a1290–1689, religion 1297–c1450, college
c1380–1513 + 1868 *now hist.,* religiousty c1530(1), monkery
1549– *chiefly contempt.,* settlement 1708–, community
1727/51–

.rule followed by: *hiersumnes, munucregol, munucdeaw,* rule
a1225–, perfection 1390–1470/85, living c1450–1513, rubric
1809(1), vinaya 1854– *Buddhist*
XR R3.1.3.0. Canonical obedience
..order observing certain: *munucregol,* order a1225–, religion
a1225–(1858), sect c1380–1814, profession c1386–1451,
congregation 1488–1530 + 1706, community 1727/51(1)
XR R3.3.3.0. Order general
...member of: *hadesmann,* religion 13..–c1325, regular 1563–,
eremite 1577/87–1773
...char of: religious c1330–, monking 1537–1650
....and reduced to stricter observance: reformed 1706–1863
...not belonging to: unordered c1386(1)
..char of: *regollic,* regular 1387–
..in manner of: religiously ?a1400–1483
..to follow: *folgian v, munuclif don vphr,* monk it *vphr* 1756(1)

.foundation for: *canoniclif, mynsterham, mynsterlif,* convent
a1225–, c(o)enoby a1475–1646 + 1882/3, monks 1556(1),
c(o)enobium 1817–1860
XR R3.3.2.3. Cœnoby
R5.5.2. Monastery
..Carthusian: charterhouse 1534–(1839)
..Hindu: math(a) 1828–
..principal: mother-house 1661–
..small: *cell*/cell OE–(1868), conventicle 1550–1603

..Tibetan: lamasery 1867–(1882)
..near Versailles: Port-Royal 1692(1)
...member of: Port-Royalist 1727/41–

XR R2.2.3.1. Jansenism

..for women only: *wifhired,* convent 1795–, canonry 1877–

XR R5.5.2. Monastery

..char of: conventual c1425*sc.* + c1475–, conventical 1765–1784
..in manner of: conventually 1814–

.manner of: *munucwise*
.custom of: *mynsterḋeaw,* monkeries *npl* 1624–, monachism
      1670(1)
.work of: *hiersumnes*

.char of: *mynsterlic, munuclic*/monkly OE–1652 + 1893,
      monastical 1401–1859, monasterial c1420–1846, cloistrose
      c1449(1), monkish 1546–(1869)*now chiefly contempt.,*
      cloisterly 1563/87–1588, cloistered 1581–1861, monac(h)al
      1587–, monastic 1600–, cloistral 1605–1868, monasterical
      1651(1), claustral 1862–
..condition of being: *munuclif, mynsterlif, regollif,*
      munuchad/monkhood OE–, religion c1200–, the habit
      c1290–(1538), religiosity c1449(1), monkery ?1536– *chiefly*
      contempt., monachism 1577–, monkship 1620–1861, monkism
      1716–1848, monasticism 1795–, monkishness 1882 + 1900,
      monkliness 1887(1)

XR R3.3.2.1. Sisterhood

...p supporting: monk-monger 1655–(1865) *hostile,* seclusionist
      1839–
....char of: monachist 1860(1)
...p opposed to: *mynsterhata*
....char of: antimonachal 1864(1)
...period passed in: monachate 1819(1)
..not: unmonkly 1833(1), unmonastic 1849 + 1869, unmonkish
      1851(1)
..and devoid of cloister: cloisterless c1386(1), uncloistered 1652–

.in manner of: *mynsterlice, munuclice*/monkly OE–, monasticly

1596(1-*SC.*), monastically 1600–, monasterially 1653(1)

R3.3.1. Religious superior

General: minister 1450–, general 1561–, minister general
    1727/41–, superior-general 1775–, mandriarch 1871(1)
.female: superioress-general 1745(1)
.Jesuit: father-general 1587–(1679), black pope 1873–
..assistant to: assistant 1622 + 1679, minister 1727/41–

Provincial: provincial 1362–(1839)
.of Knights of St John: grand prior 1703–1727/41
..office of: grand priorship 1762(1)
..territory of: priorate 1829(1), grand priory 1885(1)
.Orthodox: archimandrite 1591–
.office of: provincialship 1629–1867, provinciate 1857(1),
    provincialate 1906(1)
.territory of: province 1727/41–(1848)

Preceptor: preceptor 1710–1819
                          XR R5.5.1.1. Monastic estate

Commander: commendatory 1555–1762, commander 1611–1867,
    commendator 1669–1688
.office of: command(e)ry 1554–

Conventual head: president 1387–1557, sovereign 14..–1544,
    superior 1497–, father superior 1706–
.female: presidentress 1650(1), mother superior 1706–
.Franciscan: warden 1420–1588, guardian 1466 + 1727/41–,
    pater-guardian 1656(1)
.Orthodox: hegumen 1662–
.office of: superiority 1706–1777

Abbot: *heahfæder, mynsterfæder, abbod*/abbot OE–, father 1571–
.Buddhist: roshi 1934–
.Celtic: corb 1607(1), *coarb* 1656–
.former: *geoabbod*
.head: *heahhyrde*
.mitred: mitred abbot 1658(1)

..**jurisdiction of:** mitred abbey a1661–
.**Orthodox:** archimandrite 1591–
.**titular:** titular abbot 1934–
.**office of:** *abboddom, abbodhad, abbodrice,* abbatie c1270–1655, abbacy c1425–, abthain / abthane 1872(1), abthainry / abthanrie 1872(1), abthanage 1872(1) *(last three items all 'early Scottish Ch.')*
..**period of:** abbacy 1794–

Abbess: *abbodesse, domne, hlæfdige, moðor*/mother OE + 1603–, dame a1225–(1908), abbess 1297–, matriarch 1629(1), superioress 1671–, maternity a1693(1), domina 1751 + 1819, mother-superior 1907(1)
.**p succeeding:** coadjutrix 1725–1813, coadjutrice 1756/7(1), coadjutress 1860(1)
..**office of:** coadjutrixship 1837(1)

Prior: *ealdor, mynsterprafost, regollweard, prafost*/provost OE–, *prior*/prior OE(L)–, prevost 1483(1), *prevot* 1838(1), præpositor 1881(1)
.**office of:** *prafostfolgoð,* priory 1387 + 1879, priorate c1400 + 1737–1854, pr(a)epositure a1425–1758, priorhede c1425(1), provostry c1450–, provostship 1514–1631, priorship 1553–, prioracy 1895(1)
.**jurisdiction of:** priory c1290–, priorate 1749–1844
..**owing allegiance to foreign mother-house:** priory alien 1502–1611, alien priory 1753–1845
.**territory of:** *prafostscip*
.**assistant to:** sous-prior 1297(1), supprior 1338–1637, subprior 1340–
.**char of:** prioral 1882(1)

Prioress: dame a1225–(1908), prioress c1290–(1861)
.**office of:** priorate 1925(1)
.**assistant to:** supprioress a1400–c1534, vicaress c1613–, subprioress c1660–

Dean: *decan (L), teoðingealdor,* dean a1641–(1885)

Senior monk: *non,* chapterman 1844–

R3.3.2.0. Monk: *mynstermann, ðeow(a), ðin broderlicnes, broðer*/brother OE + c1500–, *munuc*/monk OE(L)–, clausterman c1200(1), man of religion c1200–1485, cloister-monk c1325(1), friar c1330 + 1653 + 1801, son 1416–, religion man c1430(1), monach(e) c1540–1611 *affected,* scapular a1550(1), abbey-man c1550(1), cloister-man 1581(1), pater c1630(1), monastic 1632–1864, religieux 1654–(1827), saint 1888–

.Buddhist: talapoi(n) 1586–1858, poonghie 1788–

.of age 50 or more: sempect 1865(1)

.child intended to be: *munuccild*

.discalceate: discalceate 1669 + 1706

XR R3.3.3.3. Carmelite

.fellow-: *gehada,* commoigne 1425–1612, brother c1500–(1848), conbrethren *npl* 1561(1)

.Greek (of lowest grade): rasophore 1934–

.lazy: abbey-lubber 1538–1705

.living outwith monastery: out-brother 1599(1), extern c1610–(1887)

XR R3.3.2.0. Circumcellion
R3.3.2.1. Out-sister

.Moslem: santon 1599–1873, marabout a1623–, santo 1638–1901, morbut 1769(1)

XR R3.3.2.2. Anchorite

.who is also priest: hieromonach 1882/3–

.self-ruling: *self-dema/-ere/-ende,* sarabaite 1516–(1904), idio(r)rhythmic 1934 + 1960

..char of: idiorrhythmic 1862 + 1957

.Tibetan: *lung-gom-pa* 1931–

.true: *rihtmunuc*

.wandering: *widgenge,* circumcellion 1564–, gyrovague 1801(1)

XR R3.3.2.0. Extern

..who is scholar: *vagantes npl* 1927–

.young: *munuccnapa*

.pl/coll: *broðerlicnes, broðorrædden, gebroðor, munucheap,*

observance 1486(1), monkery 1552–, *sangha* 1858– *Buddhist,*
monkdom 1862–

R3.3.2.1. Nun: *munuc, mynsterfæmne, nunfæmne,*
*mynecen(u)/*minchen OE–1611 + 1844*arch., nunne/*nun
OE–, *sweoster/*sister OE–, spouse c1230–, monial 1377–1587,
clergess 1393 + 1888*hist.,* religious 1491–1651 + 1922, moines
1513(*2q1s*), sanctimonial 1513–1838, vowess 1533–1695,
woves a1550(1), nosegent 1567(*2q1s-cant*), votaress 1589–,
votress 1590–, cloistress 1601(1), sanctimony 1630(1),
clergywoman 1673–1842, religieuse 1694–, religiose 1697(1),
monkess 1729–1861, nun-sister 1892(1)
.Japanese Buddhist: bonzess 1860(1)
.professed for choir duty: choir nun 1788/9(1), choir sister
1889(1)
.resident in convent: in-sister 1644(1)

        XR R3.3.2.3. Cœnobite
..not: out-sister 1609–1657

        XR R3.3.2.0. Extern
.pl/coll: superfluity 14..(1-*hum.*), nunnery 1651–1715

.char of: nunnish 1570–, nun-like 1611–, sisterly 1883(1)

        XR R3.3.0. Monastic
..condition of being: *nunlif,* sisterhead 14..(1), nunnishness
1570(1), sisterhood c1592–, nunship 1624–, nunnery
1650–1679, nunhood 1812–, the veil 1812–, sistership 1840–

        XR R3.3.0. Monachism
.in manner of: nun-like 1589–1755

R3.3.2.2. Anchorite: *ancor setla, ansetla, anstandende,*
*anstonde, wræcca, anc(o)r(a)/*anchor OE–, hermit c1205–,
recluse a1225–, ankerer 1407(1), incluse 1432/50 + 1868–,
solitary 1435–, anchorite/-et 1460–, anachorist a1604(1),
anchorist 1651–1662, saint 1888–

        XR R1.8.3. Contemplative
        R3.3.3.10. Paulite
.female: anchor c1230–1466, anc(ho)ress 1393–, hermitress

1611–1823, hermitess 1633–, anchorist 1651–1662, anchoritess
1655 + 1872
.**Greek (association of)**: skete 1869–
.**Indian**: *muni* 1785–, *rishi* 1808–, ashramite 1933(1)
.**Moslem**: *see R3.3.2.0. Marabout*
.**of Nitria in Egypt**: Nitrian *a* 1867–

.**life of**: *ancor lif,* reclusion c1400–1824, anchorism 1633(1),
    anchoretism 1652 + 1862, recluse 1665(1), hermitship 1825–

.**char of**: recluse a1225–, hermitical 1586–, hermitary 1633(1),
    anchoretical 1656 + 1845, anchoretic 1661 + 1829–, hermitic
    1691–, eremitical 1756/7–(1857), hermitish 1812(1)

R3.3.2.3. Cœnobite: *mynstermunuc,* c(o)enobite a1638–,
    synodite 1862(1)
                                        XR R3.3.2.1. In-sister
.**system of**: c(o)enobitism 1882/3–
.**char of**: c(o)enobitical 1636–1868, c(o)enobitic 1649–
.**in manner of**: cœnobitically 1853(1)

R3.3.2.4. Friar: friar c1290–, confrater 1583–1691 + 1897, *frater*
    1585 + 1639, bungie-bird 1591(1-*contempt.*), friarship
    1708(1-*mock*), *frate* 1722–, *breviger* 1859(2)
.**Brahmin/Buddhist**: *bhikkshu* 1811–, *bhikku* 1846–, *grihastha*
    1871–
..**in fourth stage of life**: sunnyasee/-si 1613–
.**fellow-**: co-freer a1628(1)
.**with short frock**: cutted friar 16.. + 1888, curtal friar
    c1610–a1663 + 1820*Scott* + 1888*Child*
.**Hindu**: pandaram 1711–(1859), gosain 1774–, Naga 1828–
.**mendicant**: mendinant c1386–c1400, mendivaunt c1400–1426,
    sacked friar c1400–1867, mendicant 1530–(1846), sack-friar
    1553–1772, *breviger* 1859(2), stationar c1640(1)
                                        XR R3.3.2.4. Sunnyasee
                                            R3.3.3.10. Beghard
..**licensed to beg within limits**: limiter 1377–1591, limitary

a1662(1)

..**char of:** mendiant 1535(1), mendicant 1547–(1868)

.**Moslem:** dervish 1585–, fakir 1609(1), whirler 1815(1), rufai
1832–

.**preaching:** predicator 1483–1820, pulpit-friar 1555(1), predicant
1590–1749

> XR R3.2.10. Preacher
> R3.3.3.4. Dominican
> R4.5.0. Preaching

..**district of:** limitation c1380–1552

.**who carries wallet:** walleteer 1778(1)

.**young:** friarling 1563/87(1)

.**pl/coll:** fraternity c1330–, frary 1514 + 1556, fratry 1532–1581 +
1887, friary 1538–, friarhood 1726(1), *confrerie* 1803 + 1932

.**system of:** friarage 1555(1), friary 1655 + a1661

.**char of:** friarly 1549–a1661 + 1817–, friarish 1581(1), friary 1589
+ 1605, friar-like 1600–1646, scab-shin 1607 + 1620 *contempt.*

.**in manner of:** friarly a1631(1)

.**to act as:** friar *vi* a1535 + c1645

R3.3.2.5. Monastic functionary general: obediencer
c1380–1721 + 1892, ordinar 1405–1485, ordinary 1481(1),
egomen 1591(1- *GkCh*), obedientiary 1794–, obedientiar
1892(1)

> XR R3.3.0. *Hiersumnes*

.**office of:** obedience 1727/41–

Almoner: almoner 1366–, pittancer 1426–1463 + 1706–*hist.*

Cellarer: cellarer a1300–1662 + 1820–*hist.*, cellaress *nf* 1802 +
1825 *hist.*

.**assistant to:** suthselerere c1430(1), subcellarer c1475–c1702

Chapel officer: chaplain c1386 + 1884, hebdomadary 1432/50–,
hebdomary c1450–, septimarian 1661(1), septimanarian
1882(1), hebdomadarian 1898 + 1949

Definitor: search *nf* c1450–1652, definitor 1648–(1867), zelator *nf*
1851(1)

.pl/coll: definitory 1898–
Dortourer: dortourer c1430(1)
Hordarian: procurator c1290–1645, proctor 1494(1), procuratrix
    nf 1851–, hordarian 1892(1), procureur 1907(1-*hist.*)
Hosteller: hosteler c1290–1483 + 1877–*hist.*, hospitaller 1483–,
    terrar/terrer 1593 + 1864–*hist.*, hospitalarian 1745(1), guest
    master 1897(1)
Infirmarer: enfermer c1325(1), fermerer c1386 + 1483, infirmarer
    c1430–, infirmarian 1669–, infirmaress *nf* 1802 + 1896
Kitchener: kitchener c1440 + 1820*Scott*, focary c1550(1)
Particularius: *twiccere*
Porteress: nun-porteress *nf* 1768(1)
Refectarian: fraterer c1430 + 1483, refectorian 1660–(1869),
    refectorer 1794 + 1892, refectioner 1820–, refectorary
    1844(1), refectorarian 1886 + 1892
Servant for a week: *wucdegn*
Tailor: vestment-maker 1405–1537/8, wardrober 1526(1)

R3.3.3.0. Religious order general: *munucregol,* order a1225–,
    religion a1225–(1858), sect c1380–1814, profession
    c1386–1451, congregation 1488–1530 + 1706, community
    1727/51(1)

                              XR R3.3.0. Religious general
.strict: reform 1727/41–
.less austere: mitigated *a* 1671–
.to found: make *vt* c1124–c1380

R3.3.3.1. Augustinian: Austin c1384(1), Augustin(e)
    c1400–(1708), Austiner 1466(1), Augustinian 1602(1), black
    monk c1630(1), Augustinianess *nf* 1853(1), O.S.A. *abbrev.*
    1907–
.char of: Austin 1861(1), Augustinian 1875–

.Antonine: Anthonin 1536 + 1753, Antonine a1550–, Antonian
    1907–
..char of: Antonine 1898–, Antonian 1904–
.Assumptionist: Assumptionist 1898–

.Gilbertine: *see R3.3.3.2. Gilbertine*

.Guillemin: Guillemin a1300 + 1844, Willemin c1483(1), Williamite 1668–1693

.Premonstratensian: Premonster c1440(1), Premonstratense c1440(1), Premonstratenser 1550(1), Premonstrate 1550–1631, *Premonstratensis* c1630–1805, Norbertine 1674–, Premonstratensian 1695–, Premonstrant 1700–1747, White friar 1762(1)

..char of: *Premonstratensis* 1387(1), Premonster c1425(1-*Sc.*), Premonstrense c1425(1-*Sc.*), Premonstratense 1432/50(1), Premonstratensian 1695–, Premonstrensian 1715(1), Norbertine 1865–, Premonstrant 1895–

.Scopetine: Scopetines *npl* 1537(1)

.Somaschian: Somasque 1686–1706, Somaschian 1882/3(1)

.Ursuline: Ursulines *npl* 1693–

..char of: Ursuline 1739–

R3.3.3.2. Benedictine: dame *nf* a1225–(1908), black monk c1290–1766, Benedictine 1602–(1866), O.S.B. *abbrev.* 1798–, Benedictiness *nf* 1872 + 1909

.system of: Benedictinism 1826 + 1884

.char of: Benedictine 1630 + 1861

.Camaldolite: Camaldulian / Camaldolite 1764(1), Camaldolese / Camaldulese 1828–, Camaldolensian 1882/3(1), Camaldule 1882/3(1)

.Carthusian: Charthous c1387–c1394 *occas.pl.*, Carthusian c1394–(1847), *Chartreux* c1430–1732, Charter Friar 1686(1)

..char of: Carthusian 1563/87–(1828), Charterhouse 1577–1641, *Chartreux* 1613(1)

.Casinese: Cas(s)inese 1878–

..char of: Cas(s)inese 1881–

.Celestine: Celestine 1530–1836

.Cistercian: gray monk c1290–c1300, white monk 1387–, pied monk 1530–1537, Cistercian 1616 + 1876, ?white-cloak 1621(1), Bernardine 1676 + 1797, white nun *nf* 1877 + 1954

..pl/coll: grey monks c1290–(c1300)

..system of: Cistercianism 1895–

..**char of:** Cistercian 1602–(1837), Bernardine 1792 + 1864
..**Trappist:** Trappist 1814–
...**char of:** Trappist 1847–
...**Trappistine:** Trappistine *nf* 1884–(1896)
.**Cluniac:** Cluner 1514(1), Cluniac 1631–, Cluniacensian
      1882/3(1), Clunist 1888(1)
.**Conceptionist:** Blue nun a1700–, Conceptionist 1800–(1857)
.**Gilbertine:** Gilbertine c1540 + 1693
..**char of:** Gilbertine 1631–(1885)
.**Humiliate:** Humiliate 1611 + 1656, Humilist 1611(1)
..**char of:** Humiliate 1880(1)
.**Maurist:** Maurist c1800–
.**Olivetan:** Olivetan 1691–
.**Sylvestrin:** Sylvestrin(e) 1693–1753, Sylvestrian 1882/3(1)
..**char of:** Sylvestrin 1693(1), Sylvestrian 1905(1)
.**Valliscaulian:** Valliscaulians *npl* 1888(1)
..**char of:** Valliscaulian 1882(1)

R3.3.3.3. Carmelite: Carme c1380–1797, friars of the pie *npl*
    c1394(1), white friar 1412–, Carmelite c1500–(1766),
    Carmelitan 1599(1), Carmelitess *nf* 1669(1), Carmelite *nf*
    1670–
.**char of:** Carme c1394–1479, Carmelite 1505–(1823), Carmelin
    1631–1655, Carmelitan 1736(1)

.**Calceate:** Father Calceate 1669(1), Calceate 1669(1)
..**char of:** calceate 1669(*2q1s*), calced 1884(1)
..**not:** Discalceate 1669 + 1706, O.D.C. *abbrev.* 1922–
...**char of:** discalced 1631–, discalceate 1658–
.**Teresian:** T(h)eresian 1629–

R3.3.3.4. Dominican: (friar) preacher 1297–1544, Jacobin
    a1325–, Black friar c1500–(1786), Dominic c1540(1), Jacobite
    c1550–1614 + 1818, Dominican a1632–, preaching friar
    1700–1855 *hist.*, cherubic 1826(1), cherubic friar 1826(1),
    Dominicaness *nf* 1857(1) O.P *abbrev.* 1891–
XR R3.2.10. Preacher

R4.5.0. Preaching
.**char of:** Dominical 1600(1), Dominic 1674(1), Dominican 1680–

R3.3.3.5. Franciscan: Friar Minor 1297–(1862), Minor 13..–1700,
grey friar a1310–, Minor Friar c1440–1727/51, Minorite
1577/87–, Franciscan 1599–(1856), Seraphic 1659 + 1699,
Seraphic Friar 1826–, Minorist 1835(1), thong-wearer 1901(1)
.**system of:** Franciscanism 1855(1)
.**char of:** seraphical a1540–1721, Minorite 1563/87–, Franciscan
1592–, seraphic 1826–

.**Annunciade:** Annunciade 1706(1)
.**Capuchin:** Capuc(c)ian 1597/8–1645, Capuchin 1599–,
O.S.F.(C.) *abbrev.* 1798–
.**Conventual:** Conventual 1533–(1868)
..**char of:** Conventual 1533–(1868)
.**Cordelier:** Cordelin c1330(1), Cordelier c1400–(1827)
.**Grey Sister:** Grey Sisters *npl* 1567–(1796)
.**Minim:** Minim 1546–, Bonhomme 1656–1678, Minimite 1879(1)
.**Observant:** Observant 1474–, Observantine 1646–,
Minor-Observantine 1761(1)
..**Recollect:** Recollect 1631–, *Recollet* 1760–
...**char of:** Recollect 1655–, *Recollet* 1695–
.**Poor Clare:** Minoress *nf* 1395–1451 + 1631–*hist.*, Clare *nf* 1608–
..**Urbanist:** Urbanist 1687–
.**Sarabaite:** Sarabaite 138.(1)
.**Spiritualist:** Spiritualist 1716–, Spiritual c1791–

R3.3.3.6. Jesuit: Jesuit 1559–, Jesuitess *nf* 1600–1645 +
1898*hist.*, Jesuist 1602 + c1645, Jebusite 1604 + 1681 *hostile*,
Judasite 1605(1-*hostile*), Ignatian 1613–c1683, Jesuitrice /
Jesuitrix *nf* 1629 + c1665, Loyolist 1640(*3q1s*), Loyolite
a1670–, Inig(h)ist 1686 + 1741, Ignatianist 1716(1), S.J.
abbrev. 1822–
.**writing 'Acta Sanctorum':** Bollandist 1751–
XR R1.6.1.0. Hagiography
.**resident in particular place:** ledger-Jesuit 1606(1)

.of St Paul's, Goa: Paulist 1678–1757, Paulistine 1698(2)

.system of: Jesuitism 1609–, Loyolism 1880(1)

.char of: Jebusitish 16..(1), Jesuitish 1600–1695, Jesuitical 1600–,
  Jesuited 1601–1834, Ignatian 1605–1679, Jebusitical 1613(1),
  Jesuit 1613–, Jesuital 1672(1), Jebusitic 1681 + 1898,
  Jesuitic 1804 + 1888

.to imbue with principles of: Jesuit *vt* 1601 + 1621

.to act as: jebusite *vt* 1608(1), jesuitize *vi* 1644 + 1825

R3.3.3.7. Trinitarian: Mathurin 1611–, Trinitarian 1628–,
  Trinitary 1693(1)

.char of: Trinitarian 1628–(1885)

Mercenarian: Mercenarian 1648–1740

..char of: Mercenarian 1648(1)

.Ransomer: Ransomer 1745(1), Redemptionist 1866(1)

R3.3.3.8. Greek religious

Athonite: Athonite 1887(1)

.char of: Athonite 1935–, Athoan 1939(1)

Caloyer: *Caloyer* 1615–

Hesychast: Hesychast 1835–, Palamite 1859–

.char of: Palamite 1877–

Rasophore: *see R3.3.2.0. Rasophore*

Studite: Studite 1693–

R3.3.3.9. Religio-military religious

Hospitaller: Hospitaller c1386–, spittler a1550(1), Rhodian 1550
  + 1551

.pl/coll: (Knights) Hospitallers c1330–, Hospitalaries 1598(1)

.char of: Rhodian 1592 + 1843

Knight of St John: Johannite 1563/87 + 1708

Knight of the Sepulchre: *see R3.3.4.3. Knight of Holy
  Sepulchre*

Knight Sword-bearer: Port-glaive 1656–1755, Sword-bearer

1693–1841

Knight Templar: Templar c1290–, Templary 1432/50–1656
.pl/coll: Templary Knights *npl* 1617(2)
.order of: temple a1131–1656, order 1387–, templary a1661–(1904)
..branch of: language 1727/52–1885, langue 1799–1888
.practice/belief of: Templarism 1888(1-*hist.*)
.char of: templarian 1600 + 1612, templar-like 1612(1)
Knight Teutonic: Stellifer a1550(1)
.pl/coll: white mantles c1500(1)
.char of: starred 1537–1563/83

R3.3.3.10. Other religious
Barnabite: Barnabite 1706(1)
Basilian: Basilian *a* 1780–
Beghard: Beggar c1384 + c1400, Beguine *nf* 1483–(1851),
    Beghard 1656–(1863)

> XR R3.3.2.4. Mendicant

.pl/coll: Begadores 1586(1)
.establishment of: Beguinage 1815–1854
Bridgetine: Bridget(t)ine 1533–
Brother/sister of charity: Brother of Charity 1706(1), Sister of
    Charity 1848–
Immaculate Conceptionist: Order of the (Immaculate)
    Conception *ncoll* 1727–1840
Cowley Father: Cowley Father 1902–
Crossed Friar: Crossed Friars *npl* 1494–1556, Crouched Friars *npl*
    1570/6–1807, Crutched Friars *npl* 1628–1688
Culdee: Culdee c1425–
.char of: Culdean 1807–, Culdee 1880(1)

Doctrinarian: *see R3.3.4.3. Doctrinarian*
Geronomite: Hieronymian 1656(1), Hieronymite 1727/41(1),
    Geronomite 1754–, Jeronymite 1777 + 1893
.char of: Hieronymite 1843(1)
Ignorantine: Ignorants *npl* 1693(1), Ignorantine Friars *npl*
    1861(1), Ignorantines *npl* 1882/3(1)
Josephite (Mission of St Joseph): Josephite 1897–

Josephite (Russian): Josephine 1944(1), Josephite 1946–
XR R3.1.1. Josephism
Josephite (teaching order): Josephite 1846–
Lazarist: Lazarite 1725/52(1), Lazarist 1747–
Libertine: Friar Frap(art) a1535–1600

Marist: Marist 1877–
Mekhitarist: Mekhitarist 1834–
.char of: Mechitaristican 1825(1), Mekhitarist 1874–
Oblate: O.M.I. *abbrev.* 1907 + 1922
Oratorian: Oratorian 1656–, Philippine 1852–(1863)
.female: Philippine 1773(1)
.pl/coll: Congregation of the Oratory 1815(1), French Oratory
    1885(1)
.system of: Oratorianism 1847–
.char of: Oratorical 1619(1), Philippine / Filippine 1848–,
    Oratorian 1862–
.to act as: oratorianize *vi* 1848 + 1883
Pallottine: Pallottine *a* 1890–
Papey: Papey *ncoll* 1598–1790
Passionist: Passionist 1832–
.char of: Passionist 1844–
Pauline: Pauline 1362–a1550
Paulite: Paulite 1884(1)
XR R3.3.2.2. Anchorite
.char of: Paulite 1888(1)
Penitentiary: Penitentiary 1631–1683, Penitentials *npl* 1632(1),
    Penitents *npl* 1693–
Pied Friar (of Norwich): Pied Friars *npl* 1382–
Poor Priest: Poor Priests *npl* c1380 + 1880
XR R3.2.10. Street preacher

Redemptorist: Redemptorist 1835–
.female: Redemptoristine 1884–, Redemptorine 1889(1)
.char of: Redemptorist 1863–
Rosarian: Rosarian 1867 + 1871/2
Rosminian: Rosminian 1837–
.system of: Rosminianism 1874(1)
.char of: Rosminian 1843–

Salesian: Salesian 1884–
.char of: Salesian 1836–
Salvatorian: Salvatorian 1903–
Sepulchrine: Sepulchran nun *nf* 1844 + 1857, Sepulchrine (nun)
    nf 1905(2)
.char of: Sepulchrine a1800(1)
Servite: Servite a1550–, Cellite 1882(1)
.char of: Servite 1756/7–
Sulpician: Sulpician 1786–

Theatine: Theatine 1597/8–
.char of: Theatine 1693–
Vallombrosian: Vallombrosian 1884 + 1922
.char of: Vallombrosian 1851 + 1901
Vincentian: Vincentian 1854(1)
.char of: Vincentian 1896–
Visitandine: Visitandine *nf* 1747–, Visitation nun *nf* 1899(1)
.pl/coll: (Order of the) Visitation 1701–
.char of: Visitandine 1888(1)
White Father: White Father 1889–
White Sister: White Sister 1659–

R3.4. Laity

R3.4.0. Layman general: *ceorl, lǣwede, lǣwedmann,*
    woruldman, man of the world c1200(1), idiot c1380–1660,
    secular c1400–(1829), layman 1432/50–, lay-woman *nf* 1529–,
    lay c1532–1680, laic 1596–, terrestrial 1598(1-*Shakespeare*),
    beardling 1622(1)
.in gathering for worship: meeter 1646–a1713 *Quaker,*
    congregant 1886–

                            XR R4.1.0. Worshipper
..pl/coll: *ciricwaru, gefere, gesamnung, lađung*/lathing OE–c1275,
    church-folk c1200(1), congregation 1526/34–, meeting 1593–,
    assembly 1600–(a1748), society 1828/32– *U.S.,* parish 1851–,
    Samaj / Somaj 1875– *Hindi,* pew 1882–
...female part of: sorority 1645(1-*U.S.*)
...Jewish: synagogue a1175–

....**lay head of:** parnas(s) 1831–
....**attachment to system of:** synagogism 1891(1)
....**char of:** synagogical 1621–, synagogian 1632(1), synagogal
    1682/3
...**Methodist subdivision of:** class 1742–
...**non-Christian:** *cirice*
...**non-conformist:** chapelry 1707(1)
...**Quaker:** settlement 1708–
...**char of:** congregational 1639–
...**in manner of:** congregationally 1870 + 1885
...**to imbue with characteristics of:** congregationalize *vt*
    1866(1)

.**who is member of parish:** *hieremann/hierigmann, mann,*
    parishen a1225–, parishioner 1471–
XR R3.2.2.1. Parish
..**pl/coll:** parish 1851–

.**pl/coll:** *folc, heord*/herd OE–, *scæp*/sheep OE–, lay c1330–1616,
    flock a1340–, fold 1340–, clergy 1382–1736, temporalty
    1387–1874, lay-fee 1398–1641, lay people 1429–, temporality
    1456–1679, laity ?1541–, lealty 1548(1), the people 1548/9–
.**principles of:** laicity 1909–
.**concern of:** temporal 1390(2-*Gower*), temporals *npl* 1471–(1897),
    civils *npl* 1646–1717
.**jurisdiction of:** secularity c1380 + 1535
..**action of putting (xp) under:** laicization 1881–
XR R1.6.3. Unhallowing
...**to perform:** secularize *vt* 1611–, temporalize *v* 1828(1)
XR R1.6.3. Unsanctify
.**to adopt habit/custom of:** secularize *vi* 1864(1)

.**char of:** *hwilen, hwil(w)endlic, læwede*/lewd OE–1553 + 1819*Sc.*,
    woruldlic/worldly OE–, secular c1290–, lay c1330–, temporal
    c1340–, bor(r)el 1377–c1575 + 1860, common c1380–1771,
    laic 1562–, layit 1563 + 1621 *Sc.*, laical 1563/87–, mundane
    1848–(1865)
..**condition of being:** *woruldhad, woruldlif,* temporalty c1440 +
    1482, secularity 1616(1), laity 1616–1831

XR R1.8.1.2. Unregeneracy
R1.8.2. Unspirituality
.(of x:)composed of clergy and laity: clerolaical 1599–1606
.in manner of: secularly c1380–

R3.4.1. Lay functionary general: church-worker 1886(1)
.work of: *ciricđenung*

Advocate: advocate 1387 + 1751, advowee 1691–1751
                              XR R4.16.2. Advowson
Almsman: *ælmasmann*/almsman OE–, beadsman c1230–, hermit
      1588–1688
.office of: beadsmanry 1594(1)
Beadle: *see R3.4.1. Church-officer, church-warden*
Canephorus: canephorus 1849–
Caretaker: servitor 1593(1), verger 1707–, mansionary 1708/22–,
      vergeress *nf* 1889–
                              XR R3.4.1. Church-warden
.action char of: vergerism 1857(1)
Chorister: *cantere, ciricsangere, midsingende, sangere*/songer
      OE–c1200, clergion c1325–c1400, chorister c1360–, chanter
      1382–1868, quarester 1436–1450, choirman / quireman 1488–,
      child 1510/11–, singing man 1527/8–, chorist 1538–1766,
      choirer 1624(1), singing boy 1666–1682, sing-man 1691(1),
      white-boy 1691(1), white man 1691(1), singing clerk 1709(1),
      choirist 1773(1), secular 1801(1), lay-clerk 1811(1), chorister
      boy 1817–, choir-boy 1837–, songman 1883–
.chief: rector 1546–1691
                              XR R3.2.13. Precentor, psalmist, Vicar-choral
.Moslem: *muezzin* 1585–
.pl/coll: choir / quire c1380–, chapel 1420–1674, chore 1680(1)
                              XR R4.1.4.0. Church-singing
Church-officer: beadle 1594–(1884), church-officer 17..–, altarist
      1753–
.chief: arch-beadle 1693(1)
                              XR R3.2.12.4. Ostiary
Church commissioner: church commissioner 1842(1)
Church estates commissioner: church estates commissioner

1885(1)

Church-warden: *ciricweard*/church-ward OE–1496 + 1871*hist.*,
  reeve a1300–, church-reeve c1386–1688, kirk-ma(i)ster
  1429–(1876) *Sc. and N.*, warden 1439–, church-master
  1484–1566 + 1886*dial.*, churchwarden 1494–, churchman
  1523–1598, herenach 1607– *Irish*, chapelwarden 1688–1834
                                              XR R3.2.12.4. Ostiary
                                              R3.4.1. Caretaker
.assistant to: questman 1454–a1656 + 1732–*hist.*, sideman
  1570–1682, swornman 1571–1582, sidesman 1632–
.Jewish: warden 1879–
.office of: churchwardenship 1611–(1868)
.rule of: churchwardenism 1865– *contempt.*
                                        XR R5.3.9. Churchwardenism
Clerk: *cleric*/clerk OE(L)–a1555
Deacon: *see R3.2.11.0. Lay deacon*
Elder: priest 1382–1582, senior 1382–1582, ruling elder 1593–,
  lay-elder 1594–1827, presbyter 1597–1852, ?lay-presbyter
  a1663(1), presbyter-bishop 1903(1)
.female: presbyteress 1651–1682
.Methodist chief: presiding elder 1831–
.pl/coll: lay-presbytery 1640(1)
..Mormon: the seventy 1861(1)
                                        XR R4.5.3.1. Missionary
.office of: lay-eldership 1641(1), ruling eldership 1891(1)
.Jewish tradition of: deuterosy a1641–1650
Evangelist: evangelist 1382–
                                        XR R4.5.1. Evangelist
Fontwife: font-wife 1569(1)
Lay-reader: scripture-reader ?1854–, lay-reader 1883(1)
                                        XR R4.2.4.1. Celebrant
Overseer: overseer 1785–
Parish clerk: parish clerk c1386–, clerk parishenant 1534(1),
  church-clerk 1535 + a1825*dial.*, clerk 1549–, town-clerk
  1597–1879, lay-clerk 1877–
                                        XR R3.4.1. Sexton
.office of: parish-clerkship 1513(1)
.char of: parish-clerkly 1886(1)

Parnas: see *R3.4.0. Parnas*
Pew-opener: pew-keeper 1742(1), pew-opener 1782–(1853),
   pew-woman *nf* 1810(1), pew-shutter 1886(1)
Preacher: see *R3.2.10. Lay preacher*
Reader: *meterædere*
Rector: see *R3.2.3. Lay rector*
Sacristan: *mæslere*, sacristan ?1483–, sacrist 1577/87–(1883),
   secretine 1607(1)
.female: sacristan c1440 + 1896, sacristine 1832(1), sacristaness
   1866 + 1924
Sexton: sexton 1303–, sacristan c1375–(1870), segerston
   1391–1637, secriston 14..–1537, sagarston 1575/6–1687,
   dog-whipper 1592–(1888), knoller 1611 + 1877, dog-flogger
   1806(1), *fossor* 1854 + 1877 *early ch.*
                                       XR R3.4.1. Parish clerk
.assistant to: under-sexton c1450–(1829)
.female: sextress / sextrice a1400–1476, sexton c1400–c1475,
   sextoness c1420–
.Jewish: *shamas(h) / shammes / shammos* 1650–
.office of: sextonship 1511/12–, sextonry 1525(1), sextoncy
   1831(1)
Slaughterer: porger 1864–, *shochet* 1889–
                                       XR R4.9.0. Ceremonial cleanness
Teacher: teacher 1834(1)
Tract-distributor: walker 1846(1), *colporteur* 1862 + 1865
Verger: verger 1472/3–, vergerer 1566–1676, virgerer 1581–1663,
   virgifer 1629(1), virger 1671–1832, wandsman 1865–
                                       XR R3.4.1. Sexton
.office of: vergerership 1485(1), vergership 1485–
.(of xp:)unaccompanied by: vergerless 1886(1)
.action of: virging 1926–
..to perform: verge *vi* 1900–, virge *vt* 1975–
Vesturer: *hræglweard*, vesterer 1388(1), vestiarier c1440(1),
   vesturer 1779–
Vestryman: vestry-keeper 1611–1706, vestryman 1614–
.chief: arch-vestryman 1859(1)
.char of: vestrymanly 1865(1)
Virgin: virgin *nf* c1200–

XR R1.7.0. Devotee

Widow: widow 1572–, widowist 1593 (1)

XR R1.7.0. Devotee

.male: widower 1587–1610

R3.4.2. Lay brother/sister general: converse 14..–1691,
convert 1577(1), oblat 1693–1706, *conversus* 1777–1863,
donate 1804–, oblate 1864–
Lay brother: lewd frere c1380–1530, lay-brother ?14..–(1865),
convert brother 1693(1)
.Jesuit: secular 1641(1)
Lay sister: half-sister 1482(1), convert sister 1639(1), lay-sister
1709–(1825)

R3.4.3. Lay association
Apostolate: apostolate 1897–
Confraternity: confraternity c1475–
.arch-: archconfraternity 1636–
Congregation: congregation 1488–1530 + 1706*hist.*
.member of: congregationist 1848–
Doctrinarians: Doctrinarians *npl* 1747–(1794)
Fellowship-meeting: fellowship-meeting 1679 + 1806
Fraternity: *ferræden*, fraternity c1330–
Ladies' Aid: Ladies' Aid (Society) 1873–
Oratory: oratory 1644–
Pax Romana: Pax Romana 1957–
Piarist: Piarist 1842–
Sepulchrer: sepulchrer 1537(1), knight of Holy Sepulchre 1590–
Sodality: sodality 1600–
.member of: sodalist 1794–
Third Order: Third Order 1629–
.member of: tertiary a1550–
.char of: tertiary 1891–

R4.1. Worship

R4.1.0. Worship: *arweordung, begang, begangol, bigenge, greting, lof, lofbære, lofherung, lofung, ongang, samodhering, bigeng*/bigeng OE–c1175, *weordung*/worthing OE–a1327, *bletsung*/blessing OE + 1382–a1586, holiness c1205(2), (divine) service c1205–1749, reverence c1290–1340, God's service a1300–1535, shrift a1300–a1400, worship a1300–, worshipping 1303–, serving a1310(1), anour c1314 + c1330, devotion 1340–, magnifying 1382(1), praisings *npl* 1382–1561, the calves of our lips 1382 + 1629, glory 1382–(179.), worshipfulness a1400–, praise 14..–, veneration 1432/50–, ?serve c1440(1), culture 1483(1), thanksgiving 1533–(1842), common service 1534(1), adoration 1543–, reverencing 1561(1), public service 1597(1), cult 1617–1683, *cultus* 1640(1), doxology 1649 + 1660, glorifying 1746/7(1), feasting 1840(1), -(o)latry 1848– *comb. form*

XR R1.7.0. Piety

.p char by: *gebedmann, bigenga, bigengere, bigengestre (nf), bydla, weordere, wiordegend, herger*/heryer OE–1382, louter a1340(*2q1s*), honourer a1340 + 1563, worshipper c1380–, fearer 1535–1844, votaress *nf* 1589–, sectary 1591–1800, adorer 1602–(1850), praiser 1610–1765, thanksgiver 1621–, theophile c1645(1), theophilist 1677(1), church-goer 1687–, votary ?a1690–, sacricolist 1727(1), *bhakta* 1828– *Hindi*

XR R1.7.0. Devotee
R3.4.0. Congregant

..who has seat in church: sitter 1838(1), pew-holder 1845–1887, pew-renter 1885(1)

XR R5.7.8.1. Pew

...fellow: pewfellow c1524–1673, pew-mate 1596(1)
..who attends church once on Sunday: oncer 1892–
..who attends church twice on Sunday: twicer 1902–1904
..who attends a tabernacle: tabernacler 1810(1)
..quorum of required for formal Jewish worship: minyan 1753–

.char of: devote a1340–1839, devout a1340–, devotionary

1631–1808, adorative 1637(1), devotional 1648–, doxological
1655–

.char by: worshipping 1760/72–, venerant 1846(1)

XR R1.7.0. Pious

..fervently: *domhwæt*

..together: *samodherigendlic*

..not: worshipless 1765(1), unworshipping 1828 + 1906,
unworshipful 1862 + 1893

.(of x:)worthy of: *arfull, arweordlic,* blessed / blest c1230–,
venerable 1504–, adorable 1611–1794, worshipable 1840–,
worshipful 1872–

..condition of being: adorability 1637–1832, adorableness
1806(1), worshipability 1812(1)

.in manner of: reverendly c1375–1635, reverently 1382–(1635),
devotionally 1668–, reverentially 1834(1), doxologically
1891(1)

.(of x:)in manner worthy of: adorably 1806(1)

.to perform: *+arweordian v, began(gan) v, gebiddan v, breman v,
domian v, +eadmed(i)an v, healdan v, lof beran / hebban /
ræran / reccan / wyrcan vphr, lofian v, loflæcan v, +miclian
v, toweordian v, +wuldrian v, weordian*/worth *vt* OE–c1250,
herigan/hery *vt* OE–1622, *+bletsian*/bless *vt* OE–,
halgian/hallow *vt* OE–, worship *vt* c1200–, anoure *vt*
c1250–a1400, shrive *vi* a1300–a1400, serve *vt* a1300–1702,
praise *vt* a1300–, adore *vt* 1305–(1860), glorify *vt* 1340–,
reverence *vt* a1350–, enorn *vt* c1375(1), magnify *vt* 1382–1535
+ 1864, sacre *vt* 1390(1), fear *vt* a1400–, laud *vt* c1440–1812,
embrace *vt* 1490(1-*Caxton*), elevate *vt* 1513(1), laud and bless
vphr 1526(1), reverent *vt* 1565(1), adore *vi* 1582–(1843), god
vt 1595–, venerate *vt* 1623–, thanksgive *vt* a1638(1),
congratule *vt* 1657(1), doxologize *vt* a1816(1)

XR R1.6.0. To bless

..together: *samodherian v,* coadore *v* 1607–a1711

..wrongly: forworship *vi* c1380(1), misworship *vt* a1656(1)

.lack of: unworship 1860(1)

.object of: fear 1561(1), worship 1621(1), chaitya 1875– *Buddhist,* chorten 1891– *Buddhist*

R4.1.1. Kind of worship general: cult 1679–, *cultus*
  1838–(1865)
.abundant: *lofmægen*
.of ancestors: zemeism 1902–
..char of: zemeistic 1903/4(1)
.of angels: angelolatry 1847 + 1879
                                        XR R4.1.1. Dulia
.of animals: brute-worship 1738(1), zoolatry 1817–, therolatry
  1873(1), theriolatry 1897(1)
..p char by: zoolater 1891(1)
..char by: zoolatrous 1891–
.of the ass: onolatry 1903–
.of babies: baby-worship 1894(1)
.of bread: artolatry 1626–1658, bread-worship 1641(1)
                            XR R4.2.4.2. Transubstantiation
                                R5.15.5.1. Wafer-god
..p char by: bread-worshipper 1574(1), artolater 1626(1)
.of a brother: brother-worship 1864(1)
.of bulls: taurolatry 1901(1)

.conjoint: coadoration 1637(1)
.of the Cross: staurolatry 1649 + 1684
..p char by: *rodbigenga, rodwurðiend,* staurolatrian 1600(1)
.of the dead: necrolatry 1826–
.of deity/deities: theolatry 1806–(1887)
..of other/strange deities: allotheism 1660–1863
.of the earth: geolatry 1860–
.of the external world: externalism 1874(1)
.resulting from fear: fear-worship 1849–
.of fire: pyrolatry 1669–, fire-worship 1774(1)
                            XR R2.3.10.0. Zoroastrianism
..p char by: pyrolater 1801(1), ignicolist 1816 + 1859

.of heavenly bodies: zabaism 1669–1775, astrolatry 1678 + 1877,
  sabaism 1727–, sabianism 1788–(1871), uranotheism 1801(1),
  zabianism 1845(1), star-worship 1860(1), uranolatry 1877(1),

planetolatry 1964(1)
..p char by: zabian 1614(1), zabaist 1662(1), sabian 1716 + 1864,
    star-worshipper 1860(1)
..char by: zabian 1748(1)
.of humanity: *manweorðung,* anthropolatry 1658 + 1813, positive
    religion 1864(1), positivism 1866(1)
..p char by: positivist 1854–
..char by: positivist 1858–, humanitarian 1861(1), positivistic
    1875–
.of inanimate object: fetishism / fetichism 1801–
..p char by: fetishist/-ichist 1845–
.indirect: relative *a* 1660–
.joyful: joy a1300–1483
.of a locale: topolatry 18..(1)

.of martyrs: martyrolatry 1889–
                        XR R4.12.0. Martyrdom
.of nature: nature-worship 1850–, physiolatry 1860–, physitism
    1885(1), naturism 1886–(1891)
..p char by: physiolater 1882(1)
.of Negroes: negro-worship 1861(1), negrolatry 1862(1)
.of the phallus: phallus-worship 1850(1), phallism 1879(1),
    phallicism 1884–
                        XR R2.3.3.1. Sivaism
                        R5.17.1.2. Phallus
.private: parlour-worship 1623(1)
.of hereditary ruler: ruler-cult 1928– *antiq.*
.of saints: *dulia* 1617–(1865), duly 1674(1)
                        XR R1.6.1.0. Hagiolatry
                        R4.1.1. Angelolatry
..p char by: sancticolist 1615(1)
..char of: dulian 1635(1)
..in manner of: dulically 1617(1)
.of self: autolatry a1625 + 1866–
.of serpents: ophiolatry 1862–
..p char by: ophiolater 1895(1)
..char of: ophiolatrous 1887(1)
.of stones: *stanwurðung,* litholatry 1891(1)

.of the sun:
..char of: heliolithic 1915–
..and Noah's ark:
...char of: helioarkite 1804 + 1838
.supreme: latria 1526–(1859)
..char of: latrial 1550(1), latreutical 1627–1833, latrian 1635(1),
    latreutic 1845(1)

.of trees: *treowweorðung*, tree-worshipping 1840(1), tree-worship
    1860(1), tree-cultus 1871(1), dendrolatry 1891(1), tree-cult
    1905(1)
.of virgin: parthenolatry 1818(1), virgin-worship 1848(1)
..Mary: hyperdulia 1530–, Mariolatry 1612–
...p char by: Mariolater 1861(1)
...char of: hyperdulical 1664(1), Mariolatrous 1844–, hyperdulic
    1846(1)
.of water: water-worship 1871(1)
..p char by: water-worshipper 1871(1)
.of wells: well-worshipping 1810(1), well-worship 1810–
..char by: well-worshipping 1892(1)
.according to one's will: will-worship 1549–, will-worshipping
    1571(1), wit-worship a1629–1641
..p char by: will-worshipper 1660(1)
.of women: gynæcolatry 1888(1)
.wrong: misworship 1626 + 1840, misworshipping 1647(1)
..p char by: misworshipper 1640(1)

R4.1.2.0. **Ritual general:** *ciricnytt, gield, godcundnes, halignes,
    ðeaw, ðenest, gewuna,* use c1380–, divine 1480 + 1606, liturgy
    1640–, ritual 1649–, action 1825–, *opus Dei* 1887–, *Li* 1912–*
.instance of: *æ, endebyrdnes, halig, geriht(e), geryne, sidu, ðeaw,
    ðenung, ðeowdom,* service ?a1100–, church a1175–,
    observance a1225–, rite c1315–, office a1340–, sermonyal
    c1380(1), ceremony c1380–(1856), prayer(s) 1382–(a1866),
    use 1382–, ordinance 1388–, order c1400–, worshipping
    1450/1530–1674, ordinary 1494–, preaching 1508–1523 +
    1837–1861, common prayer 1526–, form 1526–, church service
    a1555–, exercise 1560/1–(1880), common service 1580(1),

right 1590–, liturgy c1593–, worship 1604–, celebrity
1609–1774, function 1640–, rituality 1654(1), ceremonial
1672/9–, hierurgy 1678–a1740, church-office 1698(1), occasion
1789–1900, religiosity 1834(1), *cursus* 1865(1), joss-pidgin
a1889–

..pl/coll: *halignes,* sacres 1542–1548, common prayers
1549/52–1631, obsequy 1550–1605, orgia 1570/6–(1830),
orgies 1598–, holies 1613(1), sacreds 1624–1749, ephemeries
1650(1), rituals a1656–, religions 1667 + 1900, officials
1768(1), ritual 1906–

.performance of: *weofoddenung,* solemnity c1290–, solemnty
1303–1382, observance c1380–, solemnization 1447–,
solennization c1450(1), solemnation 1470/85–1656,
superstition 1513(1), solemnizing 1565–, celebration 1580–,
solemnize 1590(1), solemniation 1603–1658, officiating
1651/61(1), exercitation 1655/60–1828, exercise 1658–(1781),
officiation 1798–, ritual 1867–

..frequent: frequentation 1626 + 1887
..by more than one p: concelebration 1847–
...to perform: concelebrate *vt* 1879(1)

..p perf: ecclesiast c1386(1), ministrator 1523(1), server 1530–,
solemnizer 1577–1706, exhibent 1658(1), liturge 1737(1),
officiator 1830–, celebrant 1839–, officiant 1844–, liturgist
1848 + 1890

> XR R3.2.0. Clergyman
> R3.2.2.1. Mass priest
> R3.4.1. Lay reader

...twice on Sunday: twicer 1679(1)
..char of: solemnizing 1614–, conficient 1629(1), officiating 1651–,
ministering 1654(1), liturgistical 1889(1)
...while in chancel: chancelled 1683(1)
..char by: celebrate 1471–1564, celebrated 1586(1), solemnized
1641(1), officiative 1653(1)

.meeting for: collect 1382 + 1725–1728, collection 1609–, synaxis
1624–, prayer-meeting 1831–, holiness meeting 1892(1)

> XR R3.4.0. Congregation

..**clandestine:** conventicle 1526–, conventicling 1626–1717
...**char of:** conventicling 1683–a1715, conventicular 1847–(1864),
     conventical 1872(1)
...**in manner of:** conventically 1840(1)
...**to hold/frequent:** conventicle *vi* 1659–1680
..**Collegian:** college 1727/51–1764
                                              XR R2.2.5. Collegian
..**in open air:** field-meeting 1649 + 1818–*hist.*, field-conventicle
     1678–a1806, camp-meeting 1809–1842
...**p attending:** field-meeter 1680(1), field-conventicler 1680–1687,
     camper 1806 + 1883
....**pl/coll:** field-separation 1680(1-*Sc.*)
...**to hold/frequent:** field-conventicle *vi* 1680(1)
..**Quaker:** Quaker('s)-meeting 1751–1861, sitting 1841(1)
                                              XR R3.4.0. Settlement

.**time of:** service-time c1440–(1818), service-while 1573 + 1673,
     song-tide 1853(1)
..**joining of several at convenient time:** accumulation 1865(1)

.**rule/direction concerning:** rubric c1375–, ceremonial
     1382–1621, rubrish c1386–1547, ordinary 1494–1655 +
     a1832–, cautel 1541–1641 + 1886, agend(a/s) 1629–1775
                                              XR R5.16.1. Directory *et. seq.*
..**referring to ornaments:** ornaments rubric 1872–
..**char of:** rubrical a1754–
..**(of x:)in accordance with:** rubrically 1696–

..**liberal attitude to:** enlargement 1648–(1870)
..**conformity to:** uniformity 1549–, rubricity 1876 + 1885
...**slavish:** formalizing a1656(1), rituality 1679–1683 + 1974,
     ritualism 1843–, ecclesiolatry 1847–, externalness 1667 +
     dicts., ceremonialism 1854–, externalism 1856–(1879),
     formalism 1856–, externality 1860(1), rubricism 1862 + 1978,
     exteriority a1875–, liturgism 1926–, spikery 1965–
                                              XR R1.7.1. Sanctimoniousness
....**p char by:** formalist 1609–, ritualist 1677–, ceremonialist
     1682–, formalizer a1734(1), rubrician 1843–, rubricist 1857 +
     1902, rit 1878–1909, externalist 1879(1), spike 1902–

XR R4.1.2.1. Trinketer
.....**not:** anticeremonian a1644–1657, anticeremonialist 1865(1)
....**char of:** ceremonious 1553(1), ritualistic 1850–, formalistic
1856(1), spikey 1893–
.....**not:** anticeremonial 1655 + 1668
....**to bring under influence of:** directorize *vt* 1651 + 1659,
ritualize *vt* 1847 + 1894, ceremonialize *vt* 1858(1), formalize
vt 1866–
....**to practise:** ritualize *vi* 1842 + 1892, spike up *vt* 1923–

..**restoration of lay participation in:** liturgical movement
1929–
..**study of:** liturgics *npl* 1855–, liturgiology 1863–
XR R1.5.2. Liturgics
...**p pursuing:** liturgist 1649–1812, ritualist 1657–, liturgiologist
1866–, liturgician 1889(1)
...**char of:** liturgical 1849(1), liturgiological 1887–

.**char of:** *symbellic,* solemn a1340–, ceremonial 138.–, solemny
c1420–c1450, solem 1432/50–1570, solemned c1450–1564 *Sc.,*
solemnel 1471–1647, solemnly 1482(1), ceremonious 1555–,
solennit 1562(1), ritual 1570–, rituous 1604(1), ceremonical
a1626–1661, liturgical 1641–, liturgic 1656–, levitical
1670(1-*Milton*), hierurgical 1725/44(1), sacral 1882–
..**condition of being:** solemness 1530–, ceremoniality 1621–1660,
ceremonialness a1679(1)
XR R2.1.1. Leviticalism
..**according to Pope Gelasius:** Gelasian *a* a1773–
..**not:** unliturgical 1868(1), aliturgical 1872–
..**parallel to:** paraliturgical 1977–
..**destitute of:** riteless c1611–
..**(of day:)on which R is not celebrated:** aliturgic 1898(1)
..**converted into:** ritualized 1932–

.**in manner of:** *symbellice, gewunelice,* solemnly a1300-, solemny
c1375–a1470, solenly 1393–c1400, solenny 1480–1485, ritely
1560–1675, solemniously a1578 + 1910, ceremoniously
1596–1791, ritually 1612–, ceremonially 1643–, liturgically
1864–, ritualistically 1870 + 1886

.to perform: *+breman v, +mærsian v, đeowian v,*
   weordian/worth *vt* OE–c1250, *weorcan*/work *vt* OE–c1460,
   serve *vt* c1175–(1819), serve *vi* c1200–1691, minister *vi*
   c1330–(1855), solemnize *vt* 1382–, exercise *vt* a1400–1807,
   solennize *vt* c1440–1588, officy *vt* c1449(1), office *vt*
   c1449–1502, execute *vt* 1450–1737, solemn *vt* 1483–1555,
   observe *vt* 1526–, solemnizate *vt* 1538–1585, exercise *vi*
   1561–1663, celebrate *vt* 1564–(1840), frequent *vt* 1565–1581,
   adore *vi* 1582–(1843), officiate *vt* 1631–, ceremony *vt*
   1635–1656, put up *vt* 1641–, ceremonize *vi* 1653–1663, liturgy
   vt 1716(1), liturgize *vi* 1826(1)
..again: resolemnize *vt* 1621 + 1654/66
.to assist p performing: serve *vt* 1393–
.(of R:)to take place: stand *vi* 1649–(a1868) *Sc.*

R4.1.2.1. Kinds of rite
Annual: *geardenung*
Benedictional: benediction 1812–

XR R4.1.6.1. Salut

in Chapel: chapel 1662–
Clandestine: *see R4.1.2.1. Mysteries*
Early Christian: love-feast 1580–, *agape* 1607–(1850)
.Methodist version of: love-feast 1738–
.p participating in: love-feaster 1749/51(1)
Daily: *dægsang*
Heathen general: *godgield, hædengield,* puppetry 1528–1549,
   superstition a1529–(1849), orgies *npl* 1589–, orgion 1613(1),
   orgy 1665–, fetish / fetiche 1705–1828, orgiacs *npl* a1859(1)

XR R1.1.11.0. Paganism

.p participating in: orgiast 1791/3(1)
Hindu: pooja / puja 1681–, s(h)raddha 1787–
in Home: house church 1964–
Initiatory: initiatory 1675(1), initiation ceremony / rite 1899–
Jewish: *kaddish* 1613 + 1876–, *mincha* 1819–, *tashlik / -lich*
   1880–(1902)
.for Passover: *Haggadah* 1733–

XR R4.1.5.2.2. Passover

performed as Military duty: church parade 1846–
Monastic: *mynsterđegnung*
Morning: morning service 1657–(1862)
Pontifical: pontifical 1691(2), pontificality 1840–
Private: exercise 1592–(1825)

> XR R4.1.2.0. Conventicle

Propitiatory: expiation a1627(1)

> XR R4.8.2. Expiation

Public: exercise 1574–(1888)
Roman Catholic: trinkets 1538–1655, baggage 1549–1587,
    trinkums 1699(1), trinklets 1897(1) *all derog.,* Roman 1882(2)
.attributed to St Peter: Petrine liturgy 1865(1)
Roman stational: station c1410–a1502 *hist.*
.day of: station-day 1563/83–(1898)
.time of: station time 1387–1643
.char of: stationary 1626–, stational 1826–
.to perform: go / make / perform one's stations *vphr* a1445–, go
    on / for stations *vphr* 1574–1702
Salisbury: Sarum Use 1570–
.char of: Sarum 1832–
Secret: mysteries 1643–(1849)
Snake: snake ceremony 1959(1)
Superstitious: mumming 1528–1565, trumpery 1542/5–1824,
    trumperies 1548–1704, mummery 1549–1864

> XR R1.1.9. Superstition

.char of: mummish 1563(1)
Toy: toy-service 1889(1)
of Thanksgiving: thanksgiving 1641–(1869)
Week's: *wucđenung*

R4.1.3. Part of service general:
.amplificatory: farse 1842–
..to employ: farse *vt* 1857–, farce *vt* 1857–

Processional: processional 1882/3(1)

> XR R4.1.4.1.1. Processional

Salutation: salutation 1450/1530 + 1832–
Invitatory: invitatory 1450/1530–, invitory 1483–1563/87,

invitatorium 1853(1), invitation 1883(1)
Introit: introit 1483–, office 1548/9–

Confiteor: *confiteor* a1225–
.phrase from: *mea culpa* c1374–
Kyrie: *cyrriol, halsung, kyrielle* ?a1225(1-*Ancrene Riwle, kyrie eleison / eleëson* 13..–
.musical setting of: miserere ?c1620(1)
Absolution: *misereatur* c1450–a1470 + 1845
Gloria: *gloria*/gloria OE(L) + c1420–
Comfortable words: the comfortable words 1855 + 1893

Reading: *ræde, ræding, rædo,* lesson a1225–, chapter 1450/1530–, lecture 1526–1849, lection 1608–, pericope 1695–, *capitulum* 1753 + 1885
XR R1.2.1.1.0. Text
.char of: pericopic 1888(1)
Old Testament lesson: prophecy c1440 + 1853–, parashah ?1624– *Jewish,* prophet 1832(*2q1s*), prophetic lesson 1872(1)
.for 3rd week of Lent: pistle of (sweet) Susan 1380/1400–c1425

Versicle: *fers*/verse OE(L)–, verset a1225–1641 + 1844*hist.,* versicle a1380–, stichos 1863– *GkCh*
.action of singing/saying: versling a1225(1)
..to perform: versle *vi/t* a1225–c1330, versicle *vi* 1550(1)
Response: *reps (L), respons*/response OE(L) + 1659–, respond c1555–, responsor a1649(1), responsory a1649(1), responsal a1652–1753 + 1893, *cathisma* 1850 +1880 *GkCh*
XR R4.1.4.1.1. Responsory
.char of: responsory 1641 + 1659, responsorial 1842 + 1872
.char by: responsive 1778–

Epistle: *pistolræding,* pistle c1175–1590, epistle c1440–
XR R1.2.1.2.3.3. Epistle
R3.2.11.2. Epistoler
.char of: epistolary 1722(1)

Alleluia: *graðul, alleluia*/alleluia OE–, grail 13..–, sequence 1387–, prose c1449–, gradual 1563/83–, sequency 1641(1), gradale a1746(1)
XR R4.1.4.1.1. Tract

.char of: hallelujous 1645(1), halleujatic a1818 + 1888, alleluiatic
   1844 + 18..

Gospel: *godspel*/gospel (for / of the day) OE–
                                   XR R1.2.1.2.3.1. Gospel
                                   R3.2.11.0. Deacon
Long prayer: long prayer 1897(1)
                                   XR R4.3.1. Pulpit-prayer
Homily: *cwiðe, folclar, godspell traht, lar, spell, larspell*/lorespell
   OE–13.., sermon a1200–, prone a1670–1716 + 1897
.bell indicating: sermon-bell 1646–1807

Creed: *mæssecreda*/mass-creed OE–1563/83, *credo* c1175–
                                   XR R1.1.1.0. Creed

Collect: *samnungcwiðe, collecta*/collect OE(L) + a1225–, suffrage
   c1380–1681 + 1865–, suffrages of prayers 1447–c1613,
   intercession 1508–, suffrages 1532–, *preces* 1511 + 1844–,
   bid-prayer 1691(1), bidding prayer 1753–
                                   XR R4.3.1. Deprecation

Antecommunion: ante-communion 1827–, preparation 1855–,
   pre-communion 1868(1)
.prayers used during: preparation 1650–
Offertory: *lacsang*, oblation c1450–, offertory 1539–
.hymn during: *see* R4.1.4.1.1. Offertory anthem, *Offringsang*
.washing of celebrant's hands during: lotion 1529–, *lavabo*
   1858–, lavatory 1896(1)
                                   XR R4.1.3. Lavatory (at post-communion)
                                   R4.9.1. Purification
.to mix water and wine in chalice during: make the chalice
   vphr ?1540–

Secreta: secre 1297–a1400, secret 1387–, secreta 1753–

Communion ceremony: communion 1552–1575, the usages
   1718–, communion office 1721(1), communion service 1827(1)
                                   XR R4.2.4.0. Eucharist / communion
Preface: preface 1387–, illation 1863(1)
.Sursum corda: Sursum corda 1959–
Sanctus: sanctus c1380–, tersanctus 1832–

.part of: *hosanna*/hosanna OE–
..to sing/say: hosanna *vt* 1697–
.bell indicating: sanctus bell 1479/81–(1875), saucing bell
    1600(1)
Benedictus: *Benedictus* 1880(1)

Ordinary: ordinary 1494–
Contestation: contestation 1727/41 + 1863 *Gallican*
.char of: pro-anaphoral 1850–

Canon: *swimæsse*/swimesse OE–c1200, canon a1300–, anaphora
    1744–
.first prayer of: *te igitur* 1819–
.part of, in which Christ's sacrifice is recalled: anamnesis
    1894–
.part of, mentioning the living: *famulorum* c1380–1401
.part of, commemorating the dead: memento 1401–
.other parts of: fellowship 1389–1583, embolism 1720–,
    embolismus 1872(1), epiclesis 1878–(1966)
.elevation in: levation c1375–1559, elevation 1563/87–
.ostension in: ostension 1607–
.action of breaking host in: fraction 1602–
..to perform: *husl tobrecan vphr*, break bread *vphr* 1382–
.mixing of bread and wine in: immission 1846 + 1877,
    commixture 1850–, commixtion 1872(1), intinction 1872–
                         XR R4.2.4.1.0. Mass
.doxology in: doxologue a1617(1), glorification 1660–, doxology
    1664–

Kiss of peace: *sibbecoss,* mass-kiss c1200–c1300, pax c1440–1568
    + 1853, peace 1565(1)
Agnus Dei: Agnus Dei 1400–, Agnus 1494–1674
.bell indicating: agnus-bell 1566(1)

Postcommunion: post-common a1380–1683 + 1879–,
    post-communion 1483–
.char of: post-communion 1890–
.cleaning of chalice during: rinsing c1375 + c1425, purification
    1853(1)
..to perform: rinse *va* c1375–c1425, purify *vt* 1858–

.**cleaning of celebrant's hands during:** lavatory
a1512–1563/87, lotion 1529–
XR R4.1.3. Lavatory (at offertory)
R4.9.1. Purification
Closing benediction: benediction 1549–(1856)
Return of clergy to vestry: retrocession 1877(*2q1s*)
XR R4.1.4.1.1. Recessional
.**char of:** recessional 1867–, retrocessional 1897(1)

R4.1.4.0. Service music general: mass 1597–, church music
1644/6–, service 1691–, sacred music *no quots.*

Church-singing: *ciricsang, sang,* chantry c1340(1), cantillation
1864– *Jewish*
.**char of:** sung 1526–, chanted 1649–1841
.**to engage in:** +*singan*/sing *vt* OE–, sing *vi* 1297–(1599), chant *vi*
c1440–, chant *vt* 1526–, cantillate *vt* 1864(1)

Setting out hymn for congregation: lining (out) 1863–
.**to perform:** set *vt* c1450–1742, tune *vt* 1667–1679 + 1895*hist.,*
line (out) *v* 1853–, list *vt* 1857(1)
..**as precentor:** take up *vphr* 1577–1825 *Sc.,* precent *vi* 1732–,
precent *vt* 1872–
XR R3.2.13. Precentor
..**as succentor:** succent *vt/i* 1880–
XR R3.2.13. Succentor
Continuous singing of hymn/psalm: run line 1873 + 1888 *Sc.*
To worship with organ music: pipe up *vt* a1546(1)

R4.1.4.1.0. Hymn: *cantic (L), canticsang, ciricsang, hleoðrung,
lof, ymensang, lofsang*/lofsong OE–c1320, *sealm*/psalm
OE–(1838), *ymen*/hymn OE–, canticle c1250–, cantic(k)
1483–1669, hymnic a1834(1), spiritual 1870–, kirtan 1898–
Hindi, bhajan 1914– *Hindi*
.**pl/coll:** hymnody 1864 + 1882/3

.**stanza of:** stanza 1674–
..**of four lines:** long metre 1718(1)

..model: hirmos 1850– *GkCh*
..short: troparion 1850–(1876)*GkCh*

.antiphonal refrain to: antiphon 1775–, trope 1846–(1894), *ephymnium* 1910(1-*GkCh*)

.char of: spiritual 1382–1660 + 1905, hymnish 1583(1), hymnic 1589–, hymnal 1644–
.(of p:)singing: *ymensingende,* hymning 1674 + 1874

.the singing of: hymnology a1638–(1855), hymning 1667(1), hymnody a1711–
..p char by: hymner 1816–
..to perform: hymn *vt* 1667–, hymn *va* 1715/20–

.composition of: hymnody a1711–, hymnology 1839 + 1879
XR R4.1.4.3.0. Psalmody
..p char by: hymnographer a1619–, hymnist 1621–, hymnodist a1711 + 1883, hymnologist 1796 + 1889, laudist 1890(1)

.study of: hymnology 1818–, hymnography 1864 + 1886
..p char by: hymnologist 1882/3(1)
..char of: hymnological 1882 + 1888, hymnologic 1883(1)
..in manner of: hymnologically 1892(1)

R4.1.4.1.1. Kinds of hymn
Anthemic: *capitol/-ul(a) (L), antefn (L),* anthem c1386–
.for Advent: O's (of Advent) 1729–, olerie 1892(1)
.for offertory: *offerenda (L),* offertory c1386–, offertory sentence 1724(1)
XR R4.1.3. Offertory
.for Septuagesima: tract 1387–(1877), tractus a1450–(1854)
XR R4.1.3. Alleluia
.responsory: *reps (L),* respond 1387–, respoun(d) c1400–1466, responsory 1432/50–, response 1450/1530–, responsary c1557–(1866), responsive 1855(1)
XR R4.1.3. Respond
..char of: hypophonous 1860(1), hypophonic 1882/3(1)
..in manner of: responsorially 1901–

.verse: verse anthem 1801–, verse service 1851–
..part of: verse 1801(1)
.action of singing: antheming 1829–
..to perform: anthem *vt* 1628 + a1821, anthemize *vt* 1837(1)

Antiphonal: *antefn (L),* antiphon 1500 + 1635–(1876), antiphony
  1868(1)
.used from Trinity Sunday to Advent: salve 1428–1888
.for Good Friday: improperia *npl* 1880–, reproaches *npl* 1884–

Apollonian: hyporcheme/-ema 1603 + 1873
XR R4.1.4.1.1. Io pæan

Benedictional: *bletsingsealm, benedictus* 1552 + 1641, *benedicite*
  c1661(1), prophecy 1872– *Gallican*

Cantata: cantata 1724–
Christmas: carol 1502–
Dawn: *antelucano* 1656(1)
Easter: Exultand 1519(1), *Exultet* 1869–
Invocatory: trisagion 1387–(1894)
Joyful: carol a1547–1830, mirth-song 1561(1)
Long: canon 1862(1-*OrthCh*)
Mealtime: *beodfers*
Motet: motet 1597–, *motetto* 1644–
Negro (American): (Negro) spiritual 1866–
Nunc dimittis: *nunc dimittis* 1552–
Offertory: *lacsang, offringsang,* offertory c1386–
XR R4.1.4.1.1. Offertory anthem
R4.1.4.3.1. Offerenda

Office: office hymn 1907–
Paraphrase: paraphrase 1745–
Praising: *herigendsang, herung*/herying OE–c1420, alleluia 1382–,
  laud 1530–, hallelujah 1535–, contakion 1866(1-*GkCh*),
  theody 1867(1-*Longfellow*)
.performance of: *lofsingende*
Processional: walking hymn 1599(1), prosode 1777(1), *prosodion*
  1850–, processional 1884–
XR R4.1.3. Processional

.char of: processional 1827–, prosodiac 1850(1), prosodial 1874(1)

Recessional: recessional 1867(1), recessional hymn 1867(1),
   retrocessional hymn 1897(1)

XR R4.1.3. Retrocession

Scriptural: ode 1881(1)

.longest: Great canon 1850(1-*GkCh*)

Tantum ergo: *Tantum Ergo* 1709–

Thanksgiving: *te deum*/Te Deum OE(L)–, *io pæan* 1592(1),
   pæan 1603–

.char of: Te Deum 1874–

.performance of: pæanism 1669–a1827, Te-deuming 1862 + 1864
   nonce

Trinity: Triadic canon 1862(1-*GkCh*)

for Virgin Mary: magnificat c1200–(1862)

Wedding: *brydsang,* hymen 1613–1633 + 1807, hymenean
   1667(1), hymeneal 1717–(1871)

R4.1.4.2. Plainchant: plain-song 1513–, plain-chant 1727/41–,
   Gregorian chant 1751–, plain-singing 1795(1), Gregorian
   a1873(1), vesper music 1888(1)

.p advocating: Gregorianist 1884(1), Gregorianizer 1884(1),
   plain-chantist 1888(1)

.p versed in: Gregorian 1609(*2q1s*)

.verse of: single chant 1861–

.group of notes sung to one syllable in: neume c1440 +
   1879–*hist.,* neuma 1776–, pneuma 1881(1)

.part of, lying between reciting notes: mediation 1845–

.part of, sung above or below: organum 1782–

..p singing: organist 1782–1819, organizer 1880–

...char of: organizing 1876(1)

..to sing: organize *v* 1782–

R4.1.4.3.0. Psalm: *dryhtleoð, hearpsang, sang, sealmcwide,
   sealmleoð, sealmlof, sealmsang, sealm*/psalm OE–, theody
   1867(1)

XR R1.2.1.2.1.13. Psalm
R5.16.4. Music books

.pl/coll: *sealmas,* psalmody 1554/5–

..**portion of:** *sealmgetæl, saltere*/psalter OE–c1420 + 1508*Sc.*,
nocturn 1483–1548/9, *cathisma* 1850 + 1880 *GkCh*
.**refrain of:** rear-freight c1557(1)
.**translation of:** *saltere*/psalter OE–, psaltery 1822–
..**char of:** psalterian 1893(1)
.**making and reciting of:** *sealmglig, sealmsangmærsung,
sealmsang*/psalm-song OE + 1050, psalmody a1340–,
psalmistry 1535–1650
XR R4.1.4.1.0. Hymnody
..**p char by:** *sealmsangere, sealscop, sangere*/songer OE–c1200,
sealmwyrhta/psalmwright OE–a1240, lofsonger c1175(1),
psalmister 1395–1483, psalmist 1483–, psalmograph
1542–1657, psalmographer 1611–1648, psalmodist a1652–1669
+ 1886, psalm-singer 1806–
..**char of:** *lofsingende,* psalmodic 1749–, psalmodical 1795(1),
psalm-singing 1818–, psalmodial 1848(1)
..**to perform:** *salletan v (L), sealmlofian v, sealm*/psalm *vi* OE–,
psalm *vt* a1400–1622, psalmody *vi* c1450–1491 + 1850,
psalmonize *vi* 1483(1), psalmodize *vi* 1513–1817

R4.1.4.3.1. Kinds of psalm
Chanted: chant 1856–
Eucharistic: *communia (L)*
Guest: guest-psalm 1898(1)
Joyful: *wynpsalterium*
Metrical: jig 1621–1673, metre psalm 1655–(1863), singing psalms
npl 1679–1710, metrical psalm *no quots.*
.**author of:** psalmodist 1885(1)
.**tune of:** psalm-tune 1632–1856
Offertory: *offerenda (L)*
XR R4.1.4.1.1. *Offringsang*
Seven Penitentials: *sept psaumes* c1300 + c1475, penitential
psalms 1508–, penitentials 1641–1672/5
.**one of:** *miserere* a1225–(1845)
..**musical setting of:** *miserere* 1776–(1845)
Precatory: *gebedsealm*
Prose: reading psalms *npl* 1706–a1707

95th: venite a1225–, invitatory psalm a1340–1760/5
XR R5.16.4. Venitary
98th: cantate c1550 + 1880–
100th: jubilate 1706 + 1857
.tune of: Old Hundredth 1837–
113 to 118: hallel 1702– *Jewish*
120 to 124: canticle / song of grees 1382–1483, gradual psalms
npl 1656/81 + 1864–
148 to 150: *lofsealm, lofu*

R4.1.5.0. Liturgical year: year a1400–
.jubilee: jubilee 1432/50–
XR R4.2.2.3.1. Plenary indulgence
..char of: jubilary 1537(1)
.sabbatical: sabbath 1382–

R4.1.5.1. Sabbath: *haligdæg, symbeldæg, restdæg*/rest-day
OE–c1200 + 1894, *sabat*/Sabbath OE–, *sunnandæg*/Sunday
OE–, Lord's day c1175–, Sabbath-day a1300/1400–,
ceasing-day 1382(1), Dominical day 1553–(1743), Dominical
1628–1673, *Shabbos* 1876– *Jewish, Shabbat* 1934– *Jewish*
.on which communion is held: sacrament day 1687–1826,
supper-sabbath 1690(1), sacrament Sunday 1768–(1897),
sacrament Sabbath 1816–
XR R4.2.4.0. Communion
.observance of: Sabbatism 1611–(1879), Sabbatizing 1613–(1855),
Sabbath-keeping 1643–, Sabbatization 1644–(1827), Sunday
observance 1857 + 1973
XR R2.2.4.4.1. Seventh-Day Baptist
R2.2.5. Seventh-Day Adventist
..p char by: Sabbatarian 1613–(1864), Sabbath-keeper 1854(1)
..char of: Sabbatarian a1631–(1859), Sabbatarial 1867(1)
..to practise: sabbatize *vi* 1608–(1881), sabbathize *v* 1609–(1705),
sabbatize *vt* 1609–(1906)

.non-observance of: Sabbath-breaking 1651–, Sabbath-breach
1784(1), no-Sabbathism 1882/3(1)

..p char by: Sabbath-breaker 1607–(1853), antisabbatarian
  1645(1)
..char by: sabbathless 1605–1820, antisabbatarian 1656(1),
  sabbath-breaking 1714 + 1978
                                          XR R1.7.3. Impious
.conversion of Sunday into: sabbatization 1882(1)
.Jewish ceremony marking end of: *Habdalah* 1733–
.work done on: *unrihtweorc, untidweorc,* servile work 1382(1)
..p performing: *Shabbat-goy* 1859(1), *Shabbos-goy* 1892–,
  Sabbath-goy 1977–
.lamp lit on eve of: Sabbath lamp 1850–, Sabbath candle
  1892(1)
.letter used to denote (in calendar etc.): dominical letter
  1577/87–, dominical 1588 + 1686

.char of: sabbatary 1613–1674, Sabbath 1613–, dominical
  1623–(1891), sabbatarian a1631–(1859), sabbatical
  1645–(1892), sabbatic 1649–(1882), sabbathine 1850(1)
.(of x:)discontinued during: Sabbath-ceased 1593(1)
.in manner befitting: sabbathly 1891(1)

R4.1.5.2.0. **Feast, festival:** *beboddæg, freols, freolsdæg, freolstid,*
  gereorddæg, symbel, symbeldæg, symbelnes, symbeltid,
  mæssedæg/mass-day OE–c1315 + 1867, *mæsse*/mass
  OE–1452 + 1584*Sc.*, *haligdæg*/holy day OE–, *heah tid*/high
  tide OE–c1250 + 1837–, *tid*/tide OE–, *haligtid*/holy(-)tide
  OE–, high day c1200–, feast a1225–, feast-day a1300–,
  holiday a1375–, ferie 1377–1616, festival-day 1389–(1844),
  good tide / night c1420–1620, solemnity c1435–1449, feastful
  day 1447–1671, pace c1450(1), reverence c1470(1), festial
  1483–1491 + 1725, sacre a1500(1), festival 1589–,
  supplication 1606–(1753), panegyry 1641–(1894), surplice day
  1663(1), *festa* 1818–, fiesta 1844–, church-festival 1856(2)
                                          XR R4.2.4.1.0. *Mæsse*
.of anniversary of church dedication: encænia
  1387–1721/1800, dedication c1400–(1695), dedication day
  1581–1695

.**double:** *heahfreols, heafreolsdæg, heahfreolstid,* double feast a1225
   + c1500, double c1690–(1885), great day 1710(1), red-letter
   day 1776(1), privileged *pa* 1877–, greater feria *no quots.*
.**on which parish lecture is given:** lecture-day 1616–1677
.**local annual:** Wake Sunday 1884(1)
.**lasting nine days:** novendial 1600(1), novenary 1818–1855,
   novene 1826(1), novena 1853–
.**of obligation:** holiday of obligation 1885(1)
.**periodic:** church-ale 1419–1732/8 + 1875*hist.*, kirk-ale c1570(1)
.**saint's:** *gemynd,* saint's day a1450–, memorial 1492–1613 + 1866,
   memoration 1553(1), name-day a1721–, name's day 1799–,
   fête 1805–1877, hallow-day a1825 + a1829 *dial.,* calendar-day
   1847(1), *slava* 1900– *Serbo-Croatian*
                                         XR R4.2.7.3. Commemoration
..**who is martyr:** *ðrowung, ðrowingtid,* passion-day 1672(1)
..**minor:** by-saint's-day 1624(1)
..**who is patron saint:** pardon 1477–, patron-day 1710–, pattern
   1745–, patron 1890(1)
.**semi-double:** half-holiday 1552–1631, semi-double 1850–
..**char of:** semi-double 1728–, simple 1850–
.**on which thanks are offered:** Thanksgiving Day 1674–,
   harvest festival 1882–
.**lasting three days:** triduo 1848–(1871), triduum 1885–(1910)
.**pl/coll:** *gilddagas*

.**day before:** preparation day 1557–1683, preparation 1611–1625
..**observances for:** preparation 1557–1625, parasceve 1612–1654
.**eve of:** *mæsseæfen, mæsseniht,* holinight a1225–a1300, eve c1290–
                                         XR R4.2.7.2. Vigil
.**period of eight days beginning on:** octave 1883(1)
..**last day of:** octave 13..–
.**period of two weeks beginning on:** quinzième c1430–1480
..**last day of:** quinzième 1433–1480, quinzine c1450(1), quindecim
   1472/3–1802/12, quindene 1494–, quinzane 1863–

.**service common to class of:** common 1874–
.**service for particular:** proper 1548/9–
..**char of:** proper c1400–
.**study of:** heortology 1901–

..p pursuing: heortologist 1900–

.char of: *freols, freolslic, symbel, symbellic, halig*/holy OE–,
  festival 13..–, solemn c1325–a1700, feastful a1440–, festal
  1479–1847, spiritual 1490–1526, festial 1737(1)

XR R4.1.2.0. Solemn

.in manner of: *freolslice, symbellice*

XR R4.1.2.0. Solemnly

.observance of: *freolsung, gehealden, gehealdsumnes,* celebration
  1529–(1844), observance 1785–

..to perform: *healdian v, +freolsian*/frels *vt* OE–c1200,
  +halgian/hallow *v* OE–1796, hallow *va* c1200–1496, gete *vt*
  a1300(1), keep *vt* 1432/50–, observe *vt* 1526–, celebrate *vt*
  1560–, sanctify *vt* 1604–1727/41

R4.1.5.2.1. Specific Christian seasons and feasts
Advent: *tocyme, advent*/Advent OE(L)–
.char of: Adventual 1614/25–1663

Christmas Eve (24 Dec): Midwinter('s) night c1200–a1450,
  Midwinter('s) eve 1300/1400(1), Yule-night 1303–c1475 +
  1792*Sc.,* Christmas-eve a1340–, Yule-even 1375–(1808) *Sc.,*
  Midwinter('s) even c1420(1)
Christmas (25 Dec): *symbelcennes, midwinter*/Midwinter
  OE–1590, *geol dæg*/Yule-day OE–a1774 *chiefly Sc., geol*/Yule
  OE– *now arch., cristesmæsse*/Christmas OE–, Midwinter('s)
  day 1154–1387 + 1867*arch.,* Christenmass c1340–1601 +
  1855–*dial.,* Nativity c1380–, Christmas-day 138.–, Nowel
  c1450–1599, Christenmas day 1482(1), Xmas 1551–,
  Christ-tide 1589–1656, Christmas-tide 1626–1866,
  Christmas-time 1837(1)

XR R1.2.1.5. Nativity

.according to New Style: Parliament Christmas 1837(1-*hostile*)
.season: *Middewintres tid*/Midwinter('s) tide OE–c1330, Yule-tide
  c1475 + 1860, Yule-time 1787–
.char of: Christmas a1500–
.to observe: yule *vi* a1670 + 1828 *Sc. and N.*

Season of Epiphany: *gebyrdtid,* twelfth-tide 1530–1648,
    twelve-tide 1557–1568/70, twelve-days *npl* 1693–1725
.**day in:** *gebyrdtid*
Holy Innocents' Day (28 Dec): *cildamæssedæg,*
    cildamæsse/Childermas OE–, (Holy) Innocents' Day 1548/9–
                 XR R1.2.1.3. Holy innocents
                 R4.12.0. Martyrdom
Feast of the Circumcision (1 Jan): Circumcision 14..–(1782)
Twelfth-night (5 Jan): *twelfta niht*/Twelfth-night OE–, *twelfta*
    æfen/Twelfth-even OE–1634/5, Uphali(day) even 1506–1881
    Sc., Twelve-eve 1682(1)
Epiphany: *ætywnes, ætywung, bæddæg, godes sweotolung,*
    +*sweotolungdæg, twelfta dæg*/Twelfth-day OE–, Epiphany
    a1310–, Twelfth 1472(1), Uphaliday 1478–1609 + 1884*Sc.,*
    Uphalimas 1532 + 1556 *Sc.,* Tiffany a1633(1), Apparition
    1652–1703

Feast of St Hilary (14 Jan): Hilary-mass c1330(1)
Feast of St Paul's conversion (25 Jan): Conversion
    1382/8–1501
.**season of:** St Paul's tide 1701(1)
Eve of Candlemas (1 Feb): *candelmæsseæfen*
Candlemas (2 Feb): *candelmæssedæg, Maria mæsse*/Marymass
    OE–1052, *candelmæsse*/Candlemas OE–, Saint Mary Day
    c1310–c1450, Purification (of Our Lady) 1389–, Chandry
    1478(1)

Third Sunday before Lent: Septuagesima c1380–
.**70 days following:** *behreowsungtid,* Septuagesima 1387–1483
                 XR R4.2.2.1.0. Contrition
Saturday before Lent: Egg-Saturday 1607 + 1670
Sunday before Lent: Quinquages(i)me (Sunday) c1380–c1535 +
    1658, Shrove Sunday 1463–a1662 + 1843, *Quinquagesima*
    (Sunday) 1656–
.**period following:** *Quinquagesima* 1398(1)
..**char of:** quinquagesimal 1844–
..**first week of:** Quinquagesme c1380–1387, *Quinquagesima*
    1387–1612
...**Sunday - Tuesday in:** Shrove-tide c1425–, Shrovety 1544 +

1573, Carnival 1549–, Shrove 1579–1621 + 1913*dial.*,
      Fast-mass 1866(1)
....**Sunday in:** Fastingong Sunday 1450 + 1541
....**Monday in:** Shrove Monday c1450–(1837), Merry Monday
      1565(1), Fat Monday 1585(1), Shrift Monday 1587(1)
....**Tuesday in:** Faste(v)e(n) 1375–1874, Fastin-gong 1380–1530,
      Fast-gong c1440(1), Shroveday 14..(1), Shrove Tuesday
      a1500–, Shrift's even 15..(1), Shrift Tuesday 1542(1),
      Fasten(s)-Tuesday 1585 + 1858–1877, Gut-tide 1608–,
      Sharp-Tuesday 1858– *dial.*
...**to perform observances common to:** shrove *vi* 1586–a1645

Lent: *eallencten, easterfæsten, lectentima*/Lenten time OE–c1175
      + 1563*Sc., lenctentid*/Lenten tide OE + a1300 + a1572*Sc.,*
      len(c)ten/Lenten OE–1553, *lenctenfæst*/Lenten fast
      OE–1610, Lent c1290–(1861), Quadragesme c1440(1),
      Lent-season 1573(1), *Quadragesima* 1604–1665,
      Quadragesime 1612(2), Lent-time 1721(1), Shrift-time
      1853(1-*arch.*), Great Fast 1868(1)
                                    XR R4.1.5.3. Carentane
.a day in: *lenctendæg*
.a week in: *lenctenwuce*
.first day of: Ash Wednesday 1297–, Pulver Wednesday c1454(1),
      Pulvering Day 1754(1)
                                    XR R4.15. Ashes-dodding
.first Sunday in: *(ealda) halga dæg, len(c)ten,* Quadragesima
      (Sunday) 1617–1794, Feast of Orthodoxy 1727/41– *GkCh,*
      Orthodoxy Sunday 1850– *GkCh*
.char of: *lencten*/lenten OE–, quadragesimal 1629–

Lady-even (24 Mar): Lady-even 1306–a1548, Lady-eve 1603(1)
Annunciation (25 Mar): *bodungdæg,* Lady Day 1297–1665 +
      1888, Saint Mary Day c1310–c1450, Annunciation c1400–,
      Our Lady in March c1483(1), Our Lady in Lent 1608(1)
.quarter in which A occurs: Lady-quarter 1803(1), Ladytide
      1888–

Mid-Lent: *midfæsten*/Mid-fasten OE–c1205,
      midlencten/Midlenten OE + 1513, Mid-lent 1470–1667/8

.Sunday in: Midlenten Sunday 1377 + 1538*Sc.*, Phagyphany
14..(1), mid-Lent Sunday c1450–1837, mid-fast Sunday
1480(1), Sunday of Refreshment 1710(1), Refreshment
Sunday 1841–, Mothering Sunday 1845(1), Lætare(-)Sunday
1870–, Refection Sunday 1872(1)
.last Sunday in: Care Sunday 1536–a1575 *Sc.*, Carling Sunday
c1680–1825, Carl Sunday 1688–1825, Careing Sunday 1785(1)

Holy Week: Swiwike a1225(1), Passion 1297(2), Passion Week
c1400-, Great Week 1659 + 1812, Holy Week 1710–,
Passion-Tide 1847–, Maundy-Week 1868(1)
.eve of: Palmsun even 1571–c1605
.Palm Sunday in: *palmdæg, palmsunnandæg*/Palm Sunday OE–,
Sunday of the Passion 1297(1), Passion Sunday a1400–,
Fig-Sunday 1850(1), Hosanna Sunday 1868 + 1899
..char of: Palmsun 1813(1)
.Wednesday in: Good Wednesday 1471 + 1894, Holy Wednesday
1845(1)
.last 3 days of: *swigdagas*, Triduum 1883–
..one of: *swigeniht, swidæg*/swiday OE–c1200
.Thursday in: Sheer Thursday c1200–1621, Shire Thursday
c1380–c1541, Our Lord's Supper Day c1450(1), Shore
Thursday 1454–1537, Cene Thursday 1483(1), Shrove
Thursday 1518/19 + 1530, Maundy Thursday 1530–(1840),
Begging Thursday 1546(1), Mandate Thursday 1546–1797,
Holy Thursday 1645–
.Good Friday in: *langa frigedæg*/Long Friday OE–c1200,
Good(-)Friday c1290–, Parasceve 1548–1697
..ceremony for: creeping to/of the Cross 15..–1511 + 1924–,
Three Hours' (Service) 1898–
...to perform: creep to crouch *vphr* c1200(1), creep (to) the Cross
vphr c1200–1630
.Saturday in: *easteræfen, easterniht*, Lawson eve(n) 1725–(1841)
hist.
.Sunday in: *se drihtenlica easterdæg, se forma easterdæg,
eastre*/Easter OE–, *castersunnandæg*/Easter Sunday OE–,
easterdæg/Easter day OE–, Pasch a1131–1722 + 1885*arch.*,

Pasch-day c1200–a1670 *Sc. and N.*, Resurrection c1290–1377
+ 1838, God's Sunday 14.. + 1483, Pace c1425–1809 *Sc. and
N.*, Great Day 1812(1)

XR R4.1.5.2.2. Passover

..**char of:** *easterlic*/Easterly OE–1450/1530, paschal 1432/50–
..**season of:** *eastertid*/Eastertide OE–, Pasch-tide a1300(1)
..**p adhering to Greek or Roman:** paschalist 1641(1-*Milton*)
..**p celebrating E on day of Jewish Passover:** Quartodeciman
      1624–, paschite 1890(1)

XR R3.1.4.2. Nicene council
R4.1.5.2.2. Passover

...**practice of:** Quartodecimanism 1880–
...**char of:** Quartodecimarian 1666(1), Quartodeciman 1702–

40 days between Easter and Ascension: Great Forty Days
      1844(1)
.**first week in:** *easterwucu*, pasch-week 1375(1)
..**day in:** *easterdæg*
..**Monday in:** *oðer easterdæg*, Black Monday ?1359–1700
..**1st Sunday in:** Low Sunday 1431–1866, Low Easterday 1603(1),
      Mois 1442–1491, Renewal Sunday 1862(1)
..**week following:** Low Week 1884(1)
...**Monday and Tuesday in:** Hocktide 1484–1636 + 1656–*hist.*
...**Monday in:** Hock Monday 1481/90–1677 + 1826*hist.*,
      Hop-Monday 1528(1), Hop-Tide 1558(1)
...**Tuesday in:** Hock-Day c1175–1667 + 1777–*hist.*, Hock Tuesday
      c1250–1656 + 1777*hist.*
...**observation of:** hocking 1406–1618
....**to perform:** hock *vi* 1406(1)

Invention of the Cross (3 May): (Holy) Rood Day 1297–1841,
      Crouchmas 1389–1573, Invention of the Cross 1451–
St Helena's Day (22 May): Ellenmas 1597 + 1621

Sunday before Ascension: Rogation Sunday 1662–
.**week following:** *gangwuce*/Gang-week OE–1730/6, Cross-week
      1530–1597, Rogation Week 1530–, Procession-Week
      1546/7–1570
..**char of:** rogational 1872(1)

..Monday in: Gang-Monday 1579(1)

..days in: *+beddagas, bendagas, bentid, gangdæg*/Gang-days OE–, Rogation(s) 1387–, Rogation days c1400–, Cross-days 1501–1641, Procession days 1660(1)

XR R4.3.1. Litany
R4.15. Procession

...one of: ?Bene-day 1499(1), procession-day 1668(1)

Ascension: Hallow Thursday c1290(1), Ascension Day 1366 + 1595–, Holy Thursday c1430–(1891)

XR R1.2.1.5. Ascension

.season of: *upastignestid,* Ascensiontide 1871–

Pentecost: *fiftigdæg, pentecosten*/Pentecost OE–, *hwita sunnandæg*/Whitsunday OE–, Lok-Sounday c1315(1), Lokes 1340(1), Whitsuntide 1382–1551, Whitsun Sunday 1556 + 1825, White Sunday 1655(1)

.char of: *on hwitan sunnandæg,* Whitsun 1297–, Pentecostal a1663–

.season of: Whitsuntide c1205–, Pinkster 1821– *U.S.,* Whitsun 1849–

Trinity Sunday: Trinity c1290–(1624), Trinity Sunday 1426/7–, Trinity-tide 1511–(1841)

Corpus Christi: *Corpus Christi* 1377–, Sacre 1653(1)

Feast of the Sacred Heart: Feast of the Sacred Heart 1833–
Baptist's Day (24 June): Baptist's Day 1589(1)
Petertide (29 June): Petertide 1912–
Feast of the Visitation (2 July): Visitation (of Our Lady) 1498–
Feast of Mary Magdalen (22 July): Maudlin Tide c1430(1), Maudlin Day c1470(1), Magdalen Day 1485(1)
Feast of St James (25 July): St James's Tide a1568–1701, St James's Day 1898(1)
Relic Sunday (3rd Sun after midsummer): Relic Sunday 1461–1709

Lammas (1 Aug): *petermæsse*/Petermas OE–1548, *hlafmæssedæg*/Lammas Day OE–1792, *hlafmæsse*/Lammas OE–, Gule of August 1543–(1899)

.season of: *hlafmæssetid*
1st Sunday in August: Wake Sunday 1884(1)
Feast of the Transfiguration (6 Aug): Transfiguration
    c1460–(1510/11)
Feast of Jesus's Name (7 Aug): Jesus Day 1546(1)
Assumption (15 Aug): *afangennes,* Latter Mary Day 11.. +
    15..–1541*Sc.,* Saint Mary day the Latter 1297(1), Assumption
    1297–, Saint Mary Day c1310–c1450, Our Lady in Harvest
    c1483(1), Marymass 1492– *chiefly Sc.*
                          XR R1.2.1.5. Assumption
Feast of St Bartholomew (24 Aug): Bartholomew-tide
    1552/3–1854, Bartholomew-day 1678(1)
.char of: Bartholomean 1645(1)

Nativity of Blessed Virgin (8 Sept): Nativity 1389–, Latter
    Marymass 1492–1546 *Sc.,* Latter-Lady (in Harvest) 1641(1)
Holy Rood Eve (13 Sept): Rood-even 1375(1), Holy Rood Eve
    c1400(1)
Exaltation of the Cross (14 Sept): (Holy) Rood Day
    a1225–1825, Exaltation of the Cross 1389–, Holy Rood c1400
    + 1573, Rood(s)mas (Day) c1630 + 1825, Holy Cross Day
    1662–, Rood 1814(1)
Michaelmas (29 Sept): Michaelmas c1290–, Michaelmas Day
    1359–(1864), Michael 1406–1622
Lukesmas (18 Oct): Lukesmas 1470–1671 *Sc.*

Hallowe'en (31 Oct): Hallow-e'en 1556/1698–, All Hallow Eve
    1556–1698
All Saints (1 Nov): *ealhalgamæsse* / Allhallowmas(s) OE–1725,
    Hallowmas 1389–, All Hallows' Day 1483–1552, All Hallow(s)
    1503–1647, All Saints 1580–, Hallow-day 1596–*dial.,*
    Toussaint 1930–
.season of: Hallow-tide c1450–1609, Hollantide 1573–(1870)
Soulmass (2 Nov): Soul-mass day c1450–1533 + 1876*dial.*
St Martin's Eve (10 Nov): (St) Martin's Eve 1592–1598
Martinmas (11 Nov): Martinmas 1297–, St Martin's Day
    1517(1), St Martin 1533(1)
Shoemaker's Holiday (17 Nov): Shoemaker's Holiday 1607(1)
Andrewmas (30 Nov): *andreasmæsse,* St Andrewmasse 1641(1)

Conception Day (8 Dec): Our Lady in December c1297(1), Conception Day a1300–c1380

R4.1.5.2.2. Jewish seasons and feasts

Rosh Hashana: Feast of Trumpets 1560–, Rosh Hashana *no quots.*

Yom Kippur: F(e)ast of Expiation 1674–(1886), Expiation-day a1711(1), Day of Expiation a1713(1), Day of Atonement 1819–, Yom Kippur *no quots.*

.prayer sung for: Kol Nidre 1881–

Succoth: *geteldwurðung, getimberhalgung*, Cenophe a1300(1), Scenopegia c1380–1388, Feast of Tabernacles 1382–, Xylophory 1737(1), Succoth 1882–

Simchat Torah: rejoicing of/in/over the Law 1861–, Simchat Torah 1891–

Chanukah: Chanuk(k)ah 1891–

XR R4.9.1. Purification

Purim: *Purim* 1382–

Passover: *andbita, easterdæg, easterfreolsdæg, easterðenung, eastersymbel, eastertid, færeld, færeldfreols, ðeorfsymbel, offringdagas (npl), ðeorfdagas (npl), eastre*/Easter OE–1611, Pasch c1200–1745 + 1850–*arch.*, Forthfore c1250(1), Fase 1388(2-*Wyclif*), Passover 1530–, Passing-by 1533(1), Paschal 1581–1670, Azymes *npl* 1611–(1651), the Feast 1611– *N.T. use, Pesach* 1613 + 1887–

XR R4.1.2.1. Haggadah
R4.1.5.2.1. Easter, quartodeciman

.part of service for: *Ma Nishtana* 1902–

.char of: paschal 1658–, Passoverish 1921 + 1930

.coming before: antepaschal 1660 + 1704

.supper on: paschal 1579(1), *seder* 1865–

.(of x:)including two: bipaschal 1883–1908

.(of x:)including three: tripaschal 1883(1)

.(of x:)including four: quadripaschal 1883(1)

Harvest festival: *pentecost*/Pentecost OE–, Feast of Weeks 1382–1535, *Shavuoth* 1892–

Festival of new moon: Neomeny 1382–c1449, Calends / Kalends

1382–1609, New Moon 1382–a1649, Neomenia 1398(1)
Counting of the Omer: Counting of the Omer 1871(1)
Tisha B'Av: Tisha B'Av 1938–

R4.1.5.2.3. Other seasons and feasts
Bairam: *Bairam* 1599–1687 + 1813 *Moslem*
.lesser: *id-ul-fitr* 1734–
Dewalee: Dewalee 1698– *Hindi*
Matsuri: *Matsuri* 1727– *Japanese*
Mela: Mela 1800– *Hindi*
Mithraics: Mithraics *npl* 1864(1)
Muharram: hossy gossy 1698(1), hassan/hussan hassan 1773–,
    Moharran 1861– *Moslem*, hobson jobson 1935(1)
Ramadan: *Ramadan* 1599– *Moslem*
Feast of Seven Hills:
.char of: septimontial 1606(1)
Thesmophoria: Thesmophoria 1788–
.char of: thesmophoric 1884(1)
Festival of Vertumnus: Vertumnals *npl* 1656(1)
Vesak: Vesak 1927–
Vulcanalia:
.char of: vulcanalial 1635–1654, vulcanalian 1684(1)

R4.1.5.3. Fast general: +*fæsten*/fasten OE–c1200,
    fæstendæg/fasten-day OE–a1300, *faestentid*/fasten-tide
    OE–a1300, fasten-time a1300(1), fast a1300–, fasting-day
    a1300–, fast-day c1340–1841, indiction 1641–1685
.duly appointed: *æwfæsten, rihtfæstendæg*, kirk-fast
    1814(1-*Scott*)
.all through a period: through-fast 1652(1)
.of 40 days: Lent of Pardon 1483–1535, karyn(e) 1502(1), carene
    1647(1), carentane 1647(1), quadragesimal 1660(1)
..char of: quadragesimal 1654–(1855)
                              XR R4.1.5.2.1. Lent
.period of 3 days 4 times/yr: *ymbren*/embers *npl* OE–1573,
    ymbrendagas/ember-days *npl* OE–, quater-temps 1535(1),

quater-temper 1550(1), quarter-tense 1869(1)
..one of: ymbar 1550(1)
..duly appointed: *rihtymbren, rihtymbrendagas (npl)*
..day of: *ymbrendæg*
..week of: *ymbrenwuce*/ember-week OE + 138.–(1849)
.char of: penitent 1613(1)
.the adding of one F to another: superposition 1710/22(1)
..char of: superpository 1710/22(1)
.observation of: *lacfæsten*
..to perform: *fæsten heowan (vphr), +fæstan*/fast *vi* OE–

R4.1.6.0. Canonical hours general: (divine) service
a1225–1583, hours *npl* a1225–, office c1290–, canonic hours
npl 1483(1), canonical hours *npl* 1483–, canonial hours *npl*
1502(1), course 1570 + 1839–1844, choir offices 1876 + 1898
.one of: *sealmsang, ðenung, tid*/tide OE–1557
..service at: *tidsang, tiddenung, tidwurðung*
...bell indicating: office-bell 1841(1)
....hour so marked: *belltid*

Matins: *æftersang, dædredsang, dægredsang, morgengebidtid,*
uhtgebed, uhtðegnung, uhtsang/uht-song OE–a1225, matins
c1290–, morning prayer 1552–, matutines 1655(1),
morning-office 1765(1)
.division of: *noctern*/nocturn OE(L)–, orb 1526(1), nocturnal
1670(1)
.on feast day: *mæsseuhta*
.on Sunday: *sunnanuhta*
.in Holy Week (combined with Lauds): teneblus
a1450(1-*colloq.*), tenebres a1450–1801, tenebre / teneber
1477/9–a1548, teneble 1530–1588, tenebræ 1651–(1864)
.in office of the dead: *dirige*/dirge OE–(1875)
.communion service following: second service 1654–
.char of: *æftersingallic, uhtlic, uhtsanglic*
.to perform: matins *v* 1546–1553

Lauds: *æfenlof, herung,* lauds a1340–(1843)

Prime (6 a.m.): *prim*/prime OE(L)–, *primsang*/prime-song OE

+ 1844-*hist.*

Tierce (9 a.m.): *underntid, undern*/undern OE–c1450,
   undersang/undernsong OE + 1853*hist.*, t(i)erce c1375–,
   tierce-song 1852(1)

Sext (noon): *middægsang, middæg*/midday OE–?a1400, sext
   c1425–

Nones (3 p.m.): *nonsang, non*/noon OE–1561, nones 1709–,
   none 1845–

Lychnic: lychnic 1850(1-*GkCh*)
.prayers forming part of: lychnapsia 1850(1)

Vespers, evensong: *æfen, æfengebed, æfendream, æfenlof,*
   æfendegnung, æfendeowdom, æfensang/evensong OE–,
   evesong a1225–1460, vespers 1611–, evening-song 1634–c1740,
   vespertines a1635(1), vesper 1636–(1844), vesper service
   1797–

XR R4.8.1. *Æfenlac*
.in office of the dead: placebo a1225–
.char of: vesperal 1827(1)
.bell indicating: vesper-bell 1794–, vesper 1808–1927

Compline: *forannihtsang, nihtsang,* complin(e) a1225–,
   completory c1450–1802, *completorium* 1616–, night-office
   1767 + 1909, night-song 1844–
.collatio read before: *æfencollatio, æfenræding, durhtogennes,*
   wordmittung, collation 1387–1536

R4.1.6.1. Other services
Angelus: *angelus* 1727–
.bell indicating: pardon-bell 1538 + 1872, lady-bell 1541 + 1872,
   angelus 1847–
Evening benediction (France): *salut* 1694 + 1815–
XR R4.1.2.1. Benediction

R4.1.7. Church-going: *ciricsocn, ciricgang*/church-gang
   OE–1297, church-going 1541–

XR R4.1.0. Worship

.to synagogue: synagoguing 1824(1)

.char by: church-going 1712–, go-to-meeting 1853–(1868)
   U.S.colloq., practising 1906(1)

.zealous in: *ciricgeorn*

.to perform: *gestandan v,* go to church *vphr* a1175–, kirk *vt*
   c1425– *now Sc.,* church *v; usu. pass.* 1596–1865, practise
   (religion) *vt* 1808–

..in order to hear particular minister: sit under *vphr* 1644–

Sounding of bell before service: ringing-in 1854 + 1891

.to sound: ring (all) in *vphr* 1466–1678

Dispersion of congregation after service: kirk-skail(ing) 1819
   + 1843 *Sc.*

Turn-out of fashionable church-goers after service: church
   parade 1891–

.p involved in: church parader 1907(1)

(Of x:)suitable for use at church: go-to-meeting 1790–

XR R5.13.0. Lay garments

(Of x:)taking place after service: after sermon a1470–1815,
   afterchurch 1792(1)

R4.2. Sacrament

R4.2.0. Sacrament general: *haligdom, geryne,* sacrament
   c1175–, mystery 1506–(1850), means 1642–1650

XR R1.9.0. Grace

.pl/coll: Christendom 1297 + 1635, means of grace *npl* 1650–

.x like: sacrament a1340–(1899), sacramental 1529–(1892)

.establishment of, by Christ: institution c1538–

.x necessary to effectuality of: matter c1315–, form
   1597–1727/41, intention 1690–

..p doing x with: intentionary 1619(1)

.'high' doctrine in regard to: sacramentism 1840(1),
   sacramentalism 1861–1881, sacramentarianism 1882–(1903)

..p char by: sacramentary 1595(1), sacramentarian 1651–(1870),
   sacramentalist 1880(1)

..**char of:** sacramentary 1561–1884, sacramentarian 1865–1878

.**p recognizing only three:** trisacramentarian 1727/41(1)

.**char of:** *geryn(e)lic,* sacramental c1400–(1899), sacramentary
   1594–1837
..**condition of being:** sacramentalness 1633 + 1664,
   sacramentality 1660–1887
.**char by:** sacramented 1914(1)
.**made into:** sacramentated 1651(1)
.**(of x:)based on:** sacramental 1871–(1898)
.**in manner of:** sacramentally c1380–(1884), sacramently
   c1425(*2q1s*), in sacrament 1628(1)
..**not:** unsacramentally 1840(1)
.**to administer:** sacramentize *vi* 1655(1)
.**to deprive of qualities of:** unsacrament *vt* 1642(1)

R4.2.1.0. Baptism: *gedryncnes, dyfing, fontbæð, fulwihtbæð,
   fulwihtwæter, fullwiht*/fullought OE–c1450,
   cristnung/christening OE + a1300–(1848), fulhtninge /
   fulcninge c1200(*2q1s*), christendom 1297–1680, baptizing
   1297–, baptize/-is(e) a1300 + 1460, baptism a1300–, vollouth
   c1330(1), fulling 1387–1483, illumination 1398–1725, baptiste
   1460(1), christenhead c1470(1), baptization 1470–1704,
   fountain 1526 + 1548/9 *fig.,* volowing 1528(1), washing
   c1550(1), tincture 1612(*2q1s*), baptizement 1818(1), baptistry
   1851(1)

                                   XR R1.8.1.2. Regeneration
                              R2.2.0.1. Conversion to Christianity
                                        R4.2.1.1. Christendom
                                        R4.5.4.0. Conversion
                                        R4.9.1. Purification
                                        R5.15.12. Holy water
.**p perf:** *bæzere, fulwere, fulwihtere, fulwihtfædere, fulwihtwer,
   cristnere*/christener OE + 1483–1558, baptist c1200–,
   baptizer 1483–(1865), volower 1528(1)

                                   XR R1.2.1.3. John the Baptist
.**candidate for:** competent a1655–1729, competitor 1697(1)

.p undergoing: baptizee 1871(1)

XR R4.5.2. Catechumen

..p sponsoring: *forespreca, fulwihtbena, godsib(b)*/gossip OE– *now arch. or dial.,* undertaker 1645–1697, sponsor 1651–

.p deferring B until death-bed: clinic 1666–1819

XR R4.2.1.1. Clinic baptism

.rite of: *fulwihtđeaw, fulwihtđegnung*

..part of: institution 1607–

.rite preceding: *cristnung*

..not having undergone: *ungecristnod*

.consecration of font prior to: *fanthalgung*

.consecration of water used in: *fantbletsung*

XR R1.6.2.0. *Wæterhalgung*

..char of: *fanthalig*

.time of: *fulwihttid*

.vow of: *fulwihthad*

.renunciation of devil, world, and flesh at: renunciation 1875(1)

.spiritual relation between sponsor and baptizee at: gossipred c1315–, affinity c1440–, gossiphood 1502 + 1579, cognation c1555–1649

.feast following: gossiping a1627–, christening-dinner 1805–

.char of: baptismal 1641–, baptistical 1658(1)

.performing: baptizing 1671 + 1675

.having been brought to church to receive: churched 1340/70(1)

.having undergone: *gefullwod, gemearcod*, christened c1200(1), baptized 1687 + 1831

..not: *hæđen, unfullod, ungefulwod*, ful(e)htles c1175(1), unfulhtned c1200(1), unblessed c1310(1), unbaptized c1375–, unhoven c1375 + 1456, undipped 1693–, unchristened 1725–, unkirsened a1779– *dial.*, unchrisom 1831(1), unimmersed 1835(1)

XR R1.1.11.0. Heathen
R2.2.0.2. Lack of Christianity
R4.5.4.3. Unconversion

.capable of: baptizable 1659 + 1685

.in manner of: baptismally 1850 + 1861

.to perform: *ađwean v, gefulhtnian v, +fulwiht(i)an v,*
*gefulwihtnian v, gefuntian v, đwean v, dipan/*deep *vt*
OE–1340, *+fulwian/*full *vt* OE–1483, *dyppan/*dip *vt*
OE–(1876), *+cristnian/*christen *vt* OE–, fulht(n)e / fulcne *vt*
c1175–a1225, baptize *vt* 1297–, wash *vt* a1300–1653, christen
va c1315–(1820), baptize *va* c1325 + 1670, underfo *vt* 1362 +
1377 *both Langland,* christen from *vphr* c1485(1), volow *vt*
1530(1)

.to perform ritual preceding: *+cristnian/*christen *vt* OE +
c1450–

.to sponsor p for: *onfon v,* heave *vt* c1200–1571, gossip *vt* 1601 +
1716

.to bring p to church to receive: church *vt (no quots.)*

.to reverse: unchristen *vt* 1598–, unbaptize *vt/a* 1611–(1858)

.to undergo: *fulluht underfon vphr, fulwihtes bæđ onfon vphr,*
fang cristendom *vphr* 1297 + c1386

R4.2.1.1. Kinds of baptism

.adult: after-baptism 1680(1), adult baptism 1752(1)

.of children: pædobaptism 1640–(1872), infant-baptism 1674–

..p advocating: pædobaptist 1651–(1891)

..rites of: child-rites *npl* 1823(1)

.Christian: *cristennes,* christendom 1297–1680
                     XR R2.2.0.1. Conversion to Christianity

.daily: hemerobaptization 1653(1), hemerobaptism 1897(1)

.of fire: fire-baptism 1831(1-*Carlyle*)

..having undergone: fire-baptized 1831(1-*Carlyle*)

.hourly: horabaptism *no quots.*

..p advocating: horabaptist a1641(1)

.by immersion: *bæđ/*bath OE–c1200, plunging a1450–1532,
immersion 1629–, tinction 1657(*2q1s*), mersion 1659–1691,
immersionism 1845 + 1884

..p perf: holobaptist a1641(1), immersionist 1846–

..p undergoing: baptist 1775 + c1811

..having undergone: immersed 1892(1)

...not: undipped 1693–, unimmersed 1835(1)

..to perform: *dipan*/depe *vt* OE–1340, *dyppan*/dip *vt* OE–(1876),
plunge *vt* c1380(1)
.by layman: lay-baptism 1726(1)
.by pouring water over: perfusion 1607–, infusion 1751/73 +
1879
.private (for sick p): clinic baptism 1672–, clinical baptism
1844–
XR R4.2.1.0. Clinic

..char of: clinic 1672–, clinical 1844–
..to perform: half-baptize *vt* 1836–
.second: rebaptization 1570–1780, anabaptism 1645–(1826),
anabaptizing 1660(1), rebaptism 1795–1850
..p perf: rebaptizer c1645(1), rebaptist 1651–1738
...char of: anabaptizing 1642(1)
..char by: rebaptismal 1892(1)
..to perform: rebaptize *vt* 1640–, anabaptize *vt* 1637–(1848),
redip *vt* 1736(1)
XR R2.2.4.4.0. Baptistry

.self-: se-baptism 1646 + 1881
.spiritual: *consolamentum* 1874 + 1970 *Cathar*
.by sprinkling: rantism a1626–1701, rhantism 1843(1)
..p perf: sprinkler 1895 + 1896
..not having undergone: unsprinkled 1735 + 1802/12
..to perform: rantize *vt* 1644–1701, rhantize *vt* 1843 + 1894
.uncanonical: parabaptization 1715(1), parabaptism 1890(1) *both
early ch.*
.with water (as distinct from spiritual B): water-baptism
1673–(a1879)

R4.2.2.0. Confession: *geandetnes, scriftspræc, scrift*/shrift OE–,
shriving a1225–, confession 1377–, fassion c1440(1), shriftness
c1460(1), manifestation 1657 + c1826, confessional 1816–
.instance of: *scrift*/shrift OE–, confession c1380–
.auricular: shrift of mouth a1300(1), ear-confession 1549(1),
earish confession 1554(1), ear-shrift 1554–1604
.seal of: sigillum 1927– *RCCh*

.p advocating: confessioner 1561–1581

.p perf: *see R3.2.9. Confessor*
.p undergoing: *andettere, dædbeta, dædbetende, dædbetere,*
  penant a1300–c1400, penitencer c1380(1), penancer c1490(1),
  repentant 1532–(a1814), penitentiary 1553–1654,
  penitentionary 1577(1), shrift-child 1577–1625, contrite
  a1600(1), shriveling 1603(1-*contempt.*), confessant
  a1603–1843, confitent 1606–1858, confessary 1608(1),
  repenter 1621–, penitential 1627–1828, *confessionaire*
  1748(1), mourner 1859 + 1885 *U.S.*
..who is overly scrupulous: scrupulant 1938–
..varieties of: prostrates a1600–a1711, succumbent 1661 + 1850,
  co-stander 1709–a1773, prostrators 1709–1843, consistent
  a1711–a1773, kneeler 1719 + a1773, substrator 1720(1),
  weeper 1841–
..behaviour of: penitentials *npl* 1751–1805

.char of: confessionary 1607–1864, confessional 1817–1827

.the hearing of: shriving c1400–
..to perform: *unbindan*/unbind *va/t* OE–a1450, +*scrifan*/shrive
  vt OE–, +*scrifan*/shrive *va/i* OE–1579 + 1855, soil *vt*
  a1300–1530, remit *vt* c1375–, confess *vt/a* 1377–, release *vt*
  c1380–1574, reconcile *vt* c1430(1), absoil *vt* c1450–1548, shrift
  vt 1611–1699 + 1849
.the experience of: confessing 1642(1)
..to undergo: *geandettan v, to scrifte gan*/go (come) to shrift *vphr*
  OE–, *beon gescrifen*/be shriven *vpass* OE–, shrive *vrefl*
  a1225–1641 + 1859, shrive *vt* a1300–c1450, shrive *vi* a1300–,
  be confessed *vpass* c1340–1632, confess *vrefl* 1377–(1850),
  make one's confession *vphr* c1380–, seek to shrift *vphr*
  c1400(1), confess *vi* 1592–, reconcile *vrefl* 1869(1-*Browning*)
..to beat the breast during: craw-thump *vi* 1797/1802(1)

XR R2.2.3.0. Craw-thumper
R4.15. Knock *vi*

R4.2.2.1.0. Penitence: *behreowsung, dædbot, dædbotnes,*
  fordræst(ed)ness, hreow, gehreownes, pricung, geswicennes,
  gedræstedness, gedræstnes, hreowsung/reusing OE–13..,
  sin-boot c1175–c1200, penance a1300–1699, contrition

a1300–, repenting a1300–, repentance 13..–, repentaille
c1330–a1450, compunction a1340–(1855), remorse (of
conscience) c1374–, penitency c1450–, conscience 1467(1),
repent 1590–1611, penitence 1591–, penancy 1611(1),
remorsefulness 1617 + 1887, synderesis 1639–1651, synteresis
1650(1), penitude 1657(1), synteresy 1658(1), contriteness
1692 + 1755, remordency 1717(1), penitentness 1727–1775
XR R1.10.0. Contrition, attrition
R4.1.5.2.1. Septuagesima

.**instance of:** remorse 1652–1761

.**char by:** *dædbetende, forðræsted, hreow, hreowende, geðræsted,*
under/in shrift a1175–c1400, repentant c1290–, contrite
a1340–, penitent c1375–, contrited 1483–1642 + 1816–1821,
repent a1500(1), repentable 1571(1), remorsed a1586–1649,
penitential 1592–, remorseful 1592–, remording 1614 +
a1700, repentive 1620(1), contritional 1648(1), penitentiary
1791–1817

.**producing:** compungent 1635(1), compunctive 1649(1)

.**in manner evincing:** repentantly 1556–, penitently 1570–,
repentingly 1611–, compunctually 1625(1-*erron.*),
penitentially 1648–, contritely 1829–(1868), remorsefully
1842(1)

.**to afflict p with:** *gehreowan v,* remord *vt* c1450–a1578 + 1857,
remorse *vt* 1483–1593

.**to experience:** *behreowsian v, gehreowsian v, hreowsian/*reusie *vi*
OE–c1205, *gehreowan/*i-rew *vi* OE + c1340, repent *vrefl*
c1290–1682 + 1842*arch.,* repent *vi* c1290–, do penance *v*
a1300(1), repent *vt* c1380–, be repented *vpass* a1450 + 1530,
remorse *vi* 1530–1690

R4.2.2.1.1. Impenitence: unrepentance c1410–, unforthinking
1483(1), obduration 1494–(1882/3), impenitency 1563–,
obfirmation 1592–1665, obduracy 1597–, irrepentance
1607–(1900), unrepentingness 1615(1), obdurateness
1618–1720, obdureness 1624–1634, impenitence 1624–,
obduredness 1633–1652

.**p char by:** impenitent 1532–(1734)

.char by: *unbehreowsigende,* unrepentant c1380–(1869), uncontrite c1440–, unforthinking 1483(1), impenitent 1532–, unpenitent 1546–1801, irrepentant 1583 + a1625, obdured 1585–, unrepenting a1586–(1839), unreclaimed 1602–, obdure 1608–1655 + 1844*arch.,* unremorseful c1611–, unconfessing 1641(1), repentless a1683(1), compunctionless 1830(1), unatoning 1838(1), unapologetic 1892(1)

.in manner evincing: unrepentantly a1440–(1869), irrepentantly a1631 + 1654, impenitently 1631–, obdurately a1711–, unrepentingly 1789(1), unremorsefully 1846(1)

.to imbue p with: obfirm *vt* 1563/87–1686, obfirmate *vt* 1616(1), occrustate *vt* 1653–1681

R4.2.2.2. Absolution: *lihting, liss, liŏung, onliesednes, forgiefnes*/forgiveness OE–1480, *scrift*/shrift OE–1635 + 1828–, absolution 1200–, veny a1225–1482, soiling a1300–1529, pardon a1300–, lisnisse c1305(1), remission c1325–, indulgence 1377–c1430, veyne c1400–c1450, remit 1423–1589 *chiefly Sc.,* remitting 1577–1651, remittal 1596–c1693 + 1854, remitment 1611–1670, pardoning 1828(1)
        XR R4.9.1. Purification
.divine: *godforgifnes*
.p giving: absolvant 1506(1), absolvent 1651(1), absolver 1663–
        XR R3.2.9. Confessor

.char of: absolutory 1640 + 1726
.deserving: absolvable 1865(1)
.having received: yscryve 1387(1), confessed c1450–, shriven 1846–
..not: *unandett, ungeandett,* unshriven a1225–c1450 + 1813–, unshrivel 1340(1), unassoiled c1440–, irreconciled 1599–1691, unconfessed 1607–, unshrived 1775–(1820)

.to administer: *see R4.2.2.0. Shrive vt*

R4.2.2.3.0. Penance: *bot, hreowsung, synbot, scrift*/shrift OE–a1425, penance c1290–

.**week's:** *wucubot*
.**p perf:** satisfactor 1540(1), satisfactionar 1561–1634,
 satisfactionary 1562 + 1628
XR R4.2.2.1.0. Penitent

.**char of:** penitential a1535–, penitentiary 1577–, penitent 1613(1)
.**char by:** at/in shrift c1175–1793, penitent 1590(1), penanced
 1795(1)
..**not:** penanceless 1377(1)
.**performance of:** satisfaction a1300–
..**to perform:** *dædbetan v, +hreowsian v,* do penance *vphr* c1290–

R4.2.2.3.1. Remission of penance: absolution a1674–(1726)
.**indulgentiary:** pardon c1290–(1840), indulgence 1362–, patent
 1377–c1386, indulgency 1670–1845
XR R4.1.5.2.0. Pardon

..**for drinking:** poculary 1537(1)
..**forty days':** Lent of pardon 1483–1535, karyn(e) 1502(1), carene
 1647(1), carentane 1647(1)
XR R4.1.5.4. Quadragesimal

..**partial:** partial indulgence 1885–(1890)
..**pilgrim's:** pedary 1537(1)
..**plenary:** plenary remission / pardon / indulgence 1577–, plenary
 1826(1)
...**bull proclaiming:** sabbatine bull 1826(1)
XR R3.2.1.1.4. Papal documents
R4.1.5.0. Jubilee

..**for attending station:** stationary 1537(1)
..**three years':** triennal 1362–c1380
..**p dealing in:** *see R3.2.13. Pardoner*
..**char of:** indulgential 1674(1)
..**(of x:)having:** indulgenced 1841–
..**bull conveying:** pardon bull 1556(1)
XR R3.2.1.1.4. Papal documents

..**to attach I to x:** indulgence *vt* 1866–
XR R1.6.2.0. Pardon

R4.2.3. Confirmation: *crismliesing*/chrisom-loosing OE +

1869*hist., biscopung*/bishoping OE–, confirmment
a1300–c1315, confirming a1300–1597, confirmation 1303–,
chrism 1597–, consigning 1642(1)

XR R5.13.1. Chrismale

.Jewish: bar-mitzvah 1877–

.candidate for: confirmand 1884–
..sponsor of: *godmoᵭor*/godmother OE–, god-father 1549 + 1721
...char of: godfatherly 15..(1)
...not having: ungodmothered ?1714(1), godfatherless 1859(1)
...position of: godfathership 1807(1), godmothership 1848(1),
godmotherhood 1863(1), godfatherhood 1896(1)
.p who has undergone: confirmee 1885–

.char of: confirmatory 1686(1)
.char by: confirmed *no quots.*
..not: *untrymed, unbiscopod*/unbishop(p)ed OE–c1470 + 1844*hist.*
.to perform: *biscopian*/bishop *vt* OE–1786, confirm *vt* c1315–,
bisp *vt* c1450(1), consign *vt* 1537–1683

R4.2.4.0. Communion: *godes lichama, gemænsumnes,*
+maensumung, (the) sacrament a1225–, commoning
1382–1482, Lord's supper 1382–(1755), supper of the Lord
1382–, Eucharist a1400–, communion c1440–, oblation
c1450–, sacrifice 1504–, table 1526–(1902), maundy
1533–c1555, unbloody sacrifice 1548–(1860), office 1548/9–,
mysteries *npl* 1549(1), dominical supper 1560(1), liturgy
1560– *GkCh,* banquet 1563 + 1597, communication
c1610–1672, synaxis 1624– *GkCh,* mysteriousness 1650 +
1660, second service 1654 + 1657, altar-service 1721(1),
table-service 1823(1), ordinance 1830/40–, *nagmal* 1835–
S.Afr., table-prayers 1862(1)

XR R4.1.3. Communion ceremony
R5.15.5. Elements

.while walking about: ambuling communion 1603–1655
.between members of various sects: intercommunion 1921–

XR R1.1.16. Catholicity

.by the laity: lay-communion 1847–

.attendance at/partaking of: *hlafgang, huselgang, huselhalgung, gemana, onfangennes,* commoning 1382–1482, sumption c1440–1664, communion c1440–, perception 1483–1674, receipt 1500/20*Sc.* + 1552, manducation 1551–(1850), communicating 1559(1), mastication 1601(1-*fig.*), communication c1610–1672, theanthropophagy 1654(1), theophagy 1880 + 1907

..p char by: *huselbearn, huselgenga, huslwer,* ?sacramenter 1536(1), communer 1548–1550, communicant 1552–, communionist 1644–

...while kneeling: kneeler 1665(1)

...pl/coll: houseling people 1519–1568 + 1895

..char of: theophagitic 1805(1), communicant 1834–1866, theophagous 1880(1), communing 1887(1)

..to receive: *to hlafe gan vphr, to husle gan(gan) vphr, husles onbyrgan vphr, husl dicgan vphr, gemænsumian v, onfon v, dicgan*/thig *vt* OE–c1175, be houseled *vpass* c1200–1541 + 1870, receive *vt* 1303–, use *va* a1375–c1450, common *vrefl* c1400(1), housel *vrefl* c1400(1), ask for one's saviour *vphr* a1450 + 1470/80, use *vt* c1450 + 1567, receive one's saviour *vphr* 1470/80(1), be administered *vpass* 1495(1), receive one's maker *vphr* 1539–1634, communicate *vi* 1549–, commune *vi* 1550–(1856), receive *va* 1560–, communicate *vt* 1641–1709, masticate *vt* 1651(1-*fig.*), make one's communion *vphr* 1888(1)

..to acknowledge p as entitled to: give the right hand of fellowship *vphr* 1382–

.exclusion from: non-communion 1723(1), debarrance 1861(1), debarration 1882(1)

..p char by: non-communicant 1602–, non-communionist 1644(1)

..char of: unhouseled 1532–(1865), unreceiving 1566(1), uncommunicant 1600(1), non-communicating 1691–, non-communicant 1901(1)

.refusal to partake of: non-communion 1644(1)

..p char by: non-communicant 1602–, non-communionist 1644(1)

.consecration of elements in: sacring 1297–(1871), sacry 1303–1463, consecration 1395–, using 1472–c1500, consecrating 1579(1), eucharistizing 1714(1)

XR R1.6.2.0. Consecration

..p **perf:** consecrator 1552–

...char of: consecratory 1613–1866, consecrative a1617(1)

..**having undergone:** *gehalgod,* sacred c1380 + c1450, consecrate
  1509–1709, consecrated 1662–(1756/7), eucharistized 1737(1)

..**to perform:** *husl gehalgian vphr,* sacre *vt/a* a1225–c1485, make
  the sacrament *vphr* c1400–1585, consecrate *vt* c1500–,
  embread *vt* 1548(1-*nonce*), eucharistize *vt* 1714/7–(1876)

..**at previous celebration:** presanctification 1872(1)

...**having undergone:** presanctified 1853–

.**administration of:** +*mænsumung, husel*/housel OE–1625 +
  1844–1859, *huslung*/housel(l)ing OE–1642 + 1886,
  administration 1315–

..**to perform:** *gemænsumian v,* +*huslian*/housel *vt* OE–a1650 +
  1877, common *vt* c1375–c1500, commune *vt* c1380–c1500, give
  (p) his saviour *vphr* c1400 + a1450, housel *vi/a* 1504 + 1516,
  communicate *vt* 1539–, administer *vt* 1585–, communicate *vi*
  1635(1), administrate *vt* 1651–(1855)

.**char of:** housel(l)ing 1474–1590 + 1872, eucharistical 1534–,
  sacramental 1552–(1863), eucharistic 1664–

.**worthy of:** *husles wirde*

.**in manner of:** eucharistically 1639–

R4.2.4.1.0. Mass: *sendnes, husel*/housel OE–1625, *mæsse*/mass
  OE–, office 1548/9–

.**instance of:** *mæsse*/mass OE–

.**part of:** *mæssecapitel*

.**fixed number of:** certain 1466–1496 + 1849

.**time of:** *mæssetid,* sacringtime 1482–1594

.**day of:** liturgical day 1894(1)

.**special purpose for:** special / particular intention 1849–

.**forty hours' devotion to:** *Quarant(')ore* 1623–, the forty hours
  1759–

.**sacrifice of:** immolation 1548–

XR R4.8.0. Sacrifice

.**breaking of bread in:** fraction 1504–

.**mixing of bread and wine in:** immission 1846 + 1877,
      commixture 1850(1), commixtion 1872(1), intinction 1872–
..**to perform:** commixt *vt* 1483(1)
.**preserving portions of elements in:** reservation a1551–,
      reserving 1551(1), reposition 1657(1)

XR R5.8.16. Pyx

..**to perform:** pyx *vt* 1546–1563, reserve *vt* 1548/9–
.**p using water rather than wine in:** water-drinker 1562(1),
      waterman 1577(1)

XR R2.2.5. Aquarian

.**p advocating C in both kinds:** subutraquian 1649–1662

.**celebration of:** *mæsseðenung, onsymbelnes,*
      mæssesang/mass-song OE–c1250, mass-singing 1340–1553,
      massing 1340–1661 + 1850, mass-saying c1440–1546,
      confection 1564(1), missification 1641(1)

XR R3.2.2.1. Mass-priest

..**p perf:** *see R3.2.2.1. Mass-priest, R4.2.4.0. Consecrator*
..**to perform:** *+mæssian*/mass *vi* OE–1677 + 1851, celebre *v*
      1483(1), celebrate *va* 1534–(1862), missificate *vi* 1641(1),
      sacrifice *v* 1661(1)
...**as bishop:** pontificate *vi* 1818–, pontificate *vt* 1889(1)

XR R3.2.1.8.0. Episcopize

...**twice in a day:** duplicate *va* 1865–1881

.**to attend:** *gehieran v, gemæssian v*

.**char of:** missal a1548–1793, missalian 1624(*2q1s*), missaline
      1624(1), missatical a1670–a1683
.**performing:** missifical 1604–1607, missific 1624(1), sacramenting
      1687(1-*nonce*), missificating 1694(1), sacrificing 1836(1)
.**performed:** confect 1401(1)

R4.2.4.1.1. Kinds of mass
.**bishop's:** pontifical 1923(1)
.**at which no communion is given:** private mass 1560(1)
.**of the day:** mass of the day 1898(1)

XR R4.2.4.1.1. Votive mass

.**early:** *capitolmæsse, morgenmæsse,* matins mass 1303(1),

morrow-mass c1440–1635 + 1849*hist.,* mass of the day
    c1450(1), morn-mass 1511(1-*Sc.*), cock-mass 1795(1)
..**bell indicating:** morn-bell 1568/9(1)
.**first, of young priest:** white mass 1895(1)
.**high:** *heahmæsse*/high mass OE–, great mass 1770(1), solemn
    mass 1898(1)
..**day of:** *heahmæssedæg,* liturgical day 1894(1)
.**hunter's:** hunter's mass 1595(1), hunting mass 1597 + 1845
.**later:** aftermass 1848(1)
.**low:** *swigmæsse*/swimesse OE + c1200(1), low mass 1568(1), low
    celebration 1867(1)
.**parish, principal M of day:** parish mass 1763 + 1929–, parish
    communion 1936–, parish eucharist 1936–
.**with preconsecrated elements:** liturgy / mass of the
    presanctified 1758–
.**private:** private mass 1885(1)
.**in honour of the Rood:** rood-mass 1545(1)
.**saint's:** *mæsse, mæssesang, sang*
                             XR R4.1.5.2.0. Feast
.**in honour of Scala Cæli:** scalary *a* 1536(1)
.**special:** *sundormæsse*
.**stational:** stational mass 1902–
.**at which red vestments are used:** red mass 1889–
.**in honour of the Virgin:** marymass 1532–(1852)
                         XR R3.2.2.8. Saint Mary priest
.**votive:** votive mass 1738–
                        XR R4.2.4.1.1. Mass of the day
..**in honour of Jesus's name:** Jesus mass 1540 + 1886

R4.2.4.2. Eucharistic doctrines
Presence of Christ in communion: presence 1552–
.**actual:** real presence 1559–
..**body:** *flæsc*/flesh OE–
..**blood:** sang royal 1523(1)
..**p denying:** sacramentarian 1535–, sacramentary 1538–1858,
    significatist 1585/7–1625, figurist 1585/7–1737, symbolist
    1585/7 + 1839*hist.,* adessenarian 1751–1835, sacramentarist

1828(1), sacramentalist 1840(1), sacramenter 1845(1), symbolizer 1903(1)
...fellow-: consacramentary 1565(1)
...char of: sacramentary 1563–(1830), sacramentarian 1640–1845, Capernaitical 1563/87–a1656, Capernaitish 1643(1), Capernaitic 1880–
...in manner of: capernaitically 1640(1)
.virtual: virtualism 1883–

XR R2.2.4.5.0. Calvinism
..p holding: virtualist 1897–

Concomitance: concomitance a1535–, concomitation 1563/87(1), concomitancy 1563/87–1747, compresence a1640–1657, compresentiality 1686(1-*nonce*), compresentation 1686(1-*nonce*)

Consubstantiation: companation 1582(1), consubstantiation 1597–
.p believing: synusiast 1585/7–1674, consubstantialist a1655–a1677, consubstantiationist 1813–a1834
..char of: consubstantiating 1687(1)
.char of: consubstantiative 1853(1)
.char by: consubstantiate 1633(1)
.to cause: consubstantiate *vt* 1597–1768/74
.to believe in: consubstantiate *vi* 1715(1), consubstantialize *vi* 1838(1)

Impanation: impanation 1548–, invination 1742 + 1855
.p believing: impanator 1855 + 1866
.char by: impanate 1550–, impanated 1579–a1740, invinate 1550 + 1855
.to cause: impane *vt* 1547 + 1548, invinate *vt* 1579(1)

Transaccidentation: transaccidentation 1581–(1874), transelementation 1550–(1896)
.to cause: transelement *vt* 1567–(1878), transelementate *vt* 1579–(1899)

Transubstantiation: trans-substancing c1380(1-*Wyclif*), transubstantiation 1533–, turnkind(ing) 1548(*3q1s*), transubstantiating 1586(1), adduction 1638(1), carnification

1826–1827, transubstantialism 1842(1), transubstantialization
1826(1)
.change resulting from: transfinalization 1965–, transignification
1965–

.p believing in: Capernaite 1549–1661 *hostile*, transubstantiator
a1555–1686, metusiast 1607(1), Capernaitan 1641(1-*hostile*),
Capharnite 1706(1-*hostile*), transubstantiationist a1834(1),
transubstantialist 1838–1850, transubstantiationite 1839(1),
transubstantiationalist 1884(1)
.char of: transubstantial 1567–1651, transubstantiative 1826(1),
transubstantiatory 1878(1)
.char by: transubstantiate c1450–1678, transubstantiated
1550–(1849)
.in manner of: transubstantially 1577–1579, transubstantiatively
1826(1)
.to perform: transubstantiate *vt* 1533–, transcorporate *vt* 1570(1),
transubstanite *va* 1570–1667
.to undergo: transubstantiate *vi* 1851(1)
.to believe: transubstantialize *vi* 1826–(1846)

R4.2.5. Marriage: *gemung, gi(e)fta npl, æ*/ae OE–1200,
weddung/wedding OE–, marriage 1297–, marrying a1300–,
matrimony 1303–, order c1386(1-*Chaucer*), sponsalia *npl*
1535–178., nuptials *npl* c1555–, nuptial 1590–, union 1595–,
nuptialling 1600(1)
.invalid, but contracted in good faith: putative marriage
1811–
.ceremony of: *brydgifa npl, brydðing*, marriage rites *npl* a1661(1),
matrimony 1700–1724, marriage service 1833(1), nuptialities
npl 1863(1)
..performance of: wedding c1300–, spousal a1450(1),
solemnization 1497–, solemnacy 1591(1)
...p perf: nuptialist 1650(1), marrier 1830(1)
XR R3.2.2.1. Knit-beggar
...to perform: *geæwnian v, gemungian v, weddian*/wed *vt* OE–,
sacre *vt* c1425–1485, solemnize *vt* 1476–, sacre *vi* c1440(1),
marry *vt* 1530–, espouse *vt* 1593 + 1599, unite *vt* 1728–(1882)

XR R4.1.2.0. Solemnize

.char of: nuptial 1490–, married 1588–

.char by: *geweddod*/wedded OE–, married 1362–, wed
a1400–c1440 + 1823, nuptial 1615 + 1642

..in church/chapel: parsonified 1880(1), parsoned 1886– *both
colloq.*

.in manner of: nuptially 1890(1)

.to undergo: be married *vpass* 1297–(1722), marry *vi*
a1300–(1849), go to church 1599(1), nuptialize *v* 1857(1)

.blessing in: *brydbletsung*

.bell indicating: wedding-bell a1849(1)

.hours within which ceremony can occur: canonic(al) hours
1664–1847

.music for: *see R4.1.4.1.1. Wedding hymn*

Betrothal: betrothing c1315–, betrothment 1585–1871, affiancing
1617 + 1660, affiance 1809(1), heart-bond 1823–, betrothal
1844–

.ceremony of: Kiddushin 1904– *Jewish*

.char by: betrothed 1540–, affianced 1580 + 1865

.to perform: betroth *vt* 1303–, affiance *vt* 1555–

Banns: banns c1530–

.to publish: publish the banns *vphr* 1488–, publish *vt* 1651–1678,
out-publish *v* 1719–1727, out-ask *v* 1719–1880 *dial.*, put up
the banns *vphr* 1830–, call home *vphr* 1891 + 1892 *dial.*

R4.2.6.0. Order general: *cirichad*, order a1300–

.char of: diatactical 1646(1), diatactic 1646–1688

.major (holy): *ciricæw, heahhad, had*/had OE–1375, order
13..–1620, orders *npl* 13..–, sacred orders *npl* 1726–

..char of: ordinal 1842(1)

.minor: petty orders 1727/41(1), minor orders 1844(1)

XR R3.2.12.0. *Cleric*/clerk

.intervals between reception of various: interstices *npl* 1745 +
1885

R4.2.6.1.0. Ordination: *hadung*/hading OE–c1200, orders *npl* c1290–, sacring 1297–(1902), ordering c1315–, consecration 1387–, ordination 1432/50–, ordaining 1560–

.as bishop: *biscophad, biscophadung, biscophalgung*

XR R3.2.1.8.0. Episcopation

..formal ratification of: confirmation c1330–

.as priest: priesting 1891(1)

.as rabbi: *semicha* 1866–

.a second time: reordination 1597–

.letter recommending: dimissories *npl* c1380–1725, dimissory letter(s) 1583–(1819), demissory letters *npl* a1631–1708, dismissory letters *npl* 1664(1), dismissories *npl* 1716(1), apostle 1726–1753, dismissorial 1885(1)

.time of: *hadtima*

.vows taken during: evangelical counsels *npl* 1875–

XR R4.11.0. Vow

.laying on of hands during: imposition 1382–, laying on (of hands) 1526(1)

.anniversary of: *hadungdæg*

.to nominate p for: call *vt* c1300–(1680)

.to furnish with title to: entitle *vt* 1720(1), intitule *vt* 1720(1)

.to perform: *halgian*/hallow *vt* OE–(1325), *+hadian*/hade / hode *vt* OE–c1425, sacre *vt* c1290–a1648, ordain *vt* c1290–, lay hand(s) on *vphr* a1300–1784, order *vt* 1303–, consecrate *vt* 1387–, sanctify *vt* 1390–1660, canonize *vt* 1393–c1400, ensacre *vt* 1491(1-*Caxton*), consacre *vt* 1523(1), ordinate *vt* 1562–1597, impose *vt* 1582–1658, japan *vt* 1756–(1879) *slang*

..as priest: priest *vt* 1504–, frock *vt* 1896(1)

..a second time: reorder *vt* 1593(1), reordain *vt* a1626–

.to undergo: had *underfon vphr*, take (holy) orders *vphr* 1426–

.char of: inthronistic 1725(1)

.char by: *+hadod*/haded OE–c1200, in (holy) orders 13..–, ordered 1303–1615, ordinee c1330–c1400, ordained c1440–, consecrated 1552–1659

XR R4.9.2. Tonsured

..newly: *nigehalgod*

..not: *unhadod, ungehadod*/unihoded OE + a1250(1), unordered
1588 + 1607, unordained 1653–

..to priesthood: priested 1609(1)

.candidate for: intrant 1637/50–1761/2, probationer 1645–,
postulant 1759–, ordinand 1842–, *si quis* 1864(1-*slang*)
XR R3.2.10. Stibbler, licentiate

..disqualified: irregulate 1600(1)

..without university degree: literate 1824–(1868)

..condition of being: postulancy 1882/3–

.p who has undergone: +*hadod*/haded OE–c1200, ordinee
c1330–

.p celebrating 50 years since: jubilate 1706(1), jubilarian
1782–, sempect 1865(1-*Benedictine*)

..char of: jubilated 1772(1)

.p perf: ordainer 13..–, ordinator 1609(1), ordinant 1842–

R4.2.6.1.1. Unfrocking: *bescyrung, unhadung,* disgrading
1531/2 + 1641, deraignment 1539–1668, unfrocking 1644–
XR R4.10.3. Clerical misbehaviour

.char by: degraded 1483–(1885), disgraded 1546–1641, defrocked
1581–(1891), unfrocked 1794–, disfrocked 1837–(1856)

.to carry out: *behadian v, unhadian*/unhadien *vt* OE + c1205(2),
defrock *vt* 1581–(1891), unfrock *vt* 1644–, desecrate *vt*
1674–c1800, unfrockify *vt* 1694(1), unclergy *vt* 1695(1),
disfrock *vt* 1837–(1879), disgown *vt* 1887(1)

.to undergo: be deraigned *vpass* 1574–1778

R4.2.6.2. Vocation: calling 1578 + 1864, vocation 1578–
XR R4.16.0. Advowson, inducting

.instance of: call 1666–(1859)

.char by: called 1560–

..not: uncalled 1854(1)

.to perform: call *vt* 1560–

R4.2.6.3. Induction: induction c1380–, institution c1380–,
planting 1649(1-*Sc.*), settlement 1723–, stationing 1801–

Methodist
.instance of: point c1380(1), ordinance 1387–1450, preferment 1536–
..annual list of Methodist: stations *npl* 1885(1)
.of ordained minister to charge: instal(l)ment 1788 + 1888, induction 1871(1)
..to perform: install *vt* 1788–1888
.of p to whom congregation objects: intrusionism 1841(1), intrusion 1849 + 1878
..p char by: intrusionist 1849(1)
..non-: non-intrusion 1840–(1879), non-intrusionism 1841(1)
...p char by: non-intrusionist 1841(*2q1s*)

.p perf: institutor 1804/86(1-*U.S.*)
.reading the 39 Articles upon: reading in 1858–
..to perform: read in *vi* 1828–1863, read oneself in *vphr* 1857–

.char of: institutionary 1814 + 1835
.char by: planted 1699(1), instituted 1712 + 1804/86, settled 1773–, located 1894(1)

.to perform: institute *vt* 1325–, induct *vt* c1380–, pulpit *vt* 1529–1865, plant *vt* 1574–1721 *Sc.*, settle *vt* 1719–, locate *vt* a1814– *U.S.*
..as principal cleric: incardinate *vt* 1609–

R4.2.6.4. Seminary: seminary college 1581(1), seminary 1581–, theologate 1884–(1906)
.Jesuit, for novices: noviceship 1620–, scholasticate 1875 + 1895
..p attending: tertian father 1876(1), scholastic 1876 + 1881
...condition of: tertianship 1855–(1892)
..course in: juniorate 1845–
.preparatory: proseminary 1893(1)
.priest trained in: seminary 1581–1685, seminary man 1582(1), seminary priest 1581–1821, seminarian 1584(1), seminant c1588(1), seminarist 1835–
..from Douai: seminarist 1583–(1841), seminarian 1794–
..manner of: seminarianism 1879(1)
..char of: seminaristic 1841(1)

.table companion at: convictor 1647–
.group within: camerata 1846 + 1912

.char of: seminarian 1584(1), seminarial 1762(1)

Course for Jewish priesthood: shifting c1200(1)

R4.2.6.5. Monastic profession: *ingang, mynstergang,* profession
a1225–, conversion c1340–1482, profess c1400–14.., professing
1502(1), clothing 1628–(1891) vesture 1639(1), noviciation
1797(1)
.p char by: *niwcumen, munuccild*/monk-child OE–c1205, novice
13..–, nun-novice *nf* c1400(1), probationer 1629–, noviciate /
novitiate 1655–, *chela* 1883(1-*Buddhist*)
..char of: novice 1530–
..period of being: novicery c1440–a1470, noviciate / novitiate
1600–, probation 1603–, noviceship 1639–, novitiateship
a1670(1), probationship 1822(1), chelaship 1883– *Buddhist*
...char of: noviciate / novitiate 1756/7–

.having undergone: profess 1297–1387/8, professed c1394–,
professional c1420(1)
..not: *unmunecod, ungemunecod,* unprofessed c1430–a1450 + 1808

.document containing: profess 14..(1)

XR R4.11.0. Vow

.to perform: *had on settan vphr, munucian*/monk *vt* OE–c1205,
order *vt* 1303–, profess *vt* c1430–, cowl *vt* 1536–1848, clothe *vt*
1628 + a1700, monasticize *vt* 1854–, monachize *vt* 1896(1)
.to undergo: be professed *vpass* c1315–1797, profess oneself *vrefl*
c1510–1533, profess *vi* 1745–1829, take the vows *vphr*
1845(1), monachize *vi* 1884(1)

Secularization of monks: secularization 1882/3(1)
.p char by: fugitive 1482(1)

XR R4.10.3. Apostate

.to perform: secularize *vt* 1683–(1845), unfrockify *vt* 1694(1),
unbrother *vt* 1804(1)
.to undergo: go over the wall *vphr* 1949–

To deprive (x) of monks: demonachize *vt* 1820(1)

To make p a friar: friar *vt* 1599(1)
To divest oneself of friarhood: disfriar oneself *vrefl* 1599 +
1639

To admit p to nunhood: veil *vt* 1387–, enveil *vt* 1555(1),
nunnify *v* 1624–1640
To become a nun: *hadunge underfon vphr*, take the veil *vphr*
c1325–, be wimpled *vpass* 1439/40(1), veil *vrefl* 1631(1)
To turn/let nun out of cloister: discloister *vt* 1660(1)

R4.2.7.0. (Extreme) unction: *crismsmyrels, onsmyrung,
smirung,* smerling a1300(1), chrism a1300–, nointing
13..–1647 *aphetic,* anoiling 1303–1627, aneling 1303–1650 +
1853, ointing a1340–1652/62, anointing 1382–, unction 1387–,
oiling c1440–1562, greasing c1440– *often contempt.,*
anunction 1470(1), inunction 1483–1686 + 1898, anointment
1494–1649 + 1813–, ointment 1510/20–1621, enoiling
1526–1643, chrismation 1537–, uncting 1551(1), chrismatory
1563–1581, chrisom 1725(1)
XR R4.2.3. Confirmation
R4.2.6.1.0. Ordination
R5.15.8. Oil
.of the dying: last anointing 1340–a1400, last eling c1450(1),
(extreme) unction 1513–, chrism 1635(1), last sacraments *npl*
1700–, last rites *npl* 1922–, sacrament of the sick 1972–
.with sulphur: sulphuration 1713(1)

.sacred character conferred by: *crisma*
.consecration of chrism used in: *crismhalgung*

.p perf: anointer 1591–(1845), nointer 1647(1), aneler 1656(1)
..char of: neling 1567/8(*2q1s*)

.char of: chrismatory 1555(1)
.char by: anoint 1303–c1399, anointed c1374–, ointed 1382–1855,
greasy 1545–1583, smeared 1550–1583 *contempt.,* oiled
1550–1606, aneled 1557 + 1558
..not: unaneled 1602–, unanointed 1726(1-*dict.*)

.to perform: *đurhsmyrian v, +fættian*/fat *vt* OE–a1300,
  +smierwan/smear *vt* OE–1550 + 1823*contempt.*, ele *vt*
  c1205–c1315, forsmerl *vt* a1300(1), smerl *vt* a1300(1), chrisom
  a1300–c1420, (')noint *vt* 13..–1689 + 1821–1822 *aphetic*,
  alyne *vt* c1315(1), anele *vt* c1315–1649 + 1875, anoint *vt*
  1330–, inoynt *vt* c1350 + 1499, creme *vt* 1398(1), chrism *vt*
  ?a1400–1768/74, unct *vt* 14..–1596, oil *vt* c1440 +
  c1580–(1851), inoil *vt* 1546/7(1), benoint *vt* 1594(1),
  chrismatize *vt* 1664(1)
..to an office: salve *vt* c1200(1), oil *vt* c1440–1764, enoil *vt*
  1546–1643
..for the dying: anele *vt* 1303–1558 + 1853, anoil *vt* 1303–1688,
  anoint *vt* 1366(1)

R4.2.7.1. Funeral: *gerihtu*/rights *npl* OE + c1400–1509, obit
  c1400–1708, requiem 1303–, mass of requiem a1380–,
  obsequies *npl* c1386–, burial 1453–, vigils *npl* 1483–,
  soul-mass 1488–1681 + 1828–*hist. or dial.,* funeral a1512–,
  requiem mass a1529–(1861), funeration 1625 + 1693, burial
  service 1726–, black mass 1904(1)
.held 9 days after burial: novendial a1719(1), novemdial
  1793(1)
.set of 30: trental 13..–1694 + 1813–1881*hist.,* trent 1389(1),
  tricenary 1482 + 1911, trigintal 1491–1726 + 1898*hist.,*
  tricennial 1537(1)
.set of 40: quarental 1566(1)
.number of, lasting 2 years: biennal 1362(1)
XR R4.2.7.3. Annual
.musical setting of: requiem 1789–

.bell indicating: passing-bell 1526–, soul(-)bell 1599–, death-bell
  1781–
.ceremonial washing of corpse before: *taharah* 1819– *Jewish*

.char of: funeral c1386–, funebrial 1604–, funebrious 1653–1721,
  funerary a1693–, funereal 1725–
.in manner of: funerally 1658(1), funereally 1860–

Day of mourning: *heofungdæg*

Time of mourning: *heofungtid*

R4.2.7.2. Vigil: *ciricwæcce, wæcc(e)*/watch OE–1526, waking
c1175–1710, vigil a1225–, vigily 1377–1588, pernoctation
1633–

XR R4.1.5.2.0. Eve
.**lengthy, with arms outstretched:** cross-vigil 1932(1)
.**of festival:** *fæsten*, wake 15..–a1629 + a1806–*dial.*, agrypnia
1753(1-*GkCh*)
.**Wesleyan:** watch-night 1742–
.**pl/coll:** *uhtwæcca*

.**p perf:** *haligwæcca*
.**to perform:** *weardian v, wacian*/wake *vi* OE–1483,
wæcian/watch *vi* OE–, keep (a) vigil(s) *vphr* 1555–, watch in
vphr 1828(1)

R4.2.7.3. Commemoration: *weorðung, mynd*/mind OE +
1387–1660, commendation(s) a1225–1849/53, memory
1303–1591 + 1853–*hist.*, commemoration a1400–, obit
c1400–(1851), minning c1420–1524

XR R4.1.5.2.0. Saint's day
.**of p's death:** *gewitennes, gemynddæg*/mind-day OE–1438,
min-day a1225–1532, minning-day a1330–1543, minning-date
1556(1)
.**month's:** month's mind 1466–, thirty-day 1479 + 1546, month's
day 1542(1), monthly mind 1649 + 1660, trental 1659 + 1860
.**annual:** *geargemynd*/year-mind OE–1606, annual 1382–(1753),
year's mind 1408–1561 + 1849–*hist.*, twelvemonth's mind
1428–1829, annals *npl* 1536 + 1726, anniversary 1612–(1753)

XR R4.2.7.1. Biennial
.**Roman:** parentalia 1706–1801
.**to perform:** commemorate *vt* 1844–

R4.3. Prayer

R4.3.0. Prayer: +*bedræden*, +*clipung, forben, hiernes,* *bedu*/beads *npl* OE–1741, *+ben*/bene OE–1340 + 1594+ 1807, bode c1175(1), boon c1175–1513, bidding of beads / prayers c1175–(a1746), orison c1250–, bidding 1297–c1440, prayer a1300–, beads bidding 1387–1764, sacrifice c1595–(1876), presentation 1597–1700, pray 1654(1)

XR R1.7.1. Cant

.**instance of:** *+bed,* orison c1175–, prayer a1300–, petition c1330–, oration c1375–1593 + 1849*hist.,* pray c1440 + 1470/85, vote 1626–1664, devotions *npl* 1624–, devotionals *npl* 1659(1)
..**together:** comprecation 1635–1680 + 1864

.**p perf:** beadsman a1230–(1849), prayer c1440–(1863), oratrice *nf* 1513/14(1)
..**fellow:** comprecent 1624(1)
..**paid:** beadsman a1528–1726
..**child, praying for benefactor:** bead-child ?1499(1)
..**pl/coll:** bead-folk ?1465(1), prayer ring 1846(1), prayer circle 1880(1), praying band 1883–, prayer chain 1908 + 1911

.**'amen' at end of:** amen c1230–
.**mystic formula used in Buddhist:** *om mani padme hum* 1774–, *om* 1788–
..**to employ:** *om vi* 1976(1)
.**purpose of:** special / particular intention 1849–
.**value of:** prayer value 1906–
.**list of intended recipients of:** bead-roll c1500–1849
.**hour appointed for:** *gebedtid*
..**bell indicating:** prayer-bell a1550–
.**call to:** *ezan* 1753 + 1842, *azan* 1855– *both Moslem*

XR R3.3.4.1. Muezzin

.**payment for:** *gebedbygen*
.**directing/enjoining of:** bidding (of) prayers c1550–
..**to perform:** lead the prayers *vphr* 1866(1), lead (people) in prayer *vphr* 1880(1)
.**breakfast for:** prayer breakfast 1966–

.**char of:** deprecant 1624(2), orational 1889(1), petitive 1923–
.**char by:** beadful c1200(1), praying 1483–, prayerful 1626–

XR R1.7.0. Pious

..condition of being: prayerfulness 1846–
.without: prayerless a1631–1866
..condition of being: prayerlessness a1828–
.(of x:)that is possible in: prayable 1941(1-*Eliot*)
.(of x:)that is sought in: prayed-for 1867–
.in manner of: prayerwise 1583–(1850), prayerfully 1826–
..not: prayerlessly 1847 + 1891

.to offer: *abiddan v, gebedian v, +ciegan v, +nemnan v,*
    biddan/i-bid *vi* OE–a1300, bid a bene / bead / prayer *vphr*
    c1175–1764, boon *vi* c1200(*2q1s*), ure *vi* a1225(1), pray *vi*
    a1300–, oncall *vi* 1548(*2q1s*), say one's beads *vphr*
    1656–(1870), tell / count one's beads *vphr* 1641–
..for xp: mind *vt* c1420–1688, remember *vt* 1602–1613 + 1836
..again: repray *vi* 1616 + 1891
.to raise hands in: lift (up) the hand(s) *vphr* a1300–1807,
.to excel in: outpray *vt* 1593–(1841/4)
.to overcome by: outpray *vt* a1853(1)
.to strive (with God) in: wrestle *vi* 1612–
..action of: wrestling 1722–
.to approach God in: *secan*/seek *vt* OE–a1674
.to direct P to heaven: bend *vt* 1653(1)

R4.3.1. Kinds of prayer
.of atonement: Kol Nidre 1881–
                        XR R4.1.5.2.2. Yom Kippur
.Ave Maria: Ave c1230–1596 + 1808*Scott*, Ave Mary/-ia c1230–,
    Hail Mary a1300–, (the angels' / angelical) salutation
    ?c1600–1852
                        XR R4.3.1. Stabat Mater
..time of: ave 1463(1), Ave Maria 1835(1)
...bell indicating: Ave Mary/-ia 1599(1), Ave-bell 1635 + 1849
.in adoration of the Cross: cross a1225(1)
.for the damned: refrigerium c1645 + 1652
.for deliverance: deprecation 1596–(1892), disprayer 1615(1)
                    XR R4.3.1. Intercessory prayer
..char of: deprecative 1490–1672/5, deprecatory 1586–(1738),
    depulsory 1609(1)

..to employ: deprecate *vt* 1628–1833, deprecate against *vi* 1652(1)

.for departed: suffragies *npl* a1225–1555, suffrage c1440–1596 +
1848*arch.*

> XR R4.3.1. Whom God assoil

.dedicatory: dedication 1520–(1607)

..char of: dedicative 1655–(1825), dedicatorial 1844(1), dedicatory
1846(1)

.for the dying: commendatory prayer 1661–(1865),
recommendatory prayer 1718(1), commendation 1885(1)

.evening: vespers 1814– *poet.*

> XR R4.3.1. Sandhya

.presented through another: errand c1200–c1460 + 1849/53

.beginning with 'gaude': gaudez *npl* 1653(1)

.before meal: *beodfers, benedicite* a1225 + 1725–, grace a1225–

..p using: say-grace 1788(1)

..to use: grace *vt* 1644(1), ask a blessing *vphr* 1738–, say a blessing
vphr 1884(1)

.intercessory: deprecation 1556–1633

> XR R4.1.3. Collect
> R4.3.1. Deprecation

..char of: apprecatory 1633–1649

.invocatory: oncall a1300(1), invocation c1375–

..p using: invoker a1649–

..char of: invocatory 1691–

..expressing devotion to Trinity: in the name of (the Trinity)
OE–

..action of using: invocating 1585/7(1), invoking 1611 + 1631

..to use: invoke *vt* 1490–, invocate *vt* 1526–(1848), invocate *vi*
1582–

...loudly: roup *vt* 1513(2-*Sc.*)

.for journey: itinerary 1885(1)

.including tenfold repetition of 'Jesus': Jesus psalter 1632 +
1888

.on one's knees: *cneowgebed*

..kneeling for: knee-drill 1882(1-*Salvation Army*)

.the Lord's: *dryhtlic gebed, paternoster*/paternoster OE(L)–,
pater c1330–, Lord's Prayer 1548/9–, Our Father 1882(1)

..repetition of: paternoster c1300–

...frequent: belt of Our Fathers 1849(1), belt of pater-nosters
1844(*2q1s*)
.for mercy: Lord have mercy (upon us) 1588–(1692)

XR R4.1.3. Kyrie

.morning: morning prayer 1557(1)
..or evening: sandhya 1891– *Buddhist*
.beginning with 'O': the Fifteen O's 1531–1547
.beginning with 'oremus': oremus 1795–
.private: one's prayers *npl* a1300–(1846/8)
.using the rosary: rosary 1547–

XR R5.8.18. Rosary

.for royal family: state-prayers *npl* 1831(1)
.to Sacred Heart: Sacred Heart 1815–
.secret: *see R4.1.3. Secreta*
.at sermon: sermon-prayer 1637(1), prone a1670–, pulpit-prayer
1684–1697

XR R4.1.3. Long prayer

.in service of church: *halsunggebed*
.short: jaculatory prayer 1624–1649, ejaculation 1624–1790
..for departed: whom God assoil 1426 + 1610

XR R4.3.1. Suffrage

..char of: ejaculatory 1644–1851, ejaculative 1660(1)
..use of: ejaculation a1635(1)
...to use: ejaculate *vt* 1666–1791
.spontaneous: conceived *a* 1614–1733
..use of: conception 1661(1)
...to use: conceive *vt* 1593–1614
.Stabat Mater: Stabat Mater 1867–

XR R4.3.1. Ave Maria

.supplicatory: *letania*/litany OE(L)–, Rogation(s) 1387–,
supplication 1490–

XR R4.1.5.2.1. Rogation days

..recited by deacon and choir: ectene 1850– *GkCh*
..sung in procession: procession 1543–1616 + 1904*hist.*

XR R4.1.4.1.1. Processional

..part of, introduced by 'by': obsecration 1877–
..time when used: *halsungtima*
..char of: litaneutical 1839–1847

.**for synod:** synodals *npl* 1548/9(1)

R4.4. Good works

R4.4. Good works: merit c1380–, good working c1440(1)

XR R1.9.1. Condignity, congruity

R1.9.2. Merit

.**instance of:** *gode weorc*/good work OE–, *mitzvah* 1650– *Jewish*

.**p char by:** meriter 1607–1651, meritist 1612(*2q1s*), meritorian 1689(1)

.**p expecting to be justified by:** workmonger 1549–1581 + 1882, merit-monger 1552–1846, merit-worker 1577(1), merit-merchant 1647(1) *all contempt.*

..**char of:** work-holy 1528(1)

XR R1.1.0. Workless

.**serving God with:** service c1175–

.**reliance on, for salvation:** legalness a1665(1), legality 1678–1771

.**doctrine of salvation by:** legalism 1876(1)

XR R1.12.0. Salvation

..**p adhering to:** legalist 1651–1860

.**performance of, beyond requirements:** supererogation 1526–

.**the way of:** *karma-marga* 1877– *Hindi*

XR R1.12.0. Bhakti-marga

.**char of law concerning:** legal 1640–1786

.**to advance glory of God with:** *gewuldrian v*

Works of mercy to the bodies of men: corporal works of mercy 15.. + 1871

XR R4.15. Visitation

R4.5. Preaching

R4.5.0. Preaching: *bod, forebod, forebodung, forelar, larbodung, predicung, wordpredicung, bodung*/boding OE–c1175, preaching c1275–, sermoning a1300–1657, predication c1300–1884, preachment c1330–1672 + 1889, prophecy

1382–1709, doctrine 1560/78–1600, prophesying 1560/1–1849, (the) desk 1581–1838, pulpitry 1606–1641 + 1861, predicancy 1627(1), sermonizing 1635–, predicament 1765(1), kerygma 1889–

> XR R1.5.2. Didache
> R1.7.1. Cant

.itinerant: itinerancy 1789–

> XR R3.2.10. Local

..char of: itinerant 1661–

.open-air: field-preaching 1739 + 1814–

> XR R3.2.10. Field-preacher

.tiresome: preachification 1843(1)

.instance of: *cwide, folclar, godspell traht, lar, spell, larspell*/lorespell OE–13.., sermon a1200–, predication c1300–1715, preachment c1400–1864, preaching c1449–a1548 + c1650*Sc.*, postil 1483–1710, preach c1500*Sc.* + 1597–, exercise 1594–(1868), prone a1670–1716 + 1897

> XR R4.1.3. Homily

..part of: use 1631–1816, observe 1833(1-*Sc.*)
..text of: teme a1362–1530, text 1377–, theme 1387–1618
...prefixed to sermon: antethem(e) 1494–1561
..end of: ascription 1899(1)

..paid for by endowment: gift sermon 1766(1)
..for Lent: quadragesimal 1691(1)
..short: sermonette 1814–, sermonettino 1818(1), sermuncle 1886(1)
...p preaching: sermonettist 1873(1)

..p always talking of: gospel-gossip 1711(1)
...char of: sermonish 1858(1)
..excessive devotion to: sermonolatry 1859(1)

..char of: sermonary 1657 + 1666, sermonic 1761–, sermonical 1782 + 1829, sermonish 1847/54–, sermonesque 1859–
..(of x:)capable of providing material for: preachable c1449 + 1895–
..(of Sunday:)without: sermonless 1869–

.p perf: *see R3.2.10. Preacher, R3.3.2.4. Predicator*

.study of: kerystics 1882/3(1)

.char of: pulpitable 1772(1), pulpital 1772–1846, pulpitical 1775 +
1885, pulpitary 1784(1), pulpitic 1845(1), pulpitarian
1887(1), kerygmatic 1929–
.char by: sanctiloquent 1656 + 1845, sermonizing 1714–
..not: unpreaching 1549–(1850)
.inclined to: preachy 1819–
..condition of being: preachiness 1861–

.in manner of: pulpitically 1751(1), kerygmatically 1949–
..wearisomely: preachingly 1657(1)

.to perform: *forebodian v, forecweðan v, foresecgan v, predician
(L) v, bodian*/bode *vt* OE–a1225, sermon *vt* c1175–1863,
preach *vi* a1225–, sermon *vi* a1275–a1300, preach *vt*
c1290–(1864), pulpit *vi* c1540–1867, sermonize *vi* 1635–,
pulpiteer *vi* 1812–, predicate *vt* 1822(1), sermonize *vt* 1860(1)
..(x) out of existence: outpreach *vt* 1826–a1853
..the gospel: *godspellian v*
XR R4.5.1. Evangelization
..as itinerant minister: itinerate *vi* 1775–, travel *vi* 1791–(1913)
..as Apostolic minister: prophesy *vi* 1382–1860
..to outdo in: outpreach *vt* 1643–(1854)
..in tiresome way: preach *vi* 1523–, preachify *vi* 1775–1869

R4.5.1. Evangelization: evangelism a1626–, evangelization
1651–, gospelling 1652 + 1845–, evangelizing 1862(1)
XR R1.2.1.0. Scripture-reading
R1.2.1.2.3.1. Gospel
R2.2.0.1. Conversion to Christianity
.p perf: *æboda, godspellere, evangelista*/evangelist OE(L)–,
manfisher c1305(1), vangelist a1330–1567 *mainly Sc.,*
evangelizer 1382 + 1883, vangelie a1450(1), menfisher
c1550(1), seminary 1583 + 1610, evangel 1593–(1878),
evangelic a1617(1), evangelizationer 1825(1)
XR R3.2.10. Preacher
..char of: evangelizing 1382–, gospelling 1566 + 1579, seminary
1609 + 1640, evangelical 1651 + 1794, gracy 1661(1),

evangelistic 1845–

.char by: evangelical 1768(1-*Sterne*), evangelized 1816–
..not: disgospelling 1642(1), unevangelical 1648–, ungospel 1649 +
1653, ungospelled 1674 + 1902, ungospellized 1706 + 1721,
unevangelized 1775–, unevangelic 1857(1), disgospellized
1888(1)
XR R2.2.0.2. Lack of Christianity
R4.5.4.3. Unconversion

.to perform: *godspellian*/gospel *vt* OE–1659, evangelize *vi*
1382/8–, gospelize *vt* 1643–(1884), evangelize *vt* a1652–,
gospel *vi* 1867(1), evangelize *va/i* 1882(1)

R4.5.2. Catechesis: catechism 1502–1600, catechization
16..–(1869), catechizing 1642–(1858), catechesis 1753–,
Sunday-schooling 1847(1), *mondo* 1927– *Buddhist*
XR R1.5.2. Catechetics

.undenominational: Cowper-Templeism 1906(2)
..p supporting: Cowper-Templeite 1908(1)
..char of: Cowper-Temple 1902–

.p perf: father 1393–1833, catechizer c1414–1691, mystagogue
a1550– *GkCh,* catechist a1563–, guru / gooroo 1613 + 1810–,
director 1669–(1877) *RCCh,* swami 1901– *Hindi*
..to whom p owes religious life: (spiritual) father 1382–
..char of: catechistical 1618–(1835), catechistic 1683–
..in manner of: catechistically 1645–1692

.p undergoing: *leaflhlystend,* catechumen 14..–, auditor 1483–1691
+ 1851, catechumenist 1629–1651, audient 1612–1647
XR R4.2.1.0. Competent
..of 2nd class: hearer 1697–1722, kneeler 1882/3(1)
XR R4.2.2.0. Kneeler, weeper, etc.
..char of: catechumenical 1790–1836, catechumenal 1883(1)
..in manner of: catechumenically 1840(1)

.treatise used for: catechism 1509–, catechise 1552–1715 +
1825 *U.S.dial.,* catechismy 1579(2), *catechesis* 1753–1849,
catechetics *npl* 1849(1)

..char of: catechetical 1618–1849, catechismal 1819–(1860)
.school for: Sunday-school 1783–, sabbath-school 1845(1-*Jewish*),
church school 1862–

.char by: catechized c1449–
..not: uncatechized 1619–
...condition of being: uncatechizedness 1659(1)
.capable of undergoing: catechizable 1772–1867

.to perform: +*cristnian v,* catechize *vt* 14..–, catechumenize *vt*
1676(1)

Teaching function of church: magisterium 1866–, magistery
1899(1) *both RCCh*

R4.5.3.0. Proselytization: proselytism a1660–, proselytation
1826(1), proselytization 1871–
.p perf: proselyter a1834(1), proselytizer 1848–, proselytist 1859–
.p undergoing: proselyte 1382–

XR R3.2.13. Souper

.to perform: proselyte *vt* 1624–1831, proselyte *va* 1660–,
proselytize *vi* 1679–, proselytize *vt* 1796–
.to undergo: proselyte *vi* 1657/83–1672, proselyte *vrefl* 1716(1)

R4.5.3.1. Mission: mission 1598–, missionarizing 1829–1830,
station 1834–, missioning 1886(1), missionizing 1888(1)
.in city: city-mission 1851(1)
.Jesuit, of S. Americans: reduction 1712–

.p conducting: missioner 1654–, missionary 1656–, gospeller 1673
+ 1847/9, missionizer 1901(1), missionist 1909(1)

XR R3.2.1.3. Propagandist
R3.3.4.1. The Seventy

..who first brings Xtianity to place: apostle c1425 + 1844–
..of city-mission: city-missionary 1851(1)
..pl/coll: mission 1622–, missionary 1719–1761
..status of: missionaryship 1840–
..p susceptible to: missionee 1951(1)
..to pester with: bemissionary *vt* 1884(1)

.study of: missiology 1937–
..p engaged in: missiologist 1951–
..char of: missiological 1961–

.char of: missionary 1644–, missional 1907(1)
.performing: missionizing 1804–
.having: missionized 1879(1)
..not: unmissionized 1860(1)

.to conduct: mission *vt* 1772–, missionize *vi* 1826(1), missionate
   vi/t 1828–, missionary *vi/t* 1862–(1893), missionize *vt* 1879–,
   mission *vi* 1898(1)
.to deprive M of its character as: demissionize *vt* 1883(1)

R4.5.3.2. Revival: revival 1702–, mission 1772–, rousement
   1883– *U.S.*
.p engaged in: revivalist 1820–, reviver 1824(1)
.state/form of religion char by: revivalism 1815–
.char of: revivalistic 1882 + 1886
.to bring about: revivalize *vi* 1882(1)

Retreat: retreat 1756–
.p taking part in: retreatant 1880 + 1899, retreater 1889(1)

R4.5.4.0. Conversion: *gecierrednes, +cierring,* conversion
   c1340–, conversation 1388–1535, disciplization 1657/83(1),
   discipling 1697 + 1713, converting 1819(1), conversionism
   1885(1), passover 1889(1)
                    XR R2.2.0.1. Conversion to Christianity
                       R4.2.1.0. Baptism
.a second time: reconversion 1599–1867
.to Christianity: christening a1300–c1340, inchristianation
   1654(1), christianization 1833–1847, christianizing 1859(1)

.p perf: converter 1570/6–1838, convertist 1711–1741,
   conversionist 1887–
..to Christianity: Christianizer 1806(1)
.p writing about: conversioner 1655(1)

.p who has undergone: proselyte 1382–, converse 1388–1483, convert 1561–, convertite c1592–1624 + 1839–, convertist 1611–1616, proselytess *nf* 1879(1)

..new: *niwcumen,* neophyte 1550–

...pl/coll: babes in Christ 1526 + 1771

..to Christianity: Christianizer 1652(1-*derog.*)

...Hindu: rice-Christian 1816 + 1836

..of the RC Congregation of Propaganda: propagandist 1890–

..gentile, to Judaism: proselyte c1375–, proselytess *nf* 1621–1711

..a second time: reconvert 1843(1), retrovert 1873(1)

.performing: converting 1643(1)

.having undergone: *gebogen,* convert 1622–1812, converted 1640–

..newly: *nigecyrred, nighworfen, ni(ge)hwyrfed, niwe*

..to Christianity: christened c1200–1728, Christianized 1671–1767, Christianizing 1806(1), evangelized 1816–(1819)

.capable of: convertible 1805–

..condition of being: convertibility 1809(1)

.to perform: *gebiegan to fulluhte (vphr), gebiegan to geleafan (vphr), +cierran v,* turn *vt* c1200–1692, convert *vt* a1300–, illumine *vt* c1340–1554 + 18.., fish *vi* 1413 + 1552 *fig.,* convertise/-yse *vt* 1483(2-*Caxton*), salvationize *vt* 1927–

..from paganism: unpaganize *vt* 1678 + 1801

..a second time: reconvert *vt* 1649–

..to Christianity: *cristen*/christen *vt* OE–1644 + 1880, Christian *v* 1586–1684, Christianize *vt* 1593–1851

...a second time: rechristianize *vt* 1792–1851

.to undergo: *to fulluhte (ge)bugan (vphr), geliefan v,* turn *vi* a1225–(1891), convert *vi* a1300–1649, convert *vrefl* c1400–c1430, get religion *vphr* 1772– *orig. U.S.,* see the light *vphr* 1812–, experience religion *vphr* 1837– *chiefly U.S.,* find Jesus / Christ *vphr* 1877 + 1932, find religion 1957(1)

..to Christianity: Christianize *vi* 1598–1823

.to undo: unconvert *vt* 1825 + 1887

R4.5.4.1. Moral conversion: conversion a1340–, conversation 1382–1485

XR R1.8.1.2. Regeneration
.char of p causing: verticordious 1702(1), converting 1585(1)
.char by: convert 1622–1812, converted 1640–, converting
    1646–1675 + 1846

.to perform: +*cierran v*, convert *vt* a1340–
.to undergo: convert *vi* ?a1400–1826, convert *vrefl* c1475(1-*Sc.*)

R4.5.4.2. Reconciliation: reconcilement ?1567–1600,
    reconciliation 1625–1639 + 1753–
.char by: reconciled 1820(1-*Scott*)
.capability of undergoing: reconciliability a1861(1)
.to bring about: reconcile *vt* 1387–(a1625), recounsel *vt* 1496 +
    a1578*Sc.*, recounsel *vrefl* 1572(1-*Sc.*)
.to undergo: reconcile *vpass* 1639–1840

R4.5.4.3. Unconversion: inconversion 1633(1), unconversion
    1846(1)
XR R1.8.1.2. Irregeneracy
R2.2.0.2. Lack of Christianity
.char by: *ungecyrred*, unconverted 1648–, unconvertible 1805(1)
..condition of being: unconvertibility 1804(1)

R4.6. Pilgrimage

R4.6. Pilgrimage: *eldeodignes, wræcsið,* pilgrimage c1250–,
    pel(e)rinage c1300–1390, peregrinage 1340(1), pilgrimaging
    c1449–1731, voyage 1456–1518, peregrination
    1528–(1637/50), rummery 1638(1), roomery 1665(1),
    peregrinacy 1674(1), pilgrimizing 1818(1)
XR R5.10.2. Relic
.to Rome: *sudfor*

.p making: pilgrim a1225–, palmer a1300–1674 + 1808–*hist.*,
    pelerin 1456–c1614, peregrine 1570–1654, pilgrimer
    a1581–1827, pilgrimager 1591(1), pilgrimess *nf* 1611–, visitant
    1698–(1844), palmerman 1885(1)
..to Mecca: hadji 1612–

..**Oriental Christian, to Jerusalem:** hajji 1835(1)
..**state/domain of:** pilgrimdom 1887(1)
..**char of:** pilgrimaging a1819–

.**place to which P is made:** station c1380–, pilgrimage 1517–,
   holy places *npl* 1758–, pilgrimage town / village 1889–(1895),
   pilgrimage church 1908–(1935)
.**impulse to go on:** devotion c1489 + a1533

.**to make:** *elðeod(g)ian v, wræcsiðian v, weallian*/wall *vi*
   OE–c1485, visit *vt* a1340–, pilgrimize *vi* 1598/9–, pilgrimage
   vi 1621–

R4.7. Crusade

R4.7. Crusade: crusade 1577–, crusading 1837–
.**p engaged in:** *crusado* 1575–1625, crusader 1743–(1866), crusard
   1753(*2q1s*), croisard 1766–1838, crescentader 1880(1-*Moslem*)
..**pl/coll:** croise(e)s *npl* 1656–1846

XR R4.15. Croised

.**char by:** crusading 1759–

.**to participate in:** fong the cross *vphr* c1290(1), nim the cross
   vphr 1297(1), take the cross *vphr* c1330–, crusade it *vi* 1737–,
   crusade *vi* 1759–

R4.8. Sacrifice

R4.8.0. Sacrifice: *+blot, blotung, freolac, giefu, godcundnes,
   husel, gesægednes, onsægedness, onsægnes, onsægung, tiber,
   tobrengnes, gield*/yield OE–a1225, *lac*/lake OE–c1250,
   oflæte/oflete OE–a1300 + 1881*hist., offrung*/offering OE–,
   off(e)rand c1200–a1572, sacrifice a1300–, sacrifying
   13?–c1374, obley a1340(1), host a1340–1653, manna
   1382–1611, oblation 1412/20–, hostie 1483–1681, sacrificy
   c1511(1), immolation 1534–, offredge 1548(*2q1s*), offerture
   1595–1624, litation 1623–1660, sacrificing a1639–1742,
   mactation 1640–, sacrification 1694(1), sacrificature

1779–1827

XR R1.11.0. Atonement

R4.2.4.0. Eucharist

R4.2.4.1.0. Immolation

R4.9.1. Purification

R4.16.4. Offertory

.p making: *blotere, onsecgend,* offerer 1382–, sacrificator ?1548–1859, oblationer 1593–1660, sacrificer 1597–(1884), immolater 1652–, sacrificant 1665–(1885)

..of self: self-sacrificer 1668 + 1903

..char of: sacrificing 1848(1)

.x undergoing: *cwicalmus, onsægednes, tiber, offrung*/offering OE–, off(e)rand c1200–a1572, sacrifice c1250–(1845), host a1340–1653, oblation c1430–, hostie 1483–1681, victim 1497–, present 1535–1707, offredge 1548(*2q1s*), offer 1548–(1840), idolothyte 1579 + 1703, anathema 1581–(1857), victimate 1583(2), immolation 1589–1651, deodate a1600(1), sacreds *npl* 1608 + 1624, vict 1639(1), anatheme 1654 + 1850

..that is a goat: scapegoat 1530–

..that is a lamb: paschal lamb c1430–, passover 1530–a1680, pasch-lamb 1533–1605, passover-lamb 1545(1), paschal a1655(1)

..that is a consecrated ram: *halgungram*

.fire used in: *adfyr*

..pile for: pile 1577–

.char of: sacrificatory 1581–1699, sacrificing c1586–(1709), sacrificial 1608–, oblatory 1611–, offertorial 1856 + 1887, oblational 1867–

.char by: offered c1175–, immolate 1534–1551 + 1830*arch.*, immolated 1548–, sacrificed 1597–, offertory 1641–

.suitable for: sacrificeable 1483 + 1603, sacrifiable 1603(1), sacrificable 1646 + 1973

..not: unsacrificeable 1580–1650

.used in: sacrific 1727(1)

.in manner of: sacrificially 1937–

.to perform: *blotan v, gieldan v, lac onsendan vphr, onblotan v, ongieldan v, onsecgan v, +offrian*/offer *vt* OE–, lake *vt*

c1200(*2q1s*), sacre *vt* c1250(*2q1s*), sacrifice *vi* c1290–(1818),
sacrify *vt* a1300–1590, sacrifice *vt* a1300–, teem *vt*
13..(1-*Cursor Mundi*), sacrify *vi* a1325–1555, immolate *vt*
1548–, present *vt* 1548/9–, shrine *vt* c1611(1), immolate *vi*
1628 + 1660, victim *vt* 1671–1694, victimize *vt* 1853–
..by burning: burn *vt* c1200–, holocaust *vt* 1651(1)
..by loading altar with fat: fat *vt* 1382 + 1698

R4.8.1. Kinds of sacrifice
.of animal: trespass-offering 1535–(1845) *Jewish,* sin-offering
    1535– *Jewish*
..of bull: *hriðerfreols,* tauroboly 1700–
..of horse: hippocaust 1858–
..of 100 oxen: hecatomb a1592–
...to make: hecatomb *vt* a1745 + 1808
..of 1000 oxen: chiliomb 1697–1807
..of rams: krioboly 1879–
.burnt: *bærnelac, bærning, brynegield, cwiclac, ealloffrung, tiber,*
    holocaust c1250–, burnt-sacrifice 1382–1611, burnt(-)offering
    1382–, immolation 1589–1651, fire-offering c1870(1)
..char of: holocaustal 1828(1), holocaustic 1871(1)
.in evening: *æfenlac, æfenoffrung, nihtgild*
                                    XR R4.1.6.0. Vespers
.of first fruits: prelibation 1635/56–1805
.of food: meat-offering 1535–1611, lectisternium 1597–1857
    Roman antiq., pinda 1785– *Hindi*
.on receipt of good news: evangelian sacrifice 1808(1-*Greek
    antiq.*)
.to idol: *idelgildoffrung,* idolothyte 1579–1703, idolothism
    1607–a1640
                                    XR R1.1.11.0. Idolatry
..char of: idolothyte 1562 + 1637, idolothyous 1607 + 1637
.made by Engl king at sacrament: byzantine 1605(1), bezant /
    byzant 1667 + 1762
.made when military action was imminent: ?*fyrdtiber*
.in morning: *dægredoffrung*
.for peace: peaceable 1382(1)

.of self: self-sacrifice 1805–

..char of: self-sacrificing 1817–, self-sacrificial 1855 + 1893,
     self-surrendering 1903(1)

...condition of being: self-sacrificingness 1871(1)

..char by: self-sacrificed a1711 + 1900

.for sin: sin-money 1611(1), sin-rent 1899(1)

.in thanksgiving: thank-offering 1530–1539 + 1839–,
     peace-offering 1535–, sacrifice of praise (and thanksgiving)
     1535–, thanks-offering 1921–

..char of: gratulatory a1555–1739

.voluntary: *chagigah* 1846– *Jewish*

.votive: vow 1382–a1700, devotion 1542–1662, votive 1646(1),
     devotement 1799(1), *ex voto* 1834–

..which is hung up: pendant 1621(1)

..char of: votal 1846(1), exvotive 1863(1)

..in manner of: votively 1847(1)

.made in connection with performance of vow: *corban* 1382–

.which is waved when presented: wave-offering 1530–1625,
     heave-offering 1530–1653, shake-offering 1625(1)

..x employed in: wave-breast 1530(1), wave-loaf 1530(1),
     heave-shoulder 1530–a1659, wave-sheaf 1535(1), wave-bread
     1879(1)

..to employ: wave *vt* 1530–1535

.of wine: *win tiber*, libation 1382–, drink-offering 1535(1),
     libament 1582–(1855), libature 1632(1), minne-drinking
     1880(1-*Germ.antiq.*

..p perf: libationer 1920(1)

..char of: libatory 1834–1846, libationary 1894–

..to make: wassail *vt* 1648– *local*, libate *vt/i* 1866–

.of Rajput women: johan 1802–

R4.8.2. Propitiation: propitiation 1388–, expiation 1675–(1734)

                    XR R1.11.0. Atonement

                    R4.9.1. Lustration

.p perf: propitiator 1571–(1742)

.char of: propitiatory 1551–1736, propitiatoire 1580(1-*Sc.*)

.char by: propitiate 1551(1), propitiated a1711–(1873)

.performing: propitiating a1812(1)
.capable of: propitiable 1553 + 1563
.capable of undergoing: propitiable 1557–1662
.in manner of: propitiatorily a1555 + 1853

.to perform: *gegladdian v*, propitiate *vt* 1645–

R4.9. Cleanness

R4.9.0. Cleanness (ceremonial): *clænnesse*/cleanness OE–,
　　cleanliness 1430–1489, pureness 1607–1643, purity a1661–
.char by: *clænlic*/cleanly OE–1683, *clæn*/clean OE–, pure
　　1611–(1613)
..not: *gemænlic*, common a1300–1849, foul c1400(1), impure
　　1612/15–
.in manner evincing: purely 1613(1)

R4.9.1. Purification: washing c1375–, purification c1380–,
　　expiation 1532–1651, emundation 1609 + 1652, lustration
　　1614–, purifaction 1652(1), lustrating 1653(1), purgation
　　a1711–1769, *samskara* 1807– *Hindi*
　　　　　　　　　　　　XR R1.6.2.0. Consecration
　　　　　　　　　　　　　　　R4.1.3. Lavabo
　　　　　　　　　　　　　　　R4.1.5.2.2. Chanukah
　　　　　　　　　　　　　　　R4.8.0. Sacrifice
.of church (after defilement): *mynsterclænsung,* reconciliation
　　1533–
.of feet: maundy c1290–(1850), foot-washing 1796(1), pediluvials
　　npl 1828(1)
.of women, following childbirth: *ciricgang*/church-gang OE +
　　c1200(1), purgation 1382–14.., purification c1440–1548/9,
　　churching 1523–(1837)
.bath in which P is gained: mikva 1843– *Jewish*
.char of: lustral 1533–, februate 1610(1), lustrical 1623 + 1741,
　　lustrating 1653–(1846), lustrific 1656–1732, purificatory
　　1881(1), lustrant 1895(1)
.char by: churched 1611(1)

.to perform: *clænsian*/cleanse *vt* OE–1611, +*halgian*/hallow *vt*
   OE–, clenge *vt* a1300(1-*Sc. and N.*), purify *vt* c1330–(1853),
   purge *vt* 1390–1600, sanctify *vt* a1500–1611, expiate *vt*
   1603–1655/60, housel *vt* 1607(1), lustre *vt* 1645(1), lustrate *vt*
   1655–, catharize *vt* 1832(1)

   XR R1.6.2.0. Consecration

..in regard to woman after childbirth: purify *vt*
   c1330–1548/9, church *vt* 1440–1837
..in regard to animal: porge *vt* 1864–
...p perf: porger 1773 + 1864, *shochet* 1889– *Jewish*

   XR R3.3.4.1. Slaughterer

..in regard to defiled church: reconcile *vt* c1386–, recounsel *vt*
   c1450–1496 + 1533*Sc.*

Body of Jewish law regarding fitness of food, etc.: kashrut
   1907–
.observance of: kashrut 1907–
.food prepared according to: kosher 1886–
..char of: kosher 1851–
...not: *trefa / trifa* a 1892–
..to prepare: kosher *vt* 1892(1)

R4.9.2. Tonsure: tonsure 1387–, rasure 1483–1737, shaving
   1647(1)
.instance of: *scearu,* God's mark c1200–c1205, crown c1205–1533,
   Christ's mark a1300(1), crowning 1393(1), tonsure 1430/40–,
   corona 1846/7(1)
.p char by: shaveling 1529– *contempt.,* pilpate 1530–1560,
   shorling 1538–1560
..char of: shaveling 1577–

.char by: *bescoren,* tonsured 1706–
..condition of being: tonsurate 1897(1)

   XR R4.2.6.0. Order

..not: *unbescoren,* uncrowned 1393(1-*Langland*)

.to perform: *bescieran v, scieran*/shear *vt* OE–1653, crown *vt*
   c1290–1393, shave (a p's) crown *vphr* 13..–1593, shave *vt*
   a1400/50–, tonsure *vt* 1843–(1878)

XR R4.2.6.1.0. Ordain
.to undergo: *scieran v,* be shorn in *vphr* 1565–1567/9

R4.9.3. Circumcision: *ymbceorfnes, ymbhywung, ymbsniðennes,* circumcision c1175–, circumcising a1300–1611, posthetomy 1853–
.lack of: incircumcision a1641(1)
.p perf: circumciser 1535–(1846), mohel 1650– *Jewish, mudim* 1817– *Moslem*
.p advocating: circumcisionist 1883(1)

.char by: circumcis c1250(2), circumcised 1604–, excoriate 1611(1), unforeskinned 1671(1-*Milton*)
..not: uncircumcis c1250(1), uncircumcided 1382 + 1535, uncircumcized 1387–, incircumcized 1483 + 1554
XR R1.1.11.0. Pagan
.performing: circumcizing a1711(1)

.to perform: *ymbsniðan v, ymbceorfan*/umbecarve *vt* OE + a1240, umbeclip *vt* c1200(1), umbeshear *vt* c1200(*2q1s*), circumcize *vt* c1250–, shear *vt* c1250–a1300, circumcide *vt* 1340–1609, carve *vt* c1420(1), excise *vt* 1634–1650

R4.10. Sacrilege

R4.10.0. Sacrilege: *æbrecð, ciricbræc, ciricbryce, ciricran, feondæt, forecost(n)ung, gewemming*/wemming OE–c1375, sacrilege a1300–, sacrilegy 13..–1529, pollution 1382–1726, violation 1546–, dishallowing 1552(1), profanation 1552–, profaneness 1594–, exauguration 1600 + 1651, profanism 1607(1), desecration a1717–, sacrilegiousness 1727(1), profanement 1815(1)
XR R1.6.3. Unholiness
R1.7.3. Impiety
.p char by: sacrileger c1380–(1883), defouler 14..–c1440, sacrilege 1491–1585 + 1802, defiler 1546–(1882), profaner a1572*Sc.* + 1670–a1861, violater 1577–, sacrilegist 1621–(1898), desecrator 1879–

.**char of:** sacrileging 1554(1), desecrating 1675–, profanatory
  1853(1), desecrative a1861–(1865)
.**char by:** *æbrucol, godwræclic,* sacrilegious 1582–(1864), unsacred
  1608–, desecrated a1711–, desecrate 1873(1-*Browning*)
..**not:** unprofane 1576 + 1646
.**liable to undergo:** profanable 1891(1)
..**not:** unprofanable a1641 + 1869
.**in manner evincing:** profanely 1577–(1855), sacrilegiously
  1609–(1848), unsacredly 1852(1)

.**to cause:** *ædl(i)an v, afylan v, agælan v, awidlian v, forecostian
  v, gefylan v, idlian v, oht grettan vphr, gewemman v, widlian
  v,* defoil *vt* 13..–1549/62, defoul *vt* 13..–1614, profane *vt*
  1382–, defile *vt* ?a1500–(1683), profanate *vt* 1526–1570,
  deprave *vt* a1529(1), unhallow *vt* 1535–(1860), dishallow *vt*
  1552–(1869), execrate *vt* a1572–1656, profanizate *vt* 1578(1),
  sacrilege *vt* 1578–(1866), unconsecrate *vt* 1598–1768/74,
  exaugurate *vt* 1600–1695, desecrate *vt* a1677–, profanize *vt*
  c1873(1), disenhallow *vt* 1847(1)
..**again:** reprofane *vt* 1614(1)

R4.10.1. Blasphemy: *bismer, bismersp(r)æc, bismerung,
  dysignes, hearmcwide, hierwing, hierwnes, hosp,
  leahtorcwide, tæl, widersacung, wodnes, woffung, yfelsacung,
  yfelsæc, yfelsung, cursung*/cursing OE–, blasphemy a1225–,
  blaspheme 1384–1583, blaspheming c1430–1648, blasphement
  1544(1), blasphemation 1549 + 1552, profanity 1607–
.**p char by:** *hierwend, widersacend, yfelsacend,* curser
  1303–(c1750), blaspheme 1382 + 1401, blasphemer c1386–,
  blasphematour / -ature 1483 + 1581, profane a1529–1596 +
  1891, blasphemeress *nf* 1548(1), God tearer a1550(1), tearer
  of God 1570(1)
..**addicted to oath 'Damn me!':** damme 1618–1674

.**char by:** *wod,* blaspheme 1382 + c1410, blasphemy
  c1384(2-*Wyclif*), blasphemous 1535–, blaspheming
  1569–(1805), blasphematory 1611 + 1725, sulphurous 1828–
..**condition of being:** blasphemousness 1854(1)

.**in manner evincing:** *bismerlice, wodlice,* blasphemely c1380 + 1395, blasphemously 1531–

.**to engage in:** *bismerian v, dysigan v, +hierwan v, swician v, wiðersacian v, woffian v, +yfelsacian v, +yfelsian, wiergan*/wary *vt* OE–a1500, *cursian*/curse *vt* OE–1732, last *vt* a1225–c1300, take (p's) name in vain *vphr* 13..–, forswear *vt* c1325(1), tear (the name of) God *vphr* c1325–a1624, blaspheme *vi* 1340–(1835), blaspheme *vt* 1382–, manswear *vt* 1533–1567 *Sc.,* profane *vi* 1690(1)

R4.10.2. Iconoclasm: iconomachy 1581–, iconoclasm 1797–
XR R1.1.11.0. Heathenism
.**p char by:** iconoclast 1641–, eidoloclast 1824(1-*De Quincey*)
.**char by:** iconoclastic 1640–, iconoclast 1685–

R4.10.3. Clerical misbehaviour: irregularity a1300–
XR R4.2.6.1.1. Unfrocking
.**p char by:** irregular 1619–
.**discredit to religion occasioned by:** scandal a1225–
.**char of:** irregular c1380–
.**char by:** scandalous 1631–1667

Leaving order without dispensation: apostasy 1532 + 1877
.**p char by:** apostate c1387–
XR R4.2.6.5. Fugitive

Neglect of chastity: *æwbryce*
.**p char by:** *æwbreca*

Cleric violating vow of poverty: propertary c1400–1526, proprietary c1450–1538, proprietaire c1491(1)

Nepotism: nepotism 1662–, nephewship 1669(1)
.**p perf:** nepotist 1837–
..**char of:** nepotistical 1886(1)
.**char by:** nepotic 1847–

Simony: *see R4.16.3. Simony*

R4.10.4. Controversy: controversy 1563/87–, tippet scuffle
  1641(1-*Milton*)
.p char by: controverser 1620–a1670, controversist 1626(*2q1s*),
  controverter 1636(1), controversialist 1794–
.char by: controversious 1566(1), controversed c1575–1585,
  controversial 1583–, controversary/-ory 1610 + 1628,
  controversal 1612(1), controversional 1882/3(1)
..not: uncontroversory 1641(1), uncontroversial 1861–
.in manner of: controversially 1682 + 1882
..not: uncontroversially 1847(1)

Marprelate's tenets: Martinism 1589–1597
.p adhering to: Martinist 1589–1659
.char of: Martinish 1592(1), Marprelate 1862(1), Marprelatist
  1879(1)
.to inveigh in style of: martinize *vi* 1591(1), marprelate *vi*
  1636(1)

R4.11. Vow

R4.11.0. Vow: *gehat, wilsumnes, behat*/behote OE–a1300, vow
  1297–, avow a1300–c1465
                        XR R4.2.6.1.0. Evangelical counsels
.monastic: *munucbehat*, vow c1400–, stability 1516– *Benedictine*
                        XR R4.2.6.5. Profess
..bound by: religious a1300–, vowed 1532–a1708, votary
  1564–1656, votarious a1581(1), votal 1636–1656
...not: unprofessed c1430–a1450 + 1808

.formal: solemn *a* c1315–, sacramental *a* 1460–(1863), solemned *a*
  1567(1)
.simple: simple *a* 1759–
.of silence: silence 1387–

.p bound by: votarist 1603–
                        XR R1.8.4. Votary

.worthy of: oathable 1607(1), oath-worthy 1882 + 1886
.carrying out: votive 1593(1)

.**to make:** *gieldan v, gehatan v,* avow *vt* 1382–1583, avowre *vi*
a1560(1)
..**as a religious:** *behatan v*

XR R4.2.6.1. Ordain

R4.11.1. Covenant: *ciricwaru,* testament a1300–1611, covenant
a1300–, convenaunt 1382(1), promission c1440–1560, promise
1502–1819
.**counter-:** repromission 1382–1692, repromise 1750(1)
.**of grace:** covenant of grace a1640–(1818)

XR R1.9.0. Grace
.**of works:** covenant of works a1640–(1818), covenant of life
1647(1), work-covenant 1892(1)

XR R4.4. Good works
..**char of:** federal 1645–
.**Scottish Presbyterian:** covenant 1638–
..**p adhering to:** covenanter 1638–, covenanteer/-ier 1660–1681,
gospel-lad c1679(1), hill-man c1830(1)
...**following dispossessed minister:** wanderer 1724–
...**pl/coll:** hill-folk 1816(1)

..**taking:** covenanting 1653–
...**not:** incovenanting 1640(1)
..**having subscribed to:** incovenanted 1656(1), covenanted
1660–(1855)
...**not:** uncovenanted 1818–

..**to take:** covenant *vi* 1661(1)

.**char of:** covenantal 1863–
.**included in:** covenanted 1836–
..**not:** uncovenanted 1858 + 1860
.**in manner of:** federally 1644/5–

.**p included in:** confederate 1655–a1708, covenantee 1692–1726

R4.11.2. Non-jurancy: non-swearing 1692(1), non-jurantism
1706(1), non-jurancy 1715–, non-jurorism 1882(1)
.**p char by:** non-subscriber 1599–(1727), non-scriber 1650–1651,

non-swearer 1690–c1693, non(-)juror 1691–, non-jurant
    1702–, non-juress *nf* 1723(1)
..**observing usages:** usager 1788–
...**not:** non-usager 1874(1)

.**char of:** non-jurant 1696–
.**char by:** non-swearing 1691–a1704, non-juring 1691–,
    non-juristical 1723(1), non-jurist 1871(1)

R4.12. Martyrdom

R4.12.0. Martyrdom: *đrowendhad, đrowerhad, đrowethad,
    martirdom*/martyrdom OE–, passion a1225–1754/8 +
    1901*arch.*, martyrship a1661(1), witnessdom 1877(1)
.**p who undergoes:** *cydere, đrowere, martir*/martyr OE–, witness
    1382–(1637)
                        XR R1.2.1.3. Holy innocents
                           R4.1.1. Martyrolatry
..**race of:** *martyrcynn*
..**fellow:** co-martyr / commartyr c1555–c1645
..**female:** *đrowestre*, martyress 1471–1678
..**first:** protomartyr 1433–
..**great:** megalomartyr 1756–1840
..**in holy orders:** hieromartyr 1864(1-*GkCh*)
..**Muslim:** *shahid / shaheed* 1881–

..**narrative account of passion of:** passion 1904–
..**suffering undergone by:** *đrowung,* passion c1175–, suffering
    c1340–

.**to undergo:** martyrize *vi* 1524(1)
.**to cause violent death of unbaptized M:** baptize in blood
    vphr 1861(1)
.**to cause:** *gemartyrian v*

R4.12.1. Confession: confession 1833(1)
.**p char by:** *andettere,* confessor a1175–, confessatrix *nf* 1604(1)
..**status of:** confessorship 1655–

..**suffering undergone by:** *ďrowung,* suffering c1340–

R4.13. Exorcism

R4.13. Exorcism: *halsung*/halsing OE–1387, conjurement c1315(*2q1s*), exorcism c1375–, adjuration 1386–, exorcision 1502(1), exsufflation 1502–(1858), exorcization 1502–(1856), insufflation 1580–, exorcizing 1610–, exorcizement 1782 + 1873, exorcize 1863(1)

.**p perf:** *see R3.2.12.3. Exorcist*

.**char of:** exorcistical 1664–1827, exorcisory 1836(1), exorcismal 1887(1)

.**having undergone:** conjured 1599–1634, exorcized 1664–

.**to perform:** *healsian v, halsian*/halse *vt* OE–1553, set / light / proffer a candle before / to the devil *vphr* c1461–1649, exorcize *vt* 1546–, exsuffle *vt* 1610(1)

XR R4.15. Sain *vt*

R4.14. Excommunication

R4.14.0. Excommunication: *amansumung, biscopdom, unbletsung, amansung*/amansing OE–1340, *cursung*/cursing OE–1568 + 1872, warying c1200–a1660, mansing c1290–c1425, mallok(e) a1300(*2q1s*), sequestration c1400–, commination 1460–(1868), malediction 1477–(1855), excommunication 1494–, excommengement 1495–1641, excommuny 1502(1), fulmination 1502–1861, anathemization 1549–a1555, anathem c1555–1648, anathematical 1583 + 1775, anathema 1590–, anathematization 1593–1645 + 1865, aggravation 1611–(1864), excommunion 1641–1659, excision 1647–(1879), excommunicating 1648–(1845), unchurching a1658–(1852), dischurching 1695(1), consecration 1700(1), anathematizing 1753 + 1880

XR R1.13.0. Reprobation

.**from synagogue:** *(c)herem* 1829–

.**intensified:** maranatha 1382–, anathema maranatha 1526–,
    effulmination a1670(1)

.**rite of:** *amansumung, curs*/curse OE–, sentence c1290–1523,
    malison a1300–1586, bell, book, and candle *nphr* a1300–,
    candle, book, and bell *nphr* a1300 + 1842, censure 138.–1845,
    censury 1494–1523, anathematism 1565–1753, imprecation
    1603–, excommunication 1647–, anathema 1691–

.**p perf:** banner c1440–1627, excommunicator 1643–(1855),
    anathematizer 1647 + 1649, excommunicant 1651(1),
    comminator 1682–

..**char of:** anathematizing 1653–(1833)

.**p under:** *amansumod,* publican 1303–a1651 *transf.,* anathema
    1526–, anathem c1555(1), excommunicate 1562–(1852),
    excommunicant 1586–1641 + 1887

.**p who absolves p from:** assoiler 1813(1)

.**char of:** excommunicatory 1683–(1884), excommunicative
    1825–(1876), anathematical 1882–

.**char by:** *amansumod, amansod*/amansed OE–c1220, maledight
    a1300(*6q1s - Cursor Mundi*), cursed / curst a1300–(1862),
    aggravate 1481(1-*Caxton*), excommunicate 1526–(1874) *arch.,*
    excommunicated 1580–, anathematized 1605–, devoted
    1611–(1862), thunder-struck 1649 + 1680

..**not:** *unamansumod,* unexcommunicated 1588(1),
    unexcommunicate 1680(1)

.**disposed/eager to perform:** excommunicating 1837(1),
    excommunicatory 1837(1), excommunicative 1858(1) *all*
    Carlyle

.**to perform:** *amansumian*/amanse *vt* OE–c1308, *gewiergan*/way
    vt OE–1562, *cursian*/curse *vt* OE–, forcurse *vt* 1154 + 1300,
    accurse *vt* c1175–1667 + 1868, manse *vt* c1200 + 14..,
    maledight *vt* a1300(1), ban *vt* 1303–1483 + 1814–*hist.,*
    sequester *vt* 1395–1642, excommune *vt* 1483–1608,
    excommenge *vt* 1502–1641, excommunicate *vt* 1526/34–,
    precide *vt* 1529–1537, damn *vt* 1535(1), anathematize *vt*
    1566–, malison *vt* 1588–1675 *Sc.,* consecrate *vt* 1589–1652,
    comminate *vt* 1611–1848/54, shammatize *vt* 1613–1684

Jewish, anathemate *vt* 1615(1), unchurch *vt* a1620–, innodate *vt* 1635–1655, inknot *vt* 1639(1), fulminate *vi* 1639–(1852), dischurch *vt* 1651(1), anathemize *vt* 1674–1689 + 1837, swear at *vphr* 1680–, devote *vt* 1749(1), maledict *vt* 1780–, imban *vt* 1808 + 1828, anathematize *vi* 1837 + 1847

.**to absolve p from:** assoil *vt* 1362–1691

R4.14.1. Imprecation: *halsung, onben,* imprecation 1589–
.**char by:** imprecatory 1587–, maledictive 1865–
.**to perform:** *giernan v, halsian v, healsian v,* imprecate *vt* 1613–

R4.14.2. Interdict: interdict 1297–, interdicting c1380–1523, interdiction 1494–(c1750)
.**char by:** interdict c1440–a1593
.**to apply:** interdict *vt* c1290–, suspend *vt* c1380–1561

R4.15. Other practices

R4.15. Other practices
Ashes-dodding: ashes-dodding a1564(1)
XR R4.1.5.2.1. Ash Wednesday
Aspersion: aspersion 1553/87–, asperges 1553/87 + 1884, asperging 1865(1)
XR R5.8.3. Aspergillum
.**instance of:** asperge 1579(1)
.**having undergone:** asperged 1579–
..**not:** unhallow-washed 1614(1)
Church-strewing: church-strewing 1506(1), rush-bearing 1617–
Circumgestation: circumgestation a1564–1655, *pradakshina* 1810– *Hindi*
Sign of the Cross: *bletsung, (halig) rodtacn*/(holy) rood token OE–a1225, *cruc*/crouch OE–c1315, cross a1225–(1861), sign of the cross c1315–, blessing 1562 + 1563
XR R1.6.2.2. Blessing
.**having taken:** crossed 1625(1), croised 1639(1), becrossed 1799(1)
XR R4.7. Crusade

..**not:** *ungesenod*

.**action of making:** saining 1508–1888, consignation 1537–1660 +
1822–(1868), signing 1782–

..**p char by:** crosser 1565(1)

..**to perform:** +*mearcian*/mark *vt* OE–1577, *segnian*/sain *vt*
OE–c1375, +*segnian*/sain *vrefl* OE–1828, +*bletsian*/bless *v*
OE–, croise *vt* a1225–c1380 + 1470*Sc.,* crouch *vt* a1225–1386,
sign *vt* c1305–, cross *vt* c1430–, sain *vi* c1440 + 1571, bemark
vt 1544(1), becross *vt* 1581(1)

XR R1.6.2.2. Bless *vt*

...**before baptism:** prime-sign / primsign *vt* c1200–c1425 +
1874–*hist.*

XR R4.2.1.0. Baptism
R4.5.2. Catechumen

...**by way of dedication:** consign *vt* 1533–a1713

...**by way of sanctifying vow:** croise *vt* 1297–1639, cross *vt*
1481–1610, crusado *vt* 1671(1)

XR R4.7. Crusade
R4.11.0. Vow

...**by way of protection or exorcism:** sain *vt* a1400–(1887)

XR R4.13. Exorcism

Dance: kanticoy 1670–(1866) *NAmerind,* snake-dance 1772–,
mudra 1811– *Hindi,* sun-dance 1849–, *kagura* 1884– *Shinto,*
kachina 1888– *Pueblo,* ghost dance 1890–, sun-charm 1897–,
intichiuma 1899(1), sun-spell 1907(1), *tripudium* 1909–,
ring-shout 1931–, shango 1948 + 1971

.**to perform:** kanticoy *vi* 1649–1675

Discalceation: discalceation a1638 + 1669

Ecclesiastical duty: duty 1526–, surplice duty 1824(1)

.**(of church:)served with due office:** officed 1598–1611

To exhibit x for adoration: expose *vt* 1644 + 1850

Firewalk: fire-walk 1898 + 1900, fire-walking 1899–

.**p practising:** fire-walker 1895–

Incense burning: *byrning, recelsreoce,* fumigation c1384–(1867),
incensing 1388–, subfumigation 1390–1579, thurification
1494–(1872), censing 1499–, suffumigation 1565–1856,
thurifying a1618(1), fuming 1681/6(1), incensation 1853–

XR R5.15.7. Incense

.p perf: incenser 1555 + 1775, censer 1670(1)

           XR R3.2.12.1. Thurifer

.char by: censing 1893(1)

.to perform: *steran v*, rechelen *vt* c1200(1), incense *vt* 1303–,
  incense *vi* c1385–, cense *vt* c1386–, turify *vt* c1400(1), thurible
  vt c1440(1), thurify *vi* c1440–1460, cense *vi* c1440–, sainse *vt*
  1565(1), thurify *vt* 1570–(1851), becense *vt* 1591 + 1639,
  thurificate *vt* 1623(1), censer *vt* 1625(1), fume *vt*
  1641–1849/53, perfume *vt* 1833(1)

Kneeling, bowing, prostration: kneeling c1200–, kneelings
  c1400 + 1509, genuflexion / genuflection 1526–,
  adgeniculation 1659(1), flection 1862(1)

.p perf: louter c1340(*2q1s*), genuflector 1869(1)

.char of: genuflectory 1861(1)

.char by: genuflecting 1872(1)

.to perform: +*cneowian*/knee *vi* OE–1612, *cneowlian*/kneel *vi*
  OE–, knee *vt* 1607–(1869), genuflect *vi* 1850–

.to bow: alout *vi* c1260–a1500

.to prostrate oneself: *feallan*/fall *vi* OE–, fall on one's face /
  knees *vphr* a1300–, prostrate *vi* c1400–1755, prostern *vrefl*
  c1489 + 1588 *Sc.*, prostrate *vrefl* 1530–, prostitute *vrefl*
  1620–1624 *erron.*

.to reverence (x) by visible token (general): adore *vt*
  1582–(1839)

Lung-gom-pa: *see R3.3.2.0. Lung-gom-pa (Tibetan)*

To strike upon the breast: knock *vi* 1562 + 1583

         XR R4.2.2.0. Craw-thump *vi*

Judaic practice of turning to Jerusalem in prayer: mizrach
  1892–

Phallus-carrying: phallophoria 1903–

          XR R5.17.1.2. Phallus

.p perf: phallophorus 1854–

.char of: phallophoric 1964–

Presentation: presentation c1400–, presentment 1659(1)

.to make: present *vt* 13..–

Procession: procession 1103/23–, precession 13..–1529, ganging
  1555 + 1849/53, processioning 1593–, processional 1882/3(1)

.on Pentecost: Whit walk 1959–

.**to perform:** procession *vi* 1691–1859

         XR R4.1.5.2.1. Rogation days

Redemption: redemption 14.. + 1892

.**money used in:** redemption money 1535(1)

Visitation: visitation c1430–

         XR R4.4. Corporal works of mercy

.**instance of:** visit 1724–(1727), station 1830–

R4.16. Benefice

R4.16.0. Benefice: benefice 1340–, living 1426–, benefit 1554 +
1719, church-living a1600–1797, endowment 1649–

.**p possessing:** possessioner 1377–, incumbent 1425–,
possessionary 1532(1), pensionary 1536(1), pension 1544(1),
pensioner 1578–1581 + 1742–1878 *18th and 19th c. fig. only.*,
beneficer 1621(1), beneficiary 1641–(1846)

..**non-residentiary:** non-resident 1583–1835, non-residenter
1637/50–1842

...**char of:** non-resident 1530–

         XR R3.1.4.3.1. Non-residentiary

....**condition of being:** non-residence c1380–, non-residency
1545–1696

..**properly appointed:** regular v1645(1)

..**ubiquitary:** ubiquitary 1646–1663

..**who has one:** unalist 1743(1), singularist 1799 + 1832

..**who shares revenues with another p:** portionary 1548–1778,
portioner 1670 + 1848, portionist 1743–

...**who receives his portion in a basket:** basket-clerk
1653(1-*Milton*)

.**p administering revenue of vacant:** economic 1616(2)

.**right of French kings to revenue of vacant:** *regale* 1611–1839

.**the holding of two together:** duality 1619–1647

..**p char by:** dualist a1661(1)

.**the holding of two or more together:** plurality c1440–,
pluracie 1581(1-*Sc.*), pluralism 1818–

..p char by: pluralist 1626–
...char of: plurified 1590–1604, pluralized a1875(1)
..B char by: pluralities *npl* 1362–a1715, combination 1618(1),
    plurality a1715–, plural livings *npl* 1895(1)
.the holding of three together: triplurality 1425(1) triality
    a1529–1637
..B char by: tot-quots *npl* 1583–1637
.dispensation to hold unlimited: tot-quot 1509–1637
..p holding: tot-quot 1628–1677

.induction to: inducting c1380–1684
..p perf: inductor 1726 + 1818

.reservation of: reservation 1480–, reserve 1725(1)
..to perform: reserve *vt* c1380(1)

.char of: beneficial 1592(1)
.holding: beneficed c1425–(1850), pensionary 1569(1), incumbent
    1604–a1661, stalled 1630–1829, beneficial 1660 + a1859,
    well-beneficed 1791(1)
..not: unbeneficed 1623–
.capable of being held together: compatible 1559 + 1872
.incapable of being held with fellowship: inconsistent 1690 +
    1691

.to hold income of B during vacancy: sequester *vt* 1731(1)

R4.16.1. Kinds of benefice
.commendam: command(e)ry 1536–1807, commendo 1598(1),
    commendum 1598–1650, commendam 1607–, *commenda*
    1611–, commendatory 1755–1849 *Sc.*
..p holding: commendatary 1539–1706, commendator 1561*Sc.* +
    1679–, commendatare a1651(1-*Sc.*), commendatory
    a1693–1726
..the holding of: commendam 1563/87–1836/7, commendatorship
    1861(1), commendation 1883(1)
..char of: commendatary 1611(1), commendatory 1790(1)
..holding: commendatary 1611 + 1751, commendatory 1682–
..the awarding of: commendation 1885(1)

...to perform: commend *vt/a* 1616–

.donative: donative 1564–(1877)
..char of: donative 1559–(1875)

.family-living: family-living 1798–(1883)

.impropriate: impropriation 1578–
..p holding: proprietary c1460–1661, approprietary 1547 + a1641,
   propriatory 1569–1621, appropriator 1726–(1809)
..char of: appropriate 1599 + 1751, propriate 1616–1697
..the transferrence of: appropriation c1370–a1641 + 1876,
   appropring c1380(1- *Wyclif*), propriation 1601–1840
                                    XR R4.16.4. Disappropriation
...to perform: appropre *vt* 1340–c1449, appropriate *vt*
   1528–(1809)

.mensal: mensal 1710–1847
..char of: mensal 1605–1861

.parson's: parsonage 1377–(1818), personage c1380–1642, vicarage
   1501(1), rectorage 1556(1-*Sc.*), rectory 1594–
                                    XR R3.2.4. Parson

.plural: *see R4.16.0. Plurality*

.prebendary: provend c1330–c1400, provender c1380–c1440,
   prebend c1400–(1852), provendry 1483 + 1708, prebendal
   stall 1839–(1856)
..of religio-military order: command(e)ry 1534–1866,
   commendatory 1586(1), commendam 1601–1669,
   commendum 1630–1635
..p holding: provender c1330–1387/8, provendrer 1362–1380,
   prebendary 1422–, prebender 1556–1583, prebend 1556–,
   corrodiary 1638 + 1844, corrodier 1866(1), stall-holder
   1895(1)
                                    XR R3.1.4.3.2. Scholaster
...office of: prebendship 1570–1715, prebendary 1592–(1725),
   prebendry 1611(1), prebendaryship 1639(1)
..char of: prebendal 1751–(1862)
..to present to: prebendate *vt* 1568(1)

.presentative: *see R4.16.2. Presentative*

.in a town: town-living 1832(1)

.without cure of souls: sine-cura 1662–1706, sinecure 1672–

XR R3.2.7. Cure

..p holding: sinecurist 1817–

..char of: discured 1604(1)

.triple: *see R4.16.0. Tot-quot*

.vicar's: vicarage 1425–

XR R3.2.6. Vicar

R4.16.2. Advowson: vowson 1297–1570, advowson 1297–,
presentment 1303-1641, collation c1380–, presentation
c1380–, patronage 1412–, advowry 1495–1593, advowsonage
1528–1556, voisom 1538–1560, donation 1540–(1785),
advocation 1566–1661, advowsement 1590(1), beneficial
1591(1), collating 1642(1), advocateship 1753(1), advowsance
1754(1), advocacy 1876(1)

.last: darrein presentment 1555–

.p having: presenter 1544(2), collator 1612–, presentor 1865–
.p presented to B with: presentee 1498/9–, postulate 1514–,
donative 1651(1), patronee c1807(1)
.p who wrongly profits from: advowson-monger 1660(1)

.B char by: presentative *a* 1559–, presentable *a* 1636–
.fees payable for: exhibits *npl* 1629/30–(1863)
.certificate of: title 1377–(1860)

.the utilization of: provision c1380–, impetration 1484–1494 +
1856*hist.*, postulation 1567–
..p char by: provisor 1362–
...office of: provisorship 1651(1)
..char of: provisory 1631(1), provisionary 1736–1856
..to utilize: postule *vt* c1425(1-*Sc.*), provide *vt* 1426–a1639 +
1887–*hist.*, postulate *vt* 1533/4–

.to invest with: advowson *vt* 1597(1)
.to utilize: provender *vt* 1377(1), present *vt* c1380–1856, benefice

vt c1383–(1826), collate *vt* 1558–c1670

R4.16.3. Simony: *ciricmangung,* simony a1225–, barratry
1427–(1867), giesetrye c1430(1), church-chopping 1621(1),
barratorship 1884(1), simonism 1895(1)
.p char by: simoniac 1340–, simonient c1380–a1470, simonier
c1380–1520, simonian c1380–1567/8, simonial c1386–,
chop-church 1391–1695, simoner ?a1407(2), gyesite 1426(1),
barrator 1427(1), simoniacle 1502(1), simonite 1508–1588,
balaamite 1559(1), simonist 1567–, benefice-monger 1583(1),
chopper 1585(1), church-chopper 1631–1656, chop-living
1634(1), simonaicle 1637/50–1678
.imaginary fair for: steeple fair 1597–1624

.char of: simonient 1395–a1470, simoniacal 1567–, simonical
1570–1686, simonious 1612–1648 + 1839, simoniac 1632–
.char by: simoniacre 1533(*2q1s*), simoniacal 1569–, simonical
1588–1626, simonious 1653–1670, simonian 1854(1)

.in manner evincing: simoniently c1400(1), simoniacally 1600–,
simonically 1660(1)

R4.16.4. Other financial matters
Almoign: almoi(g)n 1641(1)
.perpetual: frank almoi(g)n 1513–(1844), perpetual alms 1530(1),
frank almonage 1655 + 1656, free alms 1726(1), alms-gift
1882(1)
Altar revenue: altarage 1478–(1851)
Annates: annates *npl* 1534–
Canon: canon 1633–1726
Cathedratic: cathedratical a1670(1), cathedratic 1670–1721,
cathedraticum 1670–1846, table-rents *npl* 1701(1)
.for ordination or installation: inthronistic 1685(1)
Collection: quest 1528–, collection 1535–
.money taken in: token-money 1546–1611
..during Lent: quadragesimals *npl* 1721(1), *quadragesimalia (npl)*
1727/41–

..during mass: massing-penny 1292–1536/7, mass-penny
1362–1579 + 1849–, ?head mass penny c1460 + 1514,
mass-groat 1550(1), mass-money 1664(1), sacrament-money
1716–1860
..at religious service: offertory 1862–
..during Whitsun: smoke farthing 1444–*hist.*, pentecostal
1549–1726, whitsun farthing 1656–1797
.p taking: oblationary 1893(1)
..char of: questing 1714(1), oblationary 1872(1)
.to take: quest *vi* 1748–(1867)
Disappropriation: disappropriation 1727/51(1)

XR R4.16.1. Appropriation
.char by: disappropriate 1613 + 1765
.to carry out: disappropriate *vt* 1656–1798
Disendowment: disendowment 1867–
.p advocating: disendower 1869–(1888)
.char by: disendowed 1874(1)
Gift to godparents: gossip-money 1845(1)
.to godchild: god-bairn gift 1535–a1605
Invest: invest 1533/4(1)
Light-payment: *leohtgesc(e)ot,* candle-silver 1420(1)
Mass-money: mass-money 1897(1)
Peter's pence: *ælmesfeoh*/alms-fee OE + *hist., romfeoh,
rompenig*/Rome-penny OE–c1470 + 1674–*hist.,
romegesceot*/Rome-shot / -scot OE–a1643 + *hist.,* Peter's
Pence 1884–
Pittance: pittance a1225–c1500 + 1737–*hist.,* pittancy a1645(1)
Procuration: procurancy c1290–c1450, procuration c1450–, proxy
1534–1725
.char of: procuratory 1459(1)
Redemption money: *see R4.15. Redemption money*
Reek-penny: reek-penny 1255–1351/2 + 1735–1832 *hist.*
Settlement: settlement 1828/32– *U.S.*
Sin-money: *see R4.8.1. Sin-money*
Stewardship: stewardship 1899–
Superstitious uses: superstitious uses *npl* 1596–
Tithe: *æcerteoðung, teoðung*/tithing OE–1538, tithe c1200–, teind
c1300–c1450

.of cattle/produce: agistment tithe 1527–1808
.p supporting: tither 1653(1-*Milton*)
.p supporting: tither 1653(1-*Milton*)
.p imposing: tither 1591–
.p subject to: tither c1386–1705, tithable 1680(1)
.char of: tithal 1882/3(1)
.subject to: tithable c1440–, tithed 1607–
.without: titheless 1615 + 1850

.to impose: tithe *vt* 1382–
.to pay: *teogodian*/tithe *vt* OE–
Tribute to superior: fee c1369–1602

R5.1. Property general

R5.1. Property general: temporalties *npl* 1377–a1715,
   spiritualty c1380–1709, spiritualties *npl* c1380– *now hist.*,
   temporality 1393–1616 + 1818*hist.*, temporalty 1396/7–1651,
   spiritualities *npl* 1417– *now hist.*, temporal c1450–(1880),
   spirituality 1456–1709 + 1818*hist.*, temporalities
   c1475–(1854), sanctimonies *npl* a1547(1), temporaries *npl*
   1596–1665, *guaca* 1604– *Inca*, sanctities *npl* 1808(1), *sacra*
   npl 1819–, spirituals *npl* 1827 + 1863

R5.2. Land

R5.2.0. Land general: church-land c1205–(1807), kirkland
   c1450–(1633) *Sc. and N.*, church-piece 1827(1)
.of bishop: *biscopham, biscopland, biscoprice*
.of cleric: glebe c1380–, glebe-land(s) 1526–, kirk-shire 1844(1),
   kirk-town 1872(1-*Sc.*)

XR R4.16. Benefice

..to furnish p with: glebe *vt* 1641(1)
..to set apart land as: glebe *vt* 1797(1)
.prebend's: prebend 1422–(1868)

XR R4.16. Benefice

.sexton's: sextry land 1675–1691

.for maintenance of altar light: light-land 1879(1-*hist.*)
.for tithes: *teoðungland*

Churchyard: *cirictun*/church-town OE–1340,
  cirichege/church-hay OE–c1450 + 1880*dial.*, churchyard
  1154–, kirk-garth c1200–(1839) *N.*, kirkyard a1300– *N.*,
  purcinct 13..–1495, church-hawe c1320–1502, sanctuary garth
  1412/13–c1624, procinct 1432/50–1616 + 1822, sanctuary
  1432/50–a1450 + 1872*dial.*, church-litten c1420 + 1674–*dial.*,
  spiritualities *npl* 1470/85(1), cemetery 1485–1806, precinct
  1547–, church-garth 1570–1851, church acre 1596(1), God's
  acre 1617–(1862), church earth 1672(1)
.of cathedral: close 1371–, churchyard 1467–1577
.of chapel: chapellage 1802(1-*Scott*), chapelry 1817–a1845
.of Jewish tabernacle: court 1535–
.of temple: temenos 1820– *Gk.antiq.*
Public way leading to church: church-way 1590–1783

R5.2.1. Structures of/in land
Pueblo underground chamber: kiva 1871–, estufa 1875–
.hole within: sipapu / shipap(u) 1891–
Sacrificial mound: sacrificial mound 1862(1)
Rock at which Mass is celebrated: mass rock 1914–
Oak at which preaching is heard: gospel-tree 1648 + 1801,
  gospel-oak 1862(1)
Prayer wall: *mani* 1863–, wailing place 1878–, the wall 1895–,
  wailing wall 1919–, mendang 1925– *Buddhist*, prayer wall
  1960–
Preaching cross: preaching-cross 1882–
Holy Well: *halig wælla*/holy well OE–

R5.3. Sanctuary/Holy Place

R5.3.0. Sanctuary/holy place general: *hælnes, halig ern,*
  haligportic, haligweorc, heafodstede, hearg, spræc, stow,
  weorðungstow, halignes/holiness OE–a1300,
  haligdom/halidom OE–1839, *hus*/house (of God, prayer, etc.)
  OE–, *zion*/zion OE–, ?wike-tun a1250(1), saintuaire

a1300–a1400/50, sanctuary a1340–(1888), holy 1382(1), high
place 1388–1662, saint sepulchre 1395–1898, synagogue
c1400–1655, altar 1401–, shrine 1593–, bethel a1617–, place
of worship 1689–, *bidental* 1692– *Rom.antiq.*, barn a1721(1),
kramat 1783–, praying-house a1843(1), prayer-house
1852–1856, harim / haram 1855 + 1883 *Muslim*, holy
sepulchre 1898–, god-box 1928– *slang*
.**used as haven:** sanctuary c1374–(1863)
.**temporary:** tabernacle 1693–1739
.**(of xp:)having no:** zionless *a* 1908(1)

R5.3.1. Temple: *ealh, ealhstede, heahreced, heall, hearg, hof, hus,
selescot, tempelhus, templgeweorc, cirice*/church OE–1632,
tempel/temple OE–, minster c1200–1581 *transf.*, sacrary
1382–1652, washing-temple 1382(1), fane 14..–1850, naos
1775–

XR R5.3.6. Shrine

.**of all gods:** pantheon ?13..–
..**char of:** pantheonic 1865(1)
.**Buddhist:** varella 1588–1662, *kiack* 1599(1), varelle 1599(1),
pagoda 1634–, vihara 1681 + 1875–, wat 1844–, chaitya 1875–
.**Chinese:** joss-house 1771–
.**devil's:** *helltræf*
.**Egyptian:** *serapeum* 1841–, *speos* 1843–
.**fire-worshippers':** fire-temple 1741(1)
.**Hawaiian:** heiau 1825–
.**heathen general:** *deofolgieldhus, heargtræf,* idol-temple 1577–,
pagod 1582–1829, pagody 1588(1), swamy-house 1778–,
adoratory 1800(1)
.**hecatomped:** hecatompedon 1703–
.**Jewish:** *weorđungstow, tempel*/temple OE–, tabernacle 1388–1653
.**Mexican:** *teocalli* 1613–, *teopan* 1891(1)
.**monopteral:** monopter 1696–1775, monopteros 1706–,
monopteral 1845(1)
.**Peruvian:** huaca 1860–
.**with front and rear porticoes:** amphiprostyle 1706 + 1850
..**char of:** amphiprostylar 1875(1)

.for rain-provoking rituals: rain-temple 1904 + 1911
.Roman roofless: sacellum 1832–1848
.Shiite: imambara 1837–
.Sikh: *gurdwara* 1909–
.small: chapel c1400–1839, fanacle 1594(1), templet(te)
　　a1843–(1892)
.for snake worship: snake-temple 1891(1)
.Tibetan: *gompa* 1895–

.char of: *templic,* templary 1607(1), templar 1728–1845
.(of x:)furnished with: templed 1822–
..not: untempled 1850(1)
.(of x:)made into: templed 1839–
.(of xp:)as many/much as will fill: templeful 1909(1)
.to enclose (x) in: temple *vt* 1593–(1839)
.to make: temple *vt* 1839/41(1)

R5.3.2. Principal place of worship: *heafodcyrice,*
　　heafodmynster, mynster/minster OE–, architemple 1297(1),
　　church cathedral 1297–1597, cathedral church a1384–1593 +
　　1845, parish church c1386–1842, mother-church 1387–, see
　　1480–1665, *duomo* 1549(1-*Ital.*), basilica 1563–, cathedral
　　1587–, dome 1691–1753, basilic 1703–1840, *dom* 1861–(1888),
　　domchurch 1864(1), superchurch 1977–
.Roman (cardinal's): title c1460–(1854), cardinal church 1670(1)
.St Paul's, London: Paul's 1377–c1645
.substitute: pro-cathedral 1874–
..char of: pro-cathedral 1868(1)

.char of: basilical 1613 + 1881, basilican 1797 + 1879,
　　cathedralish 1840(1), cathedralic 1870(1), basilicate 1882(1),
　　cathedralesque 1884(1)
.(of x:)converted into: cathedralized 1861(1)
.rights and privileges of: regalities *npl* a1641–1761, *regalia npl*
　　1727/38(1)

R5.3.3. Church/place of worship: *godes hus, gesele,*

cirice/church OE–, kirk c1200– *Sc. and N.*, temple 1399–,
steeple 1555 + 1641 *fig.*, steeple-house 1644–, dominical
1659(1), church-building 1858(1)
.in country: *feldcirice*/field-kirk OE + 1857
.in which seats are free: free church 1835–(1860)
.little: churchlet 1659 + 1883
.at which marriage is performed: Hymen's fane/temple 1789
+ 1883
.Mormon: temple 1858–
.neighbouring: *neahcyrice*
.parish: mother-church c1325–1778, parish church c1380–,
parochial 1637(1), plebanian 1631(1), plebania 1706–
.Protestant (in France): temple 1566–
.in settlement: *tuncirce*
.built of staves: stave-church 1915–
.in storefront quarters: storefront church 1938–, store church
1948–
..char of: storefront 1972–
.built of wattlework: wand-kirk c1450(1)

.char of: churchlike 1852(1), churchy 1888(1)
.(of x:)occurring within: intra-ecclesiastical 1861(1)

R5.3.4. Chapel: *bedærn,* chapel a1225–

XR R5.4.27. Chapel
.of ease: chapel of ease 1538–
.of division of parish: district chapel 1838–1842
.not subject to episcopal jurisdiction: free chapel 1523–
.little: chapelet 1587–1675
.non-Conformist: conventicle 1550–, meeting-place 1589–c1710,
meeting-house 1632–, chapel 1662–, meeting 1710–1815,
pantile 1715–1785 *contempt.*, tabernacle 1768–, gospel-shop
1782 + a1791 *contempt.*, schism-shop 1801 + 1823,
schism-house 1843 + 1893, ebenezer 1849–, Salem 1857–,
praise-house 1862–, Bethel 1865–
.parochial: chapel 1491–, parochial chapel 1650 + 1873,
chapellany 1726(1)
.private: closet 1530–1868, proprietary chapel 1873(1)

.**Roman Catholic:** mass-house 1644–1809 + 1849*hist.*,
      mass-closet 1656(1), massing-closet 1656(1)
.**Salvation Army:** citadel 1889–
.**sodality:** sodality 1667–(1725)
.**enclosing holy well:** well-chapel 1858(1)
.**Zionist (Rechabite):** tent 1886–

.**(of xp:)placed/stationed in:** chapelled 1852(1)

R5.3.5. Synagogue: synagogue c1290–, church a1300(2-*Cursor
      Mundi*), habitation 1535(1), temple 1598–, *shul / shool* 1804–
.**chief:** *heah(ge)samnung*
.**reform:** reform synagogue 1844–
.**small:** *shtibl* 1929–

R5.3.6. Shrine: *scrin*/shrine OE–, feretory c1330–
                              XR R3.2.13. Feretrar
                                    R5.3.1. Temple
                                    R5.10.1. Portable shrine
.**little:** shrinelet 1884(1)
.**saint's:** memory c1400–1691, mind-place c1449(1), confession
      1670/98–, confessional 1704 + 1727/51, confessionary
      1727/51–, *confessio* 1830/8–
..**Hindi:** *samadh* 1828–, *samadhi* 1968–
..**martyred:** martyry 1708/22–, martyrion 1711–
..**Moslem:** pir 1698–, *durgah* 1793 + 1845, santon 1835(1),
      weli/wely 1838–, marabout 1859–

.**(of x:)in:** templed 1610 + 1854, faned 1633(1), enshrined 1795(1)
.**(of x:)containing:** shrined 1589(1), shrinal 1884(1)
.**(of x:)having no:** shrineless 1892–
.**visit to:** *reliquiasocn*
                              XR R5.10.2. Relic
.**placement in:** enshrining 1868(1), enshrinement 1872(1)
..**to perform:** shrine *vt* c1290–(1803), ferter *vt* c1325 + c1450,
      enshrine *vt* 1586–, temple *vt* 1593–(1839), entemple *vt*
      1603–(1858), enchase *vt* 1615–(1823)

R5.3.7. Other
Mithraic building: *mithræum* 1878– *antiq.*
Mosque: *cirice*/church OE–1632, mahomery c1320–1481, mosque
    c1400–, mesquit(a) c1564–1665, moschite 1593(1), mosged
    1594(1), muschid 1814(1), masjid 1845–
.little: mosquelet 1888(1)
.at Mecca: *caaba* 1734–, Mecca 1850– *transf. and fig.*
.char of: mesquitical 1613(1)
Polynesian sacred enclosure: *morai* 1772/84–1840 *erron.,*
    marae 1814–(1865)
Preaching building: tickling-house 1681(1), preaching-house
    1747–, preaching-station 1904(1-*Sc.*), station 1904(1-*Sc.*)
Building for sacrifice: *offrunghus*
Vigil/prayer building: wake-house 1677(1)
Ecclesiastical court building: officiality 1858(1)
Salvation Army Hostel: Sally 1931–, Sally Ann(e) 1961–

R5.3.8. Construction/measurement
Construction: fabric 1611–, church-building 1841(1)
.work at: church work c1175–(1712)
..p engaging in: *ciricwyrhta*
.science of: ecclesiology 1837–(1865), naology 1846(1)
..p pursuing: ecclesiologist 1841–(1884)
..char of: naological 1846 + 1849
Measurement: naometry 1626(1-*Jonson*)

R5.3.9. Damage: churchwardenism 1865–

                  XR R4.10.0. Sacrilege
.to cause: churchwardenize *v* 1831–(1863)

R5.4. Parts of buildings

R5.4.0. Division of building general: plage c1214(1), aisle
    1762–(1861)

R5.4.1. Door: *tempelgeat, ciricdor (-duru)*/church-door
    OE–(1865)
.at which weddings were performed: *ciricdor (-duru),*
    wedding door 1470/3–1636, wedding kirk door 1530(1),

wedding church door 1560(1)
.with grate: church-grate 1519(1)

R5.4.2. Narthex/portico: *portic (L)*, parvis c1386–, galilee
1593–, portico 1605–, *pronaos* 1613–, out-porch 1641(1),
narthex 1673–, prostyle 1697 + 1710, ante-temple 1703–,
propylæum 1706–, *choultry* 1772–1862, posticum 1776–,
propylon 1831–, *proaulion* 1842–1869, atrium 1853(1)
.inner: esonarthrex 1850(1)
.room over: parvis 1836–
.char of: narthecal 1866(1)
.(of x:)having: porticoed 1665 + 1856, prostyle 1696 + 1810–

R5.4.3. West end:
.window in: pede-window 1846(1), oculus 1848(1)
.(of x:)situated at: west *a* 1412–

R5.4.4. Antenave: ante-temple 1703–, ante nave 1829(1)

R5.4.5. Nave: body 1418–(1712), bouk c1420 + 1499, middle
pace 1499–1772, navy 1501(1), bulk 1518(1), holy place
1526–, ship 1613(1), body-stead 1623(1), nave 1673–, *cella*
1676–, nef 1687–1775, auditorium 1727/51(1), cell 1842/75(1)
.of St Paul's, London: Paul's walk 1628(1)

R5.4.6. Aisle: aisle c1370–, eyling 1400 + 1528, yele 1498–c1600,
yell 1503/4–1540, pace 1507 + 1828, alley 1508–1776, yeld(e)
1527–1535, isle 1598(1), pass 1871–(1873) *Sc.*
.main: broad alley 1731 + 1806, body stead 1623(1) *both U.S.*
.used for burial: burial-aisle 1820–1831
.(of x:)furnished with: aisled 1538–
..not: aisleless 1849–(1865)

R5.4.7. Crossing: crossing 1835–
.tower over: rood-tower 1823 + 1839

R5.4.8. Transept: cross aisle 1451–1772, porch 1522–, transept
1538/42–, plage 1593(2), cross 1658–1702
.char of: transeptal 1846–(1886)
.(of x:)built with: cruciform 1827(1)
..condition of being: cruciformity 1846(1)
.in manner of: cruciformly 1834(1), transeptally 1856(1)

R5.4.9. Screen: purpitle 1354–1453, reredos 1446–a1490 + 1861, *cancelli* 1642–1703, screen 1643–, jube 1767–, *catapetasma* 1798(1), iconostas(is) 1833–, rood-screen 1843–, pulpitum 1845–, haikal screen 1902–
.beam at top of: rood-beam c1386 + 1850, candle-beam 1463–1499 + 1849
.gallery at top of: rood-loft 1399–, rood-soller c1562(1)
.doors in: holy doors *npl* 1772– *GkCh*
.part on either side of: parabema 1850–
..char of: parabematic 1850(1)

R5.4.10. Choir: *chor(a)*/chor(e) OE(L)–1638, choir / quire 1297–, psalmody 1674(1), ritual choir 1867 + 1886
.north side of: cantorial side 1792(1)
.south side of: decanal side 1792 + 1877

R5.4.11. Chancel/sanctuary: +*scot, weofodsteall, weohsteall,* chancel 1303–, sacrary 1387–1727, sanctuary a1400/50–, presbytery 1412–, *presbyterium* 1565 + 1701, *bema* 1683–(1861), sacrarium 1727–(1887), haikal 1884–
.(of x:)containing: sanctuaried 1852 + 1897, chancelled 1881(1)
.(of xp:)placed in: chancelled 1683(1)

R5.4.12. Holy of holies: *hearg,* holy of holies 1382–, sanctuary 1382–(1875), *sanctum sanctorum* c1400–(1878), oracle c1440–, sanctum 1577–1858, adyt 1594(1), holiest 1611(1), penetral 1657(1), adytum 1673–, sacrarium a1746–1842, sanctuarium 1796(1), *sekos* 1820–, penetrale 1827–

R5.4.13. Altar rail: parclose 1513 + 1867, rail 1641–, sept 1821–, communion-rail 1847(1), sacrarium rails *npl* 1848(1), altar-rails *npl* 1860–

R5.4.14. Pavement: pavement 1899–

R5.4.15. Gradual: settle 1611(3), gradual 1693(1-*Dryden*), predella 1853–, solea 1858–, dais 1893(1), praedella 1926(1)
.painting/sculpture on: predella 1873(1)

R5.4.16.0. Altar/communion table: *gledstede, mæssesteall, weofod*/we(o)ved OE–c1425, *alter*/altar OE(L)–, God's board a1200–1526, ariel 1382(1), the Lord's table 1535–(1852), table

1550–a1751, oyster-board 1554 + 1849, communion table
1566–, aire 1581–1652, communion board 1588–a1631,
thysiastery 1657(1)

.of fire: pyree 1638(*2q1s*), fire-altar 1926–(1935)

.high/principal: *heahweofod, heahaltare*/high altar OE–

.on hill: hill-altar 1539–1602

.for incense: perfumatory 1639(1)

.in Lady chapel: lady-altar 1898(1)

.little: aultel(le) 1555–1556, altarlet 1829(1), by-altar 1882(1)

.portable: itinerary 1631(1)

..char of: portatile 1657–

.of the holy rood: rood-altar 1472–1650/1 *Sc.*

.to which sacrament is removed: altar of repose 1884(1)

.char of: altarian 1642(1)

.(of x:)furnished with: be-altared 1655(1)

.in manner/position of: altarwise 1562–, tablewise 1637–(1881)

.to make A privileged: privilege *vt* 1844(1)

R5.4.16.1. Parts of altar

XR R5.9.1. Altar cloth

Hearth: *weofodheord*

Top: altar-stone c1325–, mensa 1848–

.portable: superaltar c1380–

.seal of relics in: tomb 1886(1), seal of relics 1897(1)

Base: foot-bank 1626(1)

Projection: *horn*/horn OE–

Frontal: tablement 1446–1552, tabula 1845(1), table 1891(1)

Gradine: shelf 1496/7(1), retable 1823–, retablo 1845–, superaltar
     1858–, predella 1859(1), retabulum 1861(1), gradin(e) 1877–,
     retable 1877–, *gradino* 1883(1)

.painting/sculpture on: predella 1848–, *gradino* 1886(1)

Back: reredos 1372/3–c1541 + 1836–, lardose 1593(1), altar-piece
     1644–, retable 1823–, superaltar 1848–

Surrounding decoration: triptych 1849–, pentaptych 1854(1),
     ancona 1874–

North side of: gospel-side 1891(1)

South side of: epistle-side 1885(1)

R5.4.17. Retrochoir: retrochoir 1848–

R5.4.18. Apse: *concha* 1613/39–, tribunal 1644–1722, apsid 1670(1), *apsis* 1706–(1852), tribune a1771–(1874), *chevet* 1809–, apse 1846–, conch 1849–(1864)
.small: apsidiole 1889–
.char of: apsidal 1846–
.(of x:)having three: triapsal 1849–(1883), triapsidal 1875–(1898)

R5.4.19. Ambulatory: ambulatory 1855–, pace-aisle 1877(1)

R5.4.20. Crypt: *cruft (L)*, undercroft 1395–, crowd 1399–1658, vault c1400–1511, shrouds *npl* 1550– *now hist., crypta* 1563–1703, grot 1658–1670/98, crypt 1789–
.under high altar, containing relics: confession 1670/98–, confessional 1704–1727/51, confessionary 1727/51–
XR R5.10.1. Reliquary

.char of: cryptal 1860(1), cryptic 1878–

R5.4.21. Triforium: *upflor,* blind-story c1520 + 1848, triforium 1703–, upfloor 1879 + 1912
.arch of: blind-window 1506(1)
.char of: triforial 1848–(1861)

R5.4.22. Clerestory: clerestory 1412–c1460 + 1851–, overstory a1490(2)
.rooms in: overcroft 1425–
.char of: clerestorial 1435(1)
.(of x:)provided with: clerestoried 1449 + 1848

R5.4.23. Gallery: loft 1504–, gallery 1630–, tribune 1865–(1904)
.for women: *gynæconitis* 1850–(1865)

R5.4.24. Bell-tower: *bellhus*/bellhouse OE–(1855) *now arch. or dial.,* steeple 1154–, clocher 1354–, belfry c1440–, shaft c1450–a1700, broach 1501–(1876), bell-tower 1614 + 1879, broach-steeple 1616(1), *campanile* 1640–, *shikhara* 1829– *Hindi,* bell-gable 1845(1), bell-steeple 1847(1), broach-spire 1848(1), fleche 1848–, *vimana* 1863– *Hindi,* belfry-tower 1874(1)
.room within for bellringers: ringing-loft 1620 + 1848

.room within for bells: sollar c1305–, belfry 1549–(1823),
    bell-loft 1764(1)
..canopy within, in which bells hang: bell-cot(e) 1859 + 1877
..opening in: weather-door 1753(1), sound-hole 1848–, louver
    1858–
.part beneath (on church floor) where ringers stand: belfry
    1549–1659
Finial: finial 1448–
.(of x:)having: finialled 1870(1)

R5.4.25. Baptistry: *fulwihtstow*, baptist(e)ry 1460–,
    dipping-place 1616 + 1766

                                        XR R5.7.5. Font

R5.4.26. Sacristy/vestry: *haligdomhus, hræglhus, huselportic,
    scrudelshus*, vestiary c1290–, vestry 1388–, sextry
    a1400–1691, revestry 1413–1683 + 1844–(1880), revestiary
    c1440–1715 + 1820, sacristanry 1483(1), revesture 1527(1),
    revester 1611(1), sacristia 1630–1644, sacristy 1656–,
    vestry-room 1710–, diaconicon 1727/51–(1876), vestiarium
    1855–, paratory 1877(2), vergery 1882(1)
.(of x:)to replace in: revester *vt* 1466(1)

R5.4.27. Chapel: chapel c1330–, porch 1522–, sacellum
    1806–(1881)

                                        XR R5.3.4. Chapel
.chantry: chantry 1418–, cantuarie 1538(1), cantarie c1593(1)
                                        XR R3.2.2.1. Chantry priest
.for shrines: feretory 1449–, shrine 1833–
                                        XR R5.10.1. Portable shrine
.Sistine: Sistine 1887–
..char of: Sistine *a* 1771–
.to which indulgence is attached: *scala cæli* c1380–1583
.side: by-chapel 1562(1)
.dedicated to the Virgin: lady-chapel 1439–(1880), lady quire
    1512–1550
.west end of: ante-chapel 1703–(1814), ante church 1874(1)

R5.4.28. Oratory: *gebedstow, gebedhus*/bead-house OE–(1866),
    oratory 13..–, oratour 13..–1596, *proseucha* a1638 + 1879–,

oraculum 1845(1)

XR R5.4.27. Chapel

R5.4.29. Other
Aumbrey: a(u)mbr(e)y 1440–1590 + 1870, locker 1527–1593
Eastern arch: *eastportic*
Chapter house: *capitelhus,* chapter-house a1122–, cabildo 1880–
Church house: church-house 1484–, sabbath-day house 1876 +
    1891, church-building 1888(1)
Counting room: audit house / room 1689 + 1726
Hagioscope: hagioscope 1839–(1848), squint 1839–, lychnoscope
    1843–1866, leper('s) window 1850–, squint-hole 1889(1)
.char of: lychnoscopic 1842–1852, hagioscopic 1872–
Kneeling place: kneeling 1587–(1861)
Laver: lavatory a1375–1866, laver c1394–1552/3
Lichgate: lich-gate / lych-gate 1482/3–, corpse-gate 1855–1864
Low side window: low side window 1847–
Niche: *portic, kiblah* 1775 + 1825 *Arab.,* fenestella 1797–1843
.on slab (indicating direction of Mecca): *mihrab* 1816–
    Moslem, prayer niche 1937–
Passage: slype 1860–
Pastophorium: pastophorium 1753–
Storeroom of synagogue: genizah 1897–
Traverse: traverse 1494–1605 + 1902
Church wall: *ciricwag,* ?body-wall 1847(1)

R5.5. Monastic property

R5.5.0. Monastic property general: *mynsterding*
R5.5.1.0. Monastic land: *mynsterland,* green-yard 1578–a1656
    + 1870
R5.5.1.1. Monastic estate: preceptory 1540–, command(e)ry
    1712–1867

XR R3.3.1. Religious superiors
R3.3.3.9. Religio-military religious
R5.5.2.0. Monastery/convent: *lif, munucstow, mynstercluse,*

mynsterstede, nunhired, nun(nan)mynster,
munuclif/munec-lif OE–c1205, *mynster*/minster OE–1513,
clauster/clauster/-re OE(L)–1726, anchor-house c1230(1),
nunnery c1275–, religion c1290–a1548, house of religion
13..–1568, closter c1330–1556, house of piety 1419–1599,
cloister 1340–, house c1375–, friars *npl* 1375–1655 + 1822–,
monastery 1432/50–, nunry c1440–1639, monk-house
1483–1694, convent 1528–, minchery 1661– *hist.*, abbey-stead
1819(1-*Scott*), *kloster* 1844 + 1878, observance 1876(1)

.Benedictine principal: archabbey 1881–
.Buddhist: *pansala* 1850–
..Japanese: bonzery 1788(1)
.of dervishes: *tekke* 1668(1)
.Jesuit: residentiary 1626(1)
.neighbouring: *neahmynster, neahnun(n)mynster*
.Observant: observancy 1876(1- *Browning*)

.char of: claustral c1430–(1862), cloistral 1844–, cloisterly 1852(1)
                               XR R3.3.0. Religious

.(of x:)provided with: abbeyed 1828–
.to convert (x) into: cloister *vt* 1863(1)

R5.5.3. Parts of monastery
Calefactory: calefactory 1681–(1844)
Cell: *cleofa, cyte, cell*/cell OE(L)–, cluse 1481(1)
Cloister: *clysung,* cloister c1400–, close c1449–1628
.enclosure/study within: karol(le) 1419/20 + 1483, carol
    1593–1810
Dormitory: dorter c1290–
Guesthouse: *sprǣchus,* forastery 1604(1), xenodochium 1612–,
    hospitium 1650–
Hordary: hordary 1892(1)
Infirmary: fermery 1377–1626, farmery c1550–
Music room: service-room 1669(1)
Obedience: obedience 1727/41–(1815)
Parlour: speech-house c1205(1), colloque 1482(1), locutory
    1483–(1856), locutorium 1774–, fratry 1786 + 1874

Reception room: *auditorium* 1863(1)
Refectory: frater c1290–, refectory 1483–, frat(e)ry 1538–,
    frater-house 1546 + 1844, refectuary 1611–1694, *refectoire*
    1667(1)
Schoolroom: *spræchus*
Waxhouse: wax-house 1385/6–1472/3
Barn: sextry barn 1843(1)
Gate: *mynstergeat,* wheel 14..–1669, tapsell gate 1922–

R5.5.4. Hermitage: *ancorstow, anseld, ansetl,*
    *ancorsetl/*anchor-settle / saidell OE + 1516–1603,
    anchor-house c1230(1), cabin 1362–1571, anchorage
    1593–1598 + 1852–, anchor-hold 1631–, hermitary 1754(1),
    reclusion 1797(1), kill 1827 + 1851 *Celtic,* ashram 1917–
    Indian
.aggregation of: laura 1727/51*dict.* + 1819– *Egyptian*

R5.6. Clerical residences

R5.6.0. Clerical residence general: *preostlif,* mansion 1451 +
    1559, manse 1534–(1860), mansion-house 1546–1738,
    glebe-house a1825–, presbytery 1825–, *presbytere*
    1844–(1860), clergy house 1865–

R5.6.1. Other
Pope's: Vatican 1555–

XR R3.2.1.1.0. Pope
.char of: Vatican 1638–, Vaticanic 1898(1), Vaticanal 1899(1),
    Vaticanical 1908(1)
Patriarch's: patriarchate 1860(1)
(Arch)bishop's: *biscopstol,* palace c1290–, see-place 1553(1),
    see-house 1845–
Dean's: deanery 1598–(1855)
Archdeacon's: archdeaconry 1779(1)
Chapter's: college 14..–
Precentor's: precentory 1906(1)

Rector's: parsonage 1472–, parsonage-house 1566–1796, rectory
     1849–
Squarson's: squarsonage 1886(1)
Pastor's: pastorage 1883–, *pastorie* 1934– *S.Afr.*
Vicar's: vicarage 1530–, vicarage house a1550–
Curate's: curatage 1879–
Sacrist's: sextry 1585 + 1829
Novices': probatory 1610(1)

R5.7. Furniture

R5.7.0. Furniture general: *ciricding,* ornament *ncoll* 13..–,
     church-stuff *ncoll* 1577/87–1687, kirk-loom 1819(1)

R5.7.1. Ark of the covenant: *earce*/ark OE–1382 + 1667–,
     scrin/shrine OE–, coffer c1325–1711, arche c1450–1532,
     cybory 1483(1)
.covering for: tabernacle (of witness) c1250–(1862), propitiatory
     a1300–, mercy-seat 1530–, mercy-stool a1536–1549,
     mercy-table 1549(1), mercy-stock 1550(2)

R5.7.2. Bell: *ciricbelle*/church-bell OE–, wakerell 1485–1602,
     bearing-bell 1552/3(1), houseling-bell 1552/3(1), lich-bell
     1552/3(1), sacring-bell 1552/3(1), sanctus-bell 1552/3(1)
                         XR R4.1.3. Parts of divine service *passim*
                                   R5.8.18. Portable bell
.leather-gear of: baldric 1428–1742

R5.7.3. Canopy: celure c1340–1553, tester c1425–, cyllowre
     c1440(1), celuring 1558(1)
.over abbot's stall: tabernacle c1400 + a1400/50
.over high altar: *ciborium* 1787–, cibory 1845(1), civory 1889(1)
.over rood: rood celure 1520–1527
.over tomb: teguryon 1483(1)
.for weddings (Jewish): chuppah 1876–, wedding canopy 1892 +
     1978

.ornamental work in: tabernacle-work 1774 + 1815

R5.7.4. Confessional: shriving pew 1487/8–1589/90, shriving
  stool 1505(1), shriving seat 1545(1), shrift 1604(1),
  confessionary 1669–1792, whispering-office 1704(1),
  confessional 1727–, box 1922(1)
.having only one stool for penitents: malchus 1883(1)
.seat for priest within: reclinatory 1637 + 1640

R5.7.5. Font: *bæð, fantbæd, fantfæt*/font-vat OE–c1220,
  fantstan/font-stone OE–1682 + 1830, *fant*/font OE–,
  wanston 1297(1), lavacre 1548(1), christening font 1610(1),
  font of baptism 1611(1), lavatory 1631–a1633, baptismal font
  1865(1), fonts *pl w sing sense* 1877(1)

XR R5.4.25. Baptistry
R5.7.12. Holy water stoup

.little: fontlet 1894(1)
.char of: fonnal ?1797–1846

R5.7.6. Lectern/pulpit: *rædescamol, rædingscamol,* lectern
  c1325–, pulpit c1330–, desk 1449–, stage 1483(1), *anabathrum*
  1623 + 1759, oratorio 1631(1), ambo 1641–, tub 1643–1728 +
  1891 *contempt. or joc.,* chair 1648 + 1873, ambon 1725–,
  rostrum 1771–, tub-pulpit a1791(1- *Wesley*), mimbar
  1816(1-*Moslem*), lutrin 1837–1856, prayer-desk 1843–, wood
  1854– *slang,* praying-desk 1906(1)
.eagle-shaped: eagle 1766–
.pelican-shaped: pelican lectern 1898(1)
.portable: tent 1678–(1885)
.three-storied: three-decker 1852–1910
.steps leading to: *rædinggrad*
.(of x:)provided with: pulpited 1904(1)
.p in favour of abolishing: ambonoclast 1851(1)

R5.7.7. Matraca: *matraca* 1910– *Spanish*

R5.7.8. Seat: sitting c1400–
.**bishop's:** *biscopstol,* see 1297–(1884), chair 1480–1867, faldistory
    1675–1722, *ex(h)edra* 1725–(1875), *cathedra* 1829–(1863)
..**used in non-cathedral church:** faldstool c1050–1340 + 1849–
..**shared with presbyters:** synthronus 1861(1)
..**(of x:)containing:** cathedrate 1536(1)
.**clergy's:** stall a1400/50–, sedilia 1793–
..**to furnish (x) with:** stall *vt* 1516 + 1857
.**pope's:** *papseld/-setl,* Peter's seat 1560(1), apostolic seat 1563 +
    1588, porphyry chair 1656(1), holy seat 1673/4(1)
.**preacher's:** pew 1479–1692, reading-pew 1641–(1848), jube
    1725(1), rising seat a1890(1)
.**of repentance:** repenting stool 1567–a1722, stool of repentance /
    repentance-stool 1647–, cutty-stool a1774– *mainly Sc.,*
    anxious bench / seat 1832–
.**of singer:** singer's seat 1777 + 1861
.**shelving projection on underside of:** misericord c1515 +
    1874–, miserere 1798 + 1801–, subsellium 1806–, subsella
    1849–

R5.7.8.1. Pew: stool 1570–1616, stall 1580–, pew 1631–, box
    1709(1)
.**pl/coll:** pewing 1454 + 1840
.**gallery of:** pew-gallery 1848(1)
.**with communion table:** table-pew 1897(1)
.**with high sides:** horse-box 1884 + 1891
.**narrow doorless:** slip 1828/32– *U.S.*
.**private:** closet c1340(1), pulpit ?1370–1485, pew 1393–, parlour
    pew 1896(1), pew-bench 1898(1)
.**end of:** standard 1866(1)
..**chair fixed to:** pew-chair 1875(1)
.**arrangement/provision of:** pewage 1841(1), pewdom
    1866–(1888)

.**p who rents/owns:** seat-holder 1842–, pew-holder 1845–(1887),
    pew-renter 1885(1)
.**(of x:)having:** pewed 1848–
..**for which users pay rent:** pew-rented 1843(1), pew-renting

1872(1)

R5.7.9. Sepulchre: sepulchre 1389–(1884), sepulture 1485–1557
.frame of: sepulchre-tree 1449(1)

R5.7.10. Stations of the cross: stations (of the cross) 1553–,
    calvary 1727/51(1), way of the cross 1868(1)

R5.7.11. Holy water stoup: water-stone 1379(1), stop
    1419–1552, stock c1450–1591, stope 1500(1), holy-water stock
    1530–1566, font 1542/5(1), holy-water stone 1566(1), stoop
    1784(1), stoup 1793–, piscina 1812(1), *benitier* 1853–,
    benatura 1873 + 1891
.portable: pew-dish 1654(1)

R5.7.12. Tabernacle: *gesele, selegesceot,* tabernacle 1487/8–,
    sacrament house 1551 + 1876–
.char of: tabernaculous 1696(1)
.to place (x) in: tabernacle *vt* 1822–(1896)
XR R5.3.6. Shrine

R5.7.13. Table
.for elements: *prothesis* 1672–, credence 1804–
.at which litany is recited: fald-stool a1626–, oratory
    1697–a1771, litany-desk 1725–(1845), *prie-dieu* 1760–(1852),
    litany-stool 1845(1)
..portable: fald-stool 1603–

R5.7.14. Other
Banner: banner c1305–, labarum 1658–(1869), prayer-flag 1882–,
    tanka 1925– *Tibetan*
.of Passion: passion-banner 1552(1)
Booth: *succah / sukkah* 1875–
Chandelier: rowel 1451–1565, *corona* 1825–, crown 1845–
Cope-stand: triangle 1532–1538

Fire-bucket: church-bucket 1611–1672
Fountain: cantharus / kantharos 1842 + 1902
Prayer-wheel: praying-wheel 1889(1), prayer-wheel 1897(1)
XR R5.8.18. Prayer-wheel

Table of commandments: commandments *npl* 1560–1766
XR R1.2.1.2.1.0. Witness

Treasury: *corban* a1300–1610, almoi(g)n c1330(1), God's chest 1535(2)

R5.8. Implements

R5.8.0. Implement general: *haligdom*/halidom OE–c1561, relic a1300–1606, mass-gear *ncoll* c1300(1), chapel ?1475 + 1862*hist.*, utensil 1650–, sacreds *npl* 1665 + 1669, *bondieuserie ncoll* 1941–

R5.8.1. Vessel general: *blodorc, huselfæt,* vesselment *ncoll* 1303–13.., chapel ?1475 + 1862*hist.*, sacreds *npl* 1665 + 1669, service *ncoll* a1700(1)

R5.8.2. Ampulla/chrismatory: *elebytt, elefæt*/elvat OE–c1450, ampul 1362–(1750), chrismator c1425(1), chrismere c1450(1), chrismatory c1450–, *ampulla* 1598 + 1838–, chrismary 1844(1), thumbstall 1849–(1872), stock 1872–
XR R5.8.10. Holy water vessel

R5.8.3. Aspergillum: strenkle c1200–1584, springel 13..–1494, sprinkle 1382–1647, sprengles 1395(1), sprent 14..(1), stick 1415–1543, holy-water stick 1419–1552, strinkle c1425–1559, holy-water strinkle c1440(1), holy-water sprinkle(r) c1440–, dashel 1502–1540, stringel 1514(1), sprink 1566(1), sprinkler 1577–, *aspergillum* 1649 + 1864–, asperges 1674(1), aspergoire 1772(1), hyssop 1838(1), asperge 1848(1), *aspersoir* 1851–(1872), aspergill 1864–, aspersory 1881–, asperser 1882(1)
XR R5.8.10. Holy water vessel

R5.8.4. Calefactory: calefactory 1536(2), pome 1866(1)

R5.8.5. Cauldron: *ceac*

R5.8.6. Cruet: cruet c1290–, flagon 1485–, urceole 1824 + ?1865, burette 1856 + 1871

R5.8.7. Cup: *ciricfæt, hal wæge, symbelcalic, calic*/chalice OE(L)–, cup c1449–1662 + 1890, goblet 1519–1692, ciboir(e) 1640 + 1656, communion-cup 1642/3(1), *ciborium* 1651–
.used at coronation: regal 1603–1662
.used at Maundy Thursday liturgies: judas cup 1593(1)

R5.8.8. Fistula: *pipe,* fistula 1670 + 1848

R5.8.9. Grail: grail c1330–, sangrail a1450–1871, holy grail 1590–, saint grail 1833–

R5.8.10. Holy water vessel: *amel,* cruet c1290–, fat c1330–1571, *aspersorium* 1861–
XR R5.7.11. Holy water stoup
R5.8.3. Aspergillum

R5.8.11. Incense holder: ship 1422–1593 + 1843–*hist.,* navet 1467–1706, incense-pan 1611 + a1661, incense-boat 1853 + 1866, navicula 1853–, nef 1867(1)
XR R5.8.17. Thurible

R5.8.12. Laver (Jewish): sea 1382 + c1450 + 1899, washing-vessel 1388–c1440, laver 1535–(1869)
XR R5.8.15. Piscina

R5.8.13. Libatory: libatory 1609(1)

R5.8.14. Paten: *huseldisc, offringdisc,* paten c1300–, plat(t)en

c1450–1624, patel(le) 1546(1), patera 1658–, offertory
1672(1), altar-plate 1856(1), patina 1868(1), paten-cover
1880(1)
.**star-shaped implement placed above:** asterisk
1872(1-*Eastern Ch.*)

R5.8.15. Piscina: lavabo *no quots.,* lavatory 14..–1519, laver
1483–1593, lavatory stone 1487/8(1), piscine 1489 + 1822–,
piscina 1793–, sacrarium 1848–(1853), aquamanile 1875–
                                            XR R5.8.12. Laver

R5.8.16. Pyx: *huselbox*/housel-box OE + 1598, box 1297 + 1556,
pyx ?c1400–, sacrament-box c1440(1), eucharist 1535 + 1560,
pyxis 1536(1), little jack 1566(1-*jocular*), custode 1653(1),
altar-pyx a1683(1), eucharistial 1844(2), custodial 1860–
                                    XR R4.2.4.1.0. Reservation
.**receptacle for:** tabernacle 1487–, dove 1849/53 *Eastern and Fr.*

R5.8.17. Thurible: *gledfæt, recelsbuc, storcille, storfæt,*
recelsfæt/rekel(s)-fat OE–c1250, censer a1250–, incenser
c1380–1624, encenser 1382–1480, sensour a1400/50 + 1546,
thurible c1440–, fumatory c1530(1), saynsure 1565(1), senssar
?1571(1), incensory 1645–, thuribulum 1706 + 1851, *koro*
1822–, thymiaterion 1850–(1857) *GkCh,* thurible-boat
1853(1), *po/bo shan lu* 1915–
                                    XR R5.8.11. Incense holder

R5.8.18. Other
Axe: *labrys* 1901–(1957) *Cretan*
Bell (portable): sacring-bell 1395–(1884), skellat 1398/9–1500/20
+ 1856–, mass-bell 14.. + 1863, sacry-bell c1430 + c1460,
cross-bell c1450(1), tantonie bell 1567(1), prayer-gong
1905(1)
                            XR R4.1.3. Parts of divine service
                                            R5.7.2. Bell
Bone: soul-catcher 1932–

Candleholder: trendle 1423–1524, paschal 1427–1593, shaft
c1450(1), judas (of the paschal) 1453–1566 + 1877*hist.*, judas
staff 1488(1), trestle 1523–1546, pan 1556(1), hearse 1563(1),
judas candlestick 1566(1), menorah 1888– *Jewish*
XR R5.7.14. Chandelier

Collection box: rood-board 1556(1-*Sc.*), plate 1779–, ladle 1813–,
collecting box 1862 + 1908, offertory-box 1886(1)

Communion voucher: token 1534–(1896)

Fan: flabellum 1875–

Key of church: church-key 1393–1685

Monstrance: *mustenance* 1479/81(1), monstre c1480–1548,
monstrance 1506–1552 + 1851–, monstrant 1509(1),
monstrate 1524(1), monstral 1532(1), observator 1560(1),
remonstrance 1656–, ostensory 1722–, ostensor 1804(1)

Osculatory: paxbred 1350–1509 + 1881, pax c1375–1670 + 1826,
paxboard 1481–1500, osculary 1537(1), osculatory 1763–

Prayer-wheel: prayer-wheel 1814–, praying machine 1817–(1879),
prayer-mill 1832–, praying-wheel 1871(1), prayer-cylinder
1894 + 1897
XR R5.7.14. Prayer wheel

Rosary: Our Lady's Psalter 1380–1605/6, pardon-beads 1516(1),
beads exilia 1526–1538, pardoned beads 1547(1), rosary of
Our Lady 1570–1669, set of beads 1593 + 1634, rosary 1597–,
bead-roll 1598–(1866), rosario 1622–1748, prayer-beads 1630
+ 1852, fifteen 1688(1), comboloio 1813– *Moslem,*
paternoster 1870(1)
XR R1.6.2.0. Pardon

.1/3 of: chaplet 1653–

.1/15 of: mystery 1852(1)

.part of, corresponding to 'aves' said: ave 1463(1)

.bead of: bead 1377–, paddereen / padderine 1689 + 1849,
prayer-bead 1975–

..nut-shaped: prayer-nut 1937–

..special, indicating a Paternoster: paternoster c1250–1714,
gaud 1390–1570 + 1874, gaudy 1434–1560

...to furnish with: gaud *vt* c1386–1552, gaudy *vt* 1482–1542

.p using: rosarist 1657(1)

.(of x:)provided with: rosaried 1834(1)

Golden rose: golden rose 1560–

Staff: *preostgyrd,* thyrsus 1591–(1856), thyrse 1603–1845, thyrsus-staff 1844(1), prayer-stick 1865–, praying flag-staff 1877(1), plume-stick 1882(1)

.bishop's: *biscopstæf, stæf*/staff OE–, bagle 1330–1557, crose / croce c1330–1617, potent 1362(1), crook c1386–c1430 + 1851, bat 1387(1), croche 14..–1563, cley(k)-staff c1440(1), bacul c1449(1), cross-staff 1460(1), crosier staff 1488–1733, crosier / crozier 1500–, crosier's staff c1511–1630, pastoral staff 1548/9–, crose-staff 1549–1566, pastoral 1658–, beagle-rod 1664(1), tau 1855–(1875), tau-staff 1885–(1888)

..(of p:)having: crosiered 1727/51–1798

..(of p:)bearing: crossed 1795(1)

..piece of silk/linen on: vexillum 1877–

.surmounted by cross (archbishop's): cross c1290–(1849), cross-staff 1540–1568 + 1884, crosier / crozier 1704*dict.* + 1796– *erron.*

..pole on which cross is borne: staff 1431–a1529

R5.9. Cloths, carpets, cushions

R5.9.1. Altar cloth: *weofodhrægl, weofodsceat(a),* altar-cloth c1200–, towel ?1284–1623, rid(d)el 13..–1517 + 1908*arch.,* communion-cloth 1631–(1866)

XR R5.4.16.1. Parts of altar

.at back: reredos 1381–1552, ?rear-front 1438(1), dorser 1516(1), parafront 1641–a1670, dossal 1851–(1866), dorsal 1870(1), superfrontal 1887(1)

.at front: frontal 1381–1566 + 1874–, pall 1432/50–(1838), pendle 1501–1512, stole 1513 + 1845, ?suffront 1516–a1670, altar-cloth 1522–, front 1533–1552/3, antepend 1542–1555, altar-front 1566–, *antependium* 1696–, fronton 1749(1), altar-facing 1859(1), altar-frontal 1859(1)

..to provide A with: stole *vt* c1475 + 1848, vest *vt* 1848–(1875)

..cloth used above: frontier 1440(1), frontlet 1536–1549 + 1874–, superfrontal 1858–

.spread upon: *pæll*/pall OE(L)– *arch.,* palla 1706(1), pallium

1865(1)

.**of red silk:** boston 1534(1)

R5.9.2. Eucharistic cloth: *offringclað, offringsceatt,*
corporale/corporal OE(L)–, *pæll*/pall OE–, altar-cloth
c1200–, corporas c1200–, towel ?1284–1737, pyx-cloth 1496/7
+ 1876, sacrament-cloth 1535/6–1853, sindon 1553–1885,
communion-cloth 1631–(1866), offertory 1706–1725, offertory
veil 1849–, palla 1885(1)

.**used for cleaning vessels:** purificatory 1670 + 1885,
manutergium 1774(1), purificator 1853–, lavabo 1870(1)

.**draped over sacrament:** *ombrellino* 1847 + 1949–

..**receptacle for:** burse 1844 + 1866

R5.9.3. Sudarium (sweat-cloth): sudary a1350–1623 +
1835*arch.*, vernicle a1400–, veronicle 14..–c1450, sudarium
1601–, veronica a1700–

R5.9.4. Veil (hanging cloth): hiding-cloth c1275(1), veil
a1300–, fore-hanging 1528(1)

.**to cover crucifix:** veil 1399–, rood-cloth 1466 + 1566, cross-cloth
1541–1566

.**to cover font:** font-cloth 1553 + 1885

.**to cover images during Lent:** veil 1399–, Lenten-cloth
1485–1546/7, Lent-cloth 1495/6–1552

.**which covers Kaaba:** *Kiswa(h)* 1599– *Arab.*

.**to cover pulpit:** pulpit-cloth 1552–(1872)

.**to cover altar-rail:** ?rail-cloth 1531(1)

.**to cover shrine:** canopy 1513–1757, chanoper 1552/3(*3q1s*)

R5.9.5. Prayer carpet: praying-carpet 1844(1), praying-rug
1847(1), prayer-carpet 1861/2(1), praying-mat 1869 + 1894,
prayer-mat 1885(1), prayer-rug 1898–, ladik 1900–

R5.9.6. Cushion: hassock 1516–, tut 1553–1786 *W.dial.*, pess
1575–1702/3 + a1825*dial.*, trush 1621– *S.dial.*, passock

1680–1687, kneeler 1848–, buffet 1877 + 1866

R5.10. Portable shrines, relics

R5.10.1. Portable shrine: *scrin*/shrine OE(L)–, sacrary
  13..–1676 *fig.,* feretory c1330–, tabernacle 1382(1), sanctuary
  c1386–1481, phylactery 1398–1536 + 1869, scrine
  c1450–1591, monstrance 1522 + 1876, feretrum 1536 + 1878,
  reliquary 1656–, *chasse* 1670–1865, reliquaire 1769–, relicary
  1796 + 1829, sanctorium 1816(1), god-shelf 1876– *Shinto*
                                        XR R5.4.20. Crypt
                                        R5.4.27. Chapel
.carried in procession: neck-barrow 1847(1)
.having form of boat: navicular *a* 1774–(1819)
.casing of: *enchassure* 1716(1)
.(of x:)contained in: shrined *a* 1849(1)

R5.10.2. Relic: *halignes, liclaf, haligdom*/halidom OE–c1561,
  corsaint 1303–a1500, relief c1449(2), relict 1535–1727
.pl/coll: *haligdom, reliquias* OE(L), hallows c1200–1561
.knife containing: relic-knife 1854(1)
.water in which R has been dipped: relic water 1562(1)
.visiting of: *relicgang*
                                        XR R4.6. Pilgrimage
.devotion to: reliquation 1617(1), reliquism 1841(1)
.translation of: *oferlad,* translation 1477–
.char of: reliquian 1629(1), reliquary 1826 + 1854
.to carry in procession: *reliquias ræran vphr*

R5.11. Vestments

R5.11.0. Vestment general: *ciricwæd,* church-cloth c1200–1585,
  vestiment a1225–, vestment 13..–, vestement 1303–1566, vest
  1663–1829
.pl/coll: habiliments 1491–, suit 1495–, revesture a1548 + 1621,
  whites 1622–, canonicals 1748–(1848), clericals 1865(1)

.of priest: *preostreaf*
..used at Mass: *mæssereaf*/mass-reaf OE–c1200, mass clothes
c1440(1), massing-vestment 1612(1), mass-vestment 1879(1)
.appendages to: gear 1552(*2q1s*)

.char of: vestimental 1849(1), vestiarian 1850–
                                        XR R4.1.2.0. Ritual
.clothed in: vested 1671–
..according to canon law: canonical 1666–(1862)
.(of service:)conducted by p in: vestmented 1867(1)

.material/accessory used for: ?tays / teys 1350/51–1404
.action of clothing p in: revesting a1500(1), vesting 1648–
..to perform: revest *vt* c1290–1609, revest *vrefl* a1297–1652,
reverse *v* 13..–c1450, revesh/-vess *v* c1375–1555, vest *vrefl*
a1668–, vest *va* 1882–

R5.11.1. Particular functionaries' attire
Pope's: *see R5.11.3. Maniple, R5.11.4. Tiara*
Cardinal's: *see R5.11.4. Hat*
.(of C:)clothed in purple: purpled 1561(1), purpurate 1664(1),
purpurated 1716(1)
Archbishop's: *see R5.11.3. Pallium*

Bishop's: *biscopgegyrelan,* pontificals 13..–, pontifical c1430–1559,
pontificalia 1577/87–1754, pontificality / -ities 1601–a1645,
pontificalibus 1620–1772, magpie 1917 + 1920 *hum.*
                                XR R5.11.2. Dalmatic, tunicle
.(of p:)in: *in pontificalibus* 1387–
.ornamental embroidery on: apparel 1485 + 1844–(1849), lawn
a1732–
..sleeves made of: lawn-sleeves c1640–
..char by: lawny 1647–1742/8, lawn-sleeved 1651–a1743,
lawn-robed 1719(1), lawned 1848(1), apparel(l)ed 1849(1)
                                XR R3.2.1.8.0. Bishop
.camail: camail 1670(1)
.chimer: chimer(e) 1375–c1430 + 1563–, shemewe 1517–1548,
cymar 1673–(1868), simar 1840–

.gaiters: continuations 1825–(1858)
.gremial: gremial 1811–(1853)
.mantelletta: mantelletta 1853–, mantelet 1602(1)
.moz(z)etta: moz(z)etta 1774–, mosette 1862(1)
.rochet: rocket 1382–1686 + 1808–*dial.*, rochet 1382–

Deacon's: *diacongegyrela,* deacon 1534–1558

　　　　　　　　　　　　　　　　　XR R5.11.2. Tunicle
Subdeacon's: subdeacon 1521–1560

　　　　　　　　　　　　　　　　　XR R5.11.2. Dalmatic
Epistoler's: *pistolclað, pistolrocc*

R5.11.2. Outergarments
Alb/surplice: *albe*/alb OE(L)–, chrisom 1570–1580

　　　　　　　　　　　　　　　　　XR R5.11.2. Surplice
.girdle for: tucking-girdle 1487/8–1530, girdle 1519–1566 + 1866
.ornament for: *parure* c1425–1527
Apron: apron 1704 + 1859
Cassock/soutane: *hacele*/hackle OE–1200, frock 1350–, sotane
　　　1652(1), subucula 1660 + 1839, cassock 1663–, suttan
　　　1755(1), soutane 1838–, pelisse 1877(1)
.(of p:)in: cassocked 1780–(1853)
.to dress in: cassock *vt* 1883(1)

Chasuble: *heden, mæssehacele*/mass-hackle OE–c1200,
　　　casul/casule OE(L)–1563/87 + 1824, *planeta*/planet(a)
　　　OE(L)+1602–, mass-cope 13..(1), chasuble c1300–, chesil
　　　1563/87–1642, massing-cope 1610(1), chasule 1655(1)
.Jewish: ephod 1382–, chasuble c1430/40(1), overbody coat
　　　1535(2)
.with front like fiddle: fiddle-back 1899 + 1960
.(of p:)clad in: chasubled 1885(1)
Cauntercotte: cauntercotte 1552/3(1)

　　　　　　　　　　　　　　　　　XR R5.11.2. Cope
Cope: *cæppe, mæssehacele, cantelcap*/cantel-cape / -cope
　　　OE–1545, *cantercæppe*/cantor-cope OE + 1348–1450,
　　　cop/cope OE–, cape c1520–1561*Sc.*, pluvial 1669– *hist.*,
　　　cappa 1859–

.(of p:)wearing: coped 1447–(1852)
Corporale: *corporale*/corporal OE(L) + 1660
Dalmatic: *biscoprocc, diaconrocc, ?dalmatice*/dalmatic OE +
    c1425–, dalmatic vestment 1804(1)
                     XR R5.11.1. Deacon's attire, bishop's attire
.char of: dalmatic 1604–

Gown: gown 1564–, cloak 1641–1727, crape-gown 1682–1706,
    canting coat 1687(1), Geneva gown 1820–
.material used for: crape 1682–1798
Manciple: *handlin,* manciple *no dict. entry*
Surplice: *mæssegierela, mæssehrægl, oferslype,* surplice c1290–,
    surpcloth 1525–1778, stole 1805–, *cotta* 1848–, nighty
    1897(1-*joc.*)
                             XR R5.11.2. Alb
.(of p:)wearing: surpliced a1765–, surplice-backed a1845(1)
Tunicle: tunicle c1425–(1877), subdeacon 1521–1560, tunic
    1696–(1877) *hist.*
Waistcoat: M. B. waistcoat 1853–(1876)

R5.11.3. Neck and shoulder garb
Amice: amit(e) 1330–1811, amice 1532–, kerchief 1552/3(1),
    aumusse 1708(1), amict 1753(1), superhumeral 1868(1)
                            XR R5.11.2. Parure
Band: tippet 1530–, scarf 1555–, Geneva band 1882(1)
.to wear: tippet *vi* 1563(1-*nonce*)
Collar: dog-collar 1861– *colloq.,* Roman collar 1897(1)
Girdle: *kusti* 1860– *Pers.*
Humeral: humeral 1641(1)
Humeral veil: sudary 1431–1549 + 1891*arch.*, veil 1782–,
    humeral veil 1853 + 1885
Maniple: maniple 1346–, fanon 1418–, phanun c1475(1), fannell
    1530–1830, sudarium 1688(1)
.worn by pope: succinctory 1572–1583 + 1868, succinctorium
    1688(1)
Pallium: *arce, pallum, pallium*/pallium OE + 1670–, pallion
    c1290–1480, pall 1480–(1726), superhumeral 1606(1),

arch-pall 1848(1), omophorion 1868–
.(of p:)having: palliated 1892(1)
Scapular: *eaxlclað,* scapulary 1674–, scapular 1870–
Stock: stock 1883(1), rabat 1889–, rabbi 1909–, vestock 1975 +
     1981
Stole: stole c1025–, orarium 1706–, orary 1814–(1826)

R5.11.4. Headgear
Coif: coif 1382–1574, mitre 1382–1614 + 1878, turban 1624 +
     1885, cidaris 1797–, tiara 1868–(1890)
.**plate of gold on:** petalon 1678–
Hat: hat a1352–
.**cardinal's:** hat a1352–, cardinal('s) hat 1538–, cap 1591–(1864),
     red hat 1819–
.**of priest or doctor of divinity:** pillion 1387–a1652
..(**of p:)wearing:** pillioned 1553(1)
.**of reformed clergy:** Geneva hat 1639(1)
.**of RC priest:** biretta 1598–
.**shovel:** shovel hat 1829–, shovel 1841–
Headband: *hæcc(e),* infule 1581–1606, frontal 1611(1), infula
     1727/41 + 1869, garland 1791(1)
.(**of p:)wearing:** *gehufud*
Mitre: *biscopheafodlin,* mitre c1380–, forked cap 1514(1), tulip
     1879(1-*slang*)
.**appendage to:** label 1552–, infula 1610–(1882), phylacter
     1661(1), lappet 1869(1)
.**char of:** forked 1509–(1641), mitral 1610–1658
.(**of p:)wearing:** mitred c1420–(1863)
Orale: fanon 1844 + 1849, orale 1844 + 1849
Skull-cap: calotte 16..–1670 + 1776–, zucchetto 1853–
Tiara: triple turban 1609(1), tiar 1616–(1841), tiara 1645–
Tonsure-cap: tonsure-cap 1889(1)
Turban: turban 1610–, tarboosh 1702–, fez 1802/3–, kulah 1920–

R5.11.5. Sartorial appurtenances

Pectoral cross: *biscoprod, sweorrod,* pectoral cross 1727/35–
Glove: *chirothecæ no quots.,* episcopal glove 1849(1)
.plate on back of: monial c1540(1), tassel 1849 + 1887
Rational: breat-brooch 1382(1), rational 1382–, pectoral c1440–,
    breast-lap 1535–1581, breast-flap a1536(1), reasonal 1577(1),
    breast-plate 1581–1667 + 1868, oracle 1868(1)
.objects on: *urim and thummim* 1537–
Ring: pontifical 1507(1)
.pope's: Fisher's-ring 1689(1), Fisherman's ring 1727/41–
Shoe: sandal c1485–(1849)

R5.12. Monastic garb

R5.12.0. Monastic garb general: *munucgegyrela, munucreaf,*
    habit 1290–, weed c1400–1760/72

R5.12.1. Monk's garb: *gylece, hrægltalu, munucscrud*
.for p in third degree: great (angelic) habit 1772(1-*GkCh*)
.for p in second degree: lesser habit 1772(1-*GkCh*)

R5.12.2. Nun's garb: *nunscrud*

R5.12.3. Belonging to order wearing white habit: white *a*
    a1225–

R5.12.4. Items of attire
Amice: amice c1430–
Cloak: cope a1225–c1400
                                        XR R5.12.4. Scapular
Cornet: cornet 1891(1)
Cowl: *cugle*/cowl OE–, cuculle c1420–1677, capouch 1592–1783,
    capuccio 1596(1), capuche a1600–(1843), capuchin 1834–
.little: cowlet / coulet 1774(1)
.(of p:)wearing: cuculled c1550(1), cowled 1561–, cucullated
    1737–1860

..**not:** uncowled 1728 + 1868
Gimp: gimp 1747–
Melote: melote 1491–a1529
Scapular: scapulary a1225–, scapular 1483–

XR R5.12.4. Cloak

Shoe:
.**(of p:)furnished with:** calceate 1669(*2q1s*), calced 1884(1)
..**not:** discalced 1631–(1885), discalceated 1639–(1856), discalceate
    1658–
Veil: *haligryft*, veil a1225–, suffibulum 1753–

R5.13. Lay garments and headgear

R5.13.0. Lay garment general: *woruldgyrla*
.**worn on Sunday:** sabbath dress 1825 + 1977, go to meeting
    1841–(1881) *colloq.*
..**char of:** go to meeting 1835–, Sunday-going 1840(1)

R5.13.1. Items of attire
Apostle's robe: apostle's mantle a1586(1)
Choirmember's robe: choir-cope a1300 + 1853
Communion veil: dominical 1565 + 1727/51
Chrismale (baptismal): *crismal OE(L)*, *crismclað*/chrisom-cloth
    OE–1532, *crisma*/chrism OE–1447, code c1420(1), chrisom
    1426–(1825), cude a1455–1552 *Sc.*, cud 1483(1), christening
    blanket 1755(1), christening-dress 1807(1), chrisom-robe
    1846–1852, christening cloak 1876(1)
.**action of leaving off:** *crismliesing*/chrisom-loosing OE +
    1869*hist.*
Dagger: *kirpan* 1904(1-*Sikh*)
Kittel (Jewish robe): kittel 1891–
Phylactery: phylactery c1380–, frontlet 1578–(1825), phylacter
    1599–1651, tephillim 1613–(1863)
.**(of p:)having:** phylactered 1738(1)
Penitential garment: *witehrægl*, *hære*/haire OE–1600, *cilic*/cilice
    OE–1843, *sæcc*/sack OE–c1620, habergeon c1386(2-*Chaucer*),

shirt of hair 1430/40–1781, white sheet 1594–, sanbenito
c1560–1842, sack gown 1693(1), samarra 1731–1841,
hair-shirt 1737(1), penitential robe 1877(1)
.(of p:)wearing: in sackcloth and ashes 1526–(1885)
Skull-cap: koppel 1892– *Jewish*
Tallith (prayer shawl): tal(l)ith 1613–, prayer-scarf 1867(1),
prayer-cloak 1876(1), praying-scarf 1887(1), praying-shawl
1892(1), prayer-shawl 1905(1)
Warlock fecket: warlock fecket 1810(1-*Sc.*)
Winding sheet: *oferbrædels,* winding-cloth a1300–c1440, sudary
a1300/1400–1756/7, winding-sheet c1420–, cered cloth
1475–1608, sindon c1500–1670, cerecloth 1553–(1868), kittel
1891–
.of Turin:
..study of: sindonology 1964–
...p perf: sindonologist 1953–
...char of: sindonological 1950–

R5.14. Pilgrims' garb

R5.14.0. Pilgrims' garb general: weed c1400–1760/72

R5.14.1. Items of attire
Hat: cockle-hat ?a1600–(1834)
.shell on: shell 1362–1507
Mantle: sclaveyn c1290–1475, sclavyn a1300–1491, slaveyn
1399–c1440, slavin ?a1400–1481
Token: sign 1362–c1400, scallop ?a1400–, scallop-shell 1530–,
Jacob's shell 1756/7(1), abbey-counter 1839/42–

R5.15. Consumables

R5.15.1. Bacon: *offrungspic*

R5.15.2. Cake: mole a1517–1697, simnel 1648–, soul-mass cake
1661 + 1837, soul-mass loaf a1800 + 1817, Haman's fritters

1846(1), Shrewsbury simnel 1883(1), Haman's ears 1949 +
1961

R5.15.3. Candle: *tapor*/taper OE–, candle a1300–, cierge
a1300–(1843), trindle 1537–1559

> XR R5.7.14. Chandelier
> R5.8.18. Candle-holder

.for Easter: paschal 1427–, paschal taper 1477/9–1653,
Easter-taper 1848(1)
.burnt on frame: trestle-candle 1559(1)
.Jewish ritual: *shamas(h)* 1961–, soul-candle 1978–
.maintained by married women: wife's light 1547/8(1)
.for nativity of John Baptist: summer-game light 1464–1519
.for the rood: beam-light 1529(1)
.(of x:)lighted by: tapered 1745–18..
.use of: tapering 1599(1-*nonce*)

R5.15.4. Easter-egg: pace eggs *npl* 1579–1876 *dial.*, Easter-eggs
npl 1825–

R5.15.5.0. Eucharistic elements: *offrung, geryne, husel*/housel
OE–1625 + 1844–(1859), sacrament a1225–1660, sacring
c1290–1448, spice c1425(1), eucharist 1536–, kind 1539–,
bread and wine *nphr* 1552–, species 1579–, elements 1593–,
elementals a1655(1), mystery 1662–1854, symbol 1671–

> XR R4.2.4.0. Communion

.material part of: matter c1315–, species 1579–

R5.15.5.1. Bread: *heofenes hlaf, hlaf, husel, mæsselac, oflæthlaf,
bread*/bread OE–, *gemana*/manna OE–(1842), *oflæte*/oflete
OE–, flesh a1300–, man a1300/40–1644, host 1303–, obley
1303– *now hist.*, housel-bread c1375(1), body 1382–,
God's-body 1387–1549, singing bread 1432/3–1616, bread of
wheat a1500(1), singing loaf 1530–1546, round robin 1546 +
1555 *contempt.*, holy bread 1548/9–, singing cake 1553–1607,
bread-god a1555 + a1631 *contempt.*, jack-of-the-box
1555(1-*contempt.*), wafer 1559–, wafer-cake c1560–1630,

wafer-bread 1565–, breaden-god 1579–1839 *contempt.*, God's
bread 1592 + 1681, wafer-god 1609– *contempt.*, hostel
1624(1), maker 1635(1), hostie 1641 + a1715 + 1837,
altar-bread 1849 + 1899
.**particle of:** *husellaf,* particle 1727/41–, pearl 1847–
..**sent from papal Mass:** *fermentum* 1719 + 1884–
.**leavened:** enzyme 1850(1)

XR R2.2.2.0. Fermentarian

..**not:** *đeorf, đeorfhlaf, đeorfling,* azyme 1582–(1651), matzah
1846–, passover-bread 1858(1), passover-cake 1858(1)
...**piece of:** *afikoman* 1891– *Jewish*
...**char of:** *đeorf*/tharf OE–1483, tharfling c1200(1), sweet
1526–1593, unleavened 1530–(1867), azymous 1727–(1763)
.**for non-communicants:** holy bread a1300–, church loaf 1499(1),
holy loaf 1499–, eulogy 1709–1782, *eulogia* 1751–(1883),
antidoron 1850–
.**given to the dying:** *wegnest,* viaticum 1562–, voyage provision
1562–1564, viands *npl* 1607(1), voyage food 1610(1), journal
1629(1)
.**made into wafers:** wafered *pa* 1889(1)

R5.15.5.2. Wine: *mæssewin, win*/wine OE–, ?singing wine
1558(1), cup 1597–1681/6 + 1884, sacrament wine 1698(1)
.**mixed with water:** ablution 1846–, mixed chalice 1877(1)

R5.15.6. Herb: *maror* 1893–

R5.15.7. Incense: *anstor, beorning, cursumbor, inbærnednes,*
inbærnis, inrecels, onbærning, onbærnnes, stor (L), dimiama,
recels/rekels OE–1483, incense a1340–, holy smoke
1627(1-*fig.*)

XR R4.16. Incense burning
R5.8.17. Thurible

.**cylinder of:** joss-stick 1845–
.**ingredient of:** onycha 1382–, onyx 1611(1)
.**char of:** thural 1624 + 1714

R5.15.8. Oil: *smirels, smiring-ele, crisma*/chrism OE–, oil
c1290–(1526), smerling a1300(1), ream 13..(1), cream/creme
1303–1642 + 1883, holy oil c1305–, chrisom ?a1400–1725,
balm 1447–1623, christendom c1511(1)

XR R4.2.7.0. Unction

.used for baptism: *fulwihtele*
.char of: chrismal 1659–

R5.15.9. Palm frond: palm 1375–, lulav 1892– *Jewish*
.(of p:)carrying: palmiferous *a* 1664 + 1866

R5.15.10. Paper: joss-paper 1884(1-*Chinese*)

R5.15.11. Soma: soma 1843–

R5.15.12. Water: *halig wæter*/holy water OE–, witch water
1659(1-*contempt.*)
.used for baptism: *bæð*/bath OE–c1230 + 1548,
fantwæter/font-water OE + 1610–1656, *wæter*/water
OE–(1597), cold water 1387(2-*Trevisa*)

XR R4.2.1.0. Baptism

R5.16. Books

R5.16.0. Book general: *ciricboc*/church-book OE–

R5.16.1. Service book general: *ciricboc*/church-book OE–1555,
standard c1400–1503, book of service 1543–1566, service-book
1580–, hirmologion 1850–, church-service 1859(1)
.for baptism: christening-book c1475(1)
.for ceremonies: ceremoniary 1567(1), ceremonial 1612–1753,
ritual 1656–
.containing collects: collectar(e) 1503–1540 + 1846–,
collectarium 1844–1849, *collectaneum* 1853(1)
.Greek: euchologue 1646–1700, *euchologian* 1651–(1876),
euchology 1659–(1843)

..small: *contakion* 1875(1)
..char of: euchological 1844(1)
.containing coronation liturgy: *halgungboc*

.containing directions for worship: directory 1640–
                                    XR R4.1.2.0. Rite
..Anglican: Book of Common Prayer 1549(1), service-book 1580–,
    book 1588(1), Prayer-book 1596/7–, liturgy 1629–(1843),
    Common Prayer Book 1682/3(1), service a1700 + 1860,
    Common Prayer 1712–1796
...certified under Great Seal: sealed book 1710 + 1849
..monastic: regel-boc c1200(1), consuetudinary 1546 + 1846–,
    consuetudinal 1817(1), customary 1882(1)

..Roman Catholic: book c1340 + 1556, ordinal 1387–,
    consuetudinary 1494(1), ordinary 1494–a1832, directory
    1759–(1885), ordo 1849–
..of Salisbury: Sarum (use) 1570–(1882), Sarum rubric 1832(1),
    Sarum office 1882(1)
..char of: directorian 1661(1)

.episcopal (containing blessings): *bletsingboc,* pontifical 1584–,
    pontifical 1660 + 1920, benedictionary 1780(1),
    benedictional 1844–(1879)
.episcopal (new bishop's): synodal 1844(1)
.for exorcism: *healsungboc*
.for fast-days: fast-book 1637(1)
.for feast-days: festial 1483 + 1725, festival 1491–1610, festilogy
    1845–
..Jewish: machzor 1864–
..containing saints' lives: passionar 14..(1), passionary c1475–,
    passional 1650–
.for Mass: *đenungboc, mæsseboc*/mass-book OE–, missal c1330–,
    missal-book c1645–
                                    XR R5.16.3. Sanctorale, temporale
.for ordination of cleric: ordinal 1658–
.concerning pastorate: *hierdeboc,* pastoral 1395–
.concerning penance: *scriftboc,* confession 1535–, penitential
    1618–, penitentiary book 1678(1), penitentiary 1853(1)

.for use during procession: processioner 14..–1566, processional
14..–1846, processionary 1466–c1544, procession 1540(1)
.concerning sacraments: *handboc,* manual 1431–1549 + 1853,
sacramentary 1624–1844

R5.16.2. Lectionary: *pistolboc, ræding boc*/reading-book
OE–c1315, pistelarie 1431(1), epistolar c1530(1), lectionary
1789–, *comes* 1844(1)
.used in summer: *sumorrædingboc*
.used in winter: *winterrædingboc*
.containing epistles: *pistolboc*/pistle-book OE–1559
.containing gospel: *godspel, godspellboc*/gospel-book OE + 1849,
evangel(s) c1386–(1886), gospeller 1440–c1530 + 1885,
evangely 1494–1577, evangelist 1523–1713, evangeliar(y)
1846–(1953), *evangelistarium* 1850–(1882), evangelistary
1865–(1882/3), tetrevangelium 1898–
XR R1.2.1.2.3.1. Gospel
.containing portions of gospel: evangelistary a1646–1790,
evangeliar(y) 1846–
.containing saints' lives: legend c1440–a1746 + 1849*hist.,*
synaxarion/-ium 1850–
XR R1.6.1.0. Saint
..p compiling: synaxarist 1908(1)
.containing all gospels/epistles: plenarium 1902–1929, plenary
1909 + 1920

R5.16.3. Breviary/office book: hours a1225–, brevial 1314 +
1847*hist.,* journal 1355/6–1549, diurnal ?a1550–1686 +
1846*hist.,* breviary 1611–, horary 1631 + 1789, horologium
1724– *GkCh,* office-book 1869(1), hour-book 1896(1)
.large: coucher 1444–1559, ledger 1481–1691, ?ledger-book
1611–1759
.part of, for daily reading: ?breviate 1813(1)
.portable: portas / portes(s) / porteous 1377–, portative 1454(1),
portifolyom 1546–1550, portal 1635 + 1905, portuary a1867–,
portiforium 1880–
..part of, for moveable feasts: sanctoral 1641(1), sanctorale

1872–
..**part of, for eccl. year:** temporal 14..–1517, temporale 1872–

R5.16.4. Music books

Antiphonary: *antefnere, antemnere,* antiphoner c1370–(1823), antiphonary 1681–, antiphonal 1691 + 1872, antiphonar 1765(1)

.**containing graduals:** grail c1440–(1849), gradual 1619–

.**containing vesper-chants:** vespers book 1772(1), vesper-book 1850–, vesperal 1869–

Hymnary: *ymnere*/hymner OE–1483, *sangboc*/song-book OE + a1700–*hist., ymenboc*/hymn-book OE–, hymnal 14..–, square book 1537/8 + 1538, anthology 1775(1), hymnar 1853(1), hymnary 1888–, hymnarium 1924(1)

Litany-book: litany-book c1475(1)

Psalter: *sealmboc*/psalm-book OE + 1579/80–(1842), *saltere*/psalter OE–(1833), psalter-book c1470*Sc.* + 1551/2–1571, *psalterion* 1893(1)

.**of the Virgin:** lady-psalter c1380–1547

.**containing the 95th psalm:** venite book 1434–1559, venitary 1853(1)

Responsory: responsorial 1853(1)

Sequencer: sequencery 1483(1), sequencer 1488 + 1904, sequence 1500(1), sequentiary 1500–(1891), sequence book 1862(1), sequenciar 1904(1-*hist.*)

Troper: *tropere*/troper OE(L)–, tropary / tropery 14..–(1882)

R5.16.5. Other books

Canon law book: maniple of the curates 1706(1)
XR R1.4.1. Canon law book

Choir book (monastic): seyny book c1492(1)

Devotional book: primer 1393–(1846), ordinary 1502–1578, rosary 1526–1583, diurnal ?a1550–1686 + 1846*hist.*

Monastic book: *mynsterboc*

Mormon book: Mormon bible 1838–

Parish register: parish-book 1594(1), church-book 1632–1673, parish-register 1712(1), church-register 1846(1), vestry-book 1856–
Prayer book: missal 1651–, synopsis 1850(1-*Gk.Ch.*), *sid(d)ur / sidoor* 1864– *Jewish*
Sermon book: *cwidboc, larboc, spellboc,* postil 1566–1605 + 1888*hist.*, homiliary 1844–
Synod book: *sinodboc*
Vestry book: vestry-book 1773/4–

R5.16.6. Miscellaneous
Surrender of sacred books in time of persecution: tradition 1840–(1874), traditorship 1877(*2q1s*)
.p char by: traditor 1597–(1877)
Altar card: altar card 1849–
Red letter: red letter 14..–
.(of x:)marked with: red-lettered 1707–

R5.17. Symbols

R5.17.0. Symbol general: symbol 1590–, tetragrammaton 1601(1), santo 1834– *Mex.*

XR R1.5.2. Typology

.worship of: symbololatry 1828–, symbolatry 1871(1)

XR R1.1.11.0. Paganism

..p char by: symbolater 1916(1)
..char of: symbolatrous 1871(1)
.non-imagistic:
..worship char by: aniconism 1907(1)
..char of: aniconic 1892–

R5.17.1.0. Image: *scuccgyld, anlicnes*/anlikeness OE–c1230, *god*/god OE–, *stoc*/stock OE– simulacre c1375–, teraphim *npl* 1382–, idol 1545–, poppet 1550–1687, puppet 1555–1809, icon 1577/87–, maumet 1581–1650 *contempt.*, poppet deity a1641(1), joss 1711– *Chinese*, godling 1762–1792, teraph

1801–
.**graven:** grave 11..–a1300, graved image 1552(1), graven 1609(1)
.**paste:** paste-god 1626(1)
.**char of:** puppetish 1550 +1620, puppetly c1550 + 1653, iconical
  1652–, iconic 1656–, jossish 1834(1)

R5.17.1.1. Christian images
Christ: Jesus 1487(1), Christ a1666 + 1876–, Christ-figure 1905–
.**face of:** verony a1300(1), vernicle 1362–, vernacle a1400–,
  veronique 1624–1825, veronica 1728–

XR R5.9.3. Sudarium

.**heart of:** Sacred Heart 1931–
.**in manger:** *presepio* 1759 + 1958–, manger 1838(1), crib 1885(1)
..**figure adorning:** santon 1926–
.**transfiguration of:** transfiguration 1712–(1838)
St Christopher: Christopher c1386–1488
Cross: *cristelmæl, cristes mæl, rodetacen, sigebeacn, sigebeam,*
  sigorbeacn, cruc/crouch OE–1340, *beam*/beam OE–1720,
  treow/tree OE–(1820), *rod*/rood OE–, *wudu*/wood OE–, holy
  rood a1100–1648 + 1798*arch.*, rood-tree c1200–c1485, cross
  c1205–, crucifix a1225–, rood-wold c1250(1), holy cross
  c1290–, christ-cross / criss-cross c1430–a1659, gibbet
  c1450–1535, weeping cross a1500–, jackanapes
  1562(1-*contempt.*), whining cross 1602(1)
.**enclosed in ring:** ring-cross 1882 + 1893
.**monumental:** palm-cross 1469/70–a1568, high cross 1596–1697,
  pulpit-cross 1598(1), calvary 1815–
.**in shape of St Andrew's C:** saltire 1970–
.**to figure C in material:** sign *vt* 1825(1)
Four evangelists: tetramorph 1848–
.**char of:** tetramorphic 1901(1)
Holy Spirit: holy ghost 1520 + 1558
Papal keys: St Peter's Keys 15..(1)
Paschal lamb: agnus dei 1583–1629
Passion: paso 1923–
Tree: jesse 1463–1549 + 1706–

Trinity: trinity 1496/7–1503/4
Virgin: mariole c1330(1), mariola 1876(1)
.with Christ's body: Our Lady of Pity 1459 + 1534, *pieta no quots.*
.annunciation of: salutation (of Our Lady) 1459 + 1534

R5.17.1.2. Non-Christian images
Animal: nandi 1807– *Hindi*, sacred cow 1891–
Circle: mandala 1859– *Buddhist,* chakra 1891– *Hindi*
Phallus: priapus 1613(1), phallus 1613–, priapism 1662(1), linga(m) 1793–1857 *Hindi*, pillar-symbol 1874(1)
Tree: verbene 1533(2), vervain 1548–, verbenæ *npl* 1600–, wren-bush 1901–, tree of wisdom 1910(1)
.trunk of: asherah 1863– *Baalish*
Siva: nataraja 1911– *Hindi*
Six-pointed star: magen david 1904– *Jewish,* Star of David 1941–
Statue: *(signum) pantheum* 1706–
Stone yoke: stone yoke 1899(1)
Soulhouse: soul-house 1907(1)
Totem: totem 1791– *Amerind.*
Vagina: yoni 1799–
.char of: yonic 1879–

Chapter Four
Notes to the
Classification

R1

R1.1.0. Faith

Geleafa is perhaps somewhat more specific in reference than its successor *(y)leve,* for it often carries the additional component "Christian." The *OED* splits *belief* into several senses, the principal of which is "faith" without a Christian element (c1175–); immediately subordinate to that sense, and dating from Wyclif in the last quarter of the fourteenth century, is the sense "Christian faith." The following note, appended to the main definition of *belief* in the *OED,* is of value:

> *Belief* was the earlier word for what is now called *faith.* The latter originally meant in English (as in Old French) 'loyalty to a person to whom one is bound by promise or duty, or to one's promise or duty itself', as in 'to keep faith, to break faith', and the derivatives *faithful, faithless,* in which there is no reference to 'belief'; i.e, 'faith' was equivalent to *fidelity, fealty.* But the word *faith* being, through Old French *fei, feith,* the etymological representative of the Latin *fides,* it began in the fourteenth

century to be used to translate the latter, and in
the course of time almost superseded 'belief', especially in theological language, leaving 'belief' in
great measure to the merely intellectual process or
state [defined] in sense 2. Thus 'belief in God' no
longer means as much as 'faith in God'.

Priest in the sense of "one who believes" is based on a passage
in the Book of Revelations (Rev. i.6.) which speaks of Jesus,
who "hath made us kings and priests unto God" (cf. *priesthood*
below). The Hindi *bhakta* covers both the sense of "believer"
and that of "worshipper." *Faith-fire* in the figurative sense of
"flame of faith" carries only one citation (McCave and Breen,
1890), suggesting a slightly flippant nonce-usage: "Neighbouring bishops were expected to keep the faith-fire ablaze along
their frontiers."

R1.1.1.0. Creed

The principal sense of *creed* is given by the *OED* as "a form
of words setting forth authoritatively and concisely the general
beliefs of the Christian church, or those regarded as essential;
a brief summary of Christian doctrine (usually and properly
applied to the Apostles', Nicene, and Athanasian creeds)." For
the purposes of this section, however, the more general sense
"the faith of a community or individual, especially as expressed
or capable of expression in a definite formula" [italics mine] is
considered central.

   Politic and its paronyms in the sense of 'adiaphorist' derive
from specific reference to "an opportunist and moderate party
which arose in France c1573, and regarded peace and political
reform as more important than the religious quarrel during the
Huguenot wars." Some, if not all, of the constituents of this
category carry a pejorative component, indifference in matters
of theology more often than not being regarded as a fault rather
than a virtue.

R1.1.1.1. Kinds of creed

Irish articles refers to the "articles of belief drawn up by Archbishop Ussher in 1615"; whether they constitute a creed of the kind constituted by other members of this subgroup is debatable.

R1.1.2. Doctrine

While a creed – at least in the Christian tradition – confines itself to the presentation of a core of basic (and usually scripturally-grounded) beliefs, *doctrine* covers a wider semantic area and includes ecclesiastical pronouncements on areas not treated by scripture (*e.g.* nuclear warfare or artificial insemination).

Both *minimism* and *maximism* carry the general sense of "(lack of) insistence on close observation of doctrine"; but both also refer specifically to the question of papal infallibility. Ultramontanists insisted (for reasons both religious and political) on a rigorous interpretation of the doctrine of infallibility; hence the cross-reference.

R1.1.3. Tradition

Tradition is best defined as "the accumulation of doctrine and accepted precedent specific to a religious group." It is often used in a narrow sense wherein it is equated with "traditional liturgical practice"; hence the cross-reference to *ritualism*.

R1.1.5.1. A Religion/Church

Spouse is a figurative use reflecting the ancient conceit of a church as the bride of its founder (e.g. *bride of Christ* as a synonym for *Christian church*). *Connexion* 1757–(1859) in this sense began by being "used by Wesley of those associated or connected with him in religious work and aims; thence it gradually became with the Wesleyans equivalent to 'religious society' or 'denomination'".

R1.1.5.2. Kinds of religion

Revealed religion is that derived from revelation, and is thus complementary to *natural religion,* which derives from non-revelational sources.

R1.1.6. Orthodoxy

Diptychs is defined as "the list or register ... of the orthodox, living and dead, who were commemorated by the early Church at the celebration of the eucharist." It derives from the concrete sense of the noun, for this list originally was recorded on two tablets. Of the five citations in the *OED,* only that from Schaff (1882/3: "In the twelfth century the diptychs fell out of use in the Latin Church") might be said to refer to the concrete rather than the abstract sense.

St Vincent of Lerins, a fifth-century ecclesiastic, produced a well-known test of religious orthodoxy; hence the presence here of the adjective *Vincentian.*

R1.1.7. Heterodoxy

Heterodoxy, cacodoxy, and *unorthodoxy* are defined as "deviation from what is considered to be orthodox." *Cacodoxy,* as one might expect from its Greek root, carries strong connotations of 'wrong' rather than simply 'different' doctrine.

R1.1.8. Free-thought

Free-thought is defined as "the free exercise of reason in matters of religious belief, unrestrained by deference to authority."

R1.1.9. Superstition

Superstition is glossed as "religious belief or practice founded on fear or ignorance." *Freit* and its paronyms derive from Old Norse *frétt* ("news," "augury") and has perhaps a stronger pagan colouring than the base term *superstition* (*cf.* the citation from *Cursor Mundi*: "I folud wiche-crafte and frete, and charmyng").

R1.1.10. Heresy

Though the base definition given by the *OED* for *heresy* ("theological or religious opinion or doctrine maintained in opposition, or held to be contrary, to the 'catholic' or orthodox doctrine of the Christian church") would seem to equate it with *unorthodoxy*, its connotative meaning calls for a separate category. *Unorthodoxy* need not carry more than a vaguely pejorative element, whereas *heresy* implies a doctrine or set of doctrines considered to be damnably wrong and spiritually dangerous or fatal.

Landloper/-leaper in the sense of "heretical person" derives from the Dutch *landlooper*, "one who runs up and down the land; a vagabond," and is equated with heretics through the intermediary sense of "renegade."

Widerweard is attested until the fourteenth century, but in Middle English it appears to have widened in meaning to "hostile, inimical," losing the specific sense of "heretical."

R1.1.11.0. Paganism

The amount of lexical material in this category, much of it pejorative, is indicative of the attention concentrated on the concept "paganism." The violence of some of the pejorative material (*fornication, whoredom*) is characteristic of religious controversy. For similar material, see R2.2.3.0. ROMAN CATHOLICISM GENERAL.

Prepuce, its paronyms, and *circumcision* and its paronyms refer to uncircumcisedness "seen as an act of omission, or state of ungodliness." *Ging* is used to translate the Latin *gentes*.

R1.1.13.0. Conformity

Conformity and *nonconformity*, though mainly found in contexts concerned with the Church of England, do possess the general sense of "(non-)conformity in matters religious or ecclesiastical."

R1.1.13.1. Nonconformity

Meetinger and *meeting-house man* recall the specialized nomenclature of nonconformist gatherings and gathering-places (*cf.* R4.1.2.0. CONVENTICLE and R5.3.4. NONCONFORMIST CHAPEL). The origin of *speckle-belly* in the sense of "dissenter" is unknown, according to the *OED*, which cites the word from Hotten's 1874 slang dictionary. *Octagonian*, describing certain Liverpudlian dissenters, refers to the shape of the building in which they worshipped. *Pantile* and its paronyms refer largely to rural meeting-houses, which were frequently "roofed with pantiles."

R1.1.13.2. Recusancy

This section might have been subsumed in R1.1.13.1. NONCONFORMITY, but its specificity led to separate classification. *Recusancy* is defined as "refusal, especially on the part of Roman Catholics, to attend the services of the Church of England." In practice, its reference was restricted almost entirely to Catholic nonconformists; recusancy came to be seen as an aggravated form of nonconformity, and from "c1570 to 1791 ... was punishable by a fine and involved many disabilities."

R1.1.14. Apostasy

Postate is an aphetic form of *apostate*. *Collapsed* is used in the sense of "lapsed."

R1.2.1.0. Bible

The meaning of *halig gewrit/Holy Writ* in earlier times could extend to include non-scriptural sacred writings. *Theology* in the sense of "Holy Scripture" is given one certain citation in the *OED* (Fabyan's *Chronicles*, 1494: "This Lamfranke [*sic*] ... was perfytely lerned in the scyence of theologie or holy wrytte"). *Scripturing* and other constituents of the category "the reading of Scripture" possess both the base meaning of "reading the Bible oneself" and the extended meaning "reading the Bible to someone (as an occupation and for the purposes of evangelization)." *Scripturalist* 1725(1) is ambiguous, for the citation (from Defoe) reads "King Charles II ridiculing the warm Disputes among some Critical Scripturalists ... concerning the visible Church"; the *OED* suggests a gloss of "one well versed in Holy Scripture."

R1.2.1.1. Text of Bible

Items in the category "strict adherence to text of Bible" refer to the same concept, that of "reverence for and adherence to the text of the Bible," but reflect different perspectives: *textualism*, for example, carries a favourable or neutral value judgement, whereas *bibliolatry* embodies disapproval. The full gloss of *gymnobiblism* reads "the opinion that the bare text of the Bible, 'without note or comment,' may be safely put before the unlearned as a sufficient guide to religious truth."

R1.2.1.1.2. Canon

Canon is defined as "the collection or list of books of the Bible accepted by the Christian Church as genuine and inspired."

R1.2.1.1.3. Textual criticism, interpretation

Textualism 1888– is defined as "textual criticism of the Bible." Both *anagogy* and *tropology* deal with secondary senses of Scripture, but whereas *anagogy* concentrates on the search for hidden, mystical meanings, *tropology* concerns itself with a search for moral meaning.

R1.2.1.1.4. Versions of text

The *He Bible,* the first of two editions published in 1611, derives its name "from its rendering of Ruth iii.15."; the *She Bible* was the second edition to be printed that year, with the misprint in question corrected. *Treacle Bible* carries the gloss "an edition ... having 'treacle/triacle' where others have 'balm.'" The *Vinegar Bible* derives its name from "an error in the running title at Luke xxii, where it reads 'The Parable of the Vinegar' (Vineyard)." *Vulgate* is employed here as a low-level superordinate covering various versions of the Bible, of which the "Hieronymian" is one. At the end of R1.2.1.1.4. are grouped three kinds of Bible, not so much special editions as versions printed for a particular group of people (*e.g. Gideon Bible*) or purpose (*e.g. family Bible, hall Bible*).

R1.2.1.2.1.0. Old Testament

Ægesetnes and all other lexical items in this section with the sense-component "law" reflect the concept of the Old Testament as the vehicle of the Mosaic dispensation, the 'old' covenant in contrast to the 'new' covenant brought into being by Christ. Some of the terminology might suggest that the

Old Testament contains little other than the Mosaic dispensation; such compendious names, however, as *the Law and the Prophets* dispel this notion. *LXX*, the Roman numeral seventy, refers to the seventy translators of the Old Testament into Greek (*cf.* the preceding term *Septuagint*).

Pharisee and cognates are found at several points in the classification, in R2.1.1. because of their nature as a sect, in R1.7.1. SANCTIMONIOUSNESS because of their pretensions to superior piety, and here because of their function as interpreters of the Mosaic law. *Legalism* and *Mosaism* both denote an adherence to "the system of Mosaic law," with *Mosaism* as a neutral counterpart to the pejorative or reproachful *legalism*.

R1.2.1.2.1.2. Genesis

The restitutionalist theory of creation holds that "the Mosaic six days record the restitution of a preceding creation which had been ... overwhelmed" (Cave, *The Inspiration of the Old Testament Inductively Considered*, 1888). A visionist "supports the view that the Biblical account of Creation was revealed to the writer in a vision or series of visions"; an epochist believes "that the 'days' of Creation ... signify epochs."

R1.2.1.2.1.9. Chronicles

Paralipomena is borrowed from Greek through late Latin, and signifies "(things) left out," referring to details given in the Book of Chronicles which are omitted in the Book of Kings.

R1.2.1.2.1.13. Psalms

Extensive duplication of entries and cross-referencing between this section and R4.1.4.3. PSALM illustrate the dual nature of the psalms as both a canonic part of the Bible and the basis of Judæo-Christian hymnology. *Theody* is Longfellow's adaptation of Dante's *teodia,* and carries the wider sense of "song of praise."

R1.2.1.2.3.1. Gospel

The *great omission* in the Gospel of Mark refers to Mark vi.45 – viii.26, the account of the working of several miracles by Christ, an account puzzlingly omitted in the synoptic gospel of Luke. The *great insertion* of the gospel of Luke (Luke ix.51 – xviii.14) is a lengthy narration without a parallel in the Gospel of Mark.

R1.2.1.3. Biblical personages

On exclusions from this and the next two sections, see chapter 2.

R1.2.1.4 Biblical places

Scala cæli is glossed "a ladder from earth to heaven; a means of attaining heavenly bliss."

R1.2.1.5. Biblical events

The organization of this section is chronological from *Nativity* to *Second Coming* (events concerning or involving Christ), followed by the *Apocalypse* and the *Joys of Mary.* The full gloss for *counsel of perfection* reads "one of the advisory declarations of Christ and the apostles, in mediæval theology reckoned as twelve, which are considered not to be universally binding, but to be given as a means of attaining greater moral perfection." The Apocalypse is not, of course, a biblical event of the same kind as the other constituents of this category, but rather is a future event referred to at length in the Bible. The Joys of Mary are "special occasions of joy to the Virgin Mary," of which "the mediæval church reckoned five."

R1.2.2. Hebrew Scripture

Targumist, principally defined as "one of the translators and commentators who compiled the Targums," can also mean "one versed in the language and literature of the Targums." *Keri* is glossed as a marginal emendation "in the Hebrew text of the Old Testament ... to be substituted in reading for that standing in the text (*Kethib*), the latter having been retained by the Masoretes as evidenced by MSS. or tradition, though considered erroneous or unintelligible." Elohists and Jehovists differ in their rendering of the name of God. The *Megillah* consists of "each of five books of the Old Testament (namely the Song of Solomon, Ruth, Lamentations, Ecclesiastes, and Esther) appointed to be read ... on certain feast days." *Pseudepigrapha* refers to Jewish scriptural texts "composed about the beginning of the Christian era, but ascribed to various Old Testament patriarchs and prophets." The *Hagiographa* is "the last of the three great divisions of the Hebrew scriptures." *Genizah* is a dubious constituent of this category, carrying as it does the gloss "the old prayer books or scriptures found in genizahs"; a *genizah* in this second sense is "a store-room for damaged, discarded, or heretical books, papers, and relics, attached to most synagogues."

R1.2.3. Non-Judæo-Christian scriptures

This section is organized alphabetically. The *Granth* comprises the Sikh scriptures; *Jataka,* from the Buddhist tradition, indicates either "a story of one or other of the former births of the Buddha" or "the Pali collection of these stories." The Puranas are "sacred poetical works ... containing the mythology of the Hindus," and *shaster,* a more general term, indicates "any one of the sacred writings of the Hindus." *Tantra* carries the same non-specific reference, but is attached to pieces of scripture rather than whole units or books. *Veda* is glossed as "one or other of the four ancient sacred books of the Hindus;

the body of sacred literature contained in these books." Finally, the *Zend-Avesta* comprises the scriptures of the Parsees, scriptures "usually attributed to Zoroaster."

R1.3.1.0. Fathers of the Church

Book of the Sentences denotes "a compilation of the opinions of the Fathers on questions of Christian doctrine." *Catena* carries the gloss "a string or series of extracts from the writings of the Fathers, forming a commentary on some portion of Scripture; also, a chronological series of extracts to prove the existence of a continuous tradition on some point of doctrine."

R1.3.1.1. Individual fathers

The adjective *Ignatian* refers especially to the Ignatian epistles, works of dubious authenticity attributed to St Ignatius. *Isidorian* is particularly associated with the twenty books of *Origines* or etymologies written by St Isidore, a seventh-century Archbishop of Seville.

R1.3.1.2. Patristic writings

The *Centuries* are a church history compiled by various clerics in sixteenth-century Magdeburg. *Collations* refers to Cassian's *Collationes Patrum in Scetica Eremo,* "conferences of (and with) the Egyptian hermits." The *Didache* is "a Christian treatise of the beginning of the second century," of importance because of its function of "filling the gap between the Apostolic age and the Church of the second century" (Schaff, in the *Journal of the Society of Biblical Literature,* 1885). *Massorah* denotes "the body of traditional information relating to the text of the Hebrew Bible, compiled by Jewish scholars in the tenth and preceding centuries; the collection of critical notes in which this information is preserved."

R1.4.1. Canon law

Canon law refers to the codified system of ecclesiastical law governing the corporate life of the Roman Catholic Church (and of western Christendom in general until the Reformation), as opposed to the more general sense "church law" referred to by the two constituents of R1.4.0. The Old English adjective *preostlic* possessed the sense "canonical" during Anglo-Saxon times, but this sense did not survive into the Middle English period. The sixth book or *sext* was added to the decretals by Pope Boniface VIII.

R1.4.2. Jewish law

Rabbi is defined as "a Jewish doctor of law. In modern Jewish use, properly applied only to one who is authorized by ordination to deal with questions of law and ritual, and to perform certain functions." *Talmudist* and *Lamdan* both denote persons learned in Jewish law, but may not carry the same reference to ceremonial functions; *Morenu* is an honorific title. *Rabbinist* carries a cross-reference to R2.1.1. KARAITE to point out that the rabbinists accept the teachings of the Talmud and the rabbis, whereas the Karaites ignore this tradition. The scribes were "a class of professional interpreters of the law ... in the Gospels often coupled with the Pharisees as upholders of ceremonial tradition"; hence the cross-reference to R2.1.1. PHARISEE. *Tradition* c1380– is defined as the "unwritten code of regulations, etc., held to have been received from Moses, and embodied in the Mishnah," and *Mishna(h)* is glossed "the collection of binding precepts ... which forms the basis of the Talmud and embodies the contents of the oral law."

R1.5.0. Theology

In this, its broadest sense, *divinity* or *theology* is defined as the "study of God and things divine." *Theologue* c1425–1859 was apparently restricted to Scotland prior to c1600. *Cherubim* with the referent "learned theologian" is a transferred use of the word's main sense ("one of the second order of angels ...reputed to excel especially in knowledge"). The first citation (dated 1758) of *odium theologicum* is from Hume's *Essays and Treatises,* and indicates prior currency: "*Odium theologicum* ... is noted even to a proverb, and means that degree of rancour, which is the most furious and implacable." *Theologoumenon* carries the implicit contrastive meaning component "theological statement (*as opposed to an inspired/revealed doctrine*)."

R1.5.1. Kinds of theology

Astro-theology is defined as "that part of theology which may be deduced from the study of the stars," and is here treated as a kind rather than a department of theology. *Natural theology* is "based upon reasoning from natural facts apart from revelation." *Lithotheology* as a discipline appears to have gained no great following; its one citation is a passing mention in one of Baring-Gould's works on religion.

Rationalism, neologism, and *modernism* are terms of sufficiently indistinct and inconsistent reference to make collocation dangerous. All share the common meaning "a movement towards modifying traditional beliefs and doctrines in accordance with the findings of modern criticism and research," the implication being that superstitious elements are removed and apparently supernatural occurrences explained as fully as possible according to the dictates of modern reason (hence the duplicated entries of *rationalism* and its cognates).

R1.5.2. Departments of theology

Apologetics refers to the argumentative defence of a religious system, especially Christianity. *Didache* is glossed "the didactic element in early Christian theology." *Isagogics* indicates "that department of theology which is introductory to exegesis, and is concerned with the literary and external history of the books of the Bible." *Meta-theology* concerns itself with the study "of the nature of religious language or statements."

Among the schools of thought in the field of moral theology, *laxism* denotes the approach maintaining that "it was justifiable to follow any probability, however slight, in favour of liberty"; the probabiliorists held that "the side on which the evidence preponderates is more probably right and therefore ought to be followed." *Probabilism* denotes the Dominican doctrine that, in matters in which the guidance of authorities conflicts, "it is lawful to follow any course in support of which a recognized doctor of the church can be cited." A *rigorist* is one who believes that "in doubtful cases of conscience the strict course is always to be followed," while a *tutiorist* would choose "the course of greater moral safety."

Symbolics is the department of theology concerned with creeds and formulations of religious faith, *typology* that concerned with symbolic representation.

R1.6.0. Holiness

An important but frequently overlooked sense-component of the *holiness / sanctity / sacredness* lexical area is that of "condition of being set apart"; this component comes to the fore particularly in the cluster of lexical items around the concept of "consecration" and in verbal forms such as *consecrate* and *sequester*. *Sacrosanctity* and its paronyms might better be separately classified owing to the suggestion of "inviolability" in their meanings; usage, however, blurs the distinction so that *sanctity* and *sacrosanctity* and respective paronyms are almost equivalent, if not exactly synonymous.

Sacrality and its paronyms (*sacral, sacralization, sacralize*) share the meanings of other lexical items in their respective categories, but derive from the vocabulary of the anthropological study of religion. *Odour of sanctity* is placed here, in the midst of more rarified abstract concepts, on the basis of its link with *sanctity* and its figurative meaning of "gracious manifestation of saintliness, reputation of holiness"; its base meaning is "a sweet or balsamic odour stated to have been exhaled by the bodies of eminent saints at their death or on subsequent disinterment."

It should be noted that in the adjectival category "blessed" lexemes denoting two separate concepts are collocated, those covering the meaning "holy" (with no reference to an earlier, unhallowed state) and those denoting the concept "consecrated" (indicating the state reached consequent to the process of consecration). *Happy* 1526–1700, "blessed," was in common use well into the first quarter of the seventeenth century, and survives today only in the collocation *of happy memory*.

R1.6.1.0. Saint

Loosely, *saint* denotes "a person characterized by holiness"; more strictly, it denotes "a person who has been canonized and entered into the calendar of saints." Since a consistent distinction is impossible to make (*cf.* gloss to OE *sanct* and *holy* 1548–1648, "holy person, saint"), lexemes carrying both meanings are placed together here. *Wuldormaga/-mago* is glossed "heir of heaven, a man who will attain the glory of heaven" and is found only in poetic usage. *Rubric* in the sense of "calendar of saints" is a transferred sense from the base meaning of "red-letter entry (of a saint's name) in the church calendar." *Saint-errant(ry)* is an ironic formation on the model of *knight-errantry*, though several of the *OED* citations indicate a serious rather than mocking use (*cf.* Southey, *Vindiciæ Ecclesiæ*

Anglicanæ (1826): "The system of Saint-Errantry ... forms as conspicuous a part of history in this age, as Knight-Errantry in the succeeding centuries"). *Saintish* 1529–1840 is "chiefly contemptuous." *Savoury* is glossed "of saintly repute or memory."

R1.6.1.1. Particular saints

Saints Mamertius, Pancras, and Gervais are known as the *ice saints* because their feasts "fall on May 11th, 12th, and 13th, when a cold spell periodically occurs."

R1.6.1.2. Canonization

Canonizing is defined as "the action of placing in the canon or calendar of the saints, according to the rules and with the ceremonies observed by the Church." *Beatification,* which strictly speaking refers to a different concept (a declaration "that a deceased member of the Church is in enjoyment of heavenly bliss"), is in common usage almost synonymous with *canonization,* and thus is here placed together with it. The verb *portess* in the sense of "canonize" is derived from *portas* (see R5.16.3.), and is glossed "to include among the saints named in the breviary; to canonize."

R1.6.2.0. Consecration

Consecration is best defined as "setting apart as holy, investing with sanctity." *Freolsian* in the sense of "consecrate" refers to the action of "freeing (from secularity)." *Inaugurate* is glossed "to make auspicious or of good augury; to confer solemnity or sanctity upon; to sanctify, consecrate."

R1.6.2.2. Blessing

Though they are very close in meaning, *blessing* has been classified apart from *consecration* because of its lack of the sense-components "investing with holiness" and "setting apart." *Blessing* expresses a wish for or invocation of blessedness upon a person or thing, while *consecration* connotes a more active and actual procuration of blessedness. *Consecration* also has connotations of officiality and corporate liturgical ceremony; *blessing* is less formal, and, putatively, less efficacious. *Cardinal's blessing,* denoting "a blessing of no special efficacy," reflects the fact that a cardinal, though highly placed in the ecclesiastical hierarchy, possesses no more consecratory power (in this limited sense) than does an ordinary parish priest. *Kiddush* is glossed "a ceremony of prayer and blessing over bread and wine, performed by the head of a Jewish household at the meal ushering in the Sabbath or a holy day." The referent of *leave-giving* 1450 + 1530(1) is uncertain; the single *OED* citation reads "wyttynge well that the blyssyng, or leaue geuynge, longeth pryncypally to God."

R1.7.0. Piety

Piety, pious, piously, and their near synonyms are closely related to *religiousness, religious,* and *religiously.* A glance at R1.1.5.0. will show that the constituents of that category have been closely restricted to words carrying only the base meaning "(condition of being) characterized by religion"; most of the words in the lexical area are better seen as being conceptually closer to "devotion" or "holiness" than to "religion" itself, and are thus placed here in a category of their own. *Love-eie* and *love-dread* illustrate a further closely related concept, that of "awe" or "fear of God" (the *OED* gloss to these items is "the fear that proceeds from love; 'filial' fear; awe; mingled feeling of dread and reverence to God"). *Theopathy* is defined as "pious sentiment; sensitiveness to divine influence," and the

Hindi *bhakti* is glossed "religious devotion, piety, or devoted faith" (*bhakti-yoga* indicating specifically "devotion to God"). In current usage the adjectives *pious* and *religious* can be used interchangeably, though careful speakers will insist that a person can be described as "religious" without also being characterized as "pious." The latter term probably now reflects an assumption of sanctimoniousness except when employed in such well-worn collocations as *pious old woman*.

R1.7.1.

Sanctimoniousness can be defined as "pretended or excessive piety"; the implication, always unfavourable, is one of piety of dubious worth or veracity. *Sauntering* is of uncertain reference. Both citations are from the York mystery plays: "Thoo sawes schall rewe hym sore / For all his saunteryng sone," and "Nowe all his gaudis no thyng hym gaynes, / His sauntering schall with bale be bought." The *OED* suggests that *sauntering* in this sense of "sanctimoniousness" is a back-formation from *sauntrell*, "petty saint." *Antimacassar* is a transferred sense from the main sense, glossed "applied to that which is typical of the period when antimacassars were in general use (chiefly in the nineteenth century)."

R1.7.3. Impiety

This area of the lexical field is closely linked with those of "idolatry" and "sacrilege"; hence the cross-references.

R1.8.0. Spirituality

The Old English participial adjective *gastbrucende* is glossed "practising in the spirit." The adverb *spiritually* 13..–1559 is duplicated at R1.2.1.1.3. SCRIPTURAL INTERPRETATION because of its connection with the anagogical approach to scriptural interpretation. *Spiritualism* 1836– and animism 1880(1) denote "the belief in the existence of soul or spirit apart from matter, and in a spiritual world generally." *Exercitation* is vaguely glossed "spiritual discipline" (sense 3b in the *OED*); the 1398 citation, from Trevisa, almost suggests "mortification of the flesh": "Some beestes ben made for exercitacion of man ...and therfore ben made flyes and lyce," while the c1425 citation ("Whan spiritual exercitation is yoven of god, recieue it with gret thankinges") is of little help in determining precisely its meaning. How well distinguished this sense is from sense 5 ("devotional exercise; an act of public or private worship") is open to question.

R1.8.1.0. Soul

The Hindi terms *moksha* and *mukti* denote "the final liberation of the soul when it is exempted from further transmigration."

R1.8.1.3. Doctrines concerning the soul

Animism denotes "the doctrine that the phenomena of animal life are produced by an immaterial *anima*, soul, or vital principle distinct from matter." *Annihilationism* denotes "the doctrine of the total annihilation [that is, of both body and soul] of the wicked after death." An appropriationist "holds that the soul is an appropriation of the being of Brahma." *Conditionalism* indicates "the doctrine of conditional survival [of the soul] after death." *Creationism,* which is opposed to *traducianism,* denotes the theory "that God immediately creates a soul for every human being born"; *traducianism* indicates the doctrine "that the soul of a child is inherited from its parents." *Mortalism* signifies the doctrine that the soul is mortal, as does *thanatism; nullibilism* denotes the doctrine that denies the existence of the soul. A *pre-existentiary* believes in the pre-existence of souls; *psychopannychism* denotes the doctrine which holds that "the soul sleeps between death and the day of judgement." A *soulary* maintains the theory "of the separate existence of the soul after the death of the body."

R1.8.2.0. Unspirituality

The lexical areas both of "spirituality" and of "clericality" are in (implied) contrast with that of "unspirituality." *Timesome* refers to the finite duration of earthly things as opposed to the eternity of the spiritual realm.

R1.8.3.0. Contemplation

Meditation is glossed "private devotional exercise consisting of continuous application of the mind to the contemplation of some religious truth, mystery, or object of reverence." *Mantra* is a Hindi holy name for "meditation"; *Samadhi* denotes "the highest state of meditation, in which the distinctions between subject and object disappear and unity with creation is attained."

R1.8.3.1. Self-examination

Self-examination is a species of contemplation, in which the devotee concentrates upon his own spiritual and moral state rather than upon mysteries of faith. *Examen* is a more formal version of the same thing, though it often has the sense of "an examination of the conscience or soul conducted by a religious superior to determine the worthiness of a candidate for ordination."

R1.8.3.2. Quietism

Quietism is a form of devotion (established by the Spanish priest Molinos) "consisting in passionate devotional contemplation, with the extinction of the will and withdrawal from all things of the sense."

R1.8.5.0. Mysticism

A *mystic* is defined as "one who ... seeks by contemplation and self-surrender to obtain union with the deity, or who believes in the possibility of the spiritual apprehension of otherwise inaccessible truths."

R1.8.5.1. Mystery

Mystery is glossed as "a religious truth known only from divine revelation; usually a doctrine of the faith involving difficulties which human reason is incapable of solving." The noun *numinous* is defined as "the non-rational mystery behind religion, which is both awesome and fascinating. It is the permanent and essential feature of all religion, including Christianity." *Tauro-serpentine* is opaque, the single citation reading only "As told in mysteries tauro-serpentine."

R1.8.6.0. Inspiration

Bierht(u) is glossed "radiance, illumination" and establishes the link between the concept of "inspiration" or "revelation" and a metaphorical use of *illumination*. *Wuldorword*, a poetic term, means "glorious word" and is used in the sense of "revelation." *Entheos* is formed through Latin from the Greek adjective meaning "divinely inspired"; the *OED* carries three citations, none of which appears to refer to inspiration within the Judæo-Christian framework. *Entheasm* and *enthusiasm* suggest the bond between the concepts of "inspiration" and "prophetic or poetic frenzy." The Hindi term *muni* is of somewhat indeterminate reference, for it denotes not only "inspired person" but "holy man," "sage," "ascetic," or "hermit" as well. This indeterminacy is characteristic as well of *rishi*. *Beatrician* in the sense of "inspired" or "revelational" refers to Dante's vision of Beatrice as a type of inspiration. The Old English verb *onwreon,* "to reveal, inspire," is a metaphoric use of the main sense 'unwrap' and is conceptually linked with "revelation."

R1.8.6.1. Prophecy

With the exceptions of *mlimo, euhages,* and *sadhu,* all lexical material in this section refers to Judæo-Christian practice and functionaries. The section might at a later date be incorporated in a classification of "prophecy and prophets" in general. *His sadhuship* is a "humorous" title for the *sadhu,* an Indian prophet.

R1.8.6.2. Vision

Beatific vision is glossed "a sight of the glories of heaven, especially that first granted to a disembodied spirit." *Bethphany* refers specifically to the third divine manifestation, the miracle at Cana.

R1.9.0. Grace

Grace is defined as "the virtuous and strengthening divine influence which operates in men, regarded as a permanent force, having its seat in the soul." *Congruous grace* refers to "grace proportioned to the effect which it is to produce, or to the disposition of him who receives it," *sufficient grace* to "the grace which (merely) renders the soul capable of performing a supernatural act."

R1.9.1. Doctrines concerning grace

With reference to grace, *Augustinianism* held that it was characterized by immediate efficacy. *Condignity* denotes "that worthiness of eternal life which a man may possess through good works performed while in a state of grace." *Congruity* refers to the scholastic doctrine that "God should confer the 'first grace' in response, and in 'a certain equality of proportion,' to the performance of good works by man." *Molinism* holds that "the efficacy of grace depends simply on the will which freely accepts it." *Monergism* refers to the doctrine that "regeneration is entirely the work of the Holy Spirit," and is opposite to *synergism,* which holds that "the human will co-operates with divine grace in the work of regeneration."

R1.9.2. Merit

Merit-monger and its synonyms denote "one who trades in merits; one who seeks to merit salvation ... by good works."

R1.10.0. Sin

Offension is glossed "spiritual stumbling, or the occasion of it." *Synfah* is a poetic adjective used to denote "stained with sin." The adjective *sooty* refers to the common conceit of the soul being blackened by sin. *Attrition* denotes "an imperfect sorrow for sin, as if a bruising which does not amount to utter crushing (contrition)."

R1.10.1. Kinds of sin

Actual sin refers to "sin which is committed by a person (as opposed to inborn original sin)." A *formal sin* is one "in the full sense, as including not merely the outward act which is forbidden, but the circumstances which constitute it as sinful." Mortal sins are those which, unamended, result in spiritual death. *Original sin* is glossed "the innate depravity, corruption, or evil tendency of man's nature, in all individuals of the human race, held to be inherited from Adam in consequence of the Fall."

R1.11.0. Atonement

Atonement is defined as "the making of satisfaction for sin, the restoration of friendly relations between God and sinners." A Stancarian held that "the atonement of Christ was wrought by his human nature only."

R1.12.1. Doctrines of salvation

Absolutism denotes the "dogma of God's acting absolutely in the affair of salvation, and not being guided in this ... by any reason." *Apocatastasis* indicates "the doctrine that all free moral creatures will share in the grace of salvation." *Nationalism* refers to the odious doctrine that "certain nations are the object of divine election." A *nudifidian* holds that faith alone is sufficient for salvation. *Particularism* refers to the dogma that "divine grace is provided for or offered to a selected part, not the whole, of the human race." A *post-destinarian* believes that "one's eternal destiny is decided after death." An *infralapsarian* has the view that "God's election of some to everlasting life was consequent to his prescience of the fall of man, or that it contemplated man as already fallen, and was thus a remedial measure." *Restorationism* denotes the view that "all men will ultimately be restored to a state of happiness in the future life." *Supralapsarian* is glossed as "a name applied to those Calvinists who held the view that, in the divine decrees, the predestination of some to eternal life and of others to eternal death was antecedent to the Creation and the Fall." *Terminism* denotes "the doctrine that God has appointed a definite term or limit in the life of each individual, after which the opportunity for salvation is lost." *Universalism* refers to the view that "the whole of mankind is offered salvation."

R1.13.0. Reprobation

Reprobation is the opposite of *salvation,* and signifies "rejection by God; the state of being so rejected or cast off, and thus ordained to eternal misery." In this connection, *tinsel* ("damnation") derives from the Old Norse *týna* ("to lose, perish, destroy"), rather than from the Old French *estincelle,* the descendant of which denotes the decorative material.

R2

R2.1.0. Judaism

The placement of this category before "Christianity" has proved controversial. As mentioned in chapter 2, both the antiquity of Judaism and the fact that it gave birth to Christianity led to its present position in the classificatory structure of R2 (*cf.* also the discussion of 'family tree' classification in chapter 1). Consistency is thus maintained, though it has been suggested that "Judaism" should follow rather than precede "Christianity" in the classification, owing to the large disparity in lexical representation between the two groups.

R2.1.1. Jewish groups and sects

It is debatable whether some of the groups forming category tags here merit the *-ism* suffix. The Sephardim, for example, constitute a geographical rather than a doctrinal division. But uniform *-ism* suffixes allow a uniform set of category tags; once again the question is whether slight distortions are counterbalanced by gains in consistency of treatment.

Chasidism denotes "any of several mystical Jewish sects of various periods" and its paronym *(C)has(s)id* is synonymous with the 1834 citation of *Assidæan.* The reader will note two earlier citations of *Assidæan* in the preceding category. These denote a Jew who "defended the purity of (his) worship against

the attempts of Antiochus Epiphanes to introduce idolatry."
Mitnagged covers any Jew who is not a Chasid of the former
type. *Hebra* is not a singular noun, but rather a collective
noun covering "a religious association of Jews too poor to hold
seats in the synagogue." The gloss to *Herodian* states that the
Herodians were a "mainly political" Jewish party; the item is
included here because one characteristic of this group was its
laxness in adherence to Judaism. *Territorialist* should perhaps
be excluded; its gloss reads "a member of a Jewish organization
aiming to secure separate Jewish territory."

R2.2.0. Christianity

Several constituents of this category (*i.e. godspel/gospel, the
faith, the cross*) carry unstated contrastive elements, implying
the notion of Christianity *as opposed to* the Old Testament dispensation or other religions. *Nazarene / -ite / -ian* and *Nasrani*
are terms used by Jews and Moslems to refer to Christians.

    Lathing (OE *laðung*) survives until c1275, but in the sense of
"congregation, gathering" rather than the OE sense of "whole
body of Christians on earth, the church"; it is a paronym of the
verb *lathian,* "to invite or summon," and characterizes Christians as those who have been called by God as his chosen people. *Holy church* seems obsolete in the sense of "the whole body
of Christians," but is still occasionally found as a synonym for
"Roman Catholic Church." The *OED* makes what might be
considered an interesting sociological observation by including
in its gloss for *holy church* the addendum "in early times, often
= the clergy or ecclesiastical authority," pointing to a long-
standing tendency in established denominations of identifying
the church with its functionaries rather than seeing it as the
sum of all its members both clerical and lay (*cf.* the *OED* gloss
to *congregation* 1526–1583 and the Quaker-inspired dichotomy
between *church* and *steeple-house* in R5.3.3.).

Primitive church and *early church* both carry the implication of purity; the first centuries of the Christian church's existence are thought by some to have embodied a Christianity unvitiated by the additions and superfluities imputed to the Church in the middle ages. The *OED* provides us with only one citation (by Jowett) for *early church,* though the term is in common use today.

R2.2.0.1. Conversion to Christianity

The inclusion of lexical material covering the concept of "conversion to Christianity" here is defensible because of close conceptual links. Nonetheless, all material here has been included in R4.5.4.0. CONVERSION as well. Cross-references to R4.5.1. EVANGELIZATION and R4.2.1.0. BAPTISM display the considerable and problematic conceptual overlap existing between the three semantic areas. Conversion to various denominations is not cross-referenced.

R2.2.1. Major early Christian sects

The overall organization of this section is alphabetical, but identifiable adaptations or offshoots of main sects are appropriately subordinated. A fairly wide acceptance and marked historical significance were the two main criteria used to determine which of the early sects would find a place here rather than in R2.2.5. VARIOUS (ANTI-)CHRISTIAN SECTS AND MOVEMENTS.

R2.2.1.1. Antidicomarianism

These fourth-century Oriental Christians denied the perpetual virginity of Mary, the mother of Christ.

R2.2.1.2. Arianism

Eusebian as a synonym for *Arian* derives from the name of
Eusebius, bishop of Nicomedia, a leader of the Arians. Note
the large chronological gap between *arrianisc* and *Arian* 1642–.

R2.2.1.6.1. Cerinthian

Cerinthian finds a place here, though strictly speaking its referent is not a sect of Gnostics. Cerinthius, a first-century
heresiarch, "attempted to unite Christianity with a mixture
of Gnosticism and Judaism, the main peculiarity being the assumption that Jesus was a man and the Christ an æon who
entered into Jesus." *Encratism* is classified with "Severite" on
the basis of its close connection with Gnosticism, particularly
in the matter of abstinence from such things as wine, animal
food, and marriage. Of the Encratites, the *Catholic Encyclopædia* says "the name was given to an early Christian sect,
or rather to a tendency common to several sects, chiefly Gnostic, whose asceticism was based on heretical views regarding
the origin of matter."

R2.2.1.7. Patarin/Patarene

The *OED* gloss reads "a name applied ... to the deacon Arialdi
and his followers, who opposed the marriage of priests; in the
twelfth century applied to Albigensians, Cathari, and others;
generally employed as a term of opprobrium, identified with
Manichean, etc."

R2.2.2.0. Greek Orthodoxy

-Ism nouns are conspicuous by their absence, as is the word *Orthodoxy* in the sense of "doctrine of the Orthodox churches."
Unfortunately, only *Greekery,* a contemptuous term, can be
found for inclusion in this category. The adjective *orthodox*

"was originally assumed to distinguish (the Greek Church) from the various divisions of the Eastern Church, e.g. the Jacobite or Monophysite, Nestorian, etc., which separated on points of doctrine, and have not accepted all the decrees of the successive general councils; but it is sometimes used by historical writers as opposed to 'Catholic.'"

Fermentarian points to the use of leavened rather than unleavened bread in the Orthodox ritual, as does *Prozymite. Azymite* is used in Orthodox circles to denote the Armenians, who use unleavened bread. *Non-united* and *Uniate* denote respectively those Orthodox branches not in union with Rome and united with Rome accepting papal jurisdiction.

R2.2.3.0. Roman Catholicism

The paucity of lexical material prior to the sixteenth century denoting Roman Catholicism and its adherents *per se* is of course indicative that Christianity and Roman Catholicism were – at least for referential purposes – synonymous in the West until the eve of the Reformation. Of the forty-five lexical items denoting the concept of "adherent of Roman Catholicism," over a third are overtly hostile or derogatory. Among these, *cacolike / -leek* shows a spark of wit of a kind not often encountered in religious dispute, representing as it does a perversion of *Catholic* based on the Greek *kakós*, "bad." *Crawthumper* is an amusing reference to the practice of thrice striking the breast during a confession of sins.

It should be noted that, since the Second Vatican Council, which concluded in 1965, a *Tridentine* or *Trentist, pace* Msgr. Lefébvre, can no longer be called an orthodox Roman Catholic.

R2.2.3.1. Roman Catholic groups and sects

Baianism, a forerunner of Jansenism, is based on the teachings of de Bay and should not be confused with *Bahaism. Gallicanism* denotes the school of thought given prominence at the synod of 1862, emphasizing a less magisterial interpretation of papal authority; as such, it is opposed to *Ultramontanism,* which insists on the plenitude of papal authority and which secured in the First Vatican Council the doctrine of papal infallibility.

While *English Catholicism* refers to the Roman church in England, *German Catholic* denotes a member of a party led by Ronge which separated from the Roman communion in 1845. The Inopportunists, though not Gallicans, were opposed to the proclamation of the dogma of infallibility in 1870 on the ground that the time was not right. Jansenists held the view that the human will is characterized by "perverseness and inability for good." *Old Catholic* 1871– denotes a member of any of several groups reunited with Rome by the 1889 Declaration of Utrecht. The Ribbon Society was a party "formed in the north and north-west of Ireland early in the nineteenth century to counteract the Protestant influence."

A certain degree of indeterminacy dogs the use of *transmontane, ultramontane,* and their paronyms. *Ultramontane* 1592–1855 and the items associated with it denote first the Roman Catholic Church north of the Alps (rather than Italian ecclesiastics). This part of the church came to oppose certain philosophies (*e.g.* on the fullness of papal power) held mainly by Italian ecclesiastics – the same Italian ecclesiastics who, together with their non-Italian supporters, later came to be associated with the label *ultramontane.* As *ultramontanism* is almost always associated with the doctrine of papal supremacy and infallibility, it is perhaps best to refer to the former (non-Italian) group by the less ambiguous term *transmontane.*

R2.2.4.0. Protestantism general

Gospel as used here is "identified by Protestants with their own system of belief, as opposed to the perversions of Christianity imputed by them to their adversaries." The emphasis here (as with words such as *gospeller*) is on a claim of exclusive possession of the truth. The adjectives *evangelic* and *evangelical* are applied especially in Germany and Switzerland to Protestants.

R2.2.4.0.2. Fundamentalism

In its present form, fundamentalism "became active among various Protestant bodies in the U.S. after the war of 1914-18." The recent explosive growth of fundamentalist sects and the *odium theologicum* that characterizes their internecine disputes promise a rich outpouring of new lexical material in years to come.

R2.2.4.0.3.1. Pilgrimage of grace

This anti-reformation movement took place in northern England in 1536, and marked a protest against the religious policies of Henry VIII.

R2.2.4.1.0. Anglicanism

Anglicanism is classified with other Protestant churches on the basis of the repudiation by the English crown of papal authority in the sixteenth century. There are many views within the Anglican communion even today on the question of its exact nature. Those characterized as 'high' churchmen tend to emphasize the catholicity of the church and the similarity of many of its doctrines, practices, and offices with Roman Catholic analogues, while 'low' or 'evangelical' churchmen strongly affirm the church's Protestant features. The diffuseness and heterogeneousness of much Anglican doctrine permit widely varying conceptions of the church's nature, but as mentioned its placement here as a Protestant body is unassailable on historical grounds.

In this connection, it is well to note the *OED* gloss to the noun *Protestant* (designating a church member): "formerly

generally accepted and used by members of the established
church, and applied to them even to the exclusion of Presbyterians, Quakers, and separatists ... in more recent times the
name has been disowned by many Anglicans."

R2.2.4.1.1.2. Continuationist

A continuationist is one who believes that the English reformation made no break in the historical continuity of the English church, that "the Anglican church is the continuation of
the pre-Reformation English Catholic Church." *Henricianism*
designates the ecclesiastical policy of Henry VIII.

R2.2.4.1.1.4. High-churchism *et seq.*

There is much confusion surrounding the use of terms such as
high church, Oxford movement, latitudinarian, and *low church.*
Briefly, from the seventeenth century onward there have been
well-established groups within the Church of England, the most
prominent of which are the 'high churchmen' and the 'low
churchmen.' High churchism – in early days often found hand
in hand with political Conservatism – stands for an authori-
tarian church acting as the spiritual arm of the state, characterized by a degree of elaborate ritual and an hierarchic form
of government. The Oxford movement was originally quite
distinct from high churchism, as it was held to be tainted by
romanizing tendencies repugnant to high churchmen. In more
recent times, however, this distinction has been much blurred.
Low churchism, formerly associated with Whiggism, is Protestant and evangelical, and favours a minimum of ritual and
hierarchic panoply. *Latitudinarianism* might suggest a toler-
ance for elements from both ends of the spectrum (and thus
be quasi-synonymous with *broad church*), but in fact it usually
designates the low-church philosophy.

R2.2.4.1.1.5. Lollardy/Wyclifism

Lollardy is included here as a precursor of the reformed English church and not, as are the other subfields, as a post-Reformation group within the church (*cf.* also note to R2.2.4.1.1.2. above).

R2.2.4.1.1.6. Low-churchism

Recordite derives from the name of an evangelical Church of England newspaper, the *Record*.

R2.2.4.1.1.7. Reunionism

This party holds as its objective the reunion of Anglicanism with the Roman Catholic Church.

R2.2.4.2. Antitrinitarianism

Trinitarian and its cognates might seem unlikely constituents of this category, but they in fact denote those holding heretical or unorthodox opinions regarding the Trinity, and as such serve as hyponyms for the concept "person characterized by Antitrinitarian views." *Racovian* derives from the name *Rakow*, a Polish centre of Antitrinitarianism in the seventeenth century; *Bid(d)el(l)ian* is from the name of John Biddle, the "father of the English Unitarians."

Praxeas was a prominent third-century Antitrinitarian; hence *Praxean*. The Remonstrant Synod "separated from the general synod of Ulster in 1830" because of their Antitrinitarian views. The Socinians, an Italian-based group originating in the sixteenth century, qualify as Antitrinitarians through their denial of Christ's divinity. The godhead of the Tetradites consisted of four beings; in addition to the Christian three, they had a "Divine Being" who was a mystical composite of the other three.

R2.2.4.3. Arminianism

This group followed the doctrine of the Dutch theologian Arminius (Harmensen), who opposed Calvin on the question of predestination. *Remonstrance* denotes the "document presented in 1610 to the states of Holland by the Dutch Arminians, relative to the points of difference between themselves and the strict Calvinists."

R2.2.4.4.0. Baptistry

Into this capacious category fall all those who do not adhere to the standard catholic (*i.e.* Roman / Anglican / sacramental) view of baptism. Common to nearly all is the insistence on a (second) adult baptism, the result of a conscious choice to be accepted into the family of God. *Anabaptistry* and its cognates are largely disowned by present-day Baptists, but are found to some extent in controversial works of recent date. *Catabaptistry* best embodies the idea of wrong baptismal doctrine. *Wederdoper* derives from Dutch *weder* "again" and *doper* "dipper" (see *dipper* 1617–(1887) and *dopper* 1620–1625 + 1881).

R2.2.4.4.1. Baptist groups and sects

The Hardshell Baptists are best known for unyielding strictness of Calvinist doctrine. Muncerian Baptists comprise the sect arising c1521 under the leadership of Münzer; the Münster Anabaptists, a fanatical group following Bernhard Knipperdolling, occupied Münster in the early sixteenth century. All Seventh-Day Baptist philosophy is based on the observance of the Lord's day on the seventh day (*i.e.* Saturday) of the week rather than on the first.

R2.2.4.5. Calvinism

Calvin's theological doctrine is notable chiefly for its emphasis on the concept of grace; hence the cross-reference. *Hugueno-tism* and cognates indicate primarily the French Calvinist tradition, while *Genevanism* and its cognates recall the city in which Calvinist and Zwinglian doctrines first met with wide acceptance. *Camisar(d)* derives from the Provençal *camisa*, "shirt," and denotes an insurgent of the Cevennes "during the persecution which followed the revocation of the Edict of Nantes" (Littré). Francis Gomar of Leyden played a significant part in the defence of orthodox Calvinism against the views of the Arminians. *Hopkinsianism* and *Taylorism* are both forms of Calvinism with doctrinal modifications.

R2.2.4.6. Lutheranism

Martinist 1751(1) is from Swift's *The Tale of a Tub*; *Augustan* refers to Augsburg, "where in 1530 Luther and Melanchthon drew up their confession of Protestant principles." The Calixtins, like the Philippists, were noted for "moderate and conciliatory views." Calixtus (d. 1656), in fact, cherished the ideal of the reunification of all Protestant sects followed by a general union of all Christendom. The Confessional Church comprised "a group of German Christians who opposed the church movement sponsored by the Nazis and which claimed to stand fast by the Reformation confessions."

The Flacians, a sixteenth-century sect, "held that original sin was not an accident in human nature but belonged to its substance"; hence the synonym *substantialist*. *Pietism* arose late in the seventeenth century, and stood for a "revival and advancement of piety in the Lutheran church." The Ubiquitarians "maintained the doctrine that Christ's body was everywhere present at all times."

R2.2.4.7. Mennonism

Founded in the sixteenth century by Menno Simons, the Mennonites "are opposed to the taking of oaths, infant baptism, military service, and the holding of civic offices." As if that were not enough, the Amish are a stricter American sect of Mennonites (*Hooker* reflects their custom of fastening clothes by means of buttons and hooks). The Borborites (from a Greek root meaning "filthy") reputedly engaged in personal practices at variance with prevailing norms.

R2.2.4.8. Methodism

Swaddling and cognates as applied to Methodists (and, by extension, to Protestants in general) are explained in the following 1747 citation from the journals of Charles Wesley: "We dined with a gentleman who explained our name to us. It seems we are beholden to Mr Cennick for it, who abounds in suchlike expressions as, 'I curse and blaspheme all the gods in heaven, but the babe that lay in swaddling clouts', &c. Hence they nicknamed him, 'Swaddler, or Swaddling John'; and the word sticks to us all, not excepting the clergy." The Jumpers arose in Wales about the mid-eighteenth century and "used to jump and dance as part of religious worship"; *Ranter* as a synonym for *Primitive Methodist* is an unkind reference to this group's practice of singing in the streets following a prayer meeting. Though there is no overt connection between the two, the Shouters resemble the Jumpers in a tendency to "leap and shout in their ecstasies."

R2.2.4.9. Moravianism

Herrnhutism and cognates derive from the German *Herrnhut*, "the Lord's keeping," after "the name of their first German settlement on the estate of Count von Zinzendorf." The Inghamites were a religious body "founded about 1740 by Benjamin Ingham, on principles akin to those of the Moravians and Methodists."

R2.2.4.12. Presbyterianism

Allobrogical alludes to Geneva "as originally a town of the Allobroges." *Congregationalism* is an adaptation of Presbyterianism in which "each local congregation of believers is held to be a church independent of any external authority." *Yellow-stick* as an epithet for Hebridean Presbyterianism is dubiously explained by Blaikie (1880) thus: "A tradition that the people of the island (Ulva) were converted from being Roman Catholics 'by the laird coming round with a man having a yellow staff ... the new religion went long afterwards ... by the name of the religion of the yellow stick.'" The *Antiburgher,* a part of the Secession Church, separated in 1747 over the burgess oath, and was not reunited until 1820. *Wee Free* and cognates designate the "minority of the Free Church of Scotland which stood apart when the main body amalgamated with the United Presbyterian Church to form the United Free Church in 1900."

Covenant covers "certain bonds of agreement signed by the Scottish Presbyterians for the defence and furtherance of their religion and ecclesiastical polity," especially the national covenant of 1638 and the solemn league and covenant of 1643. All material in this area can be found at R4.11. Vow, Covenant.

R2.2.4.13. Puritanism

This rather general category covers those who profess a rigid conformity in religion. English Puritans, for example, "regarded the reformation of the church under Elizabeth as incomplete, and called for its further 'purification.'" *Catharism* and its paronyms are derived from medieval Latin *cathari,* "the pure," a label assumed by various sects.

R2.2.4.16. Waldensianism

Insabbatist, previously thought to indicate this sect's attitude toward the Sabbath, is now thought to refer to the "peculiar" shoe (*sabot*) worn by members.

R2.2.5. Various (anti-)Christian sects and movements

In this section, either the religious system itself or its adherent(s) can serve as head category, unlike the procedure employed elsewhere in R2. Thus *Acephali,* a plural noun meaning "Christian sect acknowledging no earthly head or leader," is not made subordinate to an empty category labelled *Acephalism.* Many of the groups in this category are small and poorly attested, a fact which results in a paucity of *-ism* nouns.

R2.3.1. Buddhism

Hinayana is the name given by Mahayanists to the Buddhism of Ceylon; it is from Sanskrit *hina* "lesser" and *yana* "vehicle." Jainism, strictly speaking, is not a sectarian form of Buddhism, but rather a religion whose central doctrines "closely resemble those of Buddhism."

R2.3.3. Hinduism

Gentile and *gentoo* both are borrowed from Judæo-Christian terminology, and reflect a distinction formerly made in Hindustan between the Mohammedan and the 'pagan' Hindu. *Hare Krishna,* used as an adjective absolute, designates a cult one of whose principal features is the repetition of a mantra of the same name. Their worship is apparently directed to the god Vishnu, but a separate category is assigned here because of the considerable contemporary prominence of the Hare Krishnans.

R2.3.3.2. Sanskritization

Reference here is to conversion to a high Hindu caste, as opposed to conversion to Hinduism in general.

R2.3.4. Islam

Crescent is here used in the same capacity as is *cross* for the Christian religion. As the oldest term designating Islam and its adherents, *Sarracene / Saracen* is of etymological interest. The uncertainty of its derivation is mirrored by the plethora of attested variant forms, of which the *OED* lists more than thirty. Possible Arabic derivations are discounted as uncertain; "in medieval times the name was often associated with Sarah, the wife of Abraham; St Jerome ... identifies the Saracens with the *Agareni* (Hagarens, descendants of Hagar) 'who are now called Saracens, taking to themselves the name of Sara.'" The name was in use among the Greeks and Romans, and became firmly identified with the Mohammedans during the Crusades. *Islam* means "the manifesting of humility or submission and outward conformity with the law of God." *Unitarian* points to the monotheistic nature of Islam as opposed to (what Moslems perceive as) the tritheistic godhead of Christianity.

Assassins is related to *hashish,* and refers to the "Moslem fanatics in the time of the Crusades, who were sent forth by their sheikh ... to murder the Christian leaders." A *Hadji* is a Mecca pilgrim who undertakes the 'greater' pilgrimage on the eighth to the tenth day of the twelfth month of the Moslem year.

Orthodox Moslems (Sunnites) accept tradition as well as the contents of the Koran; Shiite or unorthodox Moslems differ chiefly by "holding that Ali (Mohammed's cousin and son-in-law) was the true successor of the prophet, the three first caliphs of the Sunnites being regarded as usurpers."

R3

R3.1.1. Kinds of church government

Collegiality is defined as "the sharing of the bishops, with the pope as their head, in the supreme responsibility of the government of the church." *Conciliarism* emphasizes the "authority of representative church councils as opposed to that of monarchical papacy." *Congregationalism* insists on the autonomy of local congregations and looks askance at centralized ecclesiastical authority, while *consociation* highlights the "confederation or union" existing between individual parishes organized on a congregational basis. *Episcopacy* is a general term referring to an ecclesiastical system employing bishops with authority over specified territories; *prelacy* and its paronyms are hostile terms for the same referent (*prelate* to some extent carrying the pejorative slant more fully expressed in locutions such as "proud prelate.")

Erastianism indicates the "doctrine of the complete subordination of the ecclesiastical to the secular power"; *regalism* further specifies that this secular power is in the hands of a monarch. *Statism* is not exactly synonymous with *establishmentarianism*; the former denotes "subservience" to political expediency in religious matters," whereas *establishmentarianism* and the two remaining constituents of this class indicate the idea of a religion ordained by government, the establishment of which is enshrined in civil law. *Law-church* is a disparaging term denoting an instance of such. *Febronianism* refers to the "doctrine of the independence of national churches," and is derived from the pseudonym of J. N. von Hontheim, an eighteenth-century divine. *Free-churchism* refers to the school of thought holding that churches should shun any form of state control. *Hierocracy* refers to the exercise of temporal power by a religious body, though it is often vaguely employed to mean "the influencing of temporal affairs by churchmen."

Josephism indicates the ecclesiastical policy of the Austrian emperor Joseph II (1741–1790), which, according to the *Catholic Encyclopædia*, "is nothing else than the highest development of the craving common among secular princes after an episcopal and territorial church .... [Joseph] treated ecclesiastical institutions as public departments of the State." *Morellianism* stands for "extreme democracy in church government"; *patriarchism* indicates ecclesiastical government by patriarchs, while *Phyletism* refers to "an excessive emphasis on the principle of nationalism ... a policy which attaches greater importance to ethnic identity than to bonds of faith and worship" within the Orthodox Church. *Theocracy* denotes a system "in which God or a god is recognized as immediate ruler."

R3.1.2. Ecclesiastical authority

Prelacy a1340–1577 has the additional and more general sense of "the authority of any superior, lay or clerical." *Spiritualist* 1651(1), as well as indicating "one who supports ... spiritual or ecclesiastical authority," carries the further meaning component that such support is in opposition to or in the face of secular or temporal authority.

R3.1.3.0. Ecclesiastical discipline

Canonical obedience refers to "the obedience to be rendered by inferior clergy to the bishop or other ecclesiastical superior, according to the canons."

R3.1.3.1. Ecclesiastical court

The Roman Rota is "the supreme court for ecclesiastical and secular causes" in the Roman Catholic Church. *Prerogative court / office* denotes "the court of an archbishop for the probate of wills and trial of testamentary causes in which effects to the value of five pounds had been left in each of two (or more) dioceses within his province." *Court of audience* refers to another archiepiscopal court "at first held by the archbishop, afterwards by learned men, called auditors, on his behalf." The archiepiscopal court in the diocese of Canterbury carries the name *(Court of) Arches* because it was at one time held in "the Church of St Mary-le-Bow (or 'of the Arches'), so named from the arches that support its steeple." Of the Presbyterian ecclesiastical courts, *synod* is that "next above the presbytery, and consisting of the ministers of, or delegates from, the presbyters within its bounds," *presbytery* that "consisting of all the ministers, and representatives from each parish or congregation, within the local area, constituting the ecclesiastical court next above the kirk-session and below the synod," and *kirk-session* that "composed of the ministers and elders of the parish or congregation."

R3.1.4.1. Kinds of council

Tractory and its paronyms in the sense of "letter from a synod of bishops" are derived from late Latin *epistola tractoria*, which in turn derives from Latin *tractatus*, "a conference treating of sacred subjects."

R3.1.4.2. Historical councils

The *OED* gloss for the nouns *Trentist* and *Tridentine*, "one who accepts and conforms to the decrees of the Council of Trent, an orthodox Roman Catholic" is, since the Second Vatican Council, correct only in its first part. One who today adheres to Tridentine practice (especially in the area of liturgy) can no longer call himself an orthodox Catholic (*cf.* note to R2.2.3.0.).

R3.1.4.3.0. Chapter

The referent of *chapter* can be either secular or monastic clergy, as the *OED* gloss demonstrates: "a duly constituted general meeting or assembly of the canons of a collegiate or cathedral church, or of the members of any monastic or religious order, for consultation and the transaction of the affairs of the order."

R3.1.4.3.1. Member of chapter

Provost, a rendering of the German *propst,* refers to the Protestant equivalent of a dean of chapter; this functionary has "charge of the principal church of a town or district." A *numerary canon* is one of the "regular number" of canons in a particular chapter, as opposed to a *supernumerary canon.*

R3.1.4.3.2. Cathedral dignitaries

Chancellor is glossed "one of the four chief dignitaries in the cathedrals of old foundations," *proctor* "a deputy elected to represent the chapter of a cathedral or collegiate church, or the clergy of a diocese or archdeaconry in the lower house of convocation of either province [*i.e.* Canterbury or York]," *scholaster* "the holder of a prebend in a cathedral to which certain teaching duties were attached," *secondary* "a cathedral dignitary of second rank," and, most vaguely, *seneschal* "a cathedral official in England." The single *OED* citation of the latter term, dated 1882, casts no light on its meaning.

R3.2.0. Clergyman general

The constituents of this class denote the concept of "clergyman, ecclesiastic" in its general sense. *Godes man / God's man* is a Hebraism, as is *godes ðegn; ðegn* is a more concise expression of the same concept. *Cleric / clerk* is glossed "before the Reformation, and in the Roman Catholic Church, a member of any of the eight orders (though sometimes excluding the bishop)"; the English post-Reformation meaning (here conflated with the earlier sense) is specified as "generally equivalent to 'clerk in holy orders', i.e. a deacon, priest, or bishop."

The *OED* further states that the latter is now "chiefly a legal or formal designation." *Preost / priest* perhaps surprisingly has long had, in addition to its specific referent "clergyman with sacrificial function, clergyman of church whose eucharistic doctrine emphasizes the sacrificial rather than the commemorative aspect of communion," the more general referent "clergyman, ecclesiastic." *Secular* points to the distinction between parish or diocesan clergy and those in one of the religious orders. The principal pre-Reformation sense of *minister* is given as "a person in orders officially charged with some function in the celebration of worship." *Abbé* is of course the French equivalent of *abbot,* but its sense encompasses "everyone who wears an ecclesiastical dress." *Tippet man* is a contemptuous allusion to an article of ecclesiastical neckwear. *Cock* is metaphorical, referring to an ecclesiastic's function as "one who arouses from (spiritual) slumber." *Autem jet,* a slang phrase, refers to the black dress of clerics; *parch* is supported by two citations, both from the works of Dylan Thomas.

Strictly speaking, *biscophired* refers to "clergy subject to a bishop," but it thus also serves as a collective noun for the secular (as opposed to the regular) clergy.

R3.2.1.0. Clerical superior general

The constituents of this category cover the concept of "church dignitary," but several have more specific (though not necessarily fixed) referents. "High priest" is referred to by *biscopealder, ealdorsacerd, forebiscop, heafodbiscop, heahsacerd, biscop / bishop,* and others, though all of these terms can refer to non-Christian functionaries as well as non-sacrificial functionaries. Rather than subordinate these lexemes to *priest,* for example, it seemed advisable to place them with *prelate, ecclesiarch,* and other near-synonyms in this admittedly rather vague class. *Gentleman untrial* is markedly obscure; little elucidation is gained from its fullest citation (from a heraldry treatise of 1486): "Ther be ij dyuerse Gentylmen made of gromys that be nott gentilmen of cote-armure nother of blode. Oon is calde in armys a gentylman vntriall, that is to say made vp emong religyous men as priorys, Abbottis, or Byschoppis." The referent may not be "clerical superior," but rather "gentleman whose upbringing and education took place in a religious institution." *Archbishop* 1600(1) is here used to translate the Latin *pontifex maximus*, "high priest." *Monsignor*, a title now most often associated with domestic prelates and honorary members of the papal household, is historically an honorific title of wide application; the French *monseigneur* has long been employed as the standard mode of address for cardinals, archbishops, and bishops. *Sheikh* 1613– is a general term for a Moslem superior, "the head of a religious order or community."

The adjective *Aaronical* in the sense of "high-priestly, pontifical" derives from the name of Aaron, the "patriarch of the Jewish priesthood."

R3.2.1.1.0. Pope

The Latin loanword *domne* is employed as a title rather than as a name. Though *servant of the servants of God* is given only one citation in the *OED*, it remains among the titles of reigning popes today. I am indebted to Mr L W Collier and Dr Heather Edwards for drawing my attention to the Old English equivalent of the modern *servant of the servants of God*. It is *godes ðeowa ðeow*, and is used (translating *episcopus servus servorum Dei*) in a seventh-century privilege of Pope Sergius I to the Abbot of Malmesbury (printed in Birch, *Cartularium Saxonicum*, I. no. 106). *Decretaliarch* is a rendering of Rabelais's French equivalent. *Cægan / keys* in the sense "papal office" alludes to "the ecclesiastical authority, held by Roman Catholics to be conferred by Christ on St Peter, and transmitted to the popes as his successors." *Economacy* has the general sense of

"the position of being controller of ecclesiastical affairs," but
the single citation refers to the pope. Among the methods of
electing a pope, compromise occurs when "all cardinals agree
to entrust the election to a small committee of two or three
members of the body"; *scrutiny* indicates an ordinary tally of
ballots, and adoration takes place when the cardinals, supposedly inspired by the Holy Spirit, together acclaim one of their
number pope without resorting to a ballot or other electoral
procedures. (An interesting account of papal elections can be
found in the first chapters of Valerie Pirie's *The Triple Crown*
(1935)).

R3.2.1.1.1. Antipope

Antipope is defined as "a pope elected in opposition to one
held to be canonically chosen; specifically applied to those who
resided at Avignon during 'the great schism of the West.'"

R3.2.1.1.2. Individual popes

Hildebrandism (from the family name of Gregory VII) refers to
that pope's "unbending assertion of the power of the papacy
and hierarchy, and of the celibacy of the clergy." An Urbanist
supported Urban VI against the antipope Clement VII.

R3.2.1.1.3. Papal offices, officials

Among the officials of the pope, the plumbator is "a custodian
of the leaden seal" used to ratify documents.

R3.2.1.1.4. Papal documents

A bull is a papal edict, the name of which derives from the
leaden seal (Latin *bulla*) attached to it. An encyclical is "an
ecclesiastical epistle, intended for extensive circulation," while
a motu proprio is "an edict issued personally by the pope to the

Roman Catholic Church, or to a part of it." Finally, a provincial is a "rescript addressed to an ecclesiastical province."

R3.2.1.2. Patriarch

Patriarch is a term of wide application. In this classification it finds a place between "pope" and "cardinal" on the basis of its sense "the head of one of the eastern churches," but other senses include "a bishop second only to the pope in episcopal and to the pope and cardinals in hierarchical rank" and "the title of the bishops of the four patriarchates of Constantinople, Alexandria, Antioch, and Jerusalem, the patriarch of Constantinople being the head of the Eastern Orthodox Church." Of the officials attached to the patriarch of Constantinople, the prothonotary is the principal secretary, the chartophylax has "charge of the official documents and records"; *referendary* seems to be equivalent to the latter.

R3.2.1.3. Cardinal

Cardinal is glossed "one of the seventy ecclesiastical princes (six cardinal bishops, fifty cardinal priests, and fourteen cardinal deacons) who constitute the pope's council or sacred college, and to whom the right of electing the pope has been restricted since the Third Lateran Council of 1173." Today the size of the College of Cardinals has been increased to more than one hundred and forty members. *Carnal* is a hostile catachresis of *cardinal*, and *king-cardinal* is a Shakespearean neologism referring specifically to Thomas Wolsey.

R3.2.1.7. Primus

Primus, glossed "the presiding bishop [in the Scottish Episcopal Church], chosen by the other bishops and having certain ceremonial privileges, but no metropolitan authority," is here placed in a class of its own because of the primus's lack of metropolitan authority, which functionally separates him from archbishops and metropolitans.

R3.2.1.8. Bishop

Scirgerefa is an extension of the secular sense ("sheriff") to the ecclesiastical sphere, and occurs often in the collocation *cristes scirgerefa*. *Patriarch* 1297– is labelled "a rhetorical or honorific title of bishops generally." *Ordinary* and its paronym *ordinar* refer to the bishop's authority, which is immediate, "of his own right and not by special deputation." *Lawn sleeves* alludes to a distinctive part of episcopal attire (*cf.* R5.11.1. "lawn sleeves"). *Horned* in the sense of "episcopal" alludes to the twin peaks of the episcopal mitre.

R3.2.1.8.1. Kinds of bishop

Superintendent is a controversial synonym of *bishop* favoured by fundamentalists and later Catholics in referring to bishops of the Church of England; *superintendentship* is the accompanying title. A coadjutor is an assistant bishop, one appointed to aid the ordinary of a diocese in the administration of his see. *Prince-bishop* is glossed "bishop who is also a prince or ruler; also one who enjoyed the temporal possessions or authority of a bishop, with princely rank." A suffragan bishop is one "considered in regard to his relation to the archbishop or metropolitan, by whom he may be summoned to attend synods and give his suffrage."

R3.2.1.8.2. Bishop's officials

A commissary is "an officer exercising spiritual or ecclesiastical jurisdiction as the representative of the bishop in parts of his diocese"; similarly, the grand vicar is "the deputy or representative" of a bishop. *Syncellus* indicates "a dignitary who was associated with a prelate and succeeded to his office" in the

Orthodox Church. *Biscopweorod* is glossed "bishop's band of men." A vicar capitular is "one who takes the place of a deceased bishop until his successor is chosen," a vicar forane "a priest appointed by a bishop to exercise a limited jurisdiction in a particular part of his diocese," and a vicar general "an ecclesiastical officer ... appointed by a bishop as his representative in matters of jurisdiction or administration."

R3.2.1.11. Dean

This class is concerned with the referent "a presbyter invested with jurisdiction over a division of an archdeaconry" as opposed to the "dean of chapter" found in R3.1.4.3.1.

R3.2.2.0. Priest

Preost / priest refers to a clergyman within a hierarchical church who, in addition to the authority to administer sacraments and conduct public worship, has a sacrificial function, whether that be literal (as in the case of druids and some ancient Græco-Roman priests) or metaphorical (as in the case of Christian priests). *Beaupere* is "a term of courtesy" for a priest, *Sir John* a "familiar or contemptuous" term (*cf. Sir John Lack-Latin* in R3.2.2.1.). *Key-bearer / -keeper* alludes to the keys of "heaven and earth" as symbols of priestly power in this life and the next (*cf.* note to *cægan / keys* in R3.2.1.1.0.). *Your priestdom / -hood / -ship* are mock titles. *Flasher* is of uncertain reference, though, from the 1736 citation "a flasher of water, *aspersor*," classification with *priest* seems defensible on the basis of the priestly function of blessing people with holy water (*cf.* R5.8.3. ASPERGILLUM). The Irish noun *soggarth* is from Latin *sacerdos* through Old Irish *sacart / -ard* and Modern Irish *sagart*. *Sacerdotage* in the sense of "priestly office" is a derisive formation from *dotage* (as is the same item listed earlier in the sense of "the priesthood collectively").

R3.2.2.1. Kinds of priest

Shaman is defined "a priest or priest-doctor among various
northern tribes of Asia ... applied to similar personages in
other parts, especially a medicine-man of some of the north-
western American aborigines." *Bell-hallower* is classed here according to its literal sense, though the meaning is not clear from
the single citation (Bishop Latimer, 1549): "Preachers, not bel-
halowers." A chantry-priest "sings daily mass for the founders
[of the chantry] or others specified by them." *Pastophor / -us*
is glossed "one of the order of priests who carried shrines of the
gods in procession as frequently represented in Egyptian art";
sphragistes indicates a priest "who kept and used the temple
seal." Among the terms for the concept "priest who celebrates
mass," *Christ-maker* opprobriously refers to the consecratory
powers of this functionary. The Arval Brethren were "a college
of twelve priests in ancient Rome, who offered sacrifice to the
field lares to secure the fertility of the soil." A fetial "performed
the rites connected with the declaration of war and the con-
clusion of peace," while a flamen was a priest "devoted to the
service of a particular deity." *Pontifex* (1579/80–) and *pontiff*
(1626–) refer to "a member of the principal college of priests
in ancient Rome," and *Salian* to a priest of Mars.

R3.2.3. Rector

The semantic areas covered by "rector" and "parson" have co-
incided to such varying extent over time that it is questionable
whether it is worthwhile to separate them here. The separation
is made on the basis that the 'cores' of the sense of each term
are sufficiently different to make a valid distinction and, additionally, the two terms are less frequently confused in modern
use than in the past. *Rector* is glossed "a parson or incumbent
of a parish whose tithes are not impropriate," whereas *parson*
carries the sense "parish clergyman" with no further restricting
component. The matter can be further confused by reference

to Trollope's *Clergymen of the Church of England* (1866, pp. 54-55): "The word parson is generally supposed to be a slang term for the rector, vicar, or incumbent of a parish, and, in the present day, is not often used without some intended touch of drollery .... Parsons were so called before rectors or vicars were known .... A parson proper, indeed, was above a vicar, –who originally was simply the curate of an impersonal parson, and acted as priest in a parish as to which some abbey or chapter stood in the position of parson. The title of rector itself is newfangled in comparison with that of parson, and has no special ecclesiastical significance."

R3.2.4. Parson

Finger-post is a transferred use from the main sense of "post set up at the parting of roads ... to indicate the directions of the several roads," and is explained in Grose's *Dictionary of the Vulgar Tongue* (1785) thus: "a parson, so called, because like the finger post, he points out a way he ... will probably never go, i.e. the way to heaven."

For an account of the sense development of *parson* and *person,* see Robert J. Menner, 'Multiple Meaning and Change of Meaning in English,' *Language* 21 (1945), 61.

R3.2.5. Pastor

Angel in the sense of "pastor" is restricted to the contexts of "the apocalypse, ecclesiastical history, and in some modern sects, as the Catholic Apostolics."

R3.2.6. Vicar

Vicar is fully glossed "in early use, a person acting as priest in place of the real parson or rector, or as the representative of a religious community to which the tithes had been appropriated; hence, in late and modern use, the incumbent of a parish of which the tithes are impropriated or appropriated, in contrast to a rector." *Ficker* is an example of jocular catachresis.

R3.2.7. Curate

A curate is "a clergyman engaged for a stipend or salary, and licensed by the bishop of a diocese to perform ministerial duties as the deputy of the incumbent." The cavalry curate required his equine locomotion so as adequately "to perform his duties in an extensive and scattered parish."

R3.2.8. Chaplain

Chaplain is defined as "a clergyman who conducts religious service in the private chapel" of an individual or institution. The diocesan ordinary was "appointed to give criminals their neck-verses, and to prepare them for death."

R3.2.10. Preacher

The Anglican lecturer is "one of a class of preachers ... who deliver afternoon or evening 'lectures,' but do not have parishes." *Counting* is a quasi-jocular collective (agminal) noun: other examples include a *dignity* of canons (R3.1.4.3.1.), a *discretion* of priests (R3.2.2.0.), and a *superfluity* of nuns (R3.3.2.1.).

R3.2.11.0. Deacon

To the deacon falls the task of reading the gospel during the course of a religious service; hence the appearance in this class of *gospeller* 1506–. The Brownist reliever is "a deacon appointed to administer relief to the poor." *Ordinee* is glossed "an ordained clergyman or minister; now usually a newly-ordained deacon."

R3.2.11.1. Subdeacon

Tunicle in the sense of "subdeacon" is an allusion to the garment worn by this functionary (*cf.* R5.11.2. TUNICLE).

R3.2.12. Minor orders

This section is arranged according to the hierarchical plan employed in previous sections of R3; hence the descending order from "acolyte" as the fourth of the minor orders to "ostiary" as the first.

R3.2.12.1. Acolyte

The distinction between an acolyte bearing incense and one bearing the thurible might seem nonsensical until it is recalled that the incense is carried in a separate vessel (the *boat* or *navicula*) prior to its placement in the thurible for combustion.

R3.2.13. Other clergy

Annunciator refers to "an officer of the Greek Church who gave notice of holy days," *feretrar* to "the custodian of the shrines." The Irish Protestant souper sought "to make proselytes by means of dispensing soup in charity." A Rome-runner / -raiker was one who was "constantly journeying to Rome to obtain benefices or other advantages." A stationar(y) was "one of the clergy at a church in Rome at which stations were held." *Vicar-choral* is glossed "one of the officers of a cathedral who sings that portion of the service which can be performed by laymen or men in minor orders."

R3.3.0. Religious general

The members of this conceptual class are superordinates to "monk" and "nun," being unmarked for sex. Though *clois-*

terer and its cognates might be thought inadequate superordinates (on the basis that *hermit* or *gyrovague* could not be subsumed under them), usage illustrates that their reference is not confined to the sense"a religious living in a convent." *Professor* is perhaps further specified ("one who has made a profession; a professed member of a religious order"), but the sense-component "having been professed" is of course implicitly present in all other members of this class. All constituents of the R3.3.0. class "order observing certain rule" are reproduced as superordinate terms at the head of R3.3.3.0. RE-LIGIOUS ORDER GENERAL. *Port-Royal* is glossed "a convent near Versailles which in the seventeenth century became the home of a lay community celebrated for its connexion with Jansenism"; hence the cross-reference. *Convent* is in the main unmarked for sex, but popular use for the past two centuries prefers *monastery* for a male and *convent* for a female institution (see also R5.5.2.). Old English *hiersumnes* in the sense of "monastic work" derives from the base component "(monastic) obedience" and thus "work done according to monastic rule."

R3.3.1. Religious superior

The general of a religious order is the supreme governor (in the case of Roman Catholic orders, under the pope) of that order worldwide. The provincial is responsible for the governance of an order within a province or district. Constituents of the class "head of convent" can in general be seen as superordinates for "abbot,' "abbess," "prior," and "prioress." *Hegumen* in fact is a term of slightly wider application; it is glossed "the head of any religious community [in the Greek Church]." Celtic *corb* and *coarb* carry the additional component "successor in ecclesiastical office" (*cf.* R3.2.1.8.2. SYNCELLUS). A mitred abbot is one whom the pope has invested "with the privilege of wearing a mitre." The base meaning of *archimandrit* is "the superior of a monastery or convent," but it is "occasionally also used of a superintendent of several monasteries"; hence the duplication of entry at R3.3.1. PROVINCIAL. *Priory alien / alien priory* refers to those monastic establishments "dependent upon and owing obedience to a mother-abbey in a foreign country"; instances of such were common in England in the early middle ages (for example, various English Cistercian houses were dependent on Clairvaux). As the Old English lexemes *decan* and *teoðingealdor* suggest, a monastic dean is a superior in charge of ten monks. *Non* as "a title of senior monks" is placed with diffidence in the company of *chapterman*, "a member of the chapter of a monastic order" and thus a "senior monk" of sorts.

R3.3.2.0. Monk

Friar c1330 + 1653 + 1801 is "loosely applied to members of the monastic or of the military orders"; *monach(e)* is characterized as an "affected" synonym of *monk. Scapular* alludes to the monastic gown. *Rasophore* finds a place here rather than in R3.3.3.8. GREEK RELIGIOUS because the constituents of that category refer to members of specific orders; *rasophore* refers to "the lowest grade of monk in the Greek Orthodox Church." The sarabaite is distinguished from the anchorite by the fact that he lived in idiorhythmic groups (without rule or superior) rather than solitarily. *Lung-gom-pa* denotes "the mystical power of walking many miles at great speed without stopping," and the same word is attested from 1931 onward in the sense "monk possessing such a power."

R3.3.2.1. Nun

Spouse in the sense of "nun" refers to the spiritual relationship obtaining between Christ and a woman who has taken religious vows. *Sanctimony* 1630(1) is a misuse of *sanctimonial* 1513–1838.

R3.3.2.2. Anchorite

The Indian ashramite is the occupant of an ashram, a hermitage, and is not necessarily in any sort of holy orders.

R3.3.2.4. Friar

Bhikkshu and *bhikku* are both glossed "Brahminical or Buddhist mendicant"; *sunnyasee* is defined as a "Brahmin in the fourth stage of his life; a wandering fakir or religious mendicant."

R3.3.2.5. Monastic functionaries

Of the functionaries, the definitor is one whose function is to supervise the behaviour and discipline of conventual inmates; the care of the material property of a monastic institution falls to the hordarian. *Refectioner* and *kitchener* might be classed together; separation is made here on the basis of the respective definitions, "a person having charge of the refectory and supplies of food" and "he who had charge of the kitchen."

R3.3.3. Religious orders

The various orders are grouped where possible according to their derivation and provenance. Within the seven large families of Latin orders (R3.3.3.1. – R3.3.3.7.), offshoots are classified according to the monastic rule from which they derive, and where this is not possible, the organization is alphabetical. Derivation is displayed by means of the same system of full stops employed throughout this classification. If the reader turns to R3.3.3.2. BENEDICTINE, and examines the entry for *Trappistine*, he will see that the category tag is preceded by three full stops, indicating that the Trappistines are an offshoot of the Trappists, who in turn follow a modification of the Cistercian rule, which itself is an adaptation of the Benedictine rule.

In this section, the religious themselves form category heads, *i.e.* *Benedictinism* is subordinate to *Benedictine*, reflecting the preponderance of personal nouns over *-ism* nouns (see also chapter 2).

R3.3.4.0. Laity

There are close conceptual links between "layman" and the "secularist" or "worldling" semantic cluster classified at R1.8.2.0., and less explicitly with the concept of "unregenerate person" at R1.8.1.2. *Idiot* in the sense of "one of the laity" derives from the obsolete sense "a person without learning; an ignorant, uneducated man," more or less synonymous with *layman* in its current secular sense.

R3.3.4.1. Lay functionaries

Advocate is defined "the secular defender, protector, or 'patron' of a church, or religious house, or benefice, or ecclesiastical office." The ancient Greek canephorus was a "maiden who carried on her head a basket containing the sacred things used in the feasts of Demeter, Bacchus, and Athene." *Church commissioner* is glossed "a member of one of the boards or commissions created to manage church matters [in the Church of England]," and a church estates commissioner is "a member of the church estates commission, which controls the management of the property of the Church of England." *Herenach* is more fully glossed "in the ancient Irish church, a lay superintendent of church lands; the hereditary warden of the church." The duplication of *churchwardenism* 1865– at R5.3.9. is explained by its gloss: "the rule of churchwardens, used contemptuously in reference to the damage done to the architecture, etc., of many church buildings under the direction of illiterate churchwardens." A lay-reader is a "layman licensed to conduct re-

ligious services." The Jewish shochet is "a person officially
certified to kill cattle and poultry in the manner prescribed
by Jewish ritual." The base meaning of *verger* is "one who
carries a rod or similar symbol of office before the dignitaries
of a cathedral or church"; in current use it can also denote
'sexton,' reflecting the amalgamation of these offices in smaller
churches. *Virgin* c1200– is glossed "an unmarried or chaste
maiden or woman ... distinguished for piety or steadfastness
in religion, and regarded as having a special place among the
members of the Christian Church on account of these merits,"
while *widow* 1572– and *widowist* 1593(1) are defined "one of
a class or order of devout or consecrated widows in the early
church."

R3.3.4.2. Lay brother, sister

Converse and its paronyms are defined "a lay member of a
convent."

R3.3.4.3. Lay associations

Apostolate is glossed "society or sodality of persons having as
their object the propagation of a method or rule of faith, life,
or conduct." An archconfraternity is "a confraternity empow-
ered to aggregate or affiliate other confraternities of the same
nature, and to impart to them its indulgences and privileges."
A fellowship-meeting is "an association formed for the purpose
of religious converse," and the Piarists are "a secular order,
founded at Rome by St Joseph Calasanctus [for] the gratu-
itous instruction of the young." *Sodality* refers to "a religious
guild or brotherhood established for purposes of devotion or
mutual help or action." *Third Order* refers to the ancillary lay
order of some religious communities (*e.g.* the Franciscans).

R4

R4.1.0. Worship

In this class are found lexical items denoting several closely-related concepts, "praise," "glorification," "honouring," "reverence," and "adoration." Though in non-religious contexts these various meanings can be distinguished with some consistency, their use in the present religious context makes them synonymous with the concept referred to by *worship,* defined as "reverence or veneration paid to a divine being or power regarded as supernatural or divine." *Shrift* in this sense derives from the Latin *confessio,* "the acknowledgement of the power and glory of God" (*cf.* the intransitive verb *shrive* a1300–a1400). *Calves of our lips* is glossed as "an offering of praise," and stems from a doubtful translation of Hosea xiv.2. *Louter* derives from the verb *lout,* "to bow, make obeisance." Both *theophile* and *theophilist* can mean "one who loves God" or "one who is beloved of God."

R4.1.1. Kinds of worship

Artolatry reflects an unfavourable view of transubstantiative doctrine. Comte's positivism is the worship of "humanity considered as a single corporate being." Scholasticism's three-part characterization of worship is apparent in the latter part of this category, dulia being the lowest "veneration paid to saints and angels," hyperdulia that paid to the Virgin, and latria "the supreme worship which is due to God alone." Some theologians would dispute that dulia and hyperdulia are forms of worship at all, holding rather that they are forms of veneration as opposed to forms of worship. From the standpoint of the present classification, however, a scalar schematization is defensible. *Well-worship* is glossed "the worship of a well or of its guardian spirit," and *will-worship* "worship according to one's own will or fancy, or imposed by human will, without divine authority."

R4.1.2.0. Ritual general

Opus Dei 1887– is glossed "the Divine Office, or liturgical worship in general, seen as man's primary duty to God." The Chinese *Li* is defined as "reason; law; the rational principle, often translated by the English word 'religion'"; its meaning, however, is better defined as "ceremonial, ritual." *Right* 1590– is an erroneous spelling of *rite*; orgies 1598– is defined "any rites, ceremonies, or secret observances, religious or otherwise, with or without implication of extravagance or license."

R4.1.2.1. Kinds of rite

Kiddush is perhaps a borderline case as regards inclusion in this category. It is defined "a portion of the daily ritual of the synagogue, composed of thanksgiving and praise, concluding with a prayer for the advent of universal peace." *Mincha* denotes a specific afternoon ritual observance.

R4.1.3. Parts of service

This section is organized according to the progression of the various parts of service as set out in modern Roman ritual. Parts of non-Roman services are either matched with their Roman equivalents or are inserted at the appropriate point. In defence of this arrangement, it is clear that the great bulk of the lexical material refers to elements which are from the Roman rite or are derivations or adaptations of it. The other possible organization of this section is an alphabetical one.

Parashah ?1624– is glossed "each section of the Pentateuch read as the weekly Sabbath lesson in the synagogue." *Gradual* in the sense of "alleluia (preceding gospel)" derives from the fact that "it was sung at the steps of the altar or while the deacon was ascending the steps of the ambo."

R4.1.4.1.1. Kinds of hymn

Anthem is defined as "a composition in unmeasured prose (usually from the Scriptures or liturgy) set to music" and *antiphon* as "a composition, in prose or verse, consisting of verses or passages sung alternately by two choirs in worship." The Old English *antefn* covers both senses. The canon in the Orthodox Church consists of "eight odes, each of many stanzas"; hence the category tag "long."

R4.1.4.2. Plainchant

Plainchant is defined as "the form of vocal music believed to have been used in the Christian Church from the earliest times, consisting of melodies composed in the medieval modes, in free rhythm depending on the accentuation of the words, and sung in unison."

R4.1.4.3.1. Kinds of psalm

Jig is applied mockingly to the metrical psalms.

R4.1.5.0. The liturgical year

Year is defined "such a space of time as arranged for religious observance in the Christian Church, with special seasons and holy days, beginning with Advent." A jubilee was "first appointed to take place every one hundred years, then shortened to fifty, then less, and now can be granted at any time and not necessarily for a whole year." *Sabbath* 1382– refers to the Israelite sabbatical year.

R4.1.5.1. The Sabbath

Both the Christian Sabbath and the Jewish Sabbath (the seventh day of the week, Saturday) are included in this class.

In Old English, and until the years prior to the Reformation, *Sabbath* was most frequently used in its Jewish sense; the sense "used of Sunday by Christians" is attested from a1509 onward. The general meaning of "day of worship, rest" is also transferred to non-Judæo-Christian religions from 1613–(1704). *Sabbatarian* applies to both Jews and Christians; in relation to the former it denotes "observer of the (Saturday) Sabbath," to the latter "Christian whose opinion and practice with regard to Sunday observance are unusually strict." *Sabbath goy* is glossed "a gentile who performs for orthodox Jews tasks forbidden to the latter on the Sabbath."

R4.1.5.2.0. Feast, festival

Heah tid / high tide was current in English until c1250; its reappearance in 1837 is apparently due to translation of the German *hochzeit*. In this class (as in the rest of R4.1.5.) no distinction is made between a "feast" and the day on which it is held; thus *feast* and *feast-day* are found together in the same category. *Pace* c1450(1) has the main sense "Easter," but, like medieval Latin *pascha,* its meaning was extended to other ecclesiastical festivals. *Supplication* 1606–(1753), as employed in the study of ancient Rome, denotes a "religious solemnity decreed on the occasion of some important public event, especially in thanksgiving for victory." *Surplice day* alludes to the wearing by college members of surplices in chapel on a feast day. Among solemnities lasting nine days, the novendial is of ancient Roman provenance, and novene /-a(ry) of Roman Catholic provenance.

Fête 1805–1877 is defined as "the festival of the saint after whom a person is named; in Roman Catholic countries observed as the birthday is in England." *Pardon* in the sense of "festival of patron saint" derives from the practice of granting indulgences on such an occasion.

Preparation (day) denotes the day before the Jewish Sabbath or other festival.

R4.1.5.2.1. Specific Christian seasons and feasts

This section is organized according to the Christian liturgical year, which begins with Advent. Feasts are interspersed with liturgical seasons and, where possible, dates are provided for the moveable feasts (those associated with a particular day of the civil year rather than being calculated from Easter). *Bæddæg* for "Epiphany" refers to the baptism of Christ. A Quartodeciman was "one of those early Christians who celebrated Easter on the day of the Jewish Passover ... whether this was a Sunday or not (a practice condemned by the Council of Nice AD325)." *Pinkster* for "Whitsuntide" was carried to the eastern United States by Dutch settlers.

R4.1.5.2.2. Jewish seasons and feasts

The adjective *bipaschal*, "including two consecutive Passover feasts," is "applied to the view that limits Christ's public ministry to a little over one year."

R4.2.0. Sacrament

Sacrament is defined as "the common name for certain solemn ceremonies or religious acts belonging to the institutions of the Christian Church," the "means by which divine grace is imparted to the soul, or by which growth in grace is promoted." The noun *sacramental* 1529–(1892) is glossed "a rite, ceremony, or observance analagous to a sacrament but not in fact one." *Matter, form* and *intention* were, according to the Schoolmen, the three things necessary to the "effectual administration and validity of a sacrament." *Intentionary*, glossed as "one who does something with 'intention,'" is opaque: the single 1619 citation reads "Not lesse blame-worthy are our superstitious Votaries or Intentionaries, that walke out of Gods Church, to the Shrines of Saints, and ... the Holy Land."

R4.2.1.0. Baptism

The concepts of "baptism" and "christening" are for the most part identical, though evidence of their distinctness (at least in liturgical terms, with christening preceding the actual rite of baptism) is provided by the transitive verb *+cristnian / christen* OE + c1450–, glossed "to perform the ritual that precedes baptism." The verbal noun *cristnung / christening* is glossed "baptism." *Tincture* is described as an "affected" use.

R4.2.2.0. Confession

Manifestation is defined as "the action of making known to another the state of one's conscience." *Mourner* comes from the vocabulary of American fundamentalism, and denotes "a person at a revival meeting who mourns for his sins." The class "varieties of penitents" includes lexical items referring to the several classes of penitents distinguishable in the early church. The intransitive verb *craw-thump*, "to confess," is a derisive reference to the Roman Catholic custom of beating the breast at confession (*cf.* the note to R2.2.3.0.).

R4.2.2.3.1. Remission of penance

Indulgence is defined as "a remission of the punishment which is still due to sin after sacramental absolution, this remission being valid in the court of conscience and before God, and being made by an application of the treasure of the church on the part of a lawful superior."

R4.2.3. Confirmation

Crismliesing / *chrisom-loosing* denotes the loosing or leaving off of the chrisom or baptismal robe, an action that forms part of the confirmation ceremony. There are no citations in the *OEB* for the participial adjective *confirmed* in the sense under consideration. It would appear that a printer's error has resulted in their omission, for the present sense is listed but is unaccompanied by quotations (see *OED* 'C' p. 808, column 1, *confirmed* (*pa*), sense 3).

R4.2.4.0. Communion

It might be argued that, given historical circumstances, no Old English lexemes denoting "communion" should be placed in the present section; they should be grouped with others denoting "mass" in R4.2.4.1.0. The present arrangement can be defended on the ground that the concepts of "communion" and "mass" are distinct, and this distinction is reflected to an extent in Old English terminology (*gemænsumnes*, "communion"; *mæsse*, "mass"). Nonetheless, it should be borne in mind that in Anglo-Saxon times "the sacrament of holy communion" and 'mass" were, if not identical, then almost always co-existent (the exception being such cases as the viaticum). *Sacrifice* in the present sense is glossed "the eucharistic celebration, in accordance with the view of it as a propitiatory offering of the body and blood of Christ in perpetuation of his sacrifice of himself." *Maundy* alludes to the supper on Holy Thursday, the occasion on which Christ is held to have instituted the sacrament of the Eucharist. *Second service* refers to the fact that, in the Church of England, communion often follows the first service of the day, morning prayer. The nature and purpose of ambuling communion are not clear from the citations, but, at any rate, we find Fuller railing against the "indecency" of the practice in 1655. The few *-phagy* nouns denoting "participation in the Eucharist, partaking of communion" are pejorative in intent.

Debarrance and *debarration,* "exclusion from communion," are terms (formerly) employed in the Church of Scotland.

R4.2.4.1.1. Kinds of mass

Private mass is a term employed by sixteenth-century Protestant controversialists to a mass at which "the congregation, though present, were not allowed to communicate." *Hunter's mass* denotes a "short mass said in great haste for hunters who were eager to start for the chase."

R4.2.4.2. Eucharistic doctrine

Concomitance denotes "the co-existence of the body and blood of Christ in each of the eucharistic elements (especially in the bread)." *Consubstantiation* indicates "the introduction or existence of Christ's body along with the bread after consecration," "the real substantial presence of the body and blood of Christ together with the bread and wine in the Eucharist." *Impanation* is defined as "a local presence or inclusion of the body of Christ in the bread after consecration, one of the modifications of the doctrine of the real presence"; *invination* denotes this doctrine as applied to the wine. *Transaccidentation* indicates "a transmutation of the accidents of the bread and wine in the Eucharist" (not a frequent occurrence outside rural Italy, one would think), and *transubstantiation* the "conversion in the Eucharist of bread and wine into the body and blood of Christ," wherein the substance rather than the accidents are altered.

R4.2.5. Marriage

With regard to the relative brevity of this section, it should be noted that the larger portion of the lexis in the lexical field "marriage" will fall outside the purview of "marriage (as an ordinance and sacrament of the church)," and thus outside that of "'religion" altogether.

R4.2.6.4. Seminary

Camerata is more fully glossed "each of the groups into which students of English theological colleges at Rome are divided."

R4.2.7. (Extreme) Unction

Unction in the sense of "sacramental anointing" denotes a ritual not confined to the anointing of a person *in extremis*; it is employed as well in baptism, confirmation, and ordination. Unmodified or otherwise unspecified references, however, usually refer to the anointing of those about to die, and thus all lexical material in the field is grouped in the present section. It is not clear from the single citation of *sulphuration*, "anointing with sulphur," when or where such an ordeal takes place. Whereas *smirung* and its paronyms were neutral Old English lexemes, by the sixteenth century the participial adjective *smeared* had acquired pejorative connotations, the neutral semantic space now being occupied by *anointed.* The transitive verb *enoil* 1546–1643 is confined to the anointing of a king.

R4.3.0. Prayer

A secondary sense-component shared by many of the lexical items in this section is that of "supplication, entreaty"; this sense-component becomes explicit in words such as *litany* and *supplication* 1490–. *Beadsman* a1528–1726 is glossed "one paid or endowed to pray for others; pensioner or almsman charged with the duty of praying for his benefactors." The Moslem *azan* refers to a "call to public prayers made by the crier from the minaret of a mosque."

R4.3.1. Kinds of prayer

Errand denotes a prayer to the godhead offered through a mediator, often the Virgin Mary. The Fifteen O's are "fifteen meditations on the Passion of Christ, composed by St Bridget, each beginning with 'O.'"

R4.4. Merit

Merit is defined as "good works viewed as entitling one to reward from God," *legality* as "reliance on works for salvation rather than on free grace." *Supererogation* is more fully glossed "the performance of good works beyond what God commands or requires, which are held to constitute a store of merit which the church may dispense to others to make up for their deficiencies." The seven corporal works of mercy are, according to the *Catholic Encyclopædia*, "(1) to feed the hungry; (2) to give drink to the thirsty; (3) to clothe the naked; (4) to harbour the harbourless; (5) to visit the sick; (6) to ransom the captive; (7) to bury the dead."

R4.5.0. Preaching

Prophecy and *prophesying* find a place here on the basis of the sense "the expounding of scripture by those who spoke 'as the Spirit gave them utterance' in special meetings, or . . . preaching at public services." *Postil,* "sermon," has grown from its base sense of "homily on the gospel or epistle for the day" to the more general sense "a series of comments on a text." *Use* denotes the part of a sermon "devoted to the practical application of doctrine," while *observe* probably derives from the secular sense "a verbal observation, a remark."

R4.5.1. Evangelization

Seminary, noun and adjective, is of Roman Catholic provenance.

R4.5.2. Catechesis

Catechesis is used as a superordinate in its broad sense of "oral instruction given to catechumens," *i.e.* religious instruction in general, with no specificity regarding method or denomination involved. The Buddhist *mondo* is glossed "an instructional technique of Zen Buddhism consisting of rapid dialogue of questions and answers between master and pupil." *Cowper-Templeism* derives from the name of W. F. Cowper-Temple (1811–1888), who introduced into the 1870 Education Act a clause providing for "religious teaching of an undenominational character."

R4.5.3.1. Mission

Mission, in the sense of "the sending forth of men on missionary work," appears first to have been used in connection with the Jesuits (1598–1644) and then generally (1641–). The two are here conflated. *City-mission* is defined as "a religious and benevolent mission to the poor and abandoned classes of great cities"; *reduction* is a translation of the Spanish *reduccion,* and is also of Jesuit origin.

R4.5.3.2. Revival

Revival is defined as "a general reawakening *of* or *in* religion in a community or some part of one," and is frequently the result of a mission or series of revival meetings.

R4.5.4.2. Reconciliation

Reconciliation is glossed "reunion of a person to a church, especially the Church of Rome."

R4.6. Pilgrimage

Both *rummery* and *rommery* are derived from the Spanish *romeria,* which in turn derives from *Roma,* but the meaning seems to be confined to "pilgrimage" as opposed to "pilgrimage to Rome" (as is also the case with *romeria*). Both citations are from editions of Sir Thomas Herbert's *A Relation of some Yeares Travaile begun Anno 1626.*

   Station c1380– is glossed "each of a number of holy places visited by pilgrims in succession; especially each of those churches in the city of Rome at which 'stations' [*cf.* R4.1.2.1. STATION] were held, and to the visiting of which on certain days indulgences were attached."

R4.8.0. Sacrifice

The present sense of *sacrifice* is defined as "the surrender to God or a deity, for the purpose of propitiation or homage, of some object or possession." The literal meaning of *mactation* is "the action of killing" (from Latin *mactare,* 'to slay'), but the reference of the word has widened to include the sacrifice which such ritual killing represents (*cf.* the citation from the *Church Times* (1888): "The view gained ground that each Mass is a separate mactation," wherein *mactation* is synonymous with *sacrifice*).

R4.8.1. Kinds of sacrifice

Krioboly has the secondary meaning "bath in the blood of rams." *Lectisternium* is glossed "a sacrifice consisting of a feast in which images of the gods were placed on couches with food before them."

R4.10.0. Sacrilege

Feondæt has the literal meaning "eating of the sacrifice to an idol," but is taken to indicate "profanation, sacrilege."

R4.10.2. Iconoclasm

The placement of *iconoclasm* and its paronyms subordinate to the concept of 'sacrilege' might seem odd, in view of the fact that an iconoclast supposedly fights against the sacrilege consequent upon idolatry. That which to one man, however, is a pagan idol is to another a god, and iconoclasm is thus viewed here as a species of sacrilege.

R4.10.3. Clerical misbehaviour

Scandal is glossed "discredit to religion occasioned by the conduct of a religious person."

R4.11.1. Covenant

Covenant is defined as "an engagement entered into by the divine being with some other being or persons." *Covenant of grace* is glossed "the relation subsisting between God and man after the Fall for deliverance from the penalties of transgressing the covenant of works," *covenant of works* being defined as "that made between God and Adam for himself and his posterity upon condition of obedience." Scottish Presbyterian covenants were "certain bonds of agreement signed by the Scottish Presbyterians for the defence and furtherance of their religion and ecclesiastical polity."

R4.11.2. Non-jurancy

Non-jurancy refers to the principles of those "beneficed clergy who refused to take the oath of allegiance in 1689 to William and Mary."

R4.15. Other practices

Church-strewing refers to "the strewing of a church floor with rushes on particular festivals," *circumgestation* to "the carrying of something about" during a religious ceremony. *Discalceation* is glossed as "taking off one's shoes as a token of reverence" and *duty* as "performance of the prescribed offices or services of the church." *Fire-walk* refers to "the ceremony of walking barefoot over hot stones, performed as a religious rite by the Fijians and others, and formerly as an ordeal in European countries." *Presentation* is defined as "the formal bringing or presenting of a person before God, as a religious act," and *redemption* "the redeeming of the eldest son by an offering [in ancient Jewish law]." *Visitation* indicates the visiting of "sick or distressed persons as a work of charity or pastoral duty," and *station* 1830– "a visit of a parish priest and his curate to the house of a parishioner on a weekday, to give to those living in the neighbourhood the opportunity of confession."

R4.16.0. Benefice

Basket-clerk is glossed "clergyman rewarded by receiving his portion in a basket"; the single citation, from Milton, reads "the Clergy had thir Portions given them in Baskets, and were thence call'd *sportularii,* basket-clerks."

R4.16.1. Kinds of benefice

Commendam denotes a benefice held "in the absence of a regular incumbent." A donative is a "benefice which the founder or patron can bestow without presentation to or investment by the ordinary," a family-living "a benefice in the gift of the head of the family." *Impropriation* refers to a benefice held by or annexed to a religious house or institution. A mensal is a benefice "appropriated to the service of the bishop for the maintenance of his table."

R4.16.2. Advowson

Advowson is defined as "the 'patronage' of an ecclesiastical office; the right of presentation to a benefice or living"; darrein presentment is "the last presentation to an ecclesiastical benefice ([used] as a proof of the right to present)." *Provision* and *impetration* refer to "appointment to a see or benefice not yet vacant; especially such an appointment made by the pope in derogation of the right of the regular patron."

R4.16.3. Simony

Simony is defined as "the act or practice of buying or selling ecclesiastical preferments, benefices, or emoluments"; *giesetrye* and its paronym *gyesite* derive from the name of Gehazi (2 Kings v.), who committed this sin.

R4.16.4. Other financial matters

Almoign denotes "the tenure (of property, etc.) by virtue of performance of some religious duty." Annates are "the first fruits or entire revenue of one year, paid to the pope by bishops and other ecclesiastics of the Roman Catholic Church on their appointment to a see or benefice." *Canon* is glossed "a presentation, pension, or customary payment upon some religious account," *cathedratic* "a payment made to a bishop by the lower clergy." *Disappropriation* refers to "the severance of property from a religious corporation" and *disendowment* the stripping of endowments (including benefices) from the church.

The invest is "a payment made to the pope or head of the church by a bishop, etc., at his investiture." *Procuration* refers to "the provision of necessary entertainment for the bishop, archdeacon, or other visitor, by the incumbent, parish, or religious house visited; subsequently commuted to a payment in money." *Settlement* denotes "a sum of money or other property granted to a minister on his ordination, in addition to his salary." *Superstitious uses* refers to "the use of lands, tenements, or goods for the maintenance of persons to pray for the souls of the dead."

R5

R5.1. Property

These are terms of wide application and, with several exceptions, would serve as superordinates for nearly all of the lexical material in R5. In some cases (*e.g. spiritualty, spirituality*) denotata include non-concrete concepts such as "revenue held or received for spiritual purposes." *Guaca,* an Inca term, may be somewhat more restricted than other constituents of this category, as it seems to apply to objects employed in ritual. However, both "temples" and "grave-mounds" are given as representative hyponymic concepts of *guaca,* and thus this category would seem the best place for it.

A different problem is presented by *sanctities* and *sacra.* Both carry the sense-component of "objects actually blessed or consecrated," a sense-component only optionally present in the other constituents of this category. Yet grouping them with "consecration" would be misleading; an examination of citations shows that their use makes them quasi-synonymous with the constituents of this category (*cf.* Wordsworth (1808): "Bear it to Bolton Priory / And lay it on St. Mary's Shrine; / To wither in the sun and breeze / 'Mid those decaying sanctities").

R5.2. Land

The superordinate of this section is *church-land*. Land identified with clerics, excepting bishops and sextons, is generally a part of the grant of a benefice – hence the cross-reference. The bulk of the lexical material signifies the concept of "churchyard," the grounds or precinct of a Christian place of worship. Though *cemetery* in the sense of "churchyard" came into use only in the late fifteenth century and died out in the early nineteenth century, there is considerable overlap between this sense and that of "burial ground" owing to the widespread (but not invariable) practice of burying the dead in consecrated ground next to a church. *Cemetery* itself is a fourteenth-century borrowing from Greek through Latin and French, and was used initially for "burial ground," whether a churchyard or not (the first *OED* citation is from Trevisa, who uses it in its Latin form to signify the Roman catacombs). As such, the restriction of *cemetery* to "burial grounds" is an example of Stern's first class of sense change, substitution, in which the change is due to altered extralinguistic reality or altered perception of that reality (*cf.* Waldron, *Sense and Sense Development* (2nd ed.), pp. 192ff.).

The section concludes with a brief list of lexical items denoting various structures either under the ground, growing out of it, or forming an integral part of it.

R5.3.0. Sanctuary/holy place general

The constituents of this class are referentially quite vague, particularly in the case of the Old English material, where the referent can be anything from an ecclesiastical building to an area or place thought to have religious or mystical significance. There is no restriction of the Old English material to Christian holy places: *weorðungstow* can refer to the Jewish temple, and *heafodstede* can designate pagan ceremonial sites (*cf.* the *OED* gloss on *high place* (1388–1662): "a place of worship or sacrifice (usually idolatrous) ... "). The Old English lexeme with the sense of "place specially appointed for worship" and thus nearest the centre of this concept in later centuries is *haligdom*, whose successor *halidom* is attested until well into the nineteenth century.

Synagogue c1400–1655 in its pre-Reformation use applied mainly to non-Christian places of worship, but in the years following the Reformation it was used polemically to designate abbeys and other ecclesiastical foundations especially associated with Roman Catholicism.

R5.3.1. Temple

Both *sacrary* and *washing temple* (tr. Latin *delubrum*) contain the sense-component "shrine," and point to the semantic overlap with that concept. *Shrine* (*cf.* R5.3.6.) is best seen as having, in addition to the base component of "place of worship," the component "containing a sacred object or objects (*e.g.* remains of a saint or a non-organic relic of any sort)." Though most foreign terms (*durgah, wely, marabout*) fall into this latter category, Christian terminology is not as well distinguished; hence the cross-reference to 'shrine.'

It should be noted that the presence of a subordinate category for "heathen temple" does not imply that the referents of lexical items in the superordinate category are necessarily not heathen; rather, items in "heathen temple" are those whose definitions carry the component "heathen" or "idolatrous," whereas those in "temple" are unmarked for presence or absence of this sense-component.

R5.3.2. Principal place of worship

Ideally, constituents of this section might have been further divided, as the difference between a minster and a cathedral in some cases is pronounced. Indeterminacy, however, makes the division impossible. *Heafodmynster* and *mynster* are glossed "cathedral, minster"; the *OED* definition of *minster* widens its reference further to include "any church of considerable size or importance." Even *cathedral* is not immune to misapplication; the *OED* states that the term "has been applied loosely to a collegiate or abbey church," and in current careless usage it can denote any large or impressive church (see also the note to *church* below).

R5.3.3. Church/place of worship

Cirice / church is the superordinate of this category. The lexical items contained within it are of exclusively Christian reference, and illustrate the close link between the Christian tradition and English vocabulary. In this connection, it is worth pointing out that Old English *cirice* could have non-Christian as well as Christian referents, and indeed *church* was used to denote non-Christian places of worship until the seventeenth century. Present-day usage in this age of widespread indifference would seem to revive the duality of reference, though whether it could be said to extend to educated speakers is questionable.

Friction between the branches of Christianity has had an effect on usage as well. Regarding *church*, the *OED* notes that "the name has been only recently or partially extended to places of worship other than those of the national ... Church ... At present, its application is partly a question of social or individual taste, or of ecclesiastical principle or theory, partly (in popular apprehension) of the size and architecture of the building." Though current North American usage tends to make a distinction between *church* and *chapel* on the basis of the last criterion, that of size, certain streams of British usage continue a distinction based on religious affiliation. It is not uncommon, for example, to hear in present-day Glasgow a clear distinction between *church* (referring to places of worship administered by the national church) and *chapel* (referring to

Roman Catholic, Episcopalian, and other Christian places of
worship).

 Steeple for the concept of "church" is a metonym, but *steeple-
house* is more intriguing, and represents an attempt by Puritanic groups to emphasize a distinction between places of worship and the collective body of worshippers; only to the latter
did they consider *church* properly applied.

R5.3.4. Chapel

As mentioned on the notes to the preceding category, the semantic space occupied by *chapel* has overlapped with that of
church in different ways at different times. Current usage tends
toward restricting *chapel* to a place of worship which is attached
to or forms part of a larger building, a sense attested since the
late thirteenth century. For complications, though, see notes
to R5.3.3. For more lexical material covering the latter sense,
see R5.4.27.

R5.4.0. Division of building general

This category head is based on the *OED* definition for *aisle*
1761–1862, a definition which is perhaps slightly misleading.
None of the citations uses *aisle* to denote any part east of the
transepts; it is restricted to side aisles, the nave itself, or the
transepts. *Plage* is included here on the basis of the *OED* gloss,
which says "one of the divisions or parts of a church," though
the 1593 citations of *plage* can be assigned a more specific referent (*cf.* R5.4.8.).

R5.4.2. Narthex/portico

The main indeterminacy here lies between the referent "porch"
and the referent "anteroom." The terms *narthex* and *portico*
can apply both to a fully enclosed room between the main en-
trance of a church and the nave, and to a roofed enclosure

outside the main doors (as in the case of Peterborough Cathedral). *Posticum* denotes an identical structure at the back of a classical temple.

R5.4.5. Nave

Holy place denotes "the outer chamber of the sanctuary in the Jewish tabernacle and temple" and as such corresponds to the nave of a Christian church.

R5.4.6. Aisle

Here, a generally consistent indeterminacy exists between referent "area on either side of nave" and referent "passage between rows of pews or seats."

R5.4.8. Transept

Transept can refer to either arm of a cruciform church or to the entire crossing.

R5.4.9. Screen

Iconostas(is) and *haikal screen* are Eastern versions of the Western rood screen; though their ritual significance varies, both Eastern and Western screens serve to divide the nave from the sanctuary, or the laity from the clergy.

R5.4.12. Holy of holies

Lexical material in this section is almost wholly non-Christian, though transferred uses are not uncommon. In Jewish temples, the holy of holies is the innermost chamber, spearated from the outer areas, in which the divine presence was manifested. *Adyt, adytum,* and *sacrarium* fulfil the same function in classical temples.

R5.4.16. Altar/communion table

This section proved one of the most difficult in R5 to classify because of two problems: one, the question of whether altars and communion tables are furniture or integral parts of a church building; two, the changing views of the nature and function of an altar or communion table. In regard to the first problem, a decision was made to place "altar" with R5.4. PARTS OF BUILDINGS on the ground that most examples are substantial pieces of masonry, woodwork, or plasterwork fixed to the floor or wall of the sanctuary and are generally immoveable. Modern altars, however, are not always of this kind, and communion tables tend to be smaller, less elaborate, and more distinct from the fabric of the building itself. A further factor in the placement of this lexical material here is the preceding categories, R5.4.13. ALTAR RAIL, R5.4.14. PAVEMENT, and R5.4.15. GRADUAL, whose constituent lexemes – closely bound up with the concept of "altar / communion table" – are part of the fabric rather than furniture.

Theologians would doubtless be discomfited to find *altar* and *communion table* grouped together. From a theological standpoint, they are of vastly different signification, and, indeed, embody one of the central disputes of the Reformation. From the standpoint of the semanticist, however, the terms denote essentially the same object, an object whose connotative or affective meaning varies from speaker to speaker (*cf. antichrist* for *pope*). Finally, there is no high degree of discreteness in the use of the two terms. From 1549 *altar* has had at least limited currency as a lexical item covering the reformed sense of *communion table*.

Oyster-board is a contemptuous term for the long, narrow tables employed by early reformers.

R5.4.25. Baptistry

Early versions were sometimes located in "a separate building contiguous to the church," but most examples are an area or part of the church building itself.

R5.4.26. Sacristy/vestry

Strictly speaking, a sacristy is a room in which the implements and vessels necessary for religious service are kept, and a vestry is a room in which clergy robe themselves. The two functions, however, overlap to a considerable extent; hence the collocation of *sacristy* and *vestry* here.

R5.4.27. Chapel

Cf. the notes to R5.3.4. CHAPEL.

R5.4.28. Oratory

There is some overlap between *oratory* and R5.4.27. CHAPEL preceding. An oratory may be a chapel; I have classified it on the basis of its more general meaning of "place of prayer (within larger building)," though *proseucha*, for example, can be a free-standing structure.

R5.5.1. Monastic land

Green-yard carries the general sense of "enclosure covered with grass or turf," but the *OED* cites a specific referent in the monastery in Norwich. It is questionable whether this lexical item is worth inclusion.

R5.5.1.1. Monastic estate

Both *commandery* and *preceptory* denote property belonging to or administered by the religio-military orders. The cross-reference to R3.3.1. RELIGIOUS SUPERIOR establishes the link between the concrete nouns in this category and their abstract counterparts denoting territories under the authority of specific officials.

R5.5.2. Monastery / convent

There are three main senses covered by this category. The first is that of a monastic establishment, without reference to the sex of the inmates, and the second and third cover establishments for men only and women only respectively. Once again the ideal would be to separate the three, and once again considerable indeterminacy prevents such a separation. Though Old English *lif* is perhaps the most neutral term, denoting only "place in which the monastic way of life is followed," *cloister, monastery,* and *convent* are or have been at some time indeterminate with regard to sex. This is also the case with Old English *mynstercluse, mynsterstede, munuclif, mynster,* and *clauster.* Thus all three kinds of establishments are grouped here. *Monastery* has gradually become more restricted to institutions for males, and lexical items including the morpheme *nun-* denote exclusively female establishments.

The cross-reference to R3.3.0. RELIGIOUS GENERAL serves to point out the close connection between the concrete noun *monastery* with referent "an identifiable artefact (*i.e.* buildings and grounds)" and the collective noun *monastery* with referent "community of religious living within those buildings." There is no firm distinction between the two senses, and this species of duality of reference is one which will be found in many other areas of the vocabulary. Paronymic adjectives are affected by the duality as well (*cf. cloistral*).

R5.5.3. Parts of monastery

The organization here is alphabetical. Old English *spræchus* and *speech-house* c1205(1) should perhaps be together, but the latter is glossed "parlour," and the former "guest quarters."

R5.6. Clerical residences

The organization of subordinate categories is hierarchical, and follows the plan laid out in R3.

R5.7. Furniture

The overall organization of this category is alphabetical; the largest subgrouping contains lexical material covering various kinds of seating, and this material is arranged according to function. *Ornament* 13..– is the most suitable superordinate, and is glossed "the accessories or furnishings of a church and its worship."

R5.7.2. Bell

Difficulty is encountered in the attempt to distinguish between differing kinds of bells and bells characterized by the circumstances of their use. Some clear indications of the distinction are found, and thus *sanctus bell* (defined here as "bell rung during Mass") carries in this section the date 1552/3(1) while *sanctus bell* in R4.1.3. PARTS OF SERVICE GENERAL is dated 1479/81–(1875). Hypothetically, all of the bell-ringing during the course of a service could be performed on one bell, but different names exist to distinguish bell-ringing during communion, for example, from that at offertory.

R5.7.5. Font

The inclusion of this lexical material in the section concerned with furniture is perhaps debatable, as many baptismal fonts are integral parts of buildings.

R5.7.6. Lectern/pulpit

Though merged in popular use, *lectern* originally refers to the place from which lessons are read, while *pulpit* refers to the place of preaching. The distinction is not, however, sharp or consistent enough to justify separate categories. There appears to be no Old English lexeme carrying the sense "pulpit" to the exclusion of the sense "lectern." *Tub* and *tub-pulpit* are associated especially with non-conformist places of worship. There is no indication in the *OED* of the *raison d'être* of an ambonoclast or of any special significance attaching to the ambo; it is likely that the phenomenon is a species of churchwardenism (*cf.* R5.3.9.).

R5.7.7. Matraca

The *OED* describes this as "a kind of mechanical wooden rattle used instead of church bells on Good Friday." During the latter part of Holy Week, and especially on Good Friday, congregations are adjured to perform the services with utmost solemnity; the use of organs and bells is sharply curtailed. Hence this Spanish substitute.

R5.8.0. Implement general

An interesting example of indeterminacy is found in the case of *haligdom / halidom* and *relic*, both of which can refer either to implements or to the relics of saints, etc. *Relic* itself is here mainly applied to the sacred objects of ancient religions. The four duplicated items show the considerable overlap existing between R5.8.1. Vessel general and this category.

R5.8.1. Vessel general

With the possible exception of Old English *blodorc*, all the constituents in this category serve as suitable superordinates for the material that follows. *Blodorc* is glossed "sacrificial vessel," and might thus be thought not to belong here, but the Christian term *huselfæt* carries the gloss "sacrificial or sacramental vessel," reminding us that sacrifice in its metaphoric rather than literal sense is at the centre of Christian ritual.

R5.8.2. Ampulla / chrismatory

Poucer might have been included here, but the *OED* states that it was "perhaps never used in English," and that it appears only in modern dictionaries.

R5.8.3. Aspergillum

The aspergillum is an implement used by clerics to sprinkle holy water on a congregation, and is found in the form either of a brush or of a perforated globe at the end of a handle. This category is noteworthy for containing twenty-three almost perfectly synonymous lexical items. Of the twenty-three, five are formed from the root *asper-*, three from *aspers-*, seven from *sprin-/spren-*, and three from *strin-/stren-*. A possible explanation for this uncommonly rich set of synonyms is the fact that aspergilla were (and are) in common use, yet are not named in the course of religious services. Hence there are what might be called the clerical names for this object based on the *aspergillum* model, the French-influenced variants of this model (*aspergoire, aspersoir,*) and the layman's set of names deriving largely from the roots *stre-* or *sprinkle*. Yet we would expect to find a similar division in lexical fields covering objects of similar function, and this is only infrequently the case. For a similar set of synonyms, see R5.8.17. THURIBLE.

R5.8.4. Calefactory

Pome reflects the fact that calefactories were ball-shaped and of a size to be clasped in the hands by a priest who was to administer the Eucharist "in cold weather."

R5.8.6. Cruet

Referents of this category are employed to hold eucharistic water and wine, in distinction to the oil vessels of R5.8.2.

R5.8.9. Grail

Sangrail is glossed as "cup," reflecting the misconception that the holy grail is a drinking vessel. In fact, it is the platter with which Joseph of Arimathea collected Christ's blood after the Crucifixion. (For some extraordinary speculations on the nature and whereabouts of the Holy Grail, the reader seeking recreation might wish to consult Michael Baigent, Richard Leigh, and Henry Lincoln, *The Holy Blood and the Holy Grail* (London: Cape, 1982)).

R5.8.10. Holy water vessel

The referents of this category are portable and are used in conjunction with the aspergillum to hold holy water before it is sprinkled, in distinction to the referents of R5.7.11. HOLY WATER STOUP, which are fixed and into which the fingers are dipped.

R5.8.11. Incense holder

The relation between *aspersory* and *aspersorium* is similar to that which obtains between *thurible* and *navicula*, in that one vessel is employed to hold the consumable before use, and the other to hold it during or after use. Referents of lexical items in the present category are used to store incense before it is burned in the thurible. *Ship, navet, incense-boat* and *navicula* demonstrate that these objects were frequently made in the shape of a boat; *nef* serves to indicate the similar etymological and conceptual link with the nave of a church building.

R5.9. Cloths, carpets, cushions

There seems to be no superordinate term for any of the subsections in this lexical set.

R5.11.0. Vestments

The constituents of this section refer to vestments in a general sense (particular items of attire can be found in the sections that follow). Though the *OED* dates the general sense of *vestment* from c1440 (words carrying this general sense during the thirteenth and fourteenth centuries having the variant spellings *vestement* or *vestiment*), I have conflated an earlier meaning of *vestment*, dated 13..–, because of its proximity in meaning. *Vestment* 13..– is glossed "garment worn by a priest or ecclesiastic on the occasion of some service or ceremony; a priestly robe." The distinction thus made by the *OED* is, I think, overfine. In the case of the collective nouns, it is assumed that the referents will form a set (*i.e.* same pattern, colours, material). *Gear* might have found a niche lower in the classification were it not for the vagueness of both gloss ("appendages to a (clerical) vestment") and citations. The cross-reference between *vestiarian* and R4.1.2.0. RITUAL GENERAL establishes the important link between the question of vestments and the liturgical movements of the time, particularly that of Keble, Pusey, and Newman. Possible denotata of *tays* / *teys* are very vague; all citations come from various extracts from the account rolls of Durham Abbey, published by the Surtees Society, and are in a context of poor ecclesiastical Latin.

R5.11.1. Particular functionaries' attire

Because a proportion of ecclesiastical attire is associated with the rank of the cleric wearing it, this section is organized according to the hierarchical ranking of R3. Some items of apparel (*e.g. maniple* and *dalmatic*) are shared by two or more grades of the hierarchy; lexical material covering these can be located in subsequent lists through the use of cross-references. The various items associated with bishops are organized alphabetically. Though *continuations* finds a place in the classification, its synonym *gaiters* does not, as none of the latter's citations is concerned with ecclesiastical dress.

R5.11.2. Outergarments

There is no superordinate term for the subcategory. *Subucula* is an historical use referring to the Anglo-Saxon period. *Cauntercotte* may be a variant spelling of *cantor-cope*; because the single sixteenth-century citation is obscure, however, it has not been included with *cope*. The coat referred to by a Scottish newspaper as a *cassock* is described as a "short, light, double-breasted coat or jacket ... worn under the Geneva gown."

There is some confusion, both etymological and semantic, over the word *cope*. Old English *cæppe* comes from the Latin *cappa*, and is glossed "cope, hood" by Bosworth-Toller. This gloss is puzzling as the two referents are conceptually incompatible (etymologically, however, Modern English *cope*, *cape* and *cap* stem from the same root). For the purposes of this category *cope* is defined as "a vestment resembling a long cloak worn by ecclesiastics in procession, also at vespers and on some other occasions." The position of *cæppe* here is thus somewhat dubious; it may be referentially closer to the monastic hood or cowl (*cf.* R5.12.). For similar referential indeterminacy, see the note to *amice*, R5.12.4.

R5.11.4. Headgear

The referent of the Jewish *coif* is a low, crowned mitre or turban worn by the high priest and (in Wyclif and the Douai Bible) by ordinary priests. *Hæcce*, grouped with lexical items denoting the concept "headband," is of uncertain reference. Bosworth-Toller provides the gloss "a frontal (rather than a crozier)"; the *OED*'s first sense of *frontal* is the vague gloss "a band or ornament worn on the forehead." Of the citations, only one from Bishop Hall (1611) appears to have a religious connection, and it says nothing of the nature of a *frontal*. *Infule* and *infula* are more specifically defined as "a slightly twisted flock or fillet of red and white wool, worn on the forehead by priests." *Skull-cap* in the sense of *calotte* or *zuchetto* is not attested, though the *OED* carries an 1819 citation from Scott mentioning a Presbyterian version. As this is apparently not of ritual, liturgical, or hierarchic significance, it is not included here.

R5.12.1. Monk's garb

Clark Hall wonders whether there is an etymological connection between *gylece* and *pylece*, a possibility made more likely by the fact that the referent of *pylece* is a robe (*cf. pelisse* 1877 in R5.11.2.). *Hrægltalu* carries the more specific sense of "clothes to which the brethren of a monastery had a claim."

R5.12.4. Items of attire

Amice is defined as an article that "was originally ... a cap or covering for the head; afterwards a hood or cape with a hood."

For another example of this kind of indeterminacy, see note to *cope*, R5.11.2.

R5.15. Consumables

Included here are words denoting the eucharistic elements, several other foods, oil, water, paper which is burnt, incense, and candles. The paucity of representation in several areas (*e.g.* "candles") is of course due to the fact that only specifically religious senses find a place in this classification. There is no superordinate term for R5.15. The organization of the category is alphabetical with the exceptions of "bread" and "wine"; these both have been subsumed under "eucharistic elements" because of the dozen-odd superordinates covering them.

R5.15.1. Bacon

Offrungspic is a compound whose sense did not survive into Middle English. The citation is from Ælfric's *Lives*.

R5.15.2. Cake

The referents of this category are mixed; *simnel* and *Shrewsbury simnel* denote "a rich currant cake, usually eaten on mid-Lent Sunday." *Soul-mass cake* and *soul-mass loaf* indicate a type of "cake or loaf formerly given away on All Soul's Day."

R5.15.5. Eucharistic elements

The superordinates here denote bread and wine as the two species of a standard Christian eucharistic rite. The sense-component "consecrated" is present in most of the constituents of this category. *Offrung* as an unmodified noun seems not to have survived the Old English period in the sense of "bread and wine"; it shifted to denote "burnt offering," or, frequently, "monetary offering." Some constituents carry the sense-component "wafer," including *oflæte / oflete*. The element *singing* in several compounds is thought to refer to the singing of the Mass (see *sing* v.1. sense 3 in the *OED*). A 1616 citation of *singing bread* makes clear that no leaven is used in its preparation, but in doing so the citation distinguishes it from *obley*, which by implication is leavened. However, this may be a misapprehension, as eucharistic bread is traditionally unleavened. Among hostile and contemptuous terms for consecrated bread, *jack-of-the-box* alludes to the practice of reserving the host in a pyx before use. I cannot vouch for the equivalence of *wave-bread* and *shew-bread*, but suspect they are both synonymous with the vulgar Latin *panes propositionis*.

R5.15.10. Paper

The referent is defined as "gold and silver paper, cut into the shape of coins and ingots and sometimes inscribed with prayers, burned by the Chinese at funerals and other religious ceremonies."

R5.15.11. Soma

This is "an intoxicating drink holding a prominent place in Vedic ritual."

R5.16.1. Service book general

In this category are books used in the conducting of religious services, with the exception of those from which portions of scripture are read (see R5.16.2. LECTIONARIES). Of the superordinate terms, only *standard* is somewhat dubious; it is glossed as "some kind of service-book," and the three citations (all in ecclesiastical Latin) provide no clues to its nature. *Euchologion* and cognates carry the gloss "prayer-book," but have been classified as service books on the basis of the definition of *contakion*, "a name given to the volume containing the liturgies of St Basil, St Chrysostom, and of the pre-sanctified, in distinction from the larger service-book, the *euchologion*." *Regel-boc* is glossed "book of monastic rules," and thus finds a place beside *consuetudinary,* "a book containing the ritual and ceremonial usages of a monastic house or order." The Sarum Use is the order of service prescribed for the Salisbury diocese from shortly after the Norman invasion to the Reformation.

Between *bletsingboc* and *pontifical* 1584– exists a gap of nearly four centuries. One explanation for the gap is that this concept was for that period assigned a more general label, but even so the only likely candidate is the superordinate *church-book*.

R5.16.2. Lectionaries

The referents of constituents in this category are books containing portions of scripture and other edifying material intended to be read out at religious services and gatherings. This distinguishes them from items such as *missal* and *synopsis* in R5.16.5., books intended essentially for private use.

R5.16.3. Breviaries and office books

These books contain prayers and readings for the appointed canonical hours. *Horologium* denotes a Greek hour-book which, says the *OED*, "to some extent" corresponds to the breviary. Couchers and other large copies lie permanently in places of worship, while portable versions (and it is this sense to which *breviary* commonly fixes today) are intended for private use.

R5.16.4. Music books

Orthographical variation in the *antefn / antiphon* pair is the result of false etymology (see Vallins, *Spelling* (revised edition), p. 39). *Gradual* denotes a particular kind of antiphon originally intended to be sung by a deacon or other celebrant on the gradual or area in front of the altar (see R5.4.15. GRAD-UAL). *Square book* denotes a species of hymnal, but on the basis of dictionary information it is not possible to assign this item a more specific category tag. Initial "p" in *psalm-book* and *psalter* was introduced after the Old English period for etymological consistency.

R5.16.5. Other books

The curious item *seyny-book* denotes "a choir book provided for the use of monks who lately had been bled." *Missal* 1651– is a vitiated sense indicating any (Roman Catholic) prayer book.

R5.16.6. Miscellaneous

Altar card is defined as "one of a set of three cards placed on the altar ... containing certain portions of the eucharistic prayer." *Red letter* refers to the convention of printing the dates of festivals in red ink on ecclesiastical and some other calendars.

R5.17. Symbols

This category illustrates the problem discussed in the section on conceptual alphabetization in chapter 1.

Chapter Five
Historical and
Etymological Data

In this chapter are data concerning the chronological spread and etymological provenance of the religious vocabulary classified in chapter 3. [62] The aim has been to provide some idea of the composition of the lexis viewed diachronically. Most desirable would have been a full historical count, noting century by century accessions and obsolescences as well as accumulated appearances, all done by etymological group and semantic category. For a lexis of the present size, however, such an analysis would be beyond the scope of this study. [63]

The approach adopted here, then, consists of three separate counts. The first is strictly historical, and tallies century

---

[62] I am indebted to Professor M. L. Samuels for suggesting this line of enquiry. The figures presented in this chapter may not always tally with the number of lexical items in the classification. Late additions to the classification were made after the historical and etymological counts had been carried out.

[63] It is worth noting here that such an analysis is of necessity manual work. While a computer could be programmed to deal with a straight historical count, no facility exists to enable a computer to distinguish lexical items by etymological group. Even if the complex principles of morphology were in some way programmable, the computer would have no means of determining whether, for example, a given latinate word entered the English vocabulary directly from Latin or through the intermediary stage of French.

by century the number of appearances (see note under *I. Historical* below) and obsolescences of the lexical items. Such a count provides an indication of the changing bulk of the lexis down through the centuries, and displays clearly the points of greatest influx and retention as well as of relative stagnation. The second count is non-historical, and provides a tally of the etymological provenance of the lexis. The third and last count displays accessions and obsolescences (as distinct from the tally of appearances in the first, historical count) by etymological group in four specific areas of the lexis chosen for the disparity of their respective referents, two dealing with abstract concepts, one with clerical personages and their offices, and one with concrete nouns.

Several points need to be stressed here. First, owing to the semantic organization of the present classification, the counts contained in this chapter tally *senses* of words rather than (or better, in addition to) words themselves. Etymological treatment is generally concerned not with differing senses of a given form (except in cases of divergent etyma converging through phonological, orthographical, or semantic processes, to produce identical descendants, such as *ear* of corn, *ear* of the body) but with a word as a unit borrowed from a different or developed from an antecedent linguistic source. The semantic organization of the present classification, on the other hand, ensures the presence of a considerable number of adapted or changed senses of many words which entered the English non-religious vocabulary at an earlier stage. A simple example is the sense of the word *standards* classified at R1.1.1.0., bearing the dating 1841– and defined as "books or documents accepted by a church as the authoritative statement of its creeed." *Standard* entered the English vocabulary some seven centuries earlier, however, as a borrowing from Old French in the sense of "a flag [etc.] ... raised on a pole to indicate the rallying point of an army (or fleet), or of one of its component portions; the distinctive ensign of a king, great noble, or commander, or of a nation." In the present count, however, the former sense of *standards* is recorded as entering the lexis in the nineteenth century. This principle must be borne in mind when seeking to extrapolate from the data presented here.

Some areas of the classification have been omitted from both historical and etymological tallies. In addition to the whole of R2, the following categories have not been included in the tally on the ground that they contain a high proportion of proper nouns:

R1.2.1.3. BIBLICAL PERSONAGES
R1.2.1.4. BIBLICAL PLACES
R1.2.1.5. BIBLICAL EVENTS
R1.2.2. HEBREW SCRIPTURES
R1.2.3. NON-JUDÆO-CHRISTIAN SCRIPTURES
R1.3.1.1. INDIVIDUAL FATHERS
R1.3.1.2. PATRISTIC WRITINGS
R3.2.1.1.2. INDIVIDUAL POPES
R3.3.3.1. AUGUSTINIAN – R3.3.3.10. OTHER RELIGIOUS

The chapter concludes with a list of Old English compound terms from the religious vocabulary that did not survive into Middle and Modern English.

I. Historical

For the purposes of this historical count ten categories were established, corresponding to the Old English period (until AD 1100) and each century from the twelfth to the present. Tally marks were then placed in the appropriate categories for each lexical item. Lack of indisputable evidence that a lexical item is attested in a particular century does not prevent that item being included in the tally for that century. *Word,* for example, in the specialized sense of "the Bible ... or some part or passage of it," has *OED* citations from the following years: 1553, 1567, 1570, 1598, 1781, 1859, 1875. Neither the seventeenth century nor the twentieth has a citation, yet, following standard *Historical Thesaurus* procedure, the compiler assigns to this sense of *word* the dating 1553– . Two assumptions are made here: first, that the four sixteenth-century citations suggest that this sense of *word* was indeed in use during the seventeenth century, and, second, that it remains in use today. Following the dating assigned by the compiler, then, this historical count tallies *word* in each century from the sixteenth to the present.

Not included in the tally are obvious isolated revivals of individual words for historical purposes or for the purposes of the historical novel. *Alms-fee* occurs periodically in historical writing as a direct revival of the Old English *ælmesfeoh*, "Peter's Pence," but is not included in the tally because *ælmesfeoh* cannot be proven to have survived beyond the Old English period. Its semantic space was filled by the lexemes *Rome-penny, Rome-shot/-scot,* and finally *Peter's Pence*, and its revival is restricted to the context of scholarly research. In the same way, isolated revivals of lexical items in historical novels (including several of Walter Scott's) have not been included in the tally. When, however, an item is revived after a long period of desuetude and appears to have been accepted outside the confines of historical writing, such as *ban (vt)* 1303–1483 + 1814– in the sense of "excommunicate," its revival is included in the tally.

No obsolescences have been tallied for the twentieth century, owing to the danger of presuming lexical death before the corpse in question is quite cold. The total number of words in the tally, after omission of the sections mentioned above, is approximately 12,000, for which 32,757 appearances in the various centuries have been recorded.

OE	12c	13c	14c	15c	16c	17c	18c	19c	20c
1818	494	1002	1978	2572	4139	5681	4584	6496	3993
1315	16	165	223	440	978	1826	733	1652	—

The results set out above lead to a number of observations concerning the lexis, the principles followed by *Thesaurus* compilers in the process of preparing information for the archives, and the nature of documentation in the *OED*. With regard to the last, we can point to several interesting phenomena. [64] There is, of course, the initial difficulty caused by the *OED* policy of excluding words that were obsolete by 1150, a condition requiring the use of Bosworth-Toller and Clark Hall for much lexical material that disappeared prior to the mid-twelfth century. Excellent as these dictionaries are, coverage of the twelfth century is indisputably patchy, a shortcoming aggravated by the relative paucity of manuscripts from that early period, reflecting the small quantity of written (as opposed to spoken) English consequent upon Norman domination of both church hierarchy and the literate classes in general.

The remarkable drop in twelfth-century lexical appearances (in the religious lexis, the total number of twelfth-century tallies is but 27 per cent of the Old English number) must thus be treated with caution, even though, once again according to the present count, 72 per cent of Old English religious lexemes did not survive the Old English period. [65] Indeed, the two figures would seem almost complementary until it is remembered that a not inconsiderable number of twelfth-century appearances represent Old English survivals into the post-Conquest period, thus giving in balance a very low number of actual accessions

---

[64]On the question of *OED* methods and accuracy, Jürgen Schäfer's *Documentation in the OED* (Oxford: Clarendon, 1980) is indispensible. Note particularly his warnings regarding the distortion consequent upon *OED* policy favouring the literary works of great authors over non-literary works of lesser figures (pp. 13-15), inconsistent word categories (pp. 22-28), chronological distribution of *OED* sources (pp. 50-54), and potential antedatings (pp. 65-71).

[65]Cf. A. C. Baugh, *A History of the English Language* (3rd ed. London: Routledge and Kegan Paul, 1978), p. 55: "An examination of the words in an Old English dictionary shows that about 85 percent of them are no longer in use." The higher proportion of Old English religious lexis still in use is partially accounted for by the introduction of latinate terminology in the tenth and eleventh centuries associated with the Benedictine reform (see also note 11 below).

in the twelfth century.

Of principles of dating followed by *Thesaurus* compilers, that having the most immediate relevance to the historical count concerns the difficulty of deciding whether in fact a lexeme is obsolete, particularly in regard to the nineteenth century. Among the historical periods, the nineteenth century has the highest number of appearances (almost half again as many as even the seventeenth century), a fact due not only to the excellent *OED* coverage of this period and indeed to the ferment of theological activity at the time but also to the caution of compilers in questioning the obsolescence of an item whose last citation occurs after about 1750. The total number of both eighteenth- and nineteenth-century obsolescences is less than half of that of nineteenth-century appearances alone (2385 as opposed to 6496). One would probably be justified in thinking the true figure somewhat higher.

Having stated these points regarding the dictionary data and the approach to it taken by compilers, we can now turn to a brief consideration of what the figures indicate about the lexis itself. As might have been expected, the seventeenth century proves to have been a period of great lexical activity, with a high proportion of accessions and the continued use of terminology which entered the vocabulary in and prior to the sixteenth century. There are many reasons for this activity, most of which are not specific to the religious vocabulary and which have been discussed by Baugh and other historians of the language. [66] We might, however, point to several factors which have a special bearing on the religious lexis. Alongside the general flowering of *belles-lettres* in the seventeenth century, there is a surge of devotional and theological writing, a surge unsurpassed in range and quality, if not in quantity, by the nineteenth and twentieth centuries. Part of the surge is the direct result of the religious upheavals of the previous cen-

---

[66]See Baugh's *History*, pp. 199–251; R. F. Jones, *The Triumph of the English Language* (Palo Alto: Stanford University Press, 1953).

tury. Whereas a considerable proportion of sixteenth-century formations and neologisms is the pejorative and controversial vocabulary of writers involved not only in theological battle but in *ad hominem* attacks on opponents of all descriptions, seventeenth-century accessions tend to reflect a more settled enquiry into spiritual as opposed to sectarian concerns. [67] In the categories R1.6.0. HOLINESS to R1.13.0. REPROBATION, for example, containing lexical material concerned largely with theological abstractions, the number of appearances tallied for the seventeenth century is 1666, not far short of the nineteenth century's total of 1900 and outnumbering by some 60 per cent the sixteenth century's 990. In an area in which we might expect less contrast (*i.e.* a steadier level of interest), the results of the tally in, for example, R5 ARTEFACTS show an almost negligible gap: 710 for the sixteenth century and 732 for the seventeenth.

How much of the drop in eighteenth-century appearances, a drop visible across the entire classification, is due to the problems experienced by the *OED* in its citations for the period, [68] and how much is due to the comparative lack of interest in religion characteristic of that rationalist century, is difficult to say. In Britain, at least, theological innovation was at a low ebb; attention was focused on issues such as church-state relations rather than on fundamentals of divinity. It must be remembered, however, that the production and dissemination of sermons and tracts took place on a considerable scale. Witness, for example, the popularity of William Law's *Serious Call,* commended by that paradoxically devout rationalist Dr Johnson. Much eighteenth-century religious writing employs (as indeed does Law) the language of moral philosophy rather than that of divinity *per se,* accounting at least in part for the

---

[67]This does not mean, however, that the seventeenth century lacks in inventiveness in the pejorative and controversial domains of language, as a glance at the subfields R2 and R3 will show.

[68]See K. M. Elisabeth Murray, *Caught in the Web of Words* (New Haven and London: Yale University Press, 1977), pp. 169, 184.

low number of appearances and the even lower rate of accessions in the eighteenth century.

Extralinguistic influences on the religious lexis in the nineteenth century are exceedingly complex, but two of the most important can be singled out for attention. They are the stimulus to piety and devotion provided by the evangelical movement, and the interest in matters of liturgy, ritual, and other externals awakened by the Oxford Movement. Though on opposite ends of the theological spectrum, both developed from seventeenth-century disputes regarding Arminianism, Laudianism, and Calvinism, and both reached maturity in the second and third quarters of the nineteenth century.

Most easily discernible is the burgeoning of interest in pre-Reformation practice and paraphernalia that was part of the Oxford Movement. Many nineteenth-century accessions are revivals of medieval Latin terminology and reflect the attention paid by followers of Newman, Keble, and Froude both to pre-Reformation British liturgical manuals and to writing on ceremony from the continent, particularly that originating in France and Italy.

The influence of nineteenth-century evangelicalism on the lexis is diffuse and less easy to identify. If, however, we take perhaps the most obvious example (R4.5.0. PREACHING to R4.5.4.3. UNCONVERSION) we see that the nineteenth century has 206 appearances, half again as many as the seventeenth century's 136. This single result stands in marked contrast with R4 totals for the two centuries which, at 2197 and 2061 respectively, are quite evenly matched. The language of piety shows strength in the nineteenth century too, where the tally stands at 123 as compared to 115 for the seventeenth century (categories R1.7.0. PIETY to R1.7.3. IMPIETY). In contrast, the seventeenth-century tally for R1.9.0. GRACE to R1.9.3. RIGHTEOUSNESS stands at 49 as against 36 for the nineteenth, a gap reflecting the importance attached in the seventeenth century to the argument over the nature of grace and the means of obtaining it. It is clear that the low-church movement of the nineteenth century had an effect on the religious lexis far less marked than did the Oxford Movement.

II. Etymological data

In the etymological count thirteen categories were established: native (N) for items of Anglo-Saxon provenance; pre-Conquest borrowing from Latin into Old English (OEL); [69] direct borrowings from French (F) and other Romance languages (OR); hybrid words (H) whose roots are Latin or Romance but whose form has been anglicized (such as *sanctifiedly*) for adjectival, adverbial, or verbal use (this category also includes compounds whose elements come from disparate sources (such as *fifth-monarchist, spin-text* [70])); borrowings from German (G) and from other Germanic languages (OG); from Celtic languages (C) and from Hebrew and Yiddish (HY); borrowings from the various Hindu languages (HI) and from Arabic (A); and finally direct borrowings from other languages (O) such as Greek, Japanese, and North American Indian languages.

No attempt has been made to trace words back to an ultimate source; the tally displays only the languages from which English has directly borrowed. An area of particular difficulty in this respect is to determine whether some ecclesiastical terms

---

[69] Very early borrowings from Latin (such as *win, cirice, biscop*) are tallied as Old English lexical items (though, as has been pointed out by L. W. Collier, some of these items acquired religious significance only after the Conversion). Borrowings made during what Baugh calls the Second Period of Latin influence are tallied in the OEL column (see Baugh, *History*, pp. 84–90; also of use are A. Campbell, *Old English Grammar* (Oxford: Clarendon, 1959), pp. 199–221, and Thomas Pyles, *The Origins and Development of the English Language* (New York: Harcourt, Brace, and World, 1964), pp. 325–328.

[70] For a different approach to similar difficulties, see A. C. Baugh, "The Chronology of French Loan-Words in English," *Modern Language Notes* 50 (1935), 91.

were borrowed directly from Latin or whether French acted as the intermediary stage. In these cases the etymological information supplied by the *OED* and Skeat has been followed. [71]

N	2453 items	(19.66%)
OEL	126 items	(1.01%)
L	1103 items	(8.84%)
F	4655 items	(37.31%)
OR	47 items	(0.38%)
H	3477 items	(27.87%)
G	6 items	(0.05%)
OG	14 items	(0.11%)
C	18 items	(0.14%)
HY	121 items	(0.97%)
HI	104 items	(0.83%)
A	85 items	(0.68%)
O	267 items	(2.14%)

Of the data set out above, perhaps the most startling is the percentage of lexis of French origin. More than a third of the English religious vocabulary comes from French, nearly double the quantity represented by words of native stock. It is a commonplace of the history of English that French influence was particularly strong in areas of the lexis covering conceptual domains such as law and religion, but the present tally allows us to judge for the first time the real extent of French domination of this lexical field. The gap between French and native stock becomes even wider when it is remembered that a significant proportion of the hybrid stock (which in itself accounts for 28 per cent of the total lexis) is of French extraction. The following figures are obtained if hybrid items are excluded from the tally (reducing the total sample to 8,999):

---

[71] On this topic, see Baugh's *History*, pp. 184-186 and 226; Pyles, *op. cit.*, pp. 328-9.

Native	27.26%
OEL	1.40%
Latin	12.25%
French	51.73%
All others	7.36%

In which areas of the religious lexis does French have an especially strong influence? As might be expected, the abstract areas show most influence. In categories from R1.1.0. FAITH to R1.1.16. CATHOLICITY, for example, the tally for words of French stock is 450, for those of hybrid stock 300, and for those of native stock 180, yielding a proportion of some 2.5 French words for every native word. An almost exactly similar result is obtained in the tally of categories R1.6.0. HOLINESS to R1.13.0. REPROBATION, where the relevant figures are 788 French, 401 hybrid, and 314 native (a proportion of 2.51 French to 1 native).

The gap increases in R3: 942 French, 782 hybrid, 361 native, yielding a proportion of 2.61:1. A large part of this disparity, however, can be traced to well-defined small areas in the subfield. The categories of lexical material referring to church government and administration (R3.1.0. to R3.1.3.1., for example) yield a French/native ratio of nearly 25:1, which is quite unrepresentative of the general trend. Extensive use of French stock in the area of ritual and ceremony can be seen in the tally for R4.1.2.0. RITUAL and R4.1.2.1. KINDS OF RITE, where the figures are 162 French, 63 hybrid, and 36 native (French/native ratio of 4.5:1).

But what of areas in which French wordstock is low? The categories R4.1.6.0. CANONICAL HOURS to R4.1.7. CHURCH-GOING show ratios very much the reverse of those just cited, 3.64 native to 1 French. Examination of these categories' constituents shows a high number of Old English lexemes, including many compounds (the list for "vespers, evensong" in addition to the uncompounded root *æfen* and the standard *æfensong/evensong*, includes *æfengebed, æfendream, æfenlof,*

æfendegnung, and *æfendeowdom*) that did not survive the
Old English period. Latin vocabulary associated with tenth-
century ecclesiastical reform penetrated to some extent (*noc-
tern/nocturn, prim/prime*) and is found in a few compound
formations such as *æfencollatio,* but the bulk of Latin borrowings in these semantic categories is not attested until the
fourteenth century and later.

Anglo-Saxon interest in the concept of "sacrifice" is reflected in the etymological proportions of categories R4.8.0.
SACRIFICE to R4.8.2. PROPITIATION, which yield a ratio of
1.23 native to 1 French. There are, for the main concept "sacrifice," some sixteen Old English near-synonyms listed, a large
number even when their differing secondary components are
taken into account (*e.g.* the disparate semantic foci of *giefu*
and *blotung*). Further illustration of the same phenomenon is
found at R4.10.1. BLASPHEMY, where there are seventeen Old
English lexemes among a total of twenty-three referring to the
head concept. Again, differing foci to some extent account for
the large number of near-synonyms, but a cluster of this size
suggests more than usual interest in the concept referred to.

The last notable area in which native wordstock considerably outnumbers that from French sources is, understandably,
R5.15. CONSUMABLES. Within this area, R5.15.7. INCENSE
represents an almost complete native domination until well into
the fourteenth century. Of the thirteen lexical constituents of
this category, ten are native Old English stock (one of the ten
surviving until 1483): yet the sole French item is the only sur-
vivor beyond the fifteenth century, with the exception of an
isolated figurative use of *holy smoke* in 1627.

Direct borrowings from Latin without the intermediary
stage of French account for less than ten per cent of the religious lexis, including those items borrowed in the pre-Conquest
period.[72] In the centuries prior to the Reformation, the scope

---

[72] *cf.* Baugh, *History,* p. 90: "Some 450 Latin words appear in English
writings before the close of the Old English period ....about one hundred

of direct borrowings from Latin is wide, ranging from areas
of liturgy and artefacts to abstract concepts. The events of
the sixteenth century sharply reduced this intake. Ceremonial
books of the Roman rite were replaced by native versions, and
items of attire and equipment were modified or dropped. The
previously mentioned revival of interest in pre-Reformation
matters occasioned by the Oxford Movement, however, led in
the nineteenth century to the exhumation of some items and
the importation of others. Examples of the former are clearly
visible in datings such as *piscine* 1489 + 1822– and *sudary*
1431–1549 + 1891 *arch..* Perhaps the most concentrated example of the latter occurs in R5.4. PARTS OF BUILDINGS, where
nineteenth-century borrowings not only from Latin (*atrium,
predella, solea, gradin(e)*) but also from Greek (*proaulion,
iconostas(is), parabema*) reach a high level. Admittedly some
of these items seem to have been borrowed for no reason other
than to replace perfectly adequate but well-worn and prosaic
terms. Consider, for example, the importation of *vestiarium*
and *paratory* for "vestry." Many of these inkhorn terms are,
however, useful and colourful additions to the English religious
vocabulary.

When words of native, French, Latin, and hybrid stock have
been tallied, material from other etymological sources accounts
for only about five per cent of the religious lexis. Best represented among these sources are Hebrew and Yiddish, Hindi,
Arabic, and Greek. Of the Hebrew and Yiddish borrowings
recorded in the present tally, some 23 per cent are clustered
in the semantic categories covering Hebrew scripture and law.
Other clusters are associated with various Jewish liturgical seasons and feasts, and the concepts of "ritual purification" and
"cleanness." These areas between them account for nearly half

---

of these were purely learned or retained so much of their foreign character
as hardly to be considered part of the English vocabulary." Among such
words in the religious lexis, we might point out *corporale* (R5.9.2.) and
antefnere (R5.16.4.) as examples from the period of ninth- and tenth-
century Benedictine reforms.

of the borrowings from Hebrew and Yiddish, and provide a clear illustration of the observation made earlier that 'exotic' borrowings tend to cluster in well-defined semantic areas rather than to spread evenly across a wide range of the lexis.

A similar pattern can be observed with Hindi wordstock. About 17 per cent of this material is found in the area covering scriptures, and a similar amount in the categories covering monastic figures (R3.3.0. to R3.3.2.5.). Outside these two areas there are clusters of Hindi stock in R1.8.3.0. CONTEMPLATION to R1.8.6.2. VISION, in R4.3.0. PRAYER to R4.5.4.3. UNCONVERSION, and in R5.17. SYMBOLS. Reasons for the location of these clusters are not difficult to find. Western interest in Hindu spirituality has been evident since the seventeenth century, if not earlier, and a tally of accessions to the English religious lexis in the last twenty years would probably show a steep rate of increase in borrowings from the Hindu tradition. Items contained in the present classification largely denote methods of prayer and the spiritual states reached by means of intense contemplation.

Concentrations of Arabic words are found in several parts of the lexis, the largest being at R5.3.6. SHRINE and R5.3.7. OTHER, where loanwords referring to Moslem places of prayer and worship are classified. In contrast to the distribution of loanwords from Hindi, Hebrew, and Yiddish, there are few Arabic loanwords referring to abstract concepts or to actions and processes. The great majority are noun substantives whose referents are artefacts or religious officials.

Among other sources of exotic loanwords in the English religious lexis are the North American Indian languages (several noun substantives referring to buildings and a group denoting kinds of dances), and a scattering from Hawaiian and Japanese Buddhist traditions. Of the 267 lexical items tallied in the final 'other' column, however, the largest single source is Greek, accounting for approximately 210 items. Few of these enter the English lexis before the mid-eighteenth century, and the great majority are not attested until the nineteenth century. [73] Architectural terminology and the nomenclature of the religious hierarchy are certainly represented, but, unlike Arabic, Greek has contributed a share of abstract theological terms such as *theologoumenon* and *theopneustia* which, if patterns evident in the last half century are a reliable guide, seems a trend likely to increase.

III. Combined historical and etymological data

To provide historico-etymological data from both concrete and abstract areas of the religious vocabulary, several small, well-defined sections of the classification have been chosen and subjected to a tally. Extrapolation of the results of this very limited count will be broadly valid for etymological groups which constitute the principal sources of the vocabulary: native, French, and hybrid wordstock. It is clear, however, in the case of etymological groups whose contribution to the English lexis is limited, that extrapolation from the results set out below would be misleading. We have noted that exotic borrowings tend to cluster in certain areas of a conceptually-organized classification. In the categories chosen for the present count, the number of exotic borrowings varies from practically nothing (R1.7.0. to R1.7.3.) to a moderately high representation in R5.1. to R5.3.9.

In each case the upper figure indicates the number of accessions (as distinct from appearances) for the century and etymological group in question, and the lower figure the number of obsolescences.

The four small sections of the classification subjected above to an historico-etymological count yield several results worthy

---

[73]There are, of course, a small number of Greek words that entered the English vocabulary via Latin at an earlier stage, such as *dogma*.

of note. First, the pattern of hybridization remains fairly constant across the four sections. Each of them tallies its first accession of hybrid wordstock in the thirteenth century, and in each case the periods of highest rate of hybrid accession are the seventeenth and nineteenth centuries (with the exception of R1.7.0. - R1.7.3., where there are more accessions of hybrid stock in the sixteenth than in the seventeenth century). Accession/obsolescence ratios vary to the extent that it would be dangerous to attach special significance to them. For hybrid wordstock, the accession/obsolescence ratios are as follow:

	R1.1.0.- R1.1.5.2.	R1.7.0.- R1.7.3.	R3.3.2.0.- R3.3.2.1.	R5.1.- R5.3.9.
16c	3.20 :1	2.23 :1	1.00 :1	2.5 :1
17c	2.56 :1	1.42 :1	0.78 :1	1.82 :1
18c	0.86 :1	1.50 :1	1.80 :1	1.80 :1
19c	1.93 :1	1.46 :1	1.23 :1	0.98 :1

The ratio for R1.1.0. - R1.1.5.2. in the nineteenth century is twice as high as its counterpart for R5.1. - R5.3.9., indicating a higher degree of retention in the former, abstract area of the vocabulary than in the latter, which is concrete. As much of this disparity, however, can probably be attributed to the difficulties mentioned earlier of assigning closing dates as to a real divergence of historical patterns in the lexis.

The relative paucity of exotic borrowings in the first three sections contrasts with the accession of fourteen in R5.1. - R5.3.9. between the seventeenth and nineteenth centuries. Such a contrast illustrates what has been said several times regarding the tendency – one might almost call it a rule – for exotic loanwords to cluster in well-defined semantic areas. Predictably, the clusters here are in areas concerned with structures for worship and, to a lesser extent, in the area of the clerical functionary (nine accessions in R3.3.2.0. - R3.3.2.1., spread out from the sixteenth century to the nineteenth).

There is no discernible constant pattern of French accessions. In R1.1.0. - R1.1.5.2., the rate of accessions is roughly the same in the thirteenth and fourteenth centuries as it is in the sixteenth and seventeenth (interestingly, the fifteenth century lags here by some two thirds). In the case of R1.7.0. - R1.7.3., however, the seventeenth-century rate of accession is more than double that of other centuries, a gap not evident in either of the following categories.

In 1935, A. C. Baugh published the results he obtained in a count of French accessions to the general vocabulary. [74] Having no conceptually-organized body of lexical material available, he gathered his sample from pages throughout the *OED* numbered -00, -20, -40, -60, and -80. For the purposes of an historico-etymological tally such a sample probably possesses sufficient randomness, though it can be criticized on the ground that extracting alphabetically serial lexemes leads to skewed results, owing to the relationship between morphology and etymology.

Baugh's figures (based on a total sample of one thousand French items) are set out by half-centuries. I have conflated them to facilitate a comparison with figures gathered from the preceding historico-etymological count, which contains 268 French items.

Century	Baugh	Present count
12th	9	1
13th	134	26
14th	306	49
15th	164	27
16th	157	51
17th	98	60
18th	59	17
19th	71	33
20th	2	4

Totals for the twelfth to fifteenth centuries remain roughly proportional, but diverge widely in the sixteenth. Baugh's count of accessions in that century yields a ratio of 0.95:1 as

---

[74] Baugh, *op. cit.*, 90-93.

against the fifteenth; the present count yields a ratio of 1.88:1. To hypothesize on the basis of such figures that the religious vocabulary imported a disproportionately large amount of French wordstock in the sixteenth century would probably be untenable. Larger samples are required before valid conclusions can be drawn. A further factor contributing to the disparity is that Baugh's count is done by lemma, the present by sense. Thus a newly transferred sense acquired by an item such as *cathedral* in the sixteenth century is counted as an accession. The procedure is by no means invalidated by this anomaly because of the comparatively low ratio of transferred senses to real accessions, but it can be shown to skew individual century counts in small samples.

It is thus probably unjustified to posit general patterns on the basis of results obtained from such highly circumscribed areas of a single lexical field. We can perhaps anticipate that overall results will match those of a similarly-structured lexical field such as "law" in the case of the principal etymological constituents. But beyond this broadest of outlines there are many idiosyncratic patterns wholly dependent on the nature of the specific category being examined. It is, moreover, quite likely that even broad similarities of pattern will disappear when a disparate lexical field such as "food" or "transportation" becomes available for comparison.

IV. Unreplaced Old English compounds

The following is a list of unreplaced Old English compound terms from the religious lexis, expressing concepts now referred to by means of periphrasis.

Compound	Gloss
æwbryce	neglect of (vow of) chastity
gebedbygen	payment for prayer

gebedtid	hour for prayer
biscopgegyrelan	bishop's vestments
burhbiscop	bishop of city
ciricgeorn	zealous in church attendance
ciricðegn	priest of church; parish priest
ciricðegnung	lay work
ciricðing	ecclesiastical property
ciricwæd	church vestments
cneowgebed	prayer on one's knees
dwolbiscop	heretical bishop
efenapostol	fellow apostle
efenbiscop	fellow bishop
efenmæssepreost	fellow priest
efensacerd	fellow priest
firenearfeðe	woe of sin
fulwihtele	oil used for baptism
gearðegnung	annual rite
halgungboc	book of coronation liturgy
halsunggebed	prayer in service of the church
halsungtima	time of (supplicatory) prayer
handpreost	domestic priest
heahsynne	very sinful
helltræf	devil's temple
hlafsenung	blessing of bread
leodbiscop	suffragan bishop
lofmægen	abundant praise
gemænscipe	agreement in doctrine
munucregol	rule followed by monks
munucðeaw	monastic rule
mynsterclænsung	purification of church building
mynstergeat	monastery gate
mynsterhata	person opposed to monasteries
mynsterðegnung	monastic rite, service
neahcyrice	neighbouring church
neah(nun(an))mynster	neighbouring convent

nigecyrred	newly converted
nigehalgod	newly ordained
nighworfen	newly converted
offrungspic	sacrificial bacon
rædinggrad	steps to lectern
reliquiasocn	visit to relics
rihtfæstendæg	duly appointed fast day
samodherian	to worship together
samodherigendlic	worshipping together
sumorrædingboc	summer lectionary
sudfor	pilgrimage to Rome
synbyrden	burden of sin
syngrin	snare of sin
synnlust	desire to sin
synræs	desire to sin
synrust	foulness of sin
tuncirice	church in settlement
đeorf	unleavened bread
đeorfhlaf	unleavened bread
đeorfling	unleavened bread
underđeod	suffragan bishop
unrihtweorc	work done on the sabbath
untidweorc	work done on the sabbath
winterrædingboc	winter lectionary
woruldgyrla	lay garment
woruldriht	Ten Commandments
woruldgeđoht	worldly thought
wucđegn	weekly servant
wucđegnung	week's service

Bibliography

Abraham, Samuel, and Ferenc Kiefer. *A Theory of Structural Semantics.* The Hague and Paris: Mouton, 1966.

Aitchison, Jean. *Language Change: Progress or Decay?* London: Fontana, 1981.

Allan, Keith. *Linguistic Meaning* (2 vols.). London: Routledge and Kegan Paul, 1986.

Austin, J. L. *How To Do Things with Words* (ed. J. O. Urmson and Marina Sbisa). Oxford: Clarendon, 1962.

Baldinger, Kurt. *Semantic Theory: Towards A Modern Semantics* (ed. Roger Wright, trans. William C. Brown). Oxford: Basil Blackwell, 1980.

Bauer, Laurie. *English Word-Formation.* Cambridge: Cambridge University Press, 1983.

Bauerle, R., U. Egli, and A. von Stechow (eds.). *Semantics from Different Points of View.* Berlin: Springer Verlag, 1979.

Baugh, Albert C. 'The Chronology of French Loan-Words in English.' *Modern Language Notes* 50 (1935), 90-93.

Baugh, Albert C., and Thomas Cable. *A History of the English Language.* 3rd ed. London: Routledge and Kegan Paul, 1978.

Baylou, Christian, and Paul Fabre. *Le Sémantique.* Millau: Editions Fernand Nathan, 1978.

Bendix, Edward H. 'The Data of Semantic Description.' In Steinberg and Jakobovits (1971), pp. 393-409.

Bolinger, Dwight. 'The Atomization of Meaning.' *Language* 41 (1965), 555–573.

504

Brown, Roger. *Words and Things.* Glencoe, Illinois: The Free Press, 1958.

Burchfield, Robert. *The English Language.* Oxford: Oxford University Press, 1986.

Campbell, A. *Old English Grammar.* Oxford: Clarendon, 1959.

Carter, Ronald. 'A Note on Core Vocabulary.' *Nottingham Linguistic Circular* 11 (1982), 39-50.

Chafe, Wallace L. *Meaning and the Structure of Language.* Chicago and London: The University of Chicago Press, 1970.

Chomsky, Noam. *Aspects of the Theory of Syntax.* Cambridge, Massachusetts: The MIT Press, 1965.

Chomsky, Noam. *Language and Responsibility.* Brighton: The Harvester Press, 1979.

Chomsky, Noam. *Rules and Representations.* New York: Columbia University Press, 1979.

Collier, L. W., and Christian Kay. 'The Historical Thesaurus of English.' *Dictionaries* 2/3 (1982/3), 80-89.

Cooper, David E. *Philosophy and the Nature of Language.* London: Longman, 1973.

Coseriu, Eugenio, and Horst Geckeler. *Trends in Structural Semantics.* Tubingen: Gunter Narr Verlag, 1981.

Cowie, A. P. 'Polysemy and the Structure of Lexical Fields.' *Nottingham Linguistic Circular* 11 (1982), 51-64.

Cruse, D. A. 'Hyponymy and Lexical Hierarchies.' *Archivum Linguisticum* 6 (1975), 26-31.

Cruse, D. A. 'On Lexical Ambiguity.' *Nottingham Linguistic Circular* 11 (1982), 65-80.

Crystal, David. *Linguistics, Language and Religion.* London: Burns and Oates, 1965.

Davidson, Donald, and Gilbert Harman (eds.). *Semantics of Natural Language*. Dordrecht: Reidel, 1972.

Dutch, Robert (ed.). *Roget's Thesaurus of English Words and Phrases*. London: Longman, 1962 (rev. 1982 by S. M. Lloyd).

Ebeling, Gerhard. *Introduction to a Theological Theory of Language* (trans. R. A. Wilson). London: Collins, 1973.

Eikmeyer, Hans-Jurgen, and Hannes Reiser (eds.). *Words, Worlds, and Contexts: New Approaches in Word Semantics*. Berlin and New York: Walter de Gruyter, 1981.

Evens, Martha W., *et al*. *Lexical-Semantic Relations: A Comparative Survey*. Carbondale and Edmonton: Linguistic Research Inc., 1980.

Fodor, J. A. *The Language of Thought*. New York: Crowell, 1975.

Fodor, Janet Dean. *Semantics: Theories of Meaning in Generative Grammar*. Cambridge, Massachusetts: Harvard University Press, 1980.

Gleason, H. A. 'The Relation of Lexicon and Grammar.' In Joseph Greenberg and A. Saporta (eds.), *Problems in Lexicography*. Bloomington, Indiana: Indiana University Press, 1962.

Greenberg, Joseph. *Universals of Language*. Cambridge, Massachusetts: The MIT Press, 1963.

Halle, Morris, Joan Bresnan, and George A. Miller (eds.). *Linguistic Theory and Psychological Reality*. Cambridge, Massachusetts: The MIT Press, 1978.

Harris, Roy. *Synonymy and Linguistic Analysis*. Oxford: Basil Blackwell, 1973.

Harrison, Bernard. *An Introduction to the Philosophy of Language*. London: Macmillan, 1979.

506

Herbermann, Charles, *et al.* (eds.). *The Catholic Encyclopædia*. London: Caxton Publishing Company, 1907.

Hoeningswald, Henry M. *Language Change and Linguistic Reconstruction*. Chicago: University of Chicago Press, 1960.

Jackendoff, Ray. *Semantic Interpretation in Generative Grammar*. Cambridge, Massachusetts: The MIT Press, 1972.

Jespersen, Otto. *Language: Its Nature, Development and Origin*. London: George Allen and Unwin, 1922.

Jespersen, Otto. *Growth and Structure of the English Language*. 9th ed. Oxford: Basil Blackwell, 1956.

Johnson, Alexander Bryan. *A Treatise on Language* (ed. David Rynin). New York: Dover, 1968 (first published ?1836).

Jones, R. F. *The Triumph of the English Language*. Palo Alto, California: Stanford University Press, 1953.

Katz, Jerrold. 'Interpretative Semantics vs. Generative Semantics.' *Foundations of Language* 6 (1970), 220-259.

Katz, Jerrold. *Language and Other Abstract Objects*. Oxford: Basil Blackwell, 1981.

Katz, Jerrold, and J. A. Fodor. 'The Structure of a Semantic Theory.' *Language* 39 (1963), 170-210.

Katz, Jerrold, and Paul M. Postal. *An Integrated Theory of Linguistic Descriptions*. Cambridge, Massachusetts: The MIT Press, 1964.

Kay, Christian. 'The Historical Thesaurus of English.' In R. R. K. Hartman, ed., *LEXeter '83 Proceedings*. Tubingen: Max Niemeyer, 1984.

Kay, Christian, and Thomas Chase. 'Constructing a Thesaurus Database.' *Journal of Linguistic and Literary Computing* (forthcoming).

Kay, Christian, and M. L. Samuels. 'Componential Analysis in Semantics: Its Validity and Applications.' *Transactions of the Philological Society* (1975), 49-79.

Kempson, Ruth M. *Presupposition and the Delimitation of Semantics.* Cambridge: Cambridge University Press, 1975.

Kempson, Ruth M. *Semantic Theory.* Cambridge: Cambridge University Press, 1977.

Komlev, N. G. *Components of the Content Structure of the Word.* The Hague and Paris: Mouton, 1976.

Kress, Gunther R. (ed.). *Halliday: System and Function in Language.* London: Oxford University Press, 1976.

Leech, Geoffrey N. *Towards a Semantic Description of English.* London: Longman, 1969.

Leech, Geoffrey N. *Semantics.* 2nd ed. Harmondsworth: Penguin, 1981.

Leefrink, Frans. *Semantico-Syntax.* London: Longman, 1973.

Lehrer, Adrienne. *Semantic Fields and Lexical Structure.* Amsterdam: North-Holland, 1974.

Levin, Samuel R. 'Aspects of Semantic and Grammatical Change.' *Linguistics* 2 (1963), 26-37.

Levin, Samuel R. *The Semantics of Metaphor.* Baltimore and London: The Johns Hopkins University Press, 1977.

Lewis, C. S. *Studies in Words.* 2nd ed. Cambridge: Cambridge University Press, 1967.

von Lindheim, Bogislav. 'Problems of Old English Semantics.' In G. I. Duthie (ed.), *English Studies Today* (Series 3). Edinburgh: Edinburgh University Press, 1964.

Linsky, L. (ed.). *Semantics and the Philosophy of Language.* Urbana: The University of Illinois Press, 1952.

Lipka, Leonhard. 'Methodology and Representation in the Study of Lexical Fields.' In *Perspektiven der Lexikalischen Semantik* (proceedings of the Wuppertaler Semantikkolloquium). Bonn: Bouvier Verlag H. Grundmann, 1980.

Lyons, John. *Structural Semantics*. Oxford: Basil Blackwell, 1963.

Lyons, John. *Introduction to Theoretical Linguistics*. Cambridge: Cambridge University Press, 1968.

Lyons, John. *Semantics* (2 vols.). Cambridge: Cambridge University Press, 1977.

Lyons, John. *Language and Linguistics*. Cambridge: Cambridge University Press, 1981.

Lyons, John. *Language, Meaning and Context*. London: Fontana, 1981.

Magnusson, Ulf, and Gunnar Persson. *Facets, Phases and Foci: Studies in Lexical Relations in English*. Stockholm: Almqvist and Wiksell, 1986.

Martinet, André. *Elements of General Linguistics* (trans. Elisabeth Palmer). London: Faber and Faber, 1964.

Mates, Benson. *On the Semantics of Proper Names*. Lisse, Netherlands: The Peter de Ridder Press, 1975.

McCawley, James. 'Interpretative Semantics Meets Frankenstein.' *Foundations of Language* 7 (1971), 284-296.

McCawley, James. *Grammar and Meaning: Papers on Syntactic and Semantic Topics*. New York: Academic Press, 1976.

Menner, R. J. 'The Conflict of Homonyms in English.' *Language* 12 (1936), 231-242.

Menner, R. J. 'Multiple Meaning and Change of Meaning in English.' *Language* 21 (1945), 59-76.

Murray, K. M. Elisabeth. *Caught in the Web of Words*. New Haven and London: Yale University Press, 1977.

Nida, Eugene A. *Componential Analysis of Meaning*. The Hague and Paris: Mouton, 1975.

Nilsen, D. L. F., and A. P. Nilsen. *Semantic Theory: A Linguistic Perspective*. Rowley, Massachusetts: Newbury House, 1975.

Ogden, C. K. *Opposition*. Bloomington: Indiana University Press, 1967.

Ohman, Suzanne. 'Theories of the Linguistic Field.' *Word* 9 (1953), 123-134.

Osgood, C. E. 'Semantic Space Revisited.' *Word* 15 (1959), 192-200.

Osgood, C. E., George J. Suci, and Percy H. Tannenbaum. *The Measurement of Meaning*. Urbana and London: The University of Illinois Press, 1957.

Palmer, F. R. *Semantics*. 2nd ed. Cambridge: Cambridge University Press, 1981.

Parret, Herman, and Jacques Bouveresse (eds.). *Meaning and Understanding*. Berlin and New York: Walter de Gruyter, 1981.

Pike, E. Royston. *Encyclopædia of Religion and Religions*. London: George Allen and Unwin, 1951.

Pirie, Valerie. *The Triple Crown*. London: Sidgwick and Jackson, 1935.

Potter, Simeon. *Changing English*. 2nd rev. ed. London: Andre Deutsch, 1975.

Pyles, Thomas. *The Origins and Development of the English Language*. New York; Harcourt, Brace and World, 1964.

Quirk, Randolph. *The Use of English*. London: Longman, 1962.

Richards, I. A. *Complementarities: Uncollected Essays* (ed. J. P. Russo). Manchester: Carcanet Press, 1976.

Ricoeur, Paul. *The Rule of Metaphor.* Toronto: University of Toronto Press, 1977.

Roberts, Jane. 'Towards an Old English Thesaurus.' *Poetica* (1978), 56-72.

Roberts, Jane. 'The English Historical Thesaurus.' *Nottingham Linguistic Circular* 11 (1982), 20-29.

Robins, R. H. *A Short History of Linguistics.* 2nd ed. London: Longman, 1979.

Sampson, Geoffrey. *Making Sense.* London: Oxford University Press, 1980.

Sampson, Geoffrey. *Schools of Linguistics: Competition and Evolution.* London: Hutchinson, 1980.

Samuels, M. L. 'The Role of Functional Selection in the History of English.' *Transactions of the Philological Society* (1965), 15-40.

Samuels, M. L. *Linguistic Evolution.* Cambridge: Cambridge University Press, 1972.

Schäfer, Jürgen. *Documentation in the O.E.D.: Shakespeare and Nashe as Test Cases.* Oxford: Clarendon, 1980.

Schiffer, Stephen R. *Meaning.* Oxford: Clarendon, 1972.

Schogt, Henry G. *Sémantique Synchronique: Synonymie, Homonymie, Polysémie.* Toronto: University of Toronto Press, 1976.

Schwarz, David S. *Naming and Referring: The Semantics and Pragmatics of Singular Terms.* Berlin and New York: Walter de Gruyter, 1979.

Searle, John R. 'The Problem of Proper Names.' In Steinberg and Jakobovits (1971), pp. 134-141.

Simpson, J. M. Y. *A First Course in Linguistics.* Edinburgh: Edinburgh University Press, 1979.

Smith, Neil, and Deirdre Wilson. *Modern Linguistics: The Results of Chomsky's Revolution.* Brighton: Harvester Press, 1979.

Sparck Jones, Karen. *Synonymy and Semantic Classification.* Cambridge: Cambridge University Press, 1964.

Spence, N. C. W. 'Linguistic Fields, Conceptual Systems, and *Weltbild.*' *Transactions of the Philological Society* (1961), 87-106.

Steinberg, Danny, and Leon A. Jakobovits (eds.). *Semantics: An Interdisciplinary Reader in Philosophy, Linguistics and Psychology.* Cambridge: Cambridge University Press, 1971.

Steiner, George. *After Babel: Aspects of Language and Translation.* Oxford: Oxford University Press, 1975.

Stern, Gustaf. *Meaning and Change of Meaning.* Goteborg: Elanders Boktrycheri Aktiebolag, 1931 (repr. Indiana University Press, 1968).

Sturtevant, Edgar H. *Linguistic Change: An Introduction to the Historical Study of Language.* Chicago and London: The University of Chicago Press, 1961 (first publ. 1917).

Sullivan, John F. *The Externals of the Catholic Church.* London: Longman, 1955.

Thrane, Torben. *Referential-Semantic Analysis.* Cambridge: Cambridge University Press, 1980.

Townley, Helen M., and Ralph O. Gee. *Thesaurus-Making.* London: Andre Deutsch, 1980.

Trollope, Anthony. *Clergymen of the Church of England.* Leicester: Leicester University Press, 1974 (first publ. 1866).

Ullmann, Stephen. *The Principles of Semantics.* Glasgow: Jackson, 1951.

Ullmann, Stephen. *Semantics: An Introduction to the Science of Meaning.* Oxford: Basil Blackwell, 1962.

Vallins, G. H. *Spelling* (rev. D. G. Scragg). London: Andre Deutsch, 1965.

Vygotsky, Lev Semenovich. *Thought and Language* (trans. Eugenia Haufmann and Gertrude Vakar). Cambridge, Massachusetts: The MIT Press, 1962.

Waldron, Ronald A. *Sense and Sense Development.* 2nd ed. London: Andre Deutsch, 1979.

von Wartburg, H. *Problems and Methods in Linguistics* (trans. J. M. H. Reid). Oxford: Basil Blackwell, 1969.

Weinrich, Uriel. 'On The Semantic Structure of Language.' In Joseph Greenberg (ed.) (1963).

White, A. R. 'Synonymous Expressions.' *The Philosophical Quarterly* 8 (1958), 193-207.

Whorf, Benjamin L. *Language, Thought, and Reality* (ed. John B. Carroll). Cambridge, Massachusetts: The MIT Press, 1956.

Wierzbicka, Anna. *Semantic Primitives* (trans. by the author and John Resemeres). Frankfurt: Athenaum Verlag, 1972.

Wotherspoon, Irené A. W. *A Notional Classification of Two Parts of English Lexis.* University of Glasgow B.Litt. thesis, 1969.

Zabeeh, Farhang, E. D. Klemke, and Arthur Jacobson (eds.). *Readings in Semantics.* Urbana: University of Illinois Press, 1974.

Ziff, Paul. *Semantic Analysis.* Ithaca, New York: Cornell University Press, 1960.

Index

Absolute synonymy	15-17
Action nouns	8, 21, 42, 48
Adjectival tags	24, 25, 45-50
Adjectives, subordinated participial	13
Agent nouns	19, 21, 42
Alphabetical ordering	1
Alphabetization, conceptual	33
Analogue	22
Archisememe	9(n.18), 10, 32
Calendrical organization	65(n.60)
Category line	50
Category tag	17, 20-28, 33-35, 42-51, 59, 61, 65, 71
Category tag, subordinate	43-45
Category tags, metalanguage of	34
Causative verb, subordinate	27
Causative verbal categories	27
Cognate term	16
Collocation	15, 23
Component, redundant	9
Componential analysis	5(n.9), 9, 12
Conceptual field	3, 4(n.7), 32
Conceptual primacy	11-14
Conceptual space	9-10
Converse verbal category	27
De-adjectival abstract nouns	14
Denotata	3, 68
Derivative adjectival and adverbial forms	11, 13, 19
Diachronic	17(n.31), 33
Dialectal variants	16
Distinguisher	33
Etymological base forms	11
Etymological primacy	11, 14, 25
Family tree progression	29, 57, 63
Full stops, system of	19(n.34), 43
Functional selection	36(n.47)
Genealogical method	29-30
Governance	2, 9, 17, 23
Head category	17-22, 43-47
Head category tag	50
Head concept	21-27, 43-47
Head noun	8, 61

Headword 9-23, 35
Historical Thesaurus of English 13, 36(n.37, 38), 37-41, 45, 54, 64
Hyponym 8-9, 17-22, 33-35
Inclusion 9
Inclusion, direct 9
Inclusion, locative 31(n.44)
Indeterminacy, referential 2-3, 10(n.19), 32, 37, 53, 68, 70
Kinship terms 19
Lacunæ 34
Lemma 2
Lexeme 19, 33, 42-46
Lexical items, cognate 8
Lexical field 1-19, 22, 33, 37, 41, 54-56
Lexical semantics 1
Lexical set 1, 2, 5, 10, 14, 29
Lexical subordination 19, 43, 51
Locomotive organization 31-32
Macroclassificatory stage 44
Marker 32
Meaning, referential 1
Metalinguistic structure 59
Microclassificatory stage 19-20, 44
Nominal 12(n.21), 13, 17, 18
Nominal categories 45
Nominal head 17-18
Nominalism 6
Nominal referential indeterminacy 15
Nominal tag 45, 48
Nominative function 2
Notional approach 10, 30(n.43)
Noun, subordinate classes 25
Noun categories, non-personal 22-23
Nouns, action 8, 21, 42, 48
Nouns, de-adjectival abstract 14
Nouns, personal agent 21
Nouns, personal patient 21
Nouns, process 21, 34
Noun tags, personal 21
Onomasiology 4
Opposition 28
Opposition, bipolar 28
Opposition, morphological 28
Organic relationship 67

Organic system	4
Paradigm	2-8, 17
Paronym	11-13, 33-34
Plural inflection	50
Predicative function	2
Primacy, conceptual	11-14
Privative	27-28
Progression	64
Quasi-synonyms	8, 33
Scalar structure	29
Semantic area	10
Semantic dependence	43-51
Semantic field	3
Semantic primacy	11-12, 14, 21
Semantic primitives	12
Semantic space	4, 19, 24
Semantic spread	22
Semantically dependent modifiers	8
Semantics, combinatorial	2
Semantics, lexical	1
Semantics, syntactical	2
Sense-components	18, 21, 23-24, 67
Sense-relations	1-3, 8, 14, 19, 20-34, 50
Signification	5, 15
Signifie	4
Structural approach	1, 6(n.10), 9
Structuralism	10
Subfield	6-14, 35, 41-44
Subordinate adjectival categories	17-18, 23-24, 47-48
Subordinate adverbial categories	17-48
Subordinates, parallel	20, 23, 26, 33, 45, 64
Subordination, lexical	19, 43, 51
Subordination, low-level	33
Superordinate	2, 6-34, 52-71
Synonymy	15-18, 22, 33, 52, 61-62
Synonymy, absolute	15-17
Synonymy, Bloomfieldian view of	15, 17
Synonymy, cognitive	15, 17, 22
System, conceptual	3(n.4), 4-8, 28
Systematization	2, 6, 8
Transformational-generative grammar	1-2, 32
Trier, J.	7, 19
Unilateral implication	8, 9

Valeur 4
Verb, performative 19, 27
Verb, subordinate 17
Verbal noun 9, 13-14, 48, 50

TEXTS AND STUDIES IN RELIGION

1. Elizabeth A. Clark, **Clement's Use of Aristotle: The Aristotelian Contribution to Clement of Alexandria's Refutation of Gnosticism**

2. Richard DeMaria, **Communal Love at Oneida: A Perfectionist Vision of Authority, Property and Sexual Order**

3. David F. Kelly, **The Emergence of Roman Catholic Medical Ethics in North America: An Historical-Methodological-Bibliographical Study**

4. David Rausch, **Zionism Within Early American Fundamentalism,1878-1918: A Convergence of Two Traditions**

5. Janine Marie Idziak, **Divine Command Morality: Historical and Contemporary Readings**

6. Marcus Braybrooke, **Inter-Faith Organizations, 1893-1979: An Historical Directory**

7. L. William Countryman, **The Rich Christian in the Church of the Early Empire: Contradictions and Accommodations**

8. Irving Hexham, **The Irony of Apartheid: The Struggle for National Independence of Afrikaner Calvinism Against British Imperialism**

9. Michael Ryan, editor, **Human Responses to the Holocaust: Perpetrators and Victims, Bystanders and Resisters**

10. G. Stanley Kane, **Anselm's Doctrine of Freedom and the Will**

11. Bruce Bubacz, **St. Augustine's Theory of Knowledge: A Contemporary Analysis**

12. Anne Barstow, **Married Priests and the Reforming Papacy: The Eleventh-Century Debates**

13. Denis Janz, editor,**Three Reformation Catechisms: Catholic, Anabaptist, Lutheran**

14. David Rausch, **Messianic Judaism: Its History, Theology, and Polity**

15. Ernest E. Best, **Religion and Society in Transition: The Church and Social Change in England, 1560-1850**

16. Donald V. Stump *et al.*, editors, *Hamartia:***The Concept of Error in the Western Tradition**

17. Louis Meyer, **Eminent Hebrew Christians of the Nineteenth Century: Brief Biographical Sketches**, edited by David Rausch

18. J. William Frost, editor, **The Records and Recollections of James Jenkins**

19. Joseph R. Washington, Jr., **Anti-Blackness in English Religion 1500-1800**

20. Joyce E. Salisbury, **Iberian Popular Religion, 600 B.C. to 700 A.D., Celts, Romans and Visigoths**

21. Longinus, **On the Sublime,** translated by James A. Arieti and John M. Crossett

22. James Gollnick, *Flesh* **as Transformation Symbol in the Theology of Anselm of Canterbury,**

23. William Lane Craig, **The Historical Argument for the Resurrection of Jesus During the Deist Controversy**

24. Steven H. Simpler, **Roland H. Bainton: An Examination of His Reformation Historiography**

25. Charles W. Brockwell, **Bishop Reginald Pecock and the Lancastrian Church: Securing the Foundations of Cultural Authority**

26. Sebastian Franck, **280 Paradoxes or Wondrous Sayings,** Translated & Introduced by E. J. Furcha

27. James Heft, **John XXII and Papal Teaching Authority**

28. Shelley Baranowski, **The Confessing Church, Conservative Elites, and the Nazi State**

29. Jan Lindhardt, **Martin Luther: Knowledge and Mediation in the Renaissance**

30. Kenneth L. Campbell, **The Intellectual Struggle of the English Papists in the Seventeenth Century: The Catholic Dilemma**

31. William R. Everdell, **Christian Apologetics in France, 1730-1790: The Roots of Romantic Religion**

32. Paul J. Morman, **Noël Aubert De Versé: A Study in the Concept of Toleration**

33. Nigel M. de S. Cameron, **Biblical Higher Criticism and the Defense of Infallibilism in 19th Century Britian**

34. Samuel J. Rogal, **John Wesley's London: A Guidebook**

35. André Séguenny, **The Christology of Caspar Schwenckfeld: Spirit and Flesh in the Process of Life Transformation,** translated by Peter C. Erb and Simone S. Nieuwolt

36. Donald E. Demaray, **The Innovation of John Newton (1725-1807): Synergism of Word and Music in Eighteenth Century Evangelism**

37. Thomas Chase, **The English Religious Lexis**